CAMBRIDGE LIBRARY COLLECTION

Books of enduring scholarly value

Travel and Exploration

The history of travel writing dates back to the Bible, Caesar, the Vikings and the Crusaders, and its many themes include war, trade, science and recreation. Explorers from Columbus to Cook charted lands not previously visited by Western travellers, and were followed by merchants, missionaries, and colonists, who wrote accounts of their experiences. The development of steam power in the nineteenth century provided opportunities for increasing numbers of 'ordinary' people to travel further, more economically, and more safely, and resulted in great enthusiasm for travel writing among the reading public. Works included in this series range from first-hand descriptions of previously unrecorded places, to literary accounts of the strange habits of foreigners, to examples of the burgeoning numbers of guidebooks produced to satisfy the needs of a new kind of traveller - the tourist.

An Account of the Arctic Regions

Written by explorer, scientist and later clergyman William Scoresby (1789–1857), this two-volume guide to the Arctic regions was first published in 1820. Scoresby, himself the son of a whaler and Arctic explorer, first sailed to the polar regions at the age of eleven, and was later apprenticed to his father. He became a correspondent of Sir Joseph Banks, and his extensive research on the Arctic area included pioneering work in oceanography, magnetism, and the study of Arctic currents and waves. He surveyed 400 miles of the Greenland coast in 1822. This account was the first book published in Britain which was devoted solely to the whale fisheries. Volume 1 is a general geographical survey of the Arctic region and includes detailed observations of polar ice conditions, atmospherology, and zoology. The book also considers the much-debated question of northern sea communication between the Atlantic and Pacific oceans.

T0300535

Cambridge University Press has long been a pioneer in the reissuing of out-of-print titles from its own backlist, producing digital reprints of books that are still sought after by scholars and students but could not be reprinted economically using traditional technology. The Cambridge Library Collection extends this activity to a wider range of books which are still of importance to researchers and professionals, either for the source material they contain, or as landmarks in the history of their academic discipline.

Drawing from the world-renowned collections in the Cambridge University Library, and guided by the advice of experts in each subject area, Cambridge University Press is using state-of-the-art scanning machines in its own Printing House to capture the content of each book selected for inclusion. The files are processed to give a consistently clear, crisp image, and the books finished to the high quality standard for which the Press is recognised around the world. The latest print-on-demand technology ensures that the books will remain available indefinitely, and that orders for single or multiple copies can quickly be supplied.

The Cambridge Library Collection will bring back to life books of enduring scholarly value (including out-of-copyright works originally issued by other publishers) across a wide range of disciplines in the humanities and social sciences and in science and technology.

An Account
of the Arctic Regions

*With a History and Description of the
Northern Whale-Fishery*

VOLUME 1

WILLIAM SCORESBY

CAMBRIDGE
UNIVERSITY PRESS

CAMBRIDGE UNIVERSITY PRESS

Cambridge, New York, Melbourne, Madrid, Cape Town,
Singapore, São Paolo, Delhi, Tokyo, Mexico City

Published in the United States of America by Cambridge University Press, New York

www.cambridge.org
Information on this title: www.cambridge.org/9781108037785

© in this compilation Cambridge University Press 2011

This edition first published 1820
This digitally printed version 2011

ISBN 978-1-108-03778-5 Paperback

Drawn by R.K. Greville Esq.r after a Sketch by W. Scoresby Jun.r

REPRESENTATION of the SHIP ESK of WHITBY,

DURING AN ATTEMPT TO INVERT HER POSITION AND BRING THE

Edinburgh Published by

Eng.d by W. & D. Lizars Edinburgh

DAMAGED BY ICE AND ALMOST FULL OF WATER.
KEEL TO THE SURFACE OF THE SEA FOR REPAIRING THE DAMAGE.

A. Constable & C.º 1820.

AN

ACCOUNT

OF THE

ARCTIC REGIONS,

WITH A

HISTORY AND DESCRIPTION

OF THE

NORTHERN WHALE-FISHERY.

BY

W. SCORESBY *Jun.* F.R.S.E.

ILLUSTRATED BY TWENTY-FOUR ENGRAVINGS.

IN TWO VOLUMES.

VOL. I.

EDINBURGH:

PRINTED FOR ARCHIBALD CONSTABLE AND CO. EDINBURGH;

AND HURST, ROBINSON AND CO. CHEAPSIDE, LONDON.

1820.

P. Neill, Printer.

TO

ROBERT JAMESON, Esq.

PROFESSOR OF NATURAL HISTORY IN THE UNIVERSITY OF EDINBURGH,

PRESIDENT OF THE WERNERIAN SOCIETY,

&c. &c. &c.

AT WHOSE SUGGESTION THIS WORK WAS UNDERTAKEN,

AND TO WHOSE EARLY AND UNIFORM FRIENDSHIP THE AUTHOR

IS DEEPLY INDEBTED,

THESE VOLUMES

ARE RESPECTFULLY

INSCRIBED.

PREFACE.

THOUGH the Natural History of the Countries within the Arctic Circle, and the nature and practice of the Whale-Fishery, possess peculiar, and I may add almost universal, interest; yet it is remarkable that no original work, published in Britain, excepting a single Tract by Henry Elking, appears to have been devoted entirely to either subject. In this respect, notwithstanding our important and extensive annual adventures to the Seas of Greenland and Davis' Strait, we have been anticipated and our supineness tacitly reproved by several works that have appeared in other countries. Among foreign authors who have treated of the Regions of the North, or of the

Whale-Fishery, may be mentioned, La Marti-
niere, Pierre de Mezange, Boisgelin and Fortia,
though these are writers, it should be observed,
who cannot be altogether followed ;—M. La Pey-
ronie, and Bernard de Reste, who have given
translations in French, not altogether accurate
however, of works of some value;—and Torfæus,
Otho Fabricius, Olafsen, Olaving, Egedé, Crantz,
Zorgdrager, Eggers, Moriniere, and a few others,
who have produced works of real merit.

The Accounts of Greenland by the faithful
and enterprising Moravian Missionaries Hans
Egedé and David Crantz, whose zeal and philan-
thropy carried them into one of the most un-
comfortable and inhospitable regions of the globe,
but particularly the latter, are works of peculiar
fidelity and value ; and the account of the Whale-
Fishery given by Zorgdrager, though written
considerably above a century ago, is, perhaps, on
the whole, the best that has appeared in any
language.

The works of Egedé and Crantz have been
translated into English, and, with the article
of Sir Charles Giesecké, in Dr Brewster's En-
cyclopædia, and some others, included in works

on miscellaneous literature or science, form the principal sources of information on the Natural History of Greenland, published in the English language. The tract by Henry Elking, already alluded to, entitled " A View of the " Greenland Trade and Whale-Fishery, with " the National and Private Advantages there- " of," is, I believe, our only original work on this interesting subject.

A considerable quantity of miscellaneous information, however, relating to Arctic Countries and to the Whale-Fishery, is to be found interspersed through the Collections of Voyages, &c. by Hakluyt, Purchas, Churchill, Harris, Pickersgill, Goldson, Forster, Müller, Coxe, Pinkerton, Kerr, Clarke, Barrow, Burney, &c.; in the translations of the Voyages or Narratives of Barentz, Martens, M. Le Roy, &c.; and in the original Voyages of Ellis, James, Fox, Ross, and others, into Baffin's or Hudson's Bay; of Cook into Behring's Strait; and of Phipps towards the North Pole.

The work now submitted to the Public is in a great measure original, being chiefly derived from researches carried on during seventeen voyages to

the Spitzbergen or Greenland Whale-Fishery. It
consists of two distinct parts, each occupying a
volume. The first relates to the progress of Discovery in the Arctic Regions, and the Natural
History of Spitzbergen and the Greenland Sea;
the second is devoted to the Whale-Fishery as
conducted in the Seas of Greenland and Davis'
Strait.

Numerous authorities have been consulted in
preparing these sheets for publication, and in all
cases, as far as I am aware, a proper reference has
been made to the works from which any information has been derived. For a small but interesting *Mémoire* by M. S. B. J. Noel, *Sur l'Antiquité de la pêche de la Baleine,* from which I
have drawn some valuable historical information,
I was indebted to the kindness of M. Noel de
la Moriniere, author of an extensive work on Ancient and Modern Fisheries, now in the course of
publication in France. Access to some valuable
works which I had not in my own possession,
and different acts of kindness or assistance were
afforded me by the Right Honourable Sir Joseph
Banks, Professor Jameson, P. Neill, Esq. Dr
Traill, and my Father. By means of some va-

luable instruments, &c. furnished me by Sir Joseph Banks, whose friendly suggestions and encouragement I am happy to acknowledge, and whose kindness and liberality I shall ever remember with gratitude, I was enabled to make some experiments on sub-marine temperature, the result of which proved novel and interesting. These, with some facilities kindly given me by William Swainson, Esq. of Liverpool, the Reverend George Young, and Mr Thomas Parkin of Whitby, and occasional obligations from other friends, noticed in different parts of the work, constitute, I believe, the amount of the assistance which I have received in preparing the materials which occupy the following pages.

CONTENTS

CONTENTS

OF

VOLUME FIRST.

<hr>

ACCOUNT OF THE ARCTIC REGIONS,
&c. &c.

<hr>

Page

CHAP. I.—REMARKS on the celebrated Question, of the existence of a Sea-communication between the Atlantic and Pacific Oceans, by the North; with an Account of the Progress of Discovery in the Northern Regions, - - 1

SECT. 1. General Remarks, indicating the existence of a Sea-communication between the Atlantic and Pacific Oceans, by the North, ib.

2. Remarks on the supposed Communication between the Atlantic and Pacific Oceans, by the North-east, - - 12

3. Remarks on the supposed Communication between the Atlantic and Pacific Oceans, by the North-west; with hints for conducting Discoveries in the Polar Regions, 16

  Page

Sect. 4. Remarks on the opinion of a Sea-communi-
         cation between the Atlantic and Pacific
         Oceans, by the North Pole,   -   40

      5. Account of the Progress of Discovery in
         the North,   -   -   61

CHAP. II.—Descriptive Account of some of
    the Polar Countries,   -   -   92

Sect. 1. Account of Spitzbergen, and the Islands
         immediately adjacent,   -   ib.
              a. Spitzbergen,   -   -   ib.
              b. Moffen Island,   -   149
              c. Low Island,   -   150
              d. Hope Island,   -   151
              e. Cherie Island,   -   -   152

      2. Account of Jan Mayen Island,   -   154

CHAP. III.—Hydrographical Survey of the
    Greenland Sea,   -   -   170

Sect. 1. Situation and Extent,—Colour and degree
         of Transparency,—Quality, Specific Gra-
         vity, and Saltness of the Greenland
         Sea,   -   -   ib.

      2. Temperature, Depth, and Pressure of the
         Greenland Sea; with a Description of an
         Apparatus for bringing up Water from
         great depths; and an Account of Expe-
         riments made with it,   -   184

      3 Remarks on the Currents of the Arctic
        Sea; with Observations respecting
        Waves,   -   203

Page

CHAP. IV.—An Account of the Greenland
   or Polar Ice,   -   -   225

SECT. 1. A Description of the various kinds or de-
            nominations of Ice,   -   ib.

      2. On the Formation of Ice on the Sea,   238

      3. Description of Ice-Fields, and Remarks
         on their Formation and tremendous Con-
         cussions,   -   -   241

      4. Description of Ice-bergs, and Remarks on
         their Formation,   -   250

      5. On the Situation or general Outline of the
         Polar Ice,   -   -   262

      6. Changes which take place, with the Ad-
         vance of the Season, in the situation of
         the Ice, in the Seas of Greenland and
         Davis' Strait,   -   270

      7. Situation of the Ice in the Region visit-
         ed by the Greenland Ships, with Ob-
         servations on the Alterations which have
         occurred, during a series of Sixteen
         Years,   -   -   276

      8. Remarks on the Properties, peculiar Move-
         ments, and Drifting of the Ice,   -   284

      9. Effects of the Ice on the Atmosphere, and
         of the Ice and Sea on each other,   296

     10. Remarks on the closest Approximations to-
         wards the Poles hitherto accomplished,
         under different Meridians,   -   306

     11. Abstract of the preceding Observations
         on the Formation, Properties and Si-
         tuation of the Polar Ice,   318

Page

CHAP. V.—Observations on the Atmospherology of the Arctic Regions; particularly relating to Spitzbergen and the adjacent
Greenland Sea,   -   -   323

SECT. 1. Remarks on the Climate of the Arctic Regions, and the effects of Cold,   -   ib.

2. General Remarks on Meteorology, with an
Investigation of the Mean Monthly, and
Annual Temperature of the North Polar
Regions, including some inferences on
the constant tendency to Equalization of
Temperature in the Atmosphere,   345

3. Remarks on the Pressure of the Atmosphere,
with Observations on the Use of the Barometer in predicting the Weather.   370

4. Appearance, Colour, Transparency, Density, degree of Dryness, and state as to
Electricity, of the Atmosphere,   -   377

5. Atmospheric Phenomena, dependent on Reflection and Refraction,   -   383

6. Observations on the Winds of the Polar Regions, with some Notices respecting Meteors not aqueous,   -   395

7. Aqueous Meteors, including Observations
on Clouds, Rain, Hail, Snow, Frost-rime,
Hoar-frost, and Fog,   -   419

CHAP. VI.—A Sketch of the Zoology of the
Arctic Regions,   -   -   446

SECT. 1. A Description of Animals of the Cetaceous
Kind, frequenting the Greenland Sea,   449
Balæna Mysticetus, or Common Whale,   ib.
Balænoptera Gibbar, or Physalis,   -   478

Page

Balænoptera Rorqual,   -   482
———— Jubartes,   -   484
———— acuto-rostrata,   -   485
Monodon Monoceros,   -   486
Delphinus Deductor,   -   496
Delphinapterus Beluga,   -   500

Sect. 2. Some Account of the Quadrupeds inhabiting Spitzbergen, and the Icy Seas adjacent,   -   -   502

Trichecus Rosmarus, or Sea-horse,   ib.
Phocæ, or Seals,   -   508
Canis Lagopus, or Arctic Fox,   -   517
Ursus maritimus, or Polar Bear,   -   ib.
Cervus Tarandus, or Rein-Deer,   -   526

3. Remarks on the Birds frequenting the Sea and Coast of Spitzbergen,   -   527

Anas Bernicla,   -   ib.
—— mollissima,   -   ib.
—— arctica,   -   ib.
Alca Alle,   -   -   528
Procellaria Glacialis,   -   ib.
Colymbus Grylle,   -   532
———— Troile,   -   ib.
———— glacialis,   -   533
Sterna hirundo,   -   -   ib.
Larus Rissa,   -   534
—— parasiticus,   -   ib.
—— crepidatus,   -   ib.
—— eburneus,   -   535
—— glaucus,   -   ib.
Tringa hypoleucos,   -   537
Emberiza nivalis,   -   ib.
Fringilla Linaria,   -   ib.

b

Page

SECT. 4. A brief Account of Amphibia, Animalcules, &c. inhabiting the Spitzbergen Sea,   538

Class AMPHIBIA.

    Squalus Borealis,   -   ib.
    Cyclopterus Liparis,   -   540

Class PISCES.

    Gadus carbonarius,   -   ib.
    Mullus barbatus?   -   541

Class ARTICULATA.

    Gammarus Arcticus,   -   ib.
    Cancer Pulex,   -   -   542
    ———— Boreas,   -   ib.
    ———— Ampulla,   -   ib.
    ———— Nugax,   -   ib.
    Larunda Ceti,   -   543

Class VERMES.

    Ascaris, Echinorhynchus, Tænia, &c.   ib.
    Ascidia gelatinosa & rustica,   -   ib.
    Lernæa branchialis,   -   ib.
    Clio helicina,   -   ib.
    Clio Borealis,   -   -   544
    Sepiæ,   -   -   ib.
    Medusæ, Animalcula, &c.   -   ib.

APPENDIX.

Page

No. I.—Meteorological Tables,   -   - (1)

  II.—Meteorological Results,   -   Fronting (48)

    A. General Abstract of the foregoing Register, (ib.)

    B. Table for determining the Mean Annual Temperature of latitude 78° N., and of the North Pole,   - (49)

    C. Table for ascertaining the Mean Temperature of the month of April, lat. 78°. N. (50)

    D. Table for ascertaining the Mean Temperature of the month of July, lat, 78°. N. (ib.)

    E. Abstract of Thermometrical Observations made at the Apartments of the Royal Society, London,   - (51)

    F. Abstract of Fifty Years Observations on the Temperature of Stockholm,   - (52)

    G. Formulæ for Calculating the Mean Temperature of unobserved months,   - (53)

  III. a.—Chronological enumeration of Voyages undertaken by the different Nations of the World, in search of a Northern Communication between the Atlantic and Pacific Oceans ; including such other Voyages as have been conducive to the advancement of Discovery in the North,   - (54)

    b.—Notice respecting the Effect of the Sun's Rays, and the Decrease of Temperature on ascending in the Atmosphere,   - (72)

  IV.—Table of Latitudes and Longitudes of Capes, Bays, &c. in Spitzbergen and Jan Mayen, derived chiefly from original Surveys,   - (73)

Page

No. V.—Catalogue of Plants found in Spitzbergen,   (75)

VI.—Notice respecting the Minerals of Spitzbergen,   (76)

VII.—State of the Wind and Weather, from August to
       May, in the Island of Jan Mayen, as collect-
       ed from the Journal of Seven Dutch Sailors,
       who wintered there in the year 1633–4,   (78)

VIII.—Experiments for determining the Specific Gra-
       vity of Ice,   -   -   (81)

ACCOUNT

ACCOUNT

OF THE

ARCTIC REGIONS,

&c.

CHAPTER I.

REMARKS ON THE CELEBRATED QUESTION OF
THE EXISTENCE OF A SEA COMMUNICATION BE-
TWEEN THE ATLANTIC AND PACIFIC OCEANS,
BY THE NORTH; WITH AN ACCOUNT OF THE
PROGRESS OF DISCOVERY IN THE NORTHERN
REGIONS.

SECT. I.

General Remarks indicating the Existence of a
Sea Communication between the Atlantic and
Pacific Oceans, by the North.

PERHAPS there is no question connected with geographical science, which has been so long in agitation, without being resolved, and so often revived with the most sanguine expectations of success, and then abandoned as hopeless,—as the

question of the existence of a navigable communication between the European and the Chinese
seas, by the north. The first attempts to reach
China by sea, were made by steering along the
coast of Africa towards the south, and the next by
proceeding from the European shore in a westerly
direction. The former, which first proved successful, was accomplished by Vasquez de Gama, a Portugueze, in the year 1497-8; and the latter was
undertaken by the renowned navigator Columbus, in
1492. The notion of steering to India by the
north-west, as the shortest way, was suggested
about the middle, or latter end of the fifteenth century, by John Vaz Costa Cortereal, who performed
a voyage to Newfoundland, about the year 1463-4 [*];
or, according to a more general opinion, by John
Cabot, the father of the celebrated Sebastian Cabot,
who attempted the navigation in 1497, and perhaps
also in 1494-5 [†]. The idea of a passage to India,
by the North Pole, was suggested by Robert
Thorne, merchant, of Bristol [‡], as early as the year
1527; and the opinion of a passage by the north-
east, was proposed soon afterwards.

The universal interest which has been attached
to this question of a sea communication between

---

[*] BARROW's " Chronological History of Voyages into the
Arctic Regions," p. 37.

[†] HARRIS's Voyages, vol. ii. p. 191.

[‡] PHIPPS' Voyage towards the North Pole, p 1.

the Atlantic and Pacific Oceans, by the North,
ever since it was first suggested about 330 or 350
years ago, is fully proved by the facts,—that the
speculation has never but once been abandoned by
the nations of Europe, for more than twenty-five
years together,—and that there have been only
three or four intervals of more than fifteen years,
in which no expedition was sent out in search of
one or other of the supposed passages, from the
year 1500, down to the present time. And it is not a
little surprising, that, after nearly a hundred different
voyages have been undertaken, with the view of discovering the desired communication with the Indian
Seas, all of which have failed, Britain should again
revive and attempt the solution of this interesting
problem.

It has been advanced as a maxim, that *what we
wish to be true, we readily believe ;*—a maxim
which, however doubtful in general, has met with a
full illustration in the northern voyages of discovery.
A single trial is often sufficient for satisfying us as to
the truth of a disputed point; but, in this instance,
though nearly an hundred trials have been made,
the problem is still considered as unresolved.

Several facts may be brought forward, on which
arguments of no mean force may be founded, in
support of the opinion of the existence of a sea
communication by the north, between Europe and

A 2

China. Among these arguments, I shall only mention the nature of the currents and tides,—the fact of an amazing body of ice being yearly dissolved in the Greenland sea, above what is there generated, —the common occurrence of drift wood, and some of it worm-eaten, in most parts of the Polar seas,— the nature of the northern termination of the continents of Europe and Asia, as well as that of America, as far as yet ascertained,—and the facts of whales having passed from the Greenland sea to the Sea of Tartary, and from remote regions in the north, to the sea of Greenland; all of which circumstances I conceive to be in favour of the existence of such a communication.

I. The prevailing current in the Spitzbergen sea, flows, we are well assured, during nine months of the year, if not all the year round, from the north-east towards the south-west. The velocity of this current may be from 5 to 20 miles per day, varying in different situations, but is most considerable near the coast of Old Greenland *. The current, on the other hand, in the middle of Behring's Strait, as observed by Lieutenant Kotzebue, sets strongly to the north-east, with a velocity, as he thought, of two miles and a half an hour, which is greater,

---

* As the proofs of this current will be brought forward under the division of the Hydrography of the Polar Seas, it is needless in this place to enter into particulars.

however, by one-half, than the rate observed by
Captain Cook *.

2. By the action of the south-westerly current, a
vast quantity of ice is annually brought from the
north and east, and conducted along the east shore
of *Old* Greenland, as far as Cape Farewell, where
such masses as still remain undissolved, are soon
destroyed by the influence of the solar heat, and the
force of the sea, to which they then become exposed from almost every quarter. This ice being entirely free from salt, and very compact, appears originally to have consisted of field ice, a kind which
perhaps requires the action of frost for many years
to bring it to the thickness which it assumes. The
quantity of heavy ice, in surface, which is thus annually dissolved, may, at a rough calculation, be stated
at about 20,000 square leagues, while the quantity
annually generated in the regions accessible to the
whalefishers, is probably not more than one-fourth
of that area. As such, the ice, which is so inexhaustible, must require an immense surface of sea
for its generation, perhaps the whole or greater
part of the so-called " polar basin," the supply required for replacing what is dissolved in Behring's
Strait, where the current sets towards the north,
being probably of small moment. The current, in
opposite parts of the northern hemisphere, being

---

* Barrow's Voyages into the Arctic Regions, p. 358.

thus found to follow the same line of direction, indicates a communication between the two, across the
Poles ; and the inexhaustible supply of ice, affording
about 15,000 square leagues to be annually dissolved, above the quantity generated in the known parts
of the Spitzbergen seas, supports the same conclusion.

3. The origin of the considerable quantity of
drift wood, found in almost every part of the Greenland sea, is traced to some country beyond the Pole,
and may be brought forward in aid of the opinion of
the existence of a sea communication between the
Atlantic and Pacific ; which argument receives additional strength from the circumstance of some of
the drift-wood being worm-eaten. This last fact, I first
observed on the shores of the Island of Jan Mayen,
where I landed in August 1817, and confirmed it
by more particular observation, when at Spitzbergen
the year following. Having no axe with me when
I observed the worm-eaten wood, and having no
means of bringing it away, I could not ascertain
whether the holes observed in the timber, were the
work of a Ptinus or a Pholas. In either case, however, as it is not known that these animals ever
pierce wood in the arctic countries, it is presumed
that the worm-eaten drift-wood is derived from a
trans-polar region.

Numerous facts of this nature might be adduced,
all of which support the same conclusion. In the

Danish settlement at Disco, is a mahogany table made out of a plank which was drifted thither by the current, and is now in the possession of the governor. A tree of logwood was also picked up not far from the same place. Another log of mahogany was picked up at sea by Admiral Lowenorn, in 1786, when on his voyage attempting the re-discovery of Old Greenland. This piece of wood, which was so large that they were obliged to saw it in two before they could get it on board, they found within sight of the coast of Greenland, in latitude 65° 11′, longitude 35° 8′ west of Paris. It was much perforated by worms, which circumstance the Admiral conceived might assist in giving it suffi cient buoyancy to swim in the water [*].

These logs of wood, the produce of the Isthmus which connects North and South America, could only reach the places where they were severally found, by floating up the west coast of America, towards the north, through Behring's Strait, and so along the northern face of Asia or America, or across the Northern Pole. Had they come by the way of the Gulf of Mexico, they might have floated to the banks of Newfoundland, by the action of the Gulf Stream, and been carried from thence to any part of the western shore of Europe; but they could not possibly have passed northward from Newfound-

---

[*] Quarterly Review, No. 36. p. 445.

land into Davis' Straits, or to the east coast of
Greenland, in direct opposition to a current which
perpetually flows towards the south-west *.

4. The northern faces of the continents of Europe and Asia, as well as of that of America, so far as
yet known, are such, as renders it difficult, even to
imagine such a position for the unascertained regions,
as to cut off the communication between the frozen
sea, near the meridian of London, and that in the
opposite part of the northern hemisphere, near Behring's Strait.

5. And, another argument which goes still farther to support the opinion of the existence of the
communication in question, is the fact of whales
which have been harpooned in the Greenland seas,
having been found in the Pacific Ocean ; and whales
with stone lances sticking in their fat, (a kind of
weapon used by no nation now known,) having been
caught both in the sea of Spitzbergen, and in Davis'
Strait.   The following are some of the authorities
for this fact, which, of all other arguments yet offered in favour of a trans-polar passage, seems to me
to be the most satisfactory.

A Dutch East India captain, of the name of
Jacob Cool, of Sardam, who had been several times
at Greenland, and was of course well acquainted with
the nature of the apparatus used in the whale

---

* Quarterly Review, No. 36. p. 445

fishery, was informed by the Fischal Zeeman of
India, that in the sea of Tartary there was a whale
taken, in the back of which was sticking a Dutch
harpoon, marked with the letters W. B. This curious circumstance was communicated to Peter
Jansz Vischer, probably a Greenland whaler, who
discovered that the harpoon in question had belonged to William Bastiaanz, Admiral of the Dutch
Greenland fleet, and had been struck into the whale
in the Spitzbergen sea *.

Muller refers to a similar circumstance when re-
cording the first discovery by sea, of the peninsula
of Kamtchatka by the Russians, in the year 1716.
The crew of the discovery vessel having wintered
on the western coast of Kamtchatka, he informs us,
that during their stay there, " the sea cast upon the
shore a whale that had in its body a harpoon of
European workmanship, marked with Roman letters †." Another account of the same nature, given
by Hendrick Hamel, in his " Unfortunate Voyage
of the yacht Sparwer, in the year 1653," and published in the " Recucil des Voyages," corroborates
the testimony of Muller. Hamel, in his narrative
of the loss of this vessel on the Island of Quel-
paert, observes, that " in the sea to the north-east

* Beschryving der Walvisvangst, vol. ii. p. 38.

† MULLER's Voyages from Asia to America; Jeffrey's
Translation, p. 42.

of Korea, they take every year a great number of whales, in some of which are found harpoons (*or* striking-irons) of the French and Dutch, who practise the whale-fishery at the extremities of Europe; whence we infer (he continues) that there is surely a passage between Korea and Japan, which communicates to the Strait of Waigatz *," separating Nova Zembla from the Continent of Europe.

Other circumstances can be adduced to the same effect. The master of the Volunteer whaler of Whitby, when near the coast of Spitzbergen, July 19. 1813, shewed me part of a lance which had been taken out of the fat of a whale killed by his crew a few weeks before. It was formed of a hard grey stone, of a flinty appearance, about three inches long, two broad, and two-tenths thick. Two holes were pierced in one end of it, by which, it appeared the stock or handle had been secured. It was completely embedded in the blubber, and the wound was quite healed. A small white scar on the skin of the whale, alone marked the place where the lance had entered. In the year 1812, the crew of a Hull fisher (the Aurora) met with a whale in the same region having a harpoon made of bone, sticking in its back; and a few years ago a lance of stone, somewhat like the one above mentioned, fixed to a piece of bone, forming a socket for the stock, was like-

* Quarterly Review, No. xxxv. p. 217.

wise found in a whale by the people of another Greenlandman of Hull: this stone-lance is now deposited in the interesting collection of natural rarities belonging to Mr Hornsea of Scarbrough *. To these facts we might add many of a similar kind, together with others of whales struck in Davis' Straits having been killed near Spitzbergen, and *vice versa*; but the above will be sufficient for affording a strong confirmation of the opinion, that a sea communication between the Atlantic and Pacific Oceans by the North, does exist. For, with regard to the stone-lances and bone-harpoons found in the bodies of whales, it may be remarked, that as the Esquimaux of Davis' Straits and Hudson's Bay, have now, from their long intercourse with Europeans, become well supplied with weapons calculated for the capture of the whale made of iron, these instruments of stone and bone, so much inferior, must have been used by some other persons who have not yet had intercourse with the civilized world; but as they are precisely the kind of weapons which were in common use among the Esquimaux a century ago, it is probable that the instruments alluded to were struck by some tribe of the same nation, inhabiting the shores of the frozen ocean, on the northern face of the American Continent, yet unexplored. If so, these facts go

---

* Plate II. fig. 1. is a representation of this instrument.

far towards establishing the existence of a communication between the Spitzbergen sea and the Pacific
Ocean.

SECT. II.

*Remarks on the supposed Communication between
the Atlantic and Pacific Oceans, by the North-
East.*

THE Russians, it appears, have at intervals discovered all the navigation between Archangel and
the Strait of Behring, excepting a portion of about
200 miles, occupied by the eastern part of a noss
or promontory lying between the rivers Khatanga
and Piacina. The northern extremity of this noss,
called Cape Ceverovostochnoi, appears to have been
doubled by Lieutenant Prontschitscheff, in the
year 1735, so that ice, and perhaps some small
islands, seem in this place to form the great obstruction to the navigation. As far as can be well
substantiated, the portion of the route between
Archangel and Kamtchatka, which has been hitherto accomplished, was performed in the following
manner.

Lieutenant Morovieff accomplished the navigation from Archangel towards the river Obe, as far
as the latitude 72° 30′ on the west coast of the pe-

ninsula separating the Gulfs of Kama and Obe, in the years 1734–5. This navigation was continued in 1738 by Lieutenants Malgyin and Skurakoff, who doubled Cape Jalmal on this promontory, and sailed into the Gulf of Obe. Lieutenants Offzin and Iwan Koskeleff, the same year performed the route from the Obe to the Eniesi or Jenisei. And the pilot, Feodor Menin, sailed in the same summer from the Eniesi towards the Lena. He reached the latitude of 73° 15′, and when he came to the mouth of the Piacina, his progress was stopped by the ice ; and finding the passage completely blocked up, he returned to the Eniesi. Thus the navigation from Archangel to the Piacina, a distance of 47 degrees of longitude towards the east, was completed. Lieutenant Prontschitscheff sailed in 1735 from Yakutsk down the Lena, then to the westward to the Olonec, where, owing to numerous interruptions from the ice, he found it necessary to winter. In the month of August of the following year, he passed the rivers Anabara and Khatanga, then penetrated the ice as far as latitude 77° 25′, and coasted along the western side of the most northerly promontory of the Samoieds' country towards the Piacina, a little beyond the Bay of Taimourska, where he was stopped by an impenetrable barrier of ice *.

---

* Coxe's " Account of the Russian Discoveries between Asia and America," p. 308.—According to Muller, Prontschitscheff did not quite reach the Bay of Taimourska.

From near Taimourska, therefore, to near the Piacina, was not accomplished *. In the same summer, Lieutenant Lassenius sailed from the Lena
eastward towards Kamtchatka, and wintered in the
river Charaulack, lying between the Lena and the
Jana, where, of 52 persons composing his crew,
46 died of the scurvy. Lieutenant Dmitri Laptieff, after an attempt which failed in 1736, was
again sent from the Lena in 1739 towards the east.
He wintered in the Indighirsa, where he lost his
vessel, but prosecuted his voyage in another, the
following spring, as far as the river Kovima, from
whence he crossed the Isthmus of the Tchuktchi
country to the river Anadir, communicating with
the sea of Kamtchatka †. The navigation round
the great promontory of the Tchuktchi, constituting the north-eastern termination of Asia, was accomplished by one of three vessels which sailed from
the Kovima, in order to penetrate into the Eastern
Ocean, on the 20th of June 1648. This expedition, indeed, is said to have originally consisted of
seven kotches, four of which were never heard of
after they sailed. One of the other three, which
proceeded for some time in company, was wrecked

---

* Muller mentions, that in 1738 Lieutenant Chariton Laptieff was sent from Petersburgh, to take up the task assigned
to Prontschitscheff, and to go through with it by sea or land ;
but it appears he also failed.—Translation, p. 19.

† Muller's Voyages,—Translation, p. 19, 20.

on the great promontory : the two remaining vessels were soon afterwards separated, and one of them, commanded by Simon Deshneff, a chief of the Cossacks, after being driven about by tempestuous winds until the month of October, was wrecked near the Olutora, lying on the east side of Kamtchatka, in the 60th degree of latitude, and the crew consisting of 25 persons, afterwards reached the Anadir *.

This brief account clearly proves, that if a sea communication between the Atlantic and Pacific by the north-east, really exists, it could never be practicable in one year. As, indeed, the Russians were five or six years in performing so much of the navigation as has been described, though they employed a number of different vessels in the undertaking, it is probable that the voyage could never be performed in one vessel, unless by mere accident, in less than eight or ten years. It is therefore clear, that the discovery of a " North-East Passage," could never be of any advantage to our commerce with China or India.

Though, however, the voyages undertaken in search of a *north-east passage* by the different nations of Europe, have amounted to about twelve, besides numerous partial attempts by the Russians, and though all of them have failed in their principal intention, yet they have not been wholly lost

---

* Coxe's Russian Discoveries, p. 313,–320.

to us ; the Spitzbergen whale and seal fisheries, so
valuable to the country, with the trade to Archangel,
having arisen out of them.

SECT. III.

*Remarks on the supposed Communication between
the Atlantic and the Pacific Oceans, by the
North-West ; with Hints for conducting Discoveries in the Polar Regions.*

The voyages of Davis in the years 1585, 6 and 7,
of Hudson in 1610, and of Baffin in 1616, were the
source of the greatest part of the discoveries which
have been made in the countries situated to the northward and westward of the south point of Greenland.
To these regions, consisting of what have been called Bays and Straits, the names of these celebrated
navigators have been applied. All the voyages, indeed, since undertaken for discovery in the same
quarter, amounting to nearly thirty, have done little more than confirm the researches of these three
individuals, and show how little there was to be
found, instead of discovering any thing of moment.
    Though the secret design of some of these voy-
ages, was the hope of finding gold or other treasures,
or of making an advantageous traffic with the natives of any new country which might be found ;
yet the ostensible object of almost the whole, was

the discovery of a shorter passage to India than
that by the Cape of Good Hope, by the north-west.
But, notwithstanding the number of expeditions
which have been fitted out, the existence of a
" north-west passage," is not yet either proved or
refuted; and though much has been done towards
the decision of this question, yet so long as any corner of Hudson's Bay or Baffin's Bay remains unexplored, the question must rest in uncertainty.

A great number of papers, and some volumes,
have been written at different periods, to prove the
existence of a north-west passage, some of which
certainly possess very considerable merit*. The arguments on this subject, given by Henry Ellis, in
his account of " A voyage to Hudson's Bay," are, I
think, as satisfactory as any I have yet met with.
He infers, that such a passage, extending from the
northern part of Hudson's Bay, does exist, from the
following considerations : From the want of trees
on the west side of Hudson's Bay, beyond a certain
latitude,—from the appearance of a certain ridge of
mountains lying near the same coast, and extending
in a direction parallel to it,—from the direct testimony of the Indians, which tends to prove, that

VOL. I.   B

---

* Besides the papers published by Purchas, Hackluyt,
Churchill, and those included in the published voyages of the
navigators who have embarked in the discovery, we have
works by Pickersgill, Goldson, and others, written exclusive-
ly on the subject.

they have seen the sea beyond the mountains, and
have observed vessels navigating therein ; and, most
particularly, from the nature and peculiarities observed in the tides.   This latter argument is by far
the most conclusive, and as such will alone be considered here.   Ellis sets out with the general principles, that in inland seas, having but small outlets,
there is little or no tide ; that in such places, what
tide there is rises highest in the inlet, where the
sea is narrowest, and becomes less and less considerable, in proportion as the sea expands within ; that
the highest tides in such situations, are occasioned
by winds blowing into the inland sea, in the direction of its strait communicating with the main
ocean, or in the direction of the course of the
tide on the exterior coast; and that the time
of high-water is soonest at places near the entrance of the inland sea, and progressively later
in other situations, according to their distance
from the strait through which the tide flows.
These facts, in the very small degree in which they
are observed, he derives from observations on the
winds and tides in the Baltic, Mediterranean, and
other inland seas.   From the application of these
principles, Ellis proceeds to shew, that every
circumstance with regard to the tides in Hudson's
Bay, is different from what would take place in
an inland sea ; and then concludes, that Hudson's Bay is not such a sea, but has some opening

which communicates with the frozen ocean on the
north-west. Just within the entrance of Hudson's
Strait, at Cary-Swan's-Nest, the tide was found by
Captain Fox to rise but six feet; whereas, on the
west side of the bay, where, from the great expansion of the waters, the tide, according to theory,
ought to have been scarcely perceptible, it rises in
different places ten, thirteen and seventeen feet. The
flood-tide on the west side of Hudson's Bay flows
towards the south; and the time of high-water is
soonest the farthest towards the north; both of
which circumstances, supposing Hudson's Bay to
be an inland sea, with only one entrance from the
east, should, Ellis conceives, according to the doc-
trines of tides, have been just the contrary. And,
lastly, the highest tides on both sides of Hudson's
Bay, are produced by north and north-west winds;
whereas, were it an inland sea, it is clear, that east
or south-east winds, blowing directly through the
strait, or in the direction of the flood-tide without,
would produce the highest tides. Hence he concludes, that the tide of flood flows into Hudson's
Bay, through some other entrance than that called
Hudson's Strait; not from Baffin's Bay either, because the tide is there inconsiderable; but from the
north-west, or from the icy sea *, by which conclu-

c 2

---

* It is not at all reasonable to suppose, that the considerable tides observed in Hudson's Bay should be occasioned by

sion, all the difficulties with regard to the tides are easily solved. How far Ellis may be correct, will, perhaps, be soon determined.

Other arguments which have been offered in favour of the separation of Greenland from America, are deduced from the existence of a current setting from the north,—from the circumstance of ice-bergs and drift wood being brought down by the current, —from whales wounded in the Spitzbergen seas having been caught in Davis' Strait,—from the position of the land, as represented on skins by the native American Indians, and from the occurrence of certain plants in Greenland, which are natives of Europe, but have never been found on any part of the American continent*.

As, however, it would take up too much of this work to enlarge on, or even to enumerate all the arguments founded on the nature of the tides, currents, ice, winds, country, &c. which have been brought forward to prove the existence of a northwest passage, I shall proceed to make a few general remarks on the probable advantages of such a discov-

---

the flood flowing through some strait communicating with Baffin's Bay, where the tide is so much less, unless this bay be connected with the Frozen Ocean ; as the tides, in penetrating an extensive sea, and pursuing a long circular course, must evidently be diminished, rather than increased.

* Quarterly Review, Nº xxxvi. p. 439.

ery, and to offer a few hints for conducting discoveries in these frozen regions.

I conceive the opinion to be quite incorrect, that if a passage were discovered, it would, probably, be open above half the year; for, supposing there really be a sea communication, near the parallel of 70°, between the southern part of Baffin's Bay, or the northern part of Hudson's Bay and Behring's Strait, it would not only, I believe, (judging from the known situations occupied by the ice, and the known coldness of these regions,) not be open above half the year, but, I imagine, it would be at intervals only of years that it would be open at all; and then, perhaps, for not longer than eight or ten weeks in a season. Hence, as affording a navigation to the Pacific Ocean, the discovery of a north-west passage could be of no service; for no one would have encouragement to attempt a passage, if the chance of succeeding were so small, for the sake only of the possibility of gaining a few months in an India voyage, when it could always be accomplished in the old way with so much more certainty. Nevertheless, the expectation of improving our geographical knowledge, and the possibility of discovering something which might lead to an extension of our commerce, as well as the prospect of discovering more of the nature of several physical phenomena, which are more observable in high latitudes than in any other part of the globe, and of extending our knowledge in the several branches of natural history, relating to polar countries; these, together with the popular feeling of curiosity, peculiarly attached to every thing connected with those remote and dangerous regions, are of themselves sufficient to render the examination of those interesting countries, an object worthy of the attention of a great nation.

The advantages that have already arisen to Britain, from the voyages hitherto undertaken in search of a north-west passage, are the establishment of the Davis' Straits whale-fishery, and of the trade of the Hudson's Bay Company; so that the expence incurred, though it has certainly been great and often fruitless, has not altogether been lost to the nation.

The adventurous spirit manifested by our early navigators, in performing such hazardous voyages in small barks, in which we should be scrupulous of trusting ourselves across the German Ocean, is calculated to strike us with surprise and admiration: while the correctness of the investigations resulting from their laborious exertions, notwithstanding the many disadvantages under which they were conducted, gives us a high opinion of their perseverance and talents. These two remarks are easily illustrated. The famous voyage of Baffin, in which the bay bearing his name was discovered, was performed in a vessel of only 55 tons burden; that of Hudson, in which, also, the bay called by his name was first navigated, in the very same vessel ; and the voyages of Davis, chiefly in vessels of 50, 35, and 10 tons burden. The recent voyage of Captain Ross into Baffin's Bay, has done a degree of credit to the memory of Baffin, by substantiating his accuracy and faithfulness which were begun to be disputed, and by showing them to be greater in extent than his most sanguine advocates could have expected.

Another observation which must be made by every reader of the voyages of our old navigators, and which must be particularly gratifying to those who consider religion as the chief business of this life, is the strain of piety and dependence on Divine Providence, which runs through almost every narrative. Their honest and laudable acknowledgments of a particular interference of the Almighty, in working out deliverance for them in times of difficulty and danger ; and their frequent declarations, expressive of their reliance upon Providence, for assistance and protection in their adventurous undertakings, are worthy of our imitation. Thus, while our modern voyagers are much in the habit of attributing their most remarkable deliverances to " luck," " chance" and " fortune," those of old evidenced certainly a more Christian-like feeling under such circumstances, by referring their deliverances to that Great Being from whom alone every good thing must be derived. They only who have a similar dependence on Providence, and who have been occasionally in try-

ing situations, can duly appreciate the confidence
and comfort which this belief is calculated to afford
under the most appalling circumstances.

The class of vessels best adapted for discovery in
the Polar Seas, seems to be that of 100 to 200 tons
burden.   All the great discoveries which have been
made in the neighbourhood of Greenland, have been
effected, it may be observed, in a description of
vessels still smaller ; which kind of ships, in some
respects, possesses a material advantage over that
of larger dimensions.   They are stronger, more
easily managed, in less danger of being stove or
crushed by ice, and are less expensive. But of these
advantages of a small vessel, the most important is
its greater comparative strength ; as ships become
weaker, it can easily be shown, as they increase in
magnitude.   A small sloop, carelessly and unscien-
tifically built, can lie aground with a full lading of
heavy goods on board, on a very uneven surface, and
yet sustain little or no injury ; nay, loaded sloops,
which have been driven on shore upon a sandy
beach, in a storm, accompanied with a heavy sea,
have sometimes been launched or floated off without having sustained any material damage; whereas a frigate or a line-of-battle ship, though built of
the strongest materials, and in the most scientific
manner, if laid aground in the very best situation,
and under the most favourable circumstances, is of-

ten ruined. The fact is, that the materials of which the largest vessels are built, are only of the same strength as those used in the construction of the smallest, while the timbers and planks in a line-of-battle ship, when compared with those of a small vessel, are by no means of a thickness proportionate to its tonnage. Hence a large vessel, however firmly built, can never possess the same comparative strength as a small one. Besides, the momentum of a large heavy vessel striking a rock, a mass of ice, or other similar body with a given velocity, is so much greater than that of a small ship, that the difference of the shock is vastly greater than the difference of the strength of the two. Thus, we will suppose, the weight of two vessels with their ballast and stores, one of 400 tons and another of 100 tons burden, to be proportionate to their tonnage, and that they both strike an immoveable mass of ice with the same velocity, say, six miles *per* hour. Then the momentum of the former will be represented by the number 24, and of the latter by 6, or as four to one, being in the same relation as their tonnage. But the comparative difference of strength of the two, we know, will probably be not greater than as two to one; consequently, the capability of the smaller vessel for resisting the concussion, will be twice as great as that of the larger; or, in other words, the vessel of 100 tons burden, would bear a blow impinged with a velocity of eight miles *per* hour, as well as the larger

one would bear a stroke given under half that velocity. With regard to pressure between two sheets
of ice, it is clear, that a large vessel would have an
advantage over a small one, were it not that a small
vessel, if of a proper construction, often rises, when
squeezed, several feet above her usual floating-mark,
while a large heavy ship, under the same circumstances, remains nearly fixed, and is, consequently,
much more compressed.

In the perilous and remarkably disastrous voyage
performed by Captain James, in the years 1631
and 1632, when he wintered in Hudson's Bay, the
smallness of his vessel affording an extraordinary
degree of strength, compared with a larger vessel,
was the means of saving himself and his crew under
a variety of dangers. This vessel, of only 70 tons
burden, endured six or seven such beatings against
rocks and ice, as would doubtless have occasioned the
destruction of almost any vessel of such a size as
was lately employed for discovery in the Polar regions *. Captain James's little vessel, besides enduring its full share of heavy storms and high
seas, both under sail in the main ocean, and at
anchor in shallow water ; besides beating and driving about among ice for twenty days together, and
lying all winter, full of water, on an uneven and

* The four vessels equipped for discovery in the year 1818,
were from 250 to 380 tons burden.

stony beach,—was two or three times exposed to a dreadful beating from ice, agitated by a heavy sea, and was four times on shore upon rocks, during strong winds or considerable swells, in one of which instances, she was left by the tide hanging on the point of a sharp rock, so that the greatest apprehension was excited that she would upset; yet, after passing through all this uncommon series of dangers, the little bark took home its crew in safety *.

Hence, it is evident, that a vessel intended for discovery in the Polar Seas, should be just large enough for conveying the requisite stores and provisions, and for affording comfortable accommodation to the navigators, but no larger. Perhaps a vessel of about 150 tons burden, would be fully sufficient to answer every purpose.

The numerous disasters to which Captain James was exposed, are to be attributed to his total ignorance of the nature of the ice, and of the countries which he explored; and to his having refused, on his outset, to take along with him any persons, who, in these respects, were better informed than himself. But he soon had occasion to regret his want of practical knowledge of these peculiar regions, his deficiency in which led him into numerous difficulties. His

---

* Captain James's voyage is included in Churchill's " Collection of Voyages ;" in Clarke's " Naufragia," &c. The original edition was published by the command of King Charles I. in 1633.

first mistake, was to get entangled among the ice lying about Cape Farewell, where he had nearly lost his vessel ; and his subsequent errors were also productive of many distresses. It is strange, that any one should have imagined, that unacquaintance with the country intended to be explored, could be of advantage to the voyager. The navigation of the Polar seas, which is peculiar, requires in a particular manner, an extensive knowledge of the nature, properties, and usual motions of the ice ; and it can only be performed to the best advantage, by those who have had long experience in working a ship in icy situations. It may be remarked, in support of this assertion, that all the great discoveries to the north and west of Greenland, have been made by persons well acquainted with the navigation of the arctic seas. Baffin, when he discovered the bay bearing his name, and boldly traversed it with only one small bark, had been employed on three several voyages of discovery before, as well as on one or more voyages to the Spitzbergen whale-fishery. Davis and Hudson also had each had experience in the navigation of these seas, before they made discoveries of any consequence ; Hudson, we know, having been three voyages on discovery, and Davis two, before they found the straits and bay which are still called by their names*.

---

* Want of experience in the navigation of icy seas, is the only objection to Officers of the Royal Navy having the direc-

It might be a material assistance to those employed in completing the examination of Baffin's Bay, as well as productive of some interesting information in meteorological phenomena, were a vessel or two to remain in the northern part of this bay during the winter. Vessels having to penetrate the ice from the main sea in the usual way, cannot probably obtain a passage into the Bay before the middle or end of the month of July, when the season is so far advanced, that if the navigators intend to return, they can only calculate upon an interval of six or eight weeks, before it will be prudent for them to make their escape out of the Bay. But by wintering in the northern part of the Bay, there is little doubt but that the vessel would be released by the ice as early as May or June, and thus be afforded about double the time for research that could be obtained by wintering out of the Bay ; at

---

tion of expeditions intended for discovery in the arctic regions. No one has a higher opinion of the nautical skill and bravery of our naval commanders than I have, (having myself served some time in the Navy, and witnessed their talents,)—yet I cannot yield the palm to them for that description of talent requisite for performing to the best advantage the navigation among ice. No officer, I believe, would expect to equal the river pilots, or the masters of the Gravesend boats, in working their little vessels up or down the Thames ;—for no judgment, however profound,—no talent, however acute, could supersede the necessity of practice for performing this navigation with the beauty and correctness with which it is accomplished by these practised pilots and boatmen.

least, such we know would be the case in other similar parts of the Polar countries. In Hudson's
Bay, for instance, the ice clears away from the northern shore long before the southern part is at all
accessible * ; and at Spitzbergen, though the sea
should be so encumbered with ice as to prevent our
approaching its coasts beyond the 76th degree of
latitude until the end of May or beginning of June,
yet near the western and northern parts of the
shore, there is usually a navigable sea much earlier.
There would not, I imagine, be any very great
danger in making this experiment, provided a sufficient quantity of fresh provisions for the prevention
of the scurvy among the crew were taken out †, and
certain precautions for the preservation of the ships
adopted. An ingenious apparatus now in use at
Leith, invented by Mr Thomas Morton, ship-
builder, and for which he has recently taken out
a patent, might, I think, be made use of to advantage by any vessel proceeding to distant regions on
discovery. A trifling damage sustained by a ship
employed in such a voyage, is often sufficient for
putting a stop to any further research ; but the use

---

* See Ellis's Voyage to Hudson's Bay, p. 321.

† Fresh provisions certainly form one of the best preventives
of the scurvy, and may be taken out in any quantity to the
polar countries, without any preparation whatever ; the action
of the cold to which they soon become exposed, preventing
putrefaction.

of Mr Morton's apparatus would afford the means of repairing every ordinary damage in almost any country. The contrivance consists of a simple frame of wood, adapted for supporting a vessel in an upright position, traversing on a kind of rail-way, fixed on an inclined plane at the margin of a river or the sea, and extending from above the reach of the tide down to the low-water mark. This frame being launched into the sea, as far as the lower end of the rail-way, receives the vessel upon it at high-water, when, by the use of blocks or chocks of wood placed on the sides of the frame, moveable by means of ropes towards the centre, the vessel is supported in an upright position, and then, by the application of a mechanical purchase, consisting of a combination of wheels and axles, constituting a powerful winch, the frame and the contained vessel are drawn up together on dry land. With this apparatus, a vessel of 200 to 300 tons burden, might be taken, by 12 or 18 men, entirely beyond the reach of the tide in the course of about an hour *. The advantage of such an apparatus in a vessel bound to the

* The intention of Mr Morton's invention is to supersede the necessity of dry docks, over which it possesses several advantages. An apparatus calculated for taking up a vessel of 300 tons burden, can be built for the sum of 500l. or 600l ; and, when once fixed, vessels can be taken up for an expence of 25s. to 30s. ; whereas the common charge for putting a ship into a graving-dock, is, in some places, as high as 10l.

Polar regions on discovery, might be very great, provided, in the place where there should prove a necessity for using it, the rise of tide should be sufficient for admitting its application, and the beach should be of a sloping nature. It could be prepared in short pieces, so as to be fitted together with screws; and though intended for sustaining the weight of a ship, would be by no means very cumbrous. Indeed, any vessel of 200 tons burden or upward, might easily carry it out in her hold, without materially, if at all, interfering with the room requisite for her stores. Thus a vessel having occasion to winter in Baffin's Bay or Davis' Strait, would require only the adjustment of the frame and *ways*, which three or four skilful mechanics might effect in a few days, before she could be hauled up on dry land, quite beyond the reach of either ice or tides, where she would constitute as comfortable a dwelling as could be expected in such a country. The apparatus could even be applied where there was not a fall of tide equal to the depth of water drawn by the vessel, by the use of a small coffer-dam, sufficient only to stop out the tide at low-water, until the rail-way should be adjusted so far down that at high-water the vessel could float upon the frame while resting on the rail-way. Then the force of the ship's company would be amply sufficient for drawing the vessel up on land.

In seas perpetually encumbered with ice, and probably crowded with islands, if not divided by necks of land, the chance of great discoveries and of extensive navigations toward the north-west, even under the best arrangements, and under the boldest seamen, is but small. The most certain method of ascertaining the existence of a communication between the Atlantic and Pacific, along the northern face of America, would doubtless be by journeys on land. Men there are, who, being long used to travel upon snow in the service of the Hudson's Bay Company, would readily undertake the journey from the interior lakes of North America to the Frozen Ocean, or, in case of a continuity of land being found, to the very Pole itself; of whose success we should certainly have a reasonable ground of hope. The practicability of this mode of making discoveries has been fully proved by the journeys of Mackenzie and Hearne ; and the possibility of performing very long journeys on snow, can be attested, from personal experience, by any persons who have wintered a few times in Hudson's Bay. The mode of travelling in these northern countries, is peculiar. A long journey can best be performed when the ground is covered with snow. In this case, each traveller is provided with a pair of snowshoes, and a sledge of eight to twelve feet in length, and one foot in breadth, on which, all the apparatus and provisions requisite for the journey, are drawn by hand. Sometimes dogs are used to assist in drawing the sledges ; but as the travellers are

apt to fall short of provision for them, they cannot-
place absolute dependance on their continued help.
Without the use of dogs, a strong experienced traveller can perform, on an average, about twenty
miles a-day, dragging after him 100 to 150 pounds
weight of articles upon his sledge.   When the surface of the snow is frozen and firm, he can occasionally accomplish forty miles in a day, but this requires an effort too laborious to be continued for
many days together.   The best opportunity for
passing these almost desert countries, is when the
ground is covered with snow ; the best time of
the year, perhaps in the spring months ; and the
most favourable hour, from one or two in the
morning until sun-rise.   After sun-rise, the surface
of the snow is apt to become soft, on which the
further progress of the traveller is suspended ; he
then rests until the evening, or until the following
morning, when the snow having become encrusted
with ice, he advances with ease and celerity.   If
he finds himself much pinched with cold when he
rests, he sets out and walks until the proper heat
of his body is restored, then refreshing himself with
a little nourishment, composes himself to sleep. He
must *bivouac* on the snow.   Here, without shelter
from hut or tent, he rests, if not as comfortably, at
least as contentedly, as those accustomed to more re-
finement can, in their well-arranged couches. He
usually hollows out a place in the snow to sleep in, and

on the windward side places his sledges on their
edges for a defence against the wind ; then laying
down a few twigs of bushes or trees, when he can
meet with them, in place of a bed, he wraps himself in his blanket, covers himself with his upper
garments, which he makes a practice of throwing
off when he rests, and enjoys his repose. The
principal articles provided by the experienced traveller for his subsistence, consist of tea, oatmeal,
bacon, bread, and sometimes a few fish or fowls, but
no spirits ; and whenever he finds it necessary to
use artificial stimuli for accelerating the circulation
of the blood, and promoting the heat of the system,
instead of resorting to spiritous liquors, knowing
them to be injurious, he drinks freely of warm tea,
which the plentifulness of wood for fire in the interior of North America, generally affords him a
ready opportunity of preparing. His relish, with
his tea, consists of a bit of broiled bacon, and
perhaps a little oatmeal porridge ; which articles,
when other supplies of fowl, fish or quadruped, fail,
being effectual for his nourishment, he lives on
with contentment. With these measures and re-
sources, travelling usually in the night or morning, and bivouacking on the snow ; subsisting,
when necessary, on the scanty provision taken
out with him, but always depending on occasional supplies of birds, fishes and quadrupeds,
which seldom wholly desert these countries ; and

directing his route by the compass, with the assistance generally of Indian guides, he performs journeys of 1000 or 1500 miles in the course of two
or three months.   The *ptarmigans* or willow-partridges, which are generally plentiful in winter near
Hudson's Bay; the musk-oxen, the wild buffaloes,
the rein-deer, and the hares, which are found in certain situations throughout the northern parts of
America, even to the Frozen Ocean, together with
the quantity of fishes which occur in almost every
river and lake, afford a tolerably regular supply of
provisions *.

---

* The willow-partridges are caught in a very simple way.
They are attracted by an artificial surface of gravel spread on
a hillock of snow, on sight of which, these birds requiring
this article for assisting digestion in the winter time, when
they feed on the tops of the willows, descend in large flocks
upon it with precipitation : A net extended by poles is erected near the edge of the surface of gravel, and a string connected with the props by which it is supported, is held by a
person on watch in any neighbouring cover, who, on observing a sufficient number of birds on the gravel, pulls away the
supports of the net, so that it falls upon them, and often en-
tangles above fifty at *a haul*.   In this way 200 or 300 birds
have frequently been taken in a winter's morning.   Hares are
commonly taken with snares, sometimes to the amount of
forty or fifty in a night;—the oxen, buffaloes and deer are
hunted or shot;—and fishes are caught with nets extended beneath a surface of ice in a lake or across a river, or taken
by a baited hook introduced into a small hole made in the ice,
which, to be effectual, is kept in continual motion.

The plan of performing a journey in this way, for discovering the northern termination of the American Continent, and for tracing it round to its junction with the coasts of the same country washed by the Atlantic, might be in some measure as follows. The party intended for this expedition, which should consist of as few individuals as possible, ought, perhaps, in the course of one summer, to make their way to one of the interior settlements of the Hudson's Bay Company, or of the Canadian traders, such as Slave Fort, on the Great Slave Lake, situated in the 62d degree of latitude, or Fort Chepewyan, near the Athapescow Lake, in latitude 58° 40', from whence Sir Alexander Mackenzie embarked on his voyage to the Frozen Ocean ; and there abide during the first winter. Supposing the travellers to winter at Slave Fort, they might calculate on being within the distance of 200 leagues, or thirty or forty days journey, moderate travelling, of the Frozen Ocean *. In the month of March

---

* Mackenzie performed his voyage from the western angle of the Great Slave Lake to the island in latitude 69° 14', which formed the termination of his navigation towards the north, in fourteen days. Here, if not actually in the frozen ocean, he was evidently very near it, and in a sea communicating with it, of which we have full proof, from his having observed traces of Esquimaux, fragments of whalebone, boats covered with skins, and most particularly from the circumstance of his having seen several white-whales, (*Balæna albicans,*) animals which, though common in the rivers of Hudson's Bay, are never seen far from the sea.

or April, the party consisting of two or three Europeans, one or two Esquimaux interpreters, and two or more Indian guides, provided with every thing requisite for the undertaking, might set out towards the north. The bad effects to be apprehended from the enmity known to exist between the Indian and Esquimaux, would probably be prevented, by having persons of each nation along with them ; indeed, that enmity, which was a few years ago so implacable, and of which such a horrid instance was witnessed by Hearne in the year 1771, is now, happily, considerably assuaged *.

On the arrival of the travellers among the Esquimaux, their Indian guides, from fear of this nation, would probably desert them, but the presence of their Esquimaux interpreters would secure them a good reception. When once they should meet with these people, they would have a strong evidence of their being near the sea, as it is well

---

* Between the Indians and the Esquimaux a mortal enmity used to exist. An Indian who was unfortunate in losing his friends, or in suffering any other particular calamity, was in the habit of superstitiously attributing it to the agencies or witcheries of the Esquimaux: to revenge himself, therefore, and to soften the anger of his tutelar deity, he thought it necessary to engage in an " Esquimaux hunt," and thus glut his vile passion for bloodshed, by destroying a certain number of these unoffending people. This horrid practice, however, is now, from the advance of civilization, rapidly sinking into disuse.

known the Esquimaux never retire far from the coast. This is a strong confirmation that the waters seen both by Hearne and Mackenzie, were arms of the sea. On their arrival at the coast, it would be necessary to associate with the Esquimaux, to submit in some measure to their mode of living; and to effect any considerable discovery, it might be requisite to spend a winter or two among them; in which case they might trace the line of the Frozen Ocean to such a length, that the place where it joins the western coasts of Baffin's Bay, or Hudson's Bay, or the eastern side of Greenland, would be determined. Or, if it should be objectionable wintering among the Esquimaux, several expeditions might be sent out at the same time from different stations, and on different meridians. One, for instance, might start from the north-western part of Hudson's Bay, and proceed to the north-west, and another from the same place towards the north; a third might start from the Slave Lake towards the north-east; and a fourth from the same station towards the north or north-west; the expence of all which would probably be less than that of one expedition by sea. We have several proofs of the practicability of this plan;—from the journeys which the settlers at Hudson's Bay and the North American Indians frequently make; from the voyage of Mackenzie, and the journeys of Hearne; and from the willingness of persons well acquainted with the nature and dangers of the enterprise, to undertake it *.

SECT. IV.

Remarks on the Opinion of a Sea Communication between the Atlantic and Pacific Oceans, by the North Pole.

THE scheme suggested by Robert Thorne of Bristol, of finding a passage to India across the North Pole, about the year 1527, appears to have been immediately attempted, by an expedition con-

---

* I have conversed with some persons who have performed journeys of above 1000 miles, over a surface of snow, during the winter, in the way above described, and who would not be unwilling to undertake an expedition for making discoveries in the Frozen Ocean.

Since this sheet was sent to press, I have learned with satisfaction, from authority which is unquestionable, that Government, in concert with the Hudson's Bay Company, have taken measures for the immediate investigation of the coast of the Frozen Ocean, from the mouth of the Copper Mine River, eastward to Hudson's Bay, or Baffin's Bay, or other coast, with which it may, on examination, be found to be connected. Lieutenant Franklin, it is said, accompanied by persons experienced in the modes of travelling in that country, is to be employed on this interesting service. From this officer's known zeal and activity, and from the promising character of this mode of making discoveries, the most satisfactory results are to be anticipated ; for, whatever progress may be made in tracing the shores of the Frozen Ocean to the eastward, will be a certain step towards the completion of the discoveries which have excited such uncommon interest.

sisting of two ships, sent out by order of Henry VIII. One of the ships, we are informed, was lost: of the nature of the success of the other, we have but a very unsatisfactory account *.

After this voyage, Barentz, Heemskerke and Ryp, attempted the trans-polar navigation in 1596; Hudson in 1607; Jonas Poole in 1610 and 1611; Baffin and Fotherby in 1614; Fotherby in 1615; Phipps in 1773, and Buchan and Franklin in 1818.

The highest latitude attained by any of these navigators, did not, it would appear, exceed 81°. Hudson's highest latitude by observation, was 80° 23'. Poole's greatest latitude attained, was 79° 50' on his first voyage, and about 80° on his second. Baffin and Fotherby reached about 80° 16'. Captain Phipps 80° 48', and Captain Buchan about 80° 20'. My Father, in the ship Resolution of Whitby, in the year 1806, with whom I then served as chief-mate, sailed to a much higher latitude than any of these voyagers already enumerated. Our latitude, on three occasions, in the month of May, as derived

---

* Hackluyt's Voyages, vol. iii. p. 129. One of the ships employed in this service was called the *Dominus Vobiscum;* but as to the names of the voyagers we have no account. From the bare information Hackluyt was able to collect, it would appear that the endeavours of the commanders had been directed more towards the north-west than towards the North Pole, though the latter appears evidently to have been the original design of the voyage.

from observations taken with a sextant by myself
and my father, was 80° 50′ 28″, 81° 1′ 53″, and 81°
12′ 42″ ; after which, we sailed so far to the northward, as made it about 81° 30′ ; which is one of the
closest approximations to the Pole which I conceive
has been well authenticated. The Honourable
Daines Barrington, it is true, informs us, in his dis-
cussion on " the probability of reaching the North
Pole," of several vessels having sailed much farther
towards the north.   In his first two papers, of " instances of navigators who have reached high northern
latitudes," he produces four examples of vessels having sailed to latitude $81\frac{1}{2}$° ; seven to 82° or upward ;
three to 83° or more ; six vessels in company to 86° ;
three examples to 88° ; two ships in company to 89°,
and one to $89\frac{1}{2}$° *, besides several others brought forward in his later papers. But with regard to these examples, I may observe, that all the instances of navigations having been performed beyond the 84th degree, are given from very loose authority, such as
the vague reports of the Dutch whale-fishers ; and
in no case, I believe, from the direct communications of the voyagers themselves.   As such, I
conceive, there is no reliance whatever to be placed
upon these extraordinary instances.   It may not,
however, be so easy to get rid of the accounts of
ships having sailed as far as 82° or 83°, the instances being so very numerous, and some of them so

---

" * Miscellanies," p. 1,–40,

very particular ; but still, there is room for some remarks on them. It may be observed, that though
the latitudes in some of the cases noted by Barrington, are said to have been derived from celestial
observations, yet it appears, that they all, or nearly so,
were given from memory, by the persons who themselves performed the voyages, or by others who had
had intercourse with them. But with regard to those
accounts, communicated by the voyagers who had
themselves made the observations, we find, that
above half of them were from oral testimony only,
at the distance of eighteen to thirty years, from the
time when the several navigations were performed.

Hence, the faithfulness of their memories, after a
lapse of so many years, may reasonably be question-
ed. One of the most modern instances, indeed,
may be objected to, on very good grounds. Captain
Clarke is said to have sailed to 81½°, and Captain
Bateson to 82° 15′, in the year 1773*. Now, this
was the year in which Captain Phipps proceeded
on discovery towards the North Pole, who, notwithstanding he made apparently every exertion, and
exposed his ships in no common degree ; though he
repeatedly traced the face of the northern ice from
the longitude of 2° E., where the ice began to trend
to the southward, to 20° E., where he was so dangerously involved, was never able to proceed beyond

---

* BARRINGTON's " Miscellanies," p. 38 and 41.

80° 48′ N., and even that length only once in the
season.   Is it reasonable, therefore, to suppose, that
whale-fishers, sailing in clear water, without any
particular object to induce them to proceed far towards the north, should exceed the length to which
Captain Phipps attained in the same year, and
within a few days of the same time, by eighty-seven
miles towards the north ?   I imagine, on the contrary, that both Captain Clarke and Captain Bateson had been mistaken in their latitude, and had
not been so far as Captain Phipps, or at least not
farther.   But I by no means wish to infer, that all
the cases brought forward in Barrington's Miscellanies are equally objectionable, or that no voyager
has ever sailed beyond the latitude of 81° or 82°;
though I feel persuaded, that, among the numerous
instances produced to prove this point, few of them
can be relied on.   The prevailing desire, indeed,
to communicate extraordinary circumstances, has a
tendency, in some measure, to bias the judgment of
the most candid person, and has, no doubt, occasioned very many exaggerated statements ; for all navigators who have proceeded to a very great extent
into any unknown region, especially where they
have little opportunity of determining their real situation, naturally give the farthest point in their
opinion, when they are in doubt, rather than the
nearest.   Even so late as the year 1817, we have a
striking illustration of this fact.   The Larkins of

Leith, which succeeded in the whale-fishery in Baffin's Bay, at an unusual season, and in an unusual latitude, was reported, on her arrival in Britain, even, I believe, by the master himself, to have been as high as 80° in Baffin's Bay; but on minute inquiry being made, as to the authority on which the Captain founded the belief of his having been to so high a latitude, and so far beyond what was supposed to have constituted the limits of the Bay, he could only declare with full confidence, that he had been to about 77°*. Now, had this circumstance passed over unnoticed for fifteen or twenty years, as was the case with the greater number of the instances quoted by Barrington, the master of the Larkins himself, though without the least design to deceive, would, in all probability, have stated it as a fact, and would have believed his own statement to have been correct, that he had actually proceeded as far as the latitude of 80°. Many other illustrations might be brought forward, of the tendency to add to any thing extraordinary, rather than to detract; so that persons relating the same circumstance occasionally through a series of years, and thus preserving the recollection of the story as they last communicated it, though they might have long forgotten the original event, have, by the most trifling, and at the time apparently unimportant additions,

---

* Quarterly Review, No. xxxv. p. 212.

been carried at last to the most extravagant lengths.
And that they themselves believe to be true what
they communicate, can be shown, from the circumstance of their not scrupling to tell the story in the
presence of persons, who, they well knew, were joint-
ly with themselves, observers of the original fact.
Such cases I have often met with; and such have
probably been noticed by almost every person who
has attended to things of this nature. Hence, the
uncertainty of oral testimony.

However dubious we may be of receiving the accounts brought forward by the Honourable Daines
Barrington, to prove the occasional accessibility of the
83d or 84th parallel of north latitude, to enterprising voyagers, of this, I conceive, we may be assured, that the opinion of an open sea round the
Pole, is altogether chimerical. We must allow,
indeed, that when the atmosphere is free from
clouds, the influence of the sun, notwithstanding
its obliquity, is, on the surface of the earth or sea,
about the time of the summer solstice, greater
at the Pole, by nearly one-fourth, than at the
equator*. Hence it is urged, that this extraordinary power of the sun, destroys all the ice generated in the winter season, and renders the temperature of the Pole, warmer and more congenial to feeling, than it is in some places lying nearer the equa-

* Edinburgh Review, No. LIX. p. 11.

tor. Now, if it be admitted, that the influence of the sun at the time of the summer solstice be nearly one-fourth greater at the Pole than it is at the equator, it must be allowed, from the same principle, that this influence in the parallel of 78°, where it is only about one forty-fifth part less than what it is at the Pole*, must also be considerably greater than at the equator; and, therefore, that whatever effects are produced by the sun's peculiar action at the Pole, the same, in a proportionate degree, must be felt at the parallel of 78°. We shall endeavour to ascertain, whether the presence of the sun during several months together in the Spitzbergen sea, produces any thing like the effect presumed by the advocates of an open sea at the Pole.

From various meteorological calculations, founded on a careful investigation of the laws of tempera-

---

* As the solar influence is proportional to the sines of the sun's altitude, the power of the sun at the Pole, is to its power at the same time in any other latitude where it does not set, as the sine of the sun's altitude at the Pole, is to half the sum of the sines of the sun's greatest and least altitude during the day in the other latitude referred to, nearly. Thus the solar influence at the Pole at the solstice, on a given horizontal surface, represented by the number 1, is equivalent to the sine of $23\frac{1}{2}$, the sun's altitude (the multiplier in this case being 1, and divider or radius being also 1) or 3988. And in the latitude of 78°, the sine of $35\frac{1}{2}$, the sun's greatest altitude or 5807, added to the sine or $11\frac{1}{2}$, the sun's least altitude or 1994, and the amount divided by 2, gives 3900, for the solar influence at the solstice in latitude 78°; which is less by about $\frac{1}{45}$th part, than the solar influence at the Pole, but greater than it is at the Equator.

ture, it has been deduced by Professor Kirwan, that the means of temperature of the months of May, June and July, in latitude 78°, are respectively as high as 37°, 51°.5, 50°.5, and the mean of the year 33°.2 or, according to other meteorologists 34°.2, notwithstanding no allowance appears to have been made for the supposed extraordinary power of the sun when continually above the horizon. But from calculations founded on twelve years observations on the temperature of the icy regions, I have determined the mean temperature of the month of May, latitude 78°, to be 22°.5, of June 31°.4, of July 37°; and of the whole year 17°, being below the temperatures calculated, by 14°.5 in May, 20°.1 in June, 13°.5 in July, and 16° or 17° in the mean annual temperature *. Hence, so far from the actual influence of the sun, though acknowledged at a certain season to be greater at the Pole than at the Equator, being above what it is calculated to be by the ordinary formulæ for temperature, it is found in latitude 78° to be greatly below it,—how then can the temperature of the Pole be expected to be so very different ? From the remarks in the ensuing pages it will be shown, that ice is annually formed during nine months of the year in the Spitzbergen sea ; and that neither calm weather, nor the proximity

---

* Appendix No. I., contains the whole series of Meteorological Tables for the year 1807 to 1818 inclusive ; from whence these results, as included in No. II., are derived.

of land, is essential for its formation. Can it then
be supposed, that at the Pole, where the mean annual temperature is probably as low as 10°*, that
the sea is not full of ice? And as the quantity of
ice dissolved every summer near Spitzbergen, by
the action of the sun only, is very small when compared with the quantity that is there generated,—
can it be imagined, that the whole quantity generated at the Pole during the year should be dissolved by the power of the sun in the course of
two or three summer months? Were the mean
temperature of the Pole, indeed, above the freezing
point of sea-water, that is, as high as 31° or 32°, as it
is usually estimated, and the mean heat of latitude
78° as high as 33° or 34°, then the circumpolar seas
would have a chance of being free from ice; but
while the temperature of the former can be shown
to be about 18°, and the latter 11° below the freezing temperature of the sea, we can have no reasonable ground, I conceive, for doubting the continual presence of ice in all the regions immediately surrounding the Pole †.

VOL. I.   D

* See Appendix, No. II.

† Should there be land near the Pole, portions of open
water, or perhaps even considerable seas, might be produced by the action of the current sweeping away the ice from
one side of it almost as fast as it could be formed; and vacan-

Though the extent to which our early navigators attained in their attempts to reach the Pole, may be a little doubtful, yet the limit to which the Polar Seas are now navigable towards the north, will have a fair chance of being determined, in consequence of the alteration which has been made in the act of Parliament offering a reward of 5000 *l.* to the person who shall first sail beyond the 89th degree of north latitude. This premium was first offered by act 16th Geo. III. c. 6.; but though it has now been in force 43 years, it has never produced any discovery, nor even, perhaps, a single attempt. The reason is obvious. No one employed in the whale-fishery, who had the opportunity, would hazard his life, his property, and the success of his voyage, in seeking after a reward which he had every reason to believe was quite beyond his reach; especially as he well knew, that although he should sail to within a few miles of the extent, which would entitle him to the premium, and there be interrupted by some insurmountable obstacle, yet he could have no claim on the reward. Hence, while he considered the prize as beyond his reach, the adventurous voyager had no stimulus to lead him forward;

---

cies in such a case might also be produced on the leeward side of the land during any powerful and continued winds; but the existence of land only, I imagine, can encourage an expectation of any of the sea northward of Spitzbergen being annually free from ice.

whereas, had a proportionate reward been offered
for a proportionate success, he would have had every
encouragement to make the attempt. In the session of 1818, this subject was brought before Parliament, and the law respecting rewards for discoveries in the Polar Seas, &c. underwent revi-
sion, and was modified and improved by the passing of a new act. After the nomination of
" commissioners for discovering the longitude at
sea," and for " judging all proposals, experiments
and improvements relating to the same, and for
rewarding persons making useful discoveries and
improvements in or connected with navigation,"—
this act offers encouragements for the discovery
of the longitude, and other useful inventions tending towards the improvement of navigation, and
then gives the regulations and conditions on
which rewards may be claimed for finding a northern passage into the Pacific, and for approaching within a degree of the North Pole, or for accomplishing certain proportions of the said passage,
or approach. The act still offers a reward of
20,000 *l.* to the owners of such ship or ships, if belonging to subjects, or to the commanders, officers,
seamen and marines, of such ships, if belonging to
his Majesty, which shall first find out and sail
through any passage between the Atlantic and
Pacific Oceans, in any direction or parallel of the
Northern Hemisphere *.   And a reward of 5000 *l.*

_____

* Act 58th Geo. III. c. 20. § 10.

to the owner of any merchant vessel, or to the commander, &c. of any King's ship, which shall first approach within one degree of the Northern Pole, ($ 11).
It then provides for the reward of certain partially
successful attempts, permitting commissioners, by
memorial, to " propose to his Majesty in Council
to direct proportionate rewards to be paid to such
persons who shall first have accomplished certain
proportions of the said passage or approach," and
then directs, that if his Majesty shall sanction the
said proposal, " the same shall be published in the
London Gazette; and any person accomplishing
such passages, or the specified proportions of them,
shall be entitled, on the award of the commissioners, to receive such total or proportionate sums as
may have been offered *," ($ 12.)

Since the passing of this act, the commissioners
appointed by Parliament have arranged two scales
of premiums for discoveries towards the North
Pole, and north-west, which have received the sanction of his Royal Highness the Prince Regent, and

---

* By the next section commissioners are authorised to take
such measures as shall satisfy themselves of the correctness of such claims for rewards, on the subject of discovery, as shall be made upon them; and being fully satisfied
with the examination and proof offered, they are authorised to
pay the said rewards, or such proportion of them as the claim-
ant may under this act, or such order in Council, be entitled
to receive.—Act 58th Geo. III. c. 20. § 13.

have been published in the London Gazette accordingly *. They are to the following effect:

" 1. To the first ship belonging to any of his Majesty's subjects, or to his Majesty, that shall proceed to the longitude of 110° west, or the mouth of Hearne's or Coppermine River, by sailing within the Arctic circle, 5000*l.*; to 130° west, or the Whale Island of Mackenzie, 10,000 *l.*; to 150° west, by sailing westward, within the Arctic circle, 15,000 *l.*; to the Pacific Ocean, by a north-west passage, as before allotted, the full reward of 20,000 *l.*

" 2. To the first ship, as aforesaid, that shall sail to 83° of north latitude, 1000 *l.*; to 85°, 2000 *l.*; to 87°, 3000 *l.*; to 88°, 4000 *l.*; and to 89°, as before allotted, the full reward of 5000 *l.*"

As this scale for discoveries towards the North Pole, commences with a latitude which there may be at least a hope of attaining, there will be no doubt of attempts being made to penetrate to the farthest navigable point, and of that extreme accessible point being soon ascertained.

---

* The memorial of the commissioners, presented to the Prince Regent, includes the remark, " That the progress of discovery has (it appears) already advanced on the eastern coast of America, and within the Arctic circle, as far as 90° west longitude, or thereabouts, from Greenwich;" but that " northwards it has not yet arrived, according to any well authenticated accounts, so far as 81° of north latitude."— (*London Gazette,* 23d March 1819). This corresponds with what has been advanced in the foregoing pages, respecting the instances of high navigations, given in Barrington's Miscellanies.

If the masses of ice which usually prevent the advance of navigators beyond the 82d degree of north latitude, be extended in a continued series to the Pole, (of which, unless there be land in the way, I have no doubt),—the expectation of reaching the Pole by sea, must be altogether chimerical. But though the access by sea be effectually intercepted, I yet imagine, notwithstanding the objections which have been urged against the scheme, that it would by no means be impossible to reach the Pole by travelling across the ice from Spitzbergen. This project having been given at some length in the Memoirs of the Wernerian Society *, it may be unnecessary here to repeat the arguments in favour of its practicability. Yet it might not be well to dismiss the subject without a few brief remarks. As the journey would not exceed 1200 miles, (600 miles each way), it might be performed on sledges drawn by dogs or rein-deer, or even on foot †. Foot-travellers would require to draw the apparatus and provisions necessary for the undertaking, on sledges by hand ; and in this way, with good despatch, the journey would occupy at least two months; but with the assistance of dogs, it might

---

Vol. ii. p. 328.

† When the paper on the Polar Ice, in which this project is included, was presented to the Wernerian Society, I was not aware of the extensive journeys, occasionally performed on snow without the assistance of any quadruped, which have recently come to my knowledge.

probably be accomplished in a little less time. With favourable winds, great advantage might be derived from sails set upon the sledges ; which sails, when the travellers were at rest, would serve for the erection of tents. Small vacancies in the ice would not prevent the journey, as the sledges could be adapted so as to answer the purpose of boats ; nor would the usual unevenness of the ice, or the depth or softness of the snow, be an insurmountable difficulty, as journeys of near equal length, and under similar inconveniencies, have been accomplished.

The Russian adventurers who occasionally proceed from Archangel and neighbouring places to Spitzbergen, and spend the winter in this dreary country, for the purpose of taking sea-horses, seals, and other animals frequenting the coast, have been supposed, from their uncommon opportunities for observation, capable of giving an opinion of much weight, on the practicability of the journey to the Pole. As such, Colonel Beaufoy (who it seems entertained the same opinion as myself, that the only access to the Pole was by a journey over the ice) proposed to them several judicious queries on this subject, with others on the nature of the climate at Spitzbergen in winter, their replies to which were altogether discouraging *. But these men, it may be observed,

---

* These queries, with their answers, which are uncommonly interesting, first appeared in Dr Thomson's Annals of Philosophy, vol. ix. p. 381. ; and were afterwards (in 1818) reprinted in a small volume, including Barrington's Polar Tracts.

who know little or nothing of the nature of field-ice, must be less adequate judges of the practicability of the scheme than any of the whale-fishers; as it is in expectation that field-ice would be met with throughout, that renders the project feasible. On the kind of ice, indeed, which occurs generally on the coast of Spitzbergen, in small irregular masses, constituting what is called drift-ice, heaped one piece upon another to a considerable height, intermixed with fragments of ice-bergs, and forming as rough a surface as can well be imagined, the journey would doubtless be impracticable; but on field-ice, found commonly within a few leagues of the sea in high latitudes, in sheets of many miles in diameter, and frequently of very even surface, the difficulties of travelling would be very inferior *.

---

* Few of the Russian fishers, it is probable, who only frequent the coast, ever saw any field ice. In the answers to queries 19. and 25. of Colonel Beaufoy, we find the ice represented as mountainous; as appearing " monstrously large and lofty;" and as running flake upon flake to a great height, so as to make the passage on foot very difficult. Now, this kind of ice is peculiar to the coast, and is totally different from field ice. Indeed its roughness is chiefly occasioned by the resistance of the coast, when the ice is forcibly driven against it by the power of strong winds. And the large openings of water observed, also result from the same cause; for whenever the wind blows for a length of time from the shore, the ice, being afloat, is generally drifted away. But such effects do not take place at a distance from land. I have myself, indeed, been many times so closely fixed among ice, that not the smallest opening could be observed from the mast head, in any direction.

Were, however, the opinion ever so general, that the journey could not be accomplished, I should still conceive, that one established fact of a journey having been performed in a similar region on similar ice, and under similar disadvantages, would be a sufficient answer. But several accounts can be brought forward to establish the fact of similar journeys, and some of them equally difficult, having been accomplished. I shall mention a few instances.

Ellis informs us, in his " Voyage to Hudson's Bay*," that the North American Indians, who trade with the factories of the Hudson's Bay Company, frequently " travel 200 or 300 miles in the depth of winter, through a wide open country, without meeting with any house to receive them, or carrying any tent to protect them." And that on such journeys, when benighted on any open plain, they are forced to lie down without fire, under shelter only of the snow. He also mentions, that a man can conveniently draw a load of above an hundred weight upon a sledge, a distance of fifteen or sixteen miles, in a winter's day †.

More recent travellers and voyagers inform us, that the Indians frequently perform much longer journeys in winter ; and it is an established fact, that many persons in the service of the Hudson's Bay

---

* Page 195.   † Id. p. 163.

Company, who reside at their settlements, have travelled 1000 or 1500 miles through snow on foot, in the course of a winter.

Muller makes mention of the Tchuktchi nation, being in the habit of travelling on the ice of the sea, in sledges drawn by rein-deer*. The same author, speaking of the power of the dogs of the Kamtchadales in drawing great burdens, illustrates the fact by stating, that in the year 1718, the governor, Knees Mischewski, ordered a whole pipe of brandy to be brought from the convent of Ketskoe to the city of Beresowa, which was accomplished by sixteen dogs†.

After the lamentable death of the illustrious navigator Captain Cook, the Resolution and Discovery, on their second advance into the Polar Sea, put into the bay of Avatscha in Kamtchatka, for obtaining a supply of naval stores and provisions. No supplies, however, being to be had at the neighbouring town of St Peter and St Paul, a despatch was sent off in a sledge drawn by dogs to Bolsherietzkoi, a distance of 135 English miles, an answer to which was returned on the fourth day; so that a journey of 270 miles upon snow, was performed in little more than three days and a-half‡.

* " Voyages from Asia to America," *Transl.* p. vii.

† Id. p. xi.

‡ Cook's Third Voyage, *Journal*, 3d of May 1779.

But this speed, though so considerable, was by no means equal to what the Kamtchatka dogs are capable of performing; the governor of Kamtchatka, Major Behm, (who so liberally and so disinterestedly supplied the wants of our voyagers,) having assured the officers belonging to these discovery ships, that the journey from St Peter and St Paul to Bolsherietzkoi and back, was usually performed in two days and a-half; and that he had once received an express from the bay of Avatscha, which is the harbour of St Peter and St Paul, in twenty-three hours[*].

But the argument which goes farthest towards proving the practicability of travelling over ice, is the fact, of a Cossack having actually performed a journey of about 800 miles, in a sledge drawn by dogs, across a surface of ice lying to the northward of the Russian dominions. This remarkable exploit, as related by Muller, is to the following effect.

Alexei Markoff, a Cossack, was sent from Yakutsk, to explore the frozen ocean, in the summer of the year 1714, by order of the Russian government; but finding the sea so crowded with ice, that he was unable to make any progress in discovery, he formed the design of travelling in sledges, during the winter or spring of the year, over the ice, which might then be expected to be firm and

---

[*] Idem, *Journal*, 3d May 1779.

compact.   Accordingly, he prepared several of the
country sledges drawn by dogs; and, accompanied
by eight persons, he set out on the 10th of March *,
from the mouth of the Jana, in latitude 70° 30', and
longitude about 138° E.   He proceeded for seven
days northward, as fast as his dogs could draw, which,
under favourable circumstances, is 80 or 100 versts
a-day †, until his progress was impeded about the
78th degree of latitude, by ice elevated into prodigious mountains.   This prevented his further advance ; at the same time, falling short of provisions
for his dogs, his return was effected with difficulty :
several of his dogs died for want, and were given to
the rest for their support.   On the 3d of April he
arrived at Ust-Janskoe Simowie, the place from
whence he started, after an absence of twenty-four
days ‡, during which time, he appears to have travelled about 800 miles §.

Hence, I conceive, that Markoff must have met
with every inconvenience which could be anticipated, in a journey from Spitzbergen to the Pole, or

---

* March the 15th, according to Forster, in his " Observations made during a voyage round the World," p. 82.

† The verst, being about $5\frac{1}{2}$ furlongs, (3500 English feet,)
the average progress of 90 versts *per* day, is equal to about
62 miles, amounting to 434 miles in 7 days.

‡ According to Forster, 19 days.

§ Muller's Voyages, &c. *Transl.* p. 18.

to the nearest land in the direction of the Pole. And as this account, derived by Muller from the archives of Yakutsk, shows us that Markoff's journey, which was nearly equal in extent to the projected journey to the Pole, was accomplished with safety to the travellers, there appears no very great reason why a person equally adventurous as Markoff and better provided, might not, in a similar manner, reach the Pole.

SECT. V.

Account of the Progress of Discovery in the North.

Some brief remarks have already been made, in the foregoing pages, relative to the discovery of several of the polar countries, since the period when a northern passage to China and India became a popular speculation; but for tracing the progress of discovery in the north with any degree of fulness, it will be necessary to go back to a period of many centuries, before the passage to India in this way was, perhaps, ever thought of.

The first considerable discovery which appears to have been made in or near the Arctic Circle, was the result of accident; one of the numerous Scandinavian depredators, who, in the ninth century, cruised the northern seas in search of plunder, having been driven by a long continued storm from the eastward, upon the coast of Iceland, in the year 861. This island, from the quantity of snow seen on the mountains, was by its discoverer NADDODD, at first called *Schnee* or *Snowland*. It was visited by a Swede of the name of Gardar Suaffarson, three years after its discovery, who wintered there; and afterwards by another Swede called Flocke, who, for assisting him in the navigation to this remote country, the compass being then unknown, is said to have carried out ravens along with him, by the flight of which, when set at liberty, he directed his course, and was led to the required country. This island, which had been denominated *Iceland* by Flocke, was again visited in the year 874 by Ingolf and Lief, two Norwegians, to whom the country presented so many natural advantages, that they, with a few followers, were induced to settle there about four years afterwards. In the course of a few years, they were joined by a number of Norwegian families, who resorted thither from political oppression; so that they soon constituted a considerable colony.

The coast of Norway, to the entrance of the White Sea, was examined about this period by a person of the name of OHTHERE, a Norwegian, who himself gave an account of his voyage to Alfred the Great, by whom it has been handed down to us along with his translation of the Ormesta of Orosius.

About the middle, or towards the end of the tenth century, an extensive country to the westward of Iceland was discovered, by one of the colonists of the name of GUNBIORN *, which country was visited in the year 982, by one ERIC RAUDA, a person who had fled from Norway to Iceland, to avoid the punishment due to the crime of murder, with various other misdemeanours, of which he had been guilty. Rauda wintered in the southern part of the country; and after spending part of three years in exploring it, returned to Iceland. For the purpose of encouraging persons to become settlers in the newly discovered country, he denominated it *Greenland*, and gave a most exaggerated account of its products and appearance. In consequence of his representations, a fleet of twenty-five sail was shortly afterwards equipped, which, laden with people of both sexes, and the requisite stores and cattle for forming a settlement, put off for Greenland; but only about one-half of the fleet arrived safe at their destination. These people were soon joined by others, both from Iceland and Norway; so that, in a few years, they also became a respectable colony.

---

* Forster's " Voyages and Discoveries made in the North," p. 79.

A regular trade being now established between
Norway, Greenland and Iceland, one of the Iceland
colonists, BIORN by name, about the year 1001,
while following his father to Greenland, from
whom he had been separated while on a trading
voyage in another ship, was accidentally driven by
a storm considerably to the south-west of Greenland, where he discovered a new country covered
with wood.   This discovery being made known on
his return to Iceland, Lief, the son of Eric Rauda,
fitted out a vessel, and with Biorn as a pilot and
a crew of thirty-five men, revisited the country
just discovered.   Here he traversed a considerable
extent of coast, and sailed up a river to a lake from
which it took its rise, where he wintered.   In this
country, called by the discoverers *Winland* or *Vin-
land*, from the circumstance of grapes having been
found in it, the day was eight hours long in
winter ; from whence it appears, that they must
have been somewhere on the coast of North America, or contiguous islands, near the parallel of 50°,
probably on the shore of Newfoundland.   Lief
returned to Greenland the following spring.   His
brother Thorwald afterwards proceeded to Winland, where he pursued the discovery of the adjacent countries during two years, without seeing any
inhabitants ; but, in the third year, he met with
three boats upon the coast, covered with leather,
containing three Indians each, which he seized, and

wantonly and barbarously murdered the whole of the men in them, excepting one who made his escape. An attack was made a little while after by the injured natives upon Thorwald's vessel; and, though the assailers were repulsed, Thorwald met with a just retribution for his cruelty, by the wound of an arrow, which occasioned his death. These savages, on account of their low stature, were called Skrœllingers, signifying dwarfs. They were probably the same race of people as are at present known by the appellation of Esquimaux. Other adventurers then visited Winland, and succeeded in establishing a good understanding with the natives, and in carrying on among them an advantageous traffic for furs and other produce of the country. Thorfin, one of these adventurers, attempted to establish a colony in Winland, and allowed the people with him a free traffic with the natives in any articles excepting weapons of war, the bartering of which he expressly forbid. One of the natives, however, contrived to steal from the Icelanders a battle-axe, trial of which he presently made on one of his companions, and killed him on the spot. The dangerous weapon was immediately seized by another of his countrymen, and thrown into the sea *.

VOL. I.   E

---

* Forster's Voyages, p. 85.

The Christian Religion was introduced into Iceland and Greenland about the year 1000, and within a hundred years afterwards generally diffused.
Above sixteen churches were then built, and two
convents. These buildings, as well as the habitations of the colonists, were erected near the southern point of Greenland. They had two settlements, the most western of which increased up to
four parishes, containing one hundred farms or villages ; and the most eastern to twelve parishes, one
hundred and ninety villages, one bishop's see, and
two convents *. The intercourse between Greenland and the rest of the world, was intercepted
about the year 1406, when the seventeenth bishop
attempted to reach his see, but was prevented by
ice. Since the beginning of the fifteenth century,
these unfortunate colonists have been, of necessity,
left to themselves, and, not having been heard of,
are supposed to have perished ; but whether they
were destroyed by their enemies the Esquimaux,
who inhabit the same country, or perished for want
of their usual supplies, or were carried off by a destructive pestilence, as some have imagined, is
still matter of doubt. It is not indeed known that
none of them yet remain, though, from the circumstance of several of the ruins of their convents having been seen by the zealous missionary Hans
Egede, in the year 1723, it is clear, that the west-

---

* BARROW's Voyages, p. 12.

ern colony is not now in existence; but as to the eastern colony, Egede was of opinion, that there was a probability of some of the people being yet alive *.

Various attempts have been made by order of the Danish Government, for the recovery of this country, and for ascertaining the fate of the unfortunate colonists, but most of them were spiritless, and all of them failed in their object.

Richard Hackluyt, in his " Voyages, Navigations, Traffiques, and Discoveries of the English Nation," gives a quotation from the History of Wales, by Dr David Powel, stating the discovery of America or the West Indies by Madoc, the son of OWEN GUYNETH, prince of North Wales, in the year 1170. Madoc left his country, it is said, in consequence of family contention, and proceeded in search of adventures by sea towards the west. Leaving Iceland far to the north, he arrived at length at " a land unknown, where he saw many strange things." Here he left most of his companions, and returned home for more people " to inhabit this fair and large country," and then went out again with ten sail of ships †.

E 2

---

* One of the Iceland bishops, who was driven very near the coast of Greenland, while on a voyage to Norway, about the middle of the sixteenth century, is said to have seen the inhabitants driving their cattle in the fields.—*Thormoder Torfager.*

† Hackluyt's Voyages, &c. vol. iii. p. 1.

Near the close of the fourteenth century, NICHO-
LAS and ANTONIO ZENO, two Italians, made voyages of discovery in the north and west, from
the islands of Shetland or Faroe, as is generally
believed.   Nicholas, it appears, visited Greenland,
and Antonio, according to Forster, sailed to a
country supposed to have been that of ancient Winland, and afterwards visited Greenland and Iceland.

After this period, a new stimulus was offered to
the enterprising trader, which was the well-found-
ed hope then entertained, of performing the passage
from Europe to India by sea, from whence immense
riches were expected to be derived.

The celebrated navigator COLUMBUS, conceiving
India, to be much more extensive than it really is,
calculated, from the known spherical form of the
earth, that he should soon reach it by sailing to the
westward, and was very anxious to make the attempt.   After a number of disappointments and
much tedious delay, he was employed, for the purpose
of putting his project into execution, by the Queen of
Spain.   He sailed from Palos in August 1492;
and the result of his voyage was the discovery of
the West Indies, the islands of which were so
named, from the supposition that they lay contiguous to the coast of India.   Soon after Columbus's
voyages, the Portugueze navigator, Vasquez de Gama, succeeded in reaching India by sailing round
the Cape of Good Hope; but before this successful

attempt, another expedition by the same nation, it appears, tried the passage by the west, on a parallel far to the northward of that pursued by Columbus. This was undertaken by JOHN VAZ COSTA COR-TEREAL, about the year 1463 or 1464, in which voyage the land of Newfoundland appears to have been seen *.

After Cortereal, SEBASTIAN CABOT, a Venetian, resident in England, seems to have been the next to attempt the voyage to India by the north-west, in the year 1497, on which occasion he coasted the American shore from the parallel of $67\frac{1}{2}°$ down to that of 38°; though it is supposed his father, JOHN CABOT, made a voyage to Newfoundland, or *Prima Vista*, as he called it, in 1494, and discovered the island of *St John*, which he so named, because it was first seen on St John's day †. Sebastian Cabot having, after this time, been several years employed in the service of the King of Spain, returned to England in 1548, when he was placed at the head of the Society of Merchant Adventurers, afterwards called the Muscovy or Russia Company; and was subsequently endowed by Edward VI. with a pension of 166*l.* 13*s.* 4*d.* a-year, for good and acceptable services done and to be done by him.

GASPAR CORTEREAL, son of the voyager John Vaz Costa Cortereal above mentioned, sailed from

* Barrow's Voyages, p. 37.
† HARRIS's Voyages, vol. ii. p. 190.

Lisbon in the year 1500, on a voyage of discovery
towards the north-west, in search of a passage that
way to the Spice Islands. He first saw the promontory of Greenland, then discovered the coast of Labrador ; and after proceeding as far towards the
north as the mountains of ice with which he met
would admit, he coasted towards the south, and
discovered the *River St Lawrence*, together with
several islands contiguous to the North American coast. The following year the same navigator, with two vessels, undertook a second voyage,
when he again saw Terra Verde (Greenland) ; but
being separated from his companion in a storm,
it is apprehended his vessel was wrecked among
the ice of Cape Farewell, as his consort returned to Lisbon without him, and he was never
heard of afterwards.   Search for the unfortunate Cortereal was immediately commenced by
his brother, MICHAEL CORTEREAL, grand door-
keeper of the king Don Manuel, who sailed from
Lisbon with three vessels on the 10th of May 1502.
But the result of this voyage was as disastrous as
the former ; for, on the vessels separating, with the
view of making a more effectual search for the lost
navigator, Michael shared a similar fate as his brother, and perished.   A third brother was anxious
to renew the search, but the King determinately
refused permission for him to embark personally in
the undertaking, lest he should also be lost, but

readily permitted other individuals to pursue the humane design, though without effect *.

An unimportant voyage was undertaken by one Aubert or Hubert, a Frenchman, in the year 1508, wherein he visited Newfoundland ; and another in 1524 by Estevan Gomez, a Spaniard or Portugueze, of the result of which little or nothing is known. An English voyage was attempted three years afterwards towards the North Pole, one of the vessels employed in which was called the *Dominus Vobiscum;* but the proceedings in this first expedition undertaken entirely by the English, for sailing in a northerly direction to India, are little known.

A few more unimportant voyages undertaken by the French, Spanish, and English, bring us down to the period when the spirit for adventure among our countrymen burst forth, under the auspices of Edward VI., and under the judicious assistance and suggestions of Sebastian Cabot, with a degree of brilliancy scarcely before known. The first voyage undertaken for discovery towards the north-east, was commenced by Sir HUGH WILLOUGHBY, in the year 1553, at the charge of " The Company of Merchant Adventurers." This expedition, consisting of three ships, with a pinnace and a boat belonging to each, left Ratcliffe, and dropped down to Deptford,

---

* Barrow's Voyages, p. 46.

on the 20th of May. The following day it passed
Greenwich with great display, in view of the Court,
who were then there, and amid the warmest accla-
mations of a great number of people of all ranks,
who had assembled to witness its sailing. One of
the ships, the Edward Bonaventure, commanded by
Richard Chancellor, pilot-major of the fleet, was separated from the rest of the little squadron, in a
storm, on the 3d of August, when they were near
the northern termination of Lapland, called, by Stephen Burrough, who accompanied Chancellor, the
North Cape; on which Sir Hugh Willoughby, in
the Bona Esperanza, accompanied by the Bona
Confidentia, proceeded in search of Wardhuus, the
place appointed for a rendezvous; but, missing it,
stretched to the eastward, until the 14th of August,
when he discovered an unknown coast, lying in latitude 72°. On this coast, now called Nova Zembla *, he was unable to land, from the shoalness of

---

* As Sir Hugh Willoughby was 160 leagues, by estimation,
E. by N. from Seynam, an island on the east coast of Norway,
in latitude 70°, when he discovered land; and the distance to
Nova Zembla, according to Arrowsmith, is not more than 220
leagues, I have no doubt but the coast seen by him was Nova
Zembla. Besides, from the length of time he was in getting
to the westward, to his wintering harbour, it is evident he was
much farther to the eastward than he imagined. Indeed the
courses and distances given in his journal, imperfect as they
are, give sufficient westing for the distance between Nova
Zembla and Lapland. And had he been mistaken in his lati-

the water. After beating three days to the north-ward, and probably making very little progress, he bore up with the wind at north-east, and ran about 70 leagues towards the south-south-east, when, fall-ing into 7 fathoms water, without seeing land, he hauled by the wind to north-westward. From that time, 21st August, until the 14th September, he coasted to the westward, seeing the Russian shore occasionally; and, on the 18th, took up his winter quarters at the mouth of the river Arzina, a har-bour in the 70th degree of latitude, on the north-eastern face of Lapland. Here, owing to the seve-rity of the cold, and the want of proper food, him-self and two ships' companies, consisting of 70 per-sons, exhausted by the combined effects of cold, hunger, and disease, perished in the ensuing spring. In the mean time, Chancellor, with the Edward Bonaventure, was more fortunate. He proceed-ed to Wardhuus, the place of rendezvous, from whence, after waiting seven days, he sailed a short distance to the northward, and then changing his course, fell in with the Russian territory, on the east side of the White Sea. In one of the Russian harbours, in this region, the ship remained through-out the winter. Chancellor, during their stay, tra-velled to Moscow, where he was handsomely enter-

tude, and had the land seen been any of the islands lying near the northern part of Russia, it is evident he could not have steered 70 leagues to the S. S. E., as he afterwards did.

tained by Juan Vasilovich, Czar of Moscow, and received permission of a free trade.   He returned to
England in 1554, and the following summer was
sent out again accompanied by Richard Gray and
George Killingworth *, " factors," for establishing a
regular trade with Russia by the way of the White
Sea, which was accomplished under various privi-
leges.

STEPHEN BURROUGH also, was sent out in a small
vessel the following year (1556), for making discoveries to the eastward.   He visited Nova Zembla, and
discovered the Island of *Weigats*, near which, in fruitless endeavours to get to the eastward, he spent above
three weeks, and then, proceeding to the westward,
he wintered at Colmagro ; and, after making some
search for the Bona Esperanza, and Bona Confidentia, returned to England in 1557.

After the complete establishment of the Russian
trade, and the discovery of all the northern face of
Russia, from the White Sea to the eastward of the
Weigats, the chance of further discovery in that direction appeared so little, that a passage to Cathay or
India, by the north-west, again became a popular speculation.   MARTIN FROBISHER, who was one of the
most sanguine advocates of the practicability of this

---

* This Killingworth was remarkable for the length and
beauty of his beard.   It was of a yellowish colour, thick and
broad, measuring 5 feet 2 inches in length.

scheme, after having for above fifteen years endeavoured in vain to accomplish an expedition, was at length,
through the assistance of Dudley, Earl of Warwick,
and a few friends, enabled to effect the equipment
of two small barks of 35 and 30 tons, and a pinnace
of 10 tons, with which he proceeded on discovery,
on the 8th of June 1576. In this voyage he discovered a strait, in latitude 63° 8', afterwards named *Frobisher's Strait;* but its situation being
long supposed to be on Greenland, instead of on
the Labrador side, the name of Lumley's Inlet
was applied to the same place.

Omitting the two subsequent voyages of Frobisher, which were chiefly undertaken in search of
treasure, and others in which nothing was discovered, we come to the commencement of a period of
about thirty years, when all or the greater part of
the discoveries which have been made towards the
north-west, and north, were accomplished. The
first important voyage was performed by JOHN
DAVIS, who, with two vessels, the *Sunshine* of
50 tons, and the *Moonshine* of 35 tons, sailed
from Dartmouth in search of a north-west passage,
on the 7th of June 1585. They fell in with ice on
the east side of Greenland, on the 19th of July;
and the following day got sight of a rocky mountainous land, appearing as if above the clouds, in
form of a sugar loaf, to which Davis gave the name
of the *Land of Desolation.* After doubling Cape

Farewell, they stood to the north-westward ; and in four days saw land to the eastward, in latitude 64° 15', being the west side of Greenland. It consisted of islands, some of them inhabited, and contained many harbours, in one of which they anchored. They afterwards stretched across an open sea to the north-westward, and again discovered land in latitude 66° 40', on the 6th of August, and anchored under a mount which they named *Mount Raleigh.* To different parts of this coast, since denominated *Cumberland Island,* they applied names. The foreland to the northward of them, they called *Dier's Cape;* that to the southward *Cape Walsingham;* and a great bay between the two capes they named *Exeter Sound;* and their anchorage they called *Totness Road.* On the 11th of August, having returned a little to the southward, they sailed to the westward, in a strait 20 or 30 leagues in width, and free from ice, which has since been denominated *Cumberland Strait.* The cape which they rounded to enter this strait, they called the *Cape of God's Mercy,* as being the place of their first entrance for discovery. On proceeding 60 leagues to the westward, they fell in with a cluster of islands in the midst of the passage, which, with the commencement of fog and unfavourable weather, put an end to their discovery. After remaining six days in expectation of a change of weather, they sailed homeward, and arrived safe at Dartmouth on the 30th September. They met with a multitude of natives in the course of the voyage, whom they found a very tractable people, and liberal in their mode of trafficking.

The discovery by Davis of a nation with whom it seemed practicable to enter into an advantageous traffic, with the great expectations, excited by the open navigation of the strait into which he sailed, of a communication with the Pacific Ocean, occasioned Davis with his two barks, to which were added a trading vessel of 120 tons, and a pinnace of 10 tons, to be again dispatched the following year. They left Dartmouth on the 7th May. After making the land near Cape Farewell, they proceeded along the west coast of Greenland, where the natives came off to their ships in 40, 50, or even 100 canoes at a time, bringing with them skins, fish, fowls, and other produce of the country. Davis having, on his passage across the Atlantic, sent two of his vessels to the eastward of Greenland, with orders to seek a passage to the northward between Greenland and Iceland, as far as latitude 80°, was now deserted by his only remaining companion, and proceeded alone on his discovery, in the Moonshine of 35 tons. From the coast of Greenland, in 66° 33′, which he discovered, he sailed westward 50 leagues until he fell in with land again in latitude 66° 19′; he cruised about this coast for some time, and then stretched to the southward, examining inlets in the Labrador shore as he went, until the 11th September, when he left the

coast about the latitude of 54°, and arrived in
England in October.   The North Star of 10 tons
burden, one of the vessels sent to the eastward of
Greenland, parted from her consort in a storm on
the 3d of September, and was never afterwards
heard of.   Though this voyage was productive of
no discovery of any consequence, yet Davis was
sent out again the next year (1587) with three
vessels.   They proceeded as before along the west
coast of Greenland, but to a greater extent, having had an observation in latitude 72° 12'.   This
land, lying on the east side of the strait now called
Davis' Strait, they named the *London Coast*.
From hence, the wind shifting to the northward,
they stretched across the strait to the westward,
got entangled among ice, and made their way
through it to the southward.   After again sailing
up Cumberland Strait as far as before, they went
across the mouth of the strait discovered by Frobisher, which they named *Lumley's Inlet*, and
passed a headland called by them *Warwick's Foreland ;* then crossing a large gulf forming the entrance of the strait afterwards sailed through by
Hudson, they came to the southermost cape of the
gulf lying in latitude 61° 10', to which they applied the name of *Cape Chidley*.   Soon afterwards
they returned to England.

    A passage to India and China by the north-east,
presenting many apparent advantages, the Dutch,

as soon as relieved from the yoke of Spain, embarked in the enterprize of discovering it.   Four
ships were equipped for this purpose in the year
1594, part of which, under the command of COR-
NELIS CORNELISON, passed the strait of Weigatz,
and proceeded about 40 leagues to the eastward,
when, finding the sea clear, and every prospect of
a passage, instead of pursuing the discovery, they
turned back to communicate the news of the happy
probability!   Another part of the expedition under the direction of WILLIAM BARENTZ, examined at the same time the western side of Nova
Zembla, giving names to several remarkable parts
of the coast from latitude 77° 25′ down to 71°.

After another expedition of seven ships, expen-
sively prepared, had been sent out in the same direction, and altogether failed, two ships under the
command of Jacob Van Heemskerke and Cornelis Ryp, with WILLIAM BARENTZ as chief pilot,
were sent out from Amsterdam on the 10th May
1596, for discovering a north-east passage.   On
an island that they discovered in latitude 74° 35′,
they killed an immense bear, from which circumstance the place was called *Bear Island.*   From
hence, at the suggestion of Cornelis Ryp, they proceeded to the northward, with the hope of getting
round the ice with which the coast of Nova Zembla is encumbered, and thus discovered land when
in latitude 80° 10′, on the 17th of June, which they

named *Spitzbergen,* or *Sharp Mountains.* They examined the coast hastily, as far to the southward as latitude 76° 50′, and then saw no more land until they approached Bear Island, (afterwards called Cherry Island,) on the 1st of July. Being doubtful of the situation of the newly discovered region, with regard to the continent of Europe, or any other known land, the two ships pursued different courses, that the navigators might satisfy themselves of its true position ; and Cornelis, sailing back again from Bear Island, direct north, arrived at a place on the west coast of Spitzbergen, which they had before denominated the *Bay of Birds* *.

Barentz, in the mean time, proceeded to the eastward, with the hope of accomplishing the main object of his voyage, and reached the coast of Nova Zembla on the 17th of July. Then persevering to the northward and eastward, with the expectation of getting round Nova Zembla, they got entangled among the ice on the coast, and were brought to the dreadful necessity of wintering in this desolate and frozen country. To attempt any description of their proceedings, their observations, or their afflictions during this severe trial, would, within the limit of a few lines, to which it is my wish to confine my remarks in this place, but spoil a most interesting and affecting narrative. " The journal

---

* De Brye, Indiæ Orientalis pars undecima, tom. iii. p. 48.–51.

of the proceedings of these poor people, as Mr Barrow beautifully observes, " during their cold, comfortless, dark and dreadful winter, is intensely and painfully interesting. No murmuring escapes them in their most hopeless and afflicted situation ; but such a spirit of true piety, and a tone of such mild and subdued resignation to Divine Providence, breathe through the whole narrative, that it is impossible to peruse the simple tale of their sufferings, and contemplate their forlorn situation, without the deepest emotion *."

Part of the sufferers made their escape in two open boats from this dismal country in the following summer ; and, after a perilous and painful voyage of above 1100 miles, arrived in safety at Cola ; but Barentz, with some others, was overcome by the severity of the climate, and the extraordinary exertions which he was obliged to make, and died.

GEORGE WEYMOUTH, who was sent out by the Muscovy and Turkey Companies, with two vessels, in the year 1602, found an inlet in the land to the northward of the Labrador coast, in latitude 61° 40', into which he said he sailed W. by S. a hundred leagues. If so, he must have been in the channel now called *Hudson's Strait*, and of course was the discoverer of it.

VOL. I.   F

---

* " Chronological History of Voyages into the Arctic Regions," p. 151.

Three voyages towards the north-west by JAMES
HALL, and one by JOHN KNIGHT, were performed
after that of Weymouth, but the next discovery worth
mentioning was made by HENRY HUDSON, who, in
1607, in a voyage towards the North Pole, traced
the east coast of Greenland, from a little to the
northward of Iceland, as high as latitude 73°, which
extreme point of his navigation this way he called
Hold with Hope. He then proceeded more to
the eastward, made the coast of Spitzbergen, sailed
as high as latitude 81°, and explored a bay between
the north end of Charles' Island and the Main,
and returned home in safety. This navigation was
performed in a very small vessel, with a crew only
of ten men and a boy.

In the year 1608, Hudson was employed in search
of a north-east passage ; the year afterwards, in a northern and western voyage in the Dutch service, the
design of which is not well understood ; and in the
season of 1610, this enterprising navigator embarked
on a voyage of discovery from England, towards
the north-west, in a vessel of fifty-five tons burden.
On this occasion, which terminated fatally to himself, he passed the Strait, the mouth of which
was first observed by Davis, and said to have been
entered by Weymouth, then discovered the bay
which bears his name, hauled his ship on shore in
a convenient situation, and wintered there. The
ship being victualled only for six months, they fell

short of provisions ; and soon after the vessel was got afloat in the summer of 1611, the crew mutinied, barbarously forced their Captain, his son, and seven of the crew, mostly invalids, into a boat, with a most scanty supply of the necessaries of life, and abandoned them to a miserable fate. The chief of the mutineers, one Green, who had received the most distinguished favours from Hudson, being preserved by him from ruin, taken into his own house, and afterwards allowed to accompany him on his voyage, met with a speedy requital for his base ingratitude. He landed with some of his companions near the western extremity of Hudson's Strait, where he met with some savages, who, though at first they appeared on friendly terms, unexpectedly attacked his party, killed the base ingrate, and mortally wounded three others. Another person, said to be also among the chiefs in the mutiny, died of want on the passage homeward.

Sir Thomas Button, with two ships, proceeded towards the north-west in the year 1612, on the same track as the unfortunate Hudson pursued. He first stretched across to the western shore of *Hudson's Bay*, examined a part of the coast, and then took up his winter quarters in a creek on the north side of a river which he discovered, and named *Nelson's River*. As soon as the ice cleared away, he examined the western side of the bay, as high along *Southampton Island* as latitude 65°, gave names to several headlands and islands, and returned to England in the autumn of 1613.

In the year 1615, ROBERT BYLOT, accompanied by the celebrated William Baffin as mate and companion, with one small vessel, visited the same quarter, and examined the eastern side of Southampton Island, as high as latitude 65° 26′. After spending three months in the frozen sea, without making any considerable discovery, they returned to England. The next year, (1616), Bylot, accompanied by WILLIAM BAFFIN as Pilot, proceeded to the examination of the sea lying north and west of Davis' Strait. They had but one vessel, the *Discovery*, of fifty-five tons burden, which had before been employed in four similar voyages, under Hudson in 1610, Button in 1612, Gibbon in 1614, and Bylot in the preceding year. In this little vessel, with seventeen persons on board, Baffin traced the west coast of Greenland up Davis' Strait, as high as the extremity of the extensive sea in the 78th degree of latitude, now named after him, as the discoverer; proceeded round by the western part of the bay as near the shore as the ice would permit, and down to the latitude of 65° 40′; having seen land, probably, all the way, excepting in the openings of some of the *sounds*, and in the interval between the latitudes of 70° 30′ and 68°, where he fell in with a large body of ice, and was under the necessity of taking a circuit to the eastward.

This voyage of Baffin's being one of the most remarkable and important navigations ever accomplished in the same quarter of the globe, is worthy a more particular description. I shall, therefore, give an abstract of Baffin's narrative, as published by Purchas *.

They sailed from Gravesend on the 26th of March 1616; but owing to bad weather and contrary winds, did not clear the Channel until the 20th of April. After a good passage across the Atlantic, they proceeded without interruption, excepting from contrary winds, up Davis' Strait to latitude 70° 20', where they anchored in a " fair sound" near Davis's London Coast. Here the tides rising only eight or nine feet, and keeping no certain course, Baffin was discouraged in the hope of a passage.

After remaining two days at this place, from whence all the inhabitants had fled, they weighed and plyed to the northward. On the 26th of May they fell in with a dead whale, and made the ship fast, to secure it: after having obtained 160 fins or blades of whalebone from it, a storm ensued, and it broke away from them.

May 30th, they reached Hope Sanderson, the northernmost land visited by Davis, lying between the parallels of 72° and 73°; and on the same evening fell in with ice, which they immediately entered, and pass-

* Pilgrimes, vol. iii. p. 844.

ed through the following day. The wind then blowing very hard at N. N. E., they put in among
some islands, in latitude 72° 45', from which the inhabitants fled on their approach, leaving only a few
women behind, who hid themselves among the
rocks. From this circumstance, the group was called *Women's Islands.* The wind being moderate,
though still contrary, they sailed on the 4th and
plyed to the northward, in a channel seven or eight
leagues wide, between the ice and the land. Being
much pestered with ice on the 9th, they anchored
near three small islands, lying eight miles from the
main, in latitude 74° 4'. The flood tide here was
very weak, but the ebb ran with a considerable
stream, which Baffin attributed to the melting of
the snow on the land. From hence they attempted to get to the northward and north-westward ;
but finding the ice impervious, though in a rapid
state of dissolution, they put in among some islands in
latitude 73° 45', until there should be more room.
Here they were visited by the natives to the amount
of forty-two persons, who bartered skins and pieces
of the tusks of sea-horses, and what are usually called unicorn's-horns, for beads, iron, and such like ;
from which the anchorage was named *Horn Sound.*

On the 18th they put to sea, and found the ice
astonishingly dispersed, having stood to the westward nearly twenty leagues, and to the northward,
as far as latitude 74° 30', before they met with any

interruption. Afterwards, however, they experienced considerable inconvenience from ice, being occasionally beset, (yet never passing a day without making some progress,) until the 1st of July, when, in latitude 75° 40', they got into an open sea. Here they stood twenty leagues off shore, before they fell in with ice, and the hope of a passage was again revived; but, on trying the tide on their return to the coast, this hope was again depressed.

The wind, on the 2d of July, veered to the southeast, and blew hard; and though the weather was thick, they were bold enough to run along the land to the northward. On the morning of the 3d, they passed a headland, in latitude 76° 35', which they called *Sir Dudley Diggs' Cape;* and twelve leagues beyond it, they opened a bay, having an island in the midst, under which they anchored; but, in two hours time, the wind still blowing very hard, the ship drove, with two anchors down, and obliged them to set sail. This bay, which Baffin reckons a fit place for killing whales, he named *Wostenholme Sound.*

On the 4th, the storm veered to W. by S., and was so furious that it blew away their fore-sail, and obliged them to lie *adrift.* Finding themselves embayed when the weather cleared a little, they set sail, and stretched across to the south-eastward, into a little cove, where they attempted " to bring up;" but the squalls from the hills being violent,

they lost both anchor and cable. The wind soon
after abated, and they stood forth. This bay, lying in latitude 77° 30', abounded with whales, and
was, in consequence, named *Whale Sound.* Another large opening to the northward of this, extending beyond the latitude of 78°, they called *Sir
Thomas Smith's Sound;* an island between these
two bays was named *Hackluyt's Isle;* and a group
lying twelve or thirteen leagues from the shore,
they called *Carey's Islands.* They now stood a
considerable distance to the westward, and were becalmed on the 10th near the land, beside another
opening, which they named *Alderman Jones'
Sound.* Near this place a boat was sent on shore.
The land was now found trending to the southward, and began to show like a bay. Steering then
along shore, they opened another large sound, in latitude 74° 20', on the 12th of July, to which they
gave the name of *Sir James Lancaster's Sound.*
From this opening a ledge of ice was connected
with the shore, along which they coasted till the
14th, " by which time," says Baffin, " we were in
the latitude of 71° 16', and plainly perceived the
land to the southward of 70° 30'; then we having
so much ice round about us, were forced to stand
more eastward, supposing to have been soon clear,
and to have kept on the off side of the ice, until we
had come into 70°, then to have stood in again."
But in this they were disappointed; for they had

to run above sixty leagues to the eastward, before they got clear of the ice, and were many times so hampered that they could get no way. They were unable to approach the shore again until the 24th of July, when they were in latitude about 68° ; and then, though they saw the land, they could not get nearer than eight or nine leagues. From this situation the ice led them into the latitude of 65° 40', where, being hopeless of a passage, considering themselves in the indraft of Cumberland Islands, and the season being too far spent to return to the head of the bay to seek for whalebone, they stood across to the coast of Greenland, and put into *Cockin Sound*, in latitude 65ᵛ 45', to refresh the crew, several of whom were sickly. Here, by the use of scurvy-grass, which they found in great abundance, and other suitable regimen, they were restored to health in a few days. This sound, described by Baffin as a very good harbour, they left on the 6th of August, and anchored all well (excepting one man, who died in Davis' Strait,) on the 30th of the same month in Dover Road.

Such was the extensive nature of the discoveries made on this occasion, and such the remarkable position given to the land, that, combined with the meagerness of all published accounts of the voyage, and the suppression of the chart and tables to which Baffin refers, occasioned a considerable doubt

both as to the truth of the narrative and the extent
of the navigation. The late voyage, however, by Captain Ross and Lieutenant Parry, how much soever
the public may feel disappointed as to the general issue, affords a pleasing confirmation of the faithfulness
and accuracy of Baffin ; and when we observe the
brief and unostentatious manner in which he nar-
rates the transactions of this important voyage,
we cannot withhold our warmest admiration.

After the voyage of Baffin, it would be tedious
even to enumerate the various expeditions which
have been sent out on discovery into the Arctic
seas, all of which have failed in their principal object. I shall therefore close this brief and imperfect sketch of the progress of northern discovery,
with observing, that, whatever has been added to
the discoveries of Willoughby, Davis, Hudson and
Baffin, among English voyagers, and to the discoveries of Barentz, Heemskerke, and Ryp, a-
mong the Dutch, consists only in the explorations
by the Russians and the Dutch of the northern
shores of the Continent of Europe and Asia, and
in the researches by the British about the shores of
Spitzbergen, and in the bays of Hudson and Baffin.
A tabular enumeration of all the voyages undertaken in search of a northern communication between the Atlantic and Pacific, with a brief view

of the result of each expedition, which is included
in the Appendix to this volume, No. III., will afford all the information requisite to be given in
this work, with regard to those voyages that I
have passed over without notice.

CHAPTER II.

DESCRIPTIVE ACCOUNT OF SOME OF THE PO-
LAR COUNTRIES *.

SECT. I.

*Account of Spitzbergen and the Islands im-
mediately adjacent.*

SPITZBERGEN extends farthest towards the north
of any country yet discovered.   It is surrounded
by the Arctic Ocean or Greenland Sea ; and though

---

* When I first formed the design of presenting to the public
the result of my observations, made in the course of repeated
visits to the coast of Spitzbergen, and neighbouring regions,
it was my intention to give a general description of all the
countries lying within the Arctic Zone ; but the excellent
works of Sir George Mackenzie, and of the Reverend Ebenezer
Henderson, on Iceland, which have recently appeared, and the
voyages of our navigators into Baffin's Bay, and the work of
Professor Giesecké on Greenland, which have been announced,
render it unnecessary for me to give any account of these
countries.   I now, therefore, abridge my original plan, by excluding the intended description of Iceland and West Greenland, and confine my remarks to those regions, of which, from
personal observation in general, I am better able to give an
original description

the occasional resort of persons, drawn thither for purposes of hunting and fishing, does not appear to have ever been inhabited. It lies between the latitudes 76° 30' and 80° 7' N., and between the longitudes of 9° and perhaps 22° E.; but some of the neighbouring islands extend at least as far north as 80° 40', and still farther towards the east than the mainland of Spitzbergen. The western part of this country was discovered by BARENTZ, Heemskerke and Ryp, in two vessels fitted out of Amsterdam, on the 19th of June 1596, who, from the numerous peaks and acute mountains observed on the coast, gave it the appropriate name of *Spitzbergen*, signifying *sharp mountains*. It was afterwards named *Newland*, or *King James' Newland*, and then *Greenland*, being supposed to be a continuation towards the east of the country so called by the Icelanders. It was rediscovered by Henry Hudson, an English navigator, in 1607, and four years afterwards became the resort of the English, for the purpose of taking whales, since which period, its shores have annually been visited by one or other of the nations of Europe, with the same object, to the present time. And though the soil of the whole of this remote country does not produce vegetables suitable or sufficient for the nourishment of a single human being, yet its coasts and adjacent seas have afforded riches and independence to thousands.

This country exhibits many interesting views, with numerous examples of the sublime. Its stupendous hills rising by steep acclivities from the very margin of the ocean to an immense height; its surface, contrasting the native protruding dark-coloured rocks, with the burden of purest snow and magnificent ices, altogether constitute an extraordinary and beautiful picture.

The whole of the western coast is mountainous and picturesque; and though it is shone upon by a four months' sun every year, its snowy covering is never wholly dissolved, nor are its icy monuments of the dominion of frost ever removed The valleys opening towards the coast, and terminating in the back ground with a transverse chain of mountains, are chiefly filled with everlasting ice. The inland valleys, at all seasons, present a smooth and continued bed of snow, in some places divided by considerable rivulets, but in others exhibiting a pure unbroken surface for many leagues in extent. Along the west coast, the mountains take their rise from within a league of the sea, and some from its very edge. Few tracts of table-land of more than a league in breadth are to be seen, and in many places the blunt termination of mountain-ridges project beyond the regular line of the coast, and overhang the waters of the ocean. The southern part of Spitzbergen consists of groups of insulated mountains, little disposed in chains, or in any determinate order, having conical, pyramidal, or ridged

summits, sometimes round-backed, frequently terminating in points, and occasionally in acute peaks,
not unlike spires. An arm of a short mountain-
chain, however, forms the southern Cape or Point-
look-out; but a low flat, in the form of a fish's
tail, of about forty square miles in surface, constitutes the termination of the coast. Other promontories lying nearly north and south, are of a similar
nature. The middle of Charles' Island is occupied
by a mountain-chain of about thirty miles in length,
rising on the west side from the sea, and on the
east from a small stripe of table-land, only a few
feet above the level of the ocean. In some parts
of the coast, indeed, the table-land, from which the
mountains take their rise, is even below the level
of the high water mark, and is only prevented
from being covered, by a natural sea-bank of shingle,
thrown up in many places to the height of ten or
fifteen feet.

To the northward of Charles' Island, the mountains are more disposed in chains than they are to
the southward. The principal ridge lies nearly
north and south; and the principal valley extends from the head of Cross Bay to the northern
face of the country, a distance of 40 or 50 miles.
An inferior chain of hills, two or three leagues
from the coast, runs parallel with the shore, from
which lateral ridges project into the sea, and terminate in mural precipices. Between these lateral

ridges, some of the most remarkable icebergs on the
coast occur.   Along the northern shore of Spitzbergen, and towards the north-east, the land is
neither so elevated, nor are the hills so sharp-pointed, as on the western coast.   Indeed, some of the
islands, and considerable tracts of the main, consist
of comparatively low land.   With regard to the
land about Red Hill, it has been observed, that
there is more natural earth and clay, though with
even less vegetation, than on almost any other part
of the coast which has been visited.   The most
remarkable mountains I have seen, are situated
near Horn Sound, on Charles' Island, and near
King's Bay.   *Horn Mount,* or Hedge-hog Mount,
so called from an appearance of spines on the top
when seen in some positions, takes its rise from a
small tract of alpine land, on the southern side of
Horn Sound.   It has different summits, chiefly in
the form of spires, one of which is remarkably
acute and elevated.   I had an opportunity of determining its height in the year 1815.   From one set
of observations, its altitude came out 1457 yards,
and from another 1473, the mean of which is 1465
yards, or 4395 feet *.   Another peak, a few miles
farther to the northward, appeared to be 3306 feet
high.

---

* See a representation of this Mountain in Plate 3.

On Charles' Island is a curious peak, which juts into the sea. It is crooked, perfectly naked, being equally destitute of snow and verdure, and, from its black appearance or pointed figure, has been denominated the *Devil's Thumb.* Its height may be about 1500 or 2000 feet. The *Middle-Hook of the Foreland,* as the central part of the chain of mountains in Charles' Island is called, is a very interesting part of the coast. These mountains, which are, perhaps, the highest land adjoining the sea which is to be met with, take their rise at the water's edge, and by a continued ascent of an angle at first of about 30°, and increasing to 45° or more, each comes to a point, with the elevation of about six-sevenths of an English mile. This portion of the chain exhibits five distinct summits, the elevation of the highest of which, as determined by Captain Phipps, is 4500 feet, and of the lowest, by estimation, above 4000 feet. Some of these summits are, to appearance, within half a league, horizontal distance, of the margin of the sea. The points formed by the top of two or three of them, are so fine, that the imagination is at a loss to conceive of a place, on which an adventurer, attempting the hazardous exploit of climbing one of the summits, might rest *. Were such an undertaking practicable, it is evident it could not be effected without imminent danger.

---

* See Plate 3. fig. 3.

Besides extraordinary courage and strength requisite in the adventurer, such an attempt would need the utmost powers of exertion, as well as the most irresistible perseverance.   Frederick Martens, in his excellent account of a " Voyage to Spitzbergen," undertaken in the year 1671, describes some of the cliffs as consisting of but one stone from the bottom to the top, or as appearing like an old decayed wall, and as smelling very sweet, where covered with lichens. In Magdalene Bay, the rocks he describes as lying in a semicircular form, having at each extremity two high mountains, with natural excavations, " after the fashion of a breast-work," and at their summits, points and cracks like battlements.

Some of the mountains of Spitzbergen are well proportioned four-sided pyramids, rising out of a base of a mile or a mile and a half, to a league square ; others form angular chains, resembling the roof of a house, which recede from the shore in parallel ridges, until they dwindle into obscurity in the distant perspective.   Some exhibit the exact resemblance of art, but in a style of grandeur exceeding the famed pyramids of the East, or even the more wonderful Tower of Babel, the presumptive design and arrogant continuation of which, was checked by the miraculous confusion of tongues.   An instance of such a regular and magnificent work of Nature, is seen near the head of King's Bay, consisting of three piles of rocks, of a regular form, known by

the name of the *Three Crowns*. They rest on
the top of the ordinary mountains, each commencing with a square table or horizontal stratum of
rock, on the top of which is another of similar form
and height, but of a smaller area; this is continued
by a third, a fourth, and so on, each succeeding
stratum being less than the next below it, until it
forms a pyramid of steps, almost as regular, to appearance, as if worked by art. I do not know that
the Three Crowns have ever been visited, or what
may be their actual form; but the appearance I
have attempted to describe, is that which they
exhibit at the distance of from five to ten leagues.
In Plate 3. is a representation of these interesting objects, seen at the distance of at least thirty
miles.

Many of the mountains of Spitzbergen are inaccessible. The steepness of the ascent, and the looseness of the rocks, with the numerous lodgments of
ice in the clefts or sides of the cliffs, constitute, in
many places, insurmountable obstacles. Some hills,
indeed, may be climbed with tolerable safety, but
generally the attempt is hazardous. Martens notices the necessity of marking every step with chalk,
as the adventurer climbs the rugged mountain,
otherwise he will not know how to get down. In
advancing, he observes, it seems easy enough to be
done, but in descending, it is found so difficult and

G 2

dangerous, that many have fallen and lost their lives in the attempt *.

When Barentz and Heemskerke discovered Cherry Island, on their advance towards the north, when they also discovered Spitzbergen, some daring fellows among their sailors, who had been collecting birds' eggs, climbed a high steep mountain, resembling those of Spitzbergen, where they unexpectedly found themselves in a most perilous situation; for, on turning to descend, the way by which they had advanced presented a dismal assemblage of pointed rocks, perpendicular precipices, and yawning chasms. The view of the danger of the descent struck them with terror. No relief, however, could be afforded them, and they were obliged to make the attempt. They soon lost the track by which they had reached the summit, and were bewildered among the rocks. At length, after a most anxious and painful exercise, in which they found it necessary to slide down the rocks, while lying flat on their bodies, they reached the foot of the cliff in safety. Barentz, who had observed their conduct from the shore, gave them a sharp reproof for their rash temerity †.

---

* Martens' Voyage, originally printed in the Dutch language, has been translated into English, and published in "An Account of several late Voyages and Discoveries to the South and North." *London*, 1694, 8vo.

† Beschryving, &c. vol. iii.

A merchant of Holland, of the name of Kiin, who accompanied the first Dutch ship which sailed to the Spitzbergen whale-fishery, in the year 1612, undertook the dangerous achievement of climbing one of the principal mountains on Charles' Island. He made some progress in the bold attempt, but slipping his foot, he fell down the steep acclivity and broke his neck.

One of the most interesting appearances to be found in Spitzbergen, is the Iceberg. This term, written Ysberg by the Dutch, signifies ice-mountain. I speak not here of the islands of ice which are borne to southern climates on the bosom of the ocean, but of those prodigious lodgments of ice which occur in the valleys adjoining the coast of Spitzbergen and other Polar countries, from which the floating icebergs seem to be derived. Where a chain of hills lies parallel to the line of the coast, and within a few miles distance of the sea-beach, having lateral ridges jutting towards the sea, at intervals of a league or two, we have a most favourable situation for the formation of icebergs. Such is precisely the nature of the situation a little to the northward of Charles' Island, where the conspicuous bodies of ice noticed by Martens, Phipps and others, and known by the name of the *Seven Icebergs*, occur. Each of these occupies a deep valley, opening towards the sea, formed by hills of about 2000 feet elevation on the sides, and termina-

ted in the interior by the chain of mountains, of
perhaps 3000 to 3500 feet in height, which follows
the line of the coast.   They are exactly of the nature and appearance of glaciers; they commence
at the margin of the sea, where they frequently constitute a considerable precipice, and extend along
the valley, which commonly rises with a gentle
slope, until they are either terminated by the brow
of the mountain in the back-ground, or interrupted
by a precipitous summit.   Besides these icebergs,
there are some, equally large, near the north-west
angle of Spitzbergen, in King's Bay and in Cross
Bay, and some of much greater magnitude near
Point-look-out, besides many others of various sizes,
in the large sounds on the western side, and along
the northern and eastern shores of this remarkable
country.

The Seven Icebergs are each, on an average,
about a mile in length, and perhaps near 200 feet
in height at the sea-edge; but some of those to the
southward are much greater.   A little to the northward of Horn Sound, is the largest iceberg I have
seen.   It occupies eleven miles in length, of the
sea-coast.   The highest part of the precipitous
front adjoining the sea is, by measurement, 402
feet, and it extends backward toward the summit
of the mountain, to about four times that elevation.
Its surface forms a beautiful inclined plane of
smooth snow : the edge is uneven and perpendicu-

lar. At the distance of fifteen miles, the front-
edge, subtended an angle of ten minutes of a degree. Near the South Cape lies another iceberg,
nearly as extensive as this. It occupies the space
between two lateral ridges of hills, and reaches the
very summit of the mountain, in the back-ground,
on which it rests.

It is not easy to form an adequate conception of
these truly wonderful productions of Nature. Their
magnitude, their beauty, and the contrast they form
with the gloomy rocks around, produce sensations
of lively interest. Their upper surfaces are generally concave; the higher parts are always covered with snow, and have a beautiful appearance; but
the lower parts, in the latter end of every summer,
present a bare surface of ice. The front of each,
which varies in height from the level of the ocean,
to 400 or 500 feet above it, lies parallel with the
shore, and is generally washed by the sea. This
part, resting on the strand, is undermined to such
an extent by the sea, when in any way turbulent,
that immense masses, loosened by the freezing
of water lodged in the recesses in winter, or by
the effect of streams of water running over its
surface and through its chasms in summer, break
asunder, and with a thundering noise fall into the
sea. But as the water is in most places shallow in
front of these icebergs, the masses which are dislodged are commonly reduced into fragments before

they can be floated away into the main sea. This fact seems to account for the rarity of icebergs in the Spitzbergen sea.

The front surface of icebergs is glistening and uneven. Wherever a part has recently broken off, the colour of the fresh fracture is a beautiful greenish-blue, approaching to emerald green; but such parts as have long been exposed to the air, are of a greenish-grey colour, and at a distance sometimes exhibit the appearance of cliffs of whitish marble. In all cases, the effect of the iceberg is to form a pleasing variety in prospect, with the magnificence of the encompassing snow-clad mountains, which, as they recede from the eye, seem to " rise crag above crag," in endless perspective.

On an excursion to one of the Seven Icebergs, in July 1818, I was particularly fortunate in witnessing one of the grandest effects which these Polar glaciers ever present. A strong north-westerly swell having for some hours been beating on the shore, had loosened a number of fragments attached to the iceberg, and various heaps of broken ice denoted recent shoots of the seaward edge. As we rowed towards it with a view of proceeding close to its base, I observed a few little pieces fall from the top, and while my eye was fixed upon the place, an immense column, probably fifty feet square, and one hundred and fifty feet high, began to leave the parent ice at the top, and leaning majestically forward with an accelerated velocity, fell with an awful crash into the sea.   The water into which it plunged was converted into an appearance of vapour or smoke, like that from a furious cannonading.   The noise was equal to that of thunder, which it nearly resembled.   The column which fell was nearly square, and in magnitude resembled a church.   It broke into thousands of pieces.   This circumstance was a happy caution; for we might inadvertently have gone to the very base of the icy cliff, from whence masses of considerable magnitude were continually breaking.   This iceberg was full of rents, as high as any of our people ascended upon it, extending in a direction perpendicularly downward, and dividing it into innumerable columns.   The surface was very uneven, being furrowed and cracked all over.   This roughness appeared to be occasioned by the melting of the snow, some streams of water being seen running over the surface; and others having worn away the superficial ice, could still be heard pursuing their course through subglacial channels to the front of the iceberg, where, in transparent streams, or in small cascades, they fell into the sea.   In some places, chasms of several yards in width were seen, in others they were only a few inches or feet across.   One of the sailors who attempted to walk across the iceberg, imprudently stept into a narrow chasm filled up with snow to the general level.   He instantly plunged up

to his shoulders, and might, but for the sudden extension of his arms, have been buried in the gulf.

In the first ages of the Spitzbergen fishery, when
the ships frequented the bays and harbours, and
sometimes moored close to the shore, many serious
disasters were occasioned by the fall of pieces of
icebergs. An instance is recorded by PURCHAS
in his " Pilgrimes." One of the Russia Company's ships, which was on the whale-fishery in the
year 1619, was driven on shore in Bell Sound, by
ice setting in from the sea. The Captain, with
most of his crew and boats, was absent at the time
of the accident ; but on the first intelligence, caused his boats to be hauled up on the ice, and proceeded on board to endeavour to get the ship off. After
they had been using every endeavour for this purpose during about an hour, a main piece of an adjoining ice-cliff came down, and almost overwhelmed the vessel and her crew in its ruins. The
shock must have been tremendous. The ice which
fell, struck the ship so high and so forcibly, that it
carried away the fore-mast, " broke the main-mast,"
sprung the bowsprit, and flung the ship over with
such violence, that a piece of ordnance was thrown
overboard from under the half-deck ; and the Captain and some of the crew were projected in the
same way. The Captain, notwithstanding his imminent danger, with fragments of ice flying in all
directions, and the masts of the ship falling around

him, escaped unhurt; but the mate, and two more of the crew, were killed, and many others were wounded*.

Icebergs are probably formed of more solid ice than glaciers; but in every other respect they are very similar. The ice of which they consist is, indeed, a little porous; but considerable pieces are found of perfect transparency. Being wholly produced from rain or snow, the water is necessarily potable. Icebergs have also the same kind of origin as glaciers. The time of their foundation, or first stratum being frozen, is probably nearly coeval with the land on which they are lodged. Their subsequent increase seems to have been produced by the congelation of the sleet of summer or autumn, and of the bed of snow annually accumulated in winter, which, being partly dissolved by the summer sun, becomes consolidated; and, on the decline of the summer heat, frozen into a new stratum of transparent ice. Snow subjected by a gentle heat to a thawing process, is first converted into large grains of ice, and these are united, and afterwards consolidated, under particular circumstances, by the water which filters through among them. If, when this imperfectly congealed mass has got cooled down below the freezing temperature by an interval of cold weather,

---

* *Letter of John Chambers to William Heley*, dated Bell Sound, 16th June 1619;—Purchas' " Pilgrimes," vol. iii. p. 734.

the sun break out and operate on the upper surface
so as to dissolve it, the water which results runs
into the porous mass, progressively fills the cavities, and being then exposed to an internal temperature sufficiently low, freezes the whole into a solid
body.   Or if, when the ice has been cooled by a
low temperature, a fog or sleet occur, it is frozen as
it falls, and encrusts the body of the iceberg with
an additional varnish of ice.

Icebergs are as permanent as the rocks on which
they rest; for though large portions may be frequently separated from the lower edge, or, by large
avalanches from the mountain summit, be hurled
into the sea, yet the annual growth replenishes the
loss, and, probably on the whole, produces a perpetual increase.   But the annual supply of ice is not
only added to the upper part, but also to the precipitous crest facing the sea; which addition being
run into, or suspended over the ocean, admits of
new fragments being detached, and of the renewal
of the vitreous surface which it presents to the eye
after each separation.   In some places, indeed,
where the sea is almost perpetually covered with
ice, the berg or glacier makes its way to a great extent into the sea, until it reaches the depth in the
water, of several hundreds of feet; and then being
capable of large dismemberments, gives rise to the
kind of mountainous masses or icebergs, found
afloat in such abundance in the sea to the westward

of Greenland. Thus, the extent of surface occupied by each iceberg, is limited by the mountains on
three sides, and by the sea, in a measure, on the
fourth; but as to its thickness, there seems no natural obstacle to its perpetual increase.

Spitzbergen and its islands, with some other
countries within the Arctic circle, exhibit a kind
of scenery which is altogether novel. The principal objects which strike the eye, are innumerable
mountainous peaks, ridges, precipices, or needles,
rising immediately out of the sea, to an elevation
of 3000 or 4000 feet, the colour of which, at a moderate distance, appears to be blackish shades of
brown, green, grey and purple; snow or ice in striæ
or patches, occupying the various clefts and hollows
in the sides of the hills, capping some of the mountain summits, and filling with extended beds the
most considerable valleys; and ice of the glacier
form, occurring at intervals all along the coast, in
particular situations as already described, in prodigious accumulations. The glistening or vitreous
appearance of the iceberg precipices; the purity,
whiteness, and beauty of the sloping expanse, formed by their snowy surfaces; the gloomy shade presented by the adjoining or intermixed mountains
and rocks, perpetually " covered with a mourning
veil of black lichens," with the sudden transitions
into a robe of purest white, where patches or beds

of snow occur, present a variety and extent of contrast altogether peculiar; which, when enlightened
by the occasional ethereal brilliancy of the Polar sky,
and harmonized in its serenity with the calmness
of the ocean,. constitute a picture both novel and
magnificent.   There is, indeed, a kind of majesty,
not to be conveyed in words, in these extraordinary
accumulations of snow and ice in the valleys, and
in the rocks above rocks, and peaks above peaks, in
the mountain groups, seen rising above the ordinary elevation of the clouds, and terminating occasionally in crests of everlasting snow, especially
when you approach the shore under shelter of the
impenetrable density of a summer fog; in which
case the fog sometimes disperses like the drawing
of a curtain, when the strong contrast of light and
shade, heightened by a cloudless atmosphere and
powerful sun, bursts on the senses in a brilliant
exhibition, resembling the production of magic.

To this strong contrast of light and shade, with
the great height and steepness of the mountains, is
to be attributed a remarkable deception in the apparent distance of the land.   Any strangers to the
Arctic countries, however well acquainted with other
regions, and however capable of judging of the distance of land generally, must be completely at a loss
in their estimations when they approach within sight
of Spitzbergen.   When at the distance of twenty
miles, it would be no difficult matter to induce even

a judicious stranger to undertake a passage in a boat
to the shore, from the belief that he was within a
league of the land. At this distance, the portions of
rock and patches of snow, as well as the contour of
the different hills, are as distinctly marked, as similar objects, in many other countries, not having
snow about them, would be at a fourth or a fifth part
of the same distance. Not, indeed, strangers only,
but persons who have been often to Spitzbergen,
such as the officers and seamen of the whale-ships,
have not unfrequently imagined, that their ship
could not stand an hour towards the land without
running aground; and yet, perhaps, the ship has
sailed three or four hours directly " in shore," and
still been remote from danger. This is a fact which
I have seen realized among my own officers repeatedly. There are circumstances, indeed, when, by a
slight change in the density of the atmosphere, a
ship, after sailing towards the land for some hours,
may appear to be as far off as at first. Thus, in
clear weather, the high land of Spitzbergen is perfectly well defined, and every thing on it appears
distinct, when at the distance of forty miles. If,
after sailing five hours towards the shore, from this
situation, at the rate of four or five knots *per* hour,
the atmosphere should become a little hazy, or even
only dark and cloudy, the land might appear to be
further distant than before. Hence we can account,
on a reasonable ground, for a curious circumstance

related in a Danish voyage, undertaken for the recovery of the last colony in Greenland, by Mogens
Heinson.   This person, who passed for a renowned
seaman in his day, was sent out by Frederick II.
King of Denmark.   After encountering many difficulties and dangers from storms and ice, he got
sight of the east coast of Greenland, and attempted
to get to it; but though the sea was quite free
from ice, and the wind favourable, and blowing a
fresh gale, he, after proceeding several hours without appearing to get any nearer the land, became
alarmed, tacked about, and returned to Denmark.
On his arrival, he attributed this extraordinary circumstance, magnified, no doubt, by his fears, to his
vessel having been stopped in its course by " some
loadstone rocks hidden in the sea."   Most authors
who have had occasion to refer to Heinson's voyage,
have speculated on this circumstance; but no one,
I believe, has satisfactorily explained the origin of
his fears.   The true cause, however, of what he
took to be a submarine magnetic influence, arose, I
doubt not, from the deceptive character of the land
as to distance, which I have attempted to describe.

From this character of Spitzbergen, there is little probability of strangers getting too near the
shore, or running into danger; for even in hazy or
snowy weather the effulgence of the land penetrates
the density of the atmosphere, to several times the
extent to which other objects are visible ; and even

in fogs, the tops of the mountains frequently appear above the region occupied by the densest stratum of mist, and warn the navigator of his advance into danger.

The same deception in the distance of terrestrial objects, and, consequently, in their real magnitude, prevails when a person is on shore, as when he views them from a station at sea. Whenever a little table land is found between the beach and the foot of the mountains, the distance across it will seldom appear above a furlong or two, though it actually should be nearly a league. Martens alluding to this deception, says, " The miles in Spitzbergen seem to be very short; but when you attempt to walk them upon the land, you will soon be weary, and unde-ceived."

Spitzbergen abounds with deep bays and exten-sive sounds, in many of which are excellent har-bours. Instead of describing the situation and ex-tent of each of these bays and sounds, which may be known by inspection of the accompanying map*, or by reference to the table of latitudes and longi-tudes in the Appendix, No. IV., I shall only no-

VOL. I.   H

* In the map of Spitzbergen, an extent of coast of above 200 miles, included between Point-look-out and Hackluyt's Headland, is laid down from an original survey. In several particular situations I found an error of 10 miles of latitude and 2 or 3 degrees of longitude, in our most approved charts.

tice such of the harbours, or other particular parts
of the coast, as have been visited by myself or described by others.

From Point-look-out to Hackluyt's Headland,
the west coast of Spitzbergen forms almost a series
of rocks and foul ground; few parts, excepting the
bays, affording anchorage for ships. In many places
the rocks run off shore, to the distance of two or
three miles, or even as many leagues, especially between Point-look-out and Horn Sound, and between
the latter and Bell Sound; also near Black Point on
the Foreland, as well as near some of the projections
of this island; at Mitre Cape on the main, and near
one of the Seven Icebergs, &c.   Some of these rocks
are dangerous to shipping, drying only at low water,
or only showing themselves when the sea is high;
others are constantly above water, or altogether so
far below the surface, that they can either be seen
and avoided, or sailed over in moderate weather
without much hazard.   On the east-side of Point-
look-out, a ridge of stony ground stretches five
leagues into the sea towards the south-east, on
which the sea occasionally breaks.

Horn Sound affords tolerable anchorage; within
Bell Sound are several anchoring places and some
rivers; and in Ice-Sound, at Green-Harbour, is
good anchorage near the bank, in ten to eight fathoms water, or less.   In several other places, when
not encumbered with ice, there is pretty good

refuge for ships. But when these places are accessible, it is generally necessary to beware of the
motions of the ice along the coast; for, in the latter end of summer or in the course of the autumn,
when the ice begins to set in from the southward,
it is time to be gone, otherwise ships are in danger
of getting blockaded with it during the winter.
On the side of Fair Foreland next the main is a
sandy bank, on which is good anchorage; also in
English Bay, West Cross Bay, Magdalena Bay,
Smeerenberg, the Norways, Vogel Sang, Love Bay,
&c. there are good roadsteads. Fair Haven, consisting of several sounds among the islands lying
on the north-west corner of Spitzbergen, was surveyed in the year 1773 by Captain Phipps. In
one of these sounds, included between Vogel Sang
and Cloven Cliff, as well as in the harbour of
Smeerenberg, the expedition under Captain Phipps
anchored. The former is represented as a good
roadstead, but open from N. E. to N. W. But
though exposed to the northward, the sound of Vogel Sang " is not liable to any inconvenience from
that circumstance, the main body of the ice lying so
near as to prevent any great sea; nor are ships in
any danger from the loose ice setting in, as this
road communicates with several others formed by
different islands, between all which there are safe

H 2

passages *." This place, called also the *North Harbour,* is easily known, from the remarkable appearance of Cloven Cliff, the north-easternmost land seen from the anchorage. Being an insulated cliff, joining the other land only by a long narrow isthmus, it preserves in all situations nearly the same form; and being nearly perpendicular, is never disguised with snow. Besides this roadstead, is Cook's Hole, about two miles to the eastward, the Norways, a league and a quarter towards the south-east, and Smeerenberg, one of the best sheltered harbours on this coast, about eleven miles towards the south-west. The latter, formed between Amsterdam and other islands, and the main, affords good anchorage in thirteen fathoms, sandy bottom, not far from the shore †. The outlets are by the north, by the west, and by the south-west, three good channels: the western one, however, is a little obstructed with rocks.

On the north and east sides of Spitzbergen, are several harbours, some of them very safe and commodious; but they are not so often free from ice as those to the westward, and therefore have seldom been visited.

---

* Phipp's Voyage towards the North Pole, p. 44.

† Idem, p. 68.

The access to some of the harbours of Spitzbergen, is, under some circumstances, and with certain
winds, somewhat difficult, if not dangerous. Calms,
from the shelter afforded by the high and precipitous mountains, are frequent in some harbours, and
eddy-winds, squalls and whirlwinds, are found occasionally to prevail.

Though the whale-fishers in the present age generally see the land of Spitzbergen every voyage,
yet not many of them visit its shores. Few opportunities indeed occur, for satisfying a rational curiosity, in the examination of this remarkable country. My Father, however, has been several times
on shore in different parts. In the year 1813, he
cruised for several days among the islands of Fair-
Haven ; and in 1816, had boats on shore at Point-
look-out. Here they observed several huts, forming
the summer residences of the Russian hunters or fishers, who frequent this remote country, one of which,
from a date marked on the side of it, appeared to
have stood ever since the year 1784. A post erected near the beach, as a mark, probably, for the best
landing place, or for a signal staff, was curiously
carved with a number of grotesque figures. They
observed something curious in the structure of the
rocks, and in the productions of the country ; but
the dangers of the coast prevented them from
making that examination which was desirable.

My first landing in an arctic country, was on Charles' Island or Fair Foreland, at the north-west point. On this occasion, I expected to have had time for a particular exploration of the country, as the weather was calm and clear when I went on shore ; but suddenly, a thick fog and breeze of wind commencing, obliged us to put off with haste, and subjected us to great anxiety before we found the ship. As nothing particular was observed, which did not occur on future excursions, it is unnecessary to give any account of the objects of interest which excited my attention. I shall only mention, that the number of birds seen in the precipices and rocks adjoining the sea, was immense ; and the noise which they made on our approach was quite deafening.

In the summer of 1818, I was several times on shore on the main near *Mitre Cape* *, and landed

---

* This being a remarkable point, and dangerous to shipping going into King's Bay or Cross Bay, being surrounded with blind rocks, and yet, as far as I could discover, without a name, I ventured to denominate it Mitre Cape, from an insulated rock about 1500 feet in height, which terminates the high land stretching towards the south, being cleft down the middle, and having the form of a mitre. For the sake of brevity in description, as well as perspicuity, I have also ventured to apply names to two or three other remarkable parts of the land, which have hitherto stood in the charts undistinguished.

once, in the same season, on the north side of King's Bay. Being near the land on the evening of the 23d of July, the weather beautifully clear, and all our sails becalmed by the hills, excepting the top-gallant sails, in which we had constantly a gentle breeze, I left the ship in charge of a principal officer, with orders to stand no nearer than into thirty fathoms water, and with two boats and fourteen men rowed to the shore. We arrived at the beach about $7\frac{1}{2}$ P. M., and landed on a track of low flat ground, extending about six miles north and south, and two or three east and west, from the east side of which, a mountain-arm takes its rise, terminating on the south with the remarkable insulated cliff constituting Mitre Cape. This table land lies so low, that it would be overflown by the sea, were it not for a natural embankment of shingle thrown up by the sea; indeed, from the sea-weed and drift-wood found upon it, it seems at no very remote period, to have been covered by the tide. The shingle forming the sea-bank consists, in general, of remarkably round pebbles; many of them being calcareous, are prettily veined.

After advancing about half a furlong from the sea, we met with mica-slate, in nearly perpendicular strata; and a little farther on, with an extensive bed of limestone in small angular fragments. Here and there we saw large ponds of fresh water, derived from melted ice and snow.;

in some places small remains of snow; and, lastly,
near the base of the mountains, a considerable morass, into which we sunk nearly to the knees.   Some
unhealthy looking mosses appeared on this swamp;
but the softest part, as well as most of the ground
we had hitherto traversed, was entirely void of vegetation.   This swamp had a moorish look, and
consisted apparently of black alluvial soil, mixed with some vegetable remains, and was curiously
marked on the surface with small polygonal ridges,
from one to three yards in diameter, so combined,
as to give the ground an appearance similar to that
exhibited by a section of honeycomb.   An ascent
of a few yards from the morass, on somewhat firm-
er ground, brought us to the foot of the first mountain to the northward of the Mitre.   Here, some
pretty specimens of Saxifraga oppositifolia and
Groenlandica, Salix herbacea, Draba alpina, Papaver
alpina (of Mr Don,) &c.; and some other plants in
full flower, were found on little tufts of soil, and
scattered about on the ascent   The first hill
rose at an inclination of 45 degrees, to the
height of about 1500 feet, and was joined on the
north side to another of about twice the elevation.
We begin to climb the acclivity on the most accessible side, at about 10 p. m,; but from the looseness of
the stones and the steepness of the ascent, we found
it a most difficult undertaking.   There was scarcely
a possibility of advancing by the common movement

of walking; for in this attempt the ground gave way at every step, and no progress was made : hence the only method of succeeding was by the effort of leaping or running, which, under the peculiar circumstances, could not be accomplished without excessive fatigue. In the direction we travelled, we met with angular fragments of limestone and quartz, chiefly of one or two pounds weight, and a few naked rocks protruding through the loose materials of which the side of the mountain, to the extent it was visible, was principally composed. These rocks appeared solid at a little distance, but on examination were found to be full of fractures in every direction, so that it was with difficulty that a specimen of five or six pounds weight, in a solid mass, could be obtained. Along the side of the first range of hills near the summit, was extended a band of ice and snow, which, in the direct ascent, we tried in vain to surmount. By great exertion, however, in tra-cing the side of the hill for about 200 yards, where it was so uncommonly steep that at every step showers of stones were precipitated to the bottom, we found a sort of angle of the hill free from ice, by which the summit was scaled.

Here we rested until I took a few angles and bearings of the most prominent parts of the coast; when, having collected specimens of the minerals, and such few plants as the barren ridge afforded, we proceeded on our excursion. In our way to the

principal mountain near us, we passed along a ridge
of the secondary mountains, which was so acute that
I sat across it with a leg on each side, as on horse-
back.   One side of it made an angle with the horizon of 50°, and the other of 40°.   To the very top,
it consisted of loose sharp limestones, of a yellowish or reddish colour, smaller in size than the
stones generally used for repairing high roads, few
pieces being above a pound in weight.   The fracture appeared rather fresh.   After passing along
this ridge about three or four furlongs, and crossing
a lodgment of ice and snow, we descended by a sort
of ravine to the side of the principal mountain,
which arose with a uniformly steep ascent, similar
to that we had already surmounted, to the very
summit.   The ascent was now even more difficult
than before : we could make no considerable progress but by the exertion of leaping and running ;
so that we were obliged to rest after every fifty or
sixty paces.   No solid rock was met with, and no
earth or soil.   The stones, however, were larger ;
appeared more decayed ; and were more uniformly
covered with black lichens ; but several plants of the
saxifraga, salix, draba, cochlearia, and juncus genera, which had been met with here and there for the
first two thousand feet of elevation, began to disappear as we approached the summit.   The invariably
broken state of the rocks appeared to have been the
effect of frost.   On calcareous rocks, some of which

are not impervious to moisture, the effect is such as might be expected; but how frost can operate in this way on quartz, is not so easily understood.

As we completed the arduous ascent, the sun had just reached the meridian below the Pole, and still shed his reviving rays of unimpaired brilliancy on a small surface of snow which capped the mountain's summit. A thermometer placed among stones in the shade of the brow of the hill, indicated a temperature as high as 37°. At the top of the first hill, the temperature was 42°; and at the foot, on the plain, 44° to 46°: so that, at the very peak of the mountain, estimated at 3000 feet elevation, the power of the sun, at midnight, produced a temperature several degrees above the freezing point, and occasioned the discharge of streams of water from the snow-capped summit.

It may appear a little remarkable, that an effect of cold, amounting to perpetual frost, that is observed in elevated situations, in temperate, and even in hot climates, does not occur on the tops of considerable mountains in Spitzbergen: and it is really extraordinary, that inferior mountains, such as Ben Nevis, in Scotland, the elevation of which is only about 4380 feet, should sometimes exhibit a crest of snow throughout the year; while, in Spitzbergen, where the mean annual temperature is about 30° lower than in Scotland, and the mountains little inferior in elevation, the snow should sometimes be wholly dissolved, at the most considerable heights. The higher Alps, excepting what is absolutely perpendicular, remain constantly covered with snow; and perhaps no instance of a thawing temperature ever occurs on any of the most elevated summits. But, in Spitzbergen, the frost relaxes in the months of July and August, and a thawing temperature prevails for considerable intervals on the greatest heights which have been visited. Martens observes, that in some of the countries of Europe, when rain falls in the valleys, snow descends upon the mountains, even in the height of summer; but that in Spitzbergen, rain falls on the tops of the highest hills.

As the capacity of air for heat increases as its density decreases, and that in such a degree that about every ninety yards of elevation in the lower atmosphere produces a depression of one degree of temperature of Fahrenheit, we find that the elevation of some of the Alps, Pyrenees, and mountains of Nepaul, in the temperate zone, and of the Andes and others in the torrid zone, is such, that their summits are above the level where a temperature of thawing can at any time prevail; and though, by the application of this principle to the mountains of Spitzbergen, we find that a thawing temperature may be occasionally expected; yet we do not see how the prevalence of a thaw should be so continual as to disperse the winter's coat of snow, where the mean temperature of the hottest month in the year must, on a mountain of 1500 feet elevation or up-ward, probably be below the freezing point *. Per-haps the difficulty is to be thus resolved : The weather in the months of June, July and August, is much clearer at Spitzbergen than it is near the neighbouring ice, where most of my observations on temperature were made ; and, as such, the tempe-rature of these months on shore must be warmer than at sea, and so much higher indeed, as is re-quisite for occasioning the dissolution of the snow even on the tops of the mountains. And this is no doubt the fact ; for, besides the increase of tempera-ture produced by the prevalent clearness of the at-mosphere, we may bring into the account the cir-cumstance that, from the steepness of the hills, the sun is always actually vertical, to one surface or other

---

* The mean temperature of July in the Greenland sea, latitude 78°, as determined from a considerable series of ob-servations (Appendix, No. II.), is no higher than 37°; and of August about 2 degrees less : as such, the mean temperature of July on a hill 500 yards high, must be below the freezing point: For 500 yards divided by 90 yards, the elevation re-quisite for producing 1 degree depression of temperature, give a product of $5\frac{5}{9}$°, which, subtracted from 37°, the tempera-ture at the level of the sea, leaves $31\frac{4}{9}$°, as the mean tem-perature at the top of the hill.

of the mountainous coast, throughout its daily course.

The highest temperature I ever observed in Spitzbergen was 48°; but in the summer of 1773, when Captain Phipps visited Spitzbergen, a temperature of 58½° once occurred *. Supposing this to be the greatest degree of heat which takes place, it will require an elevation of 7791 feet for reducing that temperature to the freezing point; and hence we may reckon this to be about the altitude of the *upper* line of congelation, where frost perpetually prevails †.

The form of the mountain-summit which I visited, is round-backed; the area of the part approaching the horizontal position not being above a quarter of an acre. The south side where we ascended, and the south-east, are the only accessible parts; the east, north and west aspects being precipitous nearly from top to bottom. What snow still remained on the summit, was but a few inches deep, and appeared to be in a state of rapid dissolution; the sides of the hill were almost entirely free from snow. The masses of stone on the brow

---

* Voyage towards the North Pole, p. 46.

† See Professor Leslie's Geometry. 2d edition, .*Table*. p. 496.

of the mountain were larger than any we had yet
met with, the fracture was less fresh, and they were
more generally covered with lichens.

From the brow of the mountain, on the side by
which we ascended, many masses of stone were dislodged by design or accident, which, whatever might
be their size, shape or weight, generally made their
way with accelerated velocity to the bottom. As
they bounded from rock to rock, they produced considerable smoke at each concussion, and setting in
motion numerous fragments in their course, they
were usually accompanied by showers of stones, all
of which were lodged in a bed of snow, lying 2000
feet below the place where the first were disengaged.
This may afford some idea of the nature of the inclination. Most of the larger stones which were set
off, broke into numbers of pieces; but some considerable masses of a tabular form, wheeled down upon
their edges, and though they made bounds of several
hundred feet at a time, and acquired a most astonishing velocity, they sometimes got to the bottom
without breaking.

The prospect was most extensive and grand. A
fine sheltered bay was seen on the east of us, an
arm of the same on the north-east, and the sea,
whose glassy surface was unruffled by a breeze,
formed an immense expanse on the west; the ice-
bergs rearing their proud crests almost to the tops
of the mountains between which they were lodged,

and, defying the power of the solar beams, were scattered in various directions about the sea-coast and in the adjoining bays. Beds of snow and ice filling extensive hollows, and giving an enamelled coat to adjoining valleys, one of which, commencing at the foot of the mountain where we stood, extended in a continued line towards the north, as far as the eye could reach; mountain rising above mountain, until by distance they dwindled into insignificancy; the whole contrasted by a cloudless canopy of deepest azure, and enlightened by the rays of a blazing sun, and the effect aided by a feeling of danger, seated as we were on the pinnacle of a rock, almost surrounded by tremendous precipices,—all united to constitute a picture singularly sublime. Here we seemed elevated into the very heavens; and though in an hazardous situation, I was sensible only of pleasing emotions, heightened by the persuasion, that, from experience in these kind of adventures, I was superior to the dangers with which I was surrounded. The effect of the elevation, and the brightness of the picture, were such, that the sea, which was at least a league from us, appeared within reach of a musket shot; mountains a dozen miles off, seemed scarcely a league from us; and our vessel which we knew was at the distance of a league from the shore, appeared in danger of the rocks.

After a short rest, in which we were much re-
freshed with a gentle breeze of wind that here
prevailed ; and after we had surveyed the surrounding scenery as long as it afforded any thing striking,
we commenced the descent. This task, however,
which, before the attempt, we had viewed with in-
difference, we found really a very hazardous, and
in some instances a painful undertaking. The way
now seemed precipitous. Every movement was a
work of deliberation. The stones were so sharp
that they cut our boots and pained our feet, and so
loose that they gave way almost at every step, and
frequently threw us backward with force against the
hill. We were careful to advance abreast of each
other, for any individual being below us would
have been in danger of being overwhelmed with
the stones, which we unintentionally dislodged in
showers. Having by much care, and with some
anxiety, made good our descent to the top of the
secondary hills, to save the fatigue of crawling along
the sharp ridge that we had before traversed, we
took down one of the steepest banks, the inclination of which was little less than fifty degrees. The
stones here being very small and loose, we sat down
on the side of the hill, and slid forward with great
facility in a sitting posture. Towards the foot of
the hill, an expanse of snow stretched across the
line of descent. This being loose and soft, we
entered upon it without fear, and our progress at

first was by no means rapid ; but on reaching the middle of it, we came to a surface of solid ice, perhaps a hundred yards across, over which we launched with astonishing velocity, but happily escaped without injury. The men whom we left below, viewed this latter movement with astonishment and fear.

On the flat of land next the sea, we met with the horns of rein-deer, many skulls and other bones of sea-horses, whales, narwhales, foxes and seals, and some human skeletons laid in chest-like coffins, exposed naked on the strand. Two Russian lodges formed of logs of pine, with a third in ruins, were also seen ; the former, from a quantity of fresh chips about them, and other appearances within them, gave evidence of their having been recently inhabited. One of them, though small, seemed a middling kind of lodging, but smelt intolerably of the smoke of wood and steam of oil. Many domestic utensils were within and about it. A new hurdle lay by the door, and traps for foxes and birds were scattered along the beach. These huts were built upon the ridge of shingle adjoining the sea.

Among the shingle on the beach, were numbers of nests, containing the eggs of terns, ducks, and burgomasters, and in some of them were young birds. One of the latter, which we took on board, was very lively, and grew rapidly ; but having taken a

fancy to a cake of white lead, with which the surgeon was finishing a drawing, he was poisoned.
The nests were all watched by the respective birds
they belonged to ; which, with loud screams and bold
attacks, defended them from the arctic gulls and
other predatory birds that hovered about the place.
They even descended within a yard or two of some
of the sailors, who were so cruel as to take their
eggs or young, and followed them for a considerable
time, screaming most violently. Several of these
eggs were afterwards hatched in warm saw-dust, but
the young birds generally died soon after they left
the shell.

The only insect I saw was a small green fly,
which swarmed upon the shingle about the beach.
The sea along the coast teemed with a species of
helix, with the clio borealis, and with small shrimps.
But no animal of the class Vermes was seen on the
shore. The birds seen were the puffin, tern, little
auk, guillemot, *black* guillemot or tyste, kittiwake,
fulmar, burgomaster, arctic gull, brent-goose, eider-
duck, crimson-headed sparrow (Fringilla flammea),
sandpiper, &c. ; but no living quadruped was observed.

Drift-wood was seen in some abundance; but all
of it seemed to have lain long on the beach, being
much battered and bleached, and some of it was
worm-eaten.

A strong north-west wind having recently prevailed, the shore was in many places covered with

deep beds of sea-weed. Among these we distinguished the Fucus vesiculosus, esculentus, saccharinus, filum, plumosus, sinuosus, clavellosus, &c. and some species of Conferva.

Of all the objects, however, that we met with in the course of our research, none excited so much interest as the carcase of a dead whale, found stranded on the beach ; which, though much swollen, and not a little putrid, at once fixed our attention, and diverted us from objects of mere curiosity. It proved a prize to us of the value of about 400 *l.*, but was not secured without much labour. Being embedded in the shingle, and surrounded by rocks, we found it would be impossible to float it off; we were, therefore, under the necessity of flensing it where it lay, and of taking its produce to the ship in boats. After the first incision was made into its side, oil sprung out in streams, and required the attention of several persons to collect it and put it into the boats. From the dangerous nature of the coast, we were unable to bring the ship within two miles of the shore ; our progress was, in consequence, uncommonly slow. The blubber and oil were put into casks as received on board. After we had secured the lading of five boats, the weather, which had hitherto been fine and calm, suddenly changed. The sky became overcast, rain-clouds appeared, and a fresh gale of wind with heavy rain, succeeded. The sixth boat had much difficulty in reaching the ship. By the

time its lading was discharged, the sea had become
high, and the ship had drifted some miles from the
place where nearly one-half of the crew were on
shore.   We were six hours before we could beat up
to this station, when, having stood within a mile of
the shore, though rocks were then on both sides of
us, we despatched two boats under shelter of the
windward rocks, and rescued the whole of the men.
They had been by this time above thirty hours absent; they amused themselves on shore by cooking
several birds which had been shot, and kept themselves warm with a fire made of drift-wood and the
fragments of the ruinous hut.   Several of them
who had the first watch after they came on board,
were so fatigued, that they actually slept as they
stood on their feet on the deck.

On the following day, the weather having mode-
rated, we set about securing the remainder of our
prize, and after about eighteen hours close attention,
we succeeded in bringing off all that was valuable.
This whale, from a harpoon found in its body, appeared to have been struck by some of the fishers
of the Elbe; and having escaped from them, it had
probably stranded itself where we found it.

During these operations, my anxiety for the safety
of the ship was considerable, as we navigated a dan
gerous shore, which had never been scientifically surveyed, and of the charts of which, such as they are,
I had no copy.   Rocks, at low-water, were seen a

mile and a quarter from the shore, and many others at smaller distances.

The next day, July 27., the weather continuing fine, we stood into King's Bay, when I was enabled to make considerable additions to a survey of the coast which I began in the year 1815, and continued throughout our stay near shore on this occasion. Six miles within the headlands forming the entrance of the bay, we had no soundings with fifty or sixty fathoms of line within a fourth of a mile of the shore on the north side; nor indeed did we ever strike the bottom while we remained in the bay.

I landed on the north side near an iceberg, where a small tract of rising ground was terminated by a perpendicular precipice of perhaps a thousand feet in height. This cliff was composed of a kind of bluish-grey marble, but, like all the rocks we had yet seen, was full of fissures in every direction. At a distance, it appeared like basaltic columns; but on nearer approach we found the resemblance was derived from deep channels formed in the perpendicular face, at intervals of a few fathoms asunder. Some of the cliffs on the opposite side of the bay had a similar appearance. The bank where we landed was covered with vegetation, and afforded beautiful specimens of several plants. A hut was erected on the beach, which appeared to have been inhabited within a few weeks. Towards the sea-edge, the stones were so small, that few pieces could

be seen of more than two or three ounces in weight.
There were several perforated rocks near the landing
place, and a cave into which we rowed with the
boat. The top was a regular arch of marble. Its
length was thirty or forty yards, breadth about eight
or ten yards, and the height of the roof about three.
We could nowhere find the bottom with an oar
eighteen feet long. Besides the common marble
rock, we found in the cave specimens of rhomboidal calcareous spar.

The weather becoming threatening about this
time, we put off, and after examining the southern
shore, and taking a few angles, proceeded to sea
While we were in King's Bay, not far from the
centre, I got an azimuth of the sun when it was
directly over the north point of the Foreland, from
whence the true bearing of that point was determined to be S. 68° W.

Two days after this, July 29., we experienced a
heavy gale of wind, during which the discovery
ships under Captain Buchan and Lieutenant Franklin, were driven into the northern ice, and narrowly
escaped being wrecked. Our latitude was then
about 79°, so that we were not far from them.

The climate of Spitzbergen is no doubt more disagreeable, to human feeling, than that of any other
country yet discovered. Extending to within ten degrees of the Pole, it is generally intensely cold, and
even in the three warmest months, the temperature

not averaging more than $34\frac{1}{2}$ degrees, it is then subject to a cold occasionally of three, four, or more degrees below the freezing point. It has the advantage, however, of being visited by the sun for an uninterrupted period of four months in each year, thus having a Summer's Day, if so long an interval between the rising and setting of the sun may be so denominated, consisting of one-third part of the year. But its winter is proportionally desolate; the sun, in the northern parts of the country, remaining perpetually below the horizon from about the 22d of October to about the 22d of February. This great Winter Night, though sufficiently dreary, is by no means so dark as might be expected, as the sun, even during its greatest south declination, approaches within $13\frac{1}{2}°$ of the horizon, and affords a faint twilight for about one-fourth part of every twenty-four hours. Added to this twilight, the aurora borealis, which sometimes exhibits a brilliancy approaching to a blaze of fire,—the stars, which shine with an uncommon degree of brightness,—and the moon, which, in north declination, appears for twelve or fourteen days together without setting,—altogether have an effect which, when heightened by the reflection of a constant surface of snow, generally give sufficient light for going abroad;—but, with the light afforded by the heavens, when the moon is below the horizon, it is seldom possible to read.

All that is known respecting the climate of Spitzbergen, or nearly so, is derived from the three or four published journals of persons having wintered by accident or design in this desolate region, together with the interesting information already alluded to, received by Colonel Beaufoy from those Russian adventurers, who not unfrequently resort hither and remain throughout the winter, for the purposes of hunting and fishing. From these sources of information, I am enabled to give the following sketch of the progress of the seasons. It is, however, designedly brief, as the climate of the arctic seas in general, which is very similar, forms a subsequent chapter of this volume.

After the sun passes the equinox, the approaches of winter, in the Polar countries, become very rapid. This gloomy season commonly sets in at the latter end of September or beginning of October, with winds from the N., N. N. W., or N. W.; or with calms, hard frost, and snow[*]. By the end of September or the beginning of October, all the birds which are only summer visitors to Spitzbergen, commence their flight towards milder regions; and by the middle of the latter month, the frost has, in some instances, been so intense, that casks of beer have been frozen in a hut, within eight feet of the fire. In November, the sun having disappeared, the frosts rapidly increase, both in frequency and intensity; but throughout the year, when strong southerly

[*] Col. Beaufoy's Queries, Nos. 2. & 33.

winds occur, they are generally accompanied with
mild weather, and sometimes with thaw. About
December and January, hard frosts with calm weather are common, but seldom a month passes without storms; storms, indeed, are so frequent, that
two-thirds of the winter may be said to be boister-
ous *. The highest winds occur about the time of
the equinoxes, and blow most frequently from the
southern quarter. Snow storms are common, often
continuing for several days, and, perhaps, once or
twice a year, for some weeks together †. Hence,
a great quantity of snow falls during the winter,
which accumulates principally in sheltered glens;
but on level ground, it seldom lies above three to
five feet deep.

Bears seem to be the only quadrupeds which stir
abroad throughout the winter; for, though foxes
and rein-deer remain constantly in the country, they
are only to be met with, in any quantity, at certain
seasons. Foxes begin to appear in the month of
February, and are to be seen in March in great
numbers. Bears, at the same time, become more
abundant, and the birds re-appear in the month of
April.

The first human beings who are known to have
passed the winter in Spitzbergen, were two parties
of seamen belonging to English whalers, who were

_____

* Beaufoy's Queries, No. 4.   † Idem, No. 26.

left on shore by accident on two different occasions;
the first party, consisting of nine persons, all perished; but the latter, composed of eight individuals,
survived the rigours of the winter of 1630-1, and
were all rescued.   In the year 1633, seven volun-
teers belonging the Dutch fleet, were induced, by
certain emoluments, to attempt the same enterprize,
and succeeded in passing the winter without sustaining any injury; but on the same hazardous
experiment being tried by seven other persons, the
following winter, they all fell a sacrifice to the ravages of the scurvy.   Some Russians seem to have
been the next to attempt this adventurous exploit,
who, from being inured to a winter little less severe
at home, were enabled to accomplish it with more
safety.   Four men who landed on an island on the
east side of Spitzbergen, in the year 1743, and
were deprived of the means of getting away by
an unexpected calamity having overtaken the
vessel to which they belonged, remained there
during six years.   Being exposed to uncommon
privations, they were led by their necessities to
adopt some most ingenious devices, for providing themselves with food and raiment, in their
long and severe banishment.   One of their number
died; but the others were relieved after a stay of
six years and three months, by a vessel providentially driven upon the coast, and restored to their

friends, enriched with skins and other produce of the country, in which they had been exiled.

In modern times, people of the same nation have been in the habit of submitting to a voluntary transportation, with the object of making some considerable advantage, by the opportunities which such a measure affords them, of hunting and fishing. These persons were formerly employed in the service of the " White Sea Fishing Company ;" but this company being now no longer in existence, the trade is conducted by private adventurers*. They now proceed from Megen, Archangel, Onega, Rala, and other places bordering the White Sea, in vessels of 60 to 160 tons, some intended for the summer fishing, and others for the winter. The former put to sea in the beginning of June, and sometimes return in September; the latter sail about a month later, and wintering in the most secure coves of Devil Bay? Bell Sound, Horn Sound, Cross Bay, Magdalena Bay, Love Bay, and others, return home in the month of August or September of the following year†.

The fishermen reside on shore during the winter, in huts of the same kind as those used by the peas-

* From a communication in answer to queries sent to Archangel by myself, in the year 1815, through Mr Edward Steward of Whitby.

† Col. Beaufoy's Queries, No. 1.

ants in Russia, which being taken out with them in pieces, are constructed with little trouble in the most convenient situations. They build their stoves with bricks, or with clay found in the country. Their largest hut, which is erected near the place where their vessels or boats are laid up, is from twenty to twenty-five feet square, and is used as a station and magazine ; but the huts used by the men who go in quest of skins, and which are erected along shore, at the distance of ten to fifty versts from each other, are only seven or eight feet square. The smaller huts are usually occupied by two or three men, who take care to provide themselves, from the store, with the necessary provisions for serving them the whole winter *.

I have visited several of these huts, some constructed of logs, others of deals two inches in thickness. The one constituting the most comfortable lodging I have seen, I met with on the north-west point of the Foreland, in the year 1809. It was built of logs of half round timber, (the original trees being slit up the middle) ; the round sides were put outward, and the ends of the timbers forming two adjoining sides stretched beyond the corner, and being notched half way into each other, formed a close joint. The logs were placed horizontally, and were built into a rectangular form, about fourteen feet

---

* Col. Beaufoy's Queries, No. 10.

long, ten broad and six high. The seams were
caulked with moss. Near the ground were two
windows, of six panes of glass each, one on the east
side and the other on the south. The roof, which
was flat, was formed of deals, and loaded with stones.
A barrel without ends composed the chimney. To
the north end of the building was attached a small
square court, open at the top, having a door-way on
the east side of it, communicating with, and affording some shelter to, the door of the hut. In the
outer court were two casks of about 100 gallons capacity each, which were found to be filled with
meal. Several tubs lay near the casks, and a quantity of pease. In the interior of the hut we found
a variety of domestic utensils, consisting of platters,
a stool, an earthen pot, horn-spoons, a tomahawk, a
boat-hook, a spear, and several small wax-tapers, with
a variety of trifling articles. On a wooden bench fixed against the west side of the apartment, were
ranged in order with pendant necks, at least twenty
ducks, with a number of eggs about them; they
were all in a state of putrefaction. From these appearances, I judged this hut had been occupied by
some Russian hunters, who, from the quantity of
provisions left behind, seemed to have either perished prematurely, or had some intention of returning.
Lest the latter should happen to be the case, I
caused the meal casks to be secured from the weather, and forbid the sailors from removing any arti-

cle of value. I only took with me the wax-tapers,
which appeared to have been intended for religious
purposes.

During the stay of the hunters, they employ
themselves in killing seals, sea-horses, &c. in the
water ; and bears, foxes, deer, or whatever else they
meet with, on land. They are furnished with provisions for eighteen months by their employers,
consisting of rye-flour for bread, oatmeal, barley-
meal, pease, salt beef, salt cod, and salt holibut,
together with curdled milk, honey, and linseed oil;
besides which, they procure for themselves *lion-
deer* in winter, and birds in summer, the use of
which is found to be very conducive to health.
Their drink chiefly consists of a liquor called *nuas,*
made from rye-flour and water; malt or spiritous
liquors being entirely forbidden, to prevent drunken-
ness, as these persons, when they were allowed it,
drank so immoderately that their work was often altogether neglected. For general purposes, they use
spring-water, when it is to be had ; or, in lieu of it,
take water from lakes: but when neither can be got,
they use melted snow *.

Their fuel, consisting of wood, is brought with
them from Russia, and landed at their station-hut,
from whence it is conveyed by water, in boats, or by
land in small hand-sledges, to the different huts

* Beaufoy's Queries, Nos. 12, 13, 18.

disposed along the coast. Drift-wood is often met with, and used for the same purpose. The hunters defend themselves from the rigour of the frost, by a covering made of skin, over which they wear a garment called *kushy*, made of the skin of rein-deer, with boots of the same. A warm cap called a *truechy*, defends the whole head and neck, and part of the face; and gloves of sheep-skin, the hands. They seldom travel far in winter; but the short excursions they have occasion to make, they perform on foot, on snow skaits, and draw their food after them on hand-sledges; but such as have dogs, employ them in this service. If surprised with a gale of wind, accompanied by snow drifts, when out of shelter, the traveller is obliged to lie down, covering himself with his kushy and his sledge, as well as he is able, until the hurricane is over; but when it continues for any length of time, the poor wretch often perishes *.

Inured to cold, as these hunters are, they seldom suffer much from its effects. And they are never prevented by cold from going abroad, though the accumulation of snow about their huts, and the fury of storms, sometimes confine them to their dwellings. They make a point of taking exercise in the air, for the prevention of the scurvy; so that when they cannot with safety or convenience walk about, they exercise themselves by throwing the snow off

---

* Col. Beaufoy's Queries, Nos. 11, 14, 15, 16, 17, & 21.

and from around their huts, which, in stormy weather, are often buried. In such cases, they are obliged to make their way through the chimney to get out. As an antiscorbutic, they make use of an herb produced in the country, a stock of which they generally provide themselves with on the approach of winter; but sometimes they are under the necessity of digging through the snow to obtain it. They either eat it without any preparation, or drink the liquor prepared from it by infusion in water. For the same purpose, they make use of a kind of raspberry, which is preserved by baking with rye-flour: this they eat, or drink the expressed juice of the fruit. A decoction of fir-tops, in water, is another beverage intended as an antidote against the scurvy *.

These men, however, hardy as they are, do not always escape the bane of these regions, the scurvy. Perhaps their hardihood in stopping so long as three years in Spitzbergen, which some of them have been known to do, might give a predisposition for this disease, and render it more fatal. In the year 1771, Mr Steward of Whitby, formerly a Greenland captain, landed on a projection of low table land, forming the south-westerly point of King's Bay, for the purpose of procuring drift wood

---

* Beaufoy's Queries, Nos. 8, & 9.

for fuel ;—a practice very common among the London fishermen, at this period, who often sailed with a very scanty stock of coals on board. Here the first wintering of the Russians, to the northward of the Foreland, had been attempted, their first hut having been built the preceding year. This hut having been seen by the party in search of wood, on their first landing, motives of curiosity led them to examine it. They hollowed as they approached it ; but no one appeared. The door being defended by a small open court, one of the party entered it ; and, applying his eye to the hole for the latch, observed a man extended on the floor, as he thought sleeping. Receiving no answer to their shouts, they at length opened the door, and found the man a corpse. His cheek, which was laid on the ground, was covered with a green concretion of mould ; and his covering, besides his clothes, was only a Russian mat. Several jackets, and other articles of clothing, were seen on a bench, on which the inmates appeared to have slept ; but no other individual, living or dead, was observed. It was supposed, that his companions had shared the same fate, and had been buried by him, who, as the last survivor, had no one to perform the same kindly office on himself. The yawl belonging to the sufferers was found hauled up on the beach ; it was fully equipped with oars, together with mast and sail.

Near the shore of Spitzbergen, the south-westerly current, so very evident at the distance of twenty or thirty leagues to the westward, is not observed. Such, indeed, is the effect of the land on this current, as well as on the tide, that the course of the stream is altogether uncertain. Captain Phipps, when in the Racehorse, in the year 1773, lying becalmed about two and a half leagues N. N. W. from Cloven Cliff, had a current setting to the westward, though his consort, the Carcass, at no great distance from him, was, at the same time, in a current running toward the eastward. Facts of a similar kind, proved by the singular movements of the closest bodies of ice, are frequently occurring. Captain Phipps observed that the tide of flood came from the southward, in latitude $79\frac{1}{2}°$, on the west coast; and that the time of high water, at full and change, was half an hour past one : this corresponds exactly with an observation made by Baffin in 1613. In the harbour of Vogel Sang, the tide was observed to rise about four feet; and at Smeerenberg, a little more : the time of high water in each, being half an hour past one, as above. At Moffen Island, the tide appeared to flow eight or nine feet perpendicular. In general, the rise of tide may be stated at about six feet during the springs, and about two feet less during the neaps. The highest tides seem to be produced by south-westerly winds; and though the most general direction of the stream of flood-tide is

K 2

from the south towards the north, yet it runs by no means regularly at all times, even in the same place.

The products of Spitzbergen, in animals, are of some worth; but in vegetables they are neither numerous, nor, as far as yet discovered, of much value; and, in minerals, they are very little known. As an account of the animals inhabiting this country, is included in the general view of the zoology of the Spitzbergen sea, it is unnecessary to notice them here.

Spitzbergen does not afford many vegetables. Of those which I was enabled to collect in the course of several excursions to the shore in 1818, I have been furnished with a catalogue, by Sir Joseph Banks, as drawn up by his librarian, Mr Robert Brown, and have given it, in full, in the Appendix *. It may be remarked, that vegetation goes on uncommonly quickly in this country. Most of the plants spring up, flower, and afford seed, in the course of a month or six weeks. They are chiefly of dwarfish size; some of the flowers are really pretty, but exhibit few colours, excepting yellow, white, and purple. And it is not unworthy of observation, that the only plant I met with in Spitzbergen, partaking of the nature of a tree, (a Salix allied to *S. herbacea,)* grows but to the height of three or four inches.

---

* See No. V.

Though Spitzbergen is probably rich in minerals,
yet the examination of it has been so partial, and
indeed trifling, that nothing of any value, excepting marble and coal, has yet been met with *. The
former is found in some parts of King's Bay, of
real beauty ; and the latter, of a tolerable quality,
near the same place. The coal is so easily procured, that many of the Dutch fishers, a few years
ago, were in the habit of laying in a stock of this
useful article, for fuel, on the passage homeward.
Captain Jacob Broerties, an intelligent whale-fisher
of Amsterdam, informed me that he had in his possession, a slab table of great beauty, manufactured
out of a block of Spitzbergen marble, which he
himself procured.

What has already been advanced concerning the
appearances and productions of Spitzbergen, applies
in general to the islands adjacent. A few remarks,
however, on the peculiarities which have been noticed, may not be superfluous.

Moffen Island, a small low island lying on the
north side of Spitzbergen, in latitude 80° 1', longitude 12° 43' E, was visited and described by Captain Phipps, who intimates that none of the old
navigators have taken any notice of it, though it is
remarkably different from any thing to be seen on
the west coast. This, considering their usual accu-

---

* A list, by my valued friend Professor Jameson, of a few
specimens of the rocks occurring in and about King's Bay,
is included in Appendix No. VI.

racy and minuteness, he deems rather extraordinary, and suggests the possibility that it had not
long existed, but might have been thrown up, by
the currents from each side of Spitzbergen meeting here.

This island is of a roundish form, about two
miles in diameter, and has a shallow lake of water
in the middle.   This lake was frozen over, except
thirty or forty yards round the edge, near the end
of July.   The whole island is covered with gravel
and small stones, without the least vegetation of
any kind.   It is but a few feet above the level of
the sea.   The only piece of drift-wood found on it
by Captain Phipps, which was about three fathoms
long, and as thick as a ship's mizen mast, had been
thrown over the sea-bank, and lay on the declivity
near the lake.   It was low water at 11 P. M. of
25th of July (1773,) when the boat landed; and
the tide appeared to flow eight or nine feet.   The
velocity of the tide, which set N. W. and S. E., was
about a mile an hour *.

Low Island, lying E. N. E. from Moffen Island,
in latitude 80° 15′, and longitude 17° 35′ E., was visited on the 29th of July 1773, by Dr Irving, who
accompanied Captain Phipps on his expedition towards the North Pole.

The island is about seven miles in length, very
flat, and covered chiefly with stones from eighteen
to thirty inches in diameter, many of them hexa-

* Phipps' Voyage, p. 53.

gons, and commodiously placed for walking on. On
the middle of the island, they found vegetation
abundant. Two rein-deer were seen feeding; and
one of them they killed. It was found to be fat,
and of a high flavour. Several large fir-trees, at
this time, lay on the shore, sixteen or eighteen feet
above the level of the sea. Some of them were seventy feet long, and had been torn up by the roots;
others had been cut down by the axe, and notched
for twelve feet lengths. This timber was not in
the least decayed; the marks of the axe indeed,
were still fresh. There were likewise some pipe-
staves, and wood fashioned for use. The beach
consisted of old timber, sand, and whalebones *.

Hope Island, on the south-east coast of Spitzbergen, lies in latitude 76°20', longitude about 20° E.
It was discovered in the year 1613, by one of the
English Russia Company's vessels, which accompanied their whale-fishing expedition. It is nine
leagues long, but scarcely a mile broad, and lies
N. E. by E. and S. W. by W. It consists of five
mountains; the northernmost one is the highest;
and those succeeding, diminish progressively in size.
On the north side is good anchorage in twenty fathoms water. About half a league from each extremity of the island, the water is very shallow; on
the south side the bottom is rocky, and unfit for anchorage; but the coast is there pretty bold.

* Phipps' Voyage, p. 58.

Cherie Island, though not immediately adjoining Spitzbergen, is, however, nearer it than any other country, and may be noticed here. It lies in latitude about 74° 30′, and longitude 20° E., being 130 miles S. S. E. (true) from Point-look-out. It was discovered in the year 1596, by the Dutch navigators Barentz, Heemskerke and Ryp, on their advance towards the north, in search of a northern passage to India, and named by them *Bear Island,* from the circumstance of a large bear, whose skin was twelve feet in length, having been killed upon it. Stephen Bennet, who was sent by Sir Francis Cherie, in the year 1603, on a voyage towards the north, partly for trading and partly for discovery, fell in with this island, and in honour of his patron and owner, called it Cherie Island. Abounding in sea-horses or morses, it soon became an important place for taking these animals, of which a thousand were once killed in seven hours. Hence it was the constant resort of adventurers in this traffic for several years, until the morses began their retreat to the northward, and the discovery of the whale-fishery presented a much more lucrative occupation.

The greatest extent of this island is about ten miles. It is somewhat of the saddle form, being high at each end, and low in the middle. On the north-east end are three regular hills of considerable elevation, covered, in general, entirely with snow; the south-west end is more irregular *. Besides morses, the island abounds with bears, foxes and sea-fowl, and its shores, at certain seasons, are said to be visited by cod and haddock. Much drift-wood also occurs on the coast. Lead-ore, in veins, at the surface of the ground, has been found here; likewise coal of a tolerable quality, and specimens of virgin silver. Lead-glance also occurs on an adjoining rock called *Gull Island*, and three different mines were discovered by one of the early morse-fishers.

Near the north-east point of this island, is a little bay, where a ship may ride in shelter, with the wind from S. E. to S. W.; but the anchorage is exposed from E. S. E. (north about) to W. S. W. There is also anchorage in some other parts, in gravelly or stony ground.

Cherie Island is often inaccessible on account of ice, which, in the spring of the year, generally stretches in a straight line from here to the southern Cape of Spitzbergen. The flood-tide about it runs from the S. W. towards the N. E., and flows about four feet.

See Plate 3. fig. 1.

SECT. II.

Account of Jan Mayen Island.

JAN MAYEN Island derived its name from that
of a Dutch navigator, who is said to have first seen
it in the year 1611 *, though it may be suspected,
as the whale-fishery of this nation did not commence until 1612, that it was not discovered until
a later period.   It was once named *Mauritius'*
Island, or *St Maurice*, in honour of Prince Maurice
of Nassau.   This country was also discovered by
the whalers of Hull about the same time, and named *Trinity Island;* in consequence of which,
when the Russia Company attempted to monopo-
lize the fishery of the whole of the Polar countries,
this island was granted by the King to the Corpo-
ration of Hull, on their petition in the year 1618,
as a fishing station.   The Dutch, who were constantly in the habit of visiting Jan Mayen from
the time of its discovery to the year 1630 or 1640,
where they derived great advantage from the whale-
fishery its coasts afforded, have given the principal
accounts of its appearance, situation and navigation which have yet appeared.   These accounts, besides being exceedingly meagre, are likewise inaccu-

---

* Beschryving der Walvisvangst, vol. ii. p. 62.

rate. They place this island in latitude 71° to
71° 23′, and longitude (corrected to Greenwich)
5° 55′ to 7° 22′ W. *; and *our* charts place it about
the same latitude, and in the longitude of 9° to 10°
or 11° W. From a survey, however, of the east
coast, which I accomplished on the 3d and 4th of
August 1817, and from solar observations for latitude and longitude (by chronometer), I found its
limits to be between the latitudes of 70° 49′ and
71° 8′ 20″ N., and between the longitudes of 7° 26′
and 8° 44′ W †.

This island, which extends in length about ten
leagues, from N. E. to S. W., is in no place above
three leagues in breadth. The northern extremity
is of a rhomboidal form, each side being about three
leagues in length, and affords a base for the remarkable peak called Beerenberg, or Bear Mountain.
The southern extremity, connected by a narrow
isthmus to one of the acute angles of the northern
land, is from 1½ to about 5 miles in breadth.

The coast affords several road-steads, with good
anchorage in five to ten fathoms water, black sandy
ground, but no harbour for a ship; all the anchorages being open to the sea in an angle of at least
ten points of the compass. Few dangers occur on

* Beschryving der Walvisvangst, Map, vol. ii. p. 64.

† The positions of several remarkable parts of the coast, are
included in the Table of Latitudes and Longitudes, Appendix,
No. IV.

the coast at a moderate offing, but what may be seen ; perhaps the greatest known danger is a rock lying about three leagues south, a little easterly, from the S. W. point of Little Wood Bay, having only eleven feet water upon it when the tide is at the lowest. It is about a stone's cast over, and was discovered by a fisher belonging to Delf-haven, who bilged his ship upon it.

The soundings about the island are very irregular, and the bottom generally consists of rocks or black sand. At the distance of eleven or twelve leagues S. S. E. from Cape South, are soundings in thirty-five and thirty-six fathoms water ; but on the northern face of the island, there are 300 fathoms depth, a cannon shot from the shore. On the north-eastern coast the depth is also great ; and also near Cape South-East ; but in most other places, the depth, at the distance of half a league from the beach, varies from ten to fifty fathoms. Between Capes North-West and North-East, between Capes North-East and South-East, and in part of the distance between Little Wood Bay and Cape South, as well as in a few portions on the west side of the island, the coast consists of a kind of wall, being generally precipitous and inaccessible. The west side affording the greatest number of anchorages, having the best convenience for landing, and being better sheltered from the most frequent storms, was selected by the Dutch for their *boiling* stations.

They had apparatus for the manufacture of oil, together with tents, cooperages and warehouses, erected
in South Bay, Rooberg, Wood Bay, English Bay,
West Cross Cove, and East Cross Cove.   In South
Bay, the Dutch once suffered the loss of three of
their tents or huts, nine oil vessels, and thirteen
boats, from the ground on which they stood being
washed away by the sea.   Mary Muss Bay, was the
first place where oil was manufactured in the island,
and was so called after an industrious woman of
that name belonging to Rotterdam, who sent the
first ship out for the purpose of reducing the blubber which might be taken, into oil on the spot.
Three places on this island, called Wood Bay,
Great Wood Bay, and Little Wood Bay, received
their names from the great quantity of drift-wood
found in them.

The western navigation of Jan Mayen is preferred to the eastern, as being less incumbered with
ice, and less subject to calms, squalls and whirlwinds, which are often encountered on passing to
the eastward of Beerenberg.   The whole island is
generally surrounded with ice in the spring of the
year; but in the autumn, or even in summer, the
ice sometimes sets so far to the westward, that it is
not visible from any part of the land.

Though the Dutch, as well as the whalers of
Hull, were, in the early part of the seventeenth
century, annual visitants to the island of Jan Mayen,
yet we have no account or description of it, except

what relates to its navigation, with a few brief notices respecting its principal mountain and glaciers.
The British fishers are now in the frequent habit of
making this land in their outward passage, but
seldom approach near the shore.   I was, therefore,
fortunate, in my passage homeward in the year 1817,
in effecting a landing upon it.   A narrative of my
excursion upon this interesting island, was read before the Wernerian Society in December 1817;
and the substance of that paper I shall now repeat
in this place.

On approaching Jan Mayen with a clear atmosphere, the first object which strikes the attention, is
the peak of Beerenberg.   This mountain rears its
icy summit to an elevation, as ascertained on this
visit, of 6870 feet above the level of the sea.   It
frequently appears above the clouds, and may be
seen, in clear weather, at the distance of thirty or
forty leagues*.   It is seated on a base, which is itself mountainous, being about 1500 feet in height;
but in a small interval between two cliffs on the
south side, the slope of the hill is continued with
little variation, at an inclination of perhaps 40° to
50°, from the summit to the margin of the sea.

The general appearance of the land, has a striking resemblance to that of Spitzbergen, both in col-

---

* I saw Beerenberg from the deck of the ship Fame, on
the 29th April 1818, when at the distance, (by observation,)
of 95 to 100 miles.

our and character. As at Spitzbergen, your approach to it, seems amazingly tardy. At the distance of ten or fifteen miles, a stranger to polar
lands would suppose himself within a league of the
rocks.

At this season (August 4th) all the high lands
were covered with snow and ice; and the low lands,
in those valleys and deep cavities, where large
beds of snow had been collected, still retained part
of their winter covering, down to the very border of
the sea.

Between Capes North-east and South-east, are
three very singular icebergs. They occupy recesses
in the cliff, where it is 1284 feet high by observation,
and nearly perpendicular, and extend from the base
of Beerenberg down to the water's edge. These
polar glaciers differed in appearance from any thing
of the kind I had before seen. They were very
rough on the surface, and of a greenish grey colour.
They presented the appearance of immense cataracts,
suddenly arrested in their progress, and congealed
on the spot, by the power of an intense frost. Like
cascades, their prominent greenish colour was variegated with snow-white patches resembling foam, which
were contrasted with the jet-black points of the most
prominent rocks peeping through their surfaces. As
in cataracts also, they seemed to follow in some measure the figure of the rocks, over which they lay,

and were marked with curvilinear striæ from top to bottom.

I left my ship (the Esk of Whitby,) at three quarters past one in the morning, accompanied by Captains Jackson and Bennet, whose ships were near at the time, and landed at half-past two, amidst a considerable surf, on a beach covered with coarse black sand. This sand, which consisted of a very thick bed, occurred through an extent of two or three miles in length, and about a furlong in breadth. It was a mixture of iron-sand, augite and pyroxene *. The black parts, which were very heavy, and readily attracted by the magnet, had an appearance exactly resembling coarse gunpowder.

This beach was the first place from Cape Northeast, four leagues distant, where the coast seemed as we passed it, to be at all accessible. Great Wood Bay was immediately to the westward of us, and Cape South east, about five miles distant to the eastward.

After a few feet rise, forming a sea-bank of black sand, the strand proceeded inland, on a horizontal level for about a fourth of a mile, where it was ter-

---

* This latter substance, which was mistaken for olivine, was pronounced by Dr Wollaston, to whom a specimen was given by the Reverend Dr Satterthwaite, to be pyroxene.— (Annals of Philosophy, by Dr Thomson, vol. xi. p. 195., Paper by Dr D. Clarke.)

minated by irregular cliffs. This strand appeared
to have been occasionally covered with the sea, as
it was strewed with drift-wood, part of which was
tolerably good timber, and the rest bruised, and a
little worm-eaten. One log, that I observed, had
been squared, and was marked with the letter G.

I had not advanced many paces, before I observed signs of a volcano. Fragments of lava were seen
at every step; blocks of burned clay were next met
with; and, nearer the cliff, large masses of red clay,
partly baked, but still in a friable state, occurred in
great abundance. Numerous pointed rocks, probably of the trap formation, were sticking through
the sand. One of these, which was vesicular basalt, had numerous beautiful crystals and grains of
augite imbedded in it. Along with this, was a rock
which appeared to be very nearly allied to the celebrated basaltic millstone of Andernach. After
leaving the sea-shore, I perceived no other mineral,
but such as bore undoubted marks of recent volcanic action, viz. cinders, earthy-slag, burned clay,
scoriæ, vesicular lava, &c. The place from whence
these substances appeared to have been discharged,
being near, we attempted to reach it. In performing the ascent, the steepness of the hill, and the
looseness of the materials, made the undertaking
not a little arduous. We frequently slid backward
several paces by the nodules of lava giving way beneath our feet; in which case, the ground generally

resounded, as if we had been travelling on empty
metallic vessels, or vaulted caverns.

The baked clay, and other loose rocks, consisted chiefly of large masses at the bottom of
the hill; but, about the middle of the ascent,
these substances were in smaller fragments.   Towards the top, blocks of half baked red clay, containing many crystals of augite, were again met
with ; and, about the southern part of the summit, a rugged wall of the same occurred, giving
the mountain a castellated form of no small magnificence.   On reaching this summit, estimated
at 1500 feet elevation above the sea, we beheld a
beautiful crater, forming a basin of 500 or 600 feet
in depth, and 600 or 700 yards in diameter.   It
was of a circular form, and both the interior and
exterior sides had a similar inclination.   The bottom of the crater was filled with alluvial matter, to
such a height that it presented a horizontal flat of
an elliptical form, measuring 400 feet by 240.   A
subterranean cavern penetrated the side of the crater at the bottom, from whence a spring of water
issued, which, after running a short distance towards the south, disappeared in the sand.

From this eminence we had a most interesting
prospect.   Towards the north appeared Beerenberg,
now first seen free from clouds, rising in majestic
importance into the region of perpetual frost.   At
the foot of the mount, on the south-east side,

near a stupendous accumulation of lava, bearing the castellated form, was another crater, of similar form to the one above described. Towards the south-west, the utmost extent of the island was visible; while, towards the north, a thick fog obscured the prospect, which, as it advanced in stately grandeur towards us, gradually shrouded the distant scenery, until the nearest mountains were wrapped in impenetrable gloom. The sea, at the same time was calm, the sun bright, and the atmosphere of half the hemisphere, without a cloud. Excepting the interest excited by the volcano, Beerenberg sunk every other object into comparative insignificance. A sketch of the appearance of this mountain from the sea, at ten miles distant, when seen above the clouds, is given among the engravings, and may afford some notion of its magnitude and beauty *.

The colour of the cliffs around, was different shades of brown or black ; and the general character of the country seemed to indicate the action of volcanic fire.

A rocky hill, with a precipitous side towards the sea, lying a little to the westward, I descended towards it, from the ridge of the crater, with the expectation of finding some other kind of rock than what had yet been met with. It was found to consist only of a cliff of yellowish grey friable earth or

* Plate 5.

clay; in which crystals of augite, along with dark roundish granular pieces of basalt lay imbedded.

A piece of iron, which appeared to have been derived from ironstone, by a smelting process conducted in the furnace of nature, was found near the volcanic mount; being very cumbrous, it was laid aside by our party as we ascended, and unfortunately left behind us when we quitted the shore. Of every other metallic, mineral, vegetable, or animal substance we met with, we took specimens.

As the icebergs observed on this island suggested the idea of frozen cascades, a poetic imagination would, in the hollow metallic sound of the earth on the volcanic mount, have conceived the cavern of Vulcan; and in the iron manufactured in the bowels of the earth, the fabrication of the same deity, for the use of his parent Jove.

The cliffs here afforded but few specimens of plants. Indeed we travelled a considerable distance before we could perceive the least sign of vegetation. As we advanced, however, we met with tufts of plants in full blossom, scattered widely about among the volcanic minerals; but under the last cliff we visited, the variety was greater, and the specimens more vigorous. Among the plants seen, we recognized the Rumex digynus, Saxifraga tricuspidata and oppositifolia, Arenaria peploides? Silene acaulis, Draba verna, &c.

A black sandy earth, or a yellowish-grey kind of clay, constituted the general soil where any occurred.

Near the sea shore, the burrows of foxes were seen, and traces of their feet below high water-mark; but none of these animals were met with. The feet-marks of white bears, and probably of rein-deer, were also perceptible. The birds were not so numerous as I anticipated. We only saw bur-gomasters, fulmars, puffins, guillemots, little auks, kittywakes, and terns. Several cetaceous animals, principally of the species Balæna Physalis, were seen, but no mysticete.

We returned to our ships at six in the morning; when the weather being clear, I took bearings of the most remarkable parts of the coast, with azi-muths and altitudes of the sun, for determining the variation of the compass, and the longitude of the island by the chronometer.

A fishing party, which I sent out, proving unsuc-cessful in the offing, approached the shore, about two miles to the eastward of the place we visited, where, though the surf was very considerable, and the strand very contracted, they effected a landing. They observed much drift-wood, a boat's oar, a ship's mast, and some other wrought wood scattered along the shore. Every mineral they noticed, and all the specimens they brought away, bore the same vol-canic character as those I observed. Near some large fissures, which here and there occurred in the rocky and precipitous cliff, immense heaps of lava were seen, which appeared to have been poured out of these chinks in the rock. Cinders, earth-slag, iron-sand, and fragments of floetz rocks, covered the beach and so much of the cliff as they had an opportunity of examining.

The volcano discovered on this excursion, I ventured to name *Esk Mount*, after the ship I commanded at the time ; and I named the first point of land to the eastward (within Cape South-east) *Cape Fishburn*, and the point within Egg Island, forming the cast side of Great Wood Bay, *Cape Brodrick*, out of respect to my friends Messrs Fishburn and Brodrick, the owners of the Esk. The intermediate Bay, where we landed, I named *Jameson Bay*, in remembrance of my respected friend Professor Jameson.

Some volcano in this neighbourhood, probably Esk Mount, was, I believe, in action in the spring of the following year. On the 29th of April 1818, we made the island of Jan Mayen, bearing north, in the ship Fame ; and having the wind from the eastward, weathered it the next day. We stretched up to the northward among bay-ice, until we came abreast of Jameson Bay, and could see distinctly Egg Island, the three icebergs, and other objects of magnitude. From about the north side of Egg Island, near Esk Mount, we were surprised with the sight of considerable jets of smoke discharged from the earth, at intervals of every three or four minutes. At first we imagined the smoke was raised by some sailors, having suffered the calamity of shipwreck; but after personally examining the phenomenon from the mast-head, for upwards of an hour, I was convinced that it could be nothing else than the feeble action of a volcano. The smoke was projected with great velocity, and seemed to rise to twice the height of the land, or about 4000 feet. On mentioning this circumstance to Captain Gilyott of the Richard of Hull, he informed me, that, while employed in killing seals in the neighbourhood of this island, in the same month of the year 1818, he observed a similar appearance. The smoke he saw frequently; and once he noticed a shining redness resembling the embers of an immense fire. He called his officers to observe it, and humorously intimated that the Moon had landed on Jan Mayen!

This fact serves to account for some strange noises heard by seven Dutch seamen, who attempted to winter here in the year 1633–4. In the beginning of the night of the 8th of September, in particular, they " were frightened by a noise, as if something had fallen very heavy upon the ground, but saw nothing." This, instead of being the fall of an iceberg, as some have supposed, was probably a volcanic phenomenon.

These seven seamen seem to have been the only human beings who ever passed the winter in Jan Mayen. They belonged to the Dutch whale-fish-

ing fleet, and voluntarily offered themselves to the
" Greenland Company," for trying the practicability of living in the winter, and establishing a colony in this island.   This scheme, masked under the
pretence of determining the true condition of the
country in winter; " concerning the nights there,
and other curious observations, disputed among
astronomers," was doubtless intended as a colonizing
experiment, with a view of facilitating the capture
of whales, and enhancing the value of the fishery to
the adventurers.   Their journal, which is given at
some length in Churchill's " Collection of Voyages
and Travels *," gives a better description of the
state of the wind and weather, from the 26th of
August to the 31st of April following, than almost
any other account of observations, made in winter,
in so high a latitude, that has yet been published.
As such, I have extracted some particulars out of
each day's remarks, and have given them, in a tabular form, in the Appendix, No. VII.   This little
party survived the severities of the winter, without
much hazard of their lives, until the scurvy began
to make its appearance among them.   The requisite
supply of fresh provisions not having been met
with, its ravages were very rapid.   One of the party died on the 16th of April; and all the rest shar-

---

* Vol. ii. p. 367,–378.

ed the same fate within about a month afterwards. Their journal terminates on the 31st of April; and, on the 4th of June, when the Dutch fleet arrived, they were all found dead in their huts.

CHAPTER III.

HYDROGRAPHICAL SURVEY OF THE GREEN-LAND SEA.

SECT. I.

Situation and Extent,—Colour and Degree of Transparency,—Quality, Specific Gravity, and Saltness of the Greenland Sea.

OF all the substances which contribute to the composition of the surface of the globe, there is none so uniform in appearance, or so similar in reality,—none more important in its application, or so general in its distribution, as the water of the ocean. In all parallels, and on all meridians, it consists of one kind of liquid, known by the general name of sea-water. From the Tropics to the Arctic Circle, its composition and its saltness, as far as yet examined, appear to be pretty nearly the same.

There are, no doubt, many circumstances which must tend to produce an inequality in the colour, saltness, and component parts of the water of the ocean;—such as the mingling of the waters of large rivers, conveying saline and earthy substances along with them; and the admixture of the soluble materials of which some parts of the bed of the sea are probably composed. But, at the same time, there are other circumstances which operate in a contrary manner, and have a tendency to equalize and combine the various qualities of sea-water, which might at one time have occurred in different regions of the globe : these are, tides along most sea-coasts,—currents in the main sea, some running superficially, some bodily, and others counter,—together with the influence of storms, and changes of temperature, causing a circulation among the particles of the water. Hence, perhaps, it is, that the difference in the degree of saltness is not, in the most distant places, very considerable. The highest specific gravity of the water of the main ocean, any where recorded, that has come to my knowledge, is 1.0297, observed by M. Lamarche, in latitude 20° 21' south, and longitude 37° 5' west of Paris * ; and the lowest 1.0259, observed by myself, in latitude 78° 0', longitude 7° 0' east †. The saline con-

---

* Annals of Phil. vol. xii. p. 32.

† In some inland seas, the degree of saltness is less than in any part of the ocean. In Baffin's Bay, for instance, the

tents of these two extremes, do not differ above one-eighth part of the whole.

As it is not my intention to consider the hydrography of the globe, but only that of a small portion of it, called the *Greenland Sea*, I shall proceed to state the limits under which this part of the Arctic Ocean is comprised.

According to a section of a public statute, intended for the regulation of the Northern Whale-fisheries, the Greenland Sea commences with the parallel of 59° 30′ of north latitude *, included between Europe and America, and extends as far towards the Pole as can be navigated. In general language, however, among the whalers, the sea adjoining Spitzbergen, in which the first considerable whale-fishery was conducted, together with the islands in this quarter, receive more particularly the title of *Greenland;* while the sea to the westward of Old Greenland, Hudson's and Baffin's Bays excepted, maintains the name of *Davis' Straits.*

In the Spitzbergen quarter, the hydrography of

surface of the sea, (into which had been poured the water from snow and ice, melted in consequence of a summer's heat,) was observed by Captain Ross to be of as low a specific gravity as 1.020; and the specific gravity of the water of the Baltic Sea, is stated at 1.014.—(Annals of Phil. vol. vii. p. 42.) In the Mediterranean, however, the specific gravity of the water appears to be greater than that of the ocean.—(Annals of Phil. vol. iv. p. 206.)

* 26th Geo. III. cap. 41. § 16.

which I have most particularly to consider, the sea
is different in colour, transparency, saltness, and
temperature, from what it generally is in the Atlantic Ocean.

The water of the main ocean is well known to
be as transparent and as colourless as that of the
most pure springs; and it is only when seen in very
deep seas, that any certain and unchangeable colour appears. This colour is commonly ultramarine
blue, differing but a shade from the colour of the
atmosphere, when free from the obscurity of cloud
or haze. Where this ultramarine blue occurs, the
rays of light seem to be absorbed in the water,
without being reflected from the bottom; the blue
rays only being intercepted. But, where the depth
is not considerable, the colour of the water is affected by the quality of the bottom. Thus, fine white
sand, in very shallow water, affords a greenish grey,
or apple-green colour, becoming of a deeper shade
as the depth increases, or as the degree of light decreases; yellow sand, in soundings, produces a dark
green colour in the water; dark sand a blackish
green; rocks a brownish or a blackish colour; and
loose sand or mud, in a tide-way, a greyish colour.
From this effect of the bottom, the names of the
White Sea, the Black Sea, and the Red Sea, have
doubtless been derived. Near the mouths of large
rivers, the sea is often of a brownish colour, owing
to the admixture of mud and other substances held
in suspension, together with vegetable or mineral dyes,

brought down with the fresh water from the land. But, in the main ocean, in deep water, the prevailing colour is blue, or greenish blue. It may be observed, that there is a good deal of deception in the colour of the sea, owing to the effect of the sun, and the colour of clouds; and its true tinge can only be observed, with accuracy, by looking downward through a long tube, reaching nearly to its surface, so as to intercept the lateral rays of light, which, by their reflection, produce the deception, and thus obtain a clear view of the interior of the sea. The trunk of the rudder answers this purpose tolerably well. When thus examined, the colour of the sea is not materially affected, either by sun or clouds. But, if examined superficially, from an exposed situation, the sea, in all places, will be found to vary in appearance with every change in the state of the atmosphere. Hence the surface generally partakes of the colour of the clouds; and, when the sky is chiefly clear, a small cloud partially intercepting the sun's rays, casts a deep brown or blackish shadow over the surface, and sometimes gives the appearance of shallow water, or rocks, and thus occasions, in the navigator, unnecessary alarm. It is not, therefore, the varying aspect of the surface of the water that is meant by the colour of the sea; but the appearance of the interior of a body of waters, when looked into through a perpendicular tube. The only effect then produced by a change in the aspect of the sky, is to give the water a lighter or darker shade; but it has little effect on its real colour. For, observed in this way, the same colours may be recognised in storm, or calm, in fine weather or foul, clear or cloudy, fair or showery, being always nearly the same.

The colour of the Greenland Sea varies from ultramarine blue to olive green, and from the most pure transparency to striking opacity. These appearances are not transitory, but permanent; not depending on the state of the weather, but on the quality of the water. Hudson, when he visited this quarter in the year 1607, noticed the changes in the colour of the sea, and made the observation, that the sea was blue where there was ice, and green where it was most open. This circumstance, however, was merely accidental. Captain Phipps does not appear to have met with any of the green water. This kind of water occurs in considerable quantity, forming, perhaps, one-fourth part of the surface of the Greenland Sea, between the parallels of 74° and 80°. It is liable to alterations in its position, from the action of the current; but still it is always renewed, near certain situations, from year to year. Often it constitutes long bands or streams, lying north and south, or north-east and south-west; but of very variable dimensions: sometimes, I have seen it extend two or three degrees of latitude in length, and from a few miles, to ten or fifteen leagues in breadth. It occurs very commonly about the meri-

dian of London, in high latitudes. In the year
1817, the sea was found to be of a blue colour, and
transparent, all the way from 12° east, in the parallel of 74° or 75°, to the longitude of 0° 12' east,
in the same parallel. It then became green, and
less transparent. The colour was nearly *grass-
green*, with a shade of black. Sometimes the
transition between the green and blue water is progressive, passing through the intermediate shades
in the space of three or four leagues; at others, it
is so sudden, that the line of separation is seen like
the rippling of a current; and the two qualities of
the water keep apparently as distinct as the waters
of a large muddy river, on first entering the sea.
In 1817, I fell in with such narrow stripes of various coloured water, that we passed streams of pale
green, olive green, and transparent blue, in the
course of ten minutes sailing.

The food of the whale occurs chiefly in the green
coloured water; it therefore affords whales in greater numbers than any other quality of the sea, and
is constantly sought after by the fishers. Besides,
whales are more easily taken in it, than in blue
water, on account of its great obscurity preventing
the whales from seeing distinctly the approach of
their enemies.

Nothing particular being observed in this kind
of water, sufficient to give it the remarkable colour
it assumes, I at first imagined that this appearance

2

was derived from the nature of the bottom of the sea. But on observing that the water was very imperfectly transparent, insomuch, that *tongues* of ice, two or three fathoms under water, could scarcely be discerned, and were sometimes invisible, and that the ice floating in the olive-green sea was often marked about the edges with an orange-yellow stain, I was convinced, that it must be occasioned by some yellow substance held in suspension by the water, capable of discolouring the ice, and of so combining with the natural blue of the sea, as to produce the peculiar tinge observed.

For the purpose of ascertaining the nature of the colouring substance, and submitting it to a future analysis, I procured a quantity of snow from a piece of ice that had been washed by the sea, and was greatly discoloured by the deposition of some peculiar substance upon it. A little of this snow, dissolved in a wine glass, appeared perfectly nebulous; the water being found to contain a great number of semi-transparent spherical substances, with others resembling small portions of fine hair. On examining these substances with a compound microscope, I was enabled to make the following observations.

The semi-transparent globules appeared to consist of an animal of the medusa kind. It was from 1-20th to 1-30th of an inch in diameter. Its surface was marked with twelve distinct patches or nebulæ, of dots of a brownish colour; these dots were disposed

in pairs, four pairs, or sixteen pairs alternately, composing one of the nebula.   The body of the me
dusa was transparent.   When the water containing these animals was heated, it emitted a very
strong odour, in some respects resembling the smell
of oysters, when thrown on hot coals, but much more
offensive.   The fibrous or hair-like substances, were
more easily examined, being of a darker colour.
They varied in length from a point to one-tenth of
an inch; and when highly magnified, were found
to be beautifully moniliform.   In the longest specimens, the number of bead-like articulations was
about thirty; hence their diameter appeared to be
about the 1-300th part of an inch.   Some of these substances seemed to vary their appearance; but whether
they were living animals, and possessed of locomotion,
I could not ascertain.   From one of the larger specimens I observed some fine collateral fibres.   They
possessed the property of decomposing light; and, in
some cases, showed all the colours of the spectrum
very distinctly.   The size of the articulations seemed
equal in all, the difference in length being occasioned
by a difference in the number of articulations.   The
whole substance had an appearance very similar to
the horns or antennæ of shrimps, fragments of which
they might possibly be, as the squillæ are very abundant in the Greenland Sea.

I afterwards examined the different qualities of
sea-water, and found these substances very abun-

dant in that of an olive-green colour; and also occurring, but in lesser quantity, in the bluish-green
water. The number of medusæ in the olive-green
sea was found to be immense. They were about
one-fourth of an inch asunder. In this proportion, a cubic inch of water must contain 64; a
cubic foot 110,592; a cubic fathom 23,887,872;
and a cubical mile about 23,888,000,000,000,000!
From soundings made in the situation where
these animals were found, it is probable the sea
is upwards of a mile in depth; but whether
these substances occupy the whole depth is uncertain. Provided, however, the depth to which
they extend be but 250 fathoms, the above immense number of one species may occur in a space
of two miles square. It may give a better conception of the amount of medusæ in this extent, if
we calculate the length of time that would be
requisite, with a certain number of persons, for
counting this number. Allowing that one person
could count a million in seven days, which is barely
possible, it would have required, that 80,000 persons should have started at the creation of the world,
to complete the enumeration at the present time!

What a stupendous idea this fact gives of the
immensity of creation, and of the bounty of Divine
Providence, in furnishing such a profusion of life in
a region so remote from the habitations of men!
But if the number of animals in a space of two

M 2

miles square be so great, what must be the amount requisite for the discolouration of the sea, through an extent of perhaps twenty or thirty thousand square miles?

These animals are not without their evident economy, as on their existence possibly depends the being of the whole race of mysticete, and some other species of cetaceous animals.   For, the minute medusæ apparently afford nourishment to the sepiæ, actiniæ, cancri, helices, and other genera of Mollusca and Aptera, so abundant in the Greenland Sea, while these latter constitute the food of several of the whale tribe inhabiting the same region; thus producing a dependant chain of animal life, one particular link of which being destroyed, the whole must necessarily perish.

Besides the minute medusæ and moniliform substances, the water of the Spitzbergen Sea, taken up in latitude 77° 30', was found to contain several species of animalcules.   Of these I discovered three kinds, full of animal life, but invisible to the naked eye.

There can be no doubt, I think, after what has been advanced, that the medusæ and other minute animals that have been described, give the peculiar colour to the sea, which is observed to prevail in these parts ; and that from their profusion, they are, at the same time, the occasion of that great diminution of transparency which always accompanies the olive-green colour.   For in the blue water.

where few of the little medusæ exist, the sea is uncommonly transparent. Captain Wood, when attempting the discovery of a north-east passage, in the year 1676, sounded near Nova Zembla in 80 fathoms water, where the bottom was not only to be seen, but even the shells lying on the ground were clearly visible.

Never having been in a very high latitude during any part of the year when the sun sets, I have never observed whether the Greenland Sea possesses the property of shining in the dark. There is, however, great reason to believe, that as the luminousness of the sea is often derived from small animals of the medusa kind, that the green-coloured water found in the Greenland Sea would be strongly phosphorescent.

The sea in the Arctic regions is of somewhat less specific gravity, than it is in temperate or torrid regions; and consequently less salt. The correct analysis of sea-water being a difficult problem, the usual measure of the saltness of the sea, is by its specific gravity; this, though but an approximation to the truth, when the quantity of any particular salt only is considered, gives the saline contents in the gross with tolerable accuracy. A quantity of sea-water taken from the surface in latitude 77° 40′, longitude 2° 30′ E., of the specific gravity of 1.0267, afforded in 1000 grains the following ingredients:

Muriate of soda, dried at temperature 212°, 30.80 grains

Magnesian salts, dried at about 212°,......   4.01

Sulphate of lime,..............................   0.81

_____

Gross saline contents,........................   35.62,

the proportion of salt in 1000 grains of sea-water,
being between 1-28th and 1-29th, or 10-286ths, or
3.56 *per cent.*

The annexed table exhibits the result of experiments on the specific gravity of the sea, in different parallels between 57° and 79°, made in various voyages to the Spitzbergen whale-fishery *.

_____

* Since this Table was sent to press, an account of the
" Quantity of Saline Matter in the Water of the North Polar
Seas," by Dr Andrew Fyfe, has been published in the Edinburgh Philosophical Journal, No. I. Several of the specimens
of sea-water examined by Dr Fyfe, having been collected by
myself, in situations included in the annexed Table, it may
be interesting to subjoin an account of the quantity of " saline
matter *per cent.*" procured from such specimens.

Lat.	Long.	Saline Matter per cent.	Lat.	Long.	Saline Matter per cent.
64°.26′	0°.38′ E	3.54	77°.30′	6°.10′ E	3.42
66.45	1.00	3.79	77.34	8.00	3.70
69.14	3.00	3.75	78.25	8.20	3.91
71.10	5.30	3.75	78.30	6.30	3.88
74.34	10.00	3.77	78.35	6.00	3.27
76.33	10.20	3.60			

Latitude.	Longitude.	Specific grav. Temp. 60°.	Temp. at Surf.	Colour.	Tem. of the Air.	Da. Mon. Yr.	Situation and Remarks.
		OBSERVATIONS on the SEA.				TIME.	
57.22	1°.16' W	1.0269	41°.0	Greenish bl.	41°	25 Mar. 1814	At sea
57.42	0.45	1.0280	43.0	Ditto	42	12 —— 1810	Ditto
57.40	4. 8	1.0231	38.0	Ditto	32	14 ·—— 1810	In Murray Fr.
57.43	4. 9	1.0244	39.0	Ditto	39	18 —— 1810	In Cromarty
59.56	1.20	1.0272	42.0	Blue	32	21 —— 1810	At sea
60.09	1. 6 ⎫	1.0278	44.0	Greenish bl.	46	4 Apr. 1814	In Brassa Sou.
——	⎬	1.0274	43.0	Ditto	55	22 Mar. 1811	Ditto
——	—— ⎭	1.0262	41.0	Ditto	29	23 —— 1810	Ditto
61.46	0.23 E	1.0268	47.0	Ultram. blue	50	29 —— 1810	At sea
64.26	0.38	1.0269	43.5	Ditto	44	3 Apr. 1815	Ditto
64.58	0.20	1.0266	48.0	Ditto	47	4 July 1810	Ditto
65.18	0.22 W	1.0264	41.0	Ditto	44	31 Mar. 1810	Ditto
66.45	1. 0 E	1.0263	43.5	Ditto	44	5 Apr. 1815	Ditto
69. 0	0. 0	1.0275	36.0	Ditto	39	2 —— 1810	Ditto
69.14	3. 0	1.0269	38.0	Ditto	39	6 —— 1815	Ditto
69.25	8.55	1.0273	42.0	Ditto	40	4 July 1810	Ditto
70. 0	5. 0	1.0274	40.0	Ditto	30	28 Apr. 1812	Ditto
70.25	1. 0 W	1.0272	37.5	Ditto	30	9 —— 1814	Ditto
70.33	1.20 E	1.0266	32.0	Ditto	35	3 —— 1810	Sea luminous
70.36	2.40	1.0271	43.0	Greenish bl.	45	17 July 1811	At sea
70.49	7.15	1.0271	36.0	Ultram. blue	33	10 Apr. 1813	Ditto
71.10	5.30	1.0269	39.0	Ditto	41	8 —— 1815	Ditto
71.17	2. 5 W	1.0271	28.5	Ditto	6	11 —— 1814	Among bay ice
71.20	2.30 E	1.0266	29.3	Blue	32	4 —— 1814	Do. in open str.
72.15	7. 5	1.0261	29.0	Greenish	25	18 —— 1814	Near a pack
72.15	10.50	1.0269	41.0	Blue	17	21 —— 1814	30 mil. from ice
73.22	8.43	1.0262	31.0	Ditto	26	7 —— 1810	Loose ice
73.42	16.50	1.0266	37.5	Ditto	11	10 —— 1810	No ice in sight
73.50	15.40	1.0271	29.3	Ditto	7	9 —— 1810	Amo. much ice
74.33	13.50	1.0272	34.5	Ditto	6	13 —— 1810	Ditto
74.34	10. 0	1.0267	32.0	Ditto	15	10 —— 1815	At sea
74.40	11.50	1.0272	32.7	Ditto	16	14 —— 1810	Ditto
74.50	10.33	1.0272	28.0	Ditto	17	14 —— 1810	Ice sludge
75.34	15. 4	1.0263	29.7	Ditto	33	17 —— 1811	Some loose ice
75.36	9.14	1.0264	28.3	Ditto	10	15 —— 1810	Sea freezing
76. 0	7. 0	1.0272	31.0	Olive green	32	25 June 1810	20 mil. from ice
76.16	9. 0	1.0261	29.0	Ultram. blue	5	17 Apr. 1810	Much drift ice
76.30	5.45 W	1.0261	30.0	Ditto	34	28 June 1817	Ice-field near
76.33	10.20 E	1.0267	33.0	Ditto	11	11 Apr. 1815	At sea
76.34	10.20	1.0265	30.0	Ditto	35	23 —— 1811	Ship beset
76.40	5.20 W	1.0266	30.0	Greenish bl.	35	26 June 1817	Near a field
76.40	9.30 E	1.0263	29.8	Ultram. blue	18	30 Apr. 1810	Ice streams
76.50	10.30	1.0260	31.0	Ditto	19	26 —— 1810	Open drift ice
77.14	10. 0	1.0267	29.0	Ditto	11	5 May 1810	Water freezing
77.15	8.20	1.0267	29.2	Ditto	16	1 —— 1811	Ship beset
77.22	8. 0	1.0267	29.5	Olive green	30	22 —— 1811	Much ice
77.23	10. 0	1.0261	31.8	Ultram. blue	26	6 —— 1810	Ice all round
77.30	6.10	1.0263	28.5	Olive green	30	17 —— 1815	Ice in sight
77.34	8. 0	1.0267	38.0	Blue	20	18 Apr. 1815	Ice streams
77.40	2. 0	1.0267	29.0	Greenish bl.	30	20 May 1813	Floes & drift ice
77.48	3. 0	1.0264	29.5	Blue	34	11 June 1810	Moored to a field
77.54	3.10	1.0261	29.0	Greenish bl.	30	7 —— 1810	Ship beset
78. 0	7. 0	1.0259	34.0	Ditto	34	24 May 1815	Ice all round
78.20	6.30	1.0265	37.5	Ditto	35	2 July 1811	Drift ice
78.25	8.20	1.0265	31.0	Olive green	26	25 Apr. 1815	Open sea
78.30	6.30	1.0265	29 0	Blue	24	26 —— 1815	Drift ice
78.34	3. 0	1.0261	30.0	Greenish bl.	22	1 June 1810	Fields and floes
78.35	5. 0	1.0254	29.0	Olive green	18	19 May 1810	Drift ice & str.
78.35	6. 0	1.0261	29.0	Ditto	16	11 —— 1815	Bay & drift ice
78.36	5.30	1.0260	31.0	Ditto	15	13 —— 1810	Drift ice & str.
79. 0	6.30	1.0271	30.0	Ditto	29	6 June 1811	Drift ice
79. 4	5.38	1.0269	29.0	Ditto	38	21 May 1816	Floes & drift ice

A glass hydrometer, with a large bulb and very slender stem, was used for determining some of these specific gravities; but others were ascertained by weighing the water in a thin glass vessel, with a ground stopper, capable of containing 1012 grains of distilled water. When the specific gravities were determined at any other temperature than 60°, they were brought to that standard by the application of a correction derived from experiment *.

---

* Table of Changes of Specific Gravity of sea-water, for every five degrees of temperature, between 30° and 100°, applicable as a correction to bring observed specific gravities to that of temperature 60°.

Temperature.	Correction subtractive.	Temperature.	Correction additive.
30 —	.0016	65 +	.0004
35	.0015	70	.0009
40	.0013	75	.0015
45	.0010	80	.0022
50	.0007	85	.0030
55	.0004	90	.0039
60	.0000	95	.0049
		100	.0060

SECT.

SECT. II.

*Temperature, Depth, and Pressure of the Green-
land Sea, with a Description of an Apparatus
for bringing up Water from great Depths, and
an Account of Experiments made with it.*

In a sea perpetually covered with ice, the temperature of the surface might be supposed to be at
or near the freezing point, in all seasons. This is
no doubt generally the case; but it is remarkable
that, in some situations, even in the keenest frost,
and in the midst of ice, the temperature of the sea,
in latitude 76° to 78°, is sometimes as high as 36° or
38° of Fahrenheit.

As far as experiments have hitherto been made,
the temperature of the sea has generally been found
to diminish on descending. But, in the Greenland
Sea, near Spitzbergen, the contrary is the fact. For
determining this interesting point, I first made use
of a cask, capable of containing about ten gallons of
water, composed of *two-inch* fir plank, as being a
bad conductor of heat. Each end of the cask was
furnished with a valve, opening and shutting simultaneously, by means of a connecting wire. With
the top of the upper valve, moveable with it, was
connected a horizontal lever, having a flat circular
extremity projecting beyond the *chime*, or edge of

the cask. This lever, on the descent of the vessel, being forced upward, lifted the valves, and allowed a free course to the water, through the cask; but, on the motion downward being suspended, the valves fell down by their weight, and prevented the water from changing. It was generally allowed to remain about half an hour at rest, that the wood might attain the temperature of the sea in that situation, and then hauled briskly up without stopping, and the temperature of the contained water immediately ascertained. In the ascent of the apparatus, the lever connected with the upper valve, met the current of water in a contrary way, pressed the valve firmly down, and secured the water more effectually within the vessel.

The results thus obtained were highly satisfactory; the water brought up being invariably warmer than that at the surface; but, after a few experiments had been made, the wood of the cask became soaked with water; several of the staves rent from end to end; and the apparatus became leaky and useless.

Sir Joseph Banks, who manifested much interest in these experiments, and favoured me with valuable hints on the subject, from time to time, then furnished me with an apparatus, made by Carey, under the inspection of Messrs Cavendish and Gilpin, both of whom, it is remarkable, died before it was completed. It was made chiefly of wood, and bound with brass. But the first time it was sent to the depth of 300 fathoms, the wood swelled, opened, and became leaky, and two plate glass illuminators, intended to admit light for reading off the degrees on a *Six's* thermometer, which accompanied it, were broken. Thus this apparatus was also rendered useless. After this, I made a model of a similar instrument, and got it cast in brass. This I fitted up, with the assistance of an ingenious mechanic, and applied to it the valves made by Carey, which then proved an elegant and useful apparatus. This instrument, which I called a *marine diver*, is represented in plate 2. fig. 2. It was 14 inches in length, 5 inches in diameter at the top, and 6 at the bottom. The illuminators, consisting of plate glass, were each 8 inches long, and 2 to $2\frac{1}{4}$ inches broad, and were placed on opposite sides. The form of the instrument was an octagonal tapering prism. A slender spring operated on a quadrant of brass, fixed to the hinge-part of each valve, and was so adjusted, as merely to support the valve, when placed in its most open position, but no more. The top of the instrument was fixed on by two thumb screws, and could be removed in a few seconds, for facilitating the examination of the water. The weight of the whole being 23 pounds, it never required any load for sinking it.

With this instrument, and the fir-cask before mentioned, I completed a series of experiments on submarine temperature, as far as contained in the following table.

TABLE.

Lat.	Long.	Depth in Feet.	Temp.	Specific gravity.	Colour.	Tem. of Air.	TIME. Da. Mo. Yr.	Situation of the Vessel.
76°.16'	9°. 0' E	Surface	26.8	1 2061	Blue	12°	19 Apr. 1810	Ship beset in ice
—	—	300	31.8	—	—	—	—	—
—	—	738	33.8	1.0270	—	—	—	—
—	—	1380	33.3	1.0269	—	—	—	—
76.16	10.50	Surface	28.3	—	—	16	23 Apr. 1810	Ship frozen up
—	—	120	28.0	—	—	—	—	—
—	—	300	28.3	—	—	—	—	—
—	—	738	30.0	—	—	—	—	—
76.34	10. 0	Surface	30.0	1.0265	—	25	23 Apr. 1811	Ship frozen up
—	—	120	31.0	1.0264	—	—	—	—
—	—	240	35.0	1.0266	—	—	—	—
—	—	360	34.0	1.0268	—	—	—	—
—	—	600	34.7	1.0267	—	—	—	—
77.15	8.10	Surface	29.3	1.0267	—	16	1 May 1811	Ship beset in ice
—	—	120	29.3	—	—	—	—	—
—	—	240	29.3	—	—	—	—	—
—	—	360	30.0	—	—	—	—	—
—	—	600	30.0	—	—	—	—	—
77.40	2.30	Surface	29.0	1.0267	Greenish	30	20 May 1813	Am. floes, &c.
—	—	300	29.3	1.0265	—	—	—	—
—	—	660	31.0	1.0262	—	—	—	—
79. 0	5.40	Surface	29.0	—	Olive gr.	34	20 May 1816	Moored to a floe
—	—	78	31.0	—	—	—	—	—
—	—	222	33.8	—	—	—	—	—
—	—	342	34.5	—	—	—	—	—
—	—	600	36.0	—	—	—	—	—
—	—	2400	36.0	—	—	—	—	—
79. 4	5.38	Surface	29.0	1.0269	—	38	21 May 1816	Am. floes & fiel.
—	—	4380	37.0	1.0265	—	—	—	—
80. 0	5. 0	Surface	29.7	—	—	40	7 June 1816	Ship beset
—	—	720	36.3	—	—	—	—	—
78. 2	0.10W	Surface	32.0	—	Blue	36	7 June 1817	Ice near
—	—	4566	38.0	—	—	—	—	—

* Down to this experiment, the apparatus used for bringing up the water, was the fir-cask ; and the mode of finding the temperature, was by a common thermometer, after it came to the surface. Hence some slight change in the temperature might possibly take place during its passage upward ; but, in all the subsequent experiments, a Six's thermometer accompanied the marine-diver, and consequently marked with accuracy the extremes of temperature through which it passed.

After these experiments were made, I applied
a wire-gauze across the upper valve of the marine-
diver, and thus converted it into a trap for insects
and small fishes; so that, whatever animals might
enter by the lower valve, in its descent, were expected to be brought up along with the water in
the instrument.   In an experiment, however, on
the specific gravity, temperature, and effects of
pressure of the sea, at the depth of 7200 feet, the
greatest depth, I believe, ever sounded, which I attempted to make on the 28th June 1817, one of
the lines broke, and the whole apparatus was lost.
This unlucky accident was occasioned by the thickest, and apparently the strongest, line of the whole
series in use, having been rotted by receiving accidental moisture.

The depth of the Greenland Sea corresponds, in
a considerable degree, both in irregularity and quantity, with the height of the Arctic lands.   But the
generally received opinion, that where a coast is
mountainous or precipitous, the sea which washes
it is deep; and where the land is low, the sea is
shallow, does not hold in every place about Spitzbergen.   Near all the headlands, stretching towards the south, indeed, where the land is usually
terminated by a flat strand, the sea is shallow to a
considerable distance, agreeably to the general principle ; and a few miles off shore, in the neighbourhood of the mountainous parts of the coast, the sea

is usually very deep, which also verifies the rule; but, in some particular cases, even at the bases of some of the highest mountains, those in Charles' Island, for instance, the sea is shallow and rocky for several miles from the shore.

Within sight of Spitzbergen, on the west side, we sometimes find instances of whales, after being harpooned, " running" perpendicularly downward, and, on their return to the surface, giving indubitable evidence of their having been at the bottom; and thus, by the quantity of line drawn out of the whale-boats, affording a good measure of the depth of the sea. In latitude 78° 53', longitude 5° 56' E. the depth was thus found to be 3600 feet; and, within a few leagues of the same place, 4000 feet. But mid-way between Spitzbergen and West Greenland, in latitude 75°, 76° or 77°, and in other situations farther to the northward, the sea has never yet been fathomed. I have attempted to sound in latitude 76° 16', longitude 9° E. with 230 fathoms of line; in latitude 79° 4', longitude 5° 35' E. with 670 fathoms; in latitude 78° 2', longitude 0° 10' W. with 721 fathoms; in latitude 75° 50', longitude 5° 50' W. with 1058 fathoms; and in latitude 76° 30', longitude 4° 48' W, with 1200 fathoms of line, without finding the bottom.

In sounding at great depths, where the pressure of the water becomes equal to, perhaps, several hundreds weight on every square inch of surface, some persons have imagined that even lead cannot sink, but will be suspended mid-way in the sea! I have conversed, indeed, with very intelligent persons, who could not be persuaded that any dependence could be placed on soundings obtained at a depth exceeding 300 fathoms. Were water a compressible substance, like air, it would be possible, that, under a certain pressure, it might become as heavy as lead; so that lead, or any other ponderous body, could only sink to a certain depth; but water being incompressible, or nearly so, it is clear, however great the pressure may be, that it must be the same downward as upward, on any body suspended in it; consequently, bodies specifically heavier, will continue to gravitate downward, whatever be the depth, or the weight of the column of water above them.

The difficulty of getting satisfactory soundings, at great depths, arises, principally, from the uncertain intimation given, when the lead strikes the bottom. This uncertainty is increased by using a thick line: for, if a lead of a hundred pounds weight were used, the rope attached to it would require to be so thick, that, at the depth of six or eight hundred fathoms, the weight of the line, even in water, would be so many times greater than that of the lead, that scarcely any effect could be observed when it should reach the bottom. Hence I always prefer a light lead, and a very small line. With a lead of 20 pounds, I have sounded in above 1000

3

fathoms, and felt assured that, if it had struck the bottom, I should have observed it; for the whole of the line in use, was not above twice as heavy as the lead; so that the diminution of one-third of the weight, would have been very observable. But, with a heavy lead and thick line, where the strength of several men is requisite to haul it up, there can be no evidence, without the test of weighing, of any trifling alteration in the strain or weight. Hence, if the lead is found to have been at the bottom, there can be no assurance that a quantity of the line, as well as the lead, has not also been on the ground. To a 20 lb. or 28 lb. lead, I generally attach 200 or 300 fathoms of common log-line, where there is no valuable apparatus along with it, and to this a small lead-line, and finish with a deep-sea line, thus increasing the line in thickness, with the increase of weight to be supported; and having the whole of such a weight that the line can be held in the hand, and the least stoppage made perceptible.

At great depths, the effect of the pressure of the sea is not a little curious. My Father met with the following singular instance, in the year 1794, which I have taken from his log-book.

On the 31st of May, the chief mate of the Henrietta of Whitby, the ship my Father then commanded, struck a whale, which " ran" all the lines out of the boat, before assistance arrived, and then dragged the boat under water, the men mean while

escaping to a piece of ice. When the fish returned
to the surface to " blow," it was struck a second
time, and soon afterwards killed. The moment it
expired, it began to sink, which not being a usual
circumstance, excited some surprise. My Father,
who was himself assisting at the capture, observing
the circumstance, seized a grapnel, fastened a rope
to it, threw it over the tail of the fish, and fortunately hooked it. It continued to sink; but the
line being held fast in the boat, at length stopped
it, though not until the " strain" was such that
the boat was in danger of sinking. The " bight"
or loop of a rope being then passed round the fish,
and allowed to drop below it, inclosed the line belonging to the sunken boat, which was found to be
the cause of the phenomenon observed. Immediately the harpoon slipped out of the whale, and
was, with the line and boat attached to it, on the
point of being lost, when it was luckily caught by
the encompassing rope. The fish being then released from the weight of the lines and boat, rose
to the surface; and the strain was transferred to the
boat connected with the disengaged harpoon. My
Father, imagining that the sunken boat was entangled among rocks at the bottom of the sea, and
that the action of a current on the line produced
the extraordinary stress, proceeded himself to assist
in hauling up the boat. The strain upon the line he
estimated at not less than three-fourths of a ton,

2

the utmost power of twenty-five men being requisite to overcome the weight. The laborious operation of hauling the line in, occupied several hours,
the weight continuing nearly the same throughout.
The sunken boat, which, before the accident, would
have been buoyant when full of water, when it came
to the surface required a boat at each end to keep
it from sinking. " When it was hoisted into the
ship, the paint came off the wood in large sheets,
and the planks, which were of wainscot, were as
completely soaked in every pore, as if they had lain
at the bottom of the sea since the Flood!" A
wooden apparatus that accompanied the boat in its
progress through the deep, consisting chiefly of a
piece of thick deal, about fifteen inches square,
happened to fall overboard, and though it originally consisted of the lightest fir, sunk in the water
like a stone. The boat was rendered useless ; even
the wood of which it was built, on being offered to
the cook as fuel, was tried and rejected as incom-
bustible.

This curious circumstance induced me to make
some experiments on the subject. I accordingly
attached some pieces of fir, elm, and hickery, containing two cubical inches of wood each, to the marine-diver, and sent them to the depth of 4000 feet.
Pieces of wood, corresponding with each of these
in shape and weight, were immersed in a bucket
of sea-water, during the time the marine-diver,

and its attached pieces, were under water, by the
way of distinguishing the degree of impregnation
produced by pressure, from the absorption which
takes place from simple immersion.   On being
brought up, they were all specifically heavier than
sea-water; and, when compared with the counterparts, the clear effect of impregnation by pressure,
was found to be 302 grains in the fir and hickery,
and 316 grains in the ash.   This experiment was
repeated in latitude 78° 2', on the 7th June 1817,
by the immersion of several articles of different
shapes * and sizes, to the depth of 4566 feet.   On
this occasion, the apparatus was 30 minutes on its
way down, rested 40 minutes, and took 36 minutes
in drawing up, being altogether 106 minutes under
water.   The degree of impregnation produced on
each of the different substances used in this experiment, is stated in the annexed Table.

---

* My friend Professor Leslie suggested this variation of
trying the relative degree of impregnation, on pieces of the
same kind of wood, of different shapes ;—a hint which I pro-
fited by in my later experiments.

TABLE.

Names of Substances.	Shape.	Solid Contents.	Specific Gravity after Immersion.	Proportion of Weight gained per Cubic Inch in consequence of Pressure.
		Cub. Inch.	W. 60°.1000	Drams Avoir.
Hickery	Wedge	1.4436	1.1760	4.606
Elm	Rectang. prism	2.0040	1.1321	5.639
Beech	Ditto	2.0040	1.1806	4.790
Fir	Thin wedge	0.9505	1.1168	4.050
Mahogany	Parallelopiped.	0.8792	1.0523	3.071
Lign. Vitæ	Rectang. prism	1.9356	1.3315	0.336
Bone	Ditto	0.1380	2.1372	0.725

This degree of impregnation is not surprising, when we consider that the pressure of water, at the depth to which these specimens of wood were sent, is equal, at least, to 2031 *lb.* or 18 *cwt.* 15 *lb.* on every square inch of surface *.

---

* According to the estimation of Sir George Shuckburgh Evelyn, (Phil. Trans. vol. lxxxviii.), corrected by Mr Fletcher, (Phil. Journ. vol. iv.), a cubic inch of distilled water, temperature 60°, weighs 252.5060 grains, being the usual unit of specific gravities, or 1.000. The mean specific gravity of the Greenland Sea, included between the parallels of 76° and 79° N, is, at temperature 60°, 1.0264, and at 30°, (the mean temperature of the water at the surface), 1.028 ; hence, As 1.000, the specific gravity of pure water, is to 252.506 grains, the weight of a cubical inch of pure water, so is 1.028, the specific gravity of the water of the Greenland Sea, to 259.5761, the

N 2

On the occasion when the marine-diver was lost, I had a very extensive and improved experiment in view, on the effect of the pressure of the sea, at one of the greatest depths ever sounded. Attached to the apparatus, were specimens of wood and other substances, to the amount of twenty articles, all carefully weighed and adjusted, that the increase of specific gravity might be accurately determined. This failing, however, by the breaking of the line, I repeated the experiment on the 18th July 1818; but having no apparatus for bringing up the water, or for ascertaining the temperature below the surface, my object was confined solely to the effect of pressure. Finding, on former trials, that pieces of fir wood sent down 4000 feet, were more impregnated with sea-water than others immersed only half that depth, I was in hopes that the degree of impregnation of similar pieces of the same kind of wood, might be applicable as a measure of depth. If this were the case, it would serve a very valuable purpose, since all the plans hitherto contrived for

weight of a cubical inch of the same, at the usual temperature of the sea. This, multiplied by 12, gives the weight of a column of sea-water, an inch square and a foot long, equal to 3114.91 grains; which, multiplied by 4566 feet, the depth to which the specimens of wood were sent, and divided by 7004, the number of Troy grains in a pound Avoirdupois, affords the result of 2030.65 lb. for the weight of a column of water an inch square, and 4565 feet high.

measuring depths from a vessel, when sailing slow-
ly, or drifting through the water, cease to be useful
beyond 200 or 300 fathoms*. With this view, I not
only attached pieces of wood of different kinds, to
the lead, and provided counterparts for immersion
in a bucket of water; but I also fastened cubes of
ash, from the same piece of timber, of about one
inch solid contents, and of the same exact weight,
to the line, at intervals of about 500 feet; by the
weight of which, when taken up, I could ascertain
whether the increase of specific gravity was in any
way proportionate to the depth. When the specimens of wood for this experiment were procured, a
clear grained piece, of double the size wanted for
sending under water, was prepared, and then cut in
two, and the two parts dressed to the same shape,
and to within a quarter of a grain of the same
weight: one of these was then adopted as a principal, and fixed to the lead or line; and the other as
a counterpart, and put into a bucket of water.
The specimens affixed to the lead were eleven in
number, and consisted of wood of different kinds,
shapes, and dimensions: they were sunk to the

---

* A very recent contrivance, for obtaining soundings from
a vessel under-way, founded on the small change in bulk which
takes place in water when strongly compressed, promises to
answer the design at still greater depths than 200 or 300 fathoms.

depth of 6348 feet.   The line was almost perpendicular for nearly an hour; and when the lead was
hauled up, I was assured, from its appearance, (the
end being covered with soft grease, that would have
retained an impression had it struck the ground,)
that it had not been at the bottom.

Each piece of wood attached to the line, was taken off as hauled in, plunged in a basin of water,
and conveyed into the cabin, where its weight in
air and in fresh water was immediately taken.
The interval between any two pieces was such,
that I had just time to determine the specific gravity of one, before the next came up.   On the arrival of the lead, the attached specimens were immediately immersed in water, and weighed as quick
as possible, together with their counterparts, which
had been secured at the bottom of a bucket of sea-
water, during the time the experiment was in progress.   As the counterparts would have floated,
they were each loaded with a piece of copper,
weighing 880 grains when under water.   Hence
the excess of 880 grains, above the weight of any
specimen in water, with this load attached, gave
the buoyancy of the wood; which excess, added to
the weight of the specimen in air, afforded the
weight of an equal bulk of water; and the comparison of the weight in air, with that of an equal bulk
of water, gave, of course, the specific gravity of the
wood.

3

The following Table exhibits the results of this experiment *.

---

* It may not be amiss to explain the method by which the calculations, in the annexed Table, were made I shall take the first line as an example. A cube of ash, weighing in air 157 grains, weighed in snow-water, temperature 60°, with a load of 880 grains attached, 797 grains, (col. v.) Hence 880— 797 $=$ 83 $+$ 157, (col. iv.) $=$ 240, (col. vi.) Then, as $252\frac{1}{2}$ grains, (the weight of a cubic inch of water, at temperature 60°,) is to 1 cubic inch, so is 240 grains, (col. vi.) to 0.951, (col. vii.) And as 240 grains, (col. vi.) is to 1.000, (the unit of specific gravity,) so is 157, (col. iv.) to 0.654, (col. viii.) The difference between col. x. and xi. gives col. xii. Then, as $252\frac{1}{2}$ grains, is to 1 cubic inch, so is 238 grains to 0.943, (col. xiii.) And as 238 grains, (col. xii.) is to 1.000, so is 278 grains, (col. x.) to 1.168, (col. xiv.) The difference between cols. iv. and x. gives col. xv. And, finally, as 0.943, (col. xiii.) is to 121 (col. xv.), so is 1.000 to 128 (col. xvi.)

All the results in columns iv, v, x, and xi, were found by means of an excellent hydrostatical balance, sensible to the twentieth of a grain. The scale-beam, which was made under my own inspection, and after a new plan, by an excellent workman, has two adjustments, derived from a perpendicular motion in the centre of the beam, and a horizontal motion in the centre of one of the ends. The former moving up and down by two opposite screws, adjusts the centre of gravity of the beam, in any way that may be required, either for a quick or a slow motion: and the latter, moving horizontally, adjusts the two arms to the same length. With this balance, most of the specific gravities, and other weights of any consequence, given in these volumes, were determined.

TABLE.

I.	II.	III.	Experiments on the Counterparts, immersed Three Hours in a Bucket of Water.					Experiments on Wood, immersed during Two or Three Hours, at Various Depths in the Sea.							
N.	Quality.	Shape.	IV. Weight in Air.	V. Weight in Water, with a load of 880 gr.	VI. Weight of an eq. bulk of Fr. Wa. Tem. 60°.	VII. Solid contents.	VIII. Spec. gravity.	IX. Depth.	X. Weight in Air.	XI. Weight in Fresh Water, T. 60°.	XII. Weight of an eq. bulk of pu. Wa. Tem. 60°.	XIII. Solid contents.	XIV. Spec. gravity.	XV. Increase of Weight by Pressure.	XVI. Proportion of Weight gained per Cubic In.
			Grains.	Grains.	Grains.	Cub. Inch.		Feet.	Grains.	Grains.	Grains.	Cub. Inch.		Grains.	Grains.
1	Ash.	Cube	157	797	240	0.951	0.654	6348	278	40	238	0.943	1.168	121	128
2	—	—	157	797	240	0.951	0.654	5868	290	41	249	0.986	1.165	133	135
3	—	—	157	797	240	0.951	0.654	5370	283	40	243	0.963	1.165	126	131
4	—	—	157	797	240	0.951	0.654	4836	278	39	239	0.947	1.163	121	128
5	—	—	157	797	240	0.951	0.654	4484	288	38	250	0.990	1.152	131	132
6	—	—	157	797	240	0.951	0.654	3708	286	39	247	0.978	1.158	129	132
7	—	—	157	797	240	0.951	0.654	3198	280	37	243	0.962	1.152	123	128
8	—	—	157	797	240	0.951	0.654	2628	277	39	238	0.943	1.164	120	127
9	—	Parallelo.	157	743	240	0.951	0.648	2058	289	35	254	1.006	1.138	132	132
10	—	Cube	252	723	389	1.541	0.669	6348	493	73	420	1.663	1.174	241	145
11	—	—	318	723	475	1.881	0.669	6348	593	88	505	2.000	1.174	275	137
12	—	—	318	723	475	1.881	0.638	3708	594	88	506	2.004	1.174	276	138
13	—	—	449	625	704	2.788	0.639	6348	868	127	741	2.934	1.171	419	143
14	—	—	606	537	949	3.758	0.639	6348	1188	177	1011	4.004	1.175	582	145
15	—	—	606	537	949	3.758	0.473	4836	1180	173	1007	3.988	1.172	574	144
16	Fir	Rect. pris.	220	631	469	1.857	0.720	6348	534	40	494	1.956	1.081	314	161
17	Oak	—	350	758	472	1.870	0.929	6348	589	92	497	1.968	1.185	239	121
18	Hickery	—	407	849	438	1.734	0.782	6348	614	119	495	1.960	1.240	207	106
19	Teak	—	370	777	473	1.873	0.693	6348	574	94	480	1.900	1.196	204	107
20	Elm	—	289	752	417	1.651	0.225	6348	538	54	484	1.917	1.112	249	129
21	Cork	Cylinder	49	711	218	0.863			86	−94	180	0.713	0.478	37	52

From this Table we may observe, that the greatest increase of specific gravity, by pressure, in the specimens of the different kinds of wood submitted to experiment, was obtained by the fir; the next greatest by the ash; the next by the elm; the next by the oak; the next by the teak; the next by the hickery; and the least by the mahogany. The cork gained still less than any of the pieces of wood. The proportion of impregnation of the same kind of wood, in specimens of different sizes and shapes, is derived from the experiments made on the ash; and it is curious to observe, that the largest cube of ash, No. 14. and the parallelopipedon of the same, No. 10. received the greatest proportional increase of weight; while the smaller pieces received less and less additional weight, *per* cubic inch, as they decreased in size. Thus, No. 14. containing about 4 solid inches of wood, gained 145 grains *per* cubic inch; No. 13. of about 3 solid inches, gained 143 grains *per* cubic inch; No. 11. of 2 solid inches, gained 137 grains *per* inch; and the specimens of 1 inch, solid contents, gained from 127 to 135 grains. It is also a little curious, that the specimens sent to the depth of 2058 feet, were as much impregnated as those sent down above 6000 feet. The cube of ash, No. 11. consisting of 2 solid inches of wood, gained 137 grains *per* inch, at the depth of 6348 feet, while a similar specimen gained 138 grains, at the inferior depth of 3708 feet. In the same way, a cube of 4 solid inches gained 145 grains *per* inch, at the extreme depth; and 144 grains *per* inch, at the depth of 4836 feet. The degree of impregnation of the one-inch cubes of ash, produced by immersion to the depth of 2058 feet to 6348 feet, varies irregularly, ·but is evidently as great at the depth of 2058 feet, as under any superior pressure; so that it is probable that the greatest permanent impregnation by pressure, of such open-grained woods as ash, elm, fir, &c. is produced at the depth of 300 or 400 fathoms. Hence it is clear that no use can be made of this effect of pressure, for determining the depth, unless it be within 2000 feet of the surface; and even in this limit, the results may be uncertain.

From a comparison of column VII. with XIII., and column IV. with XV., it appears, that an effect of the impregnation of the wood with sea-water, was to increase its dimensions, as well as its specific gravity; each specimen, on an average, having swelled 0.05 cubic inch in every solid inch of original dimensions, and gained 84 grains on every 100 grains of original weight; that is, an increase of one-twentieth in size, and twenty one twenty-fifths in weight.

I have little doubt, but the degree of impregnation always increases with the increase of pressure; but the air contained in the pores of the wood, which is never wholly disengaged, exerting an expansive force when the load of pressure is removed, forces part of the water out again. This was clearly discernible in some of the specimens used in the foregoing experiments, at the moment they were hauled up, their surfaces being covered with a thin pellicle of froth. Hence pieces of fir sometimes become buoyant, after being a few hours relieved from pressure, though kept constantly under water; but all other kinds of wood yet tried, though they lose a little of their moisture, yet remain specifically heavier than water, as long as they are kept immersed. Blocks of wood, indeed, are now in my possession, that were soaked with sea-water in the year 1817, and yet remain, at the bottom of a vessel of water, nearly as heavy as when first drawn up out of the sea.

The degree of pressure at the depth to which I sounded in my last experiment, is not a little astonishing, being, under a column of water, 6348 feet in length, at least, 2823 *lb.* or 25 *cwt.* 23 *lb.* on one square inch of surface *. Hence on the larger cubes of ash used in the experiment, though measuring only 1.59 inches in diameter, the whole pressure must have exceeded nineteen tons!

SECT. III.

Remarks on the Currents of the Arctic Sea, with Observations respecting Waves.

THE determination of the various horizontal motions in the great body of waters of the ocean, is a

---

* In this calculation, as well as others of the same nature, the weight of the column of sea-water is taken throughout, the same as at the surface, where a cubic inch, temperature 30°, weighs 259.58 grains. As, however, water is found to be somewhat compressible, its weight, at great depths, must be greater than at the surface; and consequently the whole pressure on the specimens of wood, greater than in the above estimation.

problem attended with much difficulty and uncertainty.   These motions, denominated Currents, being under the influence of some of the same principles as regulate the winds, are found to be somewhat similar to the movements of the atmosphere, though more regular and steady.   The general agents employed in the production of currents, are considered to be the rotatory motion of the Earth, the varying attractions of the Sun and Moon, differences in temperature, and particularly strong or prevailing winds.   These, when combined with the peculiarities of form in sea-coasts, and in the bed of the ocean, with other topical circumstances, may serve to account for many of the currents hitherto observed.

Currents, as regards their permanency, are either *general, particular,* or *variable ;* and, as relates to their situation, or to the depth at which they prevail in the sea, are called either *bodily, upper,* or *under* currents.

General currents are such as are always directed towards the same point of the compass.   Particular currents change their direction periodically : and variable currents are such as have no stated period, being chiefly produced by the action of the wind.

A bodily current prevails where the whole mass of waters, from the surface to the bottom, moves in the same direction, and with similar velocity.   An upper or superficial current, is where a stratum at the surface of the sea is in motion, while the lower

parts are either at rest, or have a different motion:
and an under current is where a deep stratum of
water moves in a different direction from that at
the surface.

Hence where the motions in the water are so various, there must evidently be great uncertainty
in the usual methods of ascertaining the set and
velocity of currents in deep seas. Superficial and
bodily currents, indeed, may be discovered by their
effects on the progress and course of vessels sailing
in them, or by their influence in conveying wood,
fruit, and other produce of one country, to the
shores of another; as also in conducting buoyant
articles, cast into the sea, in known situations, to
remote regions, where they may be recognized.
And, in shallow water, or wherever the depth is
such as to be fathomed with sounding lines, a heavy
body, with a line attached, being sunk to the bottom, shows, by the relative motion of a boat at the
surface, to which the weight acts as an anchor, the
true set and velocity of the current. As, however,
there are doubtless under currents, as well as superficial and bodily currents, it is evident that the
usual method of sinking a heavy bulky body, such
as an iron kettle, mid-way in the sea, and connecting it by a line to a boat, and thus forming the
kettle into a sort of floating anchor, and estimating
the set and velocity of the current by the motion of
the boat through the water, cannot be depended on
for discovering the real nature of the current, but

can only give the relative motion of the superficial water, as compared with that of the stratum of water in which the kettle is suspended. In fact, this plan for determining the course and velocity of currents, goes on the supposition that currents are only superficial, or that the waters below are always at rest, which is not true. In a deep sea, therefore, where no soundings can be obtained, the determination of currents must always be a matter of difficulty ; and, in some cases, of impracticability.

By the effects of currents on vessels and other floating bodies, the courses of many general and some particular currents, have been determined in a most satisfactory manner. That general and extensive current setting westward in tropical regions, a branch of which, after doubling the Cape of Good Hope, and extending considerably to the northward along the western coast of Africa, crosses the Atlantic, accumulates in the Gulf of Mexico, passes out by the Bahama Islands towards Newfoundland, and constitutes what has been called the Gulf Stream,—is too well known to need any proof or particular description. On the great bank of Newfoundland, this stream meets with a current setting southward from Baffin's Bay and the coasts of Greenland; and is deflected, perhaps, in two branches, towards the E. S. E. and E. N. E. By the influence of these, plants, timber, fruits, &c. the produce of America and the West Indies, are frequently washed on shore on the coasts of Ireland, the Hebrides, or Orkneys, as well as on the different shores of the continent of Europe *; and various articles belonging to vessels wrecked in Davis' Straits, or thrown overboard from vessels on the passage thither, have, by the same influence, been conducted to the shores of Britain and the adjacent islands. Thus, a bottle thrown overboard off Cape Farewell, on the 24th of May 1818, from the Alexander, (one of the ships lately employed under Captain Ross in search of a north-west passage,) was picked up on the island of Bartragh in the Bay of Killala, on the 17th of March 1819, having floated across the Atlantic at the rate of about four miles a-day †.

But as some very light substances might be drifted across the Atlantic by the prevailing westerly winds, instead of being conducted by the current, it may be of moment to mention, that among the different articles known to have drifted from Davis' Straits into the neighbourhood of Britain, were some casks and shakes ‡, which, from the marks upon them, were found to have belonged to the Royalist and London, two Hull whalers, that were wrecked between the latitudes of 61° and 62°, and

---

* Quarterly Review, No. 36. p. 441.—(Note.)

† Idem, No. 41. p. 255.

‡ For convenience in stowage, empty casks are sometimes taken to pieces, and the staves closely packed up in a cylindrical form, constituting what are called *shakes* or *packs*.

about the longitude of 56° W; the former in the
year 1814, and the latter in 1817.   The staves of
blubber casks being generally soaked with oil,
shakes formed of them float almost entirely under water, and are, therefore, defended from the
influence of the wind; and these shakes being
of a cylindrical form, are rolled over on their axes
by the force of the waves, instead of being propelled through the water.   Hence, on any reasonable calculation, founded on the influence of prevailing winds, such bodies could not be expected
to accomplish a passage across the Atlantic, unless
by the operation of a current, under the period of
many years.   But the casks above mentioned, were
picked up off the Butt of the Lewis, within twelve
months of the vessels to which they had belonged
being wrecked; and a shake that had belonged to
the London, was found by the crew of the Royal
George, drifting through the Orkneys, about eleven
months after the accident.   The latter had, therefore, performed a passage of about 1600 nautical
miles within the year; that is, at the average rate
of five miles *per* day.   It might be reasonably asked, How is it, when such a current always prevails,
that no iceberg was ever conveyed across the Atlantic to the British shore?   This does not appear to
arise from the icebergs being dissolved in their progress; because they perform a passage equally long
in other directions, having been known to drift to
the southward as far as the 40th degree of latitude,

which is as remote from Cape Farewell, as some parts of Orkney or the Western Islands; but it would seem to be owing to the circumstance, of these bodies of ice floating so deep in the sea, as to be within the influence of an under current of cold water setting out of Davis' Strait towards the south, while the upper current takes an easterly direction, and carries all light bodies along with it. If this be the fact, the heaviest or deepest icebergs should be found pursuing a southerly direction, and the lightest or shallowest should be found more to the eastward.

From the coast of Britain, the northern branch of the Gulf Stream probably extends, superficially, along the shore of Norway, towards the north-east. About the North Cape, its direction appears to be changed, by the influence of a westerly current from Nova Zembla; so that it afterwards sets towards the north-west, as high as the borders of the ice, and thus operating against the polar current setting to the south-westward, may be the means of preventing the polar ice from spreading across the North Sea. From the fact of the sea near Spitzbergen being usually six or seven degrees warmer at the depth of 100 to 200 fathoms, than it is at the surface, it seems not improbable that the water below is a still farther extension of the Gulf Stream, which, on meeting with water near the ice lighter than itself, sinks below the surface, and becomes a counter under-current.

That fresh water obtains its greatest density at a temperature a few degrees above the freezing point, and that it expands on any farther reduction of the temperature, are facts well established; but that sea-water follows a different law, and continues to contract down to the point of freezing, is a question which has not been sastisfactorily decided. Count Rumford, in his " Essays," (vol. ii. p. 302.) says, indeed, that "sea-water continues to be condensed, as it goes on to cool, even after it has passed the point at which fresh water freezes;" but from the circumstance of an under stratum of water in the Spitzbergen Sea, being generally warmer by some degrees than that at the surface, though of similar specific gravity, it would appear that the warmer water is in this case the most dense, or why does it not rise and change places with the colder water at the surface? Hence I think there is reason to believe, that sea-water follows the same law as fresh water, with regard to the extreme of density being a few degrees above the freezing temperature, and that the under-stream of comparatively warm water, observed in the Spitzbergen Sea, which is of a temperature 16° to 20° above the mean temperature of the climate, is an under-current derived from a southern region.

In some situations near Spitzbergen, the warm water not only occupies the lower and mid regions of the sea, but also appears at the surface. From inspection of the preceding Table of the Specific

Gravity, &c. of Sea-water, it will be seen, that, in some instances, even among ice, the temperature of the sea at the surface, has been as high as 36° or 38°, when that of the air has been several degrees below freezing. This circumstance, however, has chiefly occurred near the meridians of 6° to 12° east ; and we find, from observation, that the sea freezes less in these longitudes than in any other part of the Spitzbergen Sea.

Within the Arctic Circle, from the north-eastern point of Russia to the coasts of Greenland and Labrador, the prevailing current at the surface, is from east to west, from north-east to south-west, or from north to south.

In Behring's Strait, between East Cape and Cape Prince of Wales, (it has been before observed,) Lieutenant Kotzebue, the Russian navigator, found a current setting strongly to the north-east, with a velocity, as he thought, of two miles and a half an hour, which is more than double the velocity of the current observed by Captain Cook *. Along the northern face of Russia, the current is decidedly from the east towards the west, following the line of the coast †. After passing Nova Zembla, it sets westerly to Spitzbergen, where one part proceeds round Point-look-out, and along the western shore

---

* BARROW's " Voyages into the Arctic Regions," p. 358.

† Russian Voyages, pp. 339 and 391.—Quart. Rev. No. 36. p. 443, 444.   o 2

towards the north, until it meets with another branch passing to the northward of these islands; these two branches then reuniting, proceed a little to the westward; and afterwards, being deflected towards the south by the coast of Greenland, proceed regularly towards the south-west, setting with a much greater velocity near the Greenland shore than in the vicinity of Spitzbergen. Pursuing its course along the east side of Greenland, the current passes to the westward of Iceland, down to Cape Farewell. Having doubled this promontory, according to the opinion of O. Fabricius*, it is urged northward; but meeting with another current setting down the strait of Davis, before it reaches Disco Island, it is probably deflected to the westward, when the accumulation of waters on the western side of the strait, escapes to the southward, along the American shore.

The general route pursued by this current, is proved by the movements of the floating ice, which, between Spitzbergen and Greenland, being of the field or drift kind, follows, in a great measure, the motion of the superficial water.

Some illustrations of the preceding remarks shall be brought forward.

Four Greenland whalers, the Leviathan, Dauntless, Fortitude and Lion, were wrecked in the Arc-

---

* From a MS. translation of FABRICIUS, " Nye Samling af det Kongelige Danske Videnskabers Selskabs Skrivter,"— communicated to me by Sir JOSEPH BANKS.

tic ice, in latitude 78°, longitude 3° W., during a severe storm, May 5th 1817. One of these vessels, the Dauntless, after filling with water, floated in an upright position, and was drifted along with the ice towards the south-west. On the 18th of May, while the ship under my command was navigating the recesses of the ice in latitude 75° 28′, longitude 10° W., I discovered this vessel still floating, which we found had drifted 182 miles, in a S. W. by S. direction, in thirteen days, being at the rate of fourteen miles a-day. The winds, however, during this period, having prevailed chiefly from the N., E., and S. E., some of this drift must be attributed to their influence, but not a large proportion, as, on the wind becoming light, and shifting occasionally to a southerly quarter, the wreck continued to set to the southward; and before the end of May, was seen in latitude 73° 30′.

In the same season (1817,) being far immured among ice, near the main western body, we moored to a floe, and maintained our position for four days, during a strong gale of wind from the N. W., N. and N. E. When the storm subsided, we found, that we had drifted along with the ice, sixty miles to the southward, and considerably to the westward, at the average rate of near twenty miles *per* day. Our drift commenced in latitude 78° 34′, longitude 2° W. On the 1st of July following, we penetrated the ice in latitude 75° 30′, as far as the meridian of 8° W., and remained during a thick fog until the 9th, generally moored to ice, or drifting to the northward, with the wind constantly from the south-westward. As the ice was light, and had considerable drift in the water, we expected we must have set at least eighty or ninety miles to the northward; whereas, from our first observation of the sun, we found we had set nearly thirty miles to the southward. Hence, allowing for the drift of the ship by the wind, the current appeared to have set 110 or 120 miles to the southward in nine days, being twelve or thirteen miles *per* day, southing, or half a mile *per* hour, besides the distance it might have set to the westward.

In the year 1803, the Henrietta of Whitby, while prosecuting the whale-fishery, was, by a southerly storm, entangled among the ice in latitude 80° north, longitude 6° east; and afterwards accompanied it in its drift, first to the westward, and then to the south-westward or southward, at the daily rate of from five to fifteen miles. They saw bears in uncommon numbers; and at one time the coast of Greenland, they believed, was in sight. The ice pressed dreadfully around them, and accumulated in amazing heaps; but the ship always escaped the heaviest crushes, and was wonderfully preserved. After a state of complete inertion during seven weeks, the ice began to slack; when, with vigilant and laborious measures, they were enabled to make their escape, in latitude $73\frac{1}{2}°$, and longitude 9° west. In this involuntary passage along with the ice, the ship was conveyed in a S SW.$\frac{1}{2}$ W. direction, (true) a distance of about 420 miles; or with the average rate of $8\frac{1}{2}$ miles *per* day.

These facts, then, I conceive, are conclusive as to the prevalence of a south-westerly current in the Greenland sea in high latitudes; and the following, will perhaps, be considered as establishing the continuance of the same current down to Cape Farewell.

From a narrative of the loss of several of the Dutch Greenland fleet in the year 1777, we learn, that the ship Wilhelmina was moored to a field of ice on the 22d of June, in the usual fishing-station, along with a large fleet of other whalers. On the 25th, the ice having rapidly closed around, the Wilhelmina was closely *beset*. The pressure of the ice was so great, that the crew were under the necessity of working almost incessantly for eight days, in sawing a dock in the field, wherein the ship was at that time preserved. On the 25th of July, the ice slacked, and the ship was towed by the boats to the eastward. After four days laborious rowing, they reached the extremity of the opening, where they joined four ships, all of which were again beset by the ice. Shortly afterwards, they were drifted within sight of the coast of *Old* Greenland, about the parallel of $75\frac{1}{2}°$ north. On the 15th of August, nine sail were collected together; and about the 20th, after sustaining a dreadful storm, and being subjected to an immense pressure of the ice, which accumulated around them twenty or thirty feet high, two of the ships were wrecked. Two more were wrecked four or five days afterwards, together with two others at a distance from them. On the 24th, Iceland was in sight; some of the ice was in motion, and two ships seemed to escape. Another was lost on the 7th of September; and, on the 13th, the Wilhelmina was crushed to pieces, by the fall of an enormous mass of ice, which was so unexpected, that those of the crew who were in bed, had scarcely time to escape on the ice, half naked as they were. One ship now alone remained, to which the crews of four, and the surviving part of the crew of a fifth, (that was wrecked on the 30th September,) repaired. By the beginning of October, they had drifted to the latitude of 64°; and on the 11th, the last ship was overwhelmed by the ice and sunk. Thus, between three and four hundred men were driven to the ice, and exposed to the inclemency of the weather, atmost destitute of food and raiment, and without hut or tent to shield them from the piercing wind.

On the 30th of October, the miserable sufferers divided. The greater part betook themselves to the land, and attempted to travel along its rugged shores, while the rest remained on a field of ice, until it drifted as far as Staten Hook, and then procceded in their boats along shore. The want of shelter and proper clothing, exposed them to dreadful fatigue and suffering, being often under the necessity of walking to and fro on a sheet of ice during the obscurity of night, to save themselves from being frozen to death. At length, after experiencing several acts of kindness from the native Greenlanders, about 140 of the men reached the Danish settlements on the west coast of Greenland; the remainder, consisting of about 200 persons, perished*.

Thus, it appears, that the ship which survived to the latest period, set with the ice in a south-westerly direction from the usual fishing-station, (probably in latitude 78° to 80°) to the latitude of about 62°; and, at the same time, from the longitude, perhaps, of 5° to 6° east, to about 40° west; and that the ice still continued to advance along the land to the southward. This extensive drift, at the lowest calculation, must have embraced a distance of about 1300 miles, on a course S. 43° W. (true), and having been performed in about 108 days, averages twelve miles a-day exclusive of the advance that was made towards the east, from the 25th to the 28th of July.

That remarkable agitation produced in the surface of the sea by the action of the wind, called WAVES,

* Beschryving der Walvisvangst, vol. iv. p. 18.–32. &c.

is, in nautical language, distinguished into different kinds. The first effect of the wind on the water, such as that observed in small lakes or rivers in strong winds, is denominated *lipper* or *wind-lipper*, and constitutes in the high sea or in large waters, the rudiments of all larger waves. The higher waves observed in the ocean, carrying inequalities and inferior waves in all parts of their surface, are, collectively or individually, called a *sea*, and are distinguished into different kinds, according to their characters, properties or appearances ; such as, " a high sea," " a heavy sea," " a short sea," " a long sea," " a true sea," " a cross sea ;" or, as relating to the position in which a ship traverses the surges, a " head-sea," a " beam-sea," and so on. But the smooth undulations of the sea which remain after a storm, or which extend beyond the influence of the wind into a calm region, where no such waves took their rise, is most frequently denominated a *swell*. Lastly, The sublime appearance of waves in shallow water, seen also occasionally in deep seas, in which their towering summits overrunning the velocity of the hollows, are reared beyond the perpendicular, and fall over like a cascade, is, the well-known and dreaded *breakers*, or *broken water*, of the mariner.

It has been intimated by Boyle, that the highest natural or ordinary waves do not rise more than six feet above the general level of the sea. Such an elevation of the water occasioning an equal depression, produces waves of twelve feet perpendicular height. Accidental or extraordinary waves, however, such as where cross seas meet, or where parallel waves over-run one another, are sometimes much higher. The first cause of waves is doubtless the action of the wind; but the undulations which continue for many hours after the producing cause ceases to act, are attributed to the same causes as those which occasion the continuation of the vibrations of a pendulum for some time after any impulse.

The apparent progressive motion of waves has been shown, by Sir Isaac Newton, to be in the subduplicate ratio of their breadth, and the time in which a wave moves its breadth forward, (measured from the top of one wave to the top of the next), to be about the same as that in which a pendulum will perform one single oscillation, "whose length between the point of suspension and the center of oscillation, is equal to the breadth of the wave." Thus, while the particles of water have no horizontal motion whatever, the ridge of each wave may move with a velocity of 16 or 18 miles *per* hour. The progressive motion of waves resembles considerably the progress of a vibration on a very long tight cord or wire. If a cord of 20 or 30 yards in length, moderately extended in the air, be struck near one end, a vibration resembling a wave will proceed to the other extremity, with a velocity proportionate to the degree of tension. If, by putting the thumb above the cord, and a finger below, a small portion of it be made to assume the form of the letter *S*, and then the hand be suddenly withdrawn, a vibration of the very form produced by the hand will proceed to the opposite end, and from thence be reflected back, and then forward again for several successive times; and indeed, whatever impression be made on the cord, if in the form of two or three waves, the same will advance from end to end, preserving continually the same form. In this case, as well as in the case of waves, though the cord has itself no progressive motion, yet the undulations move with great freedom and celerity; not in proportion to their height, indeed, but, what operates in the same way as gravity on the water, namely, in proportion to the degree of tension of the cord. In cords of different thicknesses, with the same tension, the velocity of the vibration will of course be the greatest in the smallest cords.

As there is nothing very remarkable in the waves that occur in the Greenland Sea, excepting as to the effects produced on ice, hereafter to be noticed, any observations on this subject will equally apply to the waves in other seas.

Waves, though the entire product of the wind, are dependent, as to their magnitude, on the nature

3

and extent of the sea in which they take their rise, and on the state of dryness and degree of pressure of the atmosphere.

The natural progressive motion of waves being in the same direction as the wind, the windward or " weather-side" of a lake, river or sea, is generally almost as smooth in a storm as in a calm. Waves increase in size, accordingly as the strength of the wind and the distance from the windward-shore, become greater; but after they attain a certain magnitude, any greater distance from shore is productive of no further increase in size. Then they move forward, maintaining a similar elevation and velocity, (excepting where they are accidentally augmented by two or three waves of different elevations overtaking one another, and combining in the formation of one great sea,) to a distance often of many leagues beyond the limit to which the wind that produced them extends.

Were the atmosphere without pressure, it is probable, that no waves, unless of the smallest kind, would be produced. The pressure of the atmosphere bringing the wind and sea into immediate contact, produces more or less friction in proportion to the dryness or dampness of the air. Thus, when the air is very dry, it possesses a great attraction for water, passes over the surface of the sea with more friction, and produces more considerable waves; but whenever it is saturated with moisture, the at-

traction is diminished, and the waves are not so
high.   Most seamen will have observed, that in
strong winds accompanied with heavy rain, the sea
is seldom very high, and that much less forcible
winds, with a dry air, produce higher waves.   In
this case, it is said, " the rain keeps the sea down."
Whatever, therefore, diminishes the friction of
the wind in passing over the water, or prevents the
attraction of air and water, must operate against the
formation of waves.   Thus oil scattered on the sea,
soon spreads over a great extent of surface, intercepts the attraction between the wind and water,
and by its smoothness diminishes the friction between the two elements, so as to prevent the formation of the rudiments of waves.   By subduing
the inferior waves, it prevents the higher waves
from overrunning them and producing breakers, and
thus keeps the surface of the water, however undu-
lated, in a smooth and pretty regular surface.   A
pellicle of ice formed on the sea, interrupts the free
mobility of the superficial particles of the water,
possibly reduces the friction, and produces a similar effect.

In temperate and frigid regions, where the winds
are very variable and partial, two or three distinct
swells, pursuing different courses, are sometimes observed at the same time; and it is a very usual
circumstance, in traversing the ocean, to meet with
various swells, the evident result of powerful winds,

indicating the prevalence of storms in the immediate neighbourhood, without ever being reached
by the storms by which such swells are produced.
Thus, in latitude 68°, in the month of July 1813,
I experienced heavy swells from the E. N. E. and
W. S. W., distinctly visible at the same time, while
the wind was from the south. In latitude 63°, in
April 1815, we had strong swells from both the
northward and southward, indicating storms on
both sides of us, while we had light variable winds;
and before these subsided, an additional swell from
the eastward made its appearance ; occasionally the
three distinct swells might be observed at the same
time, but most generally only one of them was very
conspicuous. In the month of July 1816, while
crossing the North Sea, swells from the N. E., S. W.
and E. occurred together ; and in April 1817,
heavy distinct swells from the W., N. W. and
S. S. E., prevailed at the same time.

Swells in the polar seas are often the harbingers
of storms. They are more considerable near the
edge of firm ice, or among loose drift-ice, than in
the open sea. And in the same way waves are often
higher near shore and in shallow water than in the
Main Sea. In the Greenland Sea, intermitting
swells are not uncommon, especially among ice. I
call them intermitting, because several waves of remarkable magnitude appear in succession, and then,
for an interval of perhaps some minutes, the swell is
almost imperceptible.

The original direction of waves is capable of being altogether changed by a particular form of an adjoining sea-coast, body of ice, or channel of the sea. When the wind blows directly along or parallel to the line formed by the shore, the waves incline towards the land. If a high sea takes its rise where the wind blows along shore, and the coast falls gradually back, so as to bring the direction of the wind off land, the sea will usually continue to roll along shore, following the form of the land, and changing its direction with every alteration in the line of the coast. In this way, where no large points interrupt its progress, the sea makes its way along an irregular coast of ice, until in some cases it is actually so inflected, as to proceed, obliquely, against the wind.

CHAPTER IV.

AN ACCOUNT OF THE GREENLAND OR POLAR ICE.

SECT. I.

A Description of the Various Kinds or Denomi-nations of Ice.

OF the inanimate productions of the Polar Seas, none perhaps excites so much interest and astonish-ment in a stranger, as the *ice* in its great abundance and variety.   The stupendous masses, known by the name of *Ice-islands*, or *Ice-bergs*, common to Davis' Strait, and sometimes met with in the Spitz-bergen Sea, from their height, various forms, and the depth of water in which they ground, are cal-culated to strike the beholder with wonder ; yet the prodigious sheets of ice, called *fields*, more peculiar to the Spitzbergen Sea, are not less astonishing. Their deficiency in elevation, is sufficiently compensated by their amazing extent of surface. Some of them have been observed extending many leagues in length, and covering an area of several hundreds of square miles; each consisting of a single sheet of ice, having its surface raised in general four or six feet above the level of the water, and its base depressed to the depth of ten to twenty feet beneath.

The ice in general is designated by a variety of appellations, distinguishing it according to the size or shape of the pieces, their number or form of aggregation, thickness, transparency, situation, &c.

As the different denominations of ice will be frequently referred to in the course of this work, it may be useful to give definitions of the terms in use among the whale-fishers, for distinguishing them.

1. An *ice-berg* or ice-mountain, is a large insulated peak of floating ice; or a glacier, occupying a ravine or valley, generally opening towards the sea, in an arctic country.

2. A *field* is a sheet of ice so extensive, that its limits cannot be discerned from a ship's mast-head.

3. A *floe* is similar to a field, but smaller; inasmuch as its extent *can* be seen. This term, however, is seldom applied to pieces of ice of less diameter than half a mile or a mile.

4. *Drift-ice* consists of pieces less than floes, of various shapes and magnitudes.

5. *Brash-ice* is still smaller than drift-ice, con-

sisting of roundish nodules, and fragments of ice, broken off by the attrition of one piece against another. This may be considered as the wreck of other kinds of ice.

6. *Bay-ice* is that which is newly formed on the sea, and consists of two kinds, common bay-ice, and *pancake-ice*; the former occurring in smooth extensive sheets, and the latter in small circular pieces with raised edges.

7. *Sludge* consists of a stratum of detached ice-crystals, or of snow, or of the smaller fragments of brash-ice floating on the surface of the sea. This generally forms the rudiments of ice, when the sea is in agitation.

8. A *hummock* is a protuberance raised upon any plane of ice above the common level. It is frequently produced by pressure, where one piece is squeezed upon another, often set upon its edge, and in that position cemented by the frost. Hummocks are likewise formed, by pieces of ice mutually crushing each other, the wreck being heaped upon one or both of them. To hummocks, principally, the ice is indebted for its variety of fanciful shapes, and its picturesque appearance. They occur in great numbers in heavy packs, on the edges and occasionally in the middle of fields and floes, where they often attain the height of thirty feet or upwards.

9. A *calf* is a portion of ice which has been depressed by the same means as a hummock is ele-

vated.   It is kept down by some larger mass ; from
beneath which, it shows itself on one side.   I have
seen a calf so deep and broad, that the ship sailed
over it without touching, when it might be observed
on both sides of the vessel at the same time ; such
an experiment, however, is attended with considerable danger, and necessity alone can warrant it,
as calves, when disturbed by a ship sailing over
them, have not unfrequently been called from their
sub-marine situation to the surface, and with such
an accelerated velocity, as to damage the vessel, or
even to occasion shipwreck.

10. A *tongue* is a point of ice projecting nearly
horizontally from a part that is under water. Ships
have sometimes run aground upon tongues of ice.

11. A *pack* is a body of drift-ice of such magnitude, that its extent is not discernible.   A pack is
said to be *open*, when the pieces of ice, though very
near each other, do not generally touch; or *close*,
when the pieces are in complete contact.

12. A *patch* is a collection of drift or bay-ice of
a circular or polygonal form.   In point of magnitude, a pack corresponds with a field, and a patch
with a floe.

13. A *stream* is an oblong collection of drift or
bay-ice, the pieces of which are continuous.   It is
called a *sea-stream*, when it is exposed on one side
to the ocean, and affords shelter from the sea, to
whatever is within it.

14. *Open ice,* or *sailing-ice,* is where the pieces are so separate as to admit of a ship sailing conveniently among them.

15. *Heavy* and *light* are terms attached to ice, distinguishable of its thickness; heavy ice having a considerable depth in the water, and light ice very little; the former being dangerous to shipping, and the latter not. Bay-ice may be said to extend from the first pellicle of ice, up to a foot in thickness; light ice from a foot to a yard in thickness; and heavy ice from about a yard upwards.

16. *Land-ice* consists of drift-ice attached to the shore; or drift-ice, which, by being covered with mud or gravel, appears to have recently been in contact with the shore; or the flat ice, resting on the land, not having the appearance or elevation of icebergs.

17. A *bight* is a bay in the outline of the ice.

18. A *lane,* or *vein,* is a narrow channel of water in packs, or other large collections of ice.

When the sea freezes, the greatest part of the salt it contains is deposited, and the frozen mass, however spongy, probably contains no salt, but what is natural to the sea-water filling its pores. Hence the generality of ice, when dissolved, affords fresh water. As, however, the ice frozen altogether from sea-water does not appear so solid and transparent as that procured from snow or rain water, the whale-fishers distinguish it into two kinds, accordingly as it affords water that is potable, or the contrary; and accordingly as it appears to have been the product of fresh or salt water.

What is considered as *salt-water ice,* appears blackish in the water, but in the air, is of a white or grey colour, porous, and in a great measure opaque, (except when in very thin pieces), yet transmits the rays of light with a blue or bluish-green shade. When dissolved, it produces water sometimes perfectly fresh, and sometimes saltish; this depends in a great measure on the situation from whence it is taken: such parts as are raised above the surface of the sea in the form of *hummocks,* or which, though below the surface, have been long frozen, appear to gain solidity, and are commonly *fresh,* whilst those pieces taken out of the sea, that have been recently frozen, are somewhat salt. Although I have never been able to obtain, from the water of the ocean, by experiment, an ice either compact, transparent, or fresh, yet it is very probable that the retention of salt in ice, may arise from the sea-water contained in its pores; and, in confirmation of this opinion, it may be stated, that if the newest and most porous ice be removed into the air, allowed to drain for some time in a temperature of 32°, or upwards, and then be washed in fresh water, it will be found to be nearly quite free from salt, and the water produced from it may be drunk. And that sea-water has a tendency to produce fresh ice, is farther proved by the concentration observed in a quantity exposed in an open vessel to a low temperature, by the separation of the salt from the crystals of ice, in the progress of the freezing. Thus it is, that, in the coldest weather, when a ship exposed to a tempestuous sea, is washed with repeated *sprays*, and thereby covered with ice, that in different places obstructing the efflux of the water overboard, a portion always remains unfrozen, and which, on being tasted, is found to consist of salt water highly concentrated. This arises from the freezing point of water falling in a certain ratio, according to the degree of saltness; thus, though pure water, of specific gravity 1.0000, freeze with a temperature of $32°$, water of specific gravity 1.0263, containing about $5\frac{3}{4}$ *oz.* (avoird.) of salt in every gallon of 231 cubic inches ; that is, with the degree of saltness common to the Greenland Sea, freezes at $28\frac{1}{2}°$. Sea-water, concentrated by freezing, until it obtains the specific gravity of 1.1045, requires a temperature of $13\frac{2}{3}°$ for its congelation, having its freezing point reduced $18\frac{1}{3}°$ below that of pure water ; and water saturated with sea-salt remains liquid, at a temperature of zero.

Thus, we are presented with a natural process for extracting salt from the sea, or at least for greatly facilitating that process in a concentration of the saline particles, by the agency of frost.

3

Fresh-water ice of the sailors, is distinguished by its black appearance when floating in small pieces in the sea, and by its transparency when removed into the air. Large pieces may occasionally be obtained, possessing a degree of purity and transparency, equal to those of the most beautiful crystal; but generally, its transparency is interrupted by numerous small globular or pear-shaped air-bubbles : these frequently form continuous lines intersecting the ice in a direction apparently perpendicular to its plane of formation.

Fresh-water ice is fragile, but hard ; the edges of a fractured part, are frequently so keen, as to inflict a wound like glass. The most transparent pieces are capable of concentrating the rays of the sun, so as to produce a considerable intensity of heat. With a lump of ice, of by no means regular convexity, I have frequently burnt wood, fired gunpowder, melted lead, and lit the sailors' pipes, to their great astonishment ; all of whom, who could procure the needful articles, eagerly flocked around me, for the satisfaction of smoking a pipe ignited by such extraordinary means. Their astonishment was increased, on observing, that the ice remained firm and pellucid, while the solar rays emerging from it were so hot, that the hand could not be kept longer in the focus than for the space of a few seconds. In the formation of these lenses, I roughed them out with a small axe, then scraped them with a

2

knife, and polished them merely by the warmth of the hand, supporting them during the operation in a woollen glove. I once procured a piece of the purest ice, so large, that a lens of sixteen inches diameter was obtained out of it; unfortunately, however, the sun became obscured before it was completed, and never made its appearance again for a fortnight, during which time, the air being mild, the lens was spoiled.

All young ice, such as bay-ice and light ice, which form a considerable part of drift and packed ice in general, is considered by Greenland sailors as salt-water ice ; while fields, floes, bergs, and heavy ice chiefly consist of fresh-water ice. Brash-ice likewise affords fine specimens of the latter, which when taken out of the sea, are always found crowded on the surface with sharp points and conchoidal excavations.

The most porous and opaque ice, and the most solid and transparent, do not differ materially in their density; the highest specific gravity I have observed, (compared with fresh-water at a freezing temperature) being 0.925, and the lowest 0.915. And it is a little curious, that in several careful experiments for ascertaining the specific gravity of ice, recently made, the most transparent specimens have proved the lightest, and the most opaque the heaviest*. The

---

* I have made several experiments on the buoyancy of ice, by cutting it into cubical or parallelopipedonal blocks, and

mean specific gravity of ice being considered as 0.92, it will appear, that the proportion floating above to that below the surface, when plunged in fresh-water, temperature 32°, must be as 1 to 11.5. But the specific gravity of ice, when compared with the sea-water occurring on the Spitzbergen coast, temperature 35°, was ascertained to be 0.894 to 0.900; as such, when ice floats in the sea, the proportion above to that below the surface, appears, by calculation, to be as 1 to 8.2. For every solid foot of ice, therefore, which is seen above water in a

---

measuring the part that floated above the surface in rain and sea-water, at different temperatures. This method, however, was found to give discordant results, on account of different sources of error to which it was liable. As such, I tried the specific gravity, by weighing different pieces of ice in the air, when the weather was cold, and then in fresh and salt water, at a freezing temperature, with a piece of metal attached to each specimen, to sink it. The difference between the weight of the ice in water, with the load attached, and the weight in water of the load singly, showed the difference between the weight of the ice, and an equal bulk of water; consequently, this difference, added to the weight of the ice in air, afforded the weight of an equal bulk of water; and the comparison of the two latter weights, gave, in the usual way, the specific gravity of the ice.

These experiments were always performed in the open air, when the temperature was 30° to 32°. The different specimens were dried with a coarse cloth before they were weighed in air, and immediately afterwards were weighed in salt and fresh water, at a freezing temperature. The particulars of these experiments will be found in the Appendix, No. VIII.

mass floating in the sea, there must be at least
8 feet below. A cubic inch of compact ice weighs
231.5 grains, and a cubic inch of Greenland sea-
water at a freezing temperature, specific gravity
(temp. 60°) 1.0264, weighs 259.58 grains ; the
weight of ice being to the weight of sea-water as
8 to 8.97, or 8 to 9 nearly.

Water, under usual circumstances, is known to
contain a large quantity of air, amounting to per-
haps $\frac{1}{25}$th or $\frac{1}{35}$th of its bulk, which air, it is supposed is chiefly disengaged when the fluid is boiled.
It would, however, appear, that the whole of the
air contained in water is by no means disengaged
even when boiling, as water that has been boiled
and then frozen *in vacuo*, does not form a transparent ice. The following experiment on the disengagement of air from water during the freezing,
intended for observing the phenomena more minutely than can be seen on the great scale on which nature, in the expanse of the ocean, operates, was
made near Spitzbergen.

Into a 4 *oz.* clear glass-phial, I poured 2 *oz.* of
ice-water, and placing it upon the fire in a salt-
water bath, soon brought it to the boiling point.
Being removed to the front of a brisk fire, a strong
ebullition commenced, which having continued for
some time, accompanied with a copious disengagement of steam, the phial was suddenly corked and
inverted. It was then exposed to a temperature of

10°, and the ebullition continued brisk whenever the phial was plunged into cold water or snow, for a period of 15 or 20 minutes. This showed that there could be little or no air in the phial. No crystals of ice were observed, until an hour and a half after the ebullition ceased, and then the process of freezing went on briskly. In two or three hours afterwards, the whole of the water was consolidated. Air-bubbles were observed moving towards the surface, as the process advanced, and, when completed, the ice had a milky appearance throughout, and was found crowded with minute globules of air. Hence it is probable, either that water is not entirely freed from air by boiling, or that some of the water is decomposed during the progress of the freezing process.

In consequence of this disengagement of air, ice formed in small vessels, or in confined situations, cannot be altogether transparent; for whenever a pellicle of ice covers the surface, the air as it is dislodged, is prevented from escaping, but rising as high as the ice will permit, there gets inclosed by the formation of new crystals, and renders the ice obscure. But where, from accidental circumstances, the air, as it is disengaged, can make its escape, the ice which is formed may present considerable masses totally free from any visible pore. Thus, when water contained in a large cylindrical vessel, is exposed to a low temperature, the first

appearance of freezing is about the surface and
sides, in needles shooting along the surface, or
obliquely downward. The ice on the sides then
extends lower and lower, leaving a quantity of water in the middle in the form of a cone, which
forms a receptacle for the air disengaged, as the
freezing process goes on. Hence the ice on the
sides, which is formed when the evolving air has
liberty to escape towards the centre, is found purely
diaphanous, while the last formed ice, in the shape
of a cone, having its base on the bottom of the vessel and touching the surface with its apex, becomes
the receptacle for the disengaged air, and is necessarily nebulous throughout.

Ice, when rapidly dissolved, continues solid, as
long as any remains; but when exposed to the air
at a temperature of only 2 or 3 degrees above
the freezing point, its solution is effected in a very
peculiar manner. Thus a large lump of fresh-water ice, when acted on by such a process, if placed
in the plane of its formation, resolves itself into
considerable columns of a prismatic appearance.
These columns are situated in a perpendicular position, and are almost entirely detached, so that
when a blow is struck with an axe, the whole mass
frequently falls to pieces. In the land ice-bergs,
these columns are often of amazing magnitude, so
as, when separated, to form floating ice-bergs.

All the ice floating in the sea, is generally rough and uneven on the surface, and, during the greater part of the year, covered with snow. Even newly-formed ice, that is free from snow, is so rough and soft, that it cannot be skaited on.

Under water, the colour of the ice varies with the colour of the sea ; in blue water, it is blue, and in green water, green, and of deeper shades in proportion to its depth. In the thickest olive-green coloured water, its colour, far beneath the surface, appears brownish.

SECT. II.

On the Formation of Ice on the Sea.

Some naturalists have been at considerable pains to endeavour to explain the phenomena of the progressive formation of the ice in high latitudes, and the derivation of the supply which is annually furnished, for replacing the great quantity that is dissolved and dissipated by the power of the waves, and the warmth of the climate into which it drifts. It has frequently been urged, that the vicinity of land is indispensable for its formation. Whether this may be the case or not, the following observations may possibly determine.

I have often noticed the process of freezing from
the first appearance of crystals, until the ice had obtained a thickness of more than a foot; and did not
find that the land afforded any assistance or even
shelter, which could not have been dispensed with
during the operation.   It is true, that the land is
sometimes the cause of the vacancy or space free
from ice, where this new ice is generated; the ice of
older formation being driven off by easterly winds,
assisted perhaps by a current; yet this new ice frequently occurs at the distance of forty or fifty
leagues from Spitzbergen.   But I have also many
times seen ice grow to a consistence capable of stopping the progress of a ship with a brisk wind, even
when exposed to the waves of the Atlantic Ocean,
on the southern aspect of the main body of the
Greenland ice, in about the seventy-second degree
of north latitude.   In this situation, the process of
freezing is accomplished under peculiar disadvantages.   I shall attempt to describe its progress from
the commencement.

The first appearance of ice when in the state of
detached crystals, is called by the sailors *sludge*,
and resembles snow when cast into water that is too
cold to dissolve it.   This smooths the ruffled surface of the sea, and produces an effect like oil in preventing breakers.   These crystals soon unite, and
would form a continuous sheet; but, by the motion

of the waves, they are broken into very small pieces, scarcely three inches in diameter. As they strengthen, many of them coalesce, and form a larger mass. The undulations of the sea still continuing, these enlarged pieces strike each other on every side, whereby they become rounded, and their edges turned up, whence they obtain the name of *cakes* or *pancakes;* several of these again unite, and thereby continue to increase, forming larger flakes, until they become, perhaps, a foot in thickness, and many yards in circumference. Every large flake retains on its surface, the impression of the smaller flakes of which it is composed; so that, when, by the discontinuance of the swell, the whole is permitted to freeze into an extensive sheet, it sometimes assumes the appearance of a pavement.

But when the sea is perfectly smooth, the freezing process goes on more regularly, and probably more rapidly. The commencement is similar to that just described; it is afterwards continued by constant additions to its under surface. During twenty-four hours keen frost, it will have become an inch or two in thickness; and in less than forty-eight hours time, capable of sustaining the weight of a man. Both this kind and cake-ice, are termed *bay-ice.*

It is generally allowed, that all that is necessary in low temperatures for the formation of ice, is still water : Now, this is easily obtained independent of the land : for in every opening of the main body of ice at a distance from the sea, the water is always as smooth as that of a harbour ; and as I have observed, the growth of ice up to a foot in thickness in such a situation, during one month's frost, the effect of many years we might deem to be sufficient for the formation of the most ponderous fields.

There is no doubt but a large quantity of ice is annually generated in the bays, and amidst the islands of Spitzbergen ; which bays, towards the end of summer, are commonly emptied of their contents, from the thawing of the snow on the mountains causing a current outwards. But this will not account for the immense fields which are so abundant in Greenland. These evidently come from the northward, and have their origin between Spitzbergen and the Pole.

SECT. III.

Description of Ice-Fields, and Remarks on their Formation and Tremendous Concussions.

Ice-fields constitute one of the wonders of the deep. They are often met with of the diameter of twenty or thirty miles ; and when in a state of such close combination that no interstice can be seen, they sometimes extend to a length of fifty or near a hundred miles. The ice of which they are composed, is generally pure and fresh; and in heavy fields, it is probably of the average thickness of ten to fifteen feet, and then appears to be flat, low, thin ice; but where high hummocks occur, the thickness is often forty, or even fifty feet. The surface before the month of July, is always covered with a bed of snow, of perhaps a foot to a fathom in depth; this snow dissolves in the end of summer, and forms extensive pools and lakes of fresh water. Some of the largest fields are very level and smooth, though generally their surfaces are varied with hummocks. In some, these hummocks form ridges or chains, in others, they consist of insulated peaks. I once saw a field that was so free from either fissure or hummock, that I imagine, had it been free from snow, a coach might have been driven many leagues over it in a direct line, without obstruction or danger. Hummocks somewhat relieve the uniformity of intense light reflected from the surface of fields, by exhibiting shades of delicate blue in all the hollows, where the light is partly intercepted by passing through a portion of ice. When the surface of the snow on fields is frozen, or when the snow is generally dissolved, there is no difficulty in travelling over them, even without either snow skaits or sledges; but when the snow is soft and deep, travelling on foot to any distance, is a work of labour. The tribe of Esquimaux discovered by Captain Ross, made

use of sledges drawn by dogs, for conveying them
across the rough land-ice, lying between the ships
and the shore ;—a journey they performed with such
celerity, that Captain Ross conjectures " they could
travel fifty or sixty miles a-day*." Hence, if such
a distance were practicable on the drift-ice occurring
near shore, it would be much more easy on the
smoother ice of fields.

The term *field*, was given to the largest sheets of
ice by a Dutch whale-fisher. It was not until a period of many years after the Spitzbergen fishery was
established, that any navigator attempted to penetrate the ice, or that any of the most extensive sheets
of ice were seen. One of the ships resorting to
Smeerenberg for the fishery, put to sea on one occasion, when no whales were seen, persevered westward to a considerable length, and accidentally fell
in with some immense flakes of ice, which, on his return to his companions, he described as being truly
wonderful, and as resembling fields in the extent of
their surface. Hence the application of the term
Field to this kind of ice. The discoverer of it
was distinguished by the title of " Field Finder."

As strong winds are known to possess great influence in drifting off the ice, where the resistance is
not too considerable, may not such winds form open-

---

* " Voyage to Baffin's Bay," p. 133.

ings in the ice far to the north, as well as in latitudes within our reach and observation? Notwithstanding the degree in which this cause may prevail is uncertain, yet of this we are assured, that the ice on the west coast of Spitzbergen has always a tendency to drift, and actually does advance in a most surprising manner to the south or south-west; whence, some vacancy *must* assuredly be left in the place which it formerly occupied.

These openings, therefore, may be readily frozen over, whatever be their extent, and the ice may in time acquire all the characters of a massy field.

It must, however, be confessed, that from the density and transparency of the ice of fields, and the purity of the water obtained from them, it is difficult to conceive that it could possess such characters if frozen entirely from the water of the ocean ;—particularly as young ice is generally found to be porous and opaque, and does not afford a solution altogether pure.   The following theory, therefore, is perhaps more consonant to appearances; and although it may not be established, has at least probability to recommend it.

It appears from what has been advanced, that openings may occasionally occur in the ice between Spitzbergen and the Pole, and that these openings will in all probability be again frozen over.   Allowing, therefore, a thin field or a field of bay-ice to be formed in such an opening, a superstructure may

probably be added by the following process.   The
frost, which almost constantly prevails during nine
months of the year, relaxes towards the end of June or
beginning of July, whereby the covering of snow annually deposited to the depth of two or three feet
on the ice *, dissolves.   Now, as this field is supposed to arise amidst the older and heavier ice, it may
readily occupy the whole interval, and be cemented to the old ice on every side, in such a manner as
to prevent the melted snow from making its escape.
Or, whatever be the means of its retention on the
surface of the young field, whether by the adjunc-
tion of higher ice, the elevation of its border by the
pressure of the surrounding ice, or the irregularity
of its own surface, several inches of ice must be added to its thickness on the returning winter, by the
conversion of the snow-water into solid ice.   This
process repeated for many successive years, or even
ages, together with the enlargement of its under-
side from the ocean, might be deemed sufficient to
produce the most stupendous bodies of ice that have
yet been discovered ; at the same time, that the ice
thus formed would doubtless correspond, in purity and transparency, with that of fields in general.

---

* That snow is deposited on the ice in high northern latitudes, is here allowed, because no field has yet been met with
which did not support a considerable burden of it.

2

Fields may sometimes have their origin in heavy close *packs*, which, being cemented together by the intervention of new ice, may become one solid mass. In this way, are produced such fields as exhibit a rugged *hummocky* appearance.

Fields commonly make their appearance in the month of May or June, though sometimes earlier. They are frequently the resort of young whales. Strong north and westerly winds expose them to the whalers, by driving off the loose ice.

The invariable tendency of fields to drift to the south-westward, even in calms, is the means of many being yearly destroyed. They have frequently been observed to advance a hundred miles in this direction, within the space of one month, notwithstanding the occurrence of winds from every quarter. On emerging from amidst the smaller ice, which before sheltered them, they are soon broken up by the swell, are partly dissolved, and partly converted into drift-ice. The places of such, are supplied by others from the north.

The power of a swell in breaking the heaviest fields, is not a little remarkable. A *grown* swell, that is so inconsiderable as not to be observed in open water, frequently breaks up the largest fields, and converts them wholly into floes and drift-ice in the space of a few hours; while fields composed of bay-ice or light-ice, being more flexible, endure the same swell without any destructive effect.

The occasional rapid motion of fields, with the strange effects produced by such immense bodies on any opposing substance, is one of the most striking objects the polar seas present, and is certainly the most terrific.   They not unfrequently acquire a rotatory movement, whereby their circumference attains a velocity of several miles *per* hour.   A field thus in motion, coming in contact with another at rest, or more especially with another having a contrary direction of movement, produces a dreadful shock.   A body of more than ten thousand millions of tons in weight *, meeting with resistance, when in motion, produces consequences which it is scarcely possible to conceive ! The weaker field is crushed with an awful noise ; sometimes the destruction is mutual : pieces of huge dimensions and weight, are not unfrequently piled upon the top, to the height of twenty or thirty feet, while a proportionate quantity is depressed beneath.   The view of those stupendous effects in *safety*, exhibits a picture sublimely grand ; but where there is danger of being overwhelmed, ter-

---

* A field of thirty nautical miles square, and thirteen feet in thickness, would weigh somewhat more than is here mentioned.   Allowing it to displace the water in which it floats, to the depth of eleven feet, the weight would appear to be 10,182,857,142 tons nearly, in the proportion of a cubic foot of sea-water, to 64 lb.

1

ror and dismay must be the predominant feelings.
The whale-fishers at all times require unremitting
vigilance to secure their safety, but scarcely in any
situation so much, as when navigating amidst those
fields: in foggy weather, they are particularly dangerous, as their motions cannot then be distinctly
observed. It may easily be imagined, that the
strongest ship is but an insignificant impediment
between two fields in motion. Numbers of vessels,
since the establishment of the fishery, have been thus
destroyed; some have been thrown upon the ice,
some have had their hulls completely torn open,
or divided in two, and others have been overrun by
the ice, and buried beneath its heaped fragments.
The Dutch have lost as many as twenty-three sail
of ships, among the ice, in one year. In the season of 1684, fourteen of their ships were wrecked,
and eleven more remained beset during the winter.

In the year 1804, I had a good opportunity of
witnessing the effects produced by the lesser masses
in motion. Passing between two fields of bay-
ice, about a foot in thickness, they were observed
rapidly to approach each other, and before our
ship could pass the strait, they met with a velocity of three or four miles *per* hour: the one over-
laid the other, and presently covered many acres
of surface. The ship proving an obstacle to the
course of the ice, it squeezed up on both sides,
shaking her in a dreadful manner, and producing

a loud grinding, or lengthened acute tremulous
noise, accordingly as the degree of pressure was diminished or increased, until it had risen as high as
the deck. After about two hours, the motion ceased;
and soon afterwards, the two sheets of ice receded
from each other, nearly as rapidly as they had before advanced. The ship, in this case, did not
receive any injury; but had the ice been only half
a foot thicker, she might have been wrecked.

In the month of May of the year 1814, I witnessed a more tremendous scene. While navigating amidst the most ponderous ice which the
Greenland sea presents, in the prospect of making
our escape from a state of *besetment*, our progress
was unexpectedly arrested by an isthmus of ice,
about a mile in breadth, formed by the coalition of
the point of an immense field on the north, with
that of an aggregation of floes on the south. To
the north field we moored the ship, in the hope of
the ice separating in this place. I then quitted the
ship, and travelled over the ice to the point of col-
lision, to observe the state of the bar which now
prevented our release. I immediately discovered,
that the two points had but recently met; that already a prodigious mass of rubbish had been squeezed upon the top, and that the motion had not abated.
The fields continued to overlay each other with a
majestic motion, producing a noise resembling that
of complicated machinery, or distant thunder. The

pressure was so immense, that numerous fissures were occasioned, and the ice repeatedly rent beneath my feet. In one of the fissures, I found the snow on the levl to be three and a half feet deep, and the ice upwards of twelve. In one place, hummocks had been thrown up to the height of twenty feet from the surface of the field, and at least twenty-five feet from the level of the water; they extended fifty or sixty yards in length, and fifteen in breadth, forming a mass of about two thousand tons in weight The majestic unvaried movement of the ice,—the singular noise with which it was accompanied,—the tremendous power exerted,—and the wonderful effects produced, were calculated to excite sensations of novelty and grandeur, in the mind of the most careless spectator!

SECT. IV.

Description of Icebergs, and Remarks on their Formation.

THE term *Ice-bergs* has commonly been applied to the glaciers occurring in Spitzbergen, Greenland, and other arctic countries. It is also as commonly extended to the large peaks, mountains or islets of ice, that are found floating in the sea. The fixed ice-bergs, or polar glaciers, have been described in the account of Spitzbergen ; it is only necessary, therefore, in this place, to mention the floating ice-bergs.

Ice-bergs occur in many places in the Arctic and Antarctic regions ; some of them of astonishing magnitude. In the Spitzbergen sea, indeed, they are neither numerous nor bulky, compared with those of other regions ; the largest I ever met with in this quarter not exceeding 1000 yards in circumference and 200 feet in thickness. But in Hudson's Strait, Davis' Strait, and Baffin's Bay, they occur of a prodigious size. Ellis describes them as sometimes occurring of the thickness of 500 or 600 yards. Frobisher saw one ice-berg which was judged to be " near fourscore fathoms above water." Captain Middleton states the occasional size of bergs as being three or four miles in circumference, 100 fathoms under water, and a fifth or sixth part above. Captain Ross, in Davis' Strait and Baffin's Bay, observed a variety of ice-bergs ; at one time at least 700 being in sight, of which some were of astonishing magnitude, and of very singular form. One berg is described by Captain Ross as being 40 feet high and 1000 feet long; another 85 feet high and 1200 feet in circumference ; another 325 feet high and 1200 feet long; another aground in 150 fathoms water, and several together aground in 250 fathoms ; and one, he particularly describes, (the dimensions of which were

given in by Lieutenant Parry,) as having nine unequal sides, as being aground in 61 fathoms, and as
measuring 4169 yards (paces) long, 3689 yards broad,
and 51 feet high. The weight of this ice-berg, taken at somewhat smaller dimensions, was estimated
by an officer of the Alexander, at 1,292,397,673
tons. This amount, however, is greater than the
truth, the cubical inch of ice being taken at 240
grains, whereas it does not exceed 231.5 grains.

Captain Cook, when exploring the regions beyond the antarctic circle, met with ice-bergs on
every course, in great abundance, as well as of vast
size; many, according to Forster, were one or two
miles in extent, and upwards of 100 feet above the
water. On the 26th of December 1773, they count-
ed 186 ice-bergs from the mast-head, whereof none
were less than the hull of a ship.

The most abundant source of floating ice-bergs
known in the arctic regions, is Baffin's Bay. From
this remarkable sea, they constantly make their way
towards the south, down Davis' Strait, and are scattered abroad in the Atlantic to an amazing extent.
The banks of Newfoundland are occasionally crowded with these wonderful productions of the Frigid
Zone; beyond which they are sometimes conveyed,
by the operation of the southerly under-current, as
low as latitude 40° north, and even lower, a distance of at least 2000 miles from the place of their
origin.

Ice-bergs commonly float on a base which is larger in extent than the upper surface. Hence the proportion of ice appearing above water, is seldom less in elevation than one-seventh of the whole thickness ; and when the summit is conical, or of the steeple form, the elevation above water is frequently one-fourth of the whole depth of the berg.

Perhaps the most general form of ice-bergs, is with one high perpendicular side, the opposite side very low, and the intermediate surface forming a gradual slope. When of such a form, Captain Ross found that the higher end was generally to windward. Some ice-bergs have regular flat surfaces ; but most usually they have different acute summits, and occasionally exhibit the most fantastic shapes. Some have been seen that were completely perforated, or containing prodigious caverns, or having many clefts and cracks in the most elevated parts, so as to give the appearance of several distinct spires.

On some ice-bergs, where there are hollows, a great quantity of snow accumulates ; others are smooth and naked. The naked sides are often filled with conchoidal excavations of various magnitudes ; sometimes with hollows the size of the finger, and as regular as if formed by art. On some bergs pools of water occur stagnant : on others, large streams are seen oozing through crevices into the sea. In a high sea, the waves break against them as against a rock; and, in calm weather, where there is a swell, the noise made by their rising and falling is tremendous. When ice-bergs are aground, or when there is a superficial current running to leeward, the motion of other ice past them is so great, that they appear to be moving to windward. Fields of ice of considerable thickness, meeting a berg under such circumstances, are sometimes completely ripped up, and divided through the middle. Ice-bergs, when acted on by the sun, or by a temperate atmosphere, become hollow and fragile. Large pieces are then liable to be broken off, and fall into the sea with a terrible crash, which in some places produces an extraordinary echo in the neighbouring mountains. When this circumstance, called *calving*, takes place, the ice-berg loses its equilibrium, sometimes turns on one side, and occasionally is inverted. The sea is thereby put into commotion; fields of ice in the vicinity are broken up; the waves extend, and the noise is heard to the distance of several miles; and sometimes the rolling motion of the berg not ceasing, other pieces get loosened and detached, until the whole mass falls asunder, like a wreck *.

Ice-bergs differ a little in colour, according to their solidity and distance, or state of the atmosphere. A very general appearance is that of cliffs

---

* FABRICIUS, *Translation* by Sir JOSEPH BANKS.

of chalk, or of white or grey marble. The sun's
rays reflected from them, sometimes give a glistening appearance to their surfaces. Different shades
of colour occur in the precipitous parts, accordingly
as the ice is more or less solid, and accordingly as it
contains strata of earth, gravel, or sand, or is free
from any impurity. In the fresh fracture, greenish-
grey, approaching to emerald-green, is the prevailing colour.

In the night, ice-bergs are readily distinguished,
even at a distance, by their natural effulgence ; and,
in foggy weather, by a peculiar blackness in the atmosphere, by which the danger to the navigator is diminished. As, however, they occur far from land, and
often in unexpected situations, navigators crossing
the Atlantic in the gloom of night, between the parallels of 50° and 60° of latitude, or even farther to the
south, require to be always on the watch for them.
In some places, near Cape Farewell, or towards the
mouth of Davis' Strait, they sometimes occur in extensive chains ; in which case, fatal accidents have
occurred, by vessels getting involved among them
in the night, during storms. But ice-bergs occurring singly, have rarely been productive of any serious mischief.

Ice-bergs, though often dangerous neighbours, occasionally prove useful auxiliaries to the whale-fishers. Their situation, in a smooth sea, is very little
affected by the wind : under the strongest gale, they
are not perceptibly moved ; but, on the contrary, have

the appearance of advancing to windward, because
every other description of ice moves rapidly past
them, on account of its finding less resistance from
the water, and consequently drifting faster to leeward, in proportion as its depth beneath the surface
is diminished. From the ice-berg's firmness, it often
affords a stable mooring to a ship in strong adverse
winds, or when a state of rest is required for the
performance of the different operations attendant on
a successful fishery. The fisher likewise avails himself of this quiescent property, when his ship is incommoded or rendered unmanageable by the accumulation of drift ice around, when his object is to
gain a windward situation more open. He moors
under the lee of the ice-berg,—the loose ice soon
forces past,—the ship remains nearly stationary,—
and the wished-for effect seldom fails to result.
Mooring to lofty ice-bergs, is attended with considerable danger: being sometimes finely balanced,
they are apt to be overturned; and, while floating
in a tide-way, should their base be arrested by the
ground, their detrusion necessarily follows, attended
with a thundering noise, and the crushing of every
object they encounter in their descent. Thus have
vessels been often staved, and sometimes wrecked by
the fall of their icy mooring; while smaller objects,
such as boats, have been repeatedly overwhelmed,
even at a considerable distance, by the vast waves
occasioned by such events.

All ice becomes exceedingly fragile towards the close of the whale-fishing season, when the temperate air thaws its surface, and changes its solid structure into a brittle mass of imperfectly attached columns. Bergs, in this state, on being struck by an axe, for the purpose of placing a mooring anchor, have been known to rend asunder, and precipitate the careless seamen into the yawning chasm, whilst occasionally the masses are hurled apart, and fall in contrary directions with a prodigious crash, burying boats and men in one common ruin. The awful effect produced by a solid mass many thousands or even millions of tons in weight, changing its situation with the velocity of a falling body, whereby its aspiring summit is in a moment buried in the ocean, can be more easily imagined than described.

Though a blow with an edge-tool on brittle ice does not sever the mass, still it is often succeeded by a crackling noise, proving the mass to be ready to burst from the force of internal expansion, or from the destruction of its texture by a warm temperature.

It is common, when ships moor to icebergs, to lie as remote from them as their ropes will allow, and yet accidents sometimes happen, though the ship ride at the distance of a hundred yards from the ice. Thus, *calves* rising up with a velocity nearly equal to that of the descent of a falling berg, have produced destructive effects. In the year 1812, while

the Thomas of Hull, Captain Taylor, lay moored
to an ice-berg in Davis' Strait, a *calf* was detached
from beneath, and rose with such tremendous force,
that the keel of the ship was lifted on a level with
the water at the bow, and the stern was nearly immersed beneath the surface.   Fortunately the blow
was received on the keel, and the ship was not materially damaged.

From the deep pools of water formed in the summer season, on the depressed surface of some bergs,
or from the streams running down their sides, the
ships navigating where they abound, are presented
with opportunities for watering with the greatest
ease and despatch.   For this purpose, casks are
landed upon the lower bergs, filled, and rolled into
the sea ; but from the higher, the water is conveyed by means of a long tube of canvas or leather,
called a *hose*, into casks placed in the boats, at the
side of the ice, or even upon the deck of the ship.

The greater part of the ice-bergs that occur in
Davis' Strait, and on the eastern coast of North
America, notwithstanding their profusion and immense magnitude, seem to be merely fragments of
the land ice-bergs or glaciers, which exist in great
numbers on the coast, forming the boundaries of
Baffin's Bay.   These glaciers fill immense valleys,
and extend in some places several miles into the
sea ; in others, they terminate with a precipitous

edge at the general line formed by the coast. In the summer season, when they are particularly fragile, the force of cohesion is often overcome by the weight of the prodigious masses that overhang the sea ; and in winter, the same effect may be produced, by the powerful expansion of the water filling any excavation or deep-seated cavity, when its dimensions are enlarged by freezing, thereby exerting a tremendous force, and bursting the berg asunder.

Pieces thus or otherwise detached, are hurled into the sea with a dreadful crash. When they fall into sufficiently deep water, they are liable to be drifted off the land, and down Davis' Strait, according to the set of the current ; but if they fall into a shallow sea, there they must remain until sufficiently wasted to float away. In their passage down the Strait, they often ground on the reefs or shallows which occur in different situations, where they interrupt the passage of the drift-ice, and become formidable barriers to the advance of the whale-fishers into Baffin's Bay. On these reefs, and in the bays in Davis' Strait, ice-bergs have been known to take the ground, and remain stationary for some years. Fabricius and Crantz mention two immense ice-bergs having grounded in South-East Bay, where they remained several years. From their vast size, they were named by the Dutch, Amsterdam and Haarlem.

Spitzbergen is possessed of every character which is supposed to be necessary for the formation of the largest ice-bergs :—high mountains, deep extensive valleys, intense frost, occasional thaws, and great falls of sleet and snow; yet here a berg is rarely met with ; and the largest that occur are not to be compared with the productions of Baffin's Bay. The reason of the difference between Spitzbergen and Old Greenland, as to the production of ice-bergs, is perhaps this : That while the sea is generally deep, and the coast almost continually sheltered by drift-ice at the foot of the glaciers in Baffin's Bay ; in Spitzbergen, on the contrary, they usually terminate at the water's edge, or where the sea is shallow, so that no very large mass, if dislodged, can float away, and they are at the same time so much exposed to heavy swells, as to occasion dismemberments too frequently to admit of their attaining a very considerable magnitude.

Some ice-bergs, it is possible, may have their origin in deep-sheltered coves or narrow bays, which, from their contracted outlets, may prevent the ice annually formed from being disembogued, and may thus form a secure basement for a superstructure of any magnitude. Such coves being at length filled, the ice may protrude beyond its capes, and give rise to floating ice-bergs.

Müller, in his " Summary of Voyages made by the Russians on the Frozen Sea." relates a circum-

stance, from which there is reason to infer, that some
ice-bergs have their origin in the wide expanse of
the ocean.   He informs us, in a brief account, already noticed, of the expedition of Alexei Markoff,
across an extensive body of ice, in the year 1714;
that after this traveller had proceeded seven days
northward, from the mouth of the Jana, as fast as
his dogs could draw, his progress was impeded by
ice rising in the sea like mountains, from the top
of which no land could be seen, but only ice.

Here, therefore, is a fact of a continent, if we may
so speak, of mountainous ice existing, and probably
constantly increasing in the ocean, at a distance of
between three and four hundred miles from any
known land: indeed, it must, in such a situation,
be so completely sheltered by the exterior drift or
field-ice in all directions, that every facility seems
to be afforded for its growth, that a sheltered bay
in the land could supply : For if we can conceive,
from the fore-mentioned process of the enlargement
of fields by the addition of the annually deposited
humidity, that a few years may be sufficient for the
production of considerable fields of ice, what might
be the effect of fifty or sixty centuries, affording an
annual increase?   And if, to the precipitations
from the atmosphere, we add the store of ice supplied by the sea during intense frosts, and conceive
also of a state of quiescence, for the full operation
of these causes, secured for ages,—the question of

the possibility of ice-bergs being produced in the sea, would seem to have a sufficient solution.

Should this conclusion be admitted, that ice-bergs may in some cases have their origin at a distance from land, then it would appear that tl e occurrence of ice-bergs in the antarctic zone, is by no means decisive of the existence of land around the Southern Pole.

SECT. V.

On the Situation or General Outline of the Polar Ice.

That extensive body of ice, which, with occasional tracts of land, occupies the northern extremity of the earth, and prevents all access to the regions immediately surrounding the Pole, fills, it appears, on an average, a circle of above 2000 geographical miles diameter; and presents an outline which, though subject to partial variations, is found, at the same season of each succeeding year, to be generally similar, and often strikingly uniform.

The most remarkable alteration in the configuration of the polar ice on record, is that said to have taken place between Iceland and Greenland, in the beginning of the fifteenth century, whereby the intercourse between the Icelanders and the colonies in Greenland was interrupted; and although many attempts have been made on the part of Denmark, for the recovery of these colonies, and for ascertaining the fate of the colonists, they have not yet succeeded in either. It appears, that a considerable trade had been carried on between Iceland and Greenland, for upwards of 400 years, (the coasts of the latter being always accessible in the summer,) when a suspension of the intercourse took place, in consequence, it is imagined, of the polar ice having suddenly extended its usual limits, launched down by the land to Cape Farewell, and having so completely barricadoed the whole of the eastern and southern coasts, as to render them totally inaccessible. Whether this was the real and only cause of the loss of the Greenland colonies to Denmark and Iceland? Whether any of the inhabitants yet remain, or the whole race is extinct? Whether the change in the position of the ice was partial or permanent? And whether the coast where the settlements were made, may not now be approached? Are questions at present unanswerable; but which, in the main, might, perhaps, be resolved by a single examination of the coast.

In various countries, changes of climate to a certain extent, have occurred, within the limits of historical record; these changes have been commonly for the better, and have been considered as the effects of human industry, in draining marshes and

lakes, felling woods, and cultivating the earth : but
here is an occurrence, if indeed true, the reverse of
common experience, concerning the causes of which
it is not easy to offer any conjecture.

Another alteration in the position of the Greenland ice, of little importance, however, compared
with the above, took place since the year 1815 ; a
body of about 2000 square leagues of ice, having
drifted out of the Greenland Sea, from between the
parallels of 74° and 80°. This dispersion of ice,
however great as it appears to be, is probably only
temporary ; and may, in a very few years, nay, in a
season or two, be entirely replaced.

With each recurring spring, the north Polar
ice presents the following general outline. Filling
the bays of Hudson and Baffin, as well as the straits
of Hudson and part of that of Davis, it exhibits an
irregular waving, but generally continuous line, from
Newfoundland or Labrador, to Nova Zembla.

From Newfoundland it extends in a northerly direction, along the Labrador shore, generally preventing all access to the land, as high as the mouth
of Hudson's Strait ; then turning to the north-eastward, forms a bay near the coast of Greenland, in
latitude, perhaps, 66° or 67°, by suddenly passing
away to the southward, to the extremity of Greenland. The quantity of ice on the east side of Davis'
Strait, being often small, the continuity of its border is liable to be broken, so as to admit of ships

reaching the land; and sometimes the bay of the ice usually occurring in the spring, in latitude 66° or 67°, does not exist; but the sea is open up the strait to a considerable distance beyond it.

After doubling the southern promontory, or Cape Farewell, it advances in a north-eastern direction along the east coast, sometimes enveloping Iceland as it proceeds, until it reaches the island of Jan Mayen. Passing this island on the north-west, but frequently enclosing it, the edge of the ice then trends a little more to the eastward, and usually intersects the meridian of London, between the 71st and 73d degree of latitude. Having reached the longitude of 5° or 6° east, in some instances as far as 8° or 10°; in the 73d or 74th degree of north latitude, it forms a remarkable promontory, and suddenly stretches to the north, sometimes proceeding on a meridian to the latitude of 80°; at others, forming a deep sinuosity, extending two or three degrees to the northward, and then south-easterly to Cherie Island; which having passed, it assumes a more direct course a little to the southward of east, until it forms a junction with the Siberian or Nova Zemblan coast.

During the winter and spring months, the Polar ice seems closely to embrace the whole of the northern shores of Russia, to the eastward of Nova Zembla; and filling, in a great measure, Behring's Strait and the sea, to the northward of it, continues in contact with the polar face of the American continent, following the line of the coast to the eastward, until it effects a junction with the ice in the Spitzbergen Sea, or in the great north-western bays of Hudson and Baffin, or is terminated by land yet undiscovered.

That remarkable promontory, mid-way between Jan Mayen and Cherie Islands, formed by the sudden stretch of the ice to the north, constitutes the line of separation between the east or *whaling*, and west or *sealing* ice of the fishers : And the deep bay laying to the east of this promontory, which may be called *The Whale-fisher's Bight*, invariably forms the only previous track for proceeding to fishing latitudes northward.   When the ice at the extremity of this bay occurs so strong and compact, as to prevent the approach to the shores of Spitzbergen, and the advance northward beyond the latitude of 75° or 76°, it is said to be a *close season ;* and, on the contrary, it is called an *open season*, when an uninterrupted navigation extends along the western coast of Spitzbergen to Hackluyt's Headland. In an open season, therefore, a large channel of water lies between the land and the ice, from 20 to 50 leagues in breadth, extending to the latitude of 79° or 80°, and gradually approximating the coast, until it at length effects a coalition with the northwestern extremity, by a semicircular head.   When the continuity of the body of ice, intervening between Old Greenland and Nova Zembla, is thus in-

3

terrupted in an open season, the ice again makes its appearance on the south of Spitzbergen, proceeding from thence direct to Cherie Island, and then eastward as before.

Such is the general appearance of the margin or outline of the polar ice, which holds, with merely partial changes, for many successive seasons. This outline, however, is necessarily more or less affected by storms and currents; their more than ordinary prevalence in any one direction, must cause some variety of aspect in particular places, which becomes more especially apparent in the vicinity of land, where its coasts afford marks by which to estimate the advance and retreat of the ice.

The line formed by the exterior of the ice is variously indented, and very rarely appears direct or uniform. Open bays or arms occur, from a few fathoms to several miles or leagues in depth. None of them, however, have any determinate form or place, except the Whale-fisher's Bight, or great bay before described, in which the Greenlandmen always seek a passage to the fishing stations.

The place where whales occur in the greatest abundance, is generally found to be in the 78th or 79th degree of north latitude, though from the 72d to the 81st degree they have been met with. These singular animals, which, on account of their prodigious bulk and strength, might be thought entitled to reign supreme in the ocean, are harmless and timid.

They seem to prefer those situations which afford
them the most secure retreats. Among the ice,
they have an occasional shelter; but so far as it is
permeable, the security is rather apparent than real.
That they are conscious of its affording them shelter, we can readily perceive, from observing, that the
course of their flight when scared or wounded, is
generally towards the nearest or most compact ice.
The place of their retreat, however, is regulated by
various circumstances; it may sometimes depend on
the quality and quantity of food occurring, the disposition of the ice, or exemption from enemies. At
one time, their favourite haunt is amidst the huge
and extended masses of the field ice; at another, in
the open seas adjacent. Sometimes the majority of
the whales inhabiting those seas, seem collected
within a small and single circuit; at others, they
are scattered in various hordes, and numerous single
individuals, over an amazing extent of surface. To
discover and reach the haunts of the whale, is an object of the first consideration in the fishery, and occasionally the most difficult and laborious to accomplish.

In *close seasons*, though the ice joins the south
of Spitzbergen, and thereby forms a *barrier* against
the fishing-stations, yet this barrier is often of a limited extent, and terminates on the coasts of Spitzbergen in an open space, either forming, or leading
to, the retreat of the whales. Such space is some-

times frozen over until the middle or end of the month of May, but not unfrequently free of ice. The barrier here opposed to the fisher, usually consists of a body of ice from 20 to 30 or 40 leagues across, in the shortest diameter. It is generally composed of packed ice, and often cemented into a continuous field by the interference of bay ice, which incredibly augments the difficulty of navigating among it.

As the time that can be devoted to the whale-fishery is, by the nature of the climate, limited to three or four months in the year, it is of importance to pass this barrier of ice as early as possible in the season. The fisher here avails himself of every power within his command. The sails are expanded in favourable winds, and withdrawn in contrary breezes. The ship is urged forward amongst drift-ice by the force of the wind, assisted with ropes and saws. Whenever a vein of water appears in the required direction, it is if possible attained. It always affords a temporary relief, and sometimes a permanent release, by extending itself through intricate mazes, amidst ice of various descriptions, until at length it opens into the desired place, void of obstruction, constituting the usual retreat of the whales.

SECT. VI.

Changes which take place, with the advance of the Season, in the Situation of the Ice, in the Sea of Greenland and Davis' Strait.

The formidable barrier before described, when it occurs, is regularly encountered on the first arrival of the Greenland ships in the month of April, but is generally removed by natural means as the season advances. However extensive, heavy and compact it may be, it is usually found separated from the land, and divided asunder by the close of the month of June; and hence it is, that however difficult and laborious may have been the ingress into the fishing country, the egress is commonly effected without much inconvenience.

That the ice should envelope the whole coasts of Spitzbergen in the winter season, and expose the western shore about the month of June; that the ocean should be almost annually navigable on the meridians of 5° to 10° E., to the 80th degree of north latitude, while the ice in other parts of the world can rarely be penetrated beyond the 73d or 74th degree, are facts that appear to be worthy of consideration.

On the recession of the ice from the west side of the land, a lane of water must be left from one extremity to the other; while to the south of Point Look-out, a parallel motion of the ice leaves no opening or evidence of its change of place; for here, the ice meeting with no obstruction to cause it to divide, moves on in a solid body, retained firm and unbroken by the tenacious cement of the interjacent bay-ice.

In the month of May, the severity of the frost relaxes, and the temperature occasionally approaches within a few degrees of the freezing point: the salt in the sea then exerts its liquefying energy, and destroys the tenacity of the bay-ice, makes inroads in its parts by enlarging its pores into holes, diminishes its thickness, and, in the language of the whale-fisher, completely *rots* it. The packed drift-ice is then liberated; it submits to the laws of detached floating bodies, and obeys the slightest impulses of the winds or currents. The heavier having more stability than the lighter, an apparent difference of movement obtains among the pieces. Holes and lanes of water are formed, which allow the entrance and progress of the ships, without that stubborn resistance offered earlier in the spring of the year.

Bay-ice is sometimes serviceable to the whalers, in preserving them from the brunt of the heavy ice, by embedding their ships, and occasioning an equable pressure on every part of the vessel: but, in other respects, it is the greatest pest they meet with in all their labours: it is troublesome in the fishery, and in the progress to the fishing ground; it is often the means of besetment, as it is called, and thence the primary cause of every other calamity. Heavy ice, many feet in thickness, and in detached pieces of from 50 to 100 tons weight each, though crowded together in the form of a pack, may be penetrated, in a favourable gale, with tolerable despatch; whilst a sheet of bay-ice, of a few inches only in thickness, with the same advantage of wind, will often arrest the progress of the ship, and render her in a few minutes immoveable. If this ice be too strong to be broken by the weight of a boat, recourse must be had to sawing, an operation slow and laborious in the extreme.

When the warmth of the season has rotted the bay-ice, the passage to the northward can generally be accomplished with a very great saving of labour. Therefore it was, the older fishers seldom or never used to attempt it before the 10th of May, and foreign fishers in the present day, are in general late. Sometimes late arrivals are otherwise beneficial; since it frequently happens, in *close seasons*, that ships entering the ice about the middle of May, obtain an advantage over those preceding them, by gaining a situation more eligible, on account of its nearness to the land. Their predecessors, mean-

1

while, are drifted off to the westward with the
ice, and cannot recover their easting ; for they are
encompassed with a large quantity of ice, and
have a greater distance to go than when they first
entered, and on a course precisely in opposition to
the direction of the most prevailing winds. Hence
it appears, that it would be economical and beneficial to sail so late, as not to reach the *country*
before the middle of May, or to persevere on the
sealing stations until that time. There are, however, some weighty objections to this method. Open
seasons occasionally occur, and great progress may
sometimes be made in the fishery before that time.
Also, although the majority of the whalers do not
commonly succeed in passing the barrier in close
seasons before a certain period, yet some individuals, by a superior exertion, perseverance, ability, or
good fortune, accomplish the end considerably before the rest, and thereby gain a superiority in the
fishery, not to be attained by later arrivals. A
week or fortnight's solitary fishing, under these
circumstances, has frequently gained half a cargo,
—an advantage of the most interesting importance,
in a voyage of such limited duration.

The change which takes place in the ice amidst
which the whale-fisher pursues his object, is, towards the close of the *season*, indeed astonishing.
For, not only does it separate into its original individual portions,—not only does it retreat in a

body from the western coast of Spitzbergen, but in general, that barrier of ice which encloses the fishing site in the spring, which costs the fisher immense labour and anxiety to penetrate, by retarding his advance towards the north, and his progress in the fishery, for the space of several weeks,— spontaneously divides in the midst about the month of June, and on the return of the ships is not at all to be seen! Then is the sea rendered freely navigable from the very haunts of the whales, to the expanse of the Atlantic Ocean.

This quality of the ice, is of the first importance to the navigator. It is this known property which gives him confidence in his advance, and enables him to persevere without restraint, calculating on an easy return. As one-half of the fishing season is often spent in the ingress were the regress as arduous, there would be no time left for fishing: besides, the return would be rendered doubly hazardous by the prevalence of the summer fogs, which are thick in the extreme, and sometimes continue for days together, without intermission.

Were the barrier of ice not passable, the haunts of the whales could not be attained; and were the regress not favoured by natural facilities, every attempt to prosecute the whale-fishery with effect, would be attended with imminent danger; I may say, with almost certain destruction.

Similar changes as those above described, also take place in the ice of Hudson's Bay, Baffin's Bay, and Davis' Strait. The navigation of the former bay is first interrupted by ice, generally, in the month of November; but on the east side of Davis' Strait, the ice does not usually make its appearance under the land until the spring. Little progress can be made through the ice into the great bays of Hudson and Baffin, until the month of June or July, in the course of which all the bay-ice that serves as a cement to the heavy ice being dissolved, or very much reduced, a passage to the extremity of each bay is gradually opened. Baffin accomplished the navigation to the extremity of the bay called by his name, without much difficulty, in the beginning of July; but Captain Ross, in his late voyage, had much trouble in effecting the same, about the middle of August. In the months of August and September, the ice in the bays seems to be the most open, and in the Straits of Davis and Hudson almost entirely dispersed.

SECT. VII.

*Situation of the Ice in the Region visited by the
Greenland Ships, with Observations on the Alterations which have occurred during a Series
of Sixteen Years.*

WHAT has hitherto been advanced on the situation of the polar ice, refers to its most general and
permanent characters.   It will now be my object to
give a sketch of the most prominent appearances
which have annually marked the ice in the region
visited by the Spitzbergen or Greenland whale-
fishers, during a period of sixteen years.

The year 1803 was an *open* season.   So early
as the middle of April, there was no obstruction to
the navigation to the 81st degree of north latitude ;
that is, on a meridian about 5° east of Greenwich.
The weather was tempestuous ; the most prevailing
winds from the north-east.   No particular change
took place in the ice during the stay of the whalers.
The egress was consequently without obstruction.
The fishery, on the whole, was unsuccessful.

In 1804, the entrance into the northern fishing
stations, was obstructed by a barrier composed of
open drift-ice, consolidated by bay-ice of peculiar
tenacity and strength.   The bay-ice was broken up
and dispersed on the 12th of May, and a sufficient

passage for the ships opened. The fishery was tolerably good. The egress was easy.

In 1805, the fishing-stations were open, by the
end of April, up to the 78th degree of latitude.
The fishery was moderately good; the egress easy.

The singular position of the ice, in the year 1806,
was the occasion of a most interesting voyage; having afforded us the opportunity of performing an
extraordinary navigation, and of advancing nearer
to the Pole than on any other occasion since I have
been in the habit of visiting the Spitzbergen seas.
It was a close season; and the barrier of ice was so
uncommonly extensive, and continued so long, that
not more than three ships accomplished a passage
through it. This barrier extended from latitude
75° 20′ to 79° 30′; being 250 miles across. Beyond
it was an open sea, from 30 to 50 miles north and
south; from a western situation in which, we sailed in an E N E direction (true) nearly 300 miles,
without observing any signs of its termination. As
an abstract of the journal of the proceedings in this
extraordinary navigation, is given in a following section, it is unnecessary to enter into more particulars
here.

A close season again occurred in 1807. The margin of the ice was, however, pervious to a considerable extent, wherein many large whales being seen,
some ships made a successful fishing in latitude
75° or 76°; other ships, which persevered to the
northward, and passed the barrier, likewise suc-

ceeded tolerably well. The prevailing wind was from the north-east.

Though ice occurred in the place usually occupied by the barrier, in the year 1808, yet being open, and in a great measure free from bay-ice, it afforded shelter to the fishermen without obstructing their progress. Whales being plentiful, the weather fine, and the ice generally open, the fishery was uncommonly good. No difficulty was experienced by the whalers on their return, until they reached the latitude of 74°, when a remarkable barrier presented itself. It consisted of loosely packed ice, and was found to extend from the main western ice, above 100 miles to the eastward, with a general breadth of 10 to 20 leagues. A few ships forced their way through it, but most of the fleet doubled the easternmost extremity.

In 1809, we had a close season. Few ships passed the barrier before the end of May. Those which first succeeded made a prosperous fishery. At the close of the season, a free navigation led to seaward in a south-westerly direction, from latitude 79° and longitude 6° E. But near the coast of Spitzbergen, a vast body of ice was accumulated.

The season of 1810 was similar to that of 1804. Young ice cemented together the detached pieces of heavy ice that lay in the passage to the northward. A severe storm occurred on the 6th and 7th of May, which, producing a heavy swell from the northward, annihilated most of the bay-ice in one day. The retreat of the whales was soon afterwards attained, and the fishery proved partially successful. At the close of the season, an isthmus of ice stretched 50 or 60 miles from the main western body to the eastward, the extremity of which lay in longitude 12° 30′ E.

The season of 1811 was uncommonly close. Though the most arduous exertions were made by the fishers for four or five weeks, few ships passed the barrier before the 26th of May. Whales occurred in great plenty, and the fishery was generally good. During the stay of the ships, a pack of heavy ice, formed between them and the land, joining the main ice in the 80th degree of north latitude, and preserving its continuity in a southerly direction, with a breadth of 15 to 20 leagues, as far as latitude 73° 40′. In latitude 77° 30′, it approached the main ice within a few miles, but still leaving a channel leading in a south-westerly direction to seaward. This channel, however, was so narrow, that the majority of the ships did not discover it, but forced through the eastern pack, and then performed the passage to the southward along its eastern margin.

A season more singularly close than this occurred in 1812. The barrier consisted of a compact body of floes and fields. In each of the preceding years, the obstruction invariably consisted of packed ice, consolidated by the intervention of bay ice into a continuous sheet; but, on this occasion, the most ponderous field-ice barred the navigation. This singular barrier extended from the eastern pack, lying between Point-Look-out and Cherie Island, in a north-western direction to the main western ice. Much open drift ice covered the south-western side of it, and preserved the fields and floes from being destroyed by the sea. This barrier was one of the most formidable that had ever been encountered. All attempts to pass it before the close of the month of May were attended with imminent danger, and were generally nugatory. But after a week's continuance of mild calm weather, the fields and floes were released by the partial destruction of the bay-ice among them, and a winding navigation of about sixty miles in extent, opened into a clear sea adjoining the land. For some time after passing the barrier, but few whales were seen; the fishery was late, and only partially successful. The remarkable change which occasionally takes place in the polar ice, is rarely more striking than that which occurred in this season : for, notwithstanding the compact, extensive, and formidable nature of the barrier which opposed the entrance of the ships into the northern fishing stations, yet, on their return, in the month of July, they did not meet with the least obstruction, but found an open sea extending from the latitude of 79° into the Atlantic Ocean.

The year 1813 was an open season. So early as the beginning or middle of April, many ships advanced beyond the 80th degree of latitude. The weather was uncommonly tempestuous. Several of the storms prevailed with almost unabated violence for three successive days; and it was not until the month of June had commenced, that the weather became settled and moderate. In consequence of the prevalence of easterly winds, the ice was generally packed, and the fishery was bad. Scarcely more than three or four ships obtained full cargoes, and several returned without a single whale. This year, it is somewhat remarkable, the fishery in Davis' Strait was still more unsuccessful. In consequence of the failure of both fisheries, whale-oil attained a price before unequalled; having risen, towards the close of the year, as high as sixty pounds *per* ton!

In 1814, we had an open season. The ice was not packed, as in the preceding year, but was generally open and navigable. Whales occurred in great numbers in the open water; the weather was generally favourable; and the fishery proved very successful. After the middle of May, the wind prevailed from the southern and western quarters, whereby the main western ice was still more opened, and drifted up to the very shores of Spitzbergen.

Among this ice, many whales were seen and caught at a very late season.

The season of 1815 was also open in the month of April. In May a loose body of ice, partly occupied the opening in the 79th degree of latitude, and remained about a month. In June it dispersed. The fishery to the northward was closed by the middle of June; but it recommenced about the end of the month, in latitude 76°, at the edge of the ice, and continued during two or three weeks of July, a little within the borders of the ice, in the same parallel.

In 1816, we had a season partially open; the most early fishers having sailed without obstruction to a high northern latitude, while the later arrivals had to pass through a considerable open pack. The northern parts of the country were filled with bay ice most of the month of May. The fishery became general in June, but was not very prosperous.

The season of 1817 was remarkable, on account of its openness, and on account of the westerly position and peculiar penetrability of the ice. To the northward of latitude 74°, the Spitzbergen Sea is seldom navigable to the westward of the meridian of London; but, in this season, I had an opportunity of sailing as far as longitude 11° 40′ W. in latitude 75° 28′ N.; to longitude 10° W. in latitude 75° 10′ N.; and to longitude 10° 37′, (by chronometer,) in latitude 74° N. In the two first instances,

the weather was thick, and our position a little uncertain ; but, in the last, the weather was clear, and
my observations, both for latitude and longitude,
were good.   The east side of West Greenland, a
coast never, I believe, approached, excepting by ships
beset in the ice, since Hudson's voyage in 1607, was
at this time seen by myself from the mast-head ;
but the commencement of a fog put a stop to our
farther advance, otherwise the ice appeared sufficiently open to have permitted us to reach its shores.
We were then a distance of 80 or 90 miles within
the exterior limits of the ice.   In this season, from
the too great extent of the sea open to the whales,
and the wide dispersion of them, the fishery
was in general very bad.   In the month of June
the northern land-ice joined the western ice, in the
79th degree of latitude, and extended in a line to
the south-eastward, as far as Point-Look-out.   At
the point of junction of the land-ice, and main western ice, a successful but partial fishery occurred.

An open season, a good deal similar to the last
described, again occurred in 1818.   The edge of
the ice, however, lay farther to the eastward, between latitude 76° and 80°, and farther to the westward, between 73° and 76°.   On the 1st of July,
we reached the longitude of 9° W. in latitude
74° 54′, without entering the ice.   Indeed the edge
of the ice, from latitude 74° to 77°, was, about this
period, firm and impervious.   The fishery, on the

whole, was only moderately good. In the early part of the season, the prospect was excellent; but the latter fishery almost entirely failed.

In these two seasons of 1817 and 1818, the sea was more open than on any former occasion remembered by the oldest fishermen; an extent of sea amounting to about 2000 square leagues of surface, included between the parallels of 74° and 80° N. being quite void of ice, which is usually covered by it *.

SECT. VIII.

Remarks ou the Properties, peculiar Movements, and Drifting of the Ice.

1. THE ice always has a tendency to separate during calms. This property holds, both with regard to field and drift ice; and seems to arise from a repelling tendency between the individual masses, or from the action, of a very superficial current, carrying the light ice away faster than the heavy ice. Hence it is, when a body of heavy ice is released from its confinement and continuity, by the disso-

---

* Plate VII. shows the particular position of the Greenland ice, in the seasons of 1817 and 1818, as well as its general outline in close and open seasons.

lution of the intervening bay-ice, the pieces generally spread abroad in a calm, so as to allow a free
passage for ships, which before, could not be urged
on by the power of the wind, combined with every effort of art. From the same cause, it is, that ice
which, with strong winds, is formed into streams or
patches, and allows a safe and commodious navigation amidst these large aggregations, will, on the
occurrence of two or three days of calm weather, be
disseminated into every opening, and seem to occupy every space, allowing only a troublesome and si-
nuous passage for ships. In this case, the dispersion
is so general, that scarcely any two pieces can be
said to touch each other.

2. Openings in packs and among fields or floes,
frequently break out or disappear, without any apparent cause. It is often of importance to the fisher
to determine, whether any space be in the course of
diminishing or enlarging. The freezing of the water
frequently affords an intimation of its closing, as it
rarely takes place to any considerable extent, on the
extension of the bounding ice. The birds likewise
instinctively leave the closing spaces, and fly in
search of such as are in the course of opening.

The closing of heavy ice, encircling a quantity of
bay-ice, causes it to run together with such force,
that it overlaps wherever two sheets meet, until it
sometimes attains the thickness of many feet. In
this case, when a ship happens to be in the midst of

the pressure, the ice sometimes rises to the height of the gunwale, squeezing and shaking her in a terrible manner. Drift ice does not often coalesce with such a degree of force, as to endanger any ship which may happen to be beset in it ; when, however, land opposes its motion, or the ship is immured in the centre of a heavy body of it, the pressure is sometimes alarming.

3. Fields often open, close, and revolve in the most extraordinary way, in calms as well as in storms. Sometimes these motions may be accounted for ; at other times they are altogether anomalous. Fields, floes, and compact bodies of drift-ice, are disturbed by the wind, by currents and tides, or by the pressure of other ice against them. The wind forces all ice to leeward, with a velocity nearly in the inverse proportion to its depth under water ; light ice, con·· sequently, drives faster than heavy ice, loose ice faster than fields, and fields faster than bergs. Fields may approximate each other from three causes, dependent on the influence of the wind. *First,* If the lighter field be to windward, it will necessarily be impelled towards the heavier, by the influence of the wind. *Secondly,* As the wind frequently commences blowing on the windward-side of the ice, and continues several hours before it is felt a few miles distant to leeward, the windward field begins to drift, before any impression is produced on the ice to leeward of it ; and, *thirdly,* Fields

are not unfrequently impelled towards each other by winds, acting upon each from opposite quarters.

Though the set of the current in the Greenland Sea be generally towards the south-west, yet near the shore, where there are eddies and tides, it is very irregular. This irregularity produces striking effects upon the ice. Near Hackiuyt's Headland, and, indeed, at the distance of ten to twenty leagues from it, in and about the same parallel, the influence of a tide or irregular current is observed. This occasions ripplings in the water, and periodical closings and openings of the ice. At the borders of fields connected with the main body of ice, a striking movement in the drift-ice may be often observed; the loose ice adhering closely to the edge of the adjoining fields for a few hours, then moving off in a body for a short period, and alternately advancing and retreating at regular intervals.

Fields are liable also to be put in motion, by the force with which drift-ice occasionally presses against them. Thus, a body of loose ice drifting against and grazing along the side of a field in its course to leeward, becomes deflected, and its re-action causes a circular motion of the field.

4. The amazing changes which take place in the most compact ice, are often unaccountable. They astonish even those who are accustomed to their occurrence. Thus, ships immoveably fixed with regard

to the ice, have been known to perform a complete
revolution in a few hours; and two ships beset a
few furlongs apart, within the most compact pack,
have sometimes been separated to the distance of several leagues within the space of two or three days,
notwithstanding the apparent continuity of the pack
remained unbroken !

On the 7th of May 1798, the Dundee of London, (then commanded by my Father,) while forcing to the northward on the most eligible course,
was suddenly stopped by a shift of wind, and enveloped by the ice at a very short distance from the
land.   The Volunteer of Whitby, and three other
ships, were likewise arrested, a little way from the
Dundee.   During the day, three Russian hunters
visited them, coming over the ice from the nearest
shore; but as none of the crew could speak their
language, they were prevented from deriving any
information from them.

The next day, a heavy gale of wind prevailed
from the north-west; the frost was intense, and
much snow fell.   The pressure of the ice was very
severe; insomuch, that their *iron-tiller* was broken,
the ship lifted above two feet, and forced within a
mile and a-half of the land.   All the bay-ice was
squeezed upon the top of the heavy ice, and the
whole was rendered so compact, that they could not
find a hole sufficient to admit a *lead*, for the purpose of ascertaining the depth of the water.   They

got their provisions upon deck, considering the ship in great danger.

On the 9th, they were in latitude 77° 38' N. The intensity of the pressure was not diminished. The Volunteer lay beset three miles off, under a like dangerous pressure. On the 10th, the Dundee and Volunteer began to separate, though the ice continued close, and the ships were firmly beset.

In my Father's journal of the 12th, appear the following remarks : " *N. B*—I cannot, from the top-gallant-mast-head, see over the flat of ice to the north-east, into which the ship is frozen : and yet in fifty hours it has revolved from the south-south-west, westerly to north, and carried the ship with a semicircular motion 15 or 20 leagues : On the 10th instant, we were within a mile and a-half of the land, whereas our distance is now 10 leagues, and our advance to the northward even greater. The Volunteer has drifted out of sight in the south-west quarter."

On the 15th, after labouring eight and forty hours without rest, they escaped into a place of safety.

On the 17th of June 1813, I observed a strange commotion among the Greenland ice, without being able to discover any cause at all comparable with the effect. The wind had blown a fresh gale, but was now moderate ; the sea was smooth, and the situation of the ice was remote from any swells. The latitude was 78° 10' N., longitude 3° 10' E. We

VOL. I.   T

passed through a patch of drift-ice into a considerable opening, bounded by a field on the west, drift-
ice on the east, and floes and heavy drift-ice on the
north and south.   Here, the motion of the ice was
wonderful.   Large masses of drift-ice were advancing to the southward, with a velocity of two to
three miles *per* hour, leaving eddies in the sea like
those produced by a strong tide in shallow water,
while other masses of ice, similar in kind and situation, were at rest.   We passed between a floe and
some drift-ice, which actually closed as fast as the
ship sailed.   Some insulated pieces of ice astonished us with their motion; and proceeded with a
steady velocity and undeviating course across the
middle of the opening.   The ice on every side but
that on the north, being nearly at rest, the lake we
navigated was rapidly filled up; on our approach to
it, there was a space of some leagues in circumference free from ice; but in a few hours, the largest
space to be seen was not fifty yards in diameter.
With difficulty we made our escape to the eastward;
but still remaining by the edge of the packed ice,
we could observe the effect produced.   Drift-ice
continued pouring down from the north against the
side of the field; so that in the course of twelve
hours, the intervening ice formed a body of seven or
eight miles in width.

5. When speaking of the currents of the Spitzbergen Sea, I remarked, that the polar-ice, in this

situation, has a constant tendency to drift to the
south-westward. Near Spitzbergen, indeed, this
tendency is not usually observed; because the influence of the tide, eddies, peculiar pressures, &c. sometimes produce a contrary effect; but at a distance
from land, its universal prevalence can be illustrated by numerous facts of almost annual occurrence.
Some of these facts have already been given ; one
more shall suffice.

In the beginning of May 1814, we entered with
the ship Esk of Whitby, a spacious opening of the
ice, in latitude 78° 10′, longitude 4° E., to a distance
of ten or twelve leagues from the exterior, wherein
we were tempted to stay, from the appearance of a
great number of whales. On the 9th of May, the
weather, which had previously been stormy, mode-
rated, when, the frost being severe, the ship was soon
fixed in bay-ice. At the same time, the external
sheets of ice on the north-east wheeled to the south,
and forming a junction with the ice south-east from
us, completely enclosed us. Until the 16th, we
lay immoveable ; a break of the bay-ice then appeared about half a mile from us, to attain which we laboured with energy, and in eight hours accomplished a passage for the ship. On the 18th, we pursued the same opening to its eastern extremity, and
endeavoured, but without success, to force through
a narrow neck of ice, into another opening leading
farther in the same direction. On the 20th, in at-

T 2

tempting this object, we endured a heavy pressure
of the bay-ice, which shook the ship in an alarming
manner.   The next day, we made a small advance;
and on the 22d, after a fatiguing effort in passing
through the midst of an aggregation of floes, against
the wind, we reached a channel which led us several
miles to the south-eastward.   On the 23d, we lay
at rest together with four other ships.   The day following, having sawn a place for the ship in a thin
floe, we forced forward between two large masses,
where bay ice unconsolidated had been compressed,
until it had become 10 or 12 feet thick.   We were
assisted by about a hundred men from the accompanying ships, which followed close in our rear; and
after applying all our mechanical powers during
eight or nine hours, we passed the strait of about a
furlong in length, and immediately the ice collapsed and rivetted the ships of our companions to the
spot.   As they declined our proffered assistance,
(which indeed, at this time, would have been quite
unavailing), we determined to improve the advantage
we had acquired, by proceeding to the utmost limits of the opening.   Accordingly, we advanced,
on various winding courses, amidst bay-ice and
fields, in narrow obscure passages, a distance of
several miles.   We then discovered a continuation of the navigation between two immense sheets
of ice; but the channel was so narrow and intricate, that, for the distance of near a mile, it did
not appear more than 10 to 20 yards in width.   The

prospect was indeed appalling ; but, perceiving indications of the enlargement of the passage, rather
than the contrary, we advanced under a press of sail,
driving aside some disengaged lumps of ice that opposed us, and shortly accomplished our wishes in
safety.   Here, an enlivening prospect presented itself : to the extreme limits of the horizon, no interruption was visible.   We made a predetermined
signal to the ships we had left, indicative of our
hopes of a speedy release.   In two hours, however,
our sanguine expectations of an immediate escape
received a check, for we then met with fields in the
act of collapsing and completely barring our progress.   As the distance across was scarcely a mile,
and the sea to appearance clear beyond it, the interruption was most tantalizing.   We waited at the
point of union, in the hope of the separation of
the two fields ; and on the morning of the 26th of
May, our anxiety was happily relieved, by the wished-for division of the ice.   The ship, propelled by a
brisk wind, darted through the strait, and entered a
sea, which we considered the termination of our difficulties.   After steering three hours to the south-
eastward, as directed by the northern ice, we were
concerned to discover that our conclusions had been
premature.   An immense pack opened on our view,
stretching directly across our track.   There was no
alternative, but forcing through it : we therefore
pushed forward into the least connected part.   By
availing ourselves of every advantage in sailing,

where sailing was practicable, and *boring* * or
drifting, where the pieces of ice lay close together,
we at length reached the leeward part of a narrow
channel, in which we had to ply a considerable
distance against the wind.   When performing this,
the wind, which had hitherto blown a brisk breeze
from the north, increased to a strong gale.   The
ship was placed in such a critical situation, that we
could not for above an hour accomplish any reduction of the sails; and while I was personally engaged performing the duty of a pilot from the top-
mast-head, the bending of the mast was so uncommon, that I was seriously alarmed for its stability.
At length, we were enabled to reef our sails, and for
some time proceeded with less danger. We continued
to manœuvre among the ice in those situations where
its separation was most considerable.   Our direction
was now east, then north for several hours, then
easterly ten or fifteen miles ;—when, after eighteen
hours of the most difficult, and occasionally hazardous sailing, in which the ship received some
hard blows from the ice ; after pursuing a devious
course nearly ninety miles, and accomplishing a
distance on a direct north-east course of about forty

---

* *Boring* is the operation of forcing a ship through crowded
ice by the agency of the wind on the sails. The impetus of
the ship is studiously directed against the opposing pieces, and
a passage thereby effected. It can be performed only with favourable winds.

miles,—we found ourselves at the very margin of the
sea, separated only by a narrow sea-stream. The
sea was so great without, and the wind so violent,
that we durst not hazard an attempt to force
through this remaining obstacle. After waiting
about thirty hours, on the morning of the 28th of
May, the weather cleared, and the wind abated.
The sea-stream which, the preceding day, did not
exceed two hundred yards in breadth, was generally
augmented to upwards of a mile broad. One place
alone was visible, where the breadth was less considerable; to that we directed our course, forced
the ship into it, and by prompt and vigorous exertions, were enabled to surmount every difficulty, and
accomplish our final escape into the open sea.

I have been thus minute in the relation of the
progress of our extrication from an alarming, though
not very uncommon, state of besetment, both for
the purpose of giving a faint idea of the difficulties
and dangers which those engaged in the whale-
fishery have occasionally to encounter, and also more
particularly to show the extraordinary manner in
which ships are imperceptibly immured amidst the
ice, and carried away from their original situation,
by the regularity of its drift to the south-westward.

From this narrative, it will appear, that, notwithstanding we only penetrated 25 or 30 miles
on our ingress, and among ice most widely disposed: yet, before our extrication was accomplished,

we had passed on a direct course a distance of 35
or 40 leagues, whereof one-half was in contracted
channels, amidst compact and formidable ice. And,
further, that in less than a fortnight, while at rest
with regard to the ice, our drift, as ascertained by
astronomical observations, had been 60 or 70 miles
to the south, and a distance nearly as great to the
west.

SECT. IX.

*Effects of the Ice on the Atmosphere, and of the
Ice and Sea on each other.*

THE profusion of ice in the polar regions, produces peculiar and marked effects on the surrounding
elements. The sea, in consequence, exhibits some
interesting characters, and the atmosphere, some
striking phenomena. Of these, the power the ice
exerts on the wind,—on aqueous vapour,—on the
colour of the sky,—and on the temperature of the
air, are the most prominent; and of those the results are varied accordingly as the ice or swell has
the ascendency.

1. When the wind blows forcibly across a solid
pack or field of ice, its power is much diminished
ere it traverses many miles: Insomuch, that a
storm will frequently blow for several hours on

one side of a field, before it be perceptible on the other; and, while a storm prevails in open water, ships beset within sight, will not experience one-half of its severity.

2. It is not uncommon for the ice to produce the effect of repulsing and balancing an assailing wind. Thus, when a severe storm blows from the sea directly towards the main body of ice, an opposite current will sometimes prevail on the borders of the ice; and such conflicting winds have been observed to counterpoise each other, a few [furlongs distant from the ice, for several hours : the violence of the one being, as it were, subdued by the frigorific repulsion and greater density of the other. The effect resulting, is singular and manifest. For,

3. The moist and temperate gale from the southward, becomes chilled on commixture with the northern breeze, and having its capacity for moisture thereby diminished, discharges its surplus humidity in the thickest snow *. As the quantity of the snow depends considerably on the difference of temperature of the two assimilating streams of air, it follows, that the largest proportion must be precipitated on the exterior of the main body of ice,

---

* It is almost needless to say, that the foundation of this, and some of the following remarks, on the same subject, is derived from Dr HUTTON's ingenious Theory of Rain, an able and beautiful illustration of which we have in Professor LESLIE's Essay " On the Relations of Air to Heat and Moisture," p. 122.

where the contrast of temperature is the greatest :
and since that contrast must be gradually diminished, as the air passes over the gelid surface of the
ice, much of its superabundant moisture must generally be discharged before it reaches the interior.
Hence we can account for the fewness of the clouds,
—the consequent brightness of the atmosphere,—
and the rareness of storms, in situations far immured among the northern ice.

From this consideration, it might be supposed,
that after the precipitation of a certain small depth
of snow on the interior ice, the atmosphere could
alone replenish its moisture from the same surface,
and that whatever changes of temperature might
occur, it could only discharge the same again : or,
in other words, that the very same moisture would
be alternately evaporated and deposited, without a
possibility of adding to a limited depth of snow.
Now, this would assuredly be the case, if nothing
more than the same moisture evaporated from the
snowy surface of the ice, were again deposited. But,
it must be observed, that notwithstanding winds
from the north, east or west, may not furnish any
considerable quantity of snow ; and that although
those warm and humid storms which blow from the
south, may afford a large proportion of their humidity to the *exterior* ice ; yet, as the temperature
of the northern regions would be gradually elevated, by the long continuance of a southerly gale,

the advance of the wind must in consequence be farther and farther before it be reduced to the temperature of the ice; and, therefore, some snow would continue to be precipitated to an increasing and unlimited extent.

Hence, as winds blowing from the Pole must be replaced by air that is both warmer and damper, it is not possible that they should carry away more moisture from the circumpolar regions than the air which replaces them brings: but, on the contrary, as the snow deposited on the interior ice by southerly storms, (from the nature of the circumstances), must be derived from evaporations out of the sea; it is evident, that there must be an increase of snow in the icy latitudes, and that we cannot possibly determine any limit beyond which it may be affirmed that no snow can be deposited.

4. On approaching a pack, field, or other compact aggregation of ice, the phenomenon of the *ice-blink* is seen whenever the horizon is tolerably free from clouds, and in some cases even under a thick sky. The *ice-blink* consists in a stratum of a lucid whiteness, which appears over ice in that part of the atmosphere adjoining the horizon. It appears to be occasioned thus: Those rays of light which strike on the snowy surface of the ice, are reflected into the superincumbent air, where they are rendered visible, either by the reflective property of the air, simply, or by a light haze, which, on such occasions,

probably exists in the atmosphere; but the light which falls on the sea, is in a great measure absorbed, and the superincumbent air retains its native ethereal hue. Hence, when the ice-blink occurs under the most favourable circumstances, it affords to the eye a beautiful and perfect map of the ice, twenty or thirty miles beyond the limit of direct vision, but less distant in proportion as the atmosphere is more dense and obscure. The ice-blink not only shows the figure of the ice, but enables the experienced observer to judge whether the ice thus pictured be field or packed ice : if the latter, whether it be compact or open, bay or heavy ice. Field-ice affords the most lucid blink, accompanied with a tinge of yellow; that of packs is more purely white; and of bay-ice, greyish. The land, on account of its snowy covering, likewise occasions a blink, which is more yellow than that produced by the ice of fields.

5. The ice operates as a powerful equaliser of temperature. In the 80th degree of north latitude, at the edge of the main body of ice, with a northerly gale of wind, the cold is not sensibly greater than in the 70th degree, under similar circumstances.

6. Fogs are most prevalent among loose ice; but they are dispersed, and a clear sky generally produced, at the borders of a solid body of ice. The approach to solid ice is sometimes announced by this clearing of the air, and by the reduction of the tempera-

ture. On coming near a body of ice, from off which
the wind blows, a remarkable increase of cold is felt;
as much sometimes as ten degrees in an hour's sailing.

7. The reciprocal action of the ice and the sea
on each other, is particularly striking, which ever
may have the ascendancy. If, on the one hand,
the ice be arranged with a certain form of aggregation, and in due solidity, it becomes capable of resisting the turbulence of the ocean, and can, with
but little comparative diminution or breaking, sup-
press its most violent surges. Its resistance is so
effectual, that ships sheltered by it, rarely find the
sea disturbed by swells. On the other hand, the
most formidable fields yield to the slightest *grown*
swell, and become disrupted into thousands of pieces;
and ice of only a few weeks growth, on being assailed by a turbulent sea, is broken and annihilated with
incredible celerity. Bay-ice, indeed, which for weeks
has been an increasing pest to the whale-fisher, is
sometimes removed in the space of a few hours. The
destruction is in many cases so rapid, that to an unexperienced observer, the occurrence seems incredible, and rather an illusion of fancy, than a matter of
fact. Suppose a ship immoveably fixed in bay-ice,
and not the smallest opening to be seen: after a
lapse of time sufficient only for a moderate repose,
imagine a person rising from his bed,—when, be-
hold, the insurmountable obstacle has vanished !

Instead of a sheet of ice expanding unbroken to the verge of the horizon on every side, an undulating sea relieves the prospect, wherein floats, the wreck of the ice, reduced to a small fraction of its original bulk! This singular occurrence, I have more than once witnessed.

That ice should be forming or increasing, when exposed to the swells of the ocean, while the annihilation of bay-ice is so sudden and complete, might seem an anomaly or impossibility, were the circumstances passed over in silence. It must be observed, that the operation of a swell is merely to rend the bay-ice in pieces, while its destruction is principally effected, by the attrition of those pieces against each other, and the washing of the *wind-lipper* * Herein the essential difference consists : pancake ice is formed in masses so small and so strong, that the swell cannot divide them ; and the effect of the wind-lipper is repressed by the formation of sludge on its seaward margin. Hence, whenever ice does occur in agitated waters, its exterior is always sludge, and its interior pancake ice, the pieces of which gradually increase in size with the distance from the edge.

When a swell occurs in crowded yet detached ice, accompanied with thick tempestuous weather, it presents one of the most dangerous and terrific na-

---

* The first effects of a breeze of wind on smooth water is by seamen called *wind-lipper*. From it, all high seas are derived, and it is always apparent on their surfaces.

vigations that can be conceived. Each lump of ice,
by its laborious motion, and its violent concussions
of the water, becomes buried in foam, which, with
its rapid drift, and the attendant horrid noise, in-
spires the passing mariner with the most alarming
impressions; whilst the scene before him, is, if possible, rendered more awful, by his consciousness of
the many disasters which have been occasioned by
similar dangers.

When exposed to a high sea, the largest and
heaviest pieces of drift-ice are forced to leeward with
much greater velocity than small and light pieces.
Masses of ice capable of holding a ship to windward
in a storm, when the sea is smooth, frequently drive,
in a swell, with a velocity of two or three miles an
hour. This renders loose ice very dangerous in a
swell, particularly with light winds or calms. In
the season of 1818, the ship I commanded, the
Fame, was exposed to great danger by an insulated
piece of ice running against her in a calm. We
were in latitude 78°, lying at a short distance from
the western ice, at the conclusion of a gale of wind.
A fog, intensely thick, prevailed, the sea was very
high, but the wind had just subsided to a calm.
No chance of danger from ice was apprehended, until a prodigious lump was heard approaching. It was
not a hundred yards distant when it made its appearance, and, in a state of tremendous agitation,
with the sea beating, roaring, and breaking upon it

the same as on a lee shore, advanced directly towards us with a velocity of about three knots   All hands were instantly roused, the boats were manned and lowered into the water to tow the ship ; but before she could be moved from the place, the ice was alongside.   Happily the ship rolled from it at the moment the first blow was struck, which weakened the shock, and, perhaps, prevented the ship from being stove.   The succeeding blows, though all received under the ship's bottom, near the keel, proved less and less formidable, until the ship was fairly beaten out of the way; so that the ice passed to leeward, and was in a few minutes out of sight.

When a swell operates against the side of a stream or pack of ice, it washes away the snow from the surface of the most exposed pieces, as well as part of the ice, and forms every corner into a *tongue*.   These tongues, from the different depths they occupy in the sea, are forced one upon another, and so locked together, that the most violent waves, being incapable of moving them at a little distance from the edge, become totally suppressed.   Hence a stream of heavy ice, however narrow, provided it consist of half a dozen or more pieces in breadth, and be well compacted, is capable of resisting the highest swells in an astonishing degree, and for a considerable period. Under shelter of such a stream, though the waves of the Atlantic beat against it, the navigator finds a comfortable retreat, in a sea almost as smooth as a

2

river. So long as the ice hangs together, and preserves its continuity, it sustains but little loss from
the most violent surges; but whenever the sea
breaks through it, like an army dispersed and retreating in confusion before a victorious enemy, the
pieces flee before the sea, increase rather than diminish the swell, are overrun by the foaming waters,
and subjected to a rapid dissolution.

Thus, while a small stream of compact ice suppresses a swell, a large body of heavy ice, when
loose or unconnected, produces little effect, the sea
being found to penetrate with little diminution for
many leagues. A swell among ice is discovered by
the breaking of fields, or by the motions of loose
pieces, when it cannot be otherwise observed. In
some cases it becomes a useful guide to the involved navigator, by pointing out, in the direction in
which it penetrates, the way of escape. In thick
weather, especially, it is often the means of extrication to ships the most awkwardly entangled
among ice, and preserves them from being deeply
and dangerously beset.

8. A balance of power seems to be preserved be
tween the wasting influence of the waves and the
solidity and increasing property of the polar ice;
the former preventing the undue enlargement of
the boundaries of the ice, and the latter defying any
extensive, or at least permanent, inroads into the
situations usually occupied by it. For, as fast as

the borders of the ice are destroyed by the sea, or
the mildness of the climate under southerly winds,
all the losses are made up by the prevalence of the
current proceeding to the south-west, which continually brings fresh supplies of ice, and presents a
new front to the action of the waves.

SECT. X.

*Remarks on the closest Approximations towards
the Poles hitherto accomplished, under different
Meridians.*

It has already been remarked, that the 80th or
81st degree of north latitude, is generally accessible
to the Spitzbergen or Greenland whale-fishers, under
the meridian of 6° or 8° E. ; and that on some particular occasions the latitude of 80° or even 81°
has been exceeded.   None of the navigators, however, who have been sent on this or any other
track, with the express object of exploring the Polar regions, have been able to reach the parallel of
81°.   From this circumstance, from the general experience of the whale-fishers, and from an experience of seventeen voyages which I have myself
made into the Spitzbergen Sea, I think I may ven-
ture to assert, that the navigation of the North Polar
Sea is generally terminated by an impervious body of

ice, in the latitude of 80° or 81°; and that although some instances may have occurred in which vessels have proceeded a little farther, yet few of these instances can be authenticated.

One case, and only one, I can myself establish. While I served in the capacity of chief mate, in the Resolution of Whitby, commanded by my Father, (whose extraordinary perseverance is well known to all persons in the Greenland trade,) we were enabled, by astonishing efforts, and with exposure to imminent hazard, to penetrate as far as latitude 81° 30'. This being, I imagine, one of the most remarkable approximations towards the Pole yet realized, it may not be uninteresting to give an abstract of a part of my journal of this voyage.

On the 23d of March 1806, we sailed from Whitby, and, on the 12th of April, saw the first ice, near the Island of Jan Mayen, which was then in sight. The next day we penetrated the loose ice in search of seals, until we reached the edge of a solid pack; but seeing nothing to induce our stay, we made the best of our way to the eastward for the whale-fishery.

Until the 20th, the winds were mostly unfavourable; our progress was in consequence only eighty leagues on an easterly course. We then steered to the north-eastward, and soon fell in with ice, which, however, did not put us out of our course until the

u 2

following day, when we were obliged to bear more away, on account of close ice, which trended to the E., S. E., and afterwards S. S. E.

At 8 P. M. of the 24th of April, supposing ourselves near land, both from our reckoning and from the vast quantity of birds seen, the ship was laid too, the weather being thick with snow. At 10 P. M., the weather cleared, and we discovered Cherie Island ten leagues distant to the north-east, with the appearance of ice around it. This induced our prompt return along the edge of the ice, judging that direction the most prudent, though seventeen out of twenty ships in company continued to proceed to the south-eastward. Whether the masters of these ships did not see the land, or, seeing it, were determined to search for a new passage to the fishing stations on the east side of Cherie Island, we could not ascertain; but we considered it more safe to pursue the accustomed track, though apparently blocked up with an impervious body of ice.

Having surveyed the margin of the ice for four days, without discovering any material inlet, we penetrated the borders with a northerly wind, as far as practicable, and then moored to an ice-berg.

Two days afterwards, the wind veered to the south, with which we forced a little farther to the northward, and, on the 2d of May, moored to another ice-berg.

On the 4th, we observed, that some ships which, four days before, were several miles to the southward of us, had, by the peculiar set of the current, revolved to the northward.

On the 5th, with a light breeze of wind, we proceeded several miles through various intricate channels in the ice, and on the wind dying away to a calm, we advanced by *towing* *. Struck a whale, but lost it by the breaking of the line.

A heavy swell, with a strong wind from the S. W., prevailed on the 6th, by which the situation of the ship was rendered very hazardous. Lay too.

On the 7th, towed to an ice-berg, and made fast.

An opening appeared in the ice on the 9th, leading to the northward. Made sail, and pursued a devious channel during six hours, with the velocity of eight or nine miles an hour. The wind having then increased to a heavy gale, and the ice having become crowded and dangerous, we were obliged to moor. The Foreland in sight.

The next day the wind was easterly, but moderate, and the ice a little slack ; as such, we plied towards the land, and after much critical sailing

---

* The process of dragging a ship, or any other body floating in water, forward by boats, is called *towing*. The boats are all connected by ropes to the ship, and are then rowed forward, by which the ship is drawn after them.

among dangerous ice, we entered an opening so considerable, that we could not discover its extent from the top-mast-head.   We now flattered ourselves that our exertions were about to be rewarded, by having an immediate opportunity of commencing the fishery.   Our hopes, however, were soon frustrated; the open space we now navigated did not present us with a single whale, and though of an extent of 400 or 500 square miles, was, within three days, contracted to an area of a few acres.

This circumstance, so unexpected, at the same time so uncommon, would have had a tendency to paralize our efforts, had not a swell, apparently from the north, and the appearance of water in that direction by the sky, encouraged us to persevere.

On the 13th, therefore, we again pushed forward into a continuous sheet of ice; being a combination of bay-ice with scattered pieces of drift-ice. During five days we persevered in the most laborious exertions, in towing, boring, warping * and mill-dolling † ; frequently dragging heavy boats

---

* *Warping* is the process of moving a ship by means of ropes, called *warps*, which being attached to some distant fixed object, a large piece of ice, for instance, admit of the ship's being drawn forward, by the application to the ropes of the different mechanical powers on board.

† *Mill-dolling*, consists in breaking a passage through thin ice, for a ship, by a sort of *ram*, let fall from the bowsprit; or

across extensive plains of bay-ice, for the purpose of breaking a passage for the ship; scarcely allowing time for refreshment, with very limited and distant periods for rest; when, on the 18th of May, after having passed a barrier of most extraordinary extent, we accomplished our wishes, and exceeded our most sanguine expectations, by getting into a sea, to which we could see no bounds, but the ice we had passed through on the south side, and the land to the eastward. Our latitude, at this time, was about 79° 35′; Hakluyt's Headland bearing E. N. E. 35 miles distant.

We now proceeded a little towards the N., afterwards towards the N. W. or W., accordingly as appearances in the ice or sea suggested a greater probability of meeting with whales. As we advanced, we found that a pack lay to the northward, as well as to the southward of us; the two bodies of ice being ten to twenty leagues apart. The wind blowing very strong from the southward, and the sea being quite open, our progress to the westward was very rapid; so much so, indeed, that among the contracted meridians in the 80th degree of latitude, we advanced almost a degree of longitude every hour

---

by one or more boats attached to the jib-boom, having several men in each, who move from side to side, and keep them in continual motion. As the ship advances, the rope by which the boats are attached to the jib-boom, draws them forward, and prevents them from being run down.

during the day; the interval between the sun coming to the meridian, below the Pole, on the 18th,
and to the same meridian on the 19th, being nearly twenty-five hours.   When we reached the longitude of about 8° W., in latitude 79° 30', no whales
having been seen all the way, we tacked.   Our advance to the west, in this parallel, was unexampled;
and yet an expanse of sea lay before us, of which,
from the appearance of the sky, we could with confidence affirm, that neither ice, in any considerable
body, was within thirty miles, nor land within sixty
miles of us, in a westerly direction.

On stretching to the northward, from this, we
met with a compact body of ice, in latitude 80° 10',
along the edge of which we sailed on an E. or E.NE.
course (true), a distance of nearly three hundred
miles, examining every sinuosity, and keeping a vigilant watch the whole way, without seeing any
whales, excepting a dead one.   On the 23d, our
latitude, by a careful observation, at mid-night, was
81° 12' 42"; and, on the morning of the 24th, we
considered ourselves nearly a degree to the northward of Captain Phipps's farthest advance, our latitude being estimated at 81° 30', and longitude 19° E.
Here a similar expanse of sea presented itself, as on
our western reach.   The margin of the ice continued
to trend to the E. N. E., (true), as far as it was visible; and, from the appearance of the atmosphere,
it was clear that the sea was not incommoded by

2

ice, between the E. N. E. and S. E. points, within thirty miles, or limited by land within 60 or even 100 miles of the place of the ship.

Had the purport of our voyage been discovery, instead of whale-fishing, we should certainly have been enabled to add something more to our knowledge of the Globe, by the exploration of a region seldom attainable.   Discovery, however, being only in a limited degree compatible with our object, considerations of safety and prudence induced our return. Our situation was solitary indeed.   No ship, or human being, it is believed, was within 340 miles of us.   We, doubtless, occupied the most northerly situation of any individuals in the world.   The sea began to freeze, and threatened our detention.   We had made no progress in the fishery; nor could we find any whales: and the sailors began to be anxious, fearful, and troublesome.   Such were the considerations that induced us to return.

We now proceeded to the south-west, at a distance from the ice that we examined on our advance.   On the 24th, at noon, we were in latitude 81° 1′ 53″, longitude 17° 30′ E.

Having run to the south-west about 120 miles, Hakluyt's Headland was seen, bearing S. E. distant 19 or 20 leagues.   On penetrating a body of open ice encompassing the Headland, we saw a whale, and pursued it with all our boats, but without success.   From hence we steered to the westward, and found the ice, which was very compact when we passed it on the 21st of the month, now loose and navigable. The drift-ice from the north, had formed a chain of communication between the two packs, among which, on the 28th of May, in latitude 80° 8', longitude 0° 40' E., we met with whales so numerous, that, in the course of a month, we succeeded in capturing twenty-four of the species. These, with two seals, two sea-horses, two bears, and one narwhale, afforded an excellent cargo *.

On the 30th of June, we prepared for our passage home ; and the day following, entered the icy barrier that we encountered on our advance, which now consisted of an open but heavy pack. After a troublesome navigation of two or three days, we emerged from the ice into the open sea, and did not afterwards meet with any obstruction.

From the 9th of May, until the 10th of July, we saw but one ship.

On our arrival in England, we were informed, that two French frigates had cruized the fishing country during the latter end of the season, and had destroyed several of the whalers ; one of which frigates we narrowly escaped on our passage home, it having been captured near the Faroe Islands, within a day of our passing the same. This an-

---

* The whole produced upwards of 216 tons of oil.

noyance from an enemy, together with the unfavourable situation of the ice, and the scarcity of
whales on its southern aspect, was the occasion of a
very general failure in the fishery.

In no part of the Globe has any navigator been
able to approach within ten degrees of the Pole,
excepting on the west side of Spitzbergen.

In Baffin's Bay, between the longitudes of 60°
and 70° west, ships have seldom advanced beyond the
74th or 75th degree of latitude ; and only one instance is upon record, wherein the latitude of $77\frac{1}{2}$°,
near the extremity of the bay, has been reached.

Through Behring's Strait, the adventurous COOK,
on the meridian of 161° or 162° W., (very near the
American shore), advanced to the latitude of 70° 44'
N., on the 18th of August 1778 ; and, on the 26th,
in longitude 176° W., they found the ice impervious
beyond the latitude of 69° 45' N. After the lamentable death of this illustrious navigator, Captain
CLERKE directed the proceedings ; and, on the
18th of July, in the following year, reached the latitude of 70° 33', being about four leagues short of
their former advance.

Along the greater part of the extensive northern
face of the Russian dominions, the polar ice closely
adheres during two-thirds of the year ; and, in the
height of summer, seldom recedes far from any part
of the coast comprised between Nova Zembla and

2

the north-eastern termination of Asia. From some parts of the coast, indeed, it is doubtful whether the ice ever recedes at all; though, in some situations, near extensive promontories, a considerable north latitude has been obtained. Between the meridians of 60° and 70° E., along the coast of Nova Zembla, Barentz in 1596, observed in latitude 76° 15′, and is supposed, in doubling the northern Cape of this country, to have reached at least the latitude of 77° N.; and in a preceding voyage, undertaken in the year 1594, the same navigator reached the latitude of about 77° 25′, when in sight of Nova Zembla, being prevented from going further by an extensive field of ice.

In longitude about 100° E., Lieutenant Prontschitscheff, in the year 1736, penetrated the ice, near Cape Ceverovostochnoi, as far as latitude 77° 25′. And about the longitude of 175° E. a little Russian vessel, being part of an expedition of seven kotches, is said to have doubled the north-eastern promontory of Asia, in the country of the Tchuktchi, supposed to extend into a high northern latitude, at any rate considerably beyond the extent reached by Captain Cook, about 60 leagues farther to the eastward.

Hence it appears, that the nearest approach towards the North Pole, between the meridians of Nova Zembla and the north-eastern Cape of Asia, has, as might reasonably be expected, been made by the Russians; that on the meridian of Nova Zembla, the highest northern latitude has been attained by the Dutch; and that in the sea of Spitzbergen, in Hudson's and Baffin's Bay, in the sea beyond Behring's Strait, and towards the sea, washing the northern shores of America, the highest northern latitudes, have been reached by the British. Towards the southern Pole, the most careful and extensive explorations have also been made by our countrymen; Captain Cook, with indefatigable perseverance, having advanced towards the Pole on various meridians, as far as the ice would permit. On his first attempt, in the year 1772, they met with ice in about 51° S. latitude, and longitude 21° E. They saw great fields in 55° S. on the 17th January 1773; and on February the 24th, were stopped by field ice in 62° south latitude, and 95° east longitude.

Again, on the second attempt in December of the same year, they met with ice in about 62° south latitude, and 172°–173° west longitude; and on the 15th, saw field ice in latitude 66°. On the 30th of January 1774, they were stopped by immense icefields in latitude 71° 10′ 30″ S., and in longitude 107° W., which was the most considerable approximation towards the South Pole that had ever been effected.

SECT. XI.

Abstract of the preceding Observations on the Formation, Properties, and Situation of the Polar Ice.

FROM what has been advanced respecting the situation, properties, and manner of formation of the ice surrounding the Pole, the following conclusions seem naturally to result ; and as far as relates to the formation of ice, will apply generally to all situations within the Polar circles where ice occurs.

I. *Bay-ice.*—That much bay-ice is annually formed in the seas of Spitzbergen and Davis' Strait; in the Bays of Hudson and Baffin, and in other situations near the Pole, where it sometimes attains such a degree of strength and solidity, as to produce *light* fields and floes, and when broken up, light drift-ice.

That the kind of bay-ice called Pancake or Cake Ice, is frequently formed in bodies of considerable extent, and in sheets of considerable thickness on the southern face of the main body of the polar ice, even where exposed to the swells of the Atlantic Ocean; and that bay-ice is necessarily derived entirely from sea-water.

II. *Drift-ice.*—That the *light* packed or drift ice is the yearly product of the bays of the Arctic lands, and of the interstices in the body of older ice, and that it is wholly derived from the water of the ocean.

That the *heavy* packed or drift ice generally arises from the disruption of fields.

III. *Icebergs.*—That most of the ice-mountains or icebergs that occur in Baffin's Bay, Davis' Strait, Hudson's Strait, and on the eastern coast of North America, are derived from the glaciers generated on the land between the mountains of the sea-coast, and are consequently the product of snow or rain water.

That some icebergs may possibly be formed in narrow coves and deep-sheltered bays in any of the polar countries, where the set of the current or prevailing winds has not a tendency to dislodge them. Such having their bed in the waters of the ocean, must be partly the product of sea-water, and partly that of snow and rain water. And it is not improbable,

That a continent of ice-mountains may exist in regions near the Pole, yet unexplored, the nucleus of which may be as ancient as the earth itself, and its increase derived from the sea and atmosphere combined.

IV. *Fields.*—That some fields arise from the cementation, by the agency of frost, of the pieces of a closely aggregated pack, which may have consisted of light or heavy ice; and, consequently, which may have been wholly derived from the ocean, or from the sea and atmosphere combined.

That the most considerable masses are generated in openings of the far northern ice, produced by the constant recession towards the south of that body lying near the coasts of Spitzbergen; and, that such fields are at first derived from the ocean, but are indebted for a considerable portion of superstructure, to the annual addition of the whole, or part of their burden of snow.

V. *Ice in general.*—That however dependant the polar ice may have been on the land for its formation and preservation, from the time of its first appearance, to its gaining an ascendency over the waves of the ocean, sufficient to resist their utmost ravages, and to arrest the progress of maritime discovery, at a distance of perhaps from 600 to 1000 miles from the Pole,—it is now evident, that the proximity of land is not essential, either for its existence, its formation, or its increase.

VI. *Freshness of ice.*—That the ice of bergs, of heavy fields, floes, and drift-ice, and indeed of all other kinds when solid, whether formed from rain-

water or sea-water, is, excepting such parts above
water as have been recently washed by the sea during frost, perfectly free from salt.

That porous light ice, and even bay-ice, when
well drained in a mild temperature, and washed
with fresh water, generally produce potable water,
though not always entirely free from salt.

VII. *Quantity of ice.*—That an equilibrium between the quantity of new ice produced and of old
ice destroyed, is so well preserved, that the absolute quantity of ice in the polar seas is always nearly
the same; the south-westerly drift of the ice renews
the front exposed to the sea, and prevents the inroads of the swell, while the general action of the
waves of the ocean, and the influence of a comparatively mild temperature, prevent the ice from
spreading over the Atlantic.

That when the quantity of ice in any place is enlarged or diminished, the variation is only temporary and partial; the usual equality being generally restored in the course of a few years by the reversed operation of the very causes which produced
the inequality.

VIII. *Quantity of ice greater in the southern
than in the northern hemisphere.*—That there appears to exist a remarkable difference between the
two hemispheres with regard to the extent from
the Poles occupied by the ice; the ice which en-

circles the Southern Pole, being much less pervious, and extending to much lower latitudes than that around the Northern Pole.

That the 73d or 74th, and sometimes the 76th or 78th degree of North latitude, can be attained at any season of the year, and the 80th degree, if not higher, at least once in every summer; whereas the 71st degree of South latitude is probably but seldom attainable, and has only been once passed:—And,

That while the antarctic *ne plus ultra* appears to be the 72d degree of latitude, that of the arctic zone extends at least to the 82d degree, or 600 miles further, so that while the closest approach to the South Pole is not nearer than 1130 miles, the common and annual approach to the North Pole is within 600 miles.

CHAPTER V.

OBSERVATIONS ON THE ATMOSPHEROLOGY OF THE ARCTIC REGIONS; PARTICULARLY RELATING TO SPITZBERGEN AND THE ADJACENT GREENLAND SEA.

SECT. I.

Remarks on the Climate of the Arctic Regions, and the Effects of Cold.

THE climate of Spitzbergen and the adjacent sea, is, in the autumn and spring seasons, variable and tempestuous. The temperature passes through its extreme range, which probably exceeds fifty degrees in the same season, or even in the same month, with a rapidity unknown in countries situate within the temperate zones. North, west, and east winds bring with them the extreme cold of the icy regions

x 2

immediately surrounding the Pole, whilst a shift of wind to the south-west, south, or south-east, elevates the temperature towards that of the neighbouring seas.

It is not easy to associate with our ideas of summer, the view of eternal ices and snow, and the sensation of almost perpetual frost; yet, as the power of the sun is sometimes such as to produce a comfortable degree of warmth,—as much ice and snow is dissolved, and especially as on some parts of the shore vegetation appears, advances, and is perfected, —the name of Summer to such a season may, for a limited period, be applicable.

An Arctic winter consists of the accumulation of almost every thing among atmospheric phenomena, that is disagreeable to the feelings, together with the privation of those bounties of Heaven, with which other parts of the earth, in happier climates, are so plentifully endowed. Here, during the whole of the winter months, the cheering rays of the sun are neither seen nor felt, but considerable darkness perpetually prevails; this, with occasional storms of wind and snow, and a degree of cold calculated to benumb the faculties of man, give a character to those regions most repugnant to human feeling.

The most severe cold, says Crantz, that occurs in Greenland, sets in, as in temperate climates, " after the New-Year, and is so piercing in February and

March, that the stones split in twain, and the sea reeks like an oven *."

When the sun returns to enlighten the benighted north, the arctic countries become more tolerable. The months of May, June and August, are even occasionally pleasant; but with July, and partially with June and August, the densest fogs prevail. On these occasions, though the temperature of the air be mild, the feelings are much more annoyed, and the spirits much more depressed by this tedious and painful obscurity, than by the enduring of a much colder atmosphere.

The temperature of the atmosphere, in the polar seas, is, in the summer months, very uniform. In the month of July, when fogs occur, the thermometer is generally near the freezing point, and is found not to be above three or four degrees higher at mid-day than it is at mid-night, and sometimes, with steady winds and constant fog, the temperature does not vary above a degree or two for several days together. But in the spring and winter seasons, the atmospheric temperature is subject to very great and rapid alterations; and it is worthy of observation, that the most remarkable of those changes are frequently simultaneous with the greatest changes of pressure.

---

* History of Greenland, vol. i. p. 43.

The following Table affords a view of the most considerable variations of temperature which have occurred within the sphere of my own observation, but it is probable that they bear no comparison with those alterations of temperature which take place in the winter months. Those instances distinguished by an asterisk, will be found, by reference, to the Table of remarkable Barometrical Variations hereafter given, to have been attended with correspondent changes of atmospheric pressure.

TABLE

Table of Remarkable Changes of Temperature.

Year.	Month, &c.	Latitude.	Thermometric Changes.	Interval.
				Hours.
1804,	April 19.	76°.10′	17°	18
1805,	—— 30.	78.30	14	3
1811,	—— 4.	70.33	20	21
——	—— 14.	70.52	20	12
——	—— 20.	76.21	18	22
——	May 5.	77.34	14	2
——	—— 14.	77. 2	21	24
1812,	—— 3.	75.35	16	7*
——	June 11.	78.44	9	16
——	July 12.	77.56	7	11
1813,	April 23.	80. 7	11	8*
——	—— 23.	80.10	18	12*
——	—— 24.	80.10	25	24*
——	—— 24.	80.10	32	30*
——	May 22.	77.28	14	10
——	June 21.	78. 2	14	12
——	July 27.	69.45	12	16
1814,	April 10.	71. 0	25	22
——	—— 13.	71. 0	32½	24*
——	May 11.	78. 9	20	12
——	—— 13.	78. 6	11	2
——	—— 14.	78. 9	18	8
——	—— 18.	77.36	18	12
——	June 13.	78.23	12	12
1815,	April 10.	74.56	17	12
——	—— 16.	77.50	14	14
——	—— 24.	78.16	14	8
——	May 14.	77. 7	12	10
——	June 2.	79.10	8	12
——	June 14.	78.33	14	20
1816,	April 10.	71.24	19	19
——	—— 11.	73. 4	13	10
——	—— 12.	73. 5	17	24
——	—— 15.	73.55	14	11
——	May 5.	78.10	12	10
——	—— 11.	78.45	14	12
——	June 10.	79.47	15	14
1817,	April 27.	78.20	13	9
——	May 14.	76.15	8	10
——	—— 16.	75.12	13	9
——	June 16.	78.17	9	16

From the circumstance of the thermometer and the barometer frequently suffering great and rapid simultaneous changes, the thermometer becomes a valuable appendage in assisting in the prognostication of the weather. Thus, when the thermometer rises with a falling barometer, a storm may be expected from the south. When the barometer rises and the thermometer falls, during a southerly storm, the return of fine weather is indicated, with a change of wind towards the north. When the barometer falls, together with the thermometer, during a southerly or easterly breeze, a northerly or westerly wind may be expected, but not of great intensity, unless the fall of the barometer be very considerable.

The great depression of temperature which takes place in the proximity of ice with a northerly wind, appears equally as considerable to the feelings in low as in high latitudes. Thus the ice, when accumulated into a connected body, extending, apparently, from the place of observation to the Pole, causes an equalization of temperature between the two situations, so that whatever may be the latitude, it is probable, that the cold under a strong northerly gale, will be very nearly as intense as at the Pole. In confirmation of this, I may remark, that as great a degree of cold as ever I noticed, in a series of twelve years' observations, (once excepted), was in the latitude $71\frac{1}{4}°$, April 12. 1814, when the mean of three thermometers indicated the temperature of zero ; and on the same occasion, during an interval of three days, the mean temperature was less than 5°. The wind, in the mean time, was constantly from the north-eastward, generally blowing a gale, but sometimes moderate. On the 25th April 1813, latitude 80°, the thermometer fell to —4° during a hard gale from the northeast *(per* compass), but, on account of the ship being driven away from the ice, it soon rose to 10o or 15°. These are the only instances in which I have observed the thermometer at zero ; though on one occasion, in the year 1803, April 23., when we had no thermometer in the ship, I am persuaded the cold was still more intense, as I never observed its effects so apparent. Ten or fifteen men were employed on the main-yard in an operation which occupied them about a quarter of an hour ; of these, it was found, when they descended the mast, that scarcely one had escaped being frost-bitten ; some in the hands, some in the feet, and others in different parts of the face. The effect of the ice in reducing the temperature, is so considerable, that our proximity to it is often announced by the coldness, before it can be seen. In consequence of this, the difference of a few leagues in position. sometimes produces a surprising increase of cold. On the 29th of April 1815, in latitude 78° near Spitzbergen, we had a temperature of 19o to 24°, while ships at the distance of only 14 or 15 leagues to the north-west of us, had a uniform cold of 8 degrees.

The Greenland sailors being well defended from external cold, by a choice selection of warm clothing, generally support the lowest temperature, after a few days habitude, without much inconvenience. When, however, its attacks are not gradual, as when a ship, which has attained the edge of the ice under a southerly gale, is suddenly exposed to a northerly breeze, the change of temperature is so great and so rapid, that the most hardy cannot conceal their uneasiness under its first impressions. In one of the instances above quoted, in the year 1814, when a temperature of zero occurred, we reached the latitude of 70o, without experiencing any cold below 30°; but in less than twenty-four hours, the thermometer fell 25°, and indicated a temperature of 5°. Thus, between the time of my leaving the deck at night, and arising the following morning, there was an increase in the cold of about 20°. This remarkable change was attended with singular effects. The circulation of the blood was accelerated,—a sense of parched dryness was excited in the nose,—the mouth, or rather lips, were contracted in all their dimensions, as by a sphincter, and the articulation of many words was rendered difficult and imperfect ; indeed, every part of the body was more or less stimulated or disordered by the severity of the cold. The hands, if exposed, would have been frozen in a few minutes ; and even the face could not have resisted the effects of a brisk wind, continued for any length of time.   A piece of metal when applied to the tongue, instantly adhered to it, and could not be removed without its retaining a portion of the skin ; iron became brittle, and such as was at all of inferior quality, might be fractured by a blow ; brandy of English manufacture and wholesale strength, was frozen ; quicksilver, by a single process, might have been consolidated ; the sea, in some places, was in the act of freezing, and in others appeared to smoke, and produced, in the formation of *frost-rime*, an obscurity greater than that of the thickest fog.   The subtile principle of magnetism seemed to be, in some way or other, influenced by the frost ; for the deck compasses became sluggish, or even motionless, while a cabin compass traversed with celerity.   The ship became enveloped in ice ; the bows, sides, and lower rigging were loaded ; and the rudder, if not repeatedly freed, would, in a short time, have been rendered immoveable.   A considerable swell at this time prevailing, the smoke in the cabin, with the doors closed, was so intolerable, that we were under the necessity of giving free admission to the external air to prevent it.   The consequence was, that in front of a brisk fire, at the distance of a yard and a-half from it, the temperature was 25° ;

water spilt on the table froze, and, indeed, congelation took place in one situation, at the distance of
only two feet from the stove.   Hoar-frost also appeared in the sailors bed cabins, arising from their
breath, and was deposited upon their blankets.

Under a temperature such as this, the effects of
which have just been described, the whale-fishery
could not be prosecuted; for nature could not sustain any continued exposure to the pungent force of
the wind.   With a calm atmosphere, however, the
sensible effects of cold are singularly diminished;
the cold of zero then becomes equally supportable
with the temperature of 10, 15, or even 20 degrees,
when impressed by a brisk wind; hence, the sensations produced on the body, become a very equivocal
criterion for estimating the degree of cold.

The effect of cold in preventing the traversing of
compasses exposed to its influence, has been noticed
by some navigators.   Ellis, in his voyage to Hudson's Bay, in conclusion of some remarks on this
subject, states, as a remedy against this inconvenience, the propriety of removing the compasses into
a warm place, by which the needles speedily resume
their activity.

It does not appear, from experiments made on
this subject, that the inferior activity of a compass when exposed to a cold atmosphere, arises
from any diminution in the magnetic energy, but
rather from some peculiar effect produced in the
needle, or in the centre on which it turns.   For nei-

ther the attractive nor directive power of the magnet, appears to suffer any diminution by an increase
of cold. A magnet which, with difficulty, supported a weight of seven pounds in my cabin, where the
temperature was 50°, on being removed into the air,
where a cold of 8° prevailed, also supported the
same, and after some interval one pound more; but
on another pound being added, the weight fell off,
and it would then only carry seven pounds as before. Hence, the attractive property of the magnet
could not be said to be diminished, and scarcely to
be increased, by a reduction of temperature amounting to 42°. A theodolite needle, 5.55 inches in length,
when made to oscillate horizontally in the cabin,
performed ten vibrations in sixty seconds, and then
ceased. On the deck, it oscillated five times in
thirty seconds, and then ceased. Thus, the time required for performing a vibration, was the same
both in a high and in a low temperature; consequently, the directive force is unaffected by changes
in temperature; but the number of vibrations performed by the needle, though equally deflected from
the magnetic meridian when set in motion, was
much fewer in a cold situation, than it was in a
warm one. Hence, though the magnetic influence,
both as to its attractive and directive property, be
fully as great in low as in high temperatures, yet
there appears to be an increase of friction, or an in-
troduction of some unknown principle, which occa-

1

sions a diminution in the mobility of magnetic needles, when the degree of cold is very much increased.

Many remarkable effects of severe cold, are to be met with in the journals of the polar navigators, who have wintered in Spitzbergen, Nova Zembla, Greenland, Hudson's Bay, Iceland, and other situations, subject to the visits of the polar-ice, or where ice is formed on the sea.

Captain James, when wintering in Hudson's Bay, latitude 52° N., experienced such a severity of cold, that on the 10th of December, many of the sailors had their noses, cheeks, and fingers frozen as white as paper. On the 21st of the same month, their sack, vinegar, and oil, with every other thing that was liquid, were frozen so hard, that hatchets were required for cutting them with; the inside of their hut, at the same time, was lined with ice, to within a yard of the fire; and the clothes on their beds were sometimes covered with hoar-frost.

Ellis, who wintered in Hudson's Bay in 1746–7, in a creek of Haye's River, latitude 57° 30′, remarked several curious effects of cold. In the creek where the vessel lay, much ice appeared on the 5th of October; on the 8th, it was covered with a sheet of ice; and on the 31st, the river was frozen over quite hard. By the 3d of November, bottled beer, though wrapped in tow and placed near a good constant fire, was found to be frozen solid; and in the course of the winter, beer casks placed in the ground, at the depth of several feet, froze almost solid, and some of them burst; many of the sailors had their faces, ears, and toes frozen; iron adhered to the fingers; glasses used in drinking stuck to the mouth, and sometimes removed the skin from the lips or tongue; and, a sailor, who inadvertently used his finger for stopping a spirit bottle, in place of a cork, while removing it from the house to his tent, had his finger fast frozen in the bottle, in consequence of which, a part of it was obliged to be taken off, to prevent mortification.

Captain Middleton, in describing the cold of Hudson's Bay, notices the bursting of ice, rocks, trees, joists and rafters of buildings, with a noise like the firing of cannon, as an effect of severe frost. He also states, that those persons who go abroad in north winds, are liable to have their arms, hands and faces blistered and frozen in a shocking manner; in such a degree, indeed, that the skin occasionally peels off when they enter too suddenly into a warm apartment.

A Hamburgh whaler, under the command of Jacob Janzen, was beset by the ice near Spitzbergen, in the year 1769, and detained until the middle of November, during which, though they were constantly driving to the southward, a most intense cold was sometimes experienced. On one occasion, early in November, the effect of the frost was such,

1

that the seams in the upper part of the ship's sides cracked, and opened with a noise resembling the report of a pistol, so that it was apprehended the ship would either sink or fall to pieces. These openings, at first, rendered the vessel very leaky, but after she was liberated and got into open water, and into a milder climate, they closed and became again impervious to water *.

In the interesting narrative by Pelham, of the preservation of eight seamen, who were accidentally left in Spitzbergen, in the year 1630, and wintered there, are some remarks on the effects of cold. The sea of the bay where they took up their abode, froze over on the 10th of October. After the commencement of the New-Year, the frost became most intense. It raised blisters in their flesh, as if they had been burnt with fire ; and if they touched iron at such times, it would stick to their fingers like birdlime. Sometimes, when they went out of doors to procure water, they were seized in such a way by the cold, that their flesh felt as sore as if they had been cruelly beaten.

Seven Dutch sailors who wintered in Spitzbergen in the year 1633–4, were exposed to such a degree of cold, that as early as the 13th of October,

---

* Beschryving der Walvisvangst, vol. iii. p. 17. This effect, it may be observed, was probably caused by dryness rather than cold.

casks of beer placed within eight feet of the fire, froze three inches thick, and soon afterwards became almost entirely consolidated. In all cases of beer, ale, wine and spirits, freezing, it may be observed, that the aqueous parts only freeze so as to become solid; whereby, even in ale or beer, the liquor becomes concentrated in the centre, until almost as strong as spirits.

When the Dutch navigator, Barentz, wintered in Nova Zembla, in 1596–7, a most extraordinary degree of cold was sometimes felt. During the month of November, in the hut erected by the miserable sailors for their accommodation, ice two inches thick formed on the floor, and their beds were covered with hoarfrost; and when the people washed their linen indoors, it would sometimes freeze almost immediately on being taken out of the warm water. In December, wine froze in their hut, so that they were obliged to melt it every time an allowance was served out. At the close of the year, the intensity of the cold almost deprived the suffering sailors of sensation; they had recourse to hot stones, as an application to their feet and bodies, for keeping them warm; and though sitting before the fire, their backs would sometimes be white with frost, and their stockings would be burnt before they felt any warmth in their feet.

The effects of cold at Disco, as observed by M. Paul Egedé, on the 7th January 1738, and recorded by David Crantz, in his excellent "History

of Greenland," are too striking to be omitted.
" The ice and hoar-frost," says Egede, " reach
through the chimney to the stove's mouth, without
being thawed by the fire in the day-time. Over
the chimney is an arch of frost, with little holes,
through which the smoke discharges itself. The
doors and walls are as if they were plastered over
with frost, and, which is scarcely credible, beds are
often frozen to the bedsteads. The linen is frozen in
the drawers. The upper eider-down bed and the
pillows are quite stiff with frost an inch thick from
the breath."

These effects of cold, so different from any thing
experienced in Britain, are not greater than might
be expected, when we consider the lowness of the
temperature which sometimes prevails.

The morbid effects of a low temperature, in
the degree in which the Greenland sailors are
exposed to it, are principally confined to the
partial freezing of particular members. Thus the
hands, feet, or even the face, are occasionally *frost-bitten*. The prompt application of spirit of wine
with friction, or a hearty rubbing with snow, so as
to keep the temperature of the part low until the
circulation is restored, seldom fails as a specific.
The principal diseases incident to this cause, may
be comprised under the genera catarrhus and scor-
butus, although intermittents, asthmas, &c. some-

times attack persons who have been subject to such complaints. Catarrhs are very rarely followed by any dangerous consequences, but are generally expelled without proving the harbinger of other disorders.

It is a prevailing opinion, that sudden transitions from heat to cold, are very inimical to health. Where the heat is productive of copious perspiration, the sudden exposure to cold might operate unfavourably; but where no sensible perspiration prevails, I have never seen, in a healthy person, any ill effects resulting from the greatest transitions. For my own part, indeed, whenever I have occasion to expose myself to a severe cold, I like to get the body well warmed, finding that the more I am heated the longer I can resist the cold without inconvenience. Internal warmth, however, is clearly preferable to superficial heat, and the warmth produced by simple fluids, such as tea or soup, preferable to that occasioned by spirits. After the liberal use of tea, I have often sustained a cold of 10°, at the mast-head, for several hours without uneasiness. And though I have often gone from the breakfast table, where the temperature was 50 or 60 degrees, to the mast-head, where it was 10°, and without any additional clothing excepting a cap, yet I never received any injury, and seldom much inconvenience from the uncommon transition. Hence when the sea is smooth, so that the smoke of the stove can make its escape, I generally have my cabin heated as high as 50 or 60 degrees, and sometimes upward, though I am liable to be called upon deck or even to the mast-head, at a moment's warning.

In these frigid regions, the scurvy becomes a very alarming disease. It is, however, rarely seen in a Greenland ship, and is chiefly known to be destructive here, from the miserable manner in which many individuals have perished, by attempting to winter in Spitzbergen and the neighbouring countries. It seems, however, pretty certain, that this disease is not so much influenced by the severity of the climate, as by the use of improper aliment. From an excellent paper on this subject, by Dr John Aikin, published in the Memoirs of the Literary and Philosophical Society of Manchester, we may very satisfactorily deduce the conclusions following :—

That the intense cold which prevails, is probably the proximate cause of the scurvy attacking persons attempting to winter in arctic countries.

That the mode of living is nevertheless of such essential importance, as to be capable of either bringing on or repelling the attacks of the disease.

That the use of salted provisions and spirituous liquors, form a regimen the most inimical to health, by inducing a state of the body so liable to the attacks of the scurvy, that under all recorded instances, this disorder, in all its severity, has constantly followed, and has seldom failed to produce its most deleterious effects. And,

That, on the contrary, the constant use of fresh provisions, whether cured by cooking, freezing or smoking, the occasional use of oleaginous substances, together with frequent exercise, a warm dwelling and warm clothing, may be considered as a plan of living which, if judiciously pursued, would be the best calculated for the preservation of health, and so probably effectual, that there would be little danger of resisting disease throughout the severities of a Spitzbergen winter.

Though the weather in the polar regions is very damp and unpleasant in some of the summer months, yet the very equable temperature which prevails, renders this season of the year particularly healthy.

The antiseptical property of frost is rather remarkable. Animal substances, requisite as food, of all descriptions, (fish excepted), may be taken to Greenland, and there preserved any length of time, without being smoked, dried or salted. No preparation, indeed, of any kind, is necessary for their preservation, nor is any other precaution requisite, excepting suspending them in the air when taken on shipboard, shielding them a little from the sun and wet, and immersing them occasionally in sea-water, or throwing sea-water over them after heavy

rains, which will effectually prevent putrescency
on the outward passage; and in Greenland, the
cold becomes a sufficient preservative, by freezing
them as hard as blocks of wood. Beef, mutton, pork
and fowls, (the latter neither plucked nor drawn,)
are constantly taken out from England, Shetland
or Orkney, and preserved in this way. When
used, the beef cannot be divided but by an axe or
a saw; the latter instrument is generally preferred.
It is then put into cold water, from which it derives
heat by the formation of ice around it, and soon
thaws; but if put into hot water, much of the
gravy is extracted, and the meat is injured without being thawed more readily. If an attempt
be made to cook it before it is thawed, it may
be burnt on the outside, while the centre remains
raw, or actually in a frozen state. The moisture is
well preserved by freezing, a little from the surface
only evaporating, so that if cooked when three, four
or five months old, it will frequently appear as pro-
fuse of gravy as if it had been but recently killed.
But the most surprising action of the frost, on fresh
provision, is in preserving it a long time from putrefaction, even after it is thawed and returns into
a warm climate *. I have eaten unsalted mutton and

---

* In the year 1808, a leg of mutton which was taken out
to Greenland in the ship Resolution, returned to Whitby unsalted. It was then allowed to remain on board of the ship,
exposed to the sun during two remarkably hot days, when the

beef nearly five months old, which has been constantly exposed to a temperature above the freezing
point for four or five weeks in the outset, and occasionally assailed by the septical influences of rain,
fog, heat, and electricity, and yet it has proved perfectly sweet. It may be remarked, that unsalted meat
that has been preserved four or five months in a
cold climate, and then brought back to the British
coasts during the warmth of summer, must be consumed very speedily after it is cut into, or it will

thermometer in the shade was as high as 80°. After this, it
was presented to an epicure in the town; and although it was
reduced to about half its original dimensions by the loss of fat,
&c. it was declared, when cooked, to be the most exquisite morsel that he had ever tasted.

Another remarkable instance of beef and mutton being kept
a long time unsalted, under very unfavourable circumstances,
occurred in my visit to the Spitzbergen fishery, in the year
1817. Our stock of fresh provision was killed on the 17th of
March, soon after which the ship was expected to sail; but unfavourable winds detained us in port until the 1st of April.
During this interval, the weather being very mild, our fresh
meat was hung up in a large warehouse, to shelter it from the
sun and rain. Until the 21st of April, we had so little frost,
that it remained soft; but soon afterwards it was hard frozen.
After the middle of June, the weather became mild, the sum-
mer-fogs set in, and the meat soon thawed. Every day in July, but four, we had either fog or rain, with an average temperature of 36°.8. The last of this provision was cooked about
the 13th of August; and although the average temperature for
fourteen days, had been above 50°, yet it proved sweet and palatable.

fail in a day or two.   It will seldom, indeed, keep
sweet after being cooked above 20 or 30 hours.

A further antiseptical effect is produced by the
cold of the polar countries, on animal and vegetable substances, so as to preserve them, if they
remain in the same climate, unchanged for a period
of many years.   " It is observable," says Martens,
in his " Voyage to Spitzbergen," " that a dead carcase doth not easily rot or consume ; for it has been
found, that a man buried ten years before, still retained his perfect shape and dress."   An instance
corroborative of this remark, is given by M. *Bleau*,
who, in his *Atlas Historique*, informs us, that the
bodies of seven Dutch seamen, who perished in Spitzbergen in the year 1635, when attempting to pass
the winter there, were found twenty years afterwards, by some sailors who happened to land about
the place where they were interred, in a perfect
state, not having suffered the smallest degree of
putrefaction.

Wood and other vegetable substances are preserved in a similar manner.   During my exploration of the shores of Spitzbergen, in the year 1818,
several huts, and some coffins built entirely of wood,
were observed.   One of the latter appeared, by an
adjoining inscription, to contain the body of a native of Britain, who had died in the year 1788 ; and
though the coffin had lain completely exposed, excepting when covered with snow, during a period of

thirty years, the wood of which it was composed, not only was undecayed, but appeared quite fresh and new. It was painted red ; and the colour even seemed to be but little faded. Things of a similar kind, indeed, have been met with in Spitzbergen, which have resisted all injury from the weather, during the lapse of a century.

SECT. II.

General Remarks on Meteorology, with an Investigation of the Mean Monthly, and Annual Temperature of the North Polar Regions, including some Inferences on the Constant Tendency to Equalization of Temperature in the Atmosphere.

THOUGH in a state of rapid improvement, the science of Meteorology is acknowledged to be yet in its infancy.

Prior to the 17th century, no accurate mode of ascertaining the variations in atmospheric temperature was known; and, before the discovery of the weight of the atmosphere by Torricelli, about the year 1630, no means of registering its variations of pressure could be known or practised. Hence we can have no very correct idea of the relative temperature of climates, in the present and remote periods,

1

unless from occasional historical remarks of the formation of ice in particular lakes, rivers, or parts of
the sea, or from the capability of the earth, in any
region, for producing certain fruits or grain which
cannot now be raised, or the contrary.

Until after the 17th century, meteorology seems
to have been principally attended to, at least as far
as regards the indications of wind and rain, by illi-
terate persons ; the success of whose occupations depending considerably on their ability to anticipate
the most particular atmospheric changes, necessi-
tated them to study the face of the sky. The various appearances of the clouds, of the sun, moon,
and stars, together with the notes or peculiar actions of certain animals, were their principal signs.
But since the invention of the barometer, and more
particularly of late years that it has become of general use, the farmer avails himself of its oscillations, in predicting such changes as affect his inte-
rests, by endangering the fruits of his industry. In
consequence of this increased use of the thermometer and barometer,—instruments approaching so near
to perfection, that their indications in the most distant quarters of the globe can be compared, and the
comparison relied on,—meteorology, as a science, has
made a considerable advance. Not only has it received
an increased attention from professed philosophers,
but also from retired persons of a scientific turn, who,
within the last few years, have been in the habit

of attending to the phenomena which these instruments indicate, in the vicinity of their different places of abode. These records have already been useful; but, by continuing to register their observations upon the atmospheric changes, until a sufficient number shall be obtained, they will confer an important obligation on the generalizing meteorologist, and contribute to the advancement of the science of the atmosphere.

Among philosophers, Mayer, Kirwan, Hutton, Franklin, Playfair, Leslie, Wells, Forster, Halley, De Luc, Fontana, La Place, Humboldt, D'Alembert, and numerous others, have laboured in the science of meteorology with various credit and success. Among these, Professor Mayer has given us a formula for determining the temperature of any situation on the globe, where observations have not been made. Dr Hutton has presented us with a theory of rain, ingenious and plausible, and calculated to explain some phenomena, which could not before be accounted for, on any allowed principle. Kirwan, Humboldt, and others, have advanced our knowledge of the climates of different countries, by their laborious researches on atmospheric temperature. Dr Wells, by his investigation of the phenomena of dew, has accomplished a most interesting result in the discovery of the cause on which its formation depends. Professor Leslie, by the invention of several curious and useful instruments, and by his

1

profound researches on the relations of air to heat
and moisture, and on the propagation of heat and
cold through the atmosphere to distant regions, has
contributed very largely to the advancement of meteorological knowledge, and to our information on
the properties of the atmosphere ; and, in his invention of a correct hygrometer, the action of which is
dependent upon known and calculable philosophical
principles, he has presented the meteorologist with
a gift, which, when more generally known and adopted, will afford results, on the dryness and dampness
of the atmosphere, as satisfactory as those on its temperature and pressure.

Such researches as these have not been made in
vain ; yet the knowledge of atmospheric phenomena
must remain in imperfection, until the relations to
each other, of heat, electricity, pressure, &c. the
principles on which these phenomena are supposed
to depend, be ascertained, and the laws by which
they are individually governed, be fully discovered.
But when we consider the difficulty of investigating
the characters and properties of principles so obscure, and fluids so subtle as air, aqueous vapour,
electricity, light, heat, &c. there is reason to believe
that their various combinations and effects on each
other, will never be wholly elucidated.

In the economy of Nature, we find that varying
and fluctuating phenomena are produced by opposing or counteracting forces or principles ; and that

whenever one or more of these forces, by any dis-
turbing cause, gains an extraordinary advantage
over the counteracting principle, the latter, in its
turn, by a kind of oscillation produced by the prevailing tendency to equilibrium, recovers nearly an
equal advantage over the other ; and hence, whenever any extraordinary disarrangement takes place,
it is seldom evidenced by the appearance only of a
single great oscillation, or wave, as it were, which
immediately subsides; but it is usually followed by
other lesser fluctuations, until the equilibrium of
the repelling forces be in some measure restored.
Though, in some phenomena, this equilibrium never exactly takes place, yet the tendency to it is
fully evidenced by the re-action which may generally be observed. This doctrine is applicable to the
phenomena of waves, tides, winds, pressure and
temperature of the atmosphere, as well as numerous
other inequalities discoverable in the operations of
Nature.

The temperature of the atmosphere, in any particular region, is one of those phenomena, which, however
they may fluctuate, or whatever may be their daily,
monthly, or yearly variations, and however unequal
and capricious these variations may appear to be,
will, on the average of numerous corresponding periods, be found to be dependent upon some certain
laws, tending to produce equilibrium ; so that the
general results are remarkably uniform. This is a
fact now generally received ;—a fact which becomes

the more interesting and striking, the more it is investigated.

When we experience particularly cold winters, or particularly hot summers, we might suppose that the mean temperature of the years in which the former occur, would be greatly below, and that of the years in which the hot summers occur, would be greatly above the general standard. But this will seldom be found to be the case *. For here the causes, whatever they may be, which tend to produce the equilibrium, exert their influence, and compensate for the disarrangement, by an extraordinary supply or abstraction of heat, whereby the general mean is still preserved nearly uniform. Hence in temperate climates of the northern hemisphere, the mean temperature of any one year, derived from the mean of the daily extremes of heat and cold, or from any particular number of daily observations, continued

---

* When the frost was so severe in London, that the Thames was passable on the ice, in 1788, the mean temperature of the year was 50°.6, being within a small fraction of a degree of the standard; and in 1796, when the greatest cold ever observed in London occurred, the mean temperature of the year was 50°.1, which is likewise within a small fraction of a degree of the standard temperature. In the severe winter of 1813,–14, when the Thames, Tyne, and other large rivers in England were completely frozen over, the mean temperature of the two years was 49°, being a little more than a degree below the standard. And in the year 1808, when the summer was so hot that the temperature in London was as high as 93°.5, the mean heat of the year was 50°.5, which is about that of the standard.

through the course of twelve successive months, seldom differs from the general mean temperature, as
derived from the observations of a great number of
years, more than two or three degrees *.

The mean temperature of any single month, cannot be supposed to be equally uniform ; since the
uncommon prevalence of a south wind in winter, or
a north wind in summer, may cause the particular
month in which such winds occur, to be considerably
colder or warmer than the standard. This, however,
does not differ so widely from the general mean of
that month as might be expected †.

---

* From the meteorological register kept at the apartments
of the Royal Society, we find, that in twenty years, included
between 1795 and 1814, the mean annual temperature was
50°. 4. Now, in eight of these years, the mean temperature
was within 0°. 5, or half a degree of the general mean ; in thirteen years, within one degree ; in sixteen years, within two degrees ; and, in no instance, differed more than two and a half
degrees from the general mean. Hence in similar climates,
by one year's thermometric observations, we derive the mean
temperature thereof, within $2\frac{1}{2}°$, by a probability of at least
twenty to one : that is, it is more than twenty to one, in the
way of chance, but the annual mean temperature ascertained,
is within $2\frac{1}{2}°$ of the general mean, or standard temperature ;
four to one that it is within 2° ; three to two that it is within
1° ; and two to three, that it is within half a degree.

† The mean temperature in London, of the months of March,
April, May, June, July, and August, never, in one instance, differed so much from the general mean temperature of the relative month, as 5° ; and February, October, and November, never more than 6° ; but the greatest difference in December,
amounted to 8°.4 ; and in January, to 11°.4.—(Phil. Trans.
1796 to 1815.)

My object in bringing forward these facts, is, to show what degree of reliance may be placed upon a limited number of observations upon the temperature of the atmosphere of any country ; and the consequent degree of approximation to the truth, which may be reasonably inferred. As the mean annual temperature of a country is probably given, by one year's observations only, to within two or three degrees of the truth, the mean of a period of eight or ten years, will probably come within one degree of the truth.   Therefore, whenever we have a series of accurate observations conducted through such a period, we may, I think, consider the temperature of that place determined to the fraction of a degree.

Thus, by a series of thermometrical observations, continued through the space of a few years, the mean temperature of different parts of the earth, particularly of most of the capital cities, and other remarkable places in Europe, has been ascertained to the satisfaction of the philosopher.   From the comparison of the results of observations made in different countries, with each other, tracing the changes of temperature which appear, with certain changes of latitude or situation, some ingenious and philosophical men have endeavoured, by principles of analogy and induction, to determine the mean temperature of every parallel of latitude from the Equator to the North Pole.   For facilitating this purpose, Professor Mayer contrived a simple formula *, which, through the extent of the Atlantic Ocean, determined a temperature that was found to correspond with most of the observations which had been made, to a surprising nearness. For the estimation of the temperature of regions peculiarly situated as to elevation, or remoteness from the sea, either of which circumstances was found to diminish the mean heat, different philosophers have presented appropriate formulæ. From Mayer's formula, and from all the tables of the mean temperature of the polar regions, which I have met with, the temperature of the North Pole comes out about 31° or 32°, and that of latitude 78°, about 33° or 34° †. This has been considered as a near approximation; and, so long as observations were wanting, served for purposes of investigation, to complete the scale of the temperature of the globe. But though an approximation, it will be found to be very wide

---

* The following is Mayer's formula as given by Professor PLAYFAIR, in his " Outlines of Natural Philosophy," vol. i. p. 296, 3d edit. :

" Let t be the mean temperature of any parallel of which the latitude is L, M the mean temperature of the parallel of 45°, and M + E the mean temperature of the equator, then is $t = M + E \cos 2 L$. In this formula, M $=$ 58°, and E $=$ 27°. When 2 L $>$ 90, cos 2 L is negative."

† Hutton's Philosoph. and Mathem. Dictionary, edit. 1815, Art. Temperature, (by Mayer's formula from Kirwan);—

Temperature of the Pole,	31°	of lat. 78°	33°.2
According to Leslie, Elem. of			
Geometry, p. 496,	32°	—— 78°	34°.2

of the truth ; for when we reach the regions of perpetual ice, a remarkable anomaly is discovered, the
mean temperature falling below the estimation by
the formula, at once 17°! As this fact is of much
importance in generalizing our knowledge of the
temperature of the globe, I have subjoined to this volume a series of observations on the temperature, &c.
of the polar regions, conducted with care during
twelve successive voyages to the Greenland sea *,
from whence I am enabled to deduce the following
conclusions as to the probable temperature of the
polar regions, in different latitudes, during every
month of the year.

The mean temperature of the months of April,
May, June and July, are satisfactorily derived, directly from the means of the latitudes and of the
observations of temperature contained in the Appendix ;—but the mean temperature of the whole year,
and of the winter months, wherein no observations
in such high latitudes have yet been made, can only
be ascertained from analogy. From the examination
of numerous thermometrical registers, particularly
one consisting of 54,750 observations made in a succession of fifty years, at Stockholm, the valuable results of which are published in the Annals of Philosophy, (vol. i. p. 113.) it would seem, that the month of
April (Old Style) affords a temperature which, in
northern latitudes, is the mean of the year; or that
a month, of which the middle is called the 27th–28th

---

* Appendix, No. I.

of April (New Style,) furnishes a mean temperature, which does not materially differ from that of
the whole year* ;—that a month, the middle of
which falls on the 24th of July is the warmest of
the year; or that in the average of centuries, the
24th of July is probably the warmest day in the
whole year ;—that the 22d-23d of January is the
coldest of the whole year ;—that the 19th-20th of
October, and the 27th-28th of April, are each, on
a long average, of the same mean temperature as
that of the year ;—that the difference between the
mean temperature of the year and that of January,
is nearly the same, though probably not quite so
great, as the difference between the mean of the
year and that of July † ;—and that in high northern
latitudes, the progressive increase of temperature
from January to July, and the decrease from July

z 2

* From the fifty years observations at Stockholm,wherein the
mean temperature of every five days throughout the year is given,
the mean of the penthemeron, which bears the mean temperature of the year, is the 27th-28th of April, which is later by one
day only, than the middle-day of April (O. S.) And the mean
of thirty days, or fifteen preceding and fifteen following the
27th-28th of April, differs from the mean of the penthemeron
by only a small fraction of a degree; consequently, a month,
of which the 27th-28th of April is the middle, may be considered as affording a temperature corresponding with that of
the year.   The 19th of October, taken as a mean of five days,
likewise affords the mean temperature of the year.—(See Annals of Phil. vol. i. p. 114, & 266.)

† The difference between the mean temperature of the year
and that of January, in Stockholm, is one-fourteenth part less

to December, follow a similar ratio in almost every maritime situation.

Considering, then, the mean temperature of the year to be indicated by that of the 27th–28th of April, I have collated 656 observations made on 242 days, in nine different years, extending equally before and after the 27th of April, from which the mean temperature of the year in latitude 76° 45′, near the meridian of London, appears to be 18°.86. Before proceeding to the investigation of the temperature of the winter months, it will be convenient to reduce all the monthly temperatures derived from my observations to one parallel, say, to the latitude of 78° N. The observations of May, June and July, being generally made near the ice, and consequently pretty uniformly affected by its influence, are reduced to one parallel, by applying, as a correction, the difference in the temperature of the mean latitude observed and that of 78°, as determined by Mayer's formula, which, in these three instances, does not, in any one case, amount to the third of a degree; but the correction of the mean temperature of the year as well as that of April, is, I acknowledge, more arbitrary. The mean latitude of the observations for April is 75° 59′ or 2° 1′ from the parallel preferred. Considering the circumstances as similar to those above,

---

than the difference between the mean of the year, and that of July ; and in London, (from the mean of twenty years observations,) one fifty-third part less.—Append. No. II. Tables E and F.

the correction here would only have been about 0°.8 ; but as a great decrease of temperature takes place on removing from the coast to the interior of a country, much more so must be the case in passing deeper into the body of the polar ice, the frigorific effect of which on the general temperature is so striking.   Now, the observations of May, June and July, were generally made in or very near the body of ice, and mostly in similar situations ; but many of the observations of April were made at a consider-able distance from the ice, and consequently much less under its influence.   I conceive, therefore, that 3° of temperature for these 2° of latitude, as a cor-rection, is not too considerable ; and that this cor-rection is probably very nearly what it ought to be, will more fully appear, when we observe the striking conformity between this, together with all the other mean temperatures from observation, and those deriv-ed from the calculations which follow, founded upon analogy.   By the application of this correction, the temperature of April, latitude 78°, becomes 14°.23, and the mean of the year in the same proportion exactly 17° *.

The general results of all the observations on the temperature of the Greenland sea, with the cor-

* As 2° 1' (the difference of latitude between the April ob-servations and 78°), is to 3° (the correction of temperature), so is 1° 15' (the difference between the mean latitude of the ob-servations for determining the mean temperature of the year, and latitude 78°), to 1°.86 (the correction of temperature for the mean of the year.)

rections, to reduce them to one parallel, and the comparison of the reduced mean temperatures with those derived by calculation from a formula which follows *, are contained in the following Table.

Month or Period.	Mean Latitude.	Extremes of Longitude.	THERMOMETER.			Mean Temp. by Obs. reduced to lat. of 78° N.	Mean Temp. by Calc. from formu. App.G.	Differ. betw. Mean Temp. by Cal. & Obs.
			N° of Observ.	Mean Temp.	Table in App. N° II.			
April,	75.59	————	370	17°.23	C	14°.23	13°.74	0°.49
May,	77.17	15.13 E, 11.20 W.	956	22.81	A	22.52	23.28	0.76
June,	78.15	14.40 E, 10.37 W.	831	31.30	A	31.37	31.72	0.35
July,	77.18	————	548	37.28	D	37.00	——	——
Mean of year,	76.45	————	656	18.86	B	17.00	——	——

Having now discovered by observation, chiefly, the mean temperature of the months of April, May, June and July, and the probable mean temperature of the year, in the icy regions adjoining Spitzbergen, I conceive it not difficult to calculate, on very reasonable data, the temperature of the remaining months, in which no observations have yet been made. I shall still proceed on the basis of the Stockholm register, as being one of the most complete and minute registers that I have yet met with, besides having the advantage of referring to a higher latitude † than any British register.

---

* Appendix, No. II. Table G.

† Latitude 59° 20′ 31 .

The difference between the mean temperature of the year and that of July, is $21\frac{1}{2}°$ in Stockholm, and $20°$ near Spitzbergen. Finding not only that the difference of temperature between the mean of the year and July, near Spitzbergen, but that the progressive increase of temperature from April to July, also bore a strong analogy to the relative circumstances at Stockholm, I formed a scheme of decimals connected with a simple formula, by which the same proportion of change which has been observed to take place every month at Stockholm, may be very readily applied to any other country*, whence, situation and circumstances being nearly similar, the temperature of unobserved months may be calculated. The data requisite, are the temperatures of January and July, or the mean of the year and July. My observations on the temperature of the atmosphere in the Greenland sea, afford the latter data, from which, by the formula in the Appendix, I have calculated the last column but one in the foregoing table, which agrees so nearly with the results by observation, as to afford a strong presumption of the fairness of the inferences. By the same rule, the temperature of January, latitude $78°$, comes out $-1°$, that of February $0°.7$, March $6°.1$, August $34°.9$, September $27°.8$, October $18°.5$, November $9°.8$, and December $3°.1$.

It might be urged against the truth of these inferences and calculations, that southerly winds may

---

* See Appendix, No. II. Tables F and G.

prevail more in winter than in those months wherein the temperature has been tried by observation,
and consequently, that the weather would be warmer
than it is here made out. I cannot find, however,
any reason for supposing that this is the case, but
rather the contrary, as will more particularly appear
from the observations, in a following section, on the
winds.

Before I quit this speculative subject, I am naturally led to the consideration of the probable temperature of the North Pole. Following the example of every generalizing meteorologist, I may,
with some propriety, extend my speculations to the
verge of the Earth, provided I can proceed on data
not merely arbitrary or fanciful, but founded on observation and analogy.

It has been observed, that Professor Mayer's
theorem for ascertaining the temperature of every
latitude, becomes exceedingly wide of the truth,
when we approach the regions of perpetual ice, notwithstanding in most other situations on the sea,
or bordering thereon, it holds sufficiently near. The
anomaly is evidently the frigorific effect of the ice.
Admitting, then, that Mayer's formula, which has
been received with very slight limitations, by almost
every meteorologist, is founded on philosophical
principles and correct observation, and consequently that it would have applied with accuracy throughout the northern hemisphere, provided there had

been no particular cause to affect it,—then the mean temperature of latitude 76° 45′ near the western coast of Spitzbergen, would have been 33· 8 instead of 18°.8, as shown by my observations, and the mean temperature of the Pole would have been about 31°.*. Now, the difference between the mean temperature of latitude 76° 45′ by observation and calculation, which is here 15°, may be considered as the frigorific effect of the ice, because there is no other known cause why there should be any difference at all. But if the ice be the sole cause of the anomaly, it must chiefly produce its effect through the medium of those winds which brush over its surface †, whilst the mild winds from the south and east, will generally bring a temperature uninfluenced by it, and consequently tending to elevate the mean temperature above what it would be in a situation in the ice, so remote from the sea, that the milder winds could never reach it unchanged. Now, at the Pole, no wind whatever could convey the mild influence of a temperate climate, because, from

* I here follow KIRWAN, who, from Mayer's formula, calculates the temperature of latitude 77° at 33.7, and of 76° at 34.1 ; hence 76° 45′ or 76 ¾° = 33.8. Professor LESLIE, in the second edition of his Geometry, p. 496. calculates the temperature of 76° 45′ at 34°.7, assuming that of the North Pole at 32°.

† The effect of what has been called Radiation, being inconsiderable, under a dense atmosphere, subject to almost daily obscurities by snow or fog, is not here brought into consideration.

2

whatever direction it should blow, it must be cooled
down by brushing over an extensive surface of ice ;
consequently the full frigorific effect of the ice must
be greater at the Pole, than in places situated at or
near the borders of the ice. For if Mayer's formula
be well founded, and if the difference between the
observed temperature of the polar seas and that by
estimation on this formula, be entirely the frigorific
effect of the ice ;—then the frigorific effect of the
ice in the parallels which have been observed near
the sea, will be to the same at the Pole, as the
amount of frigid winds (or winds blowing over an
extensive surface of ice,) during any period in those
places whose temperatures have been observed, is to
the amount of frigid winds during the same period
at the Pole. Let us apply this proposition for examining into the frigorific effect of the ice at the Pole.

From the meteorological results, contained in the
Appendix, (No. II. Table B.), it appears, that during nine years observations made in the months of
April and May, or such parts thereof as are used in
the estimation of the mean temperature, as stated
above, the wind blew off the ice, or from the land
covered with snow and ice; that is, in the quarters
included between the S. W. b S. and N. E. points,
(north about) 147.4 days*; but in the remaining
quarters, included between N. E. and S. S. W. only
58.8 days; to the former of which, (147.4) if we

* See the next following Note.

add 25.6 days (out of 35.8) of variable winds and calms, being the proportion of frigid winds in 206.2 days, we find, that in the total period of 242 days, the temperature of the air was more or less influenced by the ice during 173 days of that period, whilst there were only 58.8 + 10.2 = 69 days, in which the winds blowing from the south and east (increased by their proportion of the variable winds and calms) could not be said to be cooled by the ice*. Hence, as 173 (the number of days in which the temperature was influenced by the ice,) is to 15°

---

* These numbers are derived from Table B in Appendix, No. II. in the manner following.

Frigid Winds, being cooled by passing over ice.	No. of days they prevailed in 9 yrs. in part of April and May.	Mild Winds, blowing out of the Sea.	No. of days they prevailed in 9 years, in part of April and May.
E N E to N E b N, (half)	17.0	S S W to S b E,	9.6
N N E to N b W	51.8	S S E to S E b E,	12.5
N N W to N W b W,	40.2	E S E to E b N,	19.7
W N W to W b S,	25.2	E N E to N E b N, (half)	17.0
W S W to S W b S,	13.2		—— 58.8
	—— 147.4		
Proportion of variable winds and calms, having their temperature reduced by the ice, - -	25.6*	Proportion of variable winds and calms *not* having their temperature reduced by the ice, - -	10.2
	173.0		69.0

* *Remark.*—As the frigid winds blew 147.4 days, whilst the milder winds blew only 58.8 days, the variable winds and calms may be considered as influenced by the frigid winds, more than the mild winds, or in the proportion of 147.4 to 58.8. Hence, as (147.4 + 58.8) = 206.2 is to 35.8, (the amount of variable winds and calms,) so is 147.4 to 25.6, the proportion of the variable winds and calms to be added to the frigid winds.

(the anomaly thereby occasioned in the mean temperature,) so is 242 the whole number of days in consideration, to 21°, the probable anomaly which might be expected, were the temperature always influenced by the ice, or the anomaly which may be supposed to occur at the Pole. Therefore, if from 31°, the calculated temperature of the Pole, we deduct 21•, we have 10° for the corrected mean temperature thereof.

This result will be farther corroborated, if we apply the same mode of investigation to another series of observations. In the former, the observations made in the Greenland Sea, in part of the months of April and May, or in the mean temperature month, have been the data for determining the frigorific effect of the ice on the temperature of the Pole; we shall now make use of the observations made in the month of *May*, during a series of twelve years, for the same purpose.

The amount of frigid winds, including the proportion of variable winds and calms, that occurred in the 78th parallel of latitude in the month of May, during a period of twelve years, comprising 372 days, was 257.2 days; and the mild winds which prevailed during the same period, amounted to 114.8 days. The mean temperature of May, latitude 78°, appears by observation to be 22°.5, but by calculations made by Kirwan, founded on Mayer's formula, it comes out 37°; so that the frigorific effect of the ice in the month of May, in this parallel, appears to be $14_o.5$. Hence, as 257.2, the number of days in which the temperature was influenced by the ice, is to $14_o.5$, the anomaly thereby occasioned in the temperature of May, so is 372, the whole number of days under consideration, to 21°, the probable anomaly which may be supposed to exist in the month of May at the Pole. Now, it is not a little pleasing, that the anomaly thus found, is precisely the same as that discovered by the former process.

As an objection to this conclusion, it might be urged, that the place where the meteorological observations were made, from whence all the deductions are derived, was not always at the margin of the solid ice, but, on the contrary, rarely so; consequently, that the northern winds would pass over a surface of water as well as one of ice, and that the full frigorific effect of the ice would be thereby diminished. The force of this argument must be allowed when singly considered; but when it is likewise remarked, that southerly winds as frequently passed over a small surface of drift-ice, as the northerly winds passed over water, the effects may perhaps be admitted to compensate each other; at least I have thus considered it, and leave the reader to determine with what degree of propriety.

Another objection to the conclusion might be suggested, on the possibility of there being a basin of water at the Pole, unencumbered with ice. But should this be the case, though I conceive we have no

good ground for imagining such a thing, I presume
the objection would not bear upon the conclusion;
because, though a basin of water might occur, it
must be entirely surrounded with ice, whereby
every general wind which could blow, must pass
over such an extent of ice, that nearly the full frigorific effect might be supposed to be produced, of
which its influence was capable.

I might, in connection with this subject, enter into an investigation of the probable range of temperature in the winter months, from a similar mode
of reasoning as has been hitherto adopted; but
the subject being so entirely speculative, I shall
content myself with mentioning the range of temperature in those months, in which my observations
have been conducted. The mean annual range of
temperature in the polar seas, observed in April during seven years, was 26º, the greatest range 41°;
the mean highest temperature 30º.6, and the mean
lowest 4º.6. The following table, however, will
show these matters more conveniently.

Month.	Nº of Years Observed.	Extremes of Latitude.	Mean Latitude.	Monthly range of Temperature.				Extremes of Temperature.			
				Mean Highest.	Mean Lowest.	Half sum of Highest & Lowest.	Mean Range.	Highest ever Observed.	Lowest ever Observed.	Greatest range.	Mean of Hig. & Lowest.
April	7	70° 0′, to 80°. 10′	76.°0′	30.6	4.6	17.6	26.0	37	— 4	41	16.5
May	12	70.50 to 80.5	77.17	34.6	10.2	22.4	24.4	40	+ 5	35	22.5
June	10	70.50 to 80.1	78.15	40.5	21.4	31.0	19.1	48	15	33	31.5
July	3	68.24 to 79.22	76.13	46.0	30.0	38.0	16.0	48	28	20	38.0

From this table we find, that as the temperature decreases, the range of the thermometer increases; hence it is probable, that in the winter months, the range is nearly, if not fully, double of what it is in summer.

That tendency to equalization, which has been observed to hold very generally in the varying appearances and effects of meteorological phenomena, derives a beautiful illustration from the investigation of the extremes of temperature and pressure of the atmosphere, as indicated by the range of the barometer and thermometer. From a great number of registers of temperature which I have had occasion to examine, I am enabled to suggest the following general inferences.

1st, That in a period of several years, the mean of the highest and lowest temperature observed in the course of each year, agrees with the mean temperature of the place, generally to the fraction of a degree.

Thus, from the twenty years register kept at the Royal Society's apartments, between 1795 and 1814, the sum of the highest temperature observed each year is 1628°, and of the lowest 372° 5, the amount of which, 2000.5, divided by 40, the number of observations, gives 50.01 for the mean of the whole, which differs only 0.39 of a degree from the mean temperature,

derived at least from 14,600 observations, supposing only two observations to have been made
each day.

2d, That in a period of years, the mean of the
extremes of temperature observed in any one month,
agrees with the mean temperature of that month,
generally, to the fraction of a degree.

In Table A of meteorological results, No. II. of
the Appendix, the sum of the highest temperatures observed in the month of *May* for
twelve years is 415°, and of the lowest 122°;
the amount, 537, divided by 24, the number
of observations, gives a mean of 22.38, differing from the mean temperature of this month,
as derived from 956 observations, only 0.43 of
a degree. From the same Table, it appears,
that the sum of the highest temperatures observed each year for ten years in *June*, is 405,
and of the lowest 214, the amount of which,
619, divided by 20, the number of observations, gives 30.95 for the mean, differing only
0.35 of a degree from the mean temperature
as derived from 831 observations. In the
same way the mean of the extremes of temperature in *April* is 17.6, differing from that
derived from the mean of 370 observations
only $1\frac{1}{2}$ degrees; and of *July*, 37.86, differing from the mean of the month, by 548
observations, only 0.89 of a degree.

3d, That the mean of the highest and lowest temperature, occurring in every month during one year, corresponds with the mean temperature of that year, generally to within two or three degrees; and in a series of years to the fraction of a degree.

At Okak, on the coast of Labrador the mean temperature of the year 1779–80, from 1460 observations, was 31°.0, the mean of the highest and lowest observations, $\left[\frac{641 + 135}{24}\right] = 32.3$, differing 1°.3 from the mean; and at the same place in 1777–8, the mean temperature was 24°.7, and that of the monthly extremes 27°.7, difference 3°.0. At Nain, on the same coast, the mean temperature in 1779–80 was 30°.3; the mean of the monthly extremes, $\left[\frac{614 + 194}{24}\right] = 30°.8$, difference 0°.5; and at the same place in 1777–8, the mean temperature was 24°.6, and the mean of the extremes 27°.9, difference 3°.3.

4th, That the mean of the greatest heat and greatest cold, which occur in any fixed place, in temperate climates, in any particular year or period of years, affords a temperature which, in many instances, corresponds very nearly, with the mean temperature of that period.

In London, from the Royal Society's register, the greatest cold which was observed in the 20 years included between 1795 and 1814, was 4°, the greatest heat 93°.5 ; the mean is 48°.75 or 1°.65 less than the mean temperature of the same period.   Even the mean of the extremes of temperature observed in any one year, does not differ so considerably from the mean of the year as might be imagined.   One year, indeed, in London, the mean of the yearly extremes was 8°.1 below that of the mean temperature ; but in the 20 years, the mean of the extremes corresponded with that of the year, 4 times to within a degree, 10 times to within 2°, 12 times to within 3°, 15 times to within 4°, 17 times to within 5°, and 19 times to within 6°.   Hence it is as great a probability that the mean of the yearly extremes of temperature is within 2° of the mean temperature of the same year, as that it differs more.

SECT. III.

Remarks on the Pressure of the Atmosphere, with Observations on the Use of the Barometer in predicting the Weather.

IN the winter and spring months, the pressure of the atmosphere, in polar latitudes, as well as its temperature, is liable to sudden and very considerable variations.   But as my observations have been

2

confined to the spring and summer seasons, I cannot give a precise account of the magnitude of
those changes. I shall, however, specify a few of
the most remarkable that have occurred within my
own observation.

Year.	Month, &c.	Latitude.	Changes of the Barometer.	Interval.
			Inches.	Hours.
1808,	April 4.	66°.59′	fell, 0.92	24
———	May 12.	77.40	fell, 0.72	24
1809,	——— 6.	73.49	fell, 0.62	24
1812,	——— 2.	75.23	fell, 0.77	12
———	——— 3.	75.35	fell, 0.92	24
1813,	April 7.	66.30	rose, 0.50	12
———	——— 13.	73.11	fell, 1.02	12
———	——— 23.	80.07	fell, 0.82	24
———	——— 24	80.10	rose, 0.86	24
1814,	——— 13.	71. 0	fell, 1.00	24
1815,	——— 12.	77.21	rose, 0.60	14
———	——— 27.	78.20	fell, 0.81	24
———	——— 28.	78.10	rose, 0.67	12
———	——— 29.	78. 0	rose, 0.80	20
1816,	——— 14.	72.54	fell, 0.53	16
1817,	——— 13.	68. 3	fell, 0.73	24
———	——— 18.	71.56	fell, 1.12	21
———	——— 20.	73.25	rose, 1.01	35

The greatest height of the mercury I ever observed during twelve Greenland voyages, was 30.57,
which occurred on the 2d of May 1815; and the
greatest depression 28.03, when near the ice in latitude 66° 50′, on the 5th of April 1808. Hence

A a 2

the greatest range of the barometer between the 1st of April and the close of July, observed within the Arctic circle during the twelve years, was 2.54 inches. It may be observed, however, that I have never seen the mercury lower than 28.75 to the northward of the 71st degree of latitude; so that the above range in the months of April to July, must be very uncommon. The greatest range of the barometer observed in the month of April during seven years, was from 28.03 to 30.48, or 2.45 inches; the greatest range in May during 12 years, was from 29.23 to 30.57, or 1.34 inches; the greatest range in June during 10 years, was from 29.25 to 30.37, or 1.12 inches; and the greatest range observed in July during six years, was from 29.30 to 30.30, or 1 inch. The average range in April is about 1.30 inches; in May 0.94, in June 0.79, and in July 0.72.

The changes in the pressure of the atmosphere, in the spring of the year, as indicated by the barometer, are not only great and rapid, but frequently portentous. I never knew the barometer mark a pressure of less than 29 inches, without its being followed or accompanied by a gale of wind, either at the place of observation, or in the immediate neighbourhood of it; and in the course of my observations of the oscillations of the mercury during sixteen successive voyages, not above five or six storms have, I think, occurred, which were not pre-

dicted by the barometer. The value of this instrument, therefore, in a country where there is frequently not an interval of five minutes between the
most perfect calm and the most impetuous storm,
is almost incalculable. The faithfulness of its indications are certainly not sufficiently appreciated,
else it would be more generally used. At one period, I amused myself by registering my predictions,
from the changes observed in the barometer ; and on
reviewing those memoranda, I find, th t of 18 predictions of atmospheric changes in the year 1812,
whereof several were remarkable, 16 or 17 proved
correct.

During the whole period in which I have been in
the habit of observing the barometer, I have never
been able to detect any small periodical changes indicative of atmospheric tides. Two remarks, however, I may offer, as being pretty general : That the
greatest fall of the mercury is frequently preceded or
followed by the greatest rise : And that the same
tendency to equality takes place in the pressure, as
has been traced in regard of the temperature of the
atmosphere ; the mean of the highest and lowest
observations in a long series corresponding to a great
minuteness with the mean pressure. The former
observation will be found frequently to hold, by
examination of the series of meterological tables
in the Appendix ; and the latter, most particularly,
if we refer to the first table of meteorological re-

sults *. In the month of May, during 12 years, the mean maximum pressure, being the mean of the highest observation each year, is 30.36, the mean minimum pressure 29.43, and the mean of the two 29.89, corresponding with the mean pressure to within two hundredth parts of an inch. And from the observations during ten years in June, a similar result is obtained: Mean maximum 30.25, mean minimum 29.47, mean of the two 29.86, and mean pressure 29.869; difference only 0.009. But the comparison of the greatest with the least pressure that occurred during the series of years, is scarcely less striking: Highest observation in June 30.37, lowest 29.25, and mean 29.81; differing from the mean pressure 0.059. And highest observation in May 30.57, lowest 29.23, mean 29.90; differing from the mean pressure, by above 1000 observations, only 0.009.

The following are the relations which, in polar latitudes, I have been enabled to trace between the barometer and the weather.

1. A hard westerly gale with snow, occasions the greatest depression of the mercury, and a light easterly wind with dry weather, the greatest elevation.

2. The rising of the mercury foretels the subsidence of wind or rain, a change of wind, or fine

---

* Appendix, No. II. Table A.

weather; and its falling, rain, snow, or a change or increase of wind.

3. The mercury rising unusually high, and then becoming stationary, indicates, in the months of April and May, a continuance of fine weather; but in June or July, foggy weather.

4. If, in the month of April, the mercury fall with some rapidity, an inch or more, a storm will most certainly succeed, however contrary appearances may be, which will probably be the more severe in proportion as it approximates the east, and will frequently continue with unabated violence for fifty or sixty hours.

5. The rising of the mercury usually precedes the cessation of a storm; but does not invariably determine the period of its continuance, as storms frequently blow for a day or two after the first rise of the mercury.

6. Sudden and repeated fluctuations in the barometer are indicative of unsettled weather; but the rapid fall of the mercury is no indication of a short gale, though in other regions the reverse is said to be the case; for before storms that continue two or three days, the barometer frequently falls an inch within twenty-four hours, and, indeed, in a gale as long and as heavy as I almost ever witnessed, the fall of the mercury was above an inch in twelve hours.

7. Before very heavy storms, when the barometer falls uncommonly low, the mercury seems to get below its natural level, and often rises two or three tenths of an inch as soon as the predicted storm commences: hence this first rise of the mercury is no indication whatever of an abatement of the wind.

8. On account of the different states of the barometer in west and east winds, the usual level of the mercury with a moderate wind at west, not being much higher than with a gale at east, a change of wind from one of these quarters to the opposite, may be accompanied with the greatest alteration in the strength of the wind, without producing any effect on the barometer. Thus a storm at east veering to west, may subside, or a gentle breeze at west veering to east, may increase to a storm, without any alteration taking place in the mercury of the barometer. But in these cases, it has already been observed, that the change which takes place in the temperature, often compensates for the imperfect action of the barometer.

SECT. IV.

Appearance, Colour, Transparency, Density, de-
gree of Dryness, and state as to Electricity, of
the Atmosphere.

THE appearance of the Greenland atmosphere,
corresponds in some degree with the winter sky of
Britain; the colour of the former is, however, of a
deeper azure; and its transparency, when clear, and
free from icy crystals, perhaps more perfect.

Far within the borders of compact ice, the atmosphere, in summer, is often cloudless, and the weather serenely pleasant, though cold. But in the
usual fishing-stations, and on the exterior of the ice
in general, a clear sky is not frequent; nevertheless, when it does occur, its transparency is peculiarly beautiful. The sun sometimes sweeps two or
three times round the Pole, without being for a moment obscured by a cloud. Objects the most remote, may be seen perfectly distinct and clear. A
ship's top-gallant-mast, at the distance of five or six
leagues, may be discerned when just appearing
above the horizon, with a common perspective glass ;
and the summits of some mountains are visible at
the distance of sixty to a hundred miles. This
perfect clearness, occurs most frequently before easterly winds. In general, however, especially in very

cold weather, objects on the horizon, when viewed
with a high magnifier, appear affected with a perpetual tremor; whence, the contemplation of distant objects is accomplished as perfectly with a good
pocket glass, as with the best telescope.   This tremulous motion, is evidently produced by the quantity of delicate icy crystals, which, in very low temperatures, are almost always seen floating in the
air.

The general obscurity of the atmosphere, arising
from clouds or fogs, is such, that the sun is frequently invisible during several successive days. At such
times, when the sun is near the northern tropic,
there is scarcely any sensible variation in the quantity of light, from noon to midnight. Hence, when
the sailors have been long abroad in the boats, or so
fully engaged as to be unable to mark the progress
of time, the inquiry, Whether it be day or night,
is not unfrequent.

There is nothing remarkable in the appearance of
the sun at midnight, excepting, that when its altitude is very small, it may be viewed with the naked
eye, without producing any painful sensation ; but
when it is more than four or five degrees above the
horizon, it generally appears as effulgent as with the
same elevation in Britain.   The force of the sun's
rays is sometimes remarkable.   Where they fall upon the snow-clad surface of the ice or land, they are,
in a great measure, reflected, without producing any

material elevation of temperature ; but when they impinge on the black exterior of a ship, the pitch on one side occasionally becomes fluid, while ice is rapidly generated on the other ; or while a thermometer, placed against the black paint-work on which the sun shines, indicates a temperature of 80 or 90 degrees, or even more, on the opposite side of the ship a cold of 20 degrees is sometimes found to prevail.

This remarkable force of the sun's rays, is accompanied with a corresponding intensity of light. A person placed in the centre of a field or other compact body of ice, under a cloudless atmosphere and elevated sun, experiences such an extraordinary intensity of light, that, if it be encountered for any length of time, is not only productive of a most painful sensation in the eyes, but sometimes of temporary, or even, as I have heard, of permanent blindness. Under such circumstances, the use of green glasses affords a most agreeable relief. Some of the Indians in North America defend their eyes by the use of a kind of wooden spectacles, having, instead of glasses, a narrow perpendicular slit, opposite to each eye. This simple contrivance, which intercepts, perhaps, nine-tenths of the light that would reach a naked eye, prevents any painful consequences from the most intense reflection of light that ever occurs.

The constant light of the sun during the summer, prevents the stars from being seen; and this, together with the frequency of cloudy or foggy weather, rarely admits a sight of the moon. Hence the longitude, which is of such essential importance in navigation, can seldom be determined by lunar observations. Chronometers, therefore, though but little used by the whale-fishers, become of enhanced value: and even a good watch, well regulated, will, where the degrees of longitude are so very contracted, point out the meridional situation of the ship for short intervals, with a very tolerable degree of accuracy.

Though the air, in the Arctic Seas, is generally in a state of dampness, approaching to complete saturation, yet, the absolute quantity of moisture cannot, when the cold is excessive, be very considerable. It is remarked by Ellis, in his voyage to Hudson's Bay, that metals are less apt to rust here than in any other climate. This observation, if we consider the relative humidity of the atmosphere, as indicated by a hygrometer, is certainly correct. Perhaps the lowness of the temperature, which, I should think, is not favourable to oxidization, and the small absolute quantity of moisture in the air, may be the occasion of this circumstance. The relative degree of dryness of the atmosphere near Spitzbergen, was ascertained by Professor Leslie's hygrometer, in the summer of the year 1817. The greatest dryness

that was observed, amounting to 27°, occurred on
the 5th of May, when the temperature was 27°.
But the average state of the hygrometer was not, I
believe, more than 5° or 6° of dryness in May, perhaps 7° or 8° in the beginning of June and end of
July; and when the foggy season prevailed, from
the 25th June to the 14th July, the greatest dryness was only 5°, and the average probably not
above 2 or 3 degrees. But though the air in the
polar regions be so generally damp, yet it is probable, that there is no habitable situation in the known
world, in which such a degree of actual dryness prevails, as in a house, or in the cabin of a ship, well
heated, when the external air is intensely cold. In
calm weather, I have frequently had my cabin heated up to 60°, when the external air was as cold as
10 or 15°. In such cases, the evaporation from
the bulb of a common thermometer, coated with
filtering paper wetted with water, has occasioned a
reduction of temperature in the instrument, of 10° to
15°; and Leslie's hygrometer has marked an extent of
dryness exceeding 150 degrees. When the external
air was at the temperature of 26°, and the cabin 50°,
'the hygrometer marked 85°; and when the temperature in the open air was 30°, and in the cabin 64°,
the hygrometer indicated 7° of dryness in the former, and 102° + in the latter. Now, Professor Leslie observes, that when the hygrometer indicates 50
or 60 degrees, we account it very dry, and from 70

3

degrees upwards, intensely dry.   In consequence of
the uncommon dryness of the cabin of a ship in cold
weather, the wainscotting sometimes shrinks as
much as half an inch in a pannel of about fifteen
inches broad, being equal to one-thirtieth of its
breadth ; but on returning to Britain, the same pannel expands again almost to its original dimensions.

Few observations, comparatively, seem to have
been made on the Electricity of the atmosphere, especially in high latitudes.   Perhaps some trials that
I made in the spring of 1818, on this subject, were
the first that have been attempted within the Arctic
circle.   On my passage towards Spitzbergen, when
in latitude 68°, I erected an insulated conductor,
eight feet above the main top-gallant-mast head,
connected by a copper wire, with a copper ball attached by a silk string to the deck.   The conductor consisted of a slender tapering tube of tinned iron,
terminated by a pointed brass wire. It was fixed in
an iron socket, supported by a large cylindrical piece
of glass, which glass, by means of another iron socket, was secured to the top of a long pole, elevated several feet above the mast head.   A tin cone
encompassed the bottom of the conductor, the mouth
of which being downward, defended the rod of glass
from getting wet, so as to injure its insulating property.   The conducting wire being kept carefully
clear of the rigging of the ship, was expected to ex-

hibit in the ball where it terminated, any difference between the state of the electricity of the ship or sea, and that of the atmosphere. The test of electricity, was a Bennet's gold-leaf electrometer, brought into contact with the ball; but though trials were made for several successive days, from latitude 68° to 75°, during clear, cloudy, and showery weather, not the least excitation was ever observed. That the effect might be rendered more perceptible, the electrometer was well dried and warmed immediately before each experiment, without which, indeed, no excitation could be produced in it, either with glass or sealing-wax. The nights being light, the aurora borealis could not be seen; but on the evening of the 20th of May, an appearance was observed very much resembling the aurora borealis, yet no signs of electricity were observed in the electrometer applied to the conductor.

SECT. V.

Atmospheric Phenomena, dependent on Reflection and Refraction.

THE production of *ice-blinks*, by the reflection of the rays of light, has already been noticed, when speaking of the ice. As a proof of the benefit that might be derived from this phenomenon, I may here

observe, that on one occasion, my Father, in the
ship Resolution, accompanied by several other vessels, was surrounded by a vast quantity of drift-ice,
aggregated so closely, that the navigation became
extremely troublesome. Observing by the blink, a
field of ice surrounded with open water, at a great
distance northward, he immediately stood towards it,
though the wind was south *, the weather tempestuous, and the intervening ice apparently closely
packed. To the astonishment of the seamen of his
own, and the masters of some accompanying ships,
he, after some hours of arduous manœuvring, gained
the edge of the field. His crew immediately began
a successful fishery, while the people belonging the
ships they left, had sufficient employment in providing for their own safety.

There are several phenomena of the atmosphere
caused by refraction, which deserve to be noticed.
Under certain circumstances, all objects seen on the
horizon, seem to be lifted above it a distance of 2
to 4, or more minutes of altitude, or so far extended in height above their natural dimensions. Ice,
land, ships, boats, and other objects, when thus enlarged and elevated, are said to *loom*. The lower
parts of *looming* objects, are sometimes connected
with the sensible horizon, by an apparent fibrous or

---

* The fishermen have a great aversion to running northward among crowded ice with a southerly wind, as it can
rarely be accomplished without considerable hazard of getting
beset.

columnar extension of their parts, which columns are always perpendicular to the horizon : at other times, they appear to be quite lifted into the air, a void space being seen between them and the horizon. This phenomenon is observed most frequently on or before an easterly wind, and is generally considered as indicative of such.

When the glaciers, lying to the south of Bern and Neufchatel, " appear nearer, plainer, and larger than usual, the country man looks for rain to follow," which commonly occurs the next day. " And the Tartars at the mouth of the river Jenisei in Siberia, look upon a magnificent appearance of the islands, as the presage of a storm *."

A most extraordinary appearance of the Foreland or Charles's Island, Spitzbergen, occurred on the 16th of July 1814†. While sailing to the southward along the coast, with an easterly wind, I observed what appeared to be a mountain, in the form of a slender but elevated monument. I was surprised that I had never seen it before; but was more astonished when I saw, not far distant, a pro-

---

* GMELIN's journey, t. iii. p. 129., from CRANTZ' Greenland, i. 50.

† Latitude of the ship 77° 50′, longitude 9° E. Thermometer at noon 46°, 6 P. M. 42°, midnight 40°. A light breeze of wind at E. S. E. Barometer 29°.79. Thick fog in the morning.

digious and perfect arch, thrown across a valley of above a league in breadth. The neighbouring mountains disclosed the cause, by exhibiting an unnatural elevation, with the columnar structure of looming objects. Presently, the scene was changed; the mountains along the whole coast, assumed the most fantastic forms; the appearance of castles with lofty spires, towers and battlements, would, in a few minutes, be converted into a vast arch or romantic bridge. These varied and sometimes beautiful metamorphoses, naturally suggested the reality of fairy descriptions; for the air was perfectly transparent, the contrast of snow and rocks was quite distinct, even in the substance of the most uncommon phantasms, though examined with a powerful telescope, and every object seemed to possess every possible stability. I never before observed a phenomenon so varied or so amusing. The land was not alone affected by this peculiar refraction, since every object between the N. E. and S. E. points of the compass, was more or less deformed by it. A mass of ice on the horizon, appeared of the height of a cliff, and the prismatic structure of its front, suggested the idea of basaltic columns. It may be remarked, that these phenomena took place on a clear evening, after an uncommonly warm afternoon.

Another similar appearance of the coast of Spitzbergen, though not quite so interesting, occurred on

2

the 14th of June 1816. The weather was clear and mild, the barometer low, the wind easterly. The lower part of the coast in sight, lying in the 80th degree of latitude, had its usual appearance; but the upper part of the hills, over which was spread in some parts, a thin stratum of visible fog, was curiously distorted. The general appearance was that of variegated basaltic columns; but the tops of some mountains were extended into the air, in the form of monumental towers. An iceberg in one place, was elevated in an extraordinary degree, and assumed the character of a prodigious cliff of alabaster pillars.

Other peculiar effects of refraction I have observed, of which some instances shall be noticed. At 6 P. M. of the 13th of May 1814*, when the ship I commanded lay beset in the ice, the wind, which for some days had blown fresh from the N. W. veered to the S. E. and subsided. A dense appearance in the atmosphere, arose to the southward of us, and advanced with the wind towards the N. W. When it came to the S. W. of us, I first noticed that the horizon, under this apparent density, was considerably elevated; and that a separation of seven

---

* Latitude 78° 6′, longitude 4° 10′ E. Barometer 30.10. Thermometer at noon 14°, at 6 P. M. 10°, at midnight 7°, and two hours afterwards, 18°.

minutes extent of the altitude, showed the division
of the true and refracted horizons. This disunion
in the horizon, was very similar in appearance to
the natural horizon, when viewed through the horizon glass of a sextant, having a considerable index
error. Viewed from the mast-head, the refracted
horizon extended about 30° farther westward than
when seen from the deck. It had the appearance
of a line drawn nearly parallel to the true horizon,
distant from it 7 minutes, with an open space between. Two ships lying beset about fourteen miles
off, the hulls of which, before the density came on,
could not be wholly seen, seemed now from the mast
head, not to be above half the distance, as the horizon was visible considerably beyond them. The appearance of these ships was singular. Their hulls
were much enlarged and elongated, and their masts
very much shortened. They had precisely the pro-
spective appearance of ships in a heeling position.

Again, on the 16th of the same month, the ship I
commanded being similarly situated with regard to
the ice, the phenomenon was repeated, with some
alteration*   The refracted portion of the horizon
appeared again in the south-east quarter : it was at

---

* Latitude 77° 56′, longitude 3° 54′ E. ; barometer 30. 51 ;
thermometer at noon 19°, at 10 P. M. 10° ; wind N. E. by N.
to N. N. W., blowing a fresh breeze.

first direct and undivided ; but, in a short time, it separated in several places, and each distinct portion was inclined at a small angle towards the true horizon. The effect of refraction was six minutes of altitude. A particular haziness was evident to the east and north of the broken horizon.

On the 28th of April 1811, I had an opportunity of ascertaining the exact effect of a singular refraction, by the alteration produced in the distance of the visible horizon. A ship, the Henrietta of Whitby, bearing easterly from us, lay beset at such a distance, that her hull was not visible ; and when viewed from an elevation of ninety feet, with a good telescope, half her lower masts were intercepted by the ice on the horizon. Now, at the elevation from which this ship was seen, the horizon, under common circumstances, would be nine miles distant ; and from the knowledge of the dimensions of her masts, I estimated the portion of the hull and masts intercepted by the horizon, at about 22 feet ; consequently, her distance beyond the horizon must have been at least $4\frac{1}{2}$ miles, and her distance from us not less than $13\frac{1}{2}$.

The day had been almost cloudless, the sun powerful. At 11 P. M.*, I was informed by the

* Latitude 77° 4′ ; longitude 8° 50′ 52″ E. ; barometer 30.17 ; thermometer at noon 26 , at 11 P. M. 16° ; the wind had been easterly, but now blew a brisk breeze from the north.

officer of the watch, that the ship to the eastward of us, appeared to be forced by the ice upon her *beam ends,* or into an heeling posture. I immediately ascended the deck, and having cleaned the glasses of a good telescope, I hastened to the mast-head. I at once attributed the cause of the deception to unequal refraction. This ship, which, two hours before, was 4½ miles beyond the visible horizon, now appeared as far within it, and was in every respect deformed like the ships above mentioned. The ice between us and the Henrietta, was compact and motionless; in confirmation of which, a few hours afterwards, we found she had resumed her former appearance; that is, she had apparently returned to her situation beyond the horizon. Now, the distance of the Henrietta, 13¼ miles, as before determined, added to about 4 miles that the horizon was visible beyond her, gives 17½ miles for its distance, which is greater by 8½ miles, than we derive from estimation, on the principle of the earth's curvature, with an elevation of 90 feet.

The horizon on this occasion, between the east and north, though continuous, appeared curiously undu lated. There appeared a difference of nearly a quarter of a degree, between the elevation of the highest and lowest portions of the circumferential boundary.

I have occasionally observed other effects of atmospheric refraction, such as produce an inverted image of distant ships; an elevation of the bow or stern, and a peculiar distortion of the masts ; a division of a ship in the middle, and a lengthening of the hull, &c. ; but the preceding having been more attentively studied in connection with the state of the atmosphere, they are more satisfactory, and consequently more worthy of particular detail.

From the whole of these facts, the following remarks may be deduced.

1st, That the curious refractions of the atmosphere in the polar regions, as far as they have been observed, have usually occurred in the evening or night, after a clear day.

2d, That they are most frequent on the commencement or approach of easterly winds. And,

3d, That they are, probably, occasioned by the commixture, near the surface of the land or sea, of two streams of air of different temperatures, so as to occasion an irregular deposition of imperfectly condensed vapour, which, when passing the verge of the horizon, may produce the phenomenon observed*.

Those phenomena, considered as the effects of refraction, &c. which remain to be mentioned, are not

---

* Perhaps the refraction of the dense vapour incumbent on the surface of the Thames, which at high water brings into the view of a spectator on the opposite bank, objects that are invisible at low water, may, in some measure, illustrate, or serve to account for this phenomenon.

peculiar to the polar seas; they may, however, be briefly noticed.

Parhelia and *coronæ* are, perhaps, not so frequent in Greenland as in some parts of America. I do not recollect to have observed these phenomena more than thrice. The first occurred on one of my earliest voyages to the fishery, and passed off merely as a wonderful appearance, without inducing me to minute the particulars. I perfectly recollect, however, that there were two or three parhelia, and four or five coloured circles. The primary one encompassed the sun, the remainder had their centres in its circumference; and some of the intersections exhibited the splendour of the parhelion. Some of the circles almost equalled in their colours the brilliancy of the rainbow; a grand arch resembling which, was at the same time displayed, in the opposite quarter. The other two instances occurred on the passage. The one, when outward bound, April 14. 1807, latitude 64° or 65°, consisted of several parhelia, which, accompanied by coloured circles and arcs of circles, and succeeded by a lunar halo, together with the aurora borealis, proved the harbingers of a tremendous tempest. The last phenomenon of this kind which I saw, appeared on the passage homeward, in July 1811. It consisted of a large circle of luminous whiteness, passing through the centre of the sun, in a direction nearly parallel to the horizon, intersected in various places with coloured circles of smal-

2

ler dimensions.   At two of the intersections of the coloured with the white circle, were exhibited bril-liant parhelia of an irregular form.

Huygens accounts for these phenomena, on the supposition that the sun's rays are refracted by cy-lindrical hail.   It is, however, probable, that such a form of hail does not occur in nature, though snow or hail of a prismatic or spicular form is not uncommon in the polar regions.   These prisms or spiculæ are so slender, that they assume the appear-ance of white hair chopped into portions of one-twentieth to one-fourth of an inch in length.   They fall most frequently when the temperature is about the freezing point, and sometimes in great profu-sion.

Several appearances resembling the rainbow, pro-duced by the refraction and reflection of the sun's rays, in particles of congealed vapour, have been observed.   On the 5th of June 1817, in particular, a beautiful iris was produced in a snow-shower; and on the 1st of June in the same year, in latitude 78° 29 , a similar arch was impressed on a shower of a kind of frozen fog.   The colours, however, were not so brilliant as those of the rainbow, and the arch was much broader.   The chord of this arch at midday, measured 50°, and its versed sine or al-titude 9°.

The *rainbow* itself is an appearance so common, that there is no need of dwelling upon it.   The *fog-bow*, or rather *fog circle*, is, on the contrary, more rarely observed, and is consequently entitled to some of our attention. The intense fogs which prevail in the polar seas, at certain seasons, occasionally rest upon the surface of the water, and reach only to an inconsiderable height. At such times, though objects situated on the water can scarcely be discerned at the distance of 100 yards, yet the sun will be visible and effulgent. Under such circumstances, on the 19th of July 1813, being at the top-mast-head, I observed a beautiful circle of about 30° diameter, with bands of vivid colours, depicted on the fog. The centre of the circle was in a line drawn from the sun through the point of vision, until it met the visible vapour in a situation exactly opposite the sun. The lower part of the circle descended beneath my feet to the side of the ship; and although it could not be an hundred feet from the eye, it was perfect, and the colours distinct. The centre of the coloured circle was distinguished by my own shadow, the head of which enveloped by a halo, was most conspicuously pourtrayed. The halo or glory was evidently impressed on the fog, but the figure appeared to be a shadow on the water, the different parts of which became obscure in proportion to their remoteness from the head, so that the lower extremities were not perceptible. I remained a long time contemplating the beautiful phenomenon before me. Notwithstanding the sun was brilliant and warm, the fog was uncommonly dense beneath. The sea and ice, within 60 yards of the ship, could scarcely be distinguished. The prospect thus circumscribed, served to fix the attention more closely on the only interesting object in sight, whose radiance and harmony of colouring, added to the singular appearance of my own image, were productive of sensations of admiration and delight.

SECT. VI.

Observations on the Winds of the Polar Regions, with some Notices respecting Meteors not aqueous.

IN my researches on the phenomena of the Greenland atmosphere, I have not attempted either to establish any particular theory, or to frame a new one ; but have principally devoted my attention to the object of forming such a combination of facts as may be applied with advantage by those naturalists who engage in the arduous task of generalizing the phenomena of nature. Excepting where my observations happen to afford an illustration of some popular or ingenious opinion, I have generally avoided theories and speculations, contenting myself with stating the plain matter of fact. At the same time, I have been careful in mentioning every little particular which has come under my own notice, that my researches may in some degree compensate for that great deficiency of observations in the polar regions, which has hitherto rendered the natural history of this part of the world so incomplete.

Respecting atmospheric temperature and pressure, I have been enabled to offer the result of several years observations, which, from the perfect nature of the instruments employed in the investigation, may be received without reserve. In the phenomena of the Winds, however, which I am now about to describe, I cannot be so precise; being able to give a correct idea only of their peculiarities and direction, whilst their relative force, founded on conjecture, I am unable to express otherwise than in the phraseology of the mariner, which, it must be allowed, is somewhat ambiguous *.

In proportion as we recede from the Equator, we find the winds become more variable, irregular, and partial. In the torrid zone, the trade-winds blow with striking regularity, and flow in a similar di-

---

* The varieties and gradations of the force of the Winds, may be comprised under the following designations: Calm, inclinable to calm, light air, gentle breeze, moderate breeze, brisk breeze, fresh breeze, strong breeze, brisk gale, fresh gale, strong gale, hard gale, very hard gale, excessive hard gale, hurricane.

rection across a great portion of the circumference of the globe. In temperate climates, the winds are capricious, and, if we except forcible gales, are in general local. A very little attention, indeed, will discover, that at certain seasons the wind blows from some particular quarter more than any other, though, in the same seasons, winds of various degrees of force and generality are observed to occur in every point of the compass. Advancing towards the polar regions, we find the irregularities of the winds increased, and their locality more striking :—storms and calms repeatedly alternate, without warning or progression ;—forcible winds blow in one place, when at the distance of a few leagues, gentle breezes prevail ;—a storm from the south, on one hand, exhausts its impetuosity upon the gentle breeze, blowing from off the ice, on the other, without prevailing in the least ;—ships within the circle of the horizon may be seen enduring every variety of wind and weather at the same moment ; some under close-reefed topsails, labouring under the force of a storm ; some becalmed and tossing about by the violence of the waves ; and others plying under gentle breezes, from quarters as diverse as the cardinal points. The cause of some of these phenomena, has, in the last chapter, been referred to the frigorific influences of the ice, the accuracy of which opinion, experience and observation confirm.

These irregularities in the arctic winds, will be now more particularly noticed, beginning with the phenomena attendant on *sudden storms*. The most general preliminaries to such are, perfect calm; curiously variable breezes with strong squalls; singular agitation of the sea; together with thick snow, which often changes from flakes to powder, and falls in such profusion as to occasion an astonishing gloominess and obscurity in the atmosphere. If the snow clear away, the gale is often at hand, whilst a luminousness on the horizon, resembling the ice-blink, sometimes points out its direction, and a noise in the upper regions of the air announces its immediate approach. As these appearances are subject to some variety, they may be more clearly explained by reference to a few of the most striking instances I have observed, in which the value of the barometer, studied in connection with the thermometer, in this variable and occasionally tempestuous climate, will be satisfactorily proved.

In the evening of the 5th of April 1811, latitude 70° 49′ N., and longitude 7° 15′ E., the wind blew a fresh gale from the northward, and the barometer which had been stationary for 35 hours, stood at 29.88 inches. At noon, on the following day, we had a moderate breeze of wind from the north-west, which, towards evening, increased to a fresh gale, exceedingly variable and squally, accompanied by thick showers of flaky snow. At 9 A. M., the thermometer stood at 10°, at 4 P. M., it had risen to 17°, and at 6 P. M. to 27°. This remarkable rise, of 17° of temperature in nine hours, indicated a southerly or easterly wind, and, because the barometer had fallen to 29.50, a severe storm was expected. Since the barometer stands highest on easterly winds, had it remained stationary, we should have expected a storm, on the veering of the wind from the N. W to the opposite quarter; but, when this change was preceded by a fall of near four-tenths of an inch in the column of mercury, a violent gale might be anticipated.

I now walked the deck somewhat alarmed at the awful appearance of the sky, in the short intervals of the showers. At one time, a luminousness resembling the ice-blink, appeared in the horizon, extending from the N. N. E. to the E. S. E *. It did not, however, proceed from any ice, as I was afterwards perfectly satisfied; neither was it likely to arise from the effects of the sun, as it was in the western quarter.

---

* A few weeks afterwards, when mentioning this circumstance to an old Greenland commander, he told me he had seen the phenomenon I described, and always considered it as the prognostic of a storm, while the position of the luminousness pointed out the quarter from whence the wind would commence.

In the midst of a thick shower, the snow was observed to clear away to leeward, which warned me
of an approaching *shift* of wind.   Immediately, all
hands were ordered on deck, to attend the sails,
and every man at his station awaited the event.   In
about ten minutes the sails gave a violent shake, and
were the next instant *taken flat aback*.   The wind,
though blowing a fresh gale, veered in a moment
from N. N. W. to E. S. E.   We steered by the
wind, after reefing sails, about an hour and a half
to the north-eastward, when the snow began to
abate, but the wind of a sudden became so violent,
that the utmost exertions of all the crew were but
just sufficient to prevent the sails from blowing to
pieces.   At length, all was made snug; a close-reefed main-topsail, and storm try-sail, were alone exposed to the fury of the tempest.   On the second
day of the storm's continuance, a heavy sea struck
the ship, and with dreadful violence mounted the
deck ; it had nearly precipitated a boat suspended
from the weather quarter, over the rail,—it lifted
and removed an eighteen pounder carronade ; —
filled two boats with water,—and stove or washed
away the whole of the bulwark, fore and aft.

During the whole of this gale, which lasted three
days, the barometer remained perfectly stationary.

On May 17. 1812, lat. 76°. 7′ long. 9½° E. the
ship which I commanded was immured among ice,
and the wind blew a hard gale from the N. N. W.

The day following it subsided, and a moderate breeze prevailed, veering from N. N. W., gradually to W., S., E., and finally settling again at N. N. W., after touching on every point of the compass. The barometer, meanwhile, was depressed. In the evening it was nearly calm. While we were in the act of towing the ship through a narrow opening between two floes, a heavy shower was observed in the N. W., advancing towards the ship. On its approach, the vane at the mast-head whirled round, the sails were violently shaken, and in a moment the snow enveloped the ship in obscurity, and a violent storm of wind dashed her, spite of every exertion, stern first, against a floe of ice which she was in the act of doubling. The concussion, though violent, was prevented, by the prompt activity of the sailors, in getting out a rope to one of the adjoining sheets of ice, from producing any particular injury. After enduring considerable pressure from the two floes, which, at the same instant, collapsed, we were enabled to make our escape, from a situation of the most perilous nature, and happily without any serious damage being sustained by the ship.

May the 10th 1813, the barometer indicated a storm ; and the singular appearance of the atmosphere strengthened the indication. After twelve or eighteen hours of calm and variable weather, occasioned evidently by conflicting winds, a sudden and impetuous storm arose, which continued with little intermission for six days

The approach of sudden storms, it has been ob
served, is sometimes announced by a noise in the
the air.   My Father once removed his ship from a
most dangerous bight in the main ice, where she
would probably have been lost, had she remained a
few minutes longer, in consequence of his having
heard the rushing of a storm in the air, when at the
mast-head.   Before the ship was out of danger, a
heavy gale commenced ; but the sails being set, and
the ship under command, she was extricated from
the perilous situation.   From this circumstance, he
imagines, that sudden storms frequently commence
at some height in the atmosphere, and gradually
descend to the surface.

A phenomenon of a description similar to that of
sudden storms, and almost equally common, is *intermitting gales*.   The nature of these winds will be
best explained, by mentioning two or three instances.

April the 22d 1814, latitude 73° 29', we had intermitting gales, snow-showers and high sea.   The
squalls continued from five minutes to half an hour
at a time ; and the intervals of calm weather were
a little longer.   During the squalls, the ship could
only bear close-reefed topsails and courses ; but in
the intervals she might have carried royals.   This
kind of weather prevailed from 8 A. M. until 3 P. M.,
when, in a shower of snow, a sudden calm occurred
and continued for an hour.   The gale then sudden-

ly recommenced with increased severity. At 9 p. m. the wind veered at once from N. N. W. to E. N. E., and then subsided. From 9 to 12 p. m., a thickness of six inches of snow fell upon the deck.

The morning of the 18th of April 1815, in the 78th degree of latitude, near Spitzbergen, was beautifully clear and serene. At 11 a. m. clouds began to obscure the face of the sky, and soon afterwards much snow fell. In the evening we experienced fresh gales from two or three quarters, with intervals of calms, in the space of an hour. North, east, and south gales, alternately prevailed, in rapid but irregular succession, during several hours. The winds not being dangerous, the appearance was uncommonly interesting.

Variable winds, and local or *partial winds*, are common in all temperate, and in some of the warmer climates : but not in that striking degree in which they occur in the frigid zone. The winds, indeed, among ice, are generally unsteady in their direction, and attended with strong gusts or squalls, particularly in very cold weather, and towards the termination of a storm. This variableness being the effect of the unequal temperature of the ice and water, is curious ; but the phenomenon that is most calculated to excite surprise is, that several distinct, and even opposite winds, with the force, in many instances, of a fresh gale, will occasionally prevail at the same moment of time, within the range of the horizon. The situation in which this circumstance occurs, would appear to be the point where conflicting winds contend for the superiority; and as in some instances their forces are effectually balanced, the winds which simultaneously blow from the southward and northward, or from the eastward and westward, have their energies almost destroyed at the place of combination. Thus, it sometimes happens, that ships within sight of each other, will, at the same period of time, experience every variety of weather, from calm to storm, from fair weather to thickest snow, together with several distinct and contrary currents of wind. An instance or two may not be uninteresting.

On the morning of the 30th of April 1810, the ship Resolution, in which I served in the capacity of chief mate and harpooner, was, during thick showers of snow, sailing by the edge of a stream of ice, with the wind from the north-westward. About 10 A. M. the snow abated, and several ships were seen within the distance of three or four miles. As all of these ships were sailing " on a wind," it was easy to ascertain the direction of the wind where they were, and curious to observe its variableness. Two ships bearing north-east from us, had the wind at N. E.; two bearing east, at E. or E. N. E.; two bearing S. E., had the wind at S. E.; while with us, it blew from the N. W. In each of these situations a fresh breeze prevailed; but in some situations, where there happened to be no ships, there appeared to be no wind at all. The clouds above us at the time, were constantly changing their forms. Showers of snow were seen in various places at a distance.

Another instance occurred also within my own observation, in April 1813. The crew of the ship Esk, under my command, were engaged in pursuit of some whales, near the edge of the main western ice, in latitude 80° 7′, during which the ship was laid-to, near the scene of the chace. In the course of the day, we had winds from every point of the compass, and with every degree of force from storm to calm. While a gentle breeze of wind from the N. prevailed with us, a heavy swell from the S. S. E. came on, and a dense black cloud appeared in the southern horizon, which rapidly arose into the zenith, and shrouded one-half of the heavens. The commixture of this dense air with the cold wind from the N., produced a copious discharge of snow. When the snow ceased, though we were nearly becalmed, we observed several ships a few miles to the south-eastward, under close-reefed topsails, having evidently a gale of wind blowing in the direction of the swell. About two hours afterwards, the southerly wind reached us, and, as we stood to the eastward, gradually increased to a gale. On returning towards the ice, however, at 5 P. M., the wind again subsided, so that when we came within four or five miles of it, the sky cleared, and we were again becalmed.

406 ACCOUNT OF THE ARCTIC REGIONS.

From the clear atmosphere to the northward and westward, and the dense sky to the southward and eastward, with the heavy swell from the S. S. E., it was evident that we were between two winds ;— a southerly storm to the southward of us, and a northerly breeze to the northward. At seven p. m. of the same day, a north-east wind commenced, and soon blew a tremendous storm. All the previous winds had been partial; this was general, and extended several degrees of latitude to the southward. This storm was particularly predicted by the barometer and thermometer; the mercury in the former, having fallen from 29.74 to 28.98 ; and in the latter from 30° to 12°, in about twelve hours.

Instances of *local storms* are not uncommon in temperate climates ; but, in the arctic regions, they are frequent and striking. Their locality is such, that a calm may occur when a storm is expected, and actually does prevail at a short distance ; so that the indications of the barometer may appear to be erroneous. In such cases, however, the reality of the storm is often proved by the agitation of the sea. Swells from various quarters make their appearance, and frequently prevail at the same time.

My Father, whose opportunities of observation have been very numerous, relates the following instance of the locality of a storm. When commanding the ship Henrietta, he was on one occasion navigating the Greenland Sea, during a tedious gale of wind, accompanied with snowy weather. As the wind began to abate, a ship appeared in sight, under all sails, and presently came up with the Henrietta. The master hailed, and inquired what had happened that my Father's ship was under close-reefed topsail in such moderate weather. On being told that a storm had just subsided, he declared that he knew nothing of it : he observed, indeed, a swell, and noticed a black cloud a-head of his ship, that seemed to advance before him, until he was over-shadowed with it, a little while before he overtook the Henrietta ; but he had had fine weather and light winds the whole day.

The last example of local storms that I shall give, occurred in the year 1817. At noon of the 4th of May, the Esk, under my command, was in latitude 78. 55′, near the ice, with a brisk breeze of wind from the E. S. E. In the evening we stood to the southward, experienced a considerable increase of wind, and at midnight tacked. We then steered under a brisk sail to the N. E., as high as latitude 80°10′, finding less wind and clearer sky as we went to the northward ; while dense clouds appeared in the southern quarter, and a heavy swell from the same direction pursued us. The wind was light in the evening of the 5th ; tacked at the edge of the northern ice, and returned to the south-westward. During the whole of the next day, we continued our course, under all sails, having a fresh breeze of wind at

S. E., heavy southerly swell, and a constant fall of snow, consisting of the most beautiful crystals I ever saw. The day following, we joined several ships, when the weather was calm and the sea fallen. We now were informed, that, while we enjoyed fine weather in the latitude of 80°, the ships in the 79th degree of latitude, during two days, had experienced a most tremendous storm; in consequence of which, some whales that had been killed before the gale came on, were lost, and four ships that were driven into the ice, were wrecked.

It is almost needless to allude to the sudden gusts and various currents of wind which occur at some elevation in the atmosphere, since they are common to all climates. As, however, it is connected with this part of my subject, it may not be amiss to quote a single instance. On a particularly fine day, my Father having landed on the northern part of Charles' Island, incited by the same curiosity which led him on shore, ascended, though not without great difficulty and fatigue, a considerable elevation, the summit of which was not broader than a common table, and which shelved on one side as steep as the roof of a house, and on the other formed a mural precipice. Engaged in admiring the extensive prospect from an eminence of about 2000 feet, he scarcely noticed the advance of a very small cloud. Its rapid approach and peculiar form, (having somewhat the appearance of a hand,) at length excited his attention; and, when it reached the place where he was seated, in a calm air, a torrent of wind assailed him with such violence, that he was obliged to throw himself on his body, and stick his hands and feet in the snow, to prevent himself from being hurled over the tremendous slope which threatened his instant destruction. The cloud having passed, the air, to his great satisfaction, again became calm, when he immediately descended, by sliding down the surface of snow, and in a few minutes reached the base of the mountain in safety.

The course of the seasons, as relates to prevailing winds, is as follows. In the spring, N., N. E. and E. winds are frequent, with severe storms from these and other quarters. The storms from the N. E., E. and S. E. are generally the most violent. When they occur in March and April, they frequently continue without intermission for two or three successive days, and rarely subside until the wind veers round to the N. or N. W. Storms, in the spring of the year, blowing from the S. E., generally change, before they abate, to the E., N. E, N. and N. W.; but storms commencing at S. W. or S. usually veer before they subside, in the contrary direction towards the N. W., and sometimes continue changing until their strength is spent in the N. or N. E. quarter. A storm beginning to blow from the western quarter, seldom continues long; when it blows hard, it commonly veers to the N. or N. E.; and it is observable, that a very hard southerly or easterly gale is frequently succeeded, within a few days, by another from the opposite quarter.

With the advance of the month of May, storms become less frequent, and the weather becomes sensibly better. The winds then begin to blow more frequently from the N. W. In June, the most common winds are N. and N. W., S. and S. W.; and in July south and south-westerly winds prevail. At this season, calms or very light winds also become frequent, and continue sometimes for several days together. In high northern latitudes, however, very heavy storms from the southward occur in July, and blow for thirty or forty hours at a time. Such storms are common about Hakluyt's Headland, when, at the same time, they are not felt to the southward of the Foreland. In August, north-east winds begin again to prevail.

In one of my Father's journals, appear the following remarks on this subject. " For sixteen out of twenty-two years, in which I have successively visited the Greenland Seas, the wind, during the months of April and May, has almost always blown from the N., N. E., E. and E. S. E., between the latitude of 74° and 81° N.; but very rarely from the westward, until about the middle of June, when winds from the W. and N. W. mostly occur *."

* These directions are *per* compass; all the others are referable to the true meridian.

In the frigid zone in general, as well as in icy regions without the Arctic Circle, winds blowing from the ice towards the open sea, are the most prevalent. In Hudson's Bay, westerly winds blow for three-fourths of the year* ; at Kamtchatka the prevailing winds are from the westward† ; in Greenland northerly winds occur during seven months in the winter ‡ ; and in a similar proportion nearly in Spitzbergen, Jan Mayen, and Nova Zembla, as far as the observations of the adventurers who have occasionally wintered in these desolate countries can testify.

In the Appendix, (No. II. Table A.) the mean duration of different winds is partly determined in the horizontal columns of " General Mean." The following Table shows the duration in days of each wind, and the number of stormy days in April, on an average of seven years; in May on an average of twelve years; in June on an average of ten years; and in July on an average of six years.

	N.	N.E.	E.	S. E.	S.	S.W.	W.	N.W.	Variable.	Calm.	Stormy Days.
April,	6.0	4.4	3.0	1.6	3.0	2.1	2.4	3.6	2.0	1.9	11.0
May,	7.4	3.7	2.0	2.3	2.1	1.6	2.1	5.6	2.4	1.8	6.1
June,	5.1	1.9	1.4	2.7	4.3	3.2	1.9	3.9	3.2	2.5	3.3
July,	2.7	2.1	1.7	1.5	5.5	5.3	2.5	2.6	3.1	4.0	3.1

* PENNANT's Arctic Zoology, *Supplement,* p. 41.

† Idem, Arctic Zoology, cxiii.

‡ Middleton's Vindication, p. 201.

The south-westerly and southerly storms of the autumn blow with particular violence, not only about Hakluyt's Headland in Spitzbergen, but in most other countries in high northern latitudes. In West Greenland, it is observed by CRANTZ, " when it once begins to be stormy, which happens mostly in autumn, the wind rages so vehemently, that the houses quiver and crack, the tents and lighter boats fly up into the air, and the sea-water scatters about in the land like snow dust. Nay, the Greenlanders say, that the storm rends off stones a couple of pounds weight, and mounts them in the air. If any one is obliged at such times to go out of the house to bring the boats into shelter, he must constantly lie and creep upon his belly, that the wind may not make him its sport. In summer, whirlwinds also spring up, that draw up the waters out of the sea, and turn a boat round several times. The most and fiercest storms rise in the south, and take a compass round to north, where they again subside and terminate in clear weather. At such times, the ice in the bays is torn from its bed, and hastens into the sea in heaps*."

Storms as tremendous as those described by Crantz, also occur in Iceland. Some facts of this nature have been given by Sir GEORGE MACKENZIE. On the 6th of November 1809, a most awful gale

---

* History of Greenland, vol. i. p. 47.

of wind occurred in Iceland, which blew from the
north during the whole twenty-four hours.   The
country, to an extent of several miles from the shore,
was covered with salt-water driven from the sea in
the form of rain; boats on the beach were taken up
into the air, and dashed to pieces*

When the countries of temperate climates suffer
under tempests in frequent succession, the polar regions enjoy a comparative tranquillity.   After the
autumn gales have passed, a series of calm weather,
attended with severe frost, frequently succeeds.
Crantz makes the general remark, that " in Disco
it is often for two or three months constantly calm,
and the air clear, though filled with vapours."   So
striking, indeed, is the stillness of the northern winter, and even that of Russia, in parts which merely
border on the frigid zone, that Dr Guthrie, in his
Dissertation on the Climate of Russia, after observing, that hail is a rare appearance in the winter season, and that tempests are equally uncommon, proceeds to remark, that nature seems " to have studied
a perfect equality in the distribution of her favours,
as it is only the parts of the earth which most enjoy
the kindly influences of the sun, that suffer by the
effects of its superior heat; so that if the atmosphere of the north is not so genial as that of the
south, at least it remains perfectly quiet and serene,

Travels in Iceland during the Summer of 1810.

without threatening destruction to man, and the product of his industry, as in what are commonly called happier climates *."

The reciprocal effects of the ice, sea, land, and
wind, on each other, have, in different places of this
work, been alluded to.   One fact which applies in
this place, yet remains to be noticed.

A striking and very singular effect of the land on
the wind, is frequently observed in Davis' Strait.
The island of Disco, lying in latitude 69° 40′ and
longitude 54° 30′ W., presents towards the sea, on
the west side, a considerable cliff, with mountainous
land beyond it.   In the season corresponding with
our summer, the sea near it is commonly open.   At
this time, when ships lying in the middle of Davis'
Strait, have a hard gale of wind blowing from the
west, on steering towards this island, which is then
a lee shore, they gradually find the force of the wind
abate, until when come within a certain distance of
the land, it subsides almost into a calm! As this circumstance is said invariably to occur, ships navigating in Davis' Strait, when oppressed by the violence
of the westerly winds, are generally enabled to attain a situation in which the wind blows with such
a diminished degree of force, as may best suit their
convenience.   Whether this effect is produced by
the height of the land, or is the effect of the repul-

* Edin. Phil. Trans., vol. ii.

sion of an off-land wind, I am not prepared to decide.

The principal meteors, not being of the aqueous
kind, that remain to be considered, are Lightning
and the Aurora borealis.   As we approach the
Pole, the former phenomenon becomes more rare, and
the latter more common.   Lightning, indeed, is
seldom seen to the northward of the arctic circle;
and when it does occur, is almost never accompanied
by thunder.   In Hudson's Bay, Ellis, James, Hudson, and other voyagers, have observed heavy storms
of thunder and lightning; but in West Greenland,
where, according to Crantz, a thunder cloud sometimes gathers, and emits flashes of lightning, thunder seldom occurs; " and when something like it is
heard, one cannot decide whether the sound proceeds
from a distant thunder clap, or from the crack of
ice and stones rending and precipitating from the
rocks."   In Spitzbergen, neither thunder nor lightning has, I believe, ever been observed.   For my
own part, I have never seen lightning to the northward of latitude 65°, and only in two instances,
when at any considerable distance from land.   July
the 25th 1815, latitude 63° longitude 0° 55′ W.,
lightning was seen in the western quarter; and on
the 4th of April in the same year, much lightning
with thunder, occurred in the latitude of 65° and
longitude 0° 10′ W.   In no other cases have I seen

3

lightning at sea, excepting when within 20 or 30 leagues of land.

The aurora borealis, on the contrary, occurs independent of land and of cold, becoming more frequent in its appearance as we approach the Pole, and enlivening by its brilliancy, and peculiar grandeur, the tedious gloom of the long winter's nights. This phenomenon having been described by many authors, some of whom have exhausted the powers of language in the elegance of their representations, renders it unnecessary for me to attempt any general description of this interesting spectacle. I shall, therefore, confine my remarks to a few particulars.

This appearance, though not very frequently seen in Britain, is very common as far south as Shetland and Feroe. In Iceland, and other countries bordering on the arctic circle, the northern lights occur almost every clear night during the winter. But in summer, the season in which I have been in the habit of visiting the polar seas, they can seldom be seen, on account of the continual presence of the sun. On the passage from England to Spitzbergen, indeed, they occur occasionally; but the general obscurity of the atmosphere in the spring of the year, prevents their frequent exhibition. It may not be altogether uninteresting, to give a table of the state of the weather, on the different occasions on which I have observed them.

TABLE *of the State of the Weather when the Aurora Borealis*
was seen.

Year.	Month & Day.	Lati- tude.	Longi- tude.	Baro- meter.	Therm.	Winds.	Weather.	Remarks.
1807,	April 15	66.10	6°.17′ W	29.64	25	E.erly	Fine, mod.	Bril. aur.; fol. by a trem. storm
1809,	Mar. 19.	58.52	1.20	30.09	—	N W	Fine, clear	Slight aur.; fine weath. contin.
1810,	April 4.	71.30	3. 0 E			S E	Moderate	Consid. aur.; follow. by storm
1811,	Mar. 28.	66.52	2. 0	30.40	16	W.erly	Boisterous	Bril. aur.; fol. by chang. wea.
—	— 29.	67.20	3 10	30.31	20	E.erly	Variable	Slight aur.; fine weath. fol.
—	— 30.	68.20	4.10	30.32	16	E N E	Fine	Bril. aur.; fine weather cont.
—	— 31.	68.50	4. 0	30.20	16	N N W	Fine & clear	Ditto ditto
1815,	April 5.	67.40	2.10	29.26	37	E b S	Boisterous	Slight aur.; windy weath. cont.
—	— 6.	69.22	3.45	29.18	36	E	Ditto	Considerable aur.; ditto
—	— 7.	70.10	4.40	29.82	30	Calm	Variable	Bril. aur.; followed by storm
1817,	— 5.	Zet	land.	30.62	46	N	Fine	Slight aur.; fine weath. cont.
—	— 8.	65. 6	1.45	29.45	28	N.erly	Stormy	Bright aur.; storm increased
1818,	— 22.	62.10	0.30 W	29.72	42	E.erly	Windy	Slight aur.; squally wea. fol.
—	— 23.	62.16	2.10 E	29.70	40	N b W	Windy	Bright aur.; do. with high sea

Among unenlightened nations, the appearance of
the northern lights is generally associated with some
curious or absurd superstition. Some uncivilized people regard them as portending national calamities;
others consider them as the effect of the merriments
of the dead *, or attribute them to causes equally
ridiculous.

However vain the notions of savage nations may
be, as to the causes or effects of the northern lights,
there is reason to believe that their connection
with other atmospheric phenomena is such, that
their occurrence, under certain circumstances or appearances, is portentous. In several of the instances
in the preceding Table, stormy weather followed the
appearance of the brilliant aurora; and one of the

---

* Robson's Account of Six Years residence in Hudson's Bay.
p. 49.

most tremendous storms I was ever exposed to, succeeded a splendid exhibition of the northern lights.
From an intelligent old man, one of the Lerwick
pilots, I received the following information on the
connection supposed to exist between certain appearances of the northern lights, and the weather.
When seen in the north-west quarter, resting near
the horizon, without extending their rays to the
zenith, they are (in winter) considered indicative
of calm frosty weather.   When they appear in brilliant display, extending towards the south-west, a
gale of wind is to be expected; or, extending towards the south-east, a southerly gale, with rain or
sleet; and, when they are seen at a considerable altitude above the horizon, having a red or copper
colour, and shooting their rays into the zenith,
they are supposed to be indicative of a violent storm.
The first and the last of these observations correspond with general experience; but of the accuracy
of the intermediate opinion, I have had no opportunity of judging.   Neither have I had opportunity of observing any agitation of the magnetic needle,
or any peculiarities of an electrical nature, in the
lower atmosphere, during the prevalence of the northern lights.   These are subjects which I yet hope
to have the means of investigating.

SECT. VII.

Aqueous Meteors, including Observations on Clouds, Rain, Hail, Snow, Frost-rime, Hoar-frost and Fog.

VERY little clear weather occurs in the Greenland Seas; for often when the atmosphere is free from any visible vapour on the land, at sea it is obscured by frost-rime in the spring of the year, and by clouds or fog in the summer; so that scarcely one-twentieth of the season devoted to the whale-fishery can be said to consist of clear weather.

The *clouds* most generally consist of a dense stratum of obscurity, composed of irregular compact patches, covering the whole expanse of the heavens. The cirrus, cirro-cumulus, and cirro-stratus, of Howard's nomenclature, are occasionally distinct; the nimbus is partly formed, but never complete; and the grandeur of the cumulus or thunder-cloud, is never seen, unless it be on the land. A cloud bearing some resemblance to the cumulus, sometimes appears near the horizon: this, when partly intercepted by the horizon, has an appearance so very similar to that of the mountains of Spitzbergen, that it is often mistaken for land. In the atmosphere over the coasts of Greenland and Spitzbergen, where the air is greatly warmed by the con-

D d 2

centration and reflection of the sun's rays in the sheltered valleys, a small imperfect cumulus is sometimes exhibited. The most common definable cloud seen at sea, is a particular modification, somewhat resembling the cirro-stratus, consisting of large patches of cloud arranged in horizontal strata, and enlightened by the sun on one edge of each stratum.

Rain is a meteor too well known to need any description; but the causes which operate so as to produce it, under the great variety of circumstances in which it occurs, are not altogether understood. The known agents made use of, in the economy of Nature, for the production of rain, are changes of temperature and electricity. The latter principle is supposed to act most powerfully in the production of thunder showers; in which case it is not unlikely but a portion of the air of the atmosphere is, by the passing of the lightning from one cloud to another, converted into water. The former seems to be the chief agent in the colder regions of the globe, where electricity is either more equal in its distribution, or not so active in its operations, as in the warmer climates. Were the capability of the atmosphere for absorbing moisture, the same at all temperatures, or were its capability increased in a similar ratio with the increase of heat, no change, however great, produced by the admixture of two streams of air of different temperatures, could occa-

sion the precipitation of any rain. But, from the
beautiful theory of the late Dr James Hutton,
supported by the able and ingenious researches of
Professor Leslie, it appears, that " while the temperature advances uniformly in arithmetical progression, the dissolving power which this communicates
to the air, mounts with the accelerating rapidity of
a geometrical series * ;" and this, in such a ratio,
that the " air has its dryness doubled at each rise
of temperature answering to fifteen centesimal degrees," or twenty-seven of Fahrenheit †.   Hence,
" whatever be the actual condition of a mass of
air, there must always exist some temperature at
which it would become perfectly damp‡;" and hence,
whenever two streams of air, saturated with moisture, of different temperatures, are mixed together,
or brush against one another, in the form of different currents of wind, there must always be a quantity of moisture precipitated.   For, if two masses of
air of different temperatures, but equal in quantity,
and both saturated with moisture, were mixed together, the resulting temperature would be nearly
the mean of the two; but, at that temperature, the
capacity of air for moisture, being less than the
quantity contained in the two commixed masses,

* LESLIE ;—" A Short Account of Experiments and Instruments, depending on the relations of Air to Heat and Moisture," p. 123.

† Idem, p. 122.   ‡ Idem, p. 123.

the surplus must be deposited. By the help of the
following Table, derived from measurements of the
curve representing the dissolving power of the air,
this subject may be more familiarly illustrated *.

Temp. of the Air by Fahrenh.	Dissolv-ingPower.	Temp. of the Air.	Dissolv-ingPower.	Temp. of the Air.	Dissolv-ingPower.	Temp. of the Air.	Dissolv-ingPower.	Temp. of the Air.	Dissolv-ingPower.
—24°	0.55	+3°	1.08	30°	2.16°	57°	4.33	84°	8.64
—21	0.60	6	1.16	33	2.34	60	4.68	87	9.33
—18	0.65	9	1.25	36	2.53	63	5.06	90	10.07
—15	0.70	12	1.35	39	2.73	66	5.47	93	10.87
—12	0.75	15	1.46	42	2.95	69	5.91	96	11.74
— 9	0.81	18	1.58	45	3.18	72	6.38	99	12.68
— 6	0.87	21	1.71	48	3.43	75	6.88	102	13.70
— 3	0.93	24	1.85	51	3.70	78	7.42	105	14.81
0	1.00	27	2.00	54	4.00	81	8.00	108	16.00

Now, a mass of air at temperature zero, can support, it appears, about one three hundred and sixty-
fifth part of its weight of moisture; or a mass of
air 365 lb. in weight, can contain, when saturated
at temperature 0°, 1 lb. of water; at temperature

---

* This Table, though very nearly correct, is yet but an
approximation. It, however, serves every purpose of illustration. What is here called the dissolving power of the
air, is perhaps, correctly speaking, the dissolving power
of caloric, the water itself that is evaporated being converted into an elastic vapour, by its combination with the
matter of heat. This vapour forms a part of the air of the atmosphere. Decrease of atmospheric pressure and increase of
temperature accelerate its formation.

27°, 2 lb. ; at temperature 54°, 4 lb. ; at temperature
81°, 8 lb. and so on. As such, the numbers in the
second column of the above Table, show the quantity of water in pounds which 365 lb. of air can
contain at any temperature between — 24° and 108°.
Suppose, then, for example, two masses of air of
365 lb. weight each, one of the temperature 18°,
the other 36°, a case quite within the limits of probability in the polar regions, to be mixed together,
the resulting temperature would be nearly the mean
of the two, or 27°. But the two masses of air before commixture, if saturated, must contain respectively 1.58 lb. and 2.53 lb. of moisture, the sum of
which, 4.11, exceeds by 0.11 lb. or one-ninth of a
pound, the quantity of water, as shown by the
Table, which twice 365 lb. of air could possibly
sustain at the mean temperature of 27°. This
0.11 lb. of water must therefore be precipitated
after the commixture of every 730 lb. of saturated
air of the temperatures proposed. At higher temperatures, however, the precipitation must be greater ; for, suppose the two assimilating streams of air
to be of the temperatures 42° and 84° ; then the
quantity of water suspended by 365 lb. of each,
would be respectively 2.95 and 8.64, amounting to
11.59 lb. ; but the quantity of moisture which
730 lb. of air could at most support, at the mean
temperature 63°, would be only 10.12 lb., so that
the excess 1.47 lb. must be precipitated.

I merely give these illustrations, for the sake of those readers who are not acquainted with the writings of Dr Hutton and Professor Leslie on this subject; considering them, at the same time, the more necessary, as this ingenious theory of rain, of which I have attempted a brief explanation, is referred to in different parts of this volume.

Rain is by no means common in the polar countries, excepting in the months of July and August, and then only with southerly or westerly winds. During all seasons of the year, however, with strong gales blowing from a southern climate, rain is occasionally observed in situations near the edge of the ice; but snow or sleet are more common even under such circumstances; and in remote situations among ice, near the 80th parallel of latitude, rain seldom or never occurs.

Hail is a much more familiar meteor in temperate than in frigid climates. In the Greenland Sea, indeed, this aqueous concretion is very rarely seen; and if we define it as consisting of pellucid spherules of ice, generated in the atmosphere, it may be said to be unknown in very high latitudes. This fact is in favour of the electrical origin of hail, as it is well known to be common in temperate climates, where the air is in a high state of electricity, and to be the frequent concomitant of thunder and lightning. The only substance resembling hail, that is generated in the frigid zone, consists of a white porous spherical concretion, of a light and snowy texture.

Snow is so very common in the arctic regions, that it may be boldly stated, that in nine days out of ten, during the months of April, May and June, more or less snow falls. With southerly winds, near the borders of the ice, or in situations where humid air blowing from the sea, assimilates with a gelid breeze from the ice, the heaviest falls of snow occur. In this case, a depth of two or three inches is sometimes deposited in an hour. The thickest precipitations also frequently precede sudden storms.

The form of the particles of snow, presents an endless variety. When the temperature of the air is within a degree or two of the freezing point, and much snow falls, it frequently consists of large irregular flakes, such as are common in Britain; sometimes it exhibits small granular, or large rough white concretions; at others, it consists of white spiculæ, or flakes composed of coarse spiculæ, or rude stellated crystals, formed of visible grains. But in severe frosts, though the sky appears perfectly clear, lamellar flakes of snow, of the most regular and beautiful forms, are always seen floating in the air, and sparkling in the sun-beams; and the snow which falls in general, is of the most elegant texture and appearance.

Snow of a reddish or brownish colour is not unfrequently seen. The brownish stain which occurs on shore, is given by an earthy substance brought from the mountains, by the streams of water derived from thawing ice and snow, or the fall of rain; the reddish colour, as far as I have observed, is given by the mute of birds; though, in the example met with by Captain Ross in Baffin's Bay, the stain appears to have been of a vegetable nature. The little auk (Alca alle), which feeds upon shrimps, is found, in some parts of the polar seas, in immense numbers. They frequently retreat to pieces of ice or surfaces of snow, and stain them all over red with their mute. Martens saw red snow in Spitzbergen, which he considered as being stained by rain-water running down by the rocks.

The extreme beauty and endless variety of the microscopic objects procured in the animal and vegetable kingdoms, are perhaps fully equalled, if not surpassed, in both the particulars of beauty and variety, by the crystals of snow. The principal configurations are the stelliform and hexagonal; though almost every shape of which, the generating angles of 60° and 120° are susceptible, may, in the course of a few years observation, be discovered. Some of the general varieties in the figures of the crystals, may be referred to the temperature of the air; but the particular and endless modifications of similar classes of crystals, can only be referred to the will and

3

pleasure of the Great First Cause, whose works, even the most minute and evanescent, and in regions the most remote from human observation, are altogether admirable.

The various modifications of crystals may be classed under five general kinds or genera. 1. Lamellar. 2. A lamellar or spherical nucleus, with spinous ramifications in different planes. 3. Fine spiculæ or six-sided prisms. 4. Hexagonal pyramids. 5. Spiculæ having one or both extremities affixed to the centre of a lamellar crystal.

1. *Lamellar crystals.* The varieties of this kind are almost infinite. They occur at all temperatures, and in the greatest abundance; and most of the specimens are extremely thin, transparent, and of an exquisitely delicate structure. They may be subdivided into several distinct species.

a. Stelliform; having six points radiating from a centre, with parallel collateral ramifications in the same plane. This species, represented in Plate VIII. Fig. 1, is the most general form met with. It varies in size from the smallest speck, to about one-third of an inch diameter. It occurs in greatest profusion when the temperature approaches the freezing point.

b. Regular hexagon. This occurs in moderate as well as in the lowest temperatures; but it becomes more delicate and thin, and diminishes in size as the cold increases. Some specimens consist of simple transparent plates, (Plate VIII. Fig. 23.)

others are beautifully variegated, within the perimeter, by white lines, forming smaller hexagons or other regular figures, in immense variety; Plate IX. Fig. 25, 27, 28, 30; Plate X. Fig. 49, &c. The size of this species is from the smallest visible speck to about one-tenth of an inch diameter.

c. Aggregations of hexagons. This beautiful species admits of immense variety. It occurs chiefly at low temperatures, and presents great limits of dimensions; Plate VIII. Figs. 2, 9, 10, 14, 17; and Plate.IX. Figs. 29, 34, 37, 39, &c. afford examples of this species.

d. Combinations of hexagons, with radii or spines, and projecting angles. This constitutes the most extensive species in the arrangement; and affords some of the most beautiful specimens. Fig. 7, Plate VIII. is an elegant combination of spines and hexagons; and Figures 50, 55, 58, 59, 60, &c. Plate X. together with all the others distinguished by the letter *s* after the numbers, constitute a novel and beautiful variety, which I have only once observed. The parallel lines that appear in these figures, are not intended as shadings, but actually occurred in the crystals, though with this difference, that the lines which appear black in the plate, were all white in the originals. Figures 56, 63, 64, and 93, were opaque crystals, and were not so thin as the others.

The latter of these, as well as Fig. 94, each having twelve spines, appear to be accidental varieties, and are produced probably by the correct application of two similar crystals upon one another.

2. *A lamellar or spherical nucleus, with spinous ramifications in different planes.*—This genus not being easily represented, is not illustrated by any figure. It consists of two or three species.

a. The fundamental figure, consisting of a lamellar crystal of any of the species above described, from the lateral and terminal planes of which arise small spines, similar to the collateral ramifications of Fig. 1. Plate VIII. These spines arise either from one or both of the lateral planes or principal surfaces, or from both lateral and terminal planes; and always maintain the usual angle of 60° with the plane from which they take their rise. The diameter of this figure sometimes exceeds the fourth of an inch. This species falls most frequently at a temperature of 20° or 25°.

b. Having a spherular nucleus, giving rise to radii in all directions. In the former species, the central figure is a transparent crystal; in this it consists of a small rough white concretion. The spines or radii are similar in both figures. The diameter of this seldom reaches a quarter of an inch. The form is echinose. This species falls when the degree of cold is near the freezing, and sometimes in rather low temperatures.

3. *Fine spiculæ or six-sided prisms.*—These are sometimes very delicate and crystalline; at others white and rough. The finest specimens,

which resemble white hair cut into lengths not exceeding a quarter of an inch, are so small and clear,
that the exact figure is not easily determined; and
the larger exhibit a fibrous or prismatic structure.
Some of these are occasionally the third of an inch
in length. This genus is only seen when the temperature is near the freezing point. When the thermometer is about 28 degrees, the finer specimens occur;
when about the freezing, the coarser appear. The
latter are very common during fog showers, and appear to be composed of aggregations of the frozen
particles of the fog, and to have their origin in the
lower parts of the atmosphere.

4. *Hexagonal pyramids.*—This kind of snow-
crystal I have but once seen. A variety, consisting
apparently of a triangular pyramid, was observed;
but whether its base was a triangular or six-sided
figure, similar to No. 96. Plate XI. is doubtful.
These pyramids were about the thirtieth part of an
inch in height, and fell along with some other curious figures, during a fresh gale of wind from the
northward, in very large quantity. Figures 44,
and 47, Plate IX. represent this kind of crystal.

5. *Spiculæ or prisms having one or both ex-*
tremities inserted in the centre of a lamellar crys-
tal.—This is the most singular genus I have ever
seen, and has been observed but twice. It resembles a pair of wheels, united by an axletree; the
wheels consisting of hexagonal or other lamellar crys-

tals, and the axle of a slender prism. Figure 43, 45, 46, and 48, represent this modification of snow-crystal. Figure 46, consists of but one tabular crystal and a prism ; and Figure 45, of three laminæ and two prisms. The length of this was one-sixth of an inch; of the other kind, from one-thirtieth to one-tenth. Some of this extraordinary figure occurred along with the last-described genus : Of which kinds, principally, a quantity of snow three or four inches in depth, once fell on the deck of the ship in which I sailed, in the course of a few hours. The temperature, when this kind of crystal fell, was in one instance 22°, and in the other 20 .

Plates VIII, IX, X, and XI. contain representations of ninety-six different snow-crystals, magnified from thirty to about four hundred times. The Italic letter following the number of the figure, refers to the second column of the annexed Table, by which, the state of the atmosphere and weather, when each crystal was observed, may be seen. The fractional number which succeeds the Italic letter, shows the diameter of the crystal in parts of an inch. The largest crystal represented was one-third of an inch diameter ; the smallest one-thirty-fifth. They were all perfect figures. Many instances, it may be observed, occur of mutilated and irregular specimens ; some wanting two or three radii, and others having radii of different sizes and shapes. But in low temperatures, the greatest proportion of crystals that fall are probably perfect geometrical figures. This constant regard to equality in the form and size of the six radii of the stellates ; the geometrical accuracy of the different parts of the hexagons ; the beauty and precision of the internal lines of the compound figures, with the proper arrangement of any attendant ramifications, and the general completion of the regular figure,— compose one of the most interesting features in the Science of Crystallography.

TABLE

A Table showing the State of the Atmosphere when each of the Figures of Snow delineated in the annexed Plates VIII, IX, X, and XI, were observed.

Date.	Reference to the Plates.	Thermometer.	Barometer.	Winds. Direction.	Winds. Force.	REMARKS.
1809, April 15.	a	21	29.92	N N E	Fresh gale	Snow very profuse.
—— 17.	b	19	29.84	N N E	Fresh gale	A considerable quantity of snow.
—— 29.	c	19	29.63	ENE,NNE	Light wind	Snow profuse.
—— May 1.	d	12	29.68	N E	Strong br.	Occasional crystals deposited.
—— 2.	e	10	29.84	N N E	Fresh gale	Delicate crystals floating in the air.
—— 3.	f	18	29.87	N E.erly	Strong gale	Snow in considerable quantity. [gran. snow.
—— 11.	g	14	30.10	N N E	Fresh br.	Profuse in quant., accomp. by much opaque small
—— 15.	h	22	29.78	E	Strong gale	Ship's deck covered with these curious crystals,
—— 30.	i	20	30.04	N E, N	Fr. or str. ga.	Slight showers of snow. [3 or 4in. deep.
—— June 16.	k	32	29.50	[Nearly calm]		Fell in great quantities.
1810, April 12.	l	22	29.80	E N E	Strong gale	A constant light shower. [opaque grains.
—— 14.	m	16	30.08	N N E	Fresh br.	Small showers. Many rough cryst. formed of
—— 20.	n	21	29.72	S.erly	Strong gale	A moderate but continued deposition of snow.
—— 21.	o	20	29.67	N E.erly	Strong gale	Snow in considerable quantity.
—— May 16.	p	19	29.70	N.	Brisk gale	Small showers ; delicate crystals.
1816, April 29.	q	23	29.95	N N W	Mod. breeze	Small showers of fine crystals.
1817, May 2.	r	17	29.75	N.erly	Fresh gale	Showers of delicate well-formed crystals.
—— 6.	s	27-26	29.80	S E	Fresh breeze	Various and beautiful figures vastly profuse ; deck of the ship covered several inches deep.

Frost-rime or frost-smoke, is a meteor peculiar to those parts of the globe, where a very low temperature prevails for a considerable time. It consists of a dense frozen vapour, apparently arising out of the sea or any large sheet of water, and ascending, in high winds and turbulent seas, to the height of 80 or 100 feet; but in light breezes and smooth water, creeping along the surface. The particles of which it consists are as small as dust, and cleave to the rigging of ships, or almost any substance against which they are driven by the wind, and afford a coating of an inch or upwards in depth. These particles adhere to one another, until the windward surface of the ropes is covered; and form long fibres, somewhat of a prismatical or pyramidal shape, having their points directed towards the wind. Frost-rime adheres readily to articles of clothing; and from the circumstance of its lodging in the hair, and giving it the appearance of being powdered, the sailors humorously style it " the barber." Such of the frost-rime as is dislodged from the rigging whenever the ship is tacked, covers the deck to a considerable thickness; and when trod upon, emits an acute sound, resembling the crushing of fine particles of glass. When collected in heaps, it has the appearance of snow dust, and if dissolved, affords pure water.

Frost-rime sometimes appears at a temperature of 20° or 22°; but generally, it is not observed until

the cold is reduced to 14°.   It is most abundant in
the lowest temperatures, with a high sea and strong
winds ; but diminishes as the swell and wind subside,
or whenever the sea begins to freeze.   When the
air is clear and apparently dry, it commences at a
higher temperature than when it is dark and damp.
Indeed, this meteor is most common when the air is
free from clouds.   Hence, though it sometimes occasions such an obscurity in the lower atmosphere,
that objects near the surface of the water cannot be
seen at the distance of 100 yards; yet, at the mast-
head, where the observer is lifted above the mist,
ships can be distinguished at the distance of five or
six miles, and high land at the distance of ten or
fifteen leagues; and when the frost-rime does not
rise above forty or fifty feet, objects on the water,
such as ice, may be discovered three or four miles off,
though they may be invisible from the deck when
within a furlong.

The cause of this phenomenon may, perhaps, be
similar to that producing rain, as it can be very well
explained on Dr Hutton's theory, already described.
The wind that brushes over the surface of the water,
and is, by the pressure of the atmosphere, brought
into immediate contact, being much colder than the
sea, must receive heat from it, and have its temperature somewhat elevated.   This increase of temperature, enables it to abstract some moisture from
the sea, and being thus rendered specifically lighter,

E e 2

it exchanges situations with the stratum of air immediately above it, and rises in the atmosphere until it gets cooled down, by admixture with other air to the common temperature. But its capacity for moisture diminishing more rapidly than its temperature, prevents it, on Dr Hutton's principle, from sustaining the water absorbed from the surface of the sea, in consequence of which, the surplus moisture is gradually deposited, and being immediately frozen, is exhibited in the air in the form of frost-rime.

An aqueous vapour, consisting of very minute frozen particles, sometimes occupies the lowest region of the atmosphere, in both temperate and frigid climates, during frosty weather ; and is deposited upon the ground, upon surfaces of ice, or almost any other substance with which it comes in contact. This vapour, which seems to be of the nature of *hoar-frost*, generally appears in the evening, after a bright sunshiny day.   When the sun declines towards the horizon, and its rays, struggling through the obliquity of a dense atmosphere, begin to lose their power, the excess of moisture evaporated during the meridian heat, is again precipitated.   The first precipitation is discovered in a slight mistiness appearing to rise from the surface of the ice : as the cold increases, this mistiness attains a greater elevation, until an obscurity, like that of frost-rime, or of a considerable fog, is produced. Such of the particles

as are borne by the breeze into contact with a ship's
rigging, affix themselves to the windward side of the
different ropes, and form a thick fringe of frozen
vapour.   In some states of the atmosphere, the coating of hoar-frost resembles the coating of frost-rime,
consisting of an irregular fringe; but in others,
every particle affixes itself in a determinate order,
so that the most delicate, and in some cases the most
beautiful crystals are produced.   I have never, however, observed more than two different forms of these
crystals; one, consisting of a combination of angular
cup-like figures, inserted into one another in an her-
baceous form, not unlike a species of erica or heath,
was seen upon the land; the other, having the form
and texture of a feather, occurred when the ship was
in the midst of a compact body of ice.   The circumstances under which the latter appeared were these.
Ice of the field kind encompassed the ship to an extent of many leagues; the latitude was 78°9 ; the longitude about 2° E.; the wind easterly.   At mid-day
a thermometer exposed to the sun's rays rose to 54°,
while the air in the shade was only 18°.   At mid-
night the temperature fell to 10°, and the frozen vapour made its appearance.   It soon increased to the
density of frost-rime, and was carried by the wind
in clouds or showers.   In the course of the night,
the rigging of the ship was most splendidly deco-
rated with a fringe of delicate crystals.   The general
form of these, was that of a feather having half of

the vane removed.   Near the surface of the ropes,
was first a small direct line of very white particles,
constituting the stem or shaft of the feather; from
whence, at an angle of 60 degrees, extended a collateral series of finer fibres in close and parallel order,
forming the vane of the feather; and from each of
these fibres in another plane, proceeded a short delicate range of spiculæ or rays, discoverable only by
the help of a microscope, with which the elegant texture and systematic construction of the feather were
completed.   Many of these crystals, possessing a perfect arrangement of the different parts corresponding with the shaft, vane, and rachis of a feather,
were upwards of an inch in length, and three-fourths
of an inch in breadth.   Some consisted of a single
flake or feather; but many of them gave rise to
other feathers, which sprung from the surface of the
vane at the usual angle.   There seemed to be no limit to the magnitude of these feathers, so long as
the producing cause continued to operate, until their
weight became so great, or the action of the wind so
forcible, that they were broken off, and fell in flakes
to the deck of the ship.

Whatever may be the predisposing cause of crystallization, it is clear, from these facts, that regular
crystals may be formed in an aerial as well as in an
aqueous menstruum; by slow and progressive additions, as well as by sudden shoots; and by a combination of visible particles, as well as by the applica-

tion of molecules to one another, when in a state of invisible solution. In the crystallization of water, and of many salts, an accurately formed needle or other regular figure, is consolidated by an instantaneous shoot or rapid progression through the substance of the crystallizing liquor ; but the formation of hoar-frost crystals is accomplished by a slow and gradual deposition of particles, brought into contact with the crystallizing surface by the motion of the air. And it is a fact worthy of notice, that a con tinued accession of new particles, adds nothing to the thickness of the crystal that first appears, but merely extends its principal surface, and as it extends, completes the several arrangements of the particles corresponding with the shaft, vane, and rachis of a feather. This principle in crystallography, which tends to produce a perfect figure, and operates so beautifully in the formation of snow flakes, as to complete each of the six-sides or radii of the crystal, after the same plan and dimensions, suggested to me not only an argument for giving to the molecules of crystals a certain polarity, or attraction for inducing them to unite together by one side rather than another, but also induced an opinion, that complete figures are formed in consequence of the mutual attractions of the crystallizing integrant particles, requiring an equilibrium of weight or of attractions round the nucleus or central particle of the crystal. Thus, in the formation of snow-crystals, it appears,

that whatever form the first few particles that combine may assume, others, which afterwards come
within their attraction, can adhere in no other than
correspondent positions, until the figure is perfected by the balancing or the neutralizing of their
united polarities.   And as the connecting of the
two poles of a magnet by a piece of iron, suppresses
its power and intercepts its attraction for other iron,
so, the perfecting of a snow-crystal, after a regular
geometrical form, it appears, suspends the attractive
property of its substance for extraneous atoms ; but
so long, it would seem, as one single particle is
wanting, the annexed surfaces exert their attraction,
until some particle comes within their influence and
completes the crystal.

Fog or mist, is the last meteor that remains to
be considered.   This is one of the greatest annoy-
ances that the arctic whalers have to encounter.   It
frequently prevails during the greater part of the
month of July, and sometimes for considerable intervals in June and August.   Its density is often
such, that it circumscribes the prospect to an area
of a few acres, not being pervious to sight at the distance of 100 yards.   It frequently lies so very low,
that the brightness of the sun is scarcely at all intercepted ; in such cases, substances warmed by the
sun's rays, give to the air immediately above them,
an increased capacity for moisture, by which evapora-

tion goes briskly on during the densest fogs. In
Newfoundland, I understand, on occasions when the
sun's rays penetrate the mist, and heat the surface
of the rocks, fish is frequently dried during the
thickest fogs. In July 1817, latitude 74°, when
the temperature of the air was 45°, Leslie's hygrometer indicated 6° of dryness, during a most intense
fog ; and on another foggy day, in the same month,
when a temperature of 40° prevailed, from 5 to 6
degrees of dryness was indicated, in a situation on
which the sun had not shone during the day. Frequently I have observed the fog to be wetting at the
height of 40 or 50 feet above the surface of the sea,
when, on the level of the ship's deck, about 14 feet
high, there was no appearance of dampness.

Fogs are more frequent and more dense at the
borders of the ice, than near the coast of Spitzbergen.
They occur principally when the mercury in the thermometer is near the freezing point ; but they are by
no means uncommon with a temperature of 40 or 45
degrees. They are most general with south-westerly,
southerly, and south-easterly winds. With northerly or north-westerly winds, they generally disperse ;
though, after a considerable continuance of southerly
winds, they sometimes prevail for a good many hours
after the wind changes to the northward. Fogs seldom occur with high winds ; yet in one or two instances, I have observed them very thick even in
storms. Rain generally disperses the fog ; but after

the rain ceases, when the air is warm and damp, the fog often returns with increased density, so that it passes the eyes like smoke, and contracts the circle of vision to a radius of fifty or sixty yards. Fogs, by increasing the apparent distance of objects, appear, sometimes, to magnify men into giants, hummocks of ice into mountains, and common pieces of drift-ice into heavy floes or bergs. When fogs prevail with a freezing temperature, they usually varnish the rigging, yards, masts, and other apparatus of ships, with transparent ice. Sometimes the ice increases to the thickness of near an inch, and is apt, when dislodged by any motion produced in the rigging, to fall in showers, and cut the hands or faces of those on deck. Columns of several yards in length often descend at once.

To navigators in general, fogs are productive of inconvenience and danger. To the whale-fisher, they prove a special annoyance, by usually putting a stop to his most important occupations, and by preventing him from discovering the nature and situation of the ice, and other dangers with which he is surrounded. They also perplex the navigator, by preventing him from obtaining observations for the correction of his latitude and longitude; so that he often sails in complete uncertainty. In icy situations, indeed, where the sea is commonly smooth, and where the sun occasionally shines through the fog, an artificial horizon may be used

3

with tolerable accuracy, even upon a ship's deck;
and upon a sheet of ice, with excellent effect.
Where, however, there is the least motion, this instrument cannot be made use of, though a very simple contrivance, which I adopted some years ago,
may often be substituted with considerable advantage.   The data for the latitude, it is well known,
are the sun's declination; the angle subtended between the sun and the horizon; and the height of
the eye of the observer.   Obtaining the correct altitude of the sun, therefore, is the principal object.
But, in fogs, the apparent horizon is brought much
nearer the observer than in clear weather; and the
angle found between it and the sun, must be too
large, and the result therefore erroneous.   The distance of the proper horizon, however, increasing with
the elevation of the observer, and decreasing as he
descends, he has it in his power, by taking a boat,
and placing his eye near the surface of the water,
to bring the horizon within less than half of the
distance at which it appears from a ship's deck.
At the height of 15 feet, the horizon is seen at the
distance of $4\frac{3}{4}$ miles; but, at the height of 3 feet,
it is reduced to about two miles.   So that, from the
latter situation, if the eye can penetrate near two
miles, a correct observation can be obtained.   But,
if not, the error of observation will be much diminished.   For, should the fog or land constitute an
apparent horizon, at the distance of a mile, the er-

ror of observation, at an elevation of 3 feet, would not be a quarter of a mile; whereas, at the height of 15 feet, the usual situation of the observer in merchant ships, the error of observation would amount to 5'. And if the visible horizon were only half a mile distant, the error of observation, at the height of 3 feet, would be still only 2'; but, at 15 feet, 13'. Again, if, by estimating the distance of the visible horizon, we attempt to make allowance for the increased dip, according to tables calculated for the purpose, we shall find that a small mistake in the estimated distance of the horizon, will be productive of a considerable error in the latitude, as deduced from an observation from the deck; but that the error at the elevation of 3 feet will be trifling. Suppose the estimated distance of the horizon to be one-fifth of a mile, but its true distance one-tenth, which is an error that might easily be committed; the dip of the sea corresponding to these two distances, at the height of 3 feet, is respectively, about 8'.4, and 16'.8, the difference 8'.4 being the error which would be produced in the latitude; but, at 15 feet elevation, the dip of the sea, at the two distances of one-fifth and one-tenth of a mile, is 42½ and 85, the difference 42½ miles being the error of the latitude; and, at 20 feet height of the eye, the error would be 56 miles. Hence, when the sea is so smooth that a boat can be lowered to the water's-edge, and the eye placed within 3 feet of the surface, there is scarcely a chance of a greater error than 8 miles ; whereas, in an observation taken upon deck, there is an equal chance of a mistake of near a degree.

This method of observing the sun's altitude, is equally useful when the horizon is intercepted by land, as when it is obscured by a fog.

Fogs are more common near the ice, than in the vicinity of land ; more frequent in open seasons than in close seasons ; and more intense and more common in the southern fishing stations, than in the most northern.

CHAPTER VI.

A SKETCH OF THE ZOOLOGY OF THE ARCTIC REGIONS.

T HE view here given of the arctic zoology, is not intended as a systematic Fauna Arctica, but merely as the skeleton of such a work ; consisting almost solely of original observations on, and descriptions of, the more remarkable animals inhabiting or frequenting Spitzbergen, and the adjacent seas. Of such animals as have already been well described, or of such as are familiar to almost every one, a simple list only is given, excepting an occasional remark, illustrative of their habits or characters. Some animals, however, of the cetaceous kind, which we occasionally meet with in the Greenland Sea, are not even named in this sketch, because, I frankly confess, that, although I have seen them more than once, I could not ascertain to what genus even they belonged. Indeed, the distinguishing characters of many of the Cetacea are so imperfectly known and described, that when any species, not very familiar, comes under the eye of the naturalist, he is often at a loss to find its place in any system of Cetology. Besides, the drawings hitherto given of many of the whale tribe are so unlike, and so preposterous, that they tend rather to mislead than to assist the practical zoologist. The mysticetus, or common whale, for instance, is figured by our most respectable naturalists with the most extravagant inconsistency. The diameter, in many of the engravings that I have seen of it, measures fully one-third of the length, making the circumference, (the body being circular), and the length of the animal, nearly equal; whereas, the actual circumference very little exceeds one-half of the length. Hence, also, as another step towards an improved system of Cetology, I have confined my engravings, as well as my descriptions, to those animals which have come immediately under my own examination, or have been sketched by persons on whose accuracy and faithfulness I could fully depend; while drawings and descriptions that I have met with, when the least doubtful, have been altogether rejected.

The arrangement I have adopted, is principally that of Linné; but, with regard to the Cetacea, I have combined Linné with La Cepède. The latter author, who has published the most voluminous and pleasing account of cetaceous animals * that has ever

* " Histoire Naturelle des Cetacées." A Paris, l'an xii. de la Republique.

appeared from the press, has, I conceive, made some judicious changes in the Linnean arrangement, though the advantage of all his alterations is not very apparent. The separation of the whales having the dorsal fin, from those without it, is certainly judicious, the difference being marked and characteristic. All whales, for instance, with horny laminæ in place of teeth, having *no* dorsal fin, are, agreeably to the arrangement of Linné, included under the generic name *Balæna* ; but those possessing the dorsal fin, are, by La Cepède, called *Balænopteræ*, signifying whales with a fin.

In a somewhat similar way, animals of the genus Delphinus of Linné, having no dorsal fin, are separated from those which possess this characteristic, and are distinguished by the name of Delphinapteri, or Dolphins without the fin. In these two particulars I have followed La Cepède *.

---

* Though La Cepède's work is evidently the result of much research, and the production of an enlarged mind, yet it is by no means accurate. In several of his departures from the Linnean arrangement, the author has fallen into great mistakes. The Balæna Mysticetus and the Balæna Nordcaper, for instance, are considered by Linné as varieties only of the same animal. La Capède makes them two species. Now, La Cepède's figure of the Baleine franche (Mysticetus), has not its counterpart in nature ; but his Baleine Nordcaper is a fair representation of the Mysticetus. A similar error occurs with

2

SECT. I.

*A Description of Animals, of the Cetaceous Kind,
frequenting the Greenland Sea.*

BALÆNA MYSTICETUS :—*The Common Whale*, *or Greenland Whale*.

THIS valuable and interesting animal, generally
called *The Whale* by way of eminence, is the object
of our most important commerce to the Polar Seas,

---

regard to the Narwal. The Narwal Vulgaire, as represented
and described by La Cepède, does not, I am persuaded, exist;
while the figure and description of the Narwal Microcéphale,
though not a little erroneous, may easily be understood as representing the common narwal. The engravings, indeed, in
general, are unlike the originals.

The style of La Cepède is animated and poetical ; and his
Histoire Naturelle des Cétacées is a most interesting work ;
but the interest, in many cases, is augmented at the expence of
truth. After this assertion, an example or two may be necessary.—One can hardly doubt, says he (p. 3.), but that the
Mysticetus may have been seen, at certain times, and in certain
seas, 100 metres, that is 328 feet, long. In the present day,
he adds, they are from 20 to 30 metres (65½ to 98½ feet) in
length, (p. 5.): They spout the water to more than the height
of 13 metres or 43 feet, (p. 8.): They swim with the velocity
of 11 metres *per* second, or 21½ nautical miles an hour, (p. 56.)
And, speaking of the narwal, (Narwal Vulgaire,) he says, it is
14 to 20 metres (47 to 66 feet) in length (p. 151), and is

—is productive of more oil than any other of the Cetacea, and, being less active, slower in its motion, and more timid than any other of the kind, of similar or nearly similar magnitude, is more easily captured.

Large as the size of the whale certainly is, it has been much over-rated ;—for such is the avidity with which the human mind receives communications of the marvellous, and such the interest attached to those researches which describe any remote and extraordinary production of nature, that the judgment of the traveller receives a bias, which, in cases of doubt, induces him to fix upon that extreme point in his opinion which is calculated to afford the greatest surprise and interest. Hence, if he perceives an animal remarkable for its minuteness, he is inclined to compare it with something still more minute ;—if remarkable for its bigness, with something fully larger. When the animal inhabits an element where he cannot examine

---

armed with a very hard, sharp weapon, measuring 5 metres or 16½ feet, (p. 151).

Now, so far from these particulars being correct, I am persuaded that the Mysticetus, which is now seldom found of a length greater than 60 feet, is as large as at any former period ; that the steam of its breath (not water) is ejected to the height of some few yards, perhaps 4 or 5 ; that it swims with a velocity, at the greatest, of 8 or 9 miles an hour ; that the average size of the narwal is only 15 feet ; and that its tusk seldom exceeds 8 or 9 feet in length.

it, or is seen under any circumstances which prevent the possibility of his determining its dimensions, his decision will certainly be in that extreme
which excites the most interest.   Thus a mistake
in the size of the whale would be easily made.   And
there is every probability of such an error having been
committed two or three centuries back, from which
period some of our present dimensions have been
derived, when we know that whales were usually
viewed with superstitious dread, and their magni
tude and powers, in consequence, highly exaggerated.   Besides, errors of this kind having a tendency to increase rather than to correct one another,
from the circumstance of each writer on the subject
being influenced by a similar bias, the most gross
and extravagant results are at length obtained.

Thus authors, we find, of the first respectability
in the present day, give a length of 80 to 100 feet,
or upwards, to the Mysticetus, and remark, with
unqualified assertion, that when the captures were
less frequent, and the animals had sufficient time
to attain their full growth, specimens were found
of 150 to 200 feet in length, or even longer; and
some ancient naturalists, indeed, have gone so far as
to assert, that whales had been seen of above 900
feet in length.

But whales, in the present day, are by no means
so bulky.   Of 322 individuals, in the capture of
which I have been personally concerned, no one, I

F f 2

believe, exceeded 60 feet in length ; and the largest I ever measured, was 58 feet from one extremity to the other, being one of the longest, to appearance, which I ever saw. An uncommon whale that was caught near Spitzbergen, about 20 years ago, the whalebone of which measured almost 15 feet, was not, I understand, so much as 70 feet in length ; and the longest actual measurement that I have met with, or heard of, is given by Sir Charles Giesecké, who informs us, that, in the spring of 1813, a whale was killed at Godhavn, of the length of 67 feet. These, however, are very uncommon instances. I therefore conceive, that 60 feet may be considered as the size of the larger animals of this species, and 65 feet in length as a magnitude which very rarely occurs.

Yet I believe that whales now occur of as large dimensions, as at any former period since the commencement of the whale-fishery. This point I endeavoured to prove, from various historical records, in a paper read before the Wernerian Society, on the 19th of December 1818, and since inserted in the " Edinburgh Philosophical Journal," No. I. p. 83.

In this paper, I brought forward the authorities of Zorgdrager, the writer of an account of the whale-fishery, and one of the early superintendants of the Dutch northern fisheries, together with opinions or remarks of Captains Anderson, Gray, Heley, and

others, who were among the earliest of the English
whalers, which satisfactorily prove, that the average
and largest produce of a whale in oil, was not greater,
near two hundred years ago, than it is at the present time; and to these are added, the testimonies
of Captains Jenkinson and Edge, as to the length of
the whale, which likewise corresponds, pretty nearly, with the measurements I have myself made.

Jenkinson, in his voyage to Russia, performed in
1557, saw a number of whales, some of which, by
estimation, were 60 feet long, and are described as
being " very monstrous." Edge, who was one of
the Russia Company's chief and earliest whalefishers,
having been ten years to Spitzbergen, prior to the
year 1625, calls the whale " a sea beaste of huge
bigness, about 65 foot long and 35 foot thick," having whalebone 10 or 11 feet long, (a common size
at present,) and yielding about 100 hogsheads of
oil; and, in a descriptive plate accompanying Captain Edge's paper on the fishery, published by
PURCHAS in 1625, is a sketch of a whale, with
this remark subjoined,—" A whale is ordinarily
about 60 foot long."

Hence I conceive we may satisfactorily conclude,
that whales of as large size are found now, as at any
former period since the Spitzbergen fishery was discovered; and I may also remark, that where any respectable authority affords actual measurements exceeding 70 feet, it will always be found that the spe-

cimen referred to, was not one of the Mysticetus
kind, but of the B. Physalis, or the B. Musculus,
animals which considerably exceed in length any of
the common whales that I have either heard of, or
met with.

When fully grown, therefore, the length of the
whale may be stated as varying from 50 to 65, and
rarely, if ever, reaching 70 feet; and its greatest
circumference from 30 to 40 feet.   It is thickest a
little behind the fins, or in the middle, between the
anterior and posterior extremes of the animal ; from
whence it gradually tapers, in a conical form, towards the tail, and slightly towards the head.   Its
form is cylindrical from the neck, to within ten feet
of the tail, beyond which it becomes somewhat
quadrangular, the greatest ridge being upward, or
on the back, and running backward nearly across
the middle of the tail.   The head has somewhat of
a triangular shape.   The under-part, the arched
outline of which is given by the jaw-bones, is flat,
and measures 16 to 20 feet in length, and 10 to 12 in
breadth. The lips, extending 15 or 20 feet in length,
and 5 or 6 in height, and forming the cavity of the
mouth, are attached to the under-jaw, and rise from
the jaw-bones, at an angle of about 80 degrees, having the appearance, when viewed in front, of the
letter U.   The upper-jaw, including the " crown-
bone," or skull, is bent down at the extremity, so as
to shut the front and upper parts of the cavity of

the mouth, and is overlapped by the lips in a squamous manner at the sides.

When the mouth is open, it presents a cavity as large as a room, and capable of containing a merchant-ship's jolly-boat, full of men, being 6 or 8 feet wide, 10 or 12 feet high (in front), and 15 or 16 feet long.

The fins, two in number, are placed between one-third and two-fifths of the length of the animal, from the snout, and about two feet behind the angle of the mouth. They are 7 to 9 feet in length, and 4 or 5 in breadth. The part by which they are attached to the body, is somewhat elliptical, and about 2 feet in diameter; the side which strikes the water is nearly flat. The articulation being perfectly spherical, the fins are capable of motion in any direction; but, from the tension of the flesh and skin below, they cannot be raised above the horizontal position. Hence the account given by some naturalists, that the whale supports its young by its fins, on its back, must be erroneous. The fins, after death, are always hard and stiff; but, in the living animal, it is presumed, from the nature of the internal structure, that they are capable of considerable flexion. The whale has no dorsal fin.

The tail, comprising, in a single surface, 80 or 100 square feet, is a formidable instrument of motion and defence. Its length is only 5 or 6 feet; but its width is 18 to 24 or 26 feet. Its position is horizontal.   In its form it is flat and semi-lunar; indented in the middle; the two lobes somewhat pointed, and turned a little backward.   Its motions are rapid and universal; its strength immense.

The eyes are situated in the sides of the head, about a foot obliquely above and behind the angle of the mouth.   They are remarkably small in proportion to the bulk of the animal's body, being little larger than those of an ox.   The whale has no external ear; nor can any orifice for the admission of sound be discovered until the skin is removed.

On the most elevated part of the head, about 16 feet from the anterior extremity of the jaw, are situated the blow-holes, or spiracles; consisting of two longitudinal apertures 6 or 8 inches in length. These are the proper nostrils of the whale.   A moist vapour, mixed with mucous, is discharged from them, when the animal breathes; but no water accompanies it, unless an expiration of the breath be made under the surface.

The mouth, in place of teeth, contains two extensive rows of " fins," or whalebone, which are suspended from the sides of the crown-bone.   These series of fins are generally curved longitudinally, although they are sometimes straight, and give an arched form to the roof of the mouth.   They are covered immediately by the lips attached to the lower jaw, and enclose the tongue between their lower extremities.   Each series, or " side of bone," as the whalefishers term it, consists of upwards of 300 laminæ *; the longest are near the middle, from whence they gradually diminish away to nothing at each extremity. Fifteen feet is the greatest length of the whalebone; but 10 or 11 feet is the average size, and 13 feet is a magnitude seldom met with. The greatest breadth, which is at the *gum*, is 10 or 12 inches. The laminæ, composing the two series of bone, are ranged side by side, two-thirds of an inch apart, (thickness of the blade included,) and resemble a frame of saws in a saw-mill. The interior edges are covered with a fringe of hair, and the exterior edge of every blade, excepting a few at each extremity of the series, is curved and flattened down, so as to present a smooth surface to the lips. In some whales, a curious hollow on one side, and ridge on the other, occurs in many of the central blades of whalebone, at regular intervals of 6 or 7 inches. May not this irregularity, like the rings in the horns of the ox, which they resemble, afford an intimation of the age of the whale? If so, twice the number of running feet in the longest lamina of whalebone in the head of a whale not full grown, would represent its age in years. In the youngest whales, called *Suckers*, the whalebone is only a few inches long; when the length reaches 6 feet or upwards, the whale is said to be *size*. The colour of the whalebone is brownish-black, or bluish-black.

---

* In a very small whale, the number was 316 or 320.

In some animals, it is striped longitudinally with white. When newly cleaned, the surface exhibits a fine play of colour. A large whale sometimes affords a ton and a half of whalebone. If the " sample blade," that is, the largest lamina in the series, weigh 7 pounds, the whole produce may be estimated at a ton ; and so on in proportion. The whalebone is inserted into the crown-bone, in a sort of rabbit. All the blades in the same series are connected together by the gum, in which the thick ends are inserted. This substance, (the gum,) is white, fibrous, tender and tasteless. It cuts like cheese. It has the appearance of the interior or kernel of the cocoa-nut.

The tongue occupies a large proportion of the cavity of the mouth, and the arch formed by the whalebone. It is incapable of protrusion, being fixed from root to tip, to the fat extending between the jaw-bones.

A slight beard, consisting of a few short scattered white hairs, surmounts the anterior extremity of both jaws.

The throat is remarkably strait.

The male organ is a large flexible member, and is concealed in a longitudinal groove, the external opening of which is 2 or 8 feet in length. This member, in the dead animal, is 8 or 10 feet in length, and about 6 inches in diameter at the root. It tapers to a point, and is perforated throughout its length by the urethra.

Two paps in the female, afford the means of rearing its young.   They are situated on the abdomen, one on each side of the pudendum, and are 2 feet apart. They appear not to be capable of protrusion, beyond the length of a few inches. ، In the dead animal, they are always found retracted.

The milk of the whale resembles that of quadrupeds in its appearance.   It is said to be rich and well-flavoured.

The vent is about 6 inches behind the pudendum of the female ; but, in the male, it is more distant from the organ of generation.

The colour of the Mysticetus is velvet-black, grey, (composed of dots of blackish-brown, on a white ground,) and white, with a tinge of yellow.   The back, most of the upper-jaw, and part of the lower jaw, together with the fins and tail, are black.   The tongue, the fore part of the under-jaw and lips, sometimes a little of the upper-jaw, at the extremity, and a portion of the belly, are white.   And the eye-lids, the junction of the tail with the body, a portion in the axillæ of the fins, &c. are grey.   I have seen whales that were all over piebald.   The older animals contain the most grey and white ; under-size whales are altogether of a bluish-black, and suckers of a pale bluish, or bluish-grey colour.

The skin of the body is slightly furrowed, like the water-lines in coarse laid paper.   On the tail, fins, &c. it is smooth.   The cuticle, or that part of the skin which can be pulled off in sheets after it has been a little dried in the air, or particularly in frost, is not thicker than parchment. The rete mucosum in adults, is about three-fourths of an inch in thickness, over most parts of the body; in suckers, nearly two inches; but on the under side of the fins, on the inside of the lips, and on the surface of the tongue, it is much thinner. This part of the integuments, is generally of the same colour throughout its thickness. The fibres of which it is composed, are perpendicular to the surface of the body. Under this lies the true skin, which is white and tough. As it imperceptibly becomes impregnated with oil, and passes gradually into the form of blubber, its real thickness cannot easily be stated. The most compact part, perhaps, may be a quarter of an inch thick.

Immediately beneath the skin lies the *blubber* or fat, encompassing the whole body of the animal, together with the fins and tail. Its colour is yellowish-white, yellow or red. In the very young animal it is always yellowish-white. In some old animals, it resembles in colour the substance of the salmon. It swims in water. Its thickness all round the body, is 8 or 10 to 20 inches, varying in different parts as well as in different individuals. The lips are composed almost entirely of blubber, and yield from one to two tons of pure oil each. The tongue is chiefly composed of a soft kind of fat, that

affords less oil than any other blubber : in the centre of the tongue, and towards the root, this fat is
intermixed with fibres of a muscular substance. The
under jaw, excepting the two jaw-bones, consists almost wholly of fat; and the crown-bone possesses a
considerable coating of it.   The fins are principally
blubber, tendons, and bones, and the tail possesses a
thin stratum of blubber.   The oil appears to be retained in the blubber in minute cells, connected together by a strong reticulated combination of tendinous
fibres.   These fibres being condensed at the surface,
appear to form the substance of the skin.   The oil is
expelled when heated ; and, in a great measure, discharges itself out of the *fenks*, whenever putrefaction in the fibrous parts of the blubber takes place.
The blubber and the whalebone are the parts of the
whale to which the attention of the fisher is directed.
The flesh and bones, excepting the jaw-bones occasionally, are rejected.   The blubber in its fresh state,
is without any unpleasant smell ; and it is not until
after the termination of the voyage, when the cargo is unstowed, that a Greenland ship becomes disagreeable.

Four tons of blubber by measure, generally afford
three tons of oil* ; but the blubber of a sucker con-

---

* The ton or tun of oil, is 252 gallons wine measure.   It
weighs, at temperature 60°, 1933 lb. 12 oz. 14 dr. avoirdupois.

tains a very small proportion. Whales have been caught that afforded nearly thirty tons of pure oil; and whales yielding twenty tons of oil, are by no means uncommon. The quantity of oil yielded by a whale, generally bears a certain proportion to the length of its longest blade of whalebone. The average quantity is expressed in the following table*.

Length of whale-bone in feet,	1	2	3	4	5	6	7	8	9	10	11	12
Oil yielded in tons - -	1½	2¼	2¾	3¼	4	5	6½	8	11	13½	17	21

Though this statement on the average be exceedingly near the truth, yet exceptions sometimes occur. A whale of 2½ feet bone, for instance, has been known to produce near ten tons of oil; and another of 12 feet bone, only nine tons. Such instances, however, are very uncommon.

A stout whale of sixty feet in length, is of the enormous weight of seventy tons; the blubber weighs about thirty tons, the bones of the head, whalebone, fins and tail, eight or ten; carcass thirty or thirty-two.

***

* This table is somewhat different from that given in Wernerian Memoirs, (vol. i. p. 582); an increased number of observations having enabled me to improve it.

3

The flesh of the young whale is of a red colour; and when cleared of fat, broiled, and seasoned with pepper and salt, does not eat unlike coarse beef; that of the old whale approaches to black, and is exceedingly coarse. An immense bed of muscles surrounding the body, is appropriated chiefly to the movements of the tail. The tail consists principally of two reticulated beds of sinewy fibres, compactly interwoven, and containing very little oil. In the central bed the fibres run in all directions; in the other, which encompasses the central one in a thinner stratum, they are arranged in regular order. These substances are extensively used, particularly in Holland, in the manufacture of glue.

Most of the bones of the whale are very porous, and contain large quantities of fine oil. The jaw-bones, which measure twenty to twenty-five feet in length, are often taken care of, principally on account of the oil that drains out of them, when they come into a warm climate. When exhausted of oil, they readily swim in water. The external surface of the most porous bones, is compact and hard. The ribs are pretty nearly solid; but the crown-bone is almost as much honeycombed as the jaw-bones. The number of ribs, according to Sir Charles Giesecké, is thirteen on each side. The bones of the fins are analogous, both in proportion and number, to those of the fingers of the human hand. From this peculiarity of structure, the fins have been denominated by Dr Flem-

ing " swimming paws." The posterior extremity of
the whale, however, is a real tail ; the termination of
the spine or os coccygis, running through the middle
of it almost to the edge.

Few opportunities of examining the internal structure of the mysticetus occur ; hence, what is known
respecting its anatomy, is deduced principally from
its analogy to other cetaceous animals.

*Table of the Comparative Dimensions of Six Mys-
ticete, from my own Measurements.*

	Ft. In.	Ft. In.	Ft. In.	Ft. In.	Ft. In.	Ft. In.
Longest blade of whalebone,	1.0	6.0	10.10	11.2	11.6	13.7
Extreme length,..............	17.0	28.0	51. 0	50.0	58.0	52.0
Length of the head,.........	5.0	8.6	16. 0	15.6	19.0	20.0
Breadth of under-jaw,......	......	......	......	9.6	12.0	......
Length from tip of lip to fin,	5.6	10.0	......	18.0	......	......
—— to greatest circumf.	7.0	......	......	24.0	......	......
Circumference at the neck,	10.0	18.6	......	31.6	......	34.0
Greatest circumference,.....	12.0	20.0	......	34.0	35.0	......
Circumfer. by the genitalia,	9.0	15.6	......	19.0	......	......
——near the tail,...	2.11	4.0	6.6	6.8	......	......
Fin,—Length,..............	2.3	......	7.0	6.4	8.6	9.0
Breadth,..............	1.3	......	4.0	4.0	5.0	......
Tail,—Length,...............	......	......	5.6	5.6	6.0	6.0
Breadth,..............	......	......	20.0	17.6	24.0	20.10
Lip,— Length,..............	4.9	8.2	15.6	15.0	18.6	19. 6
Breadth,..............	......	......	......	......	......	6. 2
Produce in oil, (tons).......	1	4	16	16	19	24
Sex,.......................	F.	M.		F.		M.

The whale seems dull of hearing. A noise in
the air, such as that produced by a person shouting,

2

is not noticed by it, though at the distance only of a ship's length; but a very slight splashing in the water, in calm weather, excites its attention, and alarms it.

Its sense of seeing is acute. Whales are observed to discover one another, in clear water, when under the surface, at an amazing distance. When at the surface, however, they do not see far.

They have no voice; but, in breathing or *blowing*, they make a very loud noise. The vapour they discharge, is ejected to the height of some yards, and appears at a distance, like a puff of smoke. When the animals are wounded, it is often stained with blood; and, on the approach of death, jets of blood are sometimes discharged alone. They blow strongest, densest, and loudest, when " running," when in a state of alarm, or when they first appear at the surface, after being a long time down. They respire or blow about four or five times a-minute.

The whale, being somewhat lighter than the medium in which it swims, can remain at the surface of the sea, with its " crown," in which the blowholes are situated, and a considerable extent of the back, above water, without any effort or motion. To descend, however, requires an exertion. The proportion of the whale that appears above water, when alive, or when recently killed, is probably not a twentieth part of the animal; but, within a day after death, when the process of putrefaction commences, the whale swells to an enormous size, until at least a third of the carcase appears above water, and sometimes the body is burst by the force of the air generated within.

By means of the tail, principally, the whale advances through the water. The greatest velocity is produced by powerful strokes against the water, impressed alternately upward and downward; but a slower motion, it is believed, is elegantly produced, by cutting the water laterally and obliquely downward, in a similar manner as a boat is forced along, with a single oar, by the operation of *skulling*. The fins are generally stretched out in an horizontal position : their chief application seems to be, the balancing of the animal, as the moment life is extinct, it always falls over on its side, or turns upon its back. They appear also to be used, in bearing off their young, in turning, and giving a direction to the velocity produced by the tail.

Bulky as the whale is, and inactive, or indeed clumsy as it appears to be, one might imagine that all its motions would be sluggish, and its greatest exertions productive of no great celerity. The fact, however, is the reverse. A whale extended motionless at the surface of the sea, can sink in the space of five or six seconds, or less, beyond the reach of its human enemies. Its velocity along the surface, or perpendicularly or obliquely downward, is the same. I have observed a whale descending, after I had harpooned it, to the depth of 400 fathoms, with the average velocity of seven or eight miles *per* hour. The usual rate at which whales swim, however, even when they are on their passage from one situation to another, seldom exceeds four miles an hour; and though, when urged by the sight of any enemy, or alarmed by the stroke of a harpoon, their extreme velocity may be at the rate of eight or nine miles an hour; yet we find this speed never continues longer than for a few minutes, before it relaxes almost to one-half. Hence, for the space of a few minutes, they are capable of darting through the water, with the velocity almost of the fastest ship under sail, and of ascending with such rapidity as to leap entirely out of the water. This feat they sometimes perform as an amusement apparently, to the high admiration of the distant spectator; but to the no small terror of the unexperienced fishers, who, even under such circumstances, are often ordered, by the foolhardy harpooner, to " pull away" to the attack. Sometimes the whales throw themselves into a perpendicular posture, with their heads downward, and, rearing their tails on high in the air, beat the water with awful violence. In both these cases, the sea is thrown into foam, and the air filled with vapours; the noise, in calm weather, is heard to a great distance; and the concentric waves produced by the concussions on the water, are communicated abroad to

a considerable extent. Sometimes the whale shakes
its tremendous tail in the air, which, cracking like a
whip, resounds to the distance of two or three miles.

When it retires from the surface, it first lifts its
head, then plunging it under water, elevates its
back like the segment of a sphere, deliberately
rounds it away towards the extremity, throws its
tail out of the water, and then disappears.

In their usual conduct, whales remain at the surface to breathe, about two minutes, seldom longer;
during which time, they "blow" eight or nine times,
and then descend for an interval usually of five or
ten minutes; but sometimes, when feeding, fifteen
or twenty. The depth to which they commonly
descend, is not known, though, from the "eddy"
occasionally observed on the water, it is evidently,
at times, only trifling. But, when struck, the quantity of line they sometimes take out of the boats, in
a perpendicular descent, affords a good measure of
the depth. By this rule, they have been known to
descend to the depth of an English mile; and with
such velocity, that instances have occurred, in which
whales have been drawn up by the line attached,
from a depth of 700 or 800 fathoms, and have been
found to have broken their jaw-bones, and sometimes crown-bone, by the blow struck against the
bottom. Some persons are of opinion, that whales
can remain under a field of ice, or at the bottom of
the sea, in shallow water, when undisturbed, for

many hours at a time. Whales are seldom found sleeping; yet, in calm weather, among ice, instances occasionally occur.

The food of the whale consists of various species of actiniæ, cliones, sepiæ, medusæ, cancri, and helices; or, at least, some of these genera are always to be seen wherever any tribe of whales is found stationary and feeding. In the dead animals, however, in the very few instances in which I have been enabled to open their stomachs, squillæ or shrimps were the only substances discovered. In the mouth of a whale just killed, I once found a quantity of the same kind of insect.

When the whale feeds, it swims with considerable velocity below the surface of the sea, with its jaws widely extended. A stream of water consequently enters its capacious mouth, and along with it, large quantities of water insects; the water escapes again at the sides; but the food is entangled and sifted, as it were, by the whalebone, which, from its compact arrangement, and the thick internal covering of hair, does not allow a particle the size of the smallest grain to escape.

There does not seem to be a sufficient dissimilarity in the form and appearance of the mysticete found in the polar seas, to entitle them to a division into other species; yet such is the difference observed in the proportions of these animals, that they may be well considered as sub-species or varieties

In some of the mysticete, the head measures four-tenths of the whole length of the animal; in others scarcely three-tenths; in some the circumference is upwards of seven-tenths of the length; in others less than six-tenths, or little more than one-half.

The sexual intercourse of whales is often observed about the latter end of summer; and females, with cubs or suckers along with them, being most commonly met with in the spring of the year, the time of their bringing forth, it is presumed, is in February or March; and their period of gestation about nine or ten months. In the latter end of April 1811, a sucker was taken by a Hull whaler, to which the funis umbilicalis was still attached. The whale has one young at a birth. Instances of two being seen with a female are very rare. The young one, at the time of parturition, is said to be at least ten, if not fourteen feet in length. It goes under the protection of its mother, for probably a year, or more; or until, by the evolution of the whalebone, it is enabled to procure its own nourishment. Supposing the criterion before mentioned, of the notches in the whalebone being indicative of the number of years growth, to be correct, then it would appear that the whale reaches the magnitude called *size*; that is, with a six feet length of whalebone, in twelve years, and attains its full growth at the age of twenty or twenty-five. Whales, doubtless, live to a great age. The marks of age are an increase in the quantity of grey colour in the skin, and a change to a yellowish tinge of the white parts about the head; a decrease in the quantity of oil yielded by a certain weight of blubber; an increase of hardness in the blubber, and in the thickness and strength of the ligamentous fibres of which it is partly composed.

The maternal affection of the whale, which, in other respects, is apparently a stupid animal, is striking and interesting. The cub, being insensible to danger, is easily harpooned; when the tender attachment of the mother is so manifested as not unfrequently to bring it within the reach of the whalers. Hence, though a cub is of little value, seldom producing above a ton of oil, and often less, yet it is sometimes struck as a snare for its mother. In this case, she joins it at the surface of the water, whenever it has occasion to rise for respiration; encourages it to swim off; assists its flight, by taking it under her fin; and seldom deserts it while life remains. She is then dangerous to approach; but affords frequent opportunities for attack. She loses all regard for her own safety, in anxiety for the preservation of her young;—dashes through the midst of her enemies;—despises the danger that threatens her;—and even voluntarily remains with her offspring, after various attacks on herself from the harpoons of the fishers. In June 1811, one of my harpooners struck a sucker, with the hope of its leading to the capture of the mother. Presently she arose close by the " fast-boat ;" and seizing the young one, dragged about a hundred fathoms of line out of the boat with remarkable force and velocity. Again she arose to the surface ; darted furiously to and fro ; frequently stopped short, or suddenly changed her direction, and gave every possible intimation of extreme agony. For a length of time, she continued thus to act, though closely pursued by the boats ; and, inspired with courage and resolution by her concern for her offspring, seemed regardless of the danger which surrounded her. At length, one of the boats approached so near, that a harpoon was hove at her. It hit, but did not attach itself. A second harpoon was struck ; this also failed to penetrate : but a third was more effectual, and held.   Still she did not attempt to escape ; but allowed other boats to approach ; so that, in a few minutes, three more harpoons were fastened ; and, in the course of an hour afterwards, she was killed.

There is something extremely painful in the destruction of a whale, when thus evincing a degree of affectionate regard for its offspring, that would do honour to the superior intelligence of human beings ; yet the object of the adventure, the value of the prize, the joy of the capture, cannot be sacrificed to feelings of compassion.

Whales, though often found in great numbers together, can scarcely be said to be gregarious ; for they are found most generally solitary, or in pairs, excepting when drawn to the same spot, by the attraction of an abundance of palatable food, or of a choice situation of the ice.

The superiority of the sexes, in point of numbers, seems to be in favour of the male. Of 124 whales which have been taken near Spitzbergen in eight years, in ships commanded by myself, 70 were males, and 54 were females, being in the proportion of five to four nearly.

The mysticetus occurs most abundantly in the frozen seas of Greenland and Davis' Strait,—in the bays of Baffin and Hudson,—in the sea to the northward of Behring's Strait, and along some parts of the northern shores of Asia, and probably America. It is never met with in the German Ocean, and rarely within 200 leagues of the British coasts: but along the coasts of Africa and South America, it is met with, periodically, in considerable numbers. In these regions, it is attacked and captured by the southern British and American whalers, as well as by some of the people inhabiting the coasts to the neighbourhood of which it resorts. Whether this whale is precisely of the same kind as that of Spitzbergen and Greenland, is uncertain, though it is evidently a mysticetus. One striking difference, possibly the effect of situation and climate, is, that the mysticetus found in southern regions, is often covered with

barnacles, (Lepas Diadema, &c.) while those of the
arctic seas are free from these shell-fish.

It would be remarkable, if an animal like the
whale, which is so timid that a bird alighting upon its back sometimes sets it off in great agitation
and terror, should be wholly devoid of enemies.
Besides man, who is doubtless its most formidable
adversary, it is subject to annoyance from sharks,
and it is also said from the narwal, sword-fish and
thrasher. With regard to the narwal, I am persuaded, that this opinion is incorrect, for so far
from its being an enemy, it is found to associate
with the whale with the greatest apparent harmony,
and its appearance indeed in the Greenland sea is
hailed by the fishers, the narwal being considered
as the harbinger of the whale. But the sword-
fish and thrasher (if such an animal there be) may
possibly be among the enemies of the whale, notwithstanding I have never witnessed their com-
bats; and the shark is known certainly to be an
enemy, though, perhaps, not a very formidable
one. Whales, indeed, flee the seas where it
abounds, and evince, by marks occasionally found on
their tails, a strong evidence of their having been
bit by the shark. A living whale may be annoyed,
though it can scarcely be supposed to be ever overcome by the shark; but a dead whale is an easy
prey, and affords a fine banquet to this insatiable
creature.

3

The whale, from its vast bulk and variety of products, is of great importance in commerce, as well as in the domestic economy of savage nations; and its oil and whalebone are of extensive application in the arts and manufactures. A description of its most valuable products, and of the uses to which they are applied, being included in the account of the whale-fishery, in the second volume of this work, it will only be necessary, in this place, to mention the purposes to which parts and products, not now objects of commerce, are or might be applied.

Though to the refined palate of a modern European, the flesh of a whale, as an article of food, would be received with abhorrence, yet we find that it is considered, by some of the inhabitants of the northern shores of Europe, Asia, and America, as well as those on the coasts of Hudson's Bay and Davis' Strait, as a choice and staple article of subsistence. The Esquimaux eat the flesh and fat of the whale, and drink the oil with greediness. Indeed, some tribes who are not familiarised with spirituous liquors, carry along with them in their canoes, in their fishing excursions, bladders filled with oil, which they use in the same way, and with a similar relish, that a British sailor does a dram*. They also eat the skin of the whale raw, both adults and children; for it is not uncommon, when the females visit the whale-ships, for them to help themselves

* Ellis's Voyage to Hudson's Bay, p. 233.

to pieces of skin, preferring those with which a
little blubber is connected, and to give it as food
to their infants suspended on their backs, who suck
it with apparent delight. Blubber, when pickled
and boiled, is said to be very palatable; the tail,
when par-boiled and then fried, is said to be not
unsavory, but even agreeable eating; and the flesh
of young whales, I know from experiment, is by no
means indifferent food.

Not only is it certain that the flesh of the whale
is now eaten by savage nations, but it is also well
authenticated that, in the 12th, 13th, 14th and
15th centuries, it was used as food by the Icelanders, the Netherlanders, the French, the Spaniards,
and probably by the English. M. S. B. Noel,
in a tract on the whale-fishery*, informs us, that
about the 13th century, the flesh, particularly the
tongue, of whales, was sold in the markets of
Bayonne, Cibourre, and Beariz, where it was esteemed as a great delicacy, being used at the best
tables; and even so late as the 15th century, he
conceives, from the authority of Charles Etienne,
that the principal nourishment of the poor in Lent,
in some districts of France, consisted of the flesh
and fat of the whale.

Besides forming a choice eatable, the inferior products of the whale are applied to other purposes by

---

* " Memoire sur l'Antiquité de la Pêche de la Baleine par
les Nations Européennes."

the Indians and Esquimaux of arctic countries,
and with some nations are essential to their comfort.
Some membranes of the abdomen are used for an
upper article of clothing, and the peritoneum in
particular, being thin and transparent, is used instead of glass in the windows of their huts; the
bones are converted into harpoons and spears, for
striking the seal, or darting at the sea-birds, and
are also employed in the erection of their tents,
and with some tribes in the formation of their
boats; the sinews are divided into filaments, and
used as thread, with which they join the seams of
their boats and tent-cloths, and sew with great
taste and nicety the different articles of dress they
manufacture; and the whalebone and other superior products, so valuable in European markets, have
also their uses among them.

I shall conclude this account of the mysticetus,
with a sketch of some of the characters which belong generally to cetaceous animals.

Whales are viviparous; they have but one young
at a time, and suckle it with teats. They are furnished with lungs, and are under the necessity of
approaching the surface of the water at intervals to
respire in the air. The heart has two ventricles
and two auricles. The blood is warmer than in the
human species; in a narwal that had been an hour
and a half dead, the temperature of the blood was 97°;
and in a mysticetus recently killed, 102°. All of

them inhabit the sea. Some of them procure their food by means of a kind of sieve, composed of two fringes of whalebone; these have no teeth. Others have no whalebone, but are furnished with teeth. They all have two lateral or pectoral fins, with concealed bones like those of a hand; and a large flexible horizontal tail, which is the principal member of motion. Some have a kind of dorsal fin, which is an adipose, or cartilaginous substance, without motion. This fin varying in form, size and position, in different species, and being in a conspicuous situation, is well adapted for a specific distinction. The appearance and dimensions of the whalebone and teeth, especially the former, are other specific characteristics. All whales have spiracles or blowholes, some with one, others with two openings, through which they breathe; some have a smooth skin all over the body; others have rugæ or sulci about the region of the thorax and on the lower jaw. And all afford, beneath the integuments, a quantity of fat or blubber, from whence a useful and valuable oil, the train-oil of commerce, is extracted.

BALÆNOPTERA *Gibbar* (La Cepède:)—*B. Physalis* of Linné, or *Razor-back* of the whalers.

This is the longest animal of the whale tribe; and, probably, the most powerful and bulky of created beings.

It differs from the mysticetus in its form being
less cylindrical, and its body longer and more slender; in its whalebone being shorter; in its produce
in blubber and oil being less; in its colour being of
a bluer tinge; in its fins being more in number; in
its breathing or blowing being more violent; in its
speed being greater; in its actions being quicker
and more restless, and in its conduct being bolder.

The length of the physalis is about 100 feet; its
greatest circumference 30 or 35.   The body is not
cylindrical, but is considerably compressed on the
sides, and angular at the back.   A transverse section near the fins is an oblong; and at the rump a
rhombus. The longest lamina of whalebone measures
about 4 feet.   It affords 10 or 12 tons of blubber.
Its colour is a pale bluish-black, or dark bluish-grey,
in which it resembles the sucking mysticetus.   Besides the two pectoral fins, it has a small horny protuberance, or rayless and immoveable fin, on the extremity of the back.   Its blowing is very violent,
and may be heard in calm weather, at the distance of
about a mile. It swims with a velocity, at the greatest, of about twelve miles an hour.   It is by no
means a timid animal; yet it does not appear to be
revengeful or mischievous.   When closely pursued
by boats, it manifests little fear, and does not attempt to outstrip them in the race; but merely endeavours to avoid them, by diving or changing its
direction.   If harpooned or otherwise wounded, it

then exerts all its energies, and escapes with its utmost velocity; but shows little disposition to retaliate on its enemies, or to repel their attacks by engaging in a combat. Though at a distance, the physalis is sometimes mistaken by the whalers for the mysticetus; yet its appearance and actions are so different, that it may be generally distinguished. It seldom lies quietly on the surface of the water when blowing, but usually has a velocity of four or five miles an hour; and when it descends, it very rarely throws its tail in the air, which is a very general practice with the mysticetus.

The great speed and activity of the physalis, render it a difficult and dangerous object of attack; while the small quantity of inferior oil it affords, makes it unworthy the general attention of the fishers. When struck, it frequently drags the fast-boat with such speed through the water, that it is liable to be carried immediately beyond the reach of assistance, and soon out of sight of both boats and ship. Hence, the striker is under the necessity of cutting the line, and sacrificing his employer's property, for securing the safety of himself and companions. I have made different attempts to capture one of these formidable creatures. In the year 1818, I ordered a general chase of them, providing against the danger of having my crew separated from the ship, by appointing a rendezvous on the shore not far distant, and preparing against the loss of much line, by dividing

2

it at 200 fathoms from the harpoon, and affixing a buoy to the end of it. Thus arranged, one of these whales was shot and another struck. The former dived with such impetuosity, that the line was broken by the resistance of the buoy as soon as it was thrown into the water, and the latter was liberated within a minute by the division of the line, occasioned, it was supposed, by its friction against the dorsal fin. Both of them escaped. Another physalis was struck by one of my inexperienced harpooners, who mistook it for a mysticetus. It dived obliquely with such velocity, that 480 fathoms of line were withdrawn from the boat in about a minute of time. This whale was also lost by the breaking of the line.

The following observations on this animal have been derived from conversations with different persons who have had opportunities of examining it when dead.

Length of a Physalis found dead in Davis' Strait, 105 feet; greatest circumference about 38. Head small compared with that of the common whale; fins long and narrow; tail about 12 feet broad, finely formed; whalebone 4 feet in length, thick, bristly and narrow; blubber 6 or 8 inches thick, of indifferent quality; colour bluish-black on the back, and bluish-grey on the belly; skin smooth, excepting about the sides of the thorax, where longitudinal rugæ or sulci occur.

The physalis occurs in great numbers in the Arctic Seas, especially along the edge of the ice, between Cherie Island and Nova Zembla, and also near Jan Mayen. Persons trading to Archangel have often mistaken it for the common whale. It is seldom seen among much ice, and seems to be avoided by the mysticetus; as such, the whale-fishers view its appearance with painful concern. It inhabits most generally in the Spitzbergen quarter, the parallels of 70 to 76 degrees; but in the months of June, July and August, when the sea is usually open, it advances along the land to the northward as high as the 80th degree of latitude. In open seasons it is seen near the Headland, at an earlier period. A whale, probably of this kind, 101 feet in length, was stranded on the banks of the Humber about the middle of September 1750.

BALÆNOPTERA *Rorqual* (La Cepède :)—*Balæna Musculus* of Linné, *or Broad-nosed Whale.*

This species of whale frequents the coasts of Scotland, Ireland, Norway, &c., and is said to feed principally upon herrings. Several characters of the musculus very much resemble those of the physalis, though, I believe, there is an essential difference between the two animals; the musculus being shorter, having a larger head and mouth, and a rounder

under-jaw than the physalis. Several individuals,
apparently of this kind, have been stranded or killed
on different parts of the coast of the united king-
dom. One, 52 feet in length, was stranded near Eye-
mouth, June 19. 1752. Another, nearly 70 feet in
length, ran ashore on the coast of Cornwall, on the
18th of June 1797. Three were killed on the north-
west coast of Ireland in the year 1762, and
two in 1763; one or two have been killed in the
Thames; and one was embayed and killed in Balta
Sound, Shetland, in the winter of 1817–18, some remains of which I saw. This latter whale was 82
feet in length; the jaw-bones were 21 feet long;
the longest lamina of whalebone about 3 feet long.
Instead of hair at the inner edge, and at the point
of each blade of whalebone, it had a fringe of bristly
fibres; and it was stiffer, harder, and more horny in
its texture than common whalebone. This whale
produced only about five tons of oil, all of it of an
inferior quality, some of it viscid and bad. It was
valued altogether, expences of removing the produce
and extracting the oil deducted, at no more than
60 *l.* Sterling. It had the usual sulci about the
thorax, and a dorsal fin.

In its blowing, swimming, and general actions, as
well as in its appearance in the water, the musculus
very much resembles the physalis, from which, indeed, while living, it can scarcely be distinguished.

н h 2

BALÆNOPTERA *Jubartes*, (La Cepède.)—*Balæna Boops*
of Linné, or *Finner* of the Whale-fishers.

Length about 46 feet; greatest circumference of
the body about 20 feet; dorsal protuberance or fin
about two feet and a half high; pectoral fins 4 or 5
feet long, externally, and scarcely a foot broad; tail
about 3 feet deep, and 10 broad; whalebone, about
300 laminæ on each side, the longest about 18 inches in length; the under-jaw about 15 feet long,
or one-third of the whole length of the animal;
sulci about two dozen in number; two external
blow-holes; blubber on the body 2 or 3 inches
thick, under the sulci none.

In the Memoirs of the Wernerian Society, a description of a whale, corresponding, in its dimensions
at least, with the Balæna Boops, has been given to
the public, by my friend Mr P. Neill, Edinburgh *
This whale was stranded on the banks of the Forth,
near Alloa, and had been considerably mutilated
before Mr Neill had an opportunity of examining
it. It is considered by him a Balæna Rostrata.
From his valuable paper part of the above description is taken, which differs so much from a Rostrata
noticed below, particularly in its larger dimensions,
and in the greater proportion which the head bears

* Vol. i. p. 201.

to the body, that it would appear to belong either to the Balæna Boops, or to an undescribed species. From the inaccuracy of the sketches of almost all the whales hitherto figured, the naturalist is rather plagued than assisted by them. As such, the figures given by La Cepède and others, can scarcely be of any service in determining the species of this whale.

BALÆNOPTERA *Acuto-rostrata*, (La Cepède).—*Balæna rostrata* of Linné, or *Beaked Whale*.

This is the last and the smallest of the whale-bone whales with which I am acquainted. In Plate 13, fig. 2. is an accurate representation of this animal, taken from an original drawing, accompanied by actual measurements, by the late James Watson, Esq. of Orkney, for the use of which I am indebted to the kindness of my friend Dr Traill of Liverpool. The animal from which this drawing was taken, was killed in Scalpa Bay, Nov. 14. 1808. Its length was $17\frac{1}{2}$ feet; circumference 20. Length from the snout to the dorsal fin $12\frac{1}{2}$ feet; from the snout to the pectoral fins 5 feet; from the snout to the eye $3\frac{1}{2}$ feet; and from the snout to the blow-holes 3 feet. Pectoral fins 2 feet long and 7 inches broad; dorsal fin 15 inches long by 9 inches high; tail 15 inches long by $4\frac{1}{2}$ feet broad. Largest whale-bone about 6 inches. Colour of the back black;

of the belly glossy-white; and of the grooves of the plicæ according to Mrs Traill, who saw it on the beach in Scalpa Bay, a sort of flesh-colour.

The Rostrata is said to inhabit, principally, the Norwegian Seas, and to grow to the length of 25 feet *. One of the species was killed near Spitzbergen, in the year 1813, some of the whalebone of which I now have in my possession. It is thin, fibrous, of a yellowish white colour, and semi-transparent, almost like lantern-horns. It is curved like a scymeter; and fringed with white hair on the convex edge and point. Its length is 9 inches; greatest breadth 2¼.

MONODON *Monoceros* (Linné:)—*Narwal,* or *Unicorn* of
the Whalers.

La Cepède notices three species of narwals; I have seen but one; and, perhaps, the other species are only imaginary, for the animal varies in appearance.

This animal, when full grown, is from 13 to 16 feet in length, exclusive of the tusk, and in circumference (two feet behind the fins, where it is thickest,) 8 to 9 feet.

The form of the head, with the part of the body before the fins, is paraboloidal, of the middle of the body nearly cylindrical, of the hinder part, to with-

---

* La Cepède states the length at 8 or 9 metres, which is 26 to 29 feet.

in two or three feet of tail somewhat conical, and from thence a ridge commencing, both at the back and belly, the section becomes first an ellipse, and then a rhombus at the junction of the tail. At the distance of 12 or 14 inches from the tail, the perpendicular diameter is about 12 inches, the transverse diameter about 7. The back and belly ridges run half way across the tail, or more; and the edges of the tail in the same way run 6 or 8 inches along the body, and form ridges on the sides of the rump. After a very slight elevation at the blowhole, the outline of the back forms a regular curve; the belly rises or seems drawn in near the vent, and expands to a perceptible bump, about two feet before the genitalia. From the neck, three or four feet backward, the back is rather depressed, and appears flat.

The head is about one-seventh of the whole length of the animal; it is small, blunt, round, and of a paraboloidal form. The mouth is small, and not capable of much extension. The under lip is wedge-shaped. The eyes are small, the largest diameter being only an inch, and are placed in a line with the opening of the mouth, about 13 inches from the snout. The blowhole, which is directly over the eyes, is a single opening, of a semicircular form, about $3\frac{1}{2}$ inches in diameter or breadth, and $1\frac{1}{2}$ radius or length. The fins, which are 12 or 14 inches long and 6 or 8 broad, are placed at one-fifth of the length of the animal from the snout.   The tail is from 15 to 20 inches long, and 3 to 4 feet broad. It has no dorsal fin ; but in place of it is an irregular sharpish fatty ridge, two inches in height, extending two and a half feet along the back, nearly mid-way between the snout and the tail.   The edge of this ridge is generally rough, and the cuticle and rete mucosum being partly wanting upon it, appear to be worn off by rubbing against ice.

The prevailing colour of the young narwal is blackish-grey on the back, variegated with numerous darker spots running into one another, and forming a dusky-black surface, paler and more open spots of grey on a white ground at the sides, disappearing altogether about the middle of the belly. In the elder animals, the ground is wholly white or yellowish-white, with dark-grey or blackish spots of different degrees of intensity.   These spots are of a roundish or oblong form : on the back, where they seldom exceed two inches in diameter, they are the darkest and the most crowded together, yet with intervals of pure white among them.   On the sides, the spots are fainter, smaller, and more open.   On the belly, they become extremely faint and few, and in considerable surfaces are not to be seen.   On the upper part of the neck, just behind the blow-hole, is often a close patch of brownish-black without any white.   The external part of the fins is also generally black at the edges, but greyish about the middle. The upper side of the tail is also blackish round the edges: but in the middle, grey, with black curvilinear streaks on a white ground, forming semicircular figures on each lobe. The under parts of the fins and tail are similar to the upper, only much paler-coloured; the middle of the fins being white, and of the tail a pale-grey. The colour of the sucklings is almost wholly a bluish-grey, or slate-colour.

The integuments are similar to those of the mysticetus, only thinner. The cuticle is about the thickness of paper: the rete mucosum three-eighths to three-tenths of an inch thick; the cutis thin, but strong and compact on the outer side.

A long prominent tusk, with which some narwals are furnished, is considered as a horn by the whale-fishers; and as such, has given occasion for the name of Unicorn being applied to this animal. This tusk occurs on the left side of the head, and is sometimes found of the length of 9 or 10 feet; according to Egede, 14 or 15*. It springs from the lower part of the upper-jaw, points forward and a little downward; being parallel in its direction to the roof of the mouth. It is spirally striated from right to left; is nearly straight, and tapers to a round blunt point; is of a yellowish-white colour, and consists of a compact kind of ivory. It is usually hollow from the base to within a few inches of

---

" Description of Greenland," p. 77.

the point.   A five feet tusk, (about the average length), is about 2¼ inches diameter at the base, 1¾ in the middle, and about ⅜ths within an inch of the end.   In such a tusk, there are five or six turns of the spiral, extending from the base to within 6 or 7 inches of the point.   Beyond this, the end is without striæ, being smooth, clean and white; the striated part is usually grey and dirty.

Besides this external tusk, which is peculiar to the male, there is another on the right side of the head, about 9 inches long, imbedded in the skull. In females, as well as in young males, in which the tooth does not appear externally, the rudiments of two tusks will almost always be found in the upper-jaw.   These are solid throughout, and are placed back in the substance of the skull, about 6 inches from its most prominent part.   They are 8 or. 9 inches in length, both in the male and female; in the former they are smooth, tapering, and terminate at.the root with an oblique truncation; in the latter they have an extremely rough surface, and finish at the base with a large irregular knob placed towards one side, which gives the tusks the form almost of pocket pistols.   Two or three instances have occurred, of male narwals having been taken, which had two large external tusks.   But this is a rare circumstance. I have never seen an external tusk on the right side of the head; though I think it not improbable, but that some which I have been shown having no perforation up the centre, might be tusks of the right side. Sir Everard Home, in his examination of the tusks of the narwal, found, on sawing one, that appeared solid, in a longitudinal direction, " a hollow tube in the middle through the greater part of its length, the point, and the portion at the root, only being solid*.

All the male narwals that I have at different times seen killed, excepting one, had a tusk of 3 to 6 feet in length, projecting from the left side of the head, of which about 8 inches in length of each, was imbedded in the skull. The perforation, in all, extended from the base to within 10 or 12 inches of the small end of the tooth.

The use of the tusk in narwals is ambiguous. It cannot be essential for procuring their food, or none of them would be without it: nor is it, perhaps, necessary for their defence, else the females and young would be subjected to the power of enemies without the means of resistance, while the male would be in possession of an admirable weapon for its protection. Dr Barclay, with whom I have communicated on this subject, is of opinion, that the tusk is principally, if not solely, a sexual distinction, similar to what occurs among some other animals. Though it cannot be essential to the existence of the animal, it may, however, be occasionally employed. From the extremity being smooth

---

* Phil. Trans. for 1813.

and clean, while all the rest is rough and dirty;
and especially from the circumstance of a broken
tusk being found, with the angles of the fractured
part rubbed down and rounded, it is not improbable
but it may be used in piercing thin ice for the convenience of respiring, without being under the necessity of retreating into open water.   It cannot, I
conceive, be used as many authors have stated, in
raking their food from the bottom of the sea;
because these animals are most commonly met with
in deep seas, where they would be incapable of surviving under the immense pressure of the column
of water resting on the bottom.

A quantity of blubber, from 2 to 3¼ inches in
thickness, and amounting sometimes to above half a
ton, encompasses the whole body.   This affords a
large proportion of very fine oil.   The skull of the
narwal, like those of the Delphinus deductor, por-
pus, beluga, grampus, dolphin, &c., is concave above,
and sends forth a large flat wedge-shaped process in
front, which affords sockets for the tusks.   Upon
this process is a bed of fat extending to the thickness of 10 or 12 inches horizontally, (as the animal
swims,) and 8 or 9 perpendicularly.   This fat gives
the round form to the head; and by its greater or
lesser deposition, occasions a considerable difference
in the shape and prominence of the forehead.   In
consequence of this, what has been called the facial

angle, is in some narwals less than 60 degrees, in others upwards of 90.

The blowhole communicates with a large double cavity or air-vessel immediately under the skin; and this is connected with the *nares* of the skull, where the opening is divided by a bony septum.

In a fine fatty substance about the internal ears of the narwal, are found multitudes of worms. They are about an inch in length, some shorter, very slender, and taper both ways, but are sharper at one end than at the other. They are transparent. Within, is the appearance of a canal; without, is a brownish ridge, running longitudinally along the body.

The vertebral column of the narwal is about 12 feet in length. The cervical vertebræ are seven in number; the dorsal twelve; the lumbar and caudal thirty-five. The whole are fifty-four, of which twelve enter the tail, and extend to within an inch of its extremity. The spinal marrow appears to run through the processes of all the vertebræ, from the head to the 40th, but does not penetrate the 41st. The spinous process diminishes in length after the 15th lumbar vertebra, until it is scarcely perceptible at the 19th. Large anterior or belly processes, on the opposite side of the column to the spinous processes, attached to two adjoining vertebræ, commence between the 30th and 31st, and terminate between the 42d and 43d vertebræ. The ribs, which are twelve on each side, six true and six false, are slender for the size of the animal. The sternum is of the shape of a heart, with the broadest part forward. Two of the false ribs on each side, joined by cartilages to the 6th true rib; the rest are detached.

The principle food of the narwal seems to be molluscous animals. In the stomachs of several that I have examined, were numerous remains of sepiæ.

Narwals are quick, active, inoffensive animals. They swim with considerable velocity. When respiring at the surface, they frequently lay motionless for several minutes, with their backs and heads just appearing above the water. They are of a somewhat gregarious disposition, often appearing in numerous little herds of half a dozen, or more, together. Each herd is most frequently composed of animals of the same sex.

When harpooned, the narwal dives in the same way, and with almost the same velocity as the mysticetus, but not to the same extent. It generally descends about 200 fathoms, then returns to the surface, and is dispatched with a lance in a few minutes.

The only good description of the common narwal hitherto published, is contained in the Memoirs of the Wernerian Society, vol. i. p. 131. It was written by Dr Fleming, who had an opportunity of inspecting a small animal of this species, that was stranded on one of the Shetland islands in the year

3

1808; and as far as one specimen could be relied on for general appearances, is uncommonly accurate and characteristic.

The following dimensions and particulars, of a male narwal, killed near Spitzbergen in the year 1817, are from my own observations.

	Feet	In.
Length, exclusive of the tusk,.........................	15	0
Length from the snout to the eyes,...............	1	$1\frac{1}{2}$
————————————— fins,...............	3	1
————————————— back-ridge,....	6	0
————————————— vent,............	9	9
Circumference, $4\frac{1}{2}$ inches from the snout,......	3	5
————————— at the eyes and blowhole,......	5	$3\frac{1}{2}$
————————— just before the fins,..............	7	5
————————— at the forepart of back-ridge,	8	5
————————— at the vent,........................	5	8
Tusk, length externally,.............................	5	$0\frac{1}{2}$
——— diameter at the base,.............	0	$2\frac{1}{4}$
Blowhole, length $1\frac{1}{2}$ in., breadth,..................	0	$3\frac{1}{2}$
Tail,————————14 in., ————, ...	3	$1\frac{1}{2}$
Fins,————————13 in., ————, ...	0	$7\frac{1}{2}$

The heart weighed 11 lb.; the blood, an hour and a-half after death, was at the temperature of 97°.

DELPHINUS *Deductor*, (Traill). — *Ca'ing* or *Leading Whale.*

Two original descriptions of this animal are before the public, the one by Mr P. Neill [*], the other by Dr Traill [†]. The paper of Dr Traill is accompanied by a drawing, taken by Mr James Watson on the spot, where 92 of the species had just been driven on shore. This drawing, judging from the known accuracy of Mr Watson, in connection with the opinion of different persons acquainted with the animal, is doubtless, in the general appearance, a faithful representation. In the engraving, Plate 13. fig. 1, this drawing is minutely copied, excepting a small reduction in the diameter, which, with the permission of Dr Traill, I was induced to make, in consequence of the comparative diameter of the figure not exactly corresponding with the actual admeasurement of the animal.

The following are the specific characters, as given by Dr Traill. Body thick, black; one short dorsal fin; pectoral fins long, narrow; head obtuse; upper jaw bent forward; teeth subconoid, sharp, and a little bent.

---

[*] " Tour through some of the Islands of Orkney and Shetland." Edin. 1806, p. 221.

[†] Nicholson's Journal, vol. xxii. p. 81.

This animal grows to the length of about 24 feet; the average length of the adults may be about 20, and their greatest circumference 10 or 11 feet. The measurements of one examined by Mr Watson, were as follow. Length 19½ feet; greatest circumference 10; pectoral fin (the external portion) 3½ feet long, by 18 inches broad; dorsal fin 15 inches high, by 2 feet 3 inches broad; breadth of the tail 5 feet. Another individual was 21½ feet in length; and a third 20 feet in length, and 11½ in circumference.

The skin is smooth, resembling oiled silk; the colour is a deep bluish-black on the back, and generally whitish on the belly; the blubber is 3 or 4 inches thick. The head is short and round; the upper-jaw projects a little over the lower. Externally it has a single spiracle. The full grown have generally 22 to 24 teeth, ⅝ths to 1¼th inches in length, in each jaw. Mr Watson observed one with 28 teeth in the upper-jaw, and 24 in the lower. In the aged animals some of the teeth are deficient; and in the sucklings none are visible. When the mouth is shut, the teeth lock between one another, like the teeth of a trap. The tail is about 5 feet broad; the dorsal fin about 15 inches high, cartilaginous and immoveable *.

This kind of dolphin sometimes appears in large herds off the Orkney, Shetland, and Feroe Islands.

* Dr Traill, MS. paper.

" Being of a gregarious disposition, the main body
of the drove follows the leading whales, as a flock of
sheep follows the wedders. This disposition is well
known by the natives of Shetland and Orkney, and
improved to their advantage; for, whenever they are
enabled to guide the leaders into a bay, they seldom fail likewise to capture a considerable number
of the followers *." From the property of following
a leader, this animal is called, in Shetland, the
Ca'ing Whale; and, for the same reason, Dr Traill
suggests the name of *Deductor.*

There is a considerable similarity between this animal and the grampus; but there are also such
marked and essential differences between the deductor and the grampus, or indeed any other animal mentioned in systems of zoology, that it is considered both by Mr Neill and Dr Traill as belonging to no species yet described.

Of these cetacea, many herds have, at different
periods, been driven on shore in Orkney, Shetland,
Feroe, Iceland, &c. In a small volume, containing
an account of the Feroe Islands †, which was put
into my hands by Dr Traill, is a description of the
method of capturing the deductor, as practised by
the natives of Feroe in the 17th century. From

* NEILL's Tour, &c.

† " Færoæ, et Færoa Reserata; that is, a description of the
islands and inhabitants of Feroe."—" Written in Danish by Lu-
cas Jacobson Debes," London, 1676, 12mo.

this work it appears, that numerous animals of this
kind, called in Feroe *grind-whales*, were frequently driven ashore by boats, and killed; and that in
this way there were taken in two places, in the year
1664, about a thousand. Many other historical
notices of the capture of shoals of these whales are
to be met with. In the year 1748, 40 individuals
were seen in Torbay, and one, 17 feet in length,
was killed; in 1799, about 200 of the deductor
species, 8 to 20 feet in length, ran themselves a-
ground at Taesta Sound, Fetlar, one of the Shetland Islands; February 25. 1805, 190 of the same
kind, 6 to 20 feet long, were driven on shore at the
Uyea Sound, Unst, Shetland; and, on the 19th of
March, in the same year, 120 more at the same spot.
In December 1806, 92 of this species were stranded in Scalpa Bay, Orkney, measuring from 5 to
21 feet in length. It was observed of the last
three shoals, that numbers of the females were
suckling their young when they were driven on
shore, and so long as they continued alive, the milk
was seen to issue from their nipples *. In the winter of 1809 and 1810, 1100 of these whales approached the shore in Hvalfiord, Iceland, and were
captured; and in the winter of 1814, 150 of the
same were driven into Balta Sound, Shetland, and
there killed. These are only a very small proportion of the instances in which, in modern times, an

---

* NEILL's Tour and DR TRAILL's MS. Notes.

extensive slaughter of the Delphinus Deductor has taken place on the shores of the British and other northern islands.

DELPHINAPTERUS *Beluga* (La Cepède:)—*Delphinus leucas* of Linné ; *Beluga* of Pennant, or *White Whale* of the fishers.

The Beluga is not unlike the narwal in its general form ; but is thicker about the middle of its body in proportion to its length.   The anterior extremity being paraboloidal, and the head small, blunt and round, give it a strong resemblance to the narwal.   Its length is equal to that of the narwal ; according to La Cepède six or seven metres.   Both jaws are furnished with teeth.   It has no dorsal fin. The skin is smooth, the colour white.   Some individuals that I have seen, were of a yellow colour, approaching to orange.

A male animal of this kind was taken in the Frith of Forth, in the month of June 1815.   Its length was 13 feet 4 inches, and its greatest circumference nearly 9 feet.   A paper relating to its capture and external appearance, by Mr P. Neill, was read before the Wernerian Society, on the 7th December 1816 ; and an account of its internal structure by Dr Barclay, was read before the same Society at its next meeting.   A beautiful drawing of

the same animal was also made by Mr Syme, paint-
er to the Wernerian Society, and author of " Illustrations of Werner's Nomenclature of Colours."
I have been favoured, through Professor Jameson,
with a copy of this drawing, as an illustration of
this article *.

The beluga is generally met with in families or
herds of five or ten together.   They are plentiful in
Hudson's Bay; Davis' Strait, and on some parts of
the northern coasts of Europe and Asia, where they
frequent some of the larger rivers.   They are taken
for the sake of the oil they produce, by harpoons or
strong nets ; in the latter case, the nets are extended across the stream, so as to prevent their escape
out of the river; and when thus interrupted in
their course to seaward, they are attacked with lances, and great numbers are sometimes killed.   I
have several times seen them on the coast of Spitzbergen ; but never in numbers of more than three
or four at a time.

---

* See Plate XIV.

SECT. II.

*Some Account of the Quadrupeds inhabiting Spitz-
bergen, and the Icy Seas adjacent.*

———

TRICHECUS *Rosmarus* :—*Walrus, Morse,* or *Sea-Horse* of
the Whale-fishers.

THIS singular animal forms the connecting link
between the mammalia of the land and the water,
corresponding, in several of its characters, both with
the bullock and the whale. It grows to the bulk
of an ox. Its canine teeth, two in number, are of
the length, externally, of 10 to 20 inches, (some
naturalists say 3 feet,) and extend downward from
the upper jaw, and include the point of the lower
jaw between them. They are incurvated inward.
Their full length, when cut out of the skull, is commonly 15 to 20 inches, sometimes almost 30 ; and
their weight 5 to 10 pounds each, or upward. The
walrus, being a slow, clumsy animal on land, its
tusks seem necessary for its defence against the
bear, and also for enabling it to raise its unweildy
body upon the ice, when its access to the shore is
prevented.

The walrus is found on the shores of Spitzbergen, 12 to 15 feet in length, and 8 to 10 feet in
circumference. The head is short, small, and flat-

tened in front. The flattened part of the face is set with strong bristles. The nostrils are on the upper part of the snout, through which it blows or breathes like a whale. The fore paws, which are a kind of webbed hand, are two-sevenths of the full length of the animal from the snout. They are from 2 to 2¼ feet in length ; and being expansive, may be stretched to the breadth of 15 to 18 inches. The hind feet, which form a sort of tail fin, extend straight backward. They are not united, as many zoologists affirm, but are detached from each other. The length of each is about 2 to 2½ feet ; the breadth, when fully extended, 2½ or 3 feet ; the termination of each toe is marked by a small nail.

The skin of the walrus is about an inch thick, and is covered with a short, yellowish-brown coloured hair. The inside of the paws, in old animals, is defended by a rough horny kind of casing, a quarter of an inch thick, probably produced by the hardening of the skin, in consequence of coarse usage in climbing over ice and rocks.

Beneath the skin, is a thin layer of fat. At some seasons, the produce is said to be considerable ; but I have never met with any that afforded above 20 or 30 gallons of oil. Excepting the head, the general form of the walrus is similar to that of the Seal. In the stomachs of walruses, I have met with shrimps, a kind of craw-fish, and the remains of young seals.

When seen at a distance, the front part of the head of the young walrus, without tusks, is not unlike the human face. As this animal is in the habit of rearing its head above water, to look at ships, and other passing objects, it is not at all improbable but that it may have afforded foundation for some of the stories of Mermaids. I have myself seen a sea-horse in such a position, and under such circumstances, that it required little stretch of imagination to mistake it for a human being; so like indeed was it, that the surgeon of the ship actually reported to me his having seen a man with his head just appearing above the surface of the water. Seals exhibit themselves in a similar way; the heads of some, at a distance, are not unlike the human head; the resemblance, however, is not so striking as that presented by the walrus.

The walrus is a fearless animal. It pays no regard to a boat, excepting as an object of curiosity. It is sometimes taken by a harpoon, when in the water. If one attack fails, it often affords an opportunity for repeating it. The capture of a walrus in the water, cannot always be accomplished without danger; for, as they go in herds, an attack made upon one individual, draws all its companions to its defence. In such cases, they frequently rally round the boat from whence the blow was struck; pierce its planks with their tusks; and, though resisted in the most determined manner, sometimes raise themselves upon the gunwale, and threaten to overset it. The best defence against these enraged animals, is, in this crisis, sea sand; which, being thrown into their eyes, occasions a partial blindness, and obliges them to disperse. When on shore, they are best killed with long sharp-pointed knives.

The tusks of the walrus, which are hard, white, and compact ivory, are employed by dentists in the fabrication of false teeth. The skin is used in place of mats, for defending the yards and rigging of ships from being chafed by friction against each other. When cut into shreds, and plaited into cordage, it answers admirably for wheel-ropes, being stronger, and wearing much longer than hemp. In ancient times, most of the ropes in ships, in northern countries, at least, would appear to have been made of this substance. When tanned, it is converted into a soft porous leather, above an inch in thickness; but it is by no means so useful, or so durable as in its *green* or raw state.

So early as the ninth century, we have accounts of the walrus being extensively fished for, on the western coast of Norway *. It now occurs in perhaps greater abundance, sometimes in troops of several hundreds together, on the shores of Spitzbergen, and neighbouring islands. It also frequents

---

* Anglo-Saxon version of OROSIUS, by ALFRED the Great. —See BARRINGTON's Translation, in his " Miscellanies," p. 462.

the ice; but seldom permits itself to be carried far from land.

Prior to the institution of the Spitzbergen whale-fishery, the capture of this animal was an object of some commercial importance. It was at first attacked by the English, on Cherie Island; but being driven from thence, if not extirpated in that quarter, by the great slaughter that was carried on, it was then pursued to Spitzbergen.

Stephen Bennet, who, on the part of the English, discovered Cherie Island in 1603, commenced the attack on the sea-horses, in this region, the year following. His first attempt, however, to capture this formidable animal, was not very successful. Of above a thousand that were seen on the beach, and attacked, only fifteen were killed: and the slaughter out of at least a thousand more which were met with on another part of the island, only increased the capture to about 50. The teeth of these animals only were taken, which, with a hogshead of loose teeth found scattered about the island, formed the principal part of the first cargo. In their attacks on the Walrus, they found muskets with ball of little service *; but, charged with pease-shot,

---

* My Father once killed a Walrus with a lance, after having fired at it in vain with a rifle; and, on examining the head which one of the balls had struck, he found it had only penetrated as far as the skull, where it was flattened and spread out like a plate of sheet lead upon the surface of the bone.

and fired into their eyes, they were more effectual, as the sailors attacked them without danger, when blinded, and dispatched them with axes, and other sharp instruments.

In the year following, another voyage was performed to Cherie Island by Mr Welden, owner of the ship which Bennet commanded. They now hit upon a better mode of attack, and killed many Sea-horses. In this instance they not only took their teeth, but also preserved their blubber, and reduced it to oil on the spot.

In 1606, Bennet was again dispatched on the same errand, having, besides the ship he commanded, a pinnace of 20 tons burden under his direction. After the ice cleared away from the island, the morses began to land; and, on their first attack, they manifested their improvement in the art of slaughtering, by capturing 700 or 800 of these animals in less than six hours. On this adventure, 22 tons of Sea-horse oil, and 3 hogsheads of teeth were obtained.

The next voyage, when Mr Welden again embarked in his own vessel, 900 or 1000 sea-horses were killed in less than seven hours. This trade was afterwards conducted in Spitzbergen and Hope Island, with equally good effect, until it was abandoned for the more important fishery of the whale.

In the present age, the Sea-horses range the coasts of Spitzbergen almost without molestation from the

British.   The Russians are their principal enemies,
who, by means of the hunting parties sent out to
winter on the coast, capture a considerable number.
The whale-fishers rarely take half a dozen in a voyage ; though my Father, in the last season, procured about 130 in Magdalane Bay.

PHOCÆ.—*Seals.*

Several species of seals occur in the Greenland Sea,
and resort to the ice in the neighbourhood of Spitzbergen and Jan Mayen in immense herds.   The
young animals, which are most frequently killed,
are found in greatest abundance on the ice near Jan
Mayen, in the spring of the year, where they become the object of a distinct fishery.   Few British
ships are fitted out for this sole purpose, though
many vessels equipped only as *sealers*, proceed annually into the Greenland Sea, from different ports
of the Elbe and Weser.

As the seal frequents the British coast, and is a
well described and well known animal, I shall not
particularise the different species that are met with
in the Arctic Seas.   A few general observations
only, will be necessary.

Seals are generally fat in the spring of the year,
and afford several gallons of blubber : even small
seals will then yield about four or five gallons of
oil.

The voice of the young seal when in pain or distress, is a whining cry, resembling that of a child. Seals appear to hear well when under water; music, or particularly a person whistling, draws them to the surface, and induces them to stretch their necks to the utmost extent, so as to prove a snare, by bringing them within reach of the shooter. The most effectual way of shooting them is by the use of small shot fired into their eyes; when killed with a bullet, they generally sink and are lost. Seals are often seen on their passage from one situation to another, in very large shoals. In such cases, for the sake of respiration, they all appear every now and then at the surface together, springing up so as to raise their heads and necks, and often their whole bodies out of the water. Their progress is pretty rapid; their actions appear frisky; and their general conduct is productive of amusement to the spectator. The sailors, when they observe such a shoal, call it a " Seal's Wedding."

The feet of seals are better adapted for their advancement in the water than on land. They cannot be said to walk, as they do not raise their bodies off the ground; yet they shuffle along, especially over ice, with a surprising speed.

Seals feed on birds, crabs, and small fishes. As, in some respects, they eat up the food required by the whale, whales are seldom to be found where they are numerous. They are very tenacious of life; so much so, that their animation is not often destroyed until after they are flayed. I have, indeed, seen them successfully attempt to swim, when in a state too shockingly mangled to be fit for description.

The uses of the seal are various ; and, to some nations, highly important. It yields train oil, which, when extracted before putrefaction has commenced, is beautifully transparent in its appearance, free from smell, and not unpleasant in taste. The skin, when tanned, is extensively employed in the making of shoes; and when dressed with the hair on, serves for the covering of trunks, &c. To the Esquimaux, the seal is of as much importance as bread is to a European. Its flesh forms their most usual food ; the fat is partly dressed for eating, and partly consumed in their lamps ; the liver when fried, is, even among sailors, esteemed as an agreeable dish. The skin, which the Esquimaux dress by processes peculiar to themselves, is made water proof. With the hair off, it is used as coverings, instead of planks, for their boats, and as outer garments for themselves; shielded with which, they can invert themselves and canoes in the water, without getting their bodies wet. A single effort with their paddle restores them to their proper position. It serves also for coverings for their tents, and for various other purposes. The jackets and trowsers made of skin by the Esquimaux are in great request among the whale-fishers for preserving them from oil and wet.

2

The Phoca Vitulina is more abundant in the Greenland Sea, than any other species, especially near Jan Mayen. The Hooded Seal is common near Spitzbergen. The usual length of the former is 4 or 5 feet ; of the latter 6 to 8 ; and it is said to grow to the length of 10 or 12 feet. The former almost always retreats before its enemies : the latter often returns their attacks ; and, being defended by his hood from the stunning effect of a blow on the nose, sometimes inflicts severe wounds on the person by whom he is attacked.

In fine weather, seals prefer the ice to the water ; and, when they find themselves dry and comfortable, have an aversion to take the water, and are sometimes easily caught. They are extremely watchful. Where a number are collected on the same piece of ice, one, if not more, is always looking round. And even a solitary seal is scarcely ever observed to allow a minute to pass without lifting its head. When seals rest on an extensive sheet of ice, they always secure their retreat, either by lying near the edge, or by keeping a hole in the ice always open before them. These precautions are necessary to preserve themselves from becoming a prey to the bear. The old animals are in general shy ; so that, when thousands are seen within the compass of a square furlong, the whole, on the approach of a boat, will perhaps make their escape. The young ones are less guarded ; and, when met with at a proper season, may sometimes be killed by a dozen at a time, on a small flake of ice.

The best situation for the seal fishery in the Arctic Sea, is in the vicinity of Jan Mayen; and the best season, the months of March and April. Ships being able to penetrate the skirts of the ice, have then a probability of meeting with them, and may occasionally make a rapid and successful fishery. The capturing of a seal is but the work of a moment. A blow with a " seal-club," (Plate XIX, fig. 6.) on the nose, immediately stuns it, and affords opportunity, by the active use of the club upon others, of arresting the flight, and making prize of many at a time. When seals are found on detached pieces of drift-ice, they are captured by the use of boats, every boat making a descent upon a different herd. When the seals are observed to be making their escape into the water, before the boat reaches the ice, the sailors give a loud continued shout, on which their victims are deluded by the amazement a sound so uncommon produces, and frequently delay their retreat until arrested by the blows of their enemies. In cases where the seals are abundant, the boat immediately pushes off, after the slaughter is finished, and proceeds to another piece of ice, for the increase of their harvest, leaving one man with their former capture, who employs himself in flaying off the skin and fat, until his companions return. But, in situations where the boats cannot navigate, the seal-fishers

2

have to pursue them over the ice, leaping from piece to piece, until they make a capture; every man then flenses his own, and drags the skin and blubber to his boat or ship.

Ships fitted out principally for the whale-fishery, have accidentally obtained, in the month of April, from 2000 to 3000 seals, and sometimes more; and vessels sent out for the seal-fishery only, have occasionally procured a cargo of 4000 or 5000, yielding near 100 tons of oil. Not above one or two vessels, at a time, have been fitted out of Britain, entirely for the seal-fishery, for many years; but from the ports of the Elbe and the Weser, a number of sealers are annually despatched.

From the exposed nature of the situation where seals are killed, and from the liability to heavy and sudden storms at the season when they are usually taken, the seal-fishery, conducted on the borders of the Spitzbergen ice, becomes a very hazardous employment.

This observation may be illustrated, by the mention of a disaster that occurred in the year 1774, as related to me by Richard Mood, a respectable old Lerwick pilot, who was himself eye-witness of the fact.

Fifty-four ships, chiefly Hamburghers, were that year fitted out for the seal fishery alone, from foreign ports. Most of these, with several English ships, had, in the spring of the year, met together on the borders of the ice, about sixty miles to the eastward of the island of Jan Mayen.   On the 29th of March, when the weather was moderate, the whole fleet penetrated within some streams of ice, and sent out their boats in search for seals.   While thus engaged, a dreadful storm suddenly arose.   So sudden and furious, indeed, was the commencement, and so tremendous and lasting the continuance, that almost all the people who were at a distance from their ships perished.   The Duke of York, Captain Petere, had two boats at that time down. The crews of these having, by their utmost exertions, rowed up to the ship, got hold of the rudder rings, but were unable to make their way along side; they held fast for some time, until the force of the sea became too great for their benumbed grasp, when they lost their hold and fell astern.   Though the ship was laid too, yet such was the increase of the sea, and such their debility from excessive cold and previous exertion, that they were unable to recover their position.   The chief mate of the ship, a resolute and noble tar, seeing that his shipmates, if not immediately succoured, would perish, determined to rescue them at the peril of his own life.   Having manned a boat with six stout seamen besides himself, he proceeded to their assistance. On reaching them, he exchanged four of his vigorous crew for two of his fainting comrades in each boat. Thus reinforced. the three boats, by the powerful exertions of their crews, were brought to the stern of the ship. Beyond this point, the increase of the sea and the rapid drift of the ship, prevented them advancing; while their comrades on board were unable to assist them, from the attention requisite for their own preservation, the ship being almost laid " on her beam ends." In this critical situation they had not remained many minutes, before a sea struck the boats, filled, and overwhelmed them, on which the whole of their crews, nineteen men in number, perished.

But this catastrophe, melancholy as it was, formed a small proportion of the disasters of the storm.

While the different ships were endeavouring to make their way clear of the ice, the Pennant was struck by such a dreadful surge that she foundered, and all hands were lost. The same sea struck the Perseverance and the Rockingham, by which one of the quarter boats of the latter was thrown upon deck, and her bulwark, fore and aft, was washed away; and five boats and five men were washed from the sides and deck of the former, while, at the same time, such damage was occasioned in the hull of the vessel, that she was under the necessity of returning home to refit.

A Dutch snow, on board of which six boats' crews of English sailors, who were unable to reach their own vessel, had taken refuge, fell to leeward against a point of ice, was wrecked, and all hands on board perished. The Rockingham, the ship in which Rich-

ard Mood, my informant, served, in passing a stream
of ice that interrupted her escape into the open sea,
received some severe blows, that carried away her
cut-water, and did considerable damage to both the
stem and bow. It was fortunate for this fleet, that,
when the gale commenced, the ships, agreeably to
the usage of the old seal-fishers, were generally under close reefed topsails, otherwise the whole might
have been dismasted.

The result of these disasters, when summed up, is
dreadful. About 400 foreign seamen, and near 200
British, are said to have been drowned ; four or five
ships were lost, and scarcely any escaped without
damage.

This storm continued in all its fury about twenty-
four hours ; and, with some small diminution of violence, prevailed about six days more before it abated.   The effect on the ice, as well as on the shipping, was striking.   Having blown the whole time
from the eastward, the ice, which before the gale
was 60 miles to the eastward of Jan Mayen, was
found on its termination, above 100 miles to the
westward.   The ship Weymouth, commanded by a
person well known by the name of French Will,
was seen at the close of the gale with a signal of
distress in the rigging.   She was found to be severely stove, and had a piece of ice several tons
weight upon deck, which had been thrown in by the
sea.   This vessel returned to Liverpool to refit, and

made such despatch out again, that she procured 2400 seals the same season.

CANIS *Lagopus.—Arctic Fox.*

This animal is seldom seen by the whale-fishers. Persons wintering in Spitzbergen sometimes find them plentiful, and make use of them as food. They are rarely found on the ice, though I have often seen the impressions of their feet on the snow ; being of a whitish colour, they are not easily distin-guished.

URSUS *maritimus.—Polar* or *Greenland Bear.*

This formidable animal is, among quadrupeds, the sovereign of the arctic countries. He is powerful and courageous ; savage and sagacious ; apparently clumsy, yet not inactive. His senses are extremely acute, especially his sight and smell. As he tra-verses extensive fields of ice, he mounts the hum-mocks and looks around for prey ; on rearing his head and snuffing the breeze, he perceives the scent of the carrion of the whale at an immense distance. A piece of *kreng* thrown into a fire, draws him to a ship from the distance of miles. The kreng of the whale, however offensive to a human nose, is to him a banquet. Seals seem to be his most usual food ; yet, from the extreme watchfulness of these crea-tures, he is often, it is believed, kept fasting for weeks together. He seems to be equally at home

on the ice as on land. He is found on field-ice,
above 200 miles from the shore. He can swim with
the velocity of three miles an hour, and can accomplish some leagues without much inconvenience.
He dives to a considerable distance, though not
very frequently.

Bears occur in Spitzbergen, Nova Zembla, Greenland, and other arctic countries, throughout the year.
In some places they are met with in great numbers.
By means of the ice, they often effect a landing on
Iceland; but as soon as they appear, they are generally attacked by the inhabitants and destroyed.
Near the east coast of Greenland, they have been
seen on the ice in such quantities, that they were
compared to flocks of sheep on a common.

The size of this animal is generally 4 or 5 feet
in height, 7 or 8 feet in length, and nearly as much
in circumference. Sometimes, however, it occurs
much larger. Barentz, in the year 1596, killed two
bears in Cherie Island, the skin of one of which
measured 12 feet, and of the other 13. Its weight
is generally from 600 lb. to above half a-ton. It is
covered with long yellowish-white hair, and is particularly shaggy about the inside of the legs. His
paws are 7 inches or more in breadth; his claws 2
inches in length. His canine teeth, exclusive of the
portion imbedded in the jaw, are about an inch and a
half in length. Having an amazing strength of jaw,
he has been known to bite a lance in two, though
made of iron half an inch in diameter.

He may be captured in the water without much danger; but, on the ice, he has such power of resistance at command, that the experiment is hazardous. When pursued and attacked, he always turns upon his enemies. If struck with a lance, he is apt to seize it in his mouth, and either bite it in two or wrest it out of the hand. If shot with a ball, unless he is struck in the head, in the heart, or in the shoulder, he is enraged rather than depressed, and falls with increased power upon his pursuers. When shot at a distance and able to escape, he has been observed to retire to the shelter of a hummock, and, as if conscious of the styptical effect of cold, apply snow with his paws to the wound.

Though possessed of courage and great means of defence, he always, unless urged by hunger, retreats before men. His general walk is slow and deliberate; but when impelled by danger or hunger, he proceeds by a galloping step; and, upon ice, can easily outrun any man.

It feeds on the kreng or carcasses of whales, in the state in which they are relinquished by the fishers; on seals, birds, foxes and deer, when it can surprise them; on eggs, and, indeed, on any animal substance that comes within its power.

The skin of the bear, when dressed with the hair on, forms beautiful mats for a hall, or the bottom of a carriage. Prepared without being ripped up, and the hairy side turned inward, it forms a warm sack-

like bed, and is used as such, in some parts of
Greenland.   The flesh, when cleared of the fat, is
well flavoured and savoury, especially the muscular
part of the ham.   I once treated my surgeon with
a dinner of bear's-ham, who knew not, for above a
month afterwards, but that it was beef-steak.   The
liver, I may observe as a curious fact, is hurtful and
even deleterious; while the flesh and liver of the
seal, on which it chiefly feeds, are nourishing and
palatable.   Sailors, who have inadvertently eaten
the liver of bears, have almost always been sick after it: some have actually died; and the effect on
others, has been to cause the skin to peel off their
bodies.   This is, perhaps, almost the only instance
known of any part of the flesh of a quadruped proving unwholesome.

Bears, though they have been known to eat one
another, are remarkably affectionate to their young.
The female, which has generally two at a birth, defends its young with such zeal, and watches over
them with such anxiety, that she sometimes falls a
sacrifice to her maternal attachment.   A pleasing
and very extraordinary instance of sagacity in a mother bear was related to me by a credible and well
informed person, who accompanied me in several
voyages to the whale-fishery, in the capacity of surgeon.   This bear, with two cubs under its protection, was pursued across a field of ice, by a party of
armed sailors.   At first she seemed to urge the

young ones to an increase of speed, by running before them, turning round, and manifesting, by a peculiar action and voice, her anxiety for their progress; but finding her pursuers gaining upon them,
she carried, or pushed, or pitched them alternately
forward, until she effected their escape. In throwing them before her, the little creatures are said to
have placed themselves across her path, to receive
the impulse; and, when projected some yards in advance, they ran onwards until she overtook them,
when they alternately adjusted themselves for a second throw.

Several instances of peculiar sagacity in these animals have been observed.

A seal, lying on the middle of a large piece of ice,
with a hole just before it, was marked out by a bear
for its prey, and secured by the artifice of diving
under the ice, and making its way to the hole by
which the seal was prepared to retreat. The seal,
however, observed its approach, and plunged into
the water; but the bear instantly sprung upon it,
and appeared, in about a minute afterwards, with
the seal in its mouth.

The captain of one of the whalers being anxious
to procure a bear, without wounding the skin, made
trial of the stratagem of laying the noose of a rope
in the snow, and placing a piece of kreng within it.
A bear, ranging the neighbouring ice, was soon en-
ticed to the spot, by the smell of burning meat.

3

He perceived the bait, approached, and seized it in his mouth; but his foot, at the same moment, by a jerk of the rope, being entangled in the noose, he pushed it off with the adjoining paw, and deliberately retired. After having eaten the piece he carried away with him, he returned. The noose, with another piece of kreng, being then replaced, he pushed the rope aside, and again walked triumphantly off with the kreng. A third time the noose was laid; but, excited to caution by the evident observation of the bear, the sailors buried the rope beneath the snow, and laid the bait in a deep hole dug in the centre. The bear once more approached, and the sailors were assured of their success. But bruin, more sagacious than they expected, after snuffing about the place for a few moments, scraped the snow away with his paw, threw the rope aside, and again escaped unhurt with his prize.

In the month of June 1812, a female bear, with two cubs, approached the ship I commanded, and was shot. The cubs, not attempting to escape, were taken alive. These animals, though at first evidently very unhappy, became at length, in some measure, reconciled to their situation; and, being tolerably tame, were allowed occasionally to go at large about the deck. While the ship was moored to a floe, a few days after they were taken, one of them, having a rope fastened round its neck, was thrown overboard. It immediately swam to the

ice, got upon it, and attempted to escape. Finding itself, however, detained by the rope, it endeavoured to disengage itself in the following ingenious
way. Near the edge of the floe was a crack in the
ice, of a considerable length, but only 18 inches, or
2 feet wide, and 3 or 4 feet deep. To this spot the
bear returned; and when, on crossing the chasm,
the bight of the rope fell into it, he placed himself
across the opening; then suspending himself by his
hind feet, with a leg on each side, he dropped his
head, and most of his body, into the chasm; and,
with a foot applied to each side of the neck, attempted, for some minutes, to push the rope over
his head. Finding this scheme ineffectual, he removed to the main ice, and running with great impetuosity from the ship, gave a remarkable pull on
the rope; then going backward a few steps he repeated the jerk. At length, after repeated attempts
to escape this way, every failure of which he announced by a significant growl, he yielded himself
to his hard necessity, and lay down on the ice in
angry and sullen silence.

Accidents with bears occasionally occur, though
not so many, by any means, as the ferocity of these
animals, and the temerity of the sailors, who embrace every opportunity of attacking them, might
lead one to expect.

Some of the early voyagers to the polar seas, had
hard conflicts with bears. Barentz' crew especially,

3

were often in danger from them, but always succeeded either in conquering or repelling them. Another party was less fortunate. Two of the crew of a vessel which had anchored near Nova Zembla, landed on an island at the mouth of the Weigats, and, impelled by curiosity, wandered some distance from the beach; but, while unconscious of danger, one of them was suddenly seized on the back by a bear, and brought to the earth. His companion ran off and gave the alarm, and a party of his shipmates came to their assistance. The bear stood over its prey during their approach, without the least appearance of fear; and, on their attack, sprung upon one of their number, and made him also a victim to its ferocity and power. The rest now fled in confusion, and could not be induced to renew the conflict. Three sailors only among the crew had sufficient courage to combat with this formidable animal; they attacked it, and after a dangerous struggle, killed it, and rescued the mangled bodies of their two unfortunate shipmates.

Captain Cook, of the Archangel of Lynn, being near the coast of Spitzbergen in the year 1788, landed, accompanied by his surgeon and mate. While traversing the shore, the captain was unexpectedly attacked by a bear, which seized him in an instant between its paws. At this awful juncture, when a moment's pause must have been fatal to him, he called to his surgeon to fire; who, with admirable resolution and steadiness, discharged his

piece as directed, and providentially shot the bear
through the head. The captain, by this prompt
assistance was preserved from being torn in pieces.

On a more recent occasion, a commander of a
whale ship was in a similar danger. Captain Haw-
kins of the Everthorpe of Hull, when in Davis'
Strait, in July 1818, seeing a very large bear, took
a boat, and pushed off in pursuit of it. On reaching it, the captain struck it twice with a lance in
the breast; and, while in the act of recovering his
weapon for another blow, the enraged animal sprung
up, and seized him by the thigh, and threw him over
its head into the water. Fortunately it did not repeat its attack, but exerted itself to escape. This
exertion, when the attention of every one was directed towards their captain, was not made in vain,
for it was allowed to swim away without further
molestation *

Various other accidents and adventures with
bears are familiar to the whale-fishers; but the
above may be sufficient as illustrations of the character of the animal. I shall only remark, with
regard to curious adventures, that, on one occasion,
a bear which was attacked by a boat's crew, in the
Spitzbergen Sea, made such a formidable resistance
that it was enabled to climb the side of the boat,

---

* This account I received in a letter from Captain Bennet,
of the Venerable of Hull.

and take possession of it, while the intimidated crew fled for safety to the water, supporting themselves by the gunwale and rings of the boat, until, by the assistance of another party from their ship, it was shot as it sat inoffensively in the stern. And, with regard to narrow escapes, I shall only add, that a sailor, who was pursued on a field of ice by a bear, when at a considerable distance from assistance, preserved his life, by throwing down an article of clothing, whenever the bear gained upon him, on which it always suspended the pursuit, until it had examined it, and thus gave him time to obtain some advance. In this way, by means of a hat, a jacket, and a neck handkerchief, successively cast down, the progress of the bear was retarded, and the sailor escaped from the danger that threatened him, in the refuge afforded him by his vessel.

CERVUS *Tarandus.—Rein-Deer.*

I have never seen this animal myself, though it is known to inhabit almost every part of Spitzbergen. It is always lean in the spring of the year; but, after the wasting of the snow, and the advance of vegetation, it feeds rapidly, and its flesh, towards the end of July, is found to be excellent venison.

SECT. III.

Remarks on the Birds frequenting the Sea and Coast of Spitzbergen.

ANAS.—*Goose, Duck,* &c.

1. ANAS *Bernicla.* Brent-goose.—Occurs in considerable numbers near the coast of Greenland, but is not seen in any quantity at Spitzbergen.

2. ANAS *mollissima.* Eider-Duck.—These birds are very abundant during the summer, in all the islands situated in the Greenland Sea. They are also met with solitary, or in pairs, near the ice, at the greatest distances from land. They fly in large flocks, near the coast, and generally arrange themselves in a regular form. Their appearance in great numbers is an intimation of the proximity of land. The variety found at Spitzbergen is not so large as generally described, exceeding very little in size the domesticated duck.

ALCA.—*Auk.* or *Penguin.*

1. ALCA *arctica.* The Puffin, or Greenland Parrot.—This bird is very common near the coast of Spitzbergen, but is rarely seen out of sight of

land. It feeds principally on shrimps, and a small species of helix *.

2. ALCA *Alle.* The Little Auk, or Roach.— This is an extremely numerous species in some situations in the Polar Seas. They occur in the water in thousands together; and sometimes in like abundance on pieces of ice. They are active in the water; but rather slow in flight. When on the ice, they generally sit in an erect posture. They dive quickly on being alarmed, and pass through the water, by the use of their wings, with great velocity. Feeding on shrimps, they are found in greatest numbers in the turbid dark-green coloured sea. On the approach of thick weather, they are particularly noisy.

PROCELLARIA *glacialis.*—*Petrel, Fulmar,* or *Mallemuk.*

The fulmar is the constant companion of the whale-fisher. It joins his ship immediately on passing the Shetland Islands, and accompanies it through the trackless ocean to the highest accessible latitudes. It keeps an eager watch for any thing thrown overboard; the smallest particle of fatty substance can scarcely escape it. As such, a hook baited with a piece of fat meat or blubber, and towed by a long twine over the ship's stern, is a means employed by

* My friend, Mr William Swainson, of Liverpool, on comparing a drawing of this bird with the British puffin, considered it as a different species. It, however, corresponds very nearly with the Alca arctica of Latham.

the sailor-boys for taking them.   In the spring of
the year, before they have glutted themselves too
frequently with the fat of the whale, they may be
eaten ; and, when carefully cleared of the skin, and
of every particle of yellow fatty substance lying beneath it, and well soaked in water, they are pretty
good, particularly in " sea-pies." They are remarkably easy and swift on the wing.   They can fly to
windward in the highest storms, and rest on the
water, with great composure, in the most tremendous seas.   But it is observed, that, in heavy gales,
they fly extremely low, generally skimming along
by the surface of the water.   The fulmar walks
awkwardly, and with the legs so bent, that the feet
almost touch the belly.   When on ice, it rests with
its body on the surface, and presents its breast to
the wind.   Like the duck, it sometimes turns its
head backward, and conceals its bill beneath its
wing.

Fulmars are extremely greedy of the fat of the
whale.   Though few should be seen when a whale
is about being captured, yet, as soon as the flensing
process commences, they rush in from all quarters,
and frequently accumulate to many thousands in
number.   They then occupy the greasy track of
the ship ; and, being audaciously greedy, fearlessly
advance within a few yards of the men employed in
cutting up the whale.   If, indeed, the fragments of
fat do not float sufficiently away, they approach so

near the scene of operations, that they are knocked
down with boat-hooks, in great numbers, and sometimes taken up by the hand.   The sea immediately
about the ship's stern, is sometimes so completely
covered with them, that a stone can scarcely be
thrown overboard, without striking one of them.
When any thing is thus cast among them, those
nearest the spot where it falls, take the alarm, and
these exciting some fear in others more remote,
sometimes put a thousand of them in motion; but
as, in rising into the air, they assist their wings, for
the first few yards, by striking the water with their
feet, there is produced by such a number of them, a
loud and most singular splashing.   It is highly amusing to observe the voracity with which they seize
the pieces of fat that fall in their way ; the size and
quantity of the pieces they take at a meal; the curious chuckling noise which, in their anxiety for
dispatch, they always make ; and the jealousy with
which they view, and the boldness with which they
attack, any of their species that are engaged in de-
vouring the finest morsels.   They frequently glut
themselves so completely, that they are unable to
fly ; in which case, when they are not relieved by a
quantity being disgorged, they endeavour to get on
the nearest piece of ice, where they rest until the
advancement of digestion restores their wonted
powers.   Then, if opportunity admit, they return
with the same gust to the banquet as before : and,

though numbers of the species may be killed, and allowed to float about among them, they appear unconscious of danger to themselves.

The fulmar never dives, but when incited to it by the appearance of a morsal of fat under water. When in close view of any men, it keeps a continual watch on both the men and its prey; having its feet continually in motion, and yet perhaps not moving at all through the water. Its boldness increases with the numbers of its species that surround it. It is a very hardy bird. Its feathers being thick, it is not easily killed with a blow. Its bite, from the crookedness, strength, and sharpness of its bill, is very severe.

Fulmars differ in colour; some are a dark dirty grey; others are much paler, and totally white on the breast and belly. In size, this bird is a little smaller than a duck. Beneath its feathers is a thick bed of fine grey down.

When carrion is scarce, the fulmars follow the living whale; and sometimes, by their peculiar motions, when hovering at the surface of the water, point out to the fisher the position of the animal of which he is in pursuit. They cannot make much impression on the dead whale, until some more powerful animal tears away the skin: the epidermis and rete mucosum they entirely remove, but the true skin is too tough for them to make way through it.

COLYMBUS. *Guillemot.*

1. COLYMBUS *grylle.*—Tysté or Doveca. This is a beautifully formed bird. It occurs in considerable numbers in icy situations, at various distances from land. I have never seen it on the ice or on land; but commonly swimming on the water. It is so remarkably watchful, and quick in diving, that if fired at without any precaution being taken to conceal the flash of the powder, it generally escapes the shot. In diving, it uses its wings under water, as in flying. It frequently dips its bill in the water, as if to keep it wet. It feeds on shrimps and small fishes. Its flesh, which is very dark-coloured, tastes a little like the liver of some animals, and is not unpleasant eating. The common colour of this species is black, with a white patch on the coverts of each wing. Some are all over grey, consisting of small alternating patches of black and white. The feet of all are red. In flying, the tail being short, the feet are used as a rudder.

2. COLYMBUS *Troile.*—Foolish guillemot or Loom. Occurs almost equally common in the Polar Seas with the doveca. It is a clumsy bird, weighing two pounds or upward, and measuring only 16 or 17 inches in length, and 28 inches across the wings, when full spread, in breadth. The colour on the back and wings is principally brownish-black; of the belly and breast, white. On ice or rocks, it sits

upright, like the penguin. It cannot rise on the wing in any direction excepting to windward. If it attempts to fly to leeward, it runs for a considerable distance along the surface of the water, and at length falls into it. It swims and dives well. It also evades the shot when fired at; but not so certainly as the doveca. Its feet compensate for the shortness of its tail in flying, and are used as a helm.

3. COLYMBUS *glacialis.*—Great northern Diver. Seen by Captain Phipps on the Coast of Spitzbergen.

STERNA *hirundo.*—*Great Tern,* or *Sea Swallow.*—This elegant bird is common on the shores of Spitzbergen, but is not met with at a distance from land. The length of its body is 7 or 8 inches, but including the tail, 14. Spread of the wings 29 or 30 inches. It flies with great ease and swiftness, and ascends to a considerable height in the air. It defends its eggs and young with great boldness from the depredations of the arctic gull; and even descends within a yard of the head of any person who ventures to molest them, and startles him with its loud screams. It lays its eggs among the shingle of the beach, above high water-mark, where the full power of the sun falls.

LARUS :—*Gull.*

1. LARUS *rissa*.   Kittywake.—Occurs in considerable numbers in the Spitzbergen Sea, and follows ships on their passage.   It is seen in every part of the Northern Atlantic from Britain to the highest latitudes ever visited.   It feeds eagerly on the blubber of the whale, but generally seizes its morsel on the wing.

2. LARUS *parasiticus*.   Arctic gull.—This predatory bird is rarely seen at a distance from the land, except about the parallel of Jan Mayen, where it is observed in constant pursuit of the kittywake.   The kittywake being a better fisher than the former, is constantly chaced until it gives up any food it may have procured, which the arctic gull generally catches before it falls into the water. The arctic gull occurs about the shores of Spitzbergen, where it not only feasts itself at the expence of other birds, on food obtained by them, but also preys upon their eggs and young.   It is rarely seen in the water; being generally on the wing.   It is easily distinguished by two tapering tail-feathers, which extend 5 or 6 inches beyond the rest of the tail.

3. LARUS *crepidatus*.—Black-toed gull or boatswain.   The habits of this are similar to those of the former species,   and it occurs in similar situations.

The two intermediate tail-feathers are much shorter than those of the parasiticus, and not so pointed.

4. LARUS *eburneus*. (Captain Phipps.)—Snowbird. This bird is not so elegantly formed as the kittywake, but is more remarkable for its immaculate whiteness. Its length is 19 or 20 inches, breadth across the wings about 3 feet. The feet and legs are black, the bill blackish-green and yellow, orbits red. The young birds have sometimes black spots on the wings.

The snow-bird, though so delicate in its appearance, is almost as ravenous as the fulmar, and as little nice in its food. It is, however, more cautious. It is a constant attendant on the flensing operations of the fishers, where it generally seizes its portion on the wing. It rarely alights in the water, but often sits on the ice, preferring the most elevated situations. Its voice is a loud and disagreeable scream.

5. LARUS *glaucus*. Burgomaster.—Larus imperiosus might perhaps be a more characteristic name for this lordly bird, and would correspond pretty nearly with the name Burgomaster or Burgermeister, as generally given to it by the Dutch. It may with propriety be called the chief magistrate of the feathered tribe in the Spitzbergen regions, as none of its *class* dares dispute its authority, when, with unhesitating superiority, it descends on its prey, though in the pos-

session of another. The burgomaster is not a numerous species, and yet it is a general attendant on
the whale-fishers whenever any spoils are to be obtained. It then hovers over the scene of action,
and, having marked out its morsel, descends upon
it and carries it off on the wing. On its descent,
the most dainty pieces must be relinquished, though
in the grasp of the fulmar, snow-bird, or kittywake. It seldom alights in the water. When
it rests on the ice, it selects a hummock, and fixes
itself on the highest pinnacle. Sometimes it con-
descends to take a more humble situation, when it
affords any advantage in procuring food. It is a
rapacious animal, and when without other food, falls
upon the smaller species of birds and eats them. I
have found the bones of a small bird in its stomach,
and have observed it in pursuit of the rotch.

The burgomaster is a large powerful bird. Its
length is about 28 inches, breadth across the wings
about 5 feet. Its colour, on the back and wing
coverts, is bluish-grey, the rest of the body beautifully white. The bill is of a yellowish colour, with
a little red on the lower mandible, and measures
$2\frac{1}{7}$ inches in length; the irides are yellow; legs
and feet yellowish flesh-red. Its eggs I have
found on the beach of Spitzbergen, deposited in the
same way as those of the tern.

The kittywake, snow-bird and burgomaster, are
sometimes shot for the sake of their feathers,which are

thickly set, fine and valuable. The two latter species being very shy, will not always approach within gunshot. From a sort of house, however, built of snow on any large sheet of ice, they may be shot with more certainty and in greater numbers than by any other contrivance that has been adopted. A piece or two of blubber or kreng being laid as a bait near the hut, which has the appearance of a hummock, they approach within gunshot without fear, and are fired at through small loop-holes made in the hut for the purpose.

TRINGA *hypoleucos*.   Sandpiper.—Seen in considerable flocks on the beach of Spitzbergen.

EMBERIZA *nivalis*.   Snow-bunting. — Occurs not only on the land, but also, less frequently however, on the ice adjacent. To some places on the shore it resorts in large flocks.

FRINGILLA *linaria*.   Lesser Redpole.—On our approach to Spitzbergen, several of this species alighted on different parts of the ship, and were so wearied apparently with being on the wing, though our distance from the land was not above ten miles, that they allowed themselves to be taken alive. How this little creature subsists, and why a bird of such apparent delicacy should resort to such a barren and gelid country, are questions of

some curiosity and difficulty. It must be migra-
tory ; and yet how such a small animal, incapable
of taking the water, can perform the journey from
Spitzbergen to a milder climate, without perishing
by the way, is difficult to conceive. Supposing it
to take advantage of a favourable gale of wind, it
must still be at least 10 hours on the wing before it could reach the nearest part of Norway, an
exertion of which one would imagine it to be totally incapable.

SECT. IV.

*A brief account of Amphibia, Fishes, Animalcules,
&c. inhabiting the Spitzbergen Sea.*

Class AMPHIBIA.

Squalus *borealis*. Greenland shark.—This animal has not, I believe, been described. The ventral fins are separate. It is without the anal fin ; but
has the temporal opening; it belongs, therefore, to
the third division of the genus. The spiracles on
the neck, are five in number on each side. The
colour is cinereous grey. The eyes are the most extraordinary part of this animal. The pupil is emerald green ; the rest of the eye blue. To the posterior edge of the pupil, is attached a white vermiform

ZOOLOGY.—GREENLAND SHARK. 539

substance, one or two inches in length. Each extremity of it consists of two filaments; but the central part is single. The sailors imagine this shark is blind, because it pays not the least attention to the presence of a man; and is, indeed, so apparently stupid, that it never draws back when a blow is aimed at it with a knife or lance. Figures 3. and 4. of Plate XV., represent this animal; and Fig. 5. shows the appearance of the eye, with its singular appendage.

The squalus borealis is 12 or 14 feet in length, sometimes more, and 6 or 8 feet in circumference. Its liver, which is remarkably oily, will fill a barrel. In its general form, it very much resembles the dog-fish. The opening of the mouth, which extends nearly across the lower part of the head, is 21 to 24 inches in width. The teeth are serrated in one jaw, and lancet-shaped and denticulated in the other. On each side, there are at least 4 or 5 rows; on one side sometimes 7 or 8.

This shark is one of the foes of the whale. It bites it and annoys it while living, and feeds on it when dead. It scoops hemispherical pieces out of its body, nearly as big as a person's head; and continues scooping and gorging lump after lump, until the whole cavity of its belly is filled. It is so insensible of pain, that though it has been run through the body with a knife and escaped; yet, after a while, I have seen it return to banquet again on the whale, at the very spot where it received its wounds. The heart is very small. It performs 6 or 8 pulsations in a minute; and continues its beating for some hours after taken out of the body. The body, also, though separated into any number of parts, gives evidence of life for a similar length of time. It is, therefore, extremely difficult to kill. It is actually unsafe to trust the hand in its mouth, though the head be separated from the body. Though the whale-fishers frequently slip into the water where sharks abound, there has been no instance that I have heard of, of their ever having been attacked by the shark. Besides dead whales, the sharks feed on small fishes and crabs. A fish, in size and form resembling a whiting, was found in the stomach of one that I killed; but the process of digestion had gone so far, that its species could not be satisfactorily discovered. In swimming, the tail only is used; the rest of its fins being spread out to balance it, are never observed in motion but when some change of direction is required.

CYCLOPTERUS *liparis*. The unctuous sucker.— Two of these animals were taken by Captain Phipps to the northward of Spitzbergen.

Class PISCES.

GADUS *carbonarius*. The Coal-fish.—This fish was also procured by Captain Phipps; which, with the species last mentioned, formed the whole of the produce of his trawling and fishing, in animals of this kind, during his stay in the vicinity of Spitzbergen. A small species of Gadus, nearly allied to the G. carbonarius, was found by myself among the arctic ice, in the parallel of 78° N*.

MULLUS *barbatus* ?—Taken by a seaman out of the mouth of a seal near Spitzbergen. The body was wholly red; the length about 12 inehes. It was boiled for our officers, and proved an excellent dish.

Class ARTICULATA.

GAMMARUS *arcticus* (Leach).—The characters of this animal (Pl. XVI. Fig. 14), I have been favoured with from Dr Leach. They are as follow : " G. oculis sublunatis ; pedum pari tertio, secundo " majori." The actions of this species suggest as a familiar name, the *mountebank shrimp*. It frequent-

---

* The only specimen I got of this fish, was put into the hands of Mr William Swainson, who considered it as a variety of the coal-fish ; though, from the contraction and change of colour produced, by the spirit in which it was preserved, the lateral line, so essential in the determination of the species, could not be traced. The number of rays in each of the fins of this specimen, was as follows : First dorsal 13, second dor. sal 18, third dorsal 20 ; first anal 22, second anal 20, &c. The third ray of the ventral fin was lengthened into a subulate point; and the hinder dorsal fin rounded, peculiarities not no. ticed by any author who has described G. Carbonarius.

ly turns over when in the water, with singular celerity, and swims with equal ease in every position.
The four feet raised in the figure above the back,
are made use of in that position, whenever its back
comes in contact with any solid substance. This
species occurs in all parts of the Spitzbergen Sea,
and at the greatest distance from land; it inhabits
the superficial water, and affords food for whales and
birds.

GAMMARUS ———— ?—Another small species of
this family, was found in large quantities in the
stomach and mouth of some mysticete. It is remarkable for the largeness of its eyes.

CANCER *Pulex* (Linné). — Taken by Captain
Phipps in a trawl, near the coast of Spitzbergen.

CANCER *Boreas* (Phipps.)—This singular species of crab, was first described and figured by Captain Phipps *. It was found in the stomach of a
seal. An animal that I have occasionally met with,
resembles this species in several of its characters. It
is figured (from an indifferent drawing, however,) in
Pl. XVI. Fig. 13.

CANCER *Ampulla* (Phipps).—Found by Captain Phipps† in the stomach of a seal; by myself in
the stomach of a shark.

CANCER *Nugax* (Phipps.)—Taken in the trawl
by Captain Phipps, near Moffen island ‡.

---

* See " Voyage towards the North Pole," p. 190.

† Idem, p. 191   ‡ Idem, p. 192.

Oniscus *Ceti*, (Lin.) Larunda *Ceti* (Leach.) *Whale's louse.*—This little animal, about half an inch in diameter, firmly fixes itself by its hooked claws, on the skin of the mysticetus. It is found principally under the fin, or in other situations where the skin is tender, and where it is not liable to be dislodged. A similar animal, but smaller, is sometimes found on the body of the narwal.

Class VERMES.

Ascaris, Echinorhynchus, Tænia, &c. *Intestina.*—Found in various animals inhabiting the northern seas.

Ascidia *gelatinosa* and A. *rustica.*—Taken by Captain Phipps, in a trawl on the north side of Spitzbergen.

Lernæa *branchialis.* — Found by Captain Phipps in the gills of the Cyclopterus liparis.

Clio *helicina.* (Phipps, p. 195.) Sea-snail.— An animal covered with a delicately beautiful shell, similar in form to that of the nautilus. The diameter is from two-eighths to three-eighths of an inch. It is found in immense quantities near the coast of Spitzbergen, but does not, I believe, occur out of sight of land *.

---

* See Fig. 11, and 12. of Pl. XVI. In these figures, this animal is magnified to about twice the natural size.

CLIO *borealis.*—Occurs in vast numbers in some situations near Spitzbergen, but is not found generally throughout the Arctic Seas. In swimming, it brings the tips of its fins almost into contact, first on one side and then on the other. I kept several of them alive in a glass of sea-water for about a month, when they gradually wasted away and died *.

SEPIA———? Cuttle-fish.—Found by myself in large quantities in the stomachs of different narwals, and appearing to constitute their principal food. The species not known.

MEDUSA, or Sea-blubber; ANIMALCULA, &c.— A great number of species of these animals occur in the Arctic Seas, and appear immediately or remotely to be the chief subsistence of the greater part of the marine and feathered animals frequenting the Polar regions.

The Greenland Sea, frozen and extensive as it is, teems with life. The variety of the animal creation is not indeed very great; but the quantity of some of the species that occur, is truly immense. A calculation of the number of minute medusæ, in a small district, has already been attempted, (p. 179. of this volume); if to these we add the number of the animalcula that I have observed, the amount, throughout the Spitz-

* See Fig. 10. Pl. XVI., natural size.

bergen Sea, if not surpassing the power of numbers, would at least exceed all the powers of the mind to conceive. The minute medusæ (Pl. XVI. fig. 16.), and moniliformes (fig. 17.), have already been described; the animalcula may be just noticed. Though I could not speak positively to the vitality of both the former substances, yet the animalcula were so active in the water, as to prevent a moment's doubt on the subject. Three kinds of animalcula are figured in Plate XVI, Nos. 18, 19, and 20. No. 18, examined by a double microscope, appeared of the size of a coarse grain of sand. It seemed of a brownish colour, and moved nearly in a direct line. No. 19, about half the size of the former, appeared globular, had a dark-coloured sort of tail, and advanced by a curious zig-zag motion. No. 20. was still smaller: It moved with amazing rapidity, by sudden starts, pausing for an instant between each impulse, and then springing in a new direction.

Besides these five minute animals, figure 15, Plate XVI, represents a beautiful creature that was brought up by the marine-diver, in the Spitzbergen Sea. Its length, excluding the antennæ, which were as long as the body, was one-tenth of an inch in one specimen, and one-fourth of an inch in another. Its body was beautifully transparent, and had quite a crystalline appearance. The antennæ and tail were red. In swimming, it proceeded by starts, and appeared very active.

VOL. I.   M m

The economy of these little creatures, as constituting the foundation of the subsistence of the largest animals in the creation, has already been noticed. The common whale feeds on medusæ, cancri, actiniæ, sepiæ, &c. and these feed probably on the minor medusæ and animalcules. The finwhales and dolphins feed principally on herrings, and other small fishes. These subsist on the smaller cancri, medusæ, and animalcules. The bear's most general food is probably the seal; the seal subsists on the cancri, and small fishes; and these on lesser animals of the tribe, or on the minor medusæ and animalcules. Thus the whole of the larger animals depend on these minute beings, which, until the year 1816, when I first entered on the examination of the sea-water, were not, I believe, known to exist in the polar seas. And thus we find a dependent chain of existence, one of the smaller links of which being destroyed, the whole must necessarily perish.

It is not a little interesting to trace the physiology of the preservation of these smaller animals. As the mean temperature of the atmosphere in the Spitzbergen Sea, has been shewn to be 10 or 12 degrees below the freezing point of salt-water, it is evident, that, were the water of the sea stationary, it must, in the course of ages, be frozen to the bottom, and along with it, as a matter of course, all the smaller animals, not having sufficient instinct or power of motion to enable them to retire into a more southern region. Now, such an event is provided against, by the constant prevalence of a current setting towards the south-west, which carries away the ice into a parallel where it can be dissolved, and occasions a circulation of water into the frozen regions, from a warmer climate. And this circulation of the water is beautifully accomplished: for, while the superficial current is performing its office, in carrying away a portion of ice, an under-current setting to the northward, is acting an equally important part, in affording warmth to the seas of the higher latitudes, and preventing the too great accumulation of the ice. But how is it, it might be asked, when a current in the waters, inhabited by the minor medusæ, is constantly setting to the southward, that these animals are not carried away into a southern region altogether? This question, if we may be allowed to argue hypothetically, admits of an easy solution. Animals, we find, when possessing any power of moving, though they be of the most imperfect kind of organization, generally employ that power by a sort of instinctive faculty, as may best serve the purposes for which they were called into existence. Now, it would be no stretch of commonly received principles, to suppose, that whenever the minor medusæ, &c. are carried to a certain extent southward, they may sink in the water, as far as the stream of the under-current, and by it be conveyed back again into their proper element. The fact of the olive-green coloured sea-water maintaining a great similarity of position, for many years together, while surface after surface of ice is carried away by the current and dissipated, is in support of this conjecture. Thus, by a most beautiful contrivance, a large portion of the surface of the globe is rendered habitable, which would otherwise be a solid mass of ice; and, by the warmth of the lower stratum of the polar sea, it is rendered congenial to many tribes of animals which must otherwise have incumbered other regions, now affording products useful for the subsistence of man.

MEDUSA ———? (Plate XVI, Fig. 3. natural size.) An extremely sensitive animal. When touched, or indeed when the vessel in which it is contained is moved, it shrinks into an irregular globular mass. It is divided into eight segments by as many rows of finny fringes. These, though only perceptible by their iridescence when in motion, are capable of moving the animal through the water. Its colour is greyish-white, but reddish, (pale lake red), in the longitudinal cavity. Occurs in the Spitzbergen Sea.

MEDUSA ———? (Pl. XVI. Fig. 5., natural size.) Eight segments. Sensitive. Iridescent fringes. Single cavity. Occurs in the Spitzbergen Sea. Colour similar to the former.

MEDUSA———? (Pl. XVI. Fig. 6. natural
size.) Form ovoidal. Eight segments. A double
cavity united by a small canal. Sensitive. Iridescent fringes. Found in latitude 75₀ 40' N., longitude 5° or 6° west. Colour similar to the former.

MEDUSA *pileus.* (Pl. XVI. Fig. 4. natural
size.) This is one of the most curious of the medusæ. It consists of eight lobes, with a beautifully iridescent finny fringe on the external edge of
each. A canal, four-fifths the length of the animal, penetrates the centre of it ; and two red cirrhi,
which may be extended to the length of nearly a
foot, proceed from a crooked cavity in opposite sides.
The animal is semi-transparent. Its colour is white,
with a blush of red ; the finny fringes of deeper red.
It is found of various sizes ; one specimen taken
up in latitude 75° 40', longitude 5° or 6° W., in a
green-coloured sea, was three inches in length.

MEDUSA ———? or Purse-shaped Medusa.
(Pl. XVI. Fig. 7. nat. size). The substance of this
is tougher than that of any other species which I
have examined. It has one large open cavity, and
is divided by the finny fringes into eight segments,
each alternate pair of which are similar. The colour is a very pale crimson, with waved purple
lines ; finny fringes deeper crimson. This animal
appeared to be almost without sensation. The only
evidence it gave of feeling was in an increased vibration of the finny fringes. Though it was cut

3

into pieces, each portion, on which there was any
of the fringe, continued, by its incessant play, to
give evidence of life during two or three days;
after which it became putrescent, and began to
waste away. This animal was found in the Spitzbergen sea. I have seen but one specimen.

MEDUSA ———— ? or Bottle-shaped Medusa.
(Pl. XVI. Fig. 8. natural size). Caught in a transparent green sea, in latitude 75° 48′, longitude
8° W. A sensitive animal. Large single cavity.
Eight segments. Finny fringes white and iridescent. Form ovoidal, with compressed mouth.

MEDUSA ? ———— ? or Orange-coloured Medusa.
(Pl. XVI. Fig. 9. natural size.) This singular species I have seen but once. It was sent me by Captain Bennet of the Venerable, being found in latitude 75° 20′, longitude 11° 50′ E. On the under-
side of the right hand extremity, (in the plate), there
was a transverse slit or opening. This animal was
convex above, and concave beneath. The length
was three inches, its breadth nearly an inch; its
thickness one-third of an inch. When slit open,
it exhibited a number of transverse bands and three
cavities. Its colour was a brilliant orange. It was
not transparent. It was not tenacious of life; having died, to appearance, soon after it was taken.

ASTERIAS: *Star-fish*. Several species of this
animal occur on the coast of Spitzbergen. Captain
Phipps procured, by means of a trawl, specimens of

ASTERIAS *papposa,* A. *rubens,* A. *ophiura,* and A. *pectinata.*

CHITON *ruber.* Coat-of-mail-shell. Taken in a trawl by Captain Phipps on the north side of Spitzbergen.

MYA *truncata* and MYTILUS *rugosus.* Found on the beach in Smeerenberg Harbour *.

BUCCINUM *carinatum.* (Phipps, p. 197.) Found also on the beach at Smeerenberg.

TURBO *helicinus.* (Phipps, p. 198.) Taken up in a trawl on the north side of Spitzbergen.

SERPULA *spirorbis* and *S. triquetra.* Found in Smeerenberg Harbour, adhering to dead shells.

SABELLA *frustulosa.* (Phipps, p. 198.) Taken up in a trawl in on the north side of Spitzbergen.

MILLEPORA *polymorpha,* and CELLEPORA *pumicosa.* Found on the beach at Smeerenberg.

SYNOICUM *turgens,* (Phipps, p. 199.) Procured by means of a trawl on the north side of Spitzbergen.

FLUSTRA *pilosa* and *F. membranacea.* Found in Smeerenberg harbour, adhering to stones.

---

* These two shells, together with the succeeding specimens of shells and zoophytes were found by Captain Phipps.

APPENDIX.

APPENDIX

TO

VOLUME FIRST.

No. I.

METEOROLOGICAL TABLES.

| 1807 | Latitude. | Therm. | Bar. | WINDS. | | Meteors and Weather. |
				Direction.	Force.	
April 1	60° 9′ N ⎫	43	29.86	N N W to N E	Fresh breezes	Snow
2	Lerwick, ⎭	47	29.90	to N N W	Ditto	Ditto
3	—	50	30.04	N.erly	Moderate breezes	Cloudy
4	60.30	41	29.79	S S W	Little wind	Ditto
5	60.43	45	29.35	to W	Strong breezes	Snow
6	Balta Sound,	48	29.65	to N b W	Strong gales	Rain
7	—	55	29.99	S erly	Moderate	Cloudy
8	—	50	29.78	W	Strong breezes	Rain
9	—	38	30.05	Variable	Fresh gales	Showers of Rain.
10	—	42	29.70	Ditto	Light airs	Rain
11	62.34	36	29.21	E S E, E N E	Fresh breezes	Ditto
12	63.26	33	29.74	E N E	Hard gales	Ditto
13	63.52	29	29.77	N E	Ditto	Dry Weather
14	64 20	28	29.90	N E	Strong gales	Cloudy
15	66.10	25	29.65	to E S E	Ditto	Ditto
16	66. 8	17	29.53	N	Hard gales	Snow
17	65.24	29	30.08	N	Ditto	Ditto
18	65.13	32	30.16	N	Light airs	Cloudy
19	67.21	39	30.00	S	Strong breezes	Ditto
20	69.47.	35	29.97	S S W	Fresh breezes	Hazy
21	72. 4	36	29.96	S S W	Ditto	Foggy
22	73.40	34	29.90	S W	Ditto	Ditto
23	75. 9	29	29.76	to W b S	Strong breezes	Clear
24	74.59	24	29.76	N W to E b N	Moderate breezes	Cloudy
25	75. 0	26	29.67	to N	Fresh breezes	Ditto
26	75.19	26	29.66	N	Ditto	Ditto
27	75.36	24	29.68	N	Light airs	Ditto
28	75.30	16	29.50	N E b E	Fresh breezes	Snow
29	75.20	20	29.48	N	Strong gales	Ditto
30	75.10	16	29.70	N	Ditto	Snow showers
May 1	75.20	18	30.05	N to N N W	Fresh gales	Much snow
2	75. 7	28	30 07	S W.erly	Light airs	Cloudy
3	74.26	20	30.16	to N.erly	Strong gales	Ditto
4	75.55	14	30.18	N b W to E N E	Strong breezes	Ditto
5	75.57	18	30.31	to N N E	Fresh gales	Clear
6	75.47	27	30.20	N N E	Moderate breeze	Ditto
7	75.51	34	30.00	N	Gentle breeze	Cloudy
8	76. 0	20	29.87	N	Fresh breeze	Ditto
9	75.31	19	29.80	N	Brisk gale	Snow
10	75.30	21	29.81	N	Fresh gale	Ditto
11	75.30	22	29.75	to E N E	Fresh breezes	Ditto
12	75.20	20	29.81	to N	Ditto	Ditto
13	75.30	17	29.48	N W.erly	Strong breezes	Ditto
14	75.22	15	29.46	W N W	Fresh breeze	Ditto
15	75.22	18	29.47	W N W	Fresh breeze	Cloudy
16	75.32	26	29.60	S S W	Light airs	Ditto
17	75.45	24	29.78	S. W.	Gentle breeze	Ditto

1807	Latitude.	Therm.	Bar.	WINDS. Direction.	Force.	Weather.
May 18	75° 50′	27	29.78	W	Gentle breeze	Snow
19	75.35	22	29.76	N W to N E	Light airs	Cloudy
20	75.55	22	29.80	N W to N E	Fresh breezes	Ditto
21	75.55	22	29.76	N	Light airs, calm	Ditto
22	76. 2	28	29 76	—	Calm	Clear
23	75.58	31	29.66	N	Moderate breeze	Cloudy
24	75.56	26	29.80	N W	Gentle breeze	Ditto
25	75.55	29	30.00	N N E	Light airs	Clear
26	75.55	26	30.01	N E	Ditto	Ditto
27	75.57	25	29.88	N b E	Fresh breeze	Cloudy
28	75.56	26	29.91	to N N W	Ditto	Snow
29	75.56	23	29.84	to N W	Ditto	Ditto
30	75.55	18	29.78	N W	Strong breeze	Ditto
31	75.51	22	29.81	N N W	Fresh breeze	Cloudy
June 1	75·48	25	29.93	Calm	Calm	Ditto
2	75.46	28	29.99	S E, W S W	Moderate breeze	Hazy
3	75.49	32	29.88	S W	Light airs	Ditto
4	75.59	33	29.82	S b W	Strong breeze	Ditto
5	76.16	32	29.97	to W S W	Brisk gales	Rain
6	76.20	′31	29.97	S E	Light airs	Rain, fog
7	76.36	30	29.83	N W	Ditto	Thick fog
8	76.35	28	29.60	S W	Ditto	Cloudy
9	76.48	32	29.78	W b N	Fresh gales	Ditto
10	76.48	32	29.79	W b N	Light airs	Foggy
11	76.50	32	29.88	W N W, S E	Nearly calm	Clear
12	76.49	32	29.93	E, E S E	Fresh breezes	Cloudy
13	76.52	29	30 00	E S E	Brisk gales	Ditto
14	77. 0	31	29.97	E	Fresh gales	Snow
15	76.54	31	29.68	to E N E	Ditto	Ditto
16	76.50	30	29.65	E N E	Fresh breeze	Ditto
17	77. 0	33	29.66	N E	Ditto	Ditto
18	77.34	32	29.72	N E	Moderate breeze	Foggy
19	76.26	34	29.81	N N E, W N W	Fresh breezes	Ditto
1808 May 1	76.17	24	29.23	N N E to E	Strong gales	Showers of snow
2	76.50	28	29.50	E to S S E	Fresh gales	Ditto
3	77. 2	28	29.40	to E S E	Ditto	Snow
4	76. 6	27	29.67	E S E	Light breeze	Cloudy
5	77.20	29	29.54	N.erly	Fresh gales	Snow
6	78. 0	28	29,73	E S E to E N E	Strong gales	Ditto
7	78. 0	26	30.20	to N N W	Fresh breezes	Cloudy
8	78. 0	27	30.23	S E to E	Moderate breeze	Snow showers
9	78. 0	28	30.10	to N N W	Strong br. calm	Ditto
10	77.50	18	30.54	N N W	Light air	Cloudy
11	77.50	26	30.45	Calm	Calm	Ditto
12	77.40	32	29.73	S	Fresh gale	Fog
13	77.45	25	29.53	Variable	Fresh breezes	Snow
14	77.50	22	29.47	W, S S W	to Moderate br.	Ditto

| 1808 | Latitude. | Therm. | Bar. | WINDS. | | Weather. |
				Direction.	Force.	
May 15	77° 50′	20	29.50	Variable.	to Calm	Hazy
16	77.40	24	29.55	W N W to N	Moderate breeze	Ditto
17	77.30	27	29.60	N	Fresh breeze	Snow
18	77.50	25	29.60	N	Ditto	Ditto
19	77.55	24	29.81	to N W b N	Strong breezes	Cloudy
20	78. 4	20	29.80	N.erly	Light airs	Ditto
21	78. 8	26	29.85	W.erly	Moderate breeze	Snow
22	78.10	29	29.98	Calm.	Calm	Cloudy
23	78.13	29	29.86	S W	Moderate breeze	Fog
24	78. 4	24	29.78	W N W to N N W	Light breezes	Clear
25	77.55	26	29.70	N.erly	Ditto	Cloudy
26	77.50	22	29.80	N W	Strong breeze	Snow
27	77.58	24	30.09	N W	Ditto	Ditto
28	78.30	25	30.00	E S E	Light breeze	Snow showers
29	78.37	24	29.90	Var. W N W	to Fresh gales	Much snow
30	78.36	32	29.93	N E	Light airs	Fog, cloudy
31	78.36	26	29.96	N E	to Calm	Snow showers
June 1	78.37	24	29.99	N E	Fresh breeze	Snow
2	78.43	36	29.97	N E	Nearly calm	Fog
3	78.43	28	29.97	Var. calm	Ditto	Fog
4	78.35	31	29.90	Calm	Calm	Clear
5	78.25	30	29.90	S S W	Fresh breeze	Hazy
6	78.20	32	29.83	S.erly	Light breeze	Fog or snow
7	78.20	29	29.87	S W	Ditto	Ditto
8	78.10	29	29.88	S.erly	Nearly calm	Fog, cloudy
9	77.50	27	29.78	Variable.	Ditto	Cloudy
10	77.18	27	29.79	W N W	Light or Mod. br.	Clear
11	77. 6	30	29.80	S	Strong breeze	Fog
12	76.37	33	29.83	S.erly	Fresh gales	Ditto
13	76.35	33	29.90	S S W	Fresh gale	Haze or fog
14	76.30	34	29.99	S S W	Strong breeze	Fog
15	75.58	34	30.06	S S W	Fresh breeze	Fog
1809						
May 1	74.15	12	29.68	N E	Moderate breeze	Frost rime
2	74. 5	10	29.84	N E b N	to Strong gale	Ditto
3	73.54	20	29.87	to N E b E	Strong gales	Snow
4	74.10	36	29.94	to S E b S	Fresh gales	Ditto
5	74.10	36	30.00	to S b E	to Light breezes	Clear
6	73.49	32	29.38	E S E to S W	Light breezes	Rain
7	73.48	25	29.53	S W, N	Fresh Gales	Snow
8	73.38	27	29.72	to W.	to Fresh b eezes	Cloudy
9	73.50	21	29.76	to N N E	Fresh gales	Snow showers
10	74.10	19	29.80	N E, calm	to Calm	Snow
11	74.45	13	30.20	N, N N E	Fresh breezes	Snow showers
12	75. 0	16	30.15	N N E, calm	Strong br. calm	Cloudy
13	75. 8	16	30.04	W N W, W S W	Fresh breezes	Ditto
14	75.48	19	30.00	Variable	Moderate breeze	Ditto
15	76. 3	20	30.02	E.erly	Nearly calm	Ditto

1809	Latitude.	Therm.	Bar.	WINDS. Direction.	WINDS. Force.	Weather.
May 16	76° 4′	22	29.78	E	to Calm	Snow
17	76. 8	30	29.35	E S E	Strong gale	Ditto
18	76. 6	23	29.79	to N N E, W N W	to Moderate br.	Snow showers
19	76.16	32	29.65	to S S W	Fresh breezes	Clear
20	76.30	31	30.03	to N W	Ditto	Fog, snow
21	76.26	31	30.12	Var. E S E	Moderate breezes	Cloudy
22	76.32	31	29.73	to S E	Ditto	Fog
23	76.24	21	30.06	to W, N	Strong gales	Cloudy
24	77. 8	17	29.98	N.erly	to Moderate br.	Ditto
25	77.20	20	29.87	N N W	Light breeze	A little snow
26	77.20	17	29.87	N W b N	to Strong gale	Snow
27	77.20	19	29.80	N N E	Strong gale	Ditto
28	77.20	19	30.04	N N E	Fresh gale	Cloudy
29	79. 0	20	30.05	N E.erly	Ditto	Ditto
30	79. 0	20	30.05	to N.	to Strong gales	Snow showers
31	79. 0	23	30.06	N E.erly	Fresh gale	Ditto
June 1	78.56	23	30.02	N N E	Ditto	Cloudy
2	79. 4	22	30.24	N N E	Fresh breeze	Ditto
3	79. 4	28	30.20	E.erly	Nearly calm	Clear
4	79. 4	26	30.10	E.erly	to Moderate br.	Cloudy
5	79. 0	24	30.06	N E	to Light airs	Ditto
6	79. 0	30	29.95	N E	Light breeze	Haze, snow
7	79. 4	31	29.88	S E.erly	Ditto	Cloudy, snow
8	79. 8	29	29.88	S E	to Calm	Snow showers
9	79. 2	27	29.86	to W	Strong gales	Ditto
10	79. 0	25	29.93	S W	Moderate breeze	Ditto
11	79. 2	30	30.06	S W.erly	Ditto	Snow
12	78.56	29	30.07	to S	Ditto	A little snow
13	78.52	31	29.97	to W	Ditto	Fog showers
14	78.56	31	29.82	W	Nearly calm	Fog
15	79. 0	30	29.68	S E	Fresh breeze	Snow showers
16	79. 0	32	29.50	to E N E	to Light breezes	Much snow, fog
17	79. 0	32	29.62	to S, S S W	to Fresh breezes	Snow, fog
18	79.30	27	29.90	N N W, S S W	Moderate breezes	Clear
19	79.30	27	29.91	S W.erly	Strong breeze	Snow showers
20	79.50	42	29.67	to E N E	Nearly calm	Clear
21	79.50	30	29.81	to S S W, S S E	to Fresh breeze	Fog
22	79.45	32	29.81	Variable	Light breeze	Fog, snow
23	79.45	32	29.82	Ditto	Ditto	Ditto
24	79.57	32	29.59	N N W, var.	Moderate breeze	Snow showers
25	79.30	34	29.64	Variable	to Fresh breeze	Fog showers
26	79. 0	32	29.84	W N W, S	Strong breezes	Snow, fog
27	78.50	32	29.94	Var. calm	Nearly calm	Ditto
28	78.48	32	29.82	Variable	Ditto	Cloudy, fog
29	78.36	32	29.82	to S.erly	to Fresh breezes	Cloudy
30	77.40	35	29.80	to W N W	Moderate breezes	Thick fog

| 1810 | Latitude. | Longitude. | THERMOMETER. | | | | BAROMETER. | | |
			Max.	Min.	No.of Obs.	Med.	Max.	Min.	Med.
April 9	74°.6	14.37 E	14	10	3	12.0	30.00	29.94	29.97
10	73.41	16. 0	12	10	3	11.0	30.14	30.00	30.07
11	74.16	14.47	20	16	3	18.0	30.00	29.88	29.94
12	73.42*	14. 0	24	14	3	20.0	29.88	29.80	29.84
13	73 59	16. 0	8	6	3	7.0	30.14	29.80	29.97
14	74.50	11.30	17	12	3	14.7	30.14	30.02	30.08
15	75. 4	9.38	14	10	2	12.0	30.02	30.26	30.14
16	75.46	9.14	15	10	3	12.6	30.26	30.08	30.17
17	76. 6	9.30	10	4	3	7.7	30.08	29.90	29.99
18	76.18	8.50	5	0	3	4.6	29.92	29.90	29.91
19	76.16*	9. 0	12	10	3	10.7	30.07	29.92	30.00
20	76.22	9. 0	21	16	3	19.3	30.07	29.60	29.83
21	76.37	11. 0	21	8	4	17.0	29.60	29.58	29.59
22	76.17	11. 0	8	5	3	6.0	29.60	30.00	29.80
23	76.16	10.50	16	11	3	13.6	30.12	30.00	30.06
24	76.20	10.30	28	19	4	23.0	30.24	29.72	29.98
25	76.30	11.10	31	18	3	26.0	29.72	29.30	29.51
26	76.25	11.15	20	17	3	18.7	29.68	29.30	29.49
27	77.10	10.20	23	17	3	20.6	29.85	29.68	29.76
28	77. 0	10.40	21	11	3	16.0	29.91	29.85	29.88
29	76.50	10. 0	18	14	3	16.0	29.98	29.91	29.95
30	76.41	9.30	22	12	3	17.7	30.04	29.98	30.01
May 1	76.58	10. 0	16	12	3	14.7	30.04	30.00	30.02
2	77.10	10. 0	14	8	3	10.7	30.00	29.96	29.98
3	77.39*	10.10	16	13	3	14.0	30.02	29.98	30.00
4	77.30	9.50	15	12	3	13.6	30.05	30.01	30.03
5	77.14	10. 0	16	16	3	16.0	30.01	29.81	29.91
6	77.20*	9.50	26	22	3	23.7	29.81	29.57	29.69
7	77.28*	10. 0	25	21	3	23.0	29.75	29.50	29.62
8	77.10	9.50	21	18	3	19.7	30.09	29.75	29.92
9	77.30	8. 0	19	17	3	18.3	30.22	30.09	30.16
10	77.50	5.40	20	17	3	18.6	30.30	30.22	30.26
11	78.15	5.35	22	19	2	20.5	30.34	30.32	30.33
12	78.15	5.30	28	19	3	23.0	30.34	30.33	30.33
13	78.25	5.50	20	15	3	18.0	30.40	30.33	30.37
14	78.48*	5.30	20	12	3	15.7	30.40	30.21	30.30
15	79. 0	5. 0	18	15	3	17.4	30.21	29.86	30.03
16	78.45	4.30	20	19	3	19.3	29.86	29.66	29.76
17	78.30	4. 0	17	16	3	16.7	29.88	29.76	29.82
18	78.25	4.10	18	16	3	17.0	29.89	29.86	29.88
19	78.35	5. 0	18	17	3	17.6	29.90	29.84	29.87

1810	WINDS.		Weather and Meteors.	Situation and Remarks.
	Direction.	Force.		
April 9	N E.erly	Hard gales	Snow showers.	At sea
10	to E S E	Fresh, light br.	Ditto	Ditto
11	to E	to Strong gales	Showers cryst. snow	Drift ice
12	E.erly	Strong gales	Ditto	At sea, no ice
13	to N N E	to Moderate br	Snow showers	Ditto
14	to N	Fresh gales	Shower cryst. snow	Bay ice
15	N to E S E	to Light airs	Snow	Ditto
16	Calm	to Calm	Showers of Snow	Bay and drift ice
17	Variable	Fresh breezes	Ditto	Crowded ice
18	N W, S W	Fresh gales	Ditto	Much ice
19	W.erly	Light br. calm	Cloudy	Very crowded ice
20	E S E, var.	Light br. fr. gales	Some cryst. snow	Ice more open.
21	E N E to N	Strong gales	Constant cryst. snow	Much bay and drift ice
22	N N W, N W	to Light breezes	Frost rime	Bay ice
23	N.erly, var.	Light breezes	Clear	Beset in bay ice
24	E S E	to Fresh gale	Snow showers	Bay and drift ice
25	Var. W N W	Strong ga. calm	Coarsely cryst. snow	Floes of Bay ice
26	W N W	to Moderate breeze	A little snow	Open drift ice
27	to N.erly	to Fresh breeze	Showers cryst. snow	Ice streams
28	W N W to W	to Light breezes	Ditto	Ditto
29	to S S W, var.	Calm to fresh br.	Much snow	Much ice near
30	Variable	Light or fresh br.	Thick snow showers	Ice streams
May 1	N W to E, S E	Calm to str. gales	Much cryst. snow	A pack of ice near
2	to N E	to Light breeze	Snow showers	Bay floes, & drift ice
3	to N N W, N N E	to Strong gales	Cryst. snow	Ditto
4	to N b W	to Moderate breeze	Some snow showers	Ditto
5	to N E	Light br. brisk ga.	Coarse cryst. snow	Much bay & drift ice
6	to N b E, N b W	Fresh or strong ga.	Clear, cloudy	Ditto
7	to N b E, N.erly	Strong gales	Snow showers	Drift ice
8	N b E to N N W	Fresh gales	Showers cryst. snow	Crowded drift ice
9	N.erly	Ditto	Ditto	Sea open
10	N W, N	to Moderate br.	Ditto	A little drift ice
11	N N W to W.erly	Light airs, calm	Clear	Near much ice
12	to N E.erly	to fresh breeze	Cloudy	Ditto
13	N N E to N N W	to Strong gales	Showers cryst. snow	Ice streams
14	to N W b N	Brisk gales	Ditto	Ditto
15	N.erly	to Strong gales	Snow showers	Ditto
16	N W b N, N	to Brisk gales	A little snow	Ditto
17	to N E	to Strong gales	Ditto	Ditto
18	N E.erly	Fresh breezes	Showers cryst. snow	Floes and drift ice
19	to Variable	Ditto	Some snow	Ice streams

—

1810	Latitude.	Longitude.	THERMOMETER.				BAROMETER.		
			Max.	Min.	No.of Obs.	Med.	Max.	Min.	Med.
May 20	79.°05 *	4. 0	24	15	3	19.7	29.97	29.90	29.93
21	79.15	3. 0	26	16	3	21.0	29.93	29.76	29.85
22	79.20	3.30	22	20	3	21.0	29.76	29.61	29.68
23	79.15	3.50	24	22	2	23.0	29.74	29.58	29.66
24	79. 0	4. 0	18	14	3	16.3	29.96	29.74	29.85
25	78.45*	4.10 E	16	12	3	13.7	30.02	29.96	29.99
26	78.53	3.40	16	12	3	13.3	29.99	29.84	29.92
27	78.57	3.28	17	16	3	16.4	29.85	29.72	29.78
28	78.50	3. 0	18	10	3	14.7	30.05	29.85	29.95
29	78.45	2.50	18	12	2	15.0	30.12	29.93	30.03
30	78.50	2.50	28	27	3	27.7	29.93	29.61	29.77
31	79. 0	2.50	36	20	2	28.0	29.75	29.47	29.61
June 1	78.34*	3. 0	24	20	3	22.0	30.04	29.75	29.89
2	78.24	4. 0	28	26	2	27.0	29.95	29.86	29.90
3	78.20	3 30	26	16	2'	21.0	29.91	29.88	29.89
4	78.15	3. 0	21	17	2	19.0	29.94	29.91	29.93
5	78.12	3.20	27	15	2	21.0	29.92	29.84	29.88
6	78. 8	3.20	26	22	2	24.0	29.84	29.75	29.80
7	78. 4	3.10	30	21	2	25.5	29.75	29.73	29.74
8	78. 0	3.10	25	24	2	24.5	29.74	29.69	29.71
9	77.55*	3. 0	30	27	2	28.5	29.68	29.64	29.66
10	77.54	3. 5	27	25	2	26.0	29.78	29.68	29.73
11	77.48*	3. 0	35	27	3	31.3	29.85	29.78	29.82
12	77.47	3.10	34	30	2	32.0	29.87	29.85	29.86
13	77.47	3.10	34	30	3	32.0	29.97	29.86	29.91
14	77.50	3. 0	34	30	3	32.3	30.12	29.97	30.05
15	77.55	3.10	35	28	2	31.5	30 20	30.12	30.16
16	77.59	3.40	30	28	2	29.0	30.25	30.20	30.23
17	78. 4	3.30	31	30	2	30.5	30.20	29.97	30.08
18	78. 7	3.20	32	30	3	30.4	29.97	29.68	29.82
19	78. 0	3.45	33	27	3	29.3	29.68	29.60	29.64
20	77.58	3.38	39	27	3	33.0	29.62	29.60	29.61
21	78. 0	3.44	32	25	3	29.3	29.72	29.62	29.67
22	77.50	4.10	28	27	2	27.5	29.93	29.72	29.82
23	76.55	7.30	31	30	2	30.5	30.06	29.93	30.00
24	76.40	6.30	35	32	3	33.7	30.04	29.94	29.99
25	76.10	7. 0	32	31	3	31.7	30.14	29.88	30.01
26	75.40	6.10	33	32	2	32.5	29.74	29.62	29.68
27	75. 0	8.30	32	32	2	32.0	29.86	29.74	29.80
28	74.20	12.30	39	35	2	37.0	29.86	29.78	29.82
29	73. 0	12.28	35	33	3	34.0	29.84	29.78	29.81
30	70.50	10.20	36	35	2	35.5	30.24	92.84	30.04

1810	WINDS.		Weather and Meteors.	Situation and Remarks.
	Direction.	Force.		
May 20	N .	to Light breeze	Some cryst. snow	Fields and floes
21	to W.erly, S S W	Light breezes	Clear	Ditto
22	to S W	to Fresh gales	Showers cryst. snow	Ditto
23	to N E or E.erly	to Calm	Coarse cryst. snow	Many floes
24	N E.erly	Brisk gales	Showers cryst. snow	Heavy drift ice
25	to N W	Ditto	Showers of snow	Floes and drift ice
26	W N W	to Light breeze	Some snow	Field and drift ice
27	N.erly, var.	Light airs	Fine cryst. snow	Fields and floes
28	E.erly, var.	Nearly calm	Cloudy	Ditto
29	E.erly, S.erly	Fresh or light br.	Some snow	Ship embayed among do.
30	S	Fresh gale	Snow showers	Ditto
31	N.erly	Calm, fresh gales	Clear	Ditto
June 1	N W b N, S.erly	Ditto	Ditto	Fields and floes
2	E to N N E	to Light breeze	Coarse cryst. snow	Floes and drift ice
3	to N b W	Light breeze	Small snow	Fields, floes, & drift ice
4	N.erly	Moderate breeze	Cloudy	Floes and drift ice
5	to N N E, N N W	Ditto	Snow	Crowded drift ice
6	N.erly	Light breeze	Snow showers	Ship beset by a field, &c.
7	N, N N W	to Strong gales	Some snow	Ditto
8	N b W to N W	to Fresh gales	Snow showers	Field and drift ice
9	W N W	Fresh gales	Ditto	Ice open, field, &c.
10	to W.	Calm, moderate br.	Some snow	Field and floes
11	N W, W b S	Light breeze	Fog	Ditto
12	to S b E, var.	to Moderate breeze	Hazy	Ditto
13	S W to S E	Light airs	Fine clear weather	Ditto
14	to W, var.	to Moderate breeze	Fog showers	Fields and drift ice
15	S S W, S E, var.	to Calm	Clear	Ditto
16	S to W, var.	to Moderate breeze	A little snow	Floes and drift ice
17	W N W, to S b W	Fresh gales	Some snow	Field, floes, &c.
18	S to W N W	to Moderate breeze	Fog, snow	Ditto
19	to N N W	Strong or light breeze	Some snow	Ditto
20	N W, N E.erly	to Calm	Cloudy	Ditto
21	N E b N	to Moderate breeze	Ditto	Floes and drift ice
22	to N W b N	to Fresh breeze	Clear	In an open pack
23	Variable	to Moderate breeze	Ditto	Ice streams
24	S.erly	Light airs, calm	Showers of snow	Sea open
25	Var. E S E	to Fresh gales	Ditto	A pack of ice near
26	to S, N W	to Fresh breeze	Snow, fog	No ice
27	to S, S W	Strong ga. mod. br.	A little snow	Much ice
28	S, N W	Fresh gales	Rain	At sea
29	S, N W	Calm to str. ga.	Some snow	Ditto
30	to S W	to Light breeze	A little snow	Ditto

1811	Latitude.	Longitude.	THERMOMETER.				BAROMETER.		
			Max.	Min.	No. of Obs.	Med.	Max.	Min.	Med.
April 1	69°.41 °	3.31 W	18	15	3	16.3	30.13	30.00	30.06
2	69.40	1.11 E	23	15	3	19.3	30.24	30.12	30.18
3	70.22°	3.23	30	27	3	28.7	29.95	29.70	29.83
4	70.33°	5. 4	30	25	3	27.7	29.88	29.77	29.82
5	70.49	7.15	14	10	3	11.6	29.88	29.69	29.79
6	71.25	10.53	27	10	3	18.0	29.69	29.50	29.60
7	71.29	10.39	28	28	3	28.0	29.50	29.50	29.50
8	70.56	10.30	30	28	3	28.7	29.70	29.50	29.60
9	70.25°	8.15	24	15	3	19.0	30.00	29.70	29.85
10	70.32°	6.58	11	8	3	10.4	30.18	30.00	30.09
11	70.44	6.26	25	17	3	21.3	30.26	30.18	30.22
12	70.52°	6. 0	27	25	3	26.0	30.25	30.19	30.22
13	70.18°	8.57	29	27	3	27.7	30.19	30.14	30.16
14	70.52°	8.59	34	25	3	28.3	30.23	30.19	30.21
15	72.36°	13.30	34	26	3	30.0	30.23	30.02	30.13
16	74.31	16.32	37	33	3	35.4	30.02	29.82	29.92
17	75.34	15. 4	34	32	3	33.0	29.82	29.74	29.78
18	75.34	13.46	34	27	3	31.3	29.89	29.66	29.77
19	75.59	12.50	32	22	3	26.3	30.12	29.89	30.01
20	76.21°	12. 0	12	10	3	10.6	30.16	30.12	30.14
21	76.32	11. 0	14	12	3	13.0	30.24	30.16	30.20
22	76.28	10.50	15	10	3	13.0	30.39	30.24	30.32
23	76.34°	10.20	25	15	3	18.4	30.47	30.31	30.39
24	76.45	10.45	27	20	3	23.0	30.31	29.97	30.14
25	76.58	10.20	22	19	3	20.3	29.97	29.82	29.89
26	77. 0°	10.20	14	5	3	9.0	30.04	29.92	29.98
27	76.58	10. 0	12	12	2	12.0	30.12	30.04	30.08
28	77. 4	8.50	26	16	3	20.7	30.17	30.10	30.14
29	77. 0	8.50	23	16	3	20.3	30.10	30.05	30.07
30	77. 8	8.48	18	16	3	17.0	30.12	30.06	30.09
May 1	77.15	8.20	21	13	3	16.7	30.17	30.12	30.15
2	77.17°	8.10	23	15	3	18.3	30.17	30.02	30.09
3	77.22	8. 0	23	19	3	21.7	30.02	29.81	29.92
4	77.27	7.50	23	19	3	21.0	29.81	29.73	29.77
5	77.34°	7.50	25	11	3	19.0	29.74	29.71	29.72
6	77.32°	7.58	12	10	3	10.6	29.79	29.74	29.77
7	77.28	8. 4	10	8	3	9.0	29.91	29.79	29.85
8	77.24	8.10	11	5	3	8.7	30.02	29.91	29.96
9	77.26	8.10	24	20	3	22.0	30.05	30.02	30.04
10	77.10°	8.10	22	14	3	18.7	30.12	30.05	30.08
11	77. 6	8. 3	10	9	3	9.3	30.15	30.07	30.11
12	77. 1°	8. 5	23	17	3	20.0	30.07	29.81	29.94
13	77. 4	8.10	31	11	3	20.0	29.81	29.63	29.72
14	77. 2	8.15	13	10	3	11.6	29.83	29.68	29.76
15	77. 2	8.56	16	12	3	13.7	29.94	29.83	29.88
16	77. 0	8.59	24	19	3	21.0	29.95	29.87	29.91

| 1811 | WINDS. | | Meteors and Weather. | Situation and Remarks. |
	Direction.	Force.		
April 1	W b N to N b W	Fresh breezes	Clear	At sea
2	Variable	to Calm	Some snow	Ice streams
3	S S W to W N W	Fresh br. to st. ga.	Much snow	Drift ice
4	W to N N W	to Moderate br.	Cloudy	Ice near
5	N N W	Fresh gales	Snow, frost rime	Ditto
6	to W N W, E	to Light br. hard ga.	Snow showers	No ice
7	to N E	Very hard gales	Some snow	At sea
8	N E	Very hard gale	Some hail	Ditto
9	to N	to Fresh gales	Snow showers	Ditto
10	to N N E	to Strong gales	Ditto	A little ice
11	to N E	to Fresh gales	Some snow showers	Drift ice
12	N E, N E b N	Fresh gales	Ditto	Ice streams
13	N N E to W N W	to Calm	Cloudy	Ditto
14	Var. E.erly	to Strong gales	Snow showers	Sea open
15	E S E to S S W	Fresh gales	Clear	Bay ice
16	to W S W	to Strong gales	Hazy	A little drift ice
17	to S S W	to Fresh gales	Rain	A pack of ice near
18	to W	Strong gales	Some snow	In a bight of ice
19	W N W to S S W	to Calm	Snow showers	Among drift ice
20	W S W to N N E	Fresh br. light br.	Clear	Much drift ice
21	E b N	Nearly calm	Ditto	Much ice
22	E.erly, W N W	to Moderate breeze	A little snow	Crowded ice
23	W N W	to Calm	Clear	Ship beset
24	E S E, W N W	to Fresh gale	Much snow	Bay and heavy ice
25	to N to E N E	Light br strong ga.	Ditto	Crowded ice
26	to N N W	to Light breeze	Some snow showers	Ditto
27	N E.erly	to Fresh gale	Ditto	Ditto
28	N E to N N W	to Light breeze	Clear	Ice more open
29	to N N E, W N W	to Calm	Snow showers	Ice crowded
30	S S W to S E	Fresh breezes	Continual snow	Ship frozen up
May 1	N N E to S E	Moderate breeze	Snow showers	Ditto
2	to E N E	Ditto	A little snow	Ship beset
3	to E S E	Fresh breezes	Snow showers	Ditto
4	to N E	Fresh gales	Much snow	Ditto
5	Variable	to Calm	Snow showers	Ditto
6	N W.erly	Fresh breezes	Ditto	Ditto
7	N W b W	Strong gales	Ditto	Ditto
8	N W	to Strong breeze	Cryst. snow	Ditto
9	S S W to W N W	Fresh gales	Snow showers	Ditto
10	to N N W	to Fresh breeze	Ditto	Ditto
11	to N W	Fresh gales	A little snow	Ditto
12	S b E to S E b S	to Light airs	Ditto	Ditto
13	to S S W, W b S	Hard gales	Snow showers	Ditto
14	to W N W	Strong gales	Ditto	Ice more open
15	W N W, var.	Fresh gales	Much small snow	Ice rather open
16	E.erly.	Calm, light breeze	Snow showers	Ditto

1811	Latitude.	Longitude.	THERMOMETER.				BAROMETER.		
			Max.	Min.	No of Obs.	Med.	Max.	Min.	Med.
May 17	77°.0′	9. 0 E	24	16	3	21.4	29.90	29.80	29.85
18	76.46	8.46	23	20	3	21.3	30.00	29.90	29.95
19	76.54	8.38	23	22	3	22.7	29.97	29.87	29.92
20	77. 5	8.30	22	20	3	21.0	29.87	29.77	29.82
21	77.20	8.28	24	20	3	22.3	29.89	29.78	29.84
22	77.22	8. 0	33	24	3	27.0	29.88	29.68	29.78
23	77.16	8.18	24	23	3	23.4	30.11	29.88	30.00
24	77.14	8.50	28	23	3	25.0	30.16	30.07	30.11
25	77.24	9.10	26	23	3	24.6	30.07	29.94	30.00
26	78. 0	9.50	27	24	3	25.7	29.94	29.88	29.91
27	78.15	9.30	23	20	3	21.7	29.88	29.86	29.87
28	78.20	9.30	25	21	3	23.0	29.99	29.88	29.94
29	78.22	9.27	24	21	3	22.3	30.08	29.99	30.03
30	78.28	5.40	23	21	3	21.6	30.09	30.03	30.06
31	78.34	5.35	29	24	3	26.7	30.03	29.98	30.01
June 1	78.34	5.38	26	24	3	25.0	30.04	30.01	30.03
2	78.36	6.10	23	22	3	22.3	30.04	30.00	30.02
3	78.34	6.10	34	28	3	31.3	30.00	29.96	29.98
4	78.38	5.58	34	24	3	28.0	29.96	29.90	29.93
5	78.29	5.54	34	23	3	29.7	29.90	29.82	29.86
6	78.40	6.10	29	28	2	28.5	29.82	29.71	29.76
7	79.20	8. 0	32	30	3	30.7	29.71	29.63	29.67
8	79.10	7.50	30	29	3	29.4	29.78	29.63	29.71
9	78.58	7. 0	31	30	3	30.3	29.94	29.78	29.86
10	78.58	6.58	38	31	3	33.6	29.95	29.94	29.94
11	78.58	6. 0	32	30	3	31.0	29.94	29.93	29.94
12	78.56	5.50	30	26	3	28.0	29.95	29.91	29.93
13	78.40	5.30	31	27	3	29.0	29.91	29.82	29.87
14	78.45	5.15	33	28	3	30.3	29.82	29.76	29.79
15	78.45	5.13	34	32	3	32.7	29.80	29.77	29.78
16	78.42	5.10	35	30	3	33.0	29.85	29.80	29.83
17	78.40	5. 8	34	30	3	32.4	29.87	29.85	29.86
18	78.36	5.10	31	30	3	30.3	29.89	29.87	29.88
19	78.15	5. 4	33	29	3	30.7	29.91	29.89	29.90
20	78.10	5. 0	37	31	3	33.6	29.92	29.77	29.84
21	78.15	5. 0	32	31	3	32.0	29.77	29.62	29.70
22	78.11	5.15	37	33	3	35.3	29.64	29.62	29.63
23	78.17	5.25	34	32	3	32.7	29.67	29.64	29.65
24	78.20	5.26	35	33	3	34.0	29.68	29.59	29.64
25	78.21	5.26	35	30	3	33.0	29.59	29.50	29.54
26	78.35	5.54	33	32	3	32.4	29.64	29.58	29.61
27	78.15	5.50	36	34	2	35.0	29.73	29.53	29.63
28	78. 4	5. 0	34	30	3	32.3	30.02	29.73	29.88
29	78. 0	5.15	35	30	3	32.7	30.10	30.02	30.06
30	78.50	6.40	37	34	3	35.3	30.02	29 94	29.98

1811	WINDS.		Meteors and Weather.	Situation and Remarks.
	Direction.	Force.		
May 17	N.erly	Moderate breezes	Much snow	Ice rather open
18	N.erly, var.	Light breezes	Ditto	Ditto
19	to S E.erly	to Strong gales	Some snow	Ditto
20	S E.erly	Hard gales	Much small snow	Ditto
21	to N E.erly	to Calm	Clear	Ditto
22	to S E.erly	Moderate breezes	A little snow	Ditto
23	N, var.	Light breezes	Clear	Ditto
24	to N W	Ditto	Cloudy	Ditto
25	N W.erly	to Fresh breezes	Some snow	Ditto
26	to N N W	to Strong gales	Clear, cloudy	Ship at liberty
27	N b W	Hard gale	Some snow showers	A little ice
28	N b W	Strong gale	Cloudy	Ditto
29	N b W	Ditto	Clear	Ditto
30	to N N W, var.	Fresh breezes	Cloudy	Near a pack of ice
31	to N W.erly	to Light breezes	Snow showers	Loose ice
June 1	W b N to N N E	Light to fresh br.	Some snow showers	Floes, loose ice
2	N.erly	to Moderate breeze	Cloudy, hazy	Drift ice
3	Variable	Light breezes, calm	Thick snow showers	Scattered drift ice
4	E.erly to N	to Light breezes	Snow showers	Ditto
5	N W.erly, var.	Fresh to light br.	Hazy, some snow	Ditto
6	N N E to E N E	to Fresh gales	Snow showers	Ditto
7	to S E	Strong gales	Snow showers, hazy	Ditto
8	to S b E	Fresh gales	Snow, hazy	Sea open, ice near
9	to S S W	to Moderate breezes	A little snow	Ditto
10	to E S E	Light breezes	Cloudy, snow	Ditto
11	to N E.erly	to Moderate breeze	Clear	Ditto
12	N E.erly	Moderate breeze	Clear, cloudy	Ditto
13	N E.erly	Light airs	Small showers snow	Ditto
14	Variable	to Calm	Rain, haze	Drift ice
15	E.erly, S E	to Light airs	Cloudy	Streams of drift ice
16	Variable	to Calm	Haze, fog	Ditto
17	N N E	to Fresh breeze	Clear, hazy	Sea open, ice in sight
18	N b E	Fresh gale	Clear, cloudy	Ditto
19	N b E	Fresh breeze	Cloudy, clear	Sea open
20	to W, S S W	to Light breezes	Fog showers	Drift ice, floes
21	S W.erly	to Calm	Ditto	Ditto
22	S E.erly, var.	Light airs, calm	Small rain	Loose ice
23	E.erly, S S W	to Moderate breeze	Fog showers	Ditto
24	to S, W.erly	Light breeze to calm	Fog, clear	Much drift ice
25	Variable	to Moderate breezes	Snow showers	Ditto
26	N W to S S E	to Fresh breezes	Snow, fog	Field, drift ice
27	to S S W, N W b W	Fresh or Mod. br.	Ditto	Ditto
28	to S W, S S E	Fresh ga. light br.	Clear, fog	Ditto
29	to E.erly	to Fresh breeze	Fog, snow	Ditto
30	E.erly	to Strong breeze	Ditto	Sea open

1811	Latitude.	Latitude.	THERMOMETER.			BAROMETER.		
			Max.	Min.	Med. of 3-4 Obs.	Max.	Min.	Med.
July 1	78°.40′	7.18 E	38	31	3	35.0	30.09	29.99	30.04
2	78.20	6.30	36	33	3	34.3	30.13	30.08	30.11
3	78. 0	6. 0	37	35	2	36.0	30.08	29.96	30.02
4	77.58	5.40	42	35	3	39.7	29.96	29.88	29.92
5	77.56	6. 0	42	41	2	41.5	29.96	29.91	29.93
6	77.48	6.58	44	36	2	40.0	30.03	29.96	30.00
7	77.48	7.20	45	36	3	41.0	30.07	30.03	30.05
8	76.36	9.20	40	38	2	39.0	30.03	29.98	30.00
9	75.40	11.36	42	39	3	40.0	29.98	29.98	29.98
10	75.15	12. 0	40	38	2	39.0	29.98	29.92	29.95
11	74.52•	11. 0	41	40	3	40.3	29.99	29.95	29.97
12	74.10	11. 0	42	40	3	41.3	29.95	29.85	29.90
13	73.10	9.40	42	39	3	40.4	29.89	29.85	29.87
14	72.17	8.27	46	36	3	41.0	29.99	29.89	29.94
15	72.10•	6.57	44	40	2	42.0	30.10	29.99	30.05
1812 May 1	74.30	15.13	28	20	3	25.0	30.28	30.20	30.24
2	75.23	14.25	30	19	3	23.7	30.37	29.60	29.98
3	75.35	10.43	14	13	3	13.3	29.70	29.40	29.55
4	74.36	10. 0	13	12	3	12.7	29.89	29.70	29.80
5	73.41	10.40	13	12	3	12.6	29.81	29.60	29.70
6	73.10	10.18	21	10	3	17.0	29.76	29.60	29.68
7	72.38	10.19	23	21	3	22.0	29.91	29.76	29.84
8	73.33	10.21	26	22	3	24.0	30.00	29.91	29.95
9	73.57	10.21	26	24	3	25.0	30.10	30.00	30.05
10	74.28	9.37	30	25	3	27.0	30.10	29.96	30.03
11	75.36•	8. 8	32	30	3	30.7	29.96	29.86	29.91
12	75.38	8.20	31	23	3	27.0	29.86	29.80	29.83
13	75.52•	9.20	24	22	4	22.7	29.83	29.77	29.80
14	76.12	10.20	26	20	4	23.3	29.88	29.79	29.84
15	76.15•	9. 0	32	30	3	30.6	29.79	29.60	29.69
16	76.20	9.40	30	30	3	30.0	29.67	29.50	29.59
17	76. 7•	9.30	22	20	3	21.0	29.85	29.67	29.76
18	76.37•	10.45	30	17	3	22.0	29.84	29.74	29.79
19	76.30	10.45	20	19	3	19.7	29.98	29.84	29.91
20	76.30	10.30	20	18	3	18.7	30.03	29.91	29.97
21	76.30	10. 0	19	19	3	19.0	29.91	29.73	29.82
22	76.20	10. 0	21	20	3	20.4	29.78	29.66	29.72
23	76.10•	10. 0	25	24	3	24.3	29.95	29.78	29.87
24	76. 5	10. 0	30	25	3	27.0	30.03	29.95	29.99
25	75.58•	10. 0	32	27	4	30.0	30.09	30.03	30.06
26	75.50•	9.40	34	32	3	32.6	30.15	30.09	30.12
27	75.57	9. 0	27	25	3	26.0	30.22	30.15	30.18
28	75.50	9.20	30	28	3	29.0	30.28	30.22	30.25
29	76. 0	9.20	31	26	3	29.0	30.30	30.28	30.29
30	76.20	10. 0	30	27	3	28.7	30.32	30.30	30.31
31	76.30	10.50	29	27	3	28.0	30.34	30.32	30.33

1811	WINDS.		Meteors and Weather.	Situation and Remarks.
	Direction.	Force.		
July 1	E.erly, N W, S W	Light to mod. br.	Snow, fog, cloudy	Sea open, a pack near
2	S W, S S W	Moderate breezes	Fog, clear	Drift ice
3	to S S E	Ditto	Cloudy, rain	Ditto
4	to S E b E	to Fresh breezes	Clear	Very loose drift ice
5	to S S W	to Moderate breeze	Clear, fog showers	Sea open, drift ice
6	S.erly	to Light breeze	Fog	Drift ice
7	S.erly var.	Light airs, calm	Fog, clear	Crowded drift ice
8	W.erly to S S W	Fresh gale	Fog	No ice
9	S W, var.	Fresh breeze, calm	Ditto	Ditto
10	S W to S S E	Fresh br. mod. br.	Hazy	Ditto
11	S W, var.	Light breeze, calm	Rain, fog	Drift ice
12	E.rly	Light breeze	Clear, fog	Ditto
13	to S E	to Fresh breeze	Fog	At sea
14	S E, W	Moderate br. calm	Very foggy	Ditto
15	to S S W	to Moderate breeze	Thick fog	Ditto
1812 May 1	W N W to N N W	Fresh gales	Cloudy	At sea
2	N N E to S E.erly	Mod. br. fresh ga.	Cloudy, snow	A pack of ice near
3	to N E b E	Very hard gales	Snow, frost rime	At sea, no ice
4	to N E b N	Hard gales	Ditto	Ditto
5	to N N E	Ditto	Frost rime	Ditto
6	N N E	Hard gale	Frost rime, snow	Ditto
7	to N	Fresh gales	Snow showers	Ditto
8	to N W	to Fresh breezes	Ditto	Streams of ice
9	to N E.erly, var.	to Light br. calm	Much cryst. snow	Ditto
10	to N W.erly, var.	to Light breeze	Snow showers	Ditto
11	E b S, E N E	to Fresh gales	Ditto	Crowded drift ice
12	to N	Light br. strong br.	Cloudy	Ditto
13	to var.	Strong breezes	Ditto	Much ice
14	W.erly to S S E	to Moderate breeze	Cloudy, snow	Ditto
15	to E N E	Fresh breezes	Cloudy, some snow	Ditto
16	to N	Strong gales	Much snow	Beset among drift ice
17	to N W	Hard gales	Cloudy	Ditto
18	Variable	to Fresh gales	Much snow	Open drift ice
19	N W b N	to Strong gales	Ditto	Large floes
20	N W b N	to Fresh gales	Ditto	Beset among floes
21	N W b N	Strong gale	Snow	Ditto
22	N W b N	Hard gale	Much snow	In an opening of ice
23	to N W b W	Strong gales	Some snow	Numerous floes
24	to W b N	to Light breezes	Clear	Ditto
25	to Var.	Light breezes	Clear, cloudy	Drift ice, floes
26	to N E.erly	Ditto	Clear	Ditto
27	to S.erly, var.	Nearly calm	Ditto	Ditto
28	to S W.erly	Ditto	Cloudy	Ditto
29	to Variable	Light breeze, calm	Clear	Ditto
30	S S E to E	Nearly calm	Ditto	Ditto
31	to S W.erly	Ditto	Clear, cloudy	Drift ice

1812	Latitude.	Longitude.	THERMOMETER.			BAROMETER.		
			Max.	Min.	Med. of 2-4 Obs.	Max.	Min.	Med.
June 1	77°.14′	9. 5 E	31	29	3	30.0	30.37	30.34	30.36
2	78.15	5.27	33	30	3	31.3	30.37	30.35	30.36
3	78.50	7. 0	32	30	3	31.0	30.35	30.15	30.25
4	78.30	5.30	33	30	3	31.7	30.15	29.93	30.04
5	78 30	5.30	34	33	3	33.3	29.93	20.89	29.91
6	78.26	5.45	35	33	3	34.0	29.89	29.87	29.88
7	78. 0	5.45	33	31	3	32.4	29.98	29.89	29.93
8	78. 0	6.45	28	23	3	25.7	30.10	29.98	30.04
9	78. 0	6.30	27	23	3	25.0	30.05	29.90	29.98
10	77.54	6.15	34	26	3	29.0	29.90	29.78	29.84
11	78.44*	6.30	26	24	4	25.0	29.83	29.77	29.80
12	78.58	6.30	26	23	4	24.3	29.88	29.78	29.83
13	78.56	6.30	28	24	3	26.0	29.78	29.68	29.73
14	78.50	6.30	28	26	3	27.0	29.78	29.72	29.75
15	78.40	6.15	30	29	3	29.3	29.80	29.78	29.79
16	79.26	6.45	28	27	3	27.4	29.81	29.77	29.79
17	78.30	6. 0	29	28	4	28.3	29.86	29.80	29.83
18	78.20	6. 0	31	29	3	32.0	29.83	29.79	29.81
19	78.10	6. 0	31	26	3	29.0	29.88	29.78	29.83
20	78.17	6. 0	27	26	3	26.3	29.88	29.74	29.81
21	78.25	6.30	30	27	3	28.6	29.74	29.70	29.72
22	78.32	6.30	29	28	3	28.4	29.76	29.72	29.74
23	78.30	6.15	32	28	3	30.0	29.80	29.68	29.74
24	78. 5	6.35	33	31	3	32.3	29.75	29.50	29.62
25	78. 9*	6.45	33	31	3	32.0	29.97	29.75	29.86
26	78.10	6.40	35	30	3	33.0	30.00	29.92	29.96
27	77.59*	6. 7	36	33	2	34.5	29.92	29.76	29.84
28	78. 0	6. 0	37	35	3	36.0	29.76	29.60	29.68
29	77.48	6.50	35	34	3	34.3	29.60	29.52	29.56
30	77.30	6.45	33	32	3	32.7	29.58	29.50	29.54
July 1	77.54	6.15	38	32	3	35.0	29.71	29.57	29.64
2	78. 9*	6.30	37	34	3	35.3	29.77	29.50	29.64
3	78.20	6.30	33	32	3	32.3	29.50	29.40	29.45
4	78.18	6.40	34	31	3	32.4	29.58	29.41	29.49
5	78.10	6.45	33	31	3	32.3	29.82	29.58	29.70
6	78. 5	6.30	32	31	3	31.3	29.96	29.82	29.89
7	78.58	6.45	34	31	3	32.7	30.00	29.96	29.98
8	77.40	6.10	33	31	3	32.0	29.96	29.86	29.91
9	77.30	6. 0	34	31	3	32.7	29.86	29.82	29.84
10	77.30	6. 0	33	31	3	32.0	29.86	29.80	29.83
11	78. 0	5.30	32	32	4	32.0	29.90	29.86	29.88
12	77.56	5.30	35	31	4	33.4	29.95	29.87	29.91
13	77.46*	5.27	40	34	3	36.6	30.03	29.95	29.99
14	78.20	6.25	34	32	3	33.0	29.97	29.83	29.90
15	77.40	5.20	34	32	3	32.7	29.83	29.67	29.75

1812	WINDS.		Meteors and Weather.	Situation and Remarks.
	Direction.	Force.		
June 1	S W.erly	Mod. breeze, calm	Cloudy	Sea open
2	S S W	Mod. or fresh br.	Much snow, fog	Drift ice and floes
3	to S E	Fresh gales	Snow showers, fog	Ditto
4	S E	Ditto	Fog showers	Ditto
5	S.erly	Fresh breezes	Fog, rain	Ditto
6	S.erly, var.	Light breezes	Constant fog, rain	Drift ice
7	N.erly	Calm to fresh br.	Fog, showers	Ditto
8	N N W to W N W	to Strong gales	Clear	Drift ice and floes
9	to W b S	to Light breezes	Ditto	Ditto
10	to N N E	Fresh breezes	Snow showers	Ditto
11	N E.erly	to Strong gales	Snow, clear	Ditto
12	N N E to N	Fresh breezes	Clear	Ditto
13	to N W, N N E	Fresh or strong ga.	Frost rime, clear	Ditto
14	N E to N	Strong gales	Clear	Ditto
15	N	Fresh or strong ga.	Some snow	Ditto
16	N b E, N	Strong gales	Cloudy, snow	Sea open
17	to W b N	to Light breeze	Cloudy	Floes and drift ice
18	to S S W, to E	to Calm	Much snow	Ditto
19	E N E to N	to Fresh breeze	Cloudy	Ditto
20	N	Fresh breeze	Fog, snow	Ditto
21	N	Strong gale	Snow, clear	Ditto
22	N	to Moderate breeze	Snow showers	Ditto
23	to W S W	Light to strong br.	Some snow	Ditto
24	to S E to N E	Strong ga. to lig. br.	Fog, much snow	Streams of ice
25	to N	Fresh gales	Snow, clear	Sea open
26	to N W b W	Light breezes	Clear	Floes
27	N to N W	Fresh breezes	Showers snow	Floes and field
28	to N	Moderate breezes	Fog, snow	Floes and drift ice
29	N N W to W N W	to Fresh breeze	Thick fog. rain	Drift ice
30	N W to S, var.	Moderate breezes	Much snow	Very open ice
July 1	E to N E	Ditto	Snow, fog	Sea stream
2	to E S E, var.	to Fresh breeze	Thick fog	Ditto
3	N E to N N W	to Hard gales	Much snow	Floes, drift ice
4	to W to S	Mod. or fresh br..	Showers of snow	Drift ice
5	S S W	to Strong breeze	Some snow	Sea open
6	to W	Moderate breezes	Snow, fog	Drift ice
7	W erly	Calm, light breeze	Ditto	Sea open
8	S S W, S W	to Fresh breeze	Cloudy, fog	No ice
9	to W to N	Fresh breeze	Hazy, cloudy	Ice streams
10	N W to N N W	Fresh gales	Fog, clear	Ditto
11	N to N W	Strong gales	Snow showers	Floes and drift ice
12	to N N E	Ditto	Ditto	Ditto
13	to N N W	Fresh breezes	Fog showers	Ditto
14	to N b E	to Strong gales	Ditto	Sea open
15	N E.erly	Strong gales	Fog, snow showers	Drift ice

1812	Latitude.	Longitude.	THERMOMETER.		Med. of 3-4 Obs.		BAROMETER.		
			Max.	Min.			Max.	Min.	Med.
July 16	77°.45′	5.30 E	33	31	3	31.7	29.85	29.60	29.73
17	77.50*	5. 7	33	31	3	31.6	30.21	29.85	30.03
18	77.59	5. 0	34	31	3	32.3	30.32	30.22	30.27
19	78. 0	5. 0	32	31	3	31.7	30.22	30.12	30.17
20	78. 0	5. 0	36	33	3	34.7	30.16	30.12	30.14
21	78. 0	4.50	35	34	3	34.3	30.22	30.16	30.19
22	78. 0	4.30	35	33	4	34.0	30.24	30.22	30.23
23	78. 0	4.30	39	37	4	38.0	30.25	30.20	30.22
24	78. 6*	5.15	38	33	3	35.4	30.20	30.14	30.17
25	78 20	6. 5	38	31	3	34.3	30.14	30.06	30.10
26	77.44	6.39	33	32	3	32.3	30.06	30.00	30.03
27	76. 4	6.48	33	32	3	32.6	30.00	29.90	29.95
28	73.26	6.45	40	37	3	38.4	29.90	29.75	29.83
29	71.18	3.45	41	39	3	40.0	29.75	29.70	29.72
30	70. 3	2. 5	42	39	3	40.7	29.80	29.70	29.75
31	68.24*	1. 7	45	44	2	44.5	29.96	29.80	29.88
1813									
April 15	76. 2	9.27	23	22		22.7	28.90	28.85	28.88
16	76.57	9.59	25	20		23.3	29.07	28.90	28.98
17	78.59	7.40	25	18		20.7	29.60	29.07	29.34
18	78.57	3.10	16	15		15.3	29.90	29.60	29.75
19	78.51*	4.30	29	14		23.4	29.90	29.83	29.86
20	79. 5	4. 0	29	25		27.0	29.83	29.53	29.68
21	79.42*	4.50	26	16		21.3	29.65	29.53	29.59
22	80. 0	4.30	22	16		18.0	29.74	29.65	29.70
23	80. 7*	4.20	30	12		20.3	29.74	28.92	29.33
24	80.10	5. 0	6	—2		2.6	29.78	28.92	29.35
25	79.15	5. 0	10	—4		5.4	29.95	29.78	29.86
26	78.20	5.20	15	14		14.3	30.15	29.95	30.05
27	78. 7*	3.30	20	14		16.7	30.33	30.15	30.24
28	78.19*	3.50	25	15		20.0	30.35	30.33	30.34
29	78.34*	4.50	21	17		18.7	30.35	30.12	30.24
30	79. 5	8.15	25	21		23.6	30.12	29.70	29.91
May 1	79.15	4.40	20	14		16.3	29.70	29.50	29.60
2	79.54*	7. 0	25	12		18.0	29.70	29.50	29.60
3	79.36*	8.15	28	13		22.0	30.20	29.70	29.95
4	78.50	5. 0	32	30		31.3	30.20	29.95	30.08
5	79.33	4.40	30	22		27.6	29.95	29.95	29.95
6	79.29*	3.20	22	21		21.7	30.10	29.95	30.02
7	78.50	2.20	25	20		23.0	30.10	29.95	30.03
8	78.47*	2. 0	22	19		20.4	29.95	29.70	29.82
9	79.16	4. 0	28	25		26.3	29.70	29.65	29.68
10	79.16	4. 0	25	22		24.0	29.65	29.50	29.57
11	79.20	5.30	16	15		15.7	29.55	29.50	29.53
12	78.59*	5.10	21	16		19.0	29.55	29.34	29.44
13	78.50	2.20	25	20		22.3	29.54	29.34	29.44
14	78.45*	2.30	27	24		25.6	29.42	29.40	29.41
15	78.25	2.10	26	13		20.4	29.40	29.40	29.40

1812	WINDS.		Weather and Meteors.	Situation and Remarks.
	Direction.	Force.		
July 16	to E S E	Strong gales	Thick fog	Drift ice
17	E S E	Ditto	Fog, snow shower	Ice near
18	to N	Moderate breeze	Much snow, fog	Ditto
19	to W, var.	Light airs, calm	Ditto	Ditto
20	S W.erly	to Fresh breeze	Fog showers	Drift ice
21	to E	Strong breezes	Clear	Embayed in ice
22	E.erly	Fresh breezes	Hazy	Ditto
23	S S E	Light airs	Fog	Ditto
24	S.erly	Ditto	Clear, fog	Ice open
25	to W	to Calm	Thick fog	Ditto
26	to N N E	Strong breezes	Ditto	Sea open
27	N E.erly	Moderate breezes	Ditto	Ditto
28	N E	Fresh gale	Cloudy	At sea
29	N E	to Strong gale	Rain	Ditto
30	to S E, var.	Light breeze	Fog, rain	Ditto
31	N W.erly	Fresh breeze, calm	Fog, clear	Ditto
1813				
April 15	E N E to E S E	Very hard gales	Much snow	At sea
16	to E N E	Hard gales	Snow, cloudy	Stream of ice
17	Variable	Light br. to fr. ga.	Ditto	Charles' Isl. in sight
18	N E	Strong gale to calm	Snow, clear	A pack of ice
19	Variable	Calm, light breeze	Clear	Ditto
20	S S E to E	Very hard gales	Constant snow	Ditto
21	to S to N W	to Calm	Snow, clear	Ditto
22	S W, var.	to Fresh breeze	Fog, cloudy	Sea open, pack
23	Variable	Calm to strong ga.	Snow showers	Pack near
24	N N E	Hard or fresh ga.	Snow, frost rime	Drift ice
25	N E b N	Hard gale	Thick frost rime	Sea open
26	to N N W	Ditto	Frost rime, snow	Ditto
27	N b W	to Moderate breeze	Clear	Streams of ice
28	N	to Calm	Ditto	Ditto
29	S W	to Strong gale	Snow, clear	Sea open
30	to S	Strong gales	Clear, cloudy	Ditto
May 1	S W to W N W	Fresh gales	Cloudy	Ice near
2	to N N E	Fresh breezes	Fog, clear	A pack in sight
3	to E, S	Mod. to fresh gales	Delightful weather	Spitzbergen in sight
4	S S E, var	Strong gale to calm	Much snow	Sea open
5	N E	Fresh gale	Clear	Ice near
6	to N W	to Light air	Ditto	Ditto
7	to S, S W	to Fresh breezes	Ditto	Ditto
8	to W, N W	Fresh breezes	Cloudy, snow	Ditto
9	S W, var.	to Light breeze	Cloudy, clear	Ditto
10	S.erly	to Fresh gales	Snow, cloudy	Spitzbergen in sight
11	N N E, N N W	Hard gales	Snow showers	Sea open
12	to N E b E	Very hard gales	Cloudy	Streams of ice
13	N N E to E S E	to Fresh gale	Thick snow	Ditto
14	N E to N b E	Strong gales	Clear, snow	Sea open
15	to N N W	Ditto	Showers of snow	Ice near

1813	Latitude.	Longitude.	THERMOMETER.			BAROMETER.		
			Max.	Min.	Med.	Max.	Min.	Med.
May 16	77°.51'*	1.50 E	20	14	17.0	29.55	29.40	29.48
17	78. 0	1.10	18	16	17.0	29.60	29.55	29.57
18	78.10	1.30	22	16	19.3	29.70	29.60	29.65
19	78. 0	2. 0	22	18	19.7	29.78	29.70	29 74
20	77.40	2. 0	30	22	24.7	29.89	29 78	29.84
21	77.35	2.30	30	20	26.6	30.02	29.89	29.95
22	77.28	2.35	32	18	27.3	30.02	29.65	29.84
23	77.19*	2.30	27	20	24.4	29.93	29.65	29.79
24	77. 9*	2.45	23	16	19.0	30.06	29.93	29.99
25	77.20	3. 0	26	25	25.7	30.06	30.04	30.05
26	77.20	3. 0	27	25	25.7	30.04	29.97	30.01
27	77.35	3.15	24	23	23.3	29.97	29.92	29.94
28	77.45	3.15	27	25	26.0	29.98	29.92	29.95
29	78. 0*	3.15	26	18	22.0	29.98	29.95	29.97
30	78.15	3.15	22	16	18.0	30.02	29.95	29.98
31	77.41*	2.45	30	20	25.0	30.02	29.95	29.99
June 1	77.25	4. 0	32	30	31.0	29.95	29.67	29.81
2	78.14*	4.50	29	29	29.0	29.77	29.67	29.72
3	78.34	5.10	31	25	28.3	29.77	29.77	29.77
4	78.45	5. 0	30	27	28.3	29.77	29.75	29.76
5	78.48	4. 0	35	31	33.0	29.83	29.75	29.79
6	78.41*	4. 0	34	32	32.7	29.85	29.75	29.80
7	78.46	3.45	44	35	38.0	29.86	29.75	29.81
8	78.54	3.40	37	35	35.7	29.87	29.80	29.83
9	78.49*	3.38	48	35	41.0	30.25	29.80	30.03
10	78.50	3.40	38	34	35.4	30.30	30.25	30.27
11	78.50	3.44	35	31	33.0	30.26	30.12	30.19
12	78.50	3.40	34	27	31.3	30.18	30.12	30.15
13	78.48	3.50	33	28	30.6	30.24	30.18	30.21
14	78.38	4.10	35	34	34.3	30.20	30.13	30.17
15	78.26*	4. 0	34	32	33.0	30.16	30.13	30 14
16	78.20	3.50	38	34	36.4	30.16	30.10	30.13
17	78.14	3.45	39	34	36.3	30.10	29.97	30.04
18	78. 1*	3.50	42	32	37.3	29.97	29.88	29.92
19	78.20	4. 5	35	32	33.4	29.88	29.76	29.82
20	78. 4	4. 5	35	28	32.0	29.90	29.73	29.82
21	78. 2*	4.40	42	35	38.3	30.00	29.90	29.95
22	78.12*	6. 0	36	32	33.7	30.02	29.88	29.95
23	78.30	6. 0	37	34	35.3	29.96	29.86	29.91
24	78.26	5.55	39	34	37.0	30.03	29.96	29.99
25	78.25	5.50	40	35	37.0	30.03	30.03	30.03
26	78.19*	5.46	40	35	37.4	30.08	30.04	30.06
27	78. 9	5.48	38	34	36.0	30. 8	30.08	30.08
28	77.44*	6.20	33	32	32.6	30.16	30.08	30.12
29	77.50	6. 0	35	32	33.3	30.28	30.16	30.22
30	77.50	6. 0	35	33	34.0	30.30	30.28	30.29

1813	WINDS.		Meteors and Weather.	Situation and Remarks.
	Direction.	Force.		
May 16	to N W	Fresh gales	Clear	Loose ice
17	to N	to Moderate gales	Cloudy	Floes and loose ice
18	to N N W	Fresh gales	Snow, cloudy	Near a pack
19	N. var.	to Calm	Ditto	Ditto
20	N. var.	Light breeze, calm	Ditto	Floes and drift ice
21	to E to S E	to Fresh gales	Much snow	Ditto
22	S S E to W N W	to Strong gale	Hazy, snow	Ditto
23	to N N W	to Light airs	Clear	Ditto
24	N	Fresh breeze	Clear, cloudy	Ditto
25	N b E	Ditto	Cloudy	Sea open
26	N. var.	Light airs	Ditto	Ditto
27	N E, N W, var.	to Moderate breeze	Ditto	Loose ice
28	N.erly, var.	Fresh breezes	Cloudy, snow	Drift ice
29	N W	to Moderate breezes	Frost rime	Ditto
30	W to S	to Calm	Ditto	Ditto
31	S.erly	Fresh breezes	Cloudy	Ditto
June 1	S b E	Strong gale, calm	Fog, rain	At sea
2	N W	Fresh br. to calm	Rain, clear	Ice near
3	S to W	Light br. to calm	Snow, cloudy	Ditto
4	W.erly	Light breeze	Cloudy, snow	Drift ice
5	S W to S	to Fresh gales	Clear, fog	Much ice
6	S S E	Fresh gale	Fog, snow	Ditto
7	to S S W	to Moderate breeze	Snow, fog	Floes and drift ice
8	to S E	Strong gales	Rain, sleet, fog	Ship beset
9	S W, E.rly	Fresh breeze, calm	Clear, fog	Do. among floes
10	S W	to Fresh breeze	Fog, cloudy	Do. floes and dr. ice
11	S W, N W, N	Light breeze, calm	Ditto	Ditto
12	N E to W N W	Fresh breeze	Fog showers	Ditto
13	S W, W S W	Calm to fresh br.	Thick fog	Open drift ice
14	to N	Moderate breeze	Cloudy	Sea open
15	to N N W	to Fresh breeze	Fog, cloudy, snow	In a bay of ice
16	N	Moderate br. calm	Fog, cloudy	Drift ice
17	N	Fresh gale	Snow showers	Ditto
18	N W	to Strong gale	Ditto	Ditto
19	N W	Strong gale	Snow, sleet	Floes and drift ice
20	N to N W	to Moderate breeze	Snow showers	Ditto
21	to S	to Fresh gales	Fog, snow	Ice streams
22	S b W	Fresh gale	Fog, cloudy	Drift ice
23	to S S E	Moderate breeze	Fog	Ditto
24	to S S W	Light breezes	Thick fog	Ditto
25	to W S W	to Moderate breeze	Fog showers	Ditto
26	to N, N E	Moderate br. calm	Snow showers	Ditto
27	Variable	to Moderate breeze	Snow, fog	Sea open
28	N N E	Fresh breeze	Fog, snow	No ice
29	N N E	Moderate breeze	Snow shower	Ice near
30	to E N E	Ditto	Ditto	Ditto

1813	Latitude.	Longitude.	THERMOMETER.			BAROMETER.		
			Max.	Min.	Med.	Max.	Min.	Med.
July 1	77°.25	3.30 E	46	35	40.0	30.30	30.30	30.30
2	77.20	3.10	36	35	35.3	30.30	30.23	30.27
3	77.18	3.20	38	33	36.3	30.23	30.03	30.13
4	77.29*	2.40	35	33	34.0	30.03	29.58	29.80
5	77.24	2. 0	35	33	34.0	29.80	29.56	29.68
6	77.26*	2.20	40	35	37.7	29.83	29.78	29.81
7	77.46	3.10	36	35	35.7	29.86	29.78	29.82
8	77.35	2. 0	38	34	35.4	30.00	29.86	29.93
9	77.38	2. 0	38	33	35.3	30.05	30.00	30.02
10	77.30	2.10	36	34	35.0	30.06	29.70	29.88
11	77.20	1.50	36	35	35.3	29.70	29.53	29.62
12	77. 0	2. 0	38	36	37.4	29.64	29.53	29.58
13	76.54	4.20	40	38	39.3	29.66	29.54	29.60
14	77.10	2.30	39	39	39.0	29.54	29.50	29.52
15	77.30	2. 0	39	36	37.3	29.77	29.48	29.63
16	78. 2*	1.10	37	34	35.6	29.92	29.77	29.84
17	78.12	1.15	37	33	34.4	29.98	29.92	29.95
18	78.20*	1. 0	33	33	33.0	29.98	29.64	29.81
19	77.40*	1.10	42	37	39.3	30.00	29.62	29.81
20	77.10	7. 0	40	38	38.7	30.04	29.70	29.87
21	76.42	7.30	40	36	37.7	29.70	29.53	29.62
22	75. 9*	7.45	37	36	36.3	29.75	29.68	29.71
1814 May 1	77.52*	6.48	15	14	14.4	29.74	29.63	29.69
2	78.20*	7.50	20	16	18.0	29.63	29.41	29.52
3	77.48*	8.30	27	17	22.0	29.50	29.40	29.45
4	77.17*	7.54	24	21	23.0	29.90	29.50	29.70
5	77.51*	6.50	25	21	23.3	30.03	29.73	29.88
6	78. 5*	5.10	27	20	23.3	29.73	29.60	29.66
7	78.10	4.50	16	10	14.0	29.63	29.61	29.62
8	78. 3	4.50	17	9	13.7	29.97	29.63	29.65
9	78. 5*	4. 0	26	13	18.4	30.13	29.97	30.05
10	78. 4	4.10	15	13	14.0	30.14	30.13	30.14
11	78. 9*	4.10	30	10	17.5	30.15	30.14	30.14
12	78. 8	4.10	18	9	14.3	30.17	30.15	30.16
13	78. 6	4.10	16	7	12.3	30.20	30 10	30.15
14	78. 9	4. 2	25	19	20.7	30.24	30.12	30.18
15	78. 2	4. 0	23	11	18.4	30.27	30.24	30.26
16	77.56*	3.54	19	10	15.0	30.51	30.27	30.39
17	77.46*	0.30	16	14	14.6	30.50	30.46	30.48
18	77.36	0. 0	30	12	21.3	30.46	30.32	30.39
19	77.34	0. 0	27	17	22.7	30.32	30.32	30.32

1813	WINDS.		Meteors and Weather.	Situation and Remarks.
	Direction.	Force.		
July 1	E to S, var.	Moderate breezes	Showers of snow	Ice near
2	S W.erly	Fresh breezes	Ditto	Sea open
3	N E to N	Light br. to str. ga.	Cloudy, snow	No ice
4	N, S	to Moderate gales	Snow and sleet	Ice near
5	S W.erly	Strong to fresh ga.	Thick snow	Ditto
6	N N E to N W	Calm to fresh br.	Snow, hazy	Ditto
7	N W to S W	to Moderate breezes	Cloudy	No ice
8	to S S W	Fresh ga. to calm	Snow, fog	A floe
9	to S	to Strong breeze	Cloudy, hazy	Ditto
10	S S E to S W	Strong gales	Fog, haze, rain	Floes and drift ice
11	S W, var.	Moderate breezes	Heavy rain, fog	Ditto
12	S W to S, var.	to Fresh breezes	Fog, rain	Drift ice
13	S b W to S S E	Fresh gales	Ditto	No ice
14	S	Ditto	Ditto	Drift ice
15	S to S S W	Ditto	Fog, rain, clear	Drift ice, streams
16	S W to W S W	Strong gales	Fog	Ditto
17	S S W, S S E	to Light breeze	Fog, rain	Ditto
18	S, var. N.	Fresh gale, to calm	Fog, snow	Floes
19	N, var.	Calm, moderate br.	Fog	Floes and drift ice
20	S S E to W S W	Fresh gales	Rain, fog	At sea
21	W S W	Ditto	Fog showers	No ice
22	W to N N W	to Moderate breeze	Cloudy	Ditto
1814 May 1	N N E to N W	Fresh gales	Snow, frost rime	Ice streams
2	N	Hard gale	Snow showers	Ditto
3	N	Ditto	Cloudy	Detached drift ice
4	N	to Moderate breeze	Cloudy, clear	Ice streams
5	Variable	to Strong gales	Clear, hazy	Ice fields and floes
6	N N W, N	to Fresh breeze	Cloudy, clear	Ditto
7	N	Fresh gale	Snow, clear	Ditto
8	N	Ditto	Frost rime	Ditto
9	N	to Light breeze	Ditto	Ditto
10	W.erly	Light breezes	Frost rime, snow	Beset among ditto
11	E.erly	Light airs, calm	Hoar frost	Ship beset
12	N.erly	Light breeze	Thick hoar frost	Ditto
13	S E	Calm to moder. br.	Great refraction	Ditto
14	S E.erly	Moderate breeze	Snow showers	Ditto
15	N E	Fresh breeze	Cloudy	Ditto
16	to N N W	Fresh breezes	Great refraction	Ditto
17	to W N W	to Strong breeze	Clear	Ditto
18	N W to E N E	to Light airs	Fine weather	Ditto
19	N W to S W	Calm to fresh br.	Hoar frost	Ditto

1814	Latitude.	Longitude.	THERMOMETER.			BAROMETER.		
			Max.	Min.	Med.	Max.	Min.	Med.
May 20	77°.35'	0. 5 E	29	15	20.2	30.33	30.32	30.32
21	77.37	0.15	28	20	24.0	30.31	30. 9	30.20
22	77.23	0.15	31	20	25.3	30. 9	30. 0	30. 5
23	77.18*	0.40	27	22	25.0	30.20	30.10	30.15
24	77.14	0.40	28	20	25.0	30.20	30.18	30.19
25	77. 6	1. 0	25	19	21.4	30.18	30.15	30.16
26	76.50	1.40	22	20	21.0	30.15	30.12	30.14
27	77. 0	4.16	25	19	22.3	30.12	30.94	30. 3
28	76.46*	4. 6	34	28	30.0	29.94	29.82	29.88
29	77.38	6. 0	28	24	26.0	29.95	29.79	29.87
30	78. 0	4. 0	30	26	28.3	30.00	29.95	29.97
31	77.50	4.20	31	30	30.4	30.00	29.62	29.81
June 1	77.45	4. 0	29	26	27.3	29.95	29.62	29.79
2	78. 0	4.39	26	21	23.3	30.01	29.95	29.98
3	78. 5	4.10	25	23	24.0	30.06	30.01	30.03
4	78.11*	4. 0	30	22	26.4	30.10	30.06	30.08
5	78. 6	5.40	29	27	28.0	30.11	30.09	30.10
6	78.25	4.55	31	29	30.0	30.09	29.90	30.00
7	78.28*	4.50	32	29	30.7	29.90	29.86	29.88
8	78.40	5.40	31	28	29.0	29.93	29.85	29.89
9	78.47	5. 0	29	27	27.7	29.93	29.84	29.88
10	78.50	5. 5	32	31	31.6	29.90	29.60	29.75
11	79. 0	5.10	34	32	33.0	29.60	29.44	29.52
12	78.25	7.30	34	28	31.7	29.84	29.42	29.63
13	78.23	6.25	40	30	35.0	30.04	29.84	29.94
14	78.40	6. 0	34	34	34.0	30.04	29.93	29.99
15	78.27	6.20	34	29	32.5	30.00	29.88	29.94
16	78.17	7.30	35	34	34.3	30.00	29.72	29.86
17	78.27	7.10	36	34	35.0	29.84	29.72	29.78
18	78.20	7.25	35	33	34.0	29.84	29.84	29.84
19	77.58	5.40	36	34	34.8	29.80	29.75	29.77
20	78.15	5.55	36	35	35.7	29.85	29.74	29.80
21	78.30	5.15	35	35	35.0	29.85	29.77	29.81
22	78.38	4.50	33	33	33.0	30.00	29.72	29.86
23	78.40	4. 0	34	33	33.3	30.04	29.86	29.95
24	78.35	4.40	34	30	32.0	29.98	29.86	29.92
25	78.28	5.20	34	33	33.4	29.98	29.76	29.87
26	78.35	4.50	34	32	33.0	29.90	29.60	29.75
27	78.50	5.25	35	34	34.3	29.80	29.54	29.67
28	78.40	5.25	34	34	34.0	29.54	29.50	29.52
29	78.20	4. 0	34	34	34.0	29.76	29.50	29.63
30	78.35	5.20	37	33	35.0	29.85	29.76	29.80

1814	WINDS.		Meteors and Weather.	Situation and Remarks.
	Direction.	Force.		
May 20	S W to S	Fresh gales	Fog	Ice rather slack
21	S W to N b W	to Strong gales	Fog, snow	Ditto
22	N, N N E,	Fresh gales	Snow, fog	Ditto
23	N, var.	Light airs	Fog	Ship partly beset
24	N E.erly	Calm to fresh br.	Fog, snow	Ditto
25	to N	to Strong gale	Snow showers	Ditto
26	N E.erly	to Fresh breeze	Snow showers	Ice more open
27	to N	to Hard gales	Thick snow	Ice slack
28	to Var.	to Moderate breeze	Snow, clear	Sea open
29	S W, W, var.	Light breezes	Rain, cloudy	Ditto
30	Variable	to Fresh gales	Constant snow	Drift ice
31	E N E, N E	Strong gales	Much snow	No ice
June 1	N E.erly	Fresh to Mod. ga.	Ditto	Near ice
2	N.erly, var.	Fresh to Mod. br.	Cloudy	No ice
3	N.erly	to Calm	Ditto	Ice near
4	Variable	Moderate breezes	Fog showers	Drift ice
5	S.erly, W.erly	Ditto	Ditto	Sea open
6	S W, var.	Fresh to light br.	Haze or fog show.	Ditto
7	N.erly, var.	Calm to moder. br.	Clear, cloudy	Ice near
8	to S W	Calm to fresh br.	Cloudy	No ice
9	S W	Fresh gale	Much small snow	In a bay of the ice
10	to S	Ditto	Thick fog	Ditto
11	to N W	Strong ga. to lig. br.	Hazy	Sea open
12	N b W	to Fresh gale	Cloudy, snow	No ice
13	Var. S W	to Calm	Clear	Charles' Island near
14	to S E, var.	Fresh br. to lig. airs	Clear, snow	Ditto
15	Var. E.erly	Calm to fresh br.	Charming weather	No ice
16	E, E S E	to Strong gales	Snow, sleet	Charles' Isl. 25 miles
17	to S S E	to Fresh gales	Fog	Ditto : no ice
18	to W S W	to Fresh breeze	Dense fog, snow	No ice
19	to S S E	to Strong gales	Fog, rain	Sea open
20	S	Strong gales	Dense fog, rain	A little ice
21	S b E, W.erly	Moderate breezes	Much rain	Ditto
22	Variable	Ditto	Fog	Ice in sight
23	S	Brisk gales	Snow, rain	Drift ice
24	S.erly, W.erly	Gentle breezes	Dense fog	Ice near
25	S S E to S S W	to Strong gales	Rain, sleet	Ditto
26	to S	Fresh gales	Fog, snow	Ice distant
27	E S E, S S W	to Strong gale	Fog, rain, snow	Ditto
28	S E to S	Fresh to Mod. br.	Fog, snow	Ice streams
29	S S E to S b W	to Strong breeze	Dense fog. snow	Much ice
30	S to E.erly	to Gentle breezes	Fog, snow, clear	Spitzbergen in sight

1814	Latitude.	Longitude.	THERMOMETER.			BAROMETER.		
			Max.	Min.	Med.	Max.	Min.	Med.
July 1	79°.30′	6. 0 E	34	33	33.7	29.85	29.60	92.72
2	79.25	6.10	33	30	32.0	29.62	29.45	29.54
3	79.22*	5.45	35	34	34.7	29.70	29.62	29.66
4	79.10	4.20	33	31	32.0	29.81	29.70	29.75
5	79.21	5.20	35	33	34.0	29.90	29.81	29.86
6	79.42*	8. 0	40	36	38.3	29.90	29.89	29.89
7	80.25	8.10	39	37	38.0	29.89	29.83	29.86
8	80.10*	8. 5	36	31	32.6	29.83	29.79	29.81
9	79.33*	7.50	42	36	39.0	30.17	29.79	29.98
10	79.23	7.55	35	34	34.7	30.17	30.07	30.12
11	79.10	6. 0	34	34	34.0	30.07	30.06	30.07
12	78.58	7.50	36	35	35.7	30.17	30.06	30.11
13	78.50*	7.10	37	33	34.6	30.17	30.15	30.16
14	78.40	8.55	34	31	32.3	30.15	29.92	30.03
15	78.20	9. 5	48	32	41.0	29.92	29.90	29.91
16	77.50	9. 0	46	40	42.5	29.90	29.79	29.85
1815								
March 23	54.29	0.30 W	—	—	——	29.20	29.06	29.13
24	——	——	—	—	——	29.55	29.06	29.31
25	56.10*	0.12	—	—	47.0	29.55	29.08	29.31
26	58.24*	0.42	45	42	43.5	29.40	29.08	29.24
27	60. 8	1. 8	46	43	44.5	29.40	28.89	29.15
28	——	——	46	44	45.0	29.07	28.91	28.99
29	——	——	49	43	46.0	29.79	29.09	29.44
30	——	——	49	43	46.0	29.79	29.64	29.71
31	——	——	49	47	47.7	29.74	29.64	29.69
April 1	61.52*	0. 7	55	50	53.0	29.84	29.74	29.79
2	62.58	0.14 E	46	46	46.0	29.80	29.50	29.65
3	64.32	0.39	44	40	42.7	29.50	29.06	29.28
4	64.55*	0.21 W	42	37	39.0	29.60	29.06	29.33
5	66.56	1. 6 E	40	37	39.0	29.60	29.38	29.49
6	69.14*	3.12	39	35	36.7	29.38	29.18	29.28
7	70. 9*	4.22	36	30	33.6	29.75	29.16	29.46
8	71.16	5.36	42	33	38.3	29.95	29.75	29.85
9	72.37*	8.31	36	34	35.0	29.95	29.36	29.65
10	74.56*	10.14	22	15	17.3	29.40	29.29	29.35
11	76.33	10.20	16	10	12.4	29.44	29.33	29.38
12	77.21	8.27	15	7	12.0	30.00	29.40	29.70
13	77.34*	7.40	10	6	8.2	30.10	29.95	30.03
14	77.56	7.25	10	8	9.3	29.95	29.82	29.88
15	78. 4*	5.25	13	7	10.0	29.82	29.82	29.82
16	77.50	6.50	20	6	12.0	29.82	29.65	29.74
17	77.40	5.50	19	17	18.0	29.65	29.50	29.57
18	77.35	8. 0	24	20	22.0	29.90	29.50	29.70
19	77.42	7.20	24	19	21.0	30.03	29.90	29.97

1814	WINDS.		Meteors and Weather.	Situation and Remarks.
	Direction.	Force.		
July 1	E.erly, var.	Moderate br calm	Rain, dense fog	Near much ice
2	S W to S	Gentle breeze	Fog, snow showers	Ditto
3	S to W.erly	Strong gales	Constant snow	Ditto
4	S W to S	Fresh gales	Snow, fog	Drift ice and floes
5	S	Strong gale	Cloudy	Ditto
6	S b E, S S W	Hard gales	Clear, cloudy, fog	Insolat. patch of ice
7	to S W	Ditto	Dense fog, clear	Ditto
8	to N W, N, N E	to Gentle breeze	Ditto	Near the N.ern ice
9	E.erly, S	Calm to fresh gale	Ditto	Ice streams
10	S, var.	to Calm	Fog, cloudy	Ditto
11	N E.erly, var.	to Light airs	Constant fog	Floes and patches
12	S	Fresh breeze	Fog, cloudy	Ice strea. and floes
13	S.erly, var.	Light breeze, calm	Fog, clear	Much drift ice
14	S.erly, var.	Mod. breeze, calm	Fog	Charles' Isl. 3 lea. off
15	Variable	Light airs, calm	Dense fog, clear	Charles' Island near
16	Variable	Light breezes	Dense fog	At sea.
1815				
March 23	S E to W, N W	Hard gales	Much rain	Whitby harbour
24	Variable	Strong to light br.	Some rain	Ditto
25	S W to N W	to Fresh gales	Showers of rain	At sea
26	W to S	Strong gales	Hazy, clear	Ditto
27	S E to S S W	Hard gales	Rain	Brassa Sound, Shet.
28	W b S	Very hard gale	Some rain	Ditto
29	N W to W, S E	Fresh gales	Much rain	Ditto
30	W S W, S W	Ditto	Cloudy, rain	Ditto
31	S b W	Fresh breeze	Clear	Ditto
April 1	S b W, S E.erly	Fresh br. light air	Clear, hazy	At sea
2	E S E to S S W	Light breezes	Hazy	Ditto
3	S S W, N N E	to Hard gale	Hazy, rain	Ditto
4	to S E.erly	to Calm, fresh br.	Thunder & lighten.	Ditto
5	E S E	Fresh gale	Showery	Ditto
6	E b S to N N E	Ditto	Aurora borealis	Ditto
7	N, N N W	Strong gale, calm	Ditto	Ditto
8	S.erly, S b W	to Strong gale	Much rain	Ditto
9	W b S to S	to Fresh gale	Hazy, snow	Ditto
10	W S W, W	Strong gales	Snow showers	Ditto
11	N W, S E to E	to Calm	Thick snow	Ditto
12	Var., N	Mod. to fresh br.	Small snow	Spitzbergen in sight
13	N N E to N	Fresh breezes	Frost rime	Ice streams
14	N b E to E N E	Fresh to mod. gale	Frost rime, clear	Charles' Isl. 15 lea.
15	to N	Str. ga. to Mod. br.	Clear	Ditto 10 lea.
16	Variable	Light airs to fr. ga.	Charm. clear weath.	Ice streams
17	N N W, N N E	Fresh gales	Snow showers	Ditto
18	E.erly, var.	Fresh gales, calm	Great fall of snow	Ditto
19	Var. E S E	Strong gales	Much snow	A little ice

1815	Latitude.	Longitude.	THERMOMETER.			BAROMETER.		
			Max.	Min.	Med.	Max.	Min.	Med.
April 20	77°.50′	7.54 E	22	18	20.3	30.33	30.03	30.18
21	78. 0	7.30	25	23	24.0	30.33	30.30	30.31
22	78.15	7.10	29	22	25.8	30.30	30.00	30.15
23	78. 0	5.50	30	25	28.0	30.00	29.95	29.98
24	78.16*	6.20	28	14	20.2	30.03	29.95	29.99
25	78.25	8.30	26	22	24.4	30.01	29.75	29.88
26	78.30	7. 0	24	20	22.3	29.75	29.65	29.70
27	78.20	8.30	30	28	29.0	29.65	29.35	29.50
28	78.10	9.35	26	23	24.3	29.46	28.79	29.12
29	77.29*	9.40	24	19	21.0	30.07	29.27	29.67
30	78.10	6.20	21	16	18.0	30.20	30.07	30.14
May 1	78.25	7.30	17	12	13.7	30.13	29.90	30.01
2	78.15	6.40	12	11	11.7	30 57	30.13	30.35
3	78. 0*	6.35	17	8	11.6	30.57	30.51	30.54
4	77.45	5.10	16	10	13.0	30.51	30.17	30.34
5	77.50	6.20	18	15	16.3	30.17	29.91	30.04
6	78.15	5.30	22	18	20.0	29.93	29.91	29.92
7	78.25	6.25	25	19	21.8	29.93	29.90	29.92
8	78.15*	6.20	22	14	18.3	29.90	29.75	29.82
9	78.35	9. 0	14	9	12.0	29.85	29.73	29.79
10	78.45*	7.45	20	14	16.8	29.83	29.73	29.78
11	78.22	6.46	16	13	14.4	29.73	29.66	29.69
12	77.50	5.50	12	10	10.6	29.83	29.66	29.75
13	77.20	4. 0	18	16	17.0	29.90	29.83	29.86
14	77. 7*	4.30	27	15	20.6	29.92	29.85	29.89
15	77.17*	4.10	20	15	17.7	29.85	29.83	29.84
16	77.40	5.10	24	21	22.2	30.04	29.85	29.94
17	77.30	6.10	32	29	30.3	30.05	29.95	30.00
18	77.20	5.45	32	17	23.3	29.95	29.89	29.92
19	76.40	4.20	23	19	20.7	30.10	29.90	30.00
20	77.20*	4.55	25	22	23.2	30.24	30.10	30.17
21	77.32	6.25	27	25	26.0	30.23	30.15	30.19
22	77.36*	6.54	33	25	30.0	30.15	30.06	30.11
23	77.48*	7.10	34	32	33.3	30.07	30.06	30.06
24	78. 0	6.56	34	31	32.4	30.18	30.06	30.12
25	78.10	5.40	32	28	29.7	30.22	30.18	30.20
26	77.26*	9.40	32	30	30.6	30.30	30.22	30.26
27	77.20	7. 0	31	28	29.3	30.30	30.15	30.23
28	77.35	5.10	31	27	29.0	30.15	30.11	30.13
29	77.27*	3.16	27	23	25.7	30.27	30.11	30.19
30	77.32	3.15	28	25	26 7	30.28	30.16	30.22
31	77.23	3.35	33	29	31.0	30.16	30.15	30.15

1815	WINDS.		Meteors and Weather.	Situation and Remarks.
	Direction.	Force.		
April 20	S E. var.	Str. ga. to Light airs	Snow, clear	Spitzbergen near
21	Var. W.erly	Light airs	Much snow, clear	Ice streams
22	S S W	to Strong gale	Snow showers	Ditto
23	S W to W	Strong gales	Ditto	Much ice
24	W N W, var.	Moderate br. calm	Charming weather	Ice streams
25	E.erly, N b E	to Fresh breeze	Ditto	Charles' Isl. 7 lea.
26	N, S.erly	to Calm	Fine clear weather	Ditto 9 lea.
27	S E to W S W	Very hard gales	Cloudy, hazy	Much ice
28	to W N W	Ditto	Snow, clear	Charles' Isl. 12 mil.
29	to W S W	Strong gales	Cloudy	No ice
30	N W to W S W	Fresh breezes	Clear	Ice streams
May 1	N W to N	Strong gales	Thick frost rime	Scattered drift ice
2	N	Fresh gale	Frost rime	Sea open
3	N N W to N W	Strong gales	Frost rime, clear	Ice near
4	to N N W	to Fresh gales	Snow showers	Patches of ice
5	to N	Strong gales	Thick snow showers	Ice streams
6	Variable	to Calm	Thick snow	Much ice
7	S E, S W	to Strong breeze	Great fall of snow	Ice streams
8	W N W to N	Light br. to fr. ga.	Snow showers	Ditto
9	N N W, var.	Strong breezes	Some snow	Charles' Isl. 3 miles
10	to W.erly, var.	Light airs	Great fall of snow	Bay ice, &c.
11	N N W	to Fresh gale	Much snow	Much bay ice
12	to N N W var.	Strong breezes	Snow showers	Scattered ice
13	N N W, N	Light airs	A little snow	Ditto
14	N.erly, var.	Ditto	Clear, snow	Ice streams
15	Var. W, S S W	Gentle breeze, calm	Some snow	Ditto
16	S to W	to Moderate breeze	Cloudy	Ditto
17	to S.erly	Calm, to light br	Ditto	Sea open
18	to Var. N.	to Strong gales	Snow showers	Some ice
19	N N W to N E	to Hard gale	Much snow	Ice streams
20	N N W, N	Mod. to fresh gale	Clear	Ditto
21	N	Fresh breeze	Ditto	Much drift ice
22	N.erly, E.erly	to Calm	Fine clear weather	Ditto
23	N.erly, var.	Calm, light breeze	Charming weather	Floes and drift ice
24	Variable	to Calm	Clear, fog	Ditto
25	N W to N N E	to Moderate breeze	Clear	Ditto
26	to Var.	to Calm	Cloudy	Spitzbergen 30 mil.
27	W, S W.erly	to Fresh breeze	Snow showers	Ice streams
28	Var. N b W	Light breeze	Cloudy	Floes and drift ice
29	W S W	Fresh breeze	Fog showers	Floes and bay ice
30	to S	to Gentle breeze	Fog	Ditto
31	S S E	Moderate breeze	Cloudy	Ditto

1815	Latitude.	Longitude.	THERMOMETER.			BAROMETER.		
			Max.	Min.	Med.	Max.	Min.	Med.
June 1	79° 0′	6.35 E	32	32	32.0	30.15	30.10	30.13
2	79.10	6.45	33	25	30.2	30.10	29.80	29.95
3	79.15*	6.45	20	16	18.3	29.80	29.72	29.76
4	78.53*	5.56	25	20	21.7	29.78	29.72	29.75
5	78.53	5.56	21	18	19.7	29.78	29.77	29.77
6	78.27*	6.50	19	18	18.6	29.77	29.73	29.75
7	78.30	5.10	21	18	19.3	29.94	29.72	29.83
8	78.34	5.15	24	18	20.7	30.06	29.94	30.00
9	78.25	5.10	30	26	28.0	30.06	30.02	30.04
10	78.20	5.30	34	32	33.0	30.02	29.94	29.98
11	78.30	7.50	34	34	34.0	30.02	29.96	29.99
12	78.15	6. 0	38	34	36.4	30.02	29.84	29.93
13	78.23*	5.40	39	34	37.0	29.90	29.80	29.85
14	78.33	6.25	26	25	25.3	29.93	29.80	29.87
15	77.57*	6. 0	31	28	29.7	29.80	29.76	29.78
16	78.11*	4.30	34	29	31.0	29.82	29.76	29.79
17	78.30	6.10	36	32	34.0	30.02	29.82	29.92
18	78.34	6.10	34	28	31.6	30.13	30.02	30.07
19	77.22*	5·40	32	30	31.0	30.21	30.09	30.15
20	75.59*	3.50	34	32	32.7	30.09	29.90	30.00
21	75.53*	3. 0	37	32	34.7	29.90	29.82	29.86
22	75.55*	3.15	37	32	34.6	29.84	29.82	29.83
23	75.48	2.55	37	34	35.7	29.94	29.84	29.89
24	76. 0	4.20	36	33	34.3	29.93	29.80	29.86
25	75.47*	5. 0	37	35	36.0	29.94	29.72	29.83
26	76.20	5.50	38	35	36.4	29.74	29.72	29.73
27	75.54	4.30	36	35	35.7	29.74	29.38	29.56
28	77.50	5.50	38	35	36.3	29.38	29.34	29.36
29	77.55	6.50	40	38	39.3	29.50	29.34	29.42
30	77.42*	8. 0	40	37	38.6	29.90	29.50	29.70
July 1	76.15	14.40	40	40	40.0	30.02	29.90	29.96
2	75.13*	12.37	41	39	40.0	30.08	30.02	30.05
3	74.53*	10.50	39	39	39.0	30.10	30.08	30.09
4	74.30	8.30	38	38	38.0	30.10	30.04	30.07
5	74.35	7.30	38	36	37.0	30.04	29.96	30.00
6	74.45	6.30	37	36	36.3	29.96	29.95	29.96
7	74.55	4.55	37	37	37.0	29.95	29.85	29.90
8	75.10*	3.10	42	37	39.0	29.85	29.81	29.83
9	75.27*	3. 0	39	36	37.3	29.81	29.76	29.78
10	75.34*	3. 0	40	37	38.7	29.76	29.72	29.74
11	76.16	3.30	40	36	38.4	29.72	29.72	29.72
12	76.36	4.25	38	32	35.7	29.77	29.72	29.75
13	76.57*	4. 5	37	31	34.0	29.90	29.77	29 83
14	75.15*	4.30	40	28	33.0	30.05	29.90	29.98
15	73.35*	4.55	40	38	39.0	30.05	29.95	30.00
16	73.06	4.15	42	40	41.0	29.95	29.84	29,89

1815	WINDS.		Weather and Meteors.	Situation and Remarks.
	Direction.	Force.		
June 1	S S E to S	Fresh gales	Hazy	Floes near
2	to W, N N W	Hard ga. fresh br.	Snow, sleet	A body of floes
3	N N W	Brisk breeze	Clear	Ditto
4	Var. S W	Gentle breeze	Fog showers	Sea 600 fath. deep
5	to N W to N N E	to Strong breeze	Fog, snow	Large floes
6	N W to N N W	to Light breeze	Snow showers	Ditto
7	to N N E	Light breeze	Fog showers	Floes and fields
8	N to S W	Ditto	Clear	Ditto
9	S. erly	Moderate breeze	Showery	Ditto
10	S S E to S W	to Light breeze	Cloudy	Ditto
11	S W to S S E	to Fresh gale	Hazy	Scattered ice
12	S to S E, var.	Hard ga. to calm	Snow, fog	Drift ice and floes
13	W.erly, var.	to Fresh breeze	Ditto	Ditto
14	N	Moderate breeze	Cloudy	Charles' Isl. 35 mil.
15	N	Fresh gale	Some snow	Crowded ice
16	to W S W	Fresh breezes	Charming weather	Ditto and floes
17	to E.erly	to Calm	Clear, cloudy	Floes
18	Var. N.erly	Light breeze, calm	Clear	Floes and drift ice
19	N	Fresh breeze	Fog, clear	Sea open
20	N W	Strong breeze	Fine clear weather	Ditto
21	W N W to N	Moderate breeze	Fog, snow	In a bay of the ice
22	N	to Calm	Thick snow showers	Ditto
23	to W, var.	Light airs	Fog	Ditto
24	N N W to S W	to Fresh gale	Fog, clear	Drift ice
25	to S S W	Strong gales	Snow, hazy	At sea
26	Variable	Light breezes	Hazy, fog	Ditto
27	S E to S	to Strong gale	Much rain, fog	A little ice
28	Variable	Fresh gale, calm	Rain, thick fog	Charles' Isl. 15 lea.
29	N E	Moderate breeze	Rain, clear	Spitzbergen near
30	N W, var.	Light breeze	Clear	Ditto
July 1	N W, W N W	Moderate breezes	Fog showers	No ice
2	to W	Light breezes	Clear	At sea
3	to N, var.	Ditto	Fog showers	A little ice
4	N E.erly	Fresh breeze	Thick fog	Drift ice
5	to N.erly	to Light breeze	Fog showers	Ditto
6	N W, N	Moderate breeze	Ditto	Open ice
7	N W to N	Fresh gales	Rain, clear	Drift ice
8	N E to E N E	Light airs	Clear	Ice near
9	E.erly	Ditto	Cloudy	Ditto
10	N W.erly	Ditto	Charm. clear weath.	Ditto
11	W N W to N W	Moderate breeze	Fog, snow	Ice streams
12	to N	to Fresh gales	Thick snow	Ice near
13	W N W	Fresh gale	Snow shower	Ditto
14	to N W	Fresh breeze	Thick show. of snow	Ditto
15	W.erly	Fresh ga. light br.	Clear, fog, rain	Ditto
16	W S W	Fresh gales	Rain, fog	Ditto

1815	Latitude.	Longitude.	THERMOMETER.			BAROMETER.		
			Max.	Min.	Med.	Max.	Min.	Med.
July 17	73°. 5′	3.45 E	41	40	40.4	29.84	29.76	29.80
18	72.45	2.40	40	39	39.3	29.86	29.77	29.81
19	72. 6	2. 0 W	38	37	37.3	29.93	29.86	29.90
20	69.12	2. 0	48	42	44.0	29.89	29.66	29.77
21	67.50	1.30	53	51	51.6	29.68	29.66	29.67
22	66.18	0.43	48	47	47.7	29.75	29.68	29.72
23	64.26	0.46	50	47	48.7	29.92	29.75	29.83
24	63 38*	0.52	52	50	51.4	30.00	29.92	29.96
25	63.28*	0.55	56	53	54.6	30.08	30.00	30.04
26	62.43*	1. 0	56	54	55.0	30.20	30.08	30.14
27	61.45*	1. 0	58	56	56.7	30.26	30.20	30.23
28	61.15	1.48 E	57	56	56.7	30.26	30.26	30.26
29	61. 7	1. 0	58	57	57.6	30.26	30.13	30.20
30	60.15*	0.25 W	56	53	54.3	30.23	30.13	30.18
31	58. 6	1. 6	54	53	53.5	30.27	30.23	30.25
1816 April 1	59.10	2. 0 W	40	40	40.0	30.36	30.10	30.23
2	60. 8	1. 8	42	38	40.0	30.10	30.00	30.05
3	60. 8	1. 8	43	39	40.3	30.20	30.00	30.10
4	61.23	0.10	43	40	41.5	30.20	30.06	30.13
5	63.59*	0 32 E*	44	40	42.0	30.06	29.86	29.96
6	66.54*	2.18	42	40	40.7	29.86	29.50	29.68
7	67.54*	3. 2	45	41	42.3	29.70	29.56	29.63
8	69.30	5. 0	42	37	39,7	29.86	29.70	29.78
9	69.50*	5.32	42	31	37.6	29.86	29.75	29.80
10	71.24*	9.10	24	21	22.7	29.80	29.75	29.78
11	73. 4	9.34	34	29	31.7	29.80	29.50	29.65
12	73 5	7. 2	20	12	16.4	29.67	29.38	29.52
13	72.45	8. 2	24	16	20.6	29.80	29.67	29.73
14	72.54	5. 0	20	20	20.0	30.00	29.78	29.89
15	73.55	7.20	28	14	20.0	29.78	29.47	29.62
16	73.30	6.30	34	27	31.0	29.62	29.56	29.59
17	73.23*	5.40	24	20	22.0	29.56	29.40	29.48
18	74.13*	2. 0	20	16	18.0	29.70	29.40	29.55
19	74.40	3. 4	26	25	25.7	29.70	29.60	29.65
20	75.17	3.47	30	28	29.0	29.65	29.60	29.63
21	75.37	4.41	32	28	30.7	29.60	29.35	29.47
22	75.50	7.44	27	26	26.3	29.85	29.43	29.64
23	76.14*	9.48	32	30	30.6	29.90	29.75	29.83
24	76.59*	9. 6	32	29	30.7	29.75	29.50	29.62
25	77. 0	8.30	29	23	26.3	29.65	29.45	29.55
26	76.55	8.35	20	17	18.4	29.55	29.45	29.50
27	76.45	8.40	21	15	17.7	29.55	29.49	29.52
28	76.28	8.40	27	14	20.6	29.60	29.49	29.55
29	76 26*	8. 9	24	21	22.7	29.95	29.60	29.77
30	76.20	8.10	30	27	28.3	30.05	29.95	30.00

1815	WINDS.		Weather and Meteors.	Situation and Remarks.
	Direction.	Force.		
July 17	S W to W	Moderate br. calm	Fog	Some ice
18	E.erly	to Fresh breeze	Fog, rain, hazy	Ice in sight
19	E S E to N E	to Strong gale	Thick fog, rain	Ditto
20	to E.erly	to Light airs	Ditto	No ice
21	E.erly, var.	to Calm	Fog, rain	At sea
22	N N W, W N W	to Fresh breeze	Cloudy	Ditto
23	to W, var.	Moderate breeze	Ditto	Ditto
24	Var.	Calm, light breeze	Ditto	Ditto
25	Var. N. W.	Moderate breeze	Rain	Ditto
26	N W.erly	Fresh breezes	Ditto	No soundings
27	to W.erly	to Calm	Clear	Soundings, 105 fa.
28	S b W	Moderate breeze	Cloudy	Soundings, 86 fa.
29	to Var.	Strong breeze, calm	Rain, hazy	Soundings, 90 fa.
30	N W to W	Fresh gales	Rain, fog	Zetland in sight
31	N	Fresh breeze	Cloudy	Kinnaird's Head, 45′
1816				
April 1	S S E	Fresh or strong ga.	Snow, sleet, hail	At sea
2	to S E	Strong gales	Show. of hail, sleet	In Brassa Sound, ⎫
3	to S S E	Fresh gales	Cloudy	Zetland ⎬
4	S	Fresh breeze	Hail, sleet	At sea ⎭
5	S to S E	to Strong gale	Showers of hail	Ditto
6	to E	to Moderate breeze	Hail, rain, sleet	Ditto
7	E	Light br. squally	Snow, rain	Ditto
8	E	Light air, calm	Snow showers	Ditto
9	N W.erly	to Fresh breeze	Clear, snow	Ditto
10	N W. E S E	Fresh gales	Snow showers	Ditto
11	W.erly, var.	Strong gale, calm	Much snow	Ditto
12	N	Hard gale	Snow showers	Ditto
13	N N E to N N W	to Fresh breeze	Snow showers	Saw a piece of ice
14	to N N E, S E	Lig. br. to hard ga.	Constant snow	Drift ice
15	to E N E	Very hard gales	Snow, sleet, haze	One piece of ice
16	to E	Hard gales	Snow showers	No ice
17	to N N E	Ditto	Thick snow	Ditto
18	to N	to Fresh breeze	Snow showers	Ice streams
19	N N E to E	to Strong gale	Ditto	Ditto
20	E N E, var.	to Light breeze	Thick snow, sleet	Ditto
21	Variable	Fresh breeze, calm	Snow, haze, sleet	A little ice
22	Ditto	Moderate br. calm	Snow, thick fog	Loose pieces of ice
23	E S E	Very hard gale	Fog, haze	Ice streams
24	S E.erly	Strong gale, calm	Thick snow	Much Drift ice.
25	E N E to N N W	Fresh gales	Cloudy	Ditto
26	N W	Fresh gale	Crystallized snow	Ditto
27	N W, E.erly	to Gentle breeze	Much crys. snow	Ditto
28	to N N W	Light airs	Snow showers	Ditto
29	N N W	Moderate breeze	Fine snow crystals	Ditto
30	N, E, S S E	Calm, strong gale	Very thick snow	Ditto

1816	Latitude.	Longitude.	THERMOMETER.			BAROMETER.		
			Max.	Min.	Med.	Max.	Min.	Med.
May 1	77°. 4′	10.30 E	26	21	23.0	30.06	29.96	30.01
2	77.30	9.10	22	18	20.3	29.96	29.78	29.87
3	77.40	9. 5	22	21	21.3	29.98	29.96	29.97
4	77.58	8.50	28	25	26.4	29.98	29.90	29.94
5	78.10	8.40	28	17	24.7	29.90	29.90	29.90
6	78. 5	8.40	14	10	12.3	29.90	29.80	29.85
7	77.59	8.30	10	8	9.5	30.03	29.83	29.93
8	78.50	8. 0	12	9	10.3	30.03	30.02	30.02
9	78.55	7.50	20	10	15.4	30.02	29.90	29.96
10	78.53	7.40	20	10	16.0	29.90	29.65	29.78
11	78.45•	7. 0	26	20	23.5	29.90	29.65	29.77
12	78.40	7.50	28	16	22.5	29.97	29.90	29.94
13	78.48	8. 0	24	18	20.0	29.92	29.86	29.89
14	78.40	8. 0	24	10	17.8	29.86	29.82	29.84
15	78.38•	7.25	15	8	10.7	29.87	29.82	29.84
16	78.40	7.35	16	15	15.6	29.85	29.80	29.83
17	78.40	8.36	23	16	19.0	29.98	29.80	29.89
18	78.30	8.50	28	22	24.7	30.20	29.98	30.09
19	78.50•	7.50	34	30	32.0	30.20	29.88	30.04
20	78.58	5.50	34	30	32.0	29.88	29.76	29.82
21	79. 4	5.55	38	33	35.0	29.96	29.76	29.86
22	79.14	5.40	35	32	33.7	29.90	29.60	29.75
23	79.23	5.30	33	30	32.0	29.63	29.55	29.59
24	79.27	4.50	35	26	31.7	29.55	29.40	29.47
25	79.32•	5.50	28	21	24.6	29.80	29.37	29.59
26	79.36	5.20	38	29	33.5	29.86	29.68	29.77
27	79.40	5.20	34	32	33.0	29.68	29.56	29.62
28	79.42•	5.30	36	33	34.3	29.63	29.60	29.61
29	79.46	5.30	37	35	36.0	29.95	29.63	29.79
30	79.50	5.20	40	34	36.0	30.03	29.95	29.99
31	79.55	5.10	36	34	35.0	30.03	29.85	29.94
June 1	80. 0	5.15	37	31	35.7	29.85	29.81	29.83
2	80. 1	5.20	41	39	40.0	29.83	29.77	29.80
3	79.59	5.25	42	34	39.0	29.77	29.59	29.68
4	79.58	5.21	39	33	35.3	29.59	29.50	29.55
5	79.58	5.20	38	33	34.7	29.50	29.42	29.46
6	80. 0	5.10	36	32	34.0	29.53	29.52	29.52
7	79.56	5. 0	37	32	34.6	29.67	29.53	29.60
8	79.53•	4.55	42	32	36.0	29.80	29.67	29.74
9	79.49	4.53	32	30	30.7	29.88	29.80	29.84
10	79.47•	4.50	45	32	37.0	29.89	29.88	29.88
11	79.46	4.56	34	30	32.0	29.89	29.64	29.77
12	79.40	4.45	34	33	33.3	29.64	29.58	29.61
13	79.44•	4.55	34	33	33.7	29.70	29.61	29.66
14	79. 0	5. 0	35	33	34.0	29.70	29.56	29.63
15	79. 0	5. 0	35	31	33.6	29.62	29.53	29.57

| 1816 | WINDS. | | Meteors and Weather. | Situation and Remarks. |
	Direction.	Force.		
May 1	S E	Very hard gale	Thick snow	Amo. heavy dr. ice, with tremend. swell, ship driv. into a heavy pack, and damaged.
2	S E	Hard gale	Ditto	
3	S E, S S E	Strong gales	Snow showers	
4	S S E, S b E	Very hard gales	Thick snow shower	Among much ice
5	S to W N W, N	to Light breezes	Constant snow	Ditto
6	N	Strong gale	Snow showers	Ditto
7	N. N W	Fresh gales	Frost rime	Sea open
8	N W to N	Moderate breeze	Cloudy	Ditto
9	Var. S E.erly	Calm, fresh breeze	Strong snow show.	Ice near
10	W N W, N N E	Strong gales	Cloudy	Surrounded by ice.
11	to N E	to Light breeze	Some snow	Sea open
12	N.erly	Light airs	Clear	Bay ice
13	N.erly	Ditto	Show. of crys. snow	Spitzbergen in sight
14	E N E to N	to Fresh gales	Clear, cloudy	Ice near
15	N to N W	to Light breeze	Clear	Drift ice
16	Var. S W	Calm, mod. breeze	A little snow	Frozen in bay ice
17	N.erly, var.	to Calm	Cloudy	Ditto
18	S	Strong gale	Clear, snow	Ice streams
19	S to S S W	Fresh gales	Much rain, fog	Floes and drift ice
20	S, S W	to Moderate breeze	Thick fog, snow	Large floes
21	S to S S E	Fresh gales	Fog shower, rain	Ditto
22	S E	to Moderate breeze	Fog, rain, snow	Many floes
23	S E to S S W	to Fresh gale	Much snow	Ditto
24	S E. var.	to Calm, str. br.	Snow, fog	Ditto
25	N W.erly, var.	Fresh breeze	Clear	Charles' Isl. 22 lea.
26	S S E	Strong gale	Snow, fog, rain	Many floes
27	to S	to Light breeze	Rain, haze, fog	Surrounded by floes
28	S S E to S S W	to Fresh gales	Fog or snow show.	Ship beset by ditto
29	S	Strong breeze	Ditto	Ditto
30	S to S W	Moderate breezes	Constant fog	Ditto
31	S S W	Fresh gale	Fog showers	Ditto
June 1	S b W to S b E	Fresh ga. mod. br.	Snow showers	Ship closely beset by
2	E b N to S	Light airs	Fog showers	floes and heavy ice
3	S E to N E	to Fresh gale	Fog, rain, sleet	Hackl. Headlan. 45
4	S E to N E	to Light airs	Fog, snow, sleet	Ship close beset
5	S E to S S W	Fresh br. str. ga.	Much snow	Made a small rem.
6	S E to S b E	to Moderate breeze	Snow, sleet	Ship immoveable
7	Variable	to Calm	Snow, fog	Ditto
8	W.erly, N.erly	to Light airs	Fog, clear	Ditto
9	N	Fresh breeze	Snow showers	Moved a little way
10	to W var.	Light breeze, calm	Fog, clear	Removed some dist.
11	N N E	Light br. to fr. gale	Fog, snow	Gained smaller ice
12	N E to N b W	to Light airs	Haze, fog, snow	Escaped to sea
13	Variable	Gentle breezes	Fog or snow show.	Drift ice
14	Var. N E.erly	to Strong breeze	Curious refraction	Ice streams
15	to N N W	Strong breeze	Fog showers	Sea open

1816	Latitude.	Longitude.	THERMOMETER.			BAROMETER.		
			Max.	Min.	Med.	Max.	Min.	Med.
June 16	79°.12 *	4.50 E	37	31	35.0	29.79	29.62	29.71
17	79.10	6.50	33	32	32.7	29.86	29.79	29.82
18	79. 0	4.40	33	31	32.4	29.96	29.86	29.91
19	78.40	5.10	34	32	33.3	30.05	29.96	30.01
20	78.20	4.45	38	33	35.7	30.23	30.05	30.14
21	78. 7	4.50	36	34	35.3	30.36	30.23	30.29
22	78.16	1. 0	34	33	33.6	30.36	30.06	30.21
23	78.24	2. 0	34	32	33.4	30.06	29.82	29.94
24	78.11	0.30	38	31	34.7	29.85	29.82	29.84
25	78.15	0. 0	31	27	28.7	30.00	29.85	29.92
26	78.20	1. 0 W	29	28	28.6	30.10	30.00	30.05
27	78.16	1.25	31	29	30.0	30.07	29.84	29.96
28	78. 8 *	1.30	33	30	31.0	29.84	29.77	29.80
29	78. 8	2. 0	34	29	32.0	29.80	29.77	29.79
30	78. 6	2. 5	38	34	36.0	29.90	29.80	29.85
1817								
April 1	54.29	0.28 W	50	44	47.0	30.57	30.43	30.50
2	56.20	1. 0	48	45	46.5	30.57	30.54	30.55
3	56.53 *	1.20 *	56	44	49.3	30.67	30.54	30.61
4	57.57 *	1.12	44	38	41.3	30.72	30.67	30.69
5	60. 8	1. 8	46	44	45.0	30.68	30.62	30.65
6	60. 8	1. 8	50	43	46.5	30.65	30.62	30.64
7	62.47	1. 1 E	46	44	45.0	30.65	30.05	30.35
8	65. 6	1.35	36	28	32.6	30.05	29.45	29.75
9	64.39 *	2. 6	28	26	27.0	29.65	29.45	29.55
10	64.29	3.30	28	26	27.0	29.95	29.65	29.80
11	65. 0	5.13	31	29	29.7	29.95	29.70	29.82
12	65.48	4.19	34	31	32.7	29.80	29.55	29.68
13	68. 3	6. 3	40	30	36.0	29.80	29.07	29.43
14	69.25	6.32	35	34	34.6	29.45	29.07	29.26
15	70.27 *	4.42	32	28	30.4	29.35	29.10	29.23
16	70. 0	6.52	30	28	29.0	29.62	29.35	29.48
17	70.12 *	9.40 *	30	28	29.0	29.85	29.62	29.74
18	71.56	10.16	32	32	32 0	29.87	29.23	29.55
19	73.13 *	11.46	35	34	34.7	29.25	28.75	29.00
20	73.25	11.30	34	28	31.0	29.76	29.25	29.50
21	76. 5 *	13.22 *	28	21	25.0	29.65	29.20	29.43
22	75.50	11.50	24	21	22.3	29.73	29.30	29.51
23	77.24	7. 0	22	18	20.7	29.90	29.73	29.82
24	78.21	2.23	21	16	19.0	29.82	29.75	29.78
25	78. 0	2.35 W	11	7	9.3	30.02	29.82	29.92
26	78.23	1.55	14	8	10.2	30.02	29.86	29.94
27	78.20	2.10	22	12	16.8	29.86	29.76	29.81
28	78. 5	4. 0 E	14	12	13.4	29.76	29.67	29.72
29	77.54	2.40 W	8	4	6.3	29.75	29.67	29.71
30	77.48	3.20	8	5	6.6	29.80	29.75	29.78

1816	WINDS.		Meteors and Weather.	Situation and Remarks.
	Direction.	Force.		
June 16	N W.erly	to Light airs	Clear	Sea open
17	W.erly, S b W	Moder. breeze, calm	Snow showers	Ice streams
18	W b N to S S W	to Moder. breeze	Ditto	Ice in sight
19	to W	Fresh or light br.	Thick fog, snow	Sea open
20	to S S W	to Fresh breeze	Snow, fog	Drift ice
21	S W	Strong breeze	Fog	Ditto
22	S W b S	Strong gale	Fog, haze, rain	Much drift ice
23	to S W b W	Fresh to light br.	Thick fog	Ditto
24	Var. N W to N E	to Fresh br. calm	Snow showers	Much heavy ice
25	to N	Fresh br. to calm	Snow, fog	Floes and drift ice
26	Var. S b W	to Moderate breeze	Snow showers	Ditto
27	S W	to Fresh breeze	Ditto	Ditto
28	to W N W	Strong breezes	Ditto	Ditto
29	Variable	Light br. calm	Some snow	{ Ship in great dis-
30	Ditto	Ditto	Fog or snow	{ tress, fills with water
1817				
April 1	S W to E S E	Gentle breezes	Clear	In Whitby harbour
2	S W, N E	Fresh br. to calm	Cloudy	At sea
3	N.erly, S.erly	Light breeze, calm	Fine clear weather	Ditto
4	S.	to Fresh gale	Dense atmosphere	Buchanness, 6 leag.
5	S S W to W N W, N	Fresh breezes	Aurora borealis	In Brassa Sound
6	N.erly to S W	Calm, fresh gale	Cloudy	Ditto
7	S W	Strong gale	Rain, haze	At sea
8	to W, N E to N	Mod. br. strong ga.	Snow, aurora bor.	Ditto
9	to N N E	Hard gales	Much snow, hail	Ditto
10	N b W, N W	Intermittent gale	Snow showers	Ditto
11	W N W to N	Ditto	Opaque hail	Ditto
12	N N E, S W	Fresh ga. light br.	Snow, sleet, rain	Ditto
13	S S W to W	Strong or fresh ga.	Sleet, rain, snow	Ditto
14	N N E to E	Mod. br. hard ga.	Ditto	Ditto
15	E N E to N N E	Very hard gale	Rain, snow	Ditto
16	to N W b N	Strong gales	Snow showers	Ditto
17	N b W to N W	Fresh breezes	Some snow	Ditto
18	S to S E, W b S	Cal. to exces. ha. ga.	Constant snow	Ditto
19	to Var.	to Calm, light br.	Showers of snow	Heavy sea, no wind
20	N.erly, S W, var.	to Fresh gale	Cloudy, snow	Temp. of sea, 35°
21	W S W to W N W	to Hard gales	Snow showers	Spitzbergen 30′, Ice
22	to N W, E, var.	to Calm	Snow	Ditto 40′, Ice
23	E S E to N E	Strong gales	Snow shower	Ice near
24	E N E to N b W	Fresh or strong ga.	Much snow	Loose drift ice
25	N N W, N W	Fresh breezes	Frost rime	Streams, &c. of ice
26	to N N E	to Light airs	Frost rime, clear	A little ice
27	to N E	to Fresh gale	Clear, snow shower	Scattered ice
28	N N E to N N W	Strong gales	A little frost rime	No ice
29	N N W	Ditto	Frost rime	Loose ice
30	N N W	Fresh gale	Thick frost rime	Ice streams

1817	Latitude.	Longitude.	THERMOMETER.			BAROMETER.		
			Max.	Min.	Med.	Max.	Min.	Med.
May 1	77°.55′	2.40 W	16	10	13.3	29.90	29.80	29.85
2	78.15	2.35	19	15	17.3	29.90	29.80	29.85
3	78.28*	1. 5	20	13	17.4	29.80	29.50	29.65
4	78.55	0.45	20	20	20.0	29.85	29.50	29.68
5	80. 5	5.50*E	30	28	28.7	29.95	29.85	29.90
6	79.18	3.58	28	26	27.0	29.95	29.80	29.87
7	78.55	0.40	31	30	30.3	29.85	29.80	29.83
8	78.50	1.20 W	30	30	30.0	29.89	29.81	29.85
9	77.20	1.40	31	30	30.3	29.80	29.43	29.61
10	77.52*	1.50	31	30	30.4	29.53	29.39	29.46
11	78. 2	2.40*	30	29	29.7	29.83	29.53	29.68
12	77.50	2.20	32	26	29.3	30.15	29.83	29.99
13	76.50	2.30	32	28	30.3	30.25	30.15	30.20
14	75.52	8. 5*	23	15	19.0	30.20	30.09	30.15
15	75.53*	6.40	18	15	16.4	30.10	30.09	30.09
16	75.12	6. 0	31	27	29.3	30.10	29.70	29.90
17	75.16	8.30	31	28	29.6	29.97	29.90	29.94
18	75.28	11.20	34	31	32.7	30.00	29.97	29.98
19	75.23	10.40	34	32	33.0	30.07	30.00	30.04
20	75.30	9.50*	32	30	31.0	30.07	30.07	30.07
21	75.30	9.40	31	31	31.0	30.07	29.85	29.96
22	75.34	9.40	31	30	30.3	29.85	29.73	29.79
23	75.45	9.10	32	29	30.4	29.95	29.73	29.84
24	75.58	8.50	29	28	28.3	30.14	29.95	30.04
25	76.15*	7.32*	30	24	27.7	30.16	30.02	30.09
26	76.37*	5.35*	38	32	35.3	30.02	30.00	30.01
27	77. 7*	3.20	32	31	31.6	30.10	30.00	30.05
28	77.25	2.50	32	30	30.7	30.25	30.10	30.18
29	77.34*	1.50	30	27	28.7	30.25	30.20	30.22
30	77.39*	1.40	27	25	26.0	30.20	29.93	30.07
31	78. 2	0.30	28	26	27.0	29.93	29.84	29.88
June 1	78.29*	1.20	28	22	24.7	29.89	29.84	29.87
2	78.15	0.25 E	30	26	28.7	29.95	29.89	29.92
3	77.56*	0.20	36	33	34.3	29.94	29.92	29.93
4	78. 0	0.20	34	33	33.6	29.96	29.87	29.91
5	77.54*	0.10	33	33	33.0	29.87	29.81	29.84
6	77.56	0.15	40	33	36.3	29.87	29.79	29.83
7	78. 2*	0.20	43	36	38.4	29.93	29.87	29.90
8	78.10	0.10	30	28	29.0	29.95	29.93	29.94
9	78.12	2. 0 W	30	27	28.3	30.04	29.95	30.00
10	78.20	0.24 E	30	27	28.3	30.06	30.04	30.05
11	78.26*	0.30 W	27	25	25.7	30.09	30.06	30.07
12	78.34	1.40	26	25	25.4	30.07	29.95	30.01
13	78.28*	1.30	28	22	25.7	29.95	29.60	29.78
14	78.17*	2. 5	29	20	25.0	29.60	29.50	29.55
15	78. 4	2.50	25	22	23.3	29.55	29.52	29.53

1817		WINDS.		Weather and Meteors.	Situation and Remarks.
		Direction.	Force.		
May	1	N b E, var.	Light or fresh br.	Frost rime, snow	Near the main ice
	2	E to N, var.	to Fresh gales	Cryst. snow	Ditto
	3	N b E, S E b E	Strong gale, calm	Much cryst. snow	Ditto
	4	S E to E N E	to Fresh gale	Snow showers	Ditto
	5	Ditto	to Light breeze	Clear, cloudy	Spitz. 40 to 50 miles
	6	E S E to S E	Fresh ga. light br.	Fine snow crystals	Near the W.rn pack
	7	S S E to E N E	Moderate breezes	Hazy weather	Ditto
	8	to S E b E	to Fresh gales	Snow, sleet, haze	Ditto
	9	E to S S E	Strong breezes	Thick fog, snow	At sea
	10	E S E to S b E	to Light breeze	Fog or snow show.	Ice in sight
	11	S W to S b E	Mod. or strong br.	Snow showers	Ditto
	12	S S W, N b E	to Calm	Fog, snow	Ditto
	13	to E N E	Fresh breezes	Thick fog, snow	No ice
	14	N b W, N N E	Mod. br. strong ga.	Fog, snow	Near a pack
	15	N b E	Very hard gale	Thick snow	Amongst loose ice
	16	to N b W	Strong gales	Haze, snow	A few pieces of ice
	17	N b E	Fresh breeze	Haze, fog	Ice streams, &c.
	18	N	Light breeze	Thick fog, snow	Much heavy ice
	19	N N E to E b N	to Fresh breeze	Fog, haze	An open pack
	20	N E	Strong gale	Haze, snow	At sea
	21	N E b N	to Fresh gale	Haze, snow, fog	Ditto
	22	N E b N	to Calm	Thick fog, snow	Brash ice
	23	N to N W	Calm to moder. br.	Snow showers	Near the W. pack
	24	to N	Moderate breezes	Ditto	Ditto
	25	N, S E b E	Moder. br. calm	Cloudy	Ditto
	26	to S S E	Light airs	Clear	Much heavy ice
	27	to E b N	Light breezes	Cloudy	Ditto
	28	E.erly	Light breeze, calm	Clear, fog	Ice near
	29	N E to N b W	Moderate breezes	Clear, cloudy	Drift ice, &c.
	30	to W	to Fresh breeze	Clear	At sea
	31	to N N W	to Moderate breeze	Cloudy	Much crowded ice
June	1	N b W to N W	Moderate breeze	Frost rime	Much ice
	2	Var. S b W	to Strong breeze	Cloudy	At sea
	3	S b W to S b E	Moderate breeze	Snow showers	A little ice
	4	to E b S, var.	Ditto	Ditto	Ditto
	5	E b S to S E b S	to Light airs	Brilliant rain-bow	Ditto
	6	to S b E	Moderate breeze	Snow showers	Ditto
	7	Variable	Light airs	Ditto	Ditto
	8	Ditto.	to Calm	Fog showers	Drift ice and floes
	9	Ditto	to Light airs	Ditto	Floes, &c.
	10	W.erly, N.erly	to Moderate breeze	Clear, cloudy	Drift ice
	11	N W to W	Fresh breeze	Clear	In a bay of the ice
	12	N W	to Hard gale	Cloudy, snow	Solid ice near
	13	N b W to W N W	to Strong breeze	Thick snow	Drift ice and floes
	14	to N	Hard gale	Snow showers	Ditto
	15	to N W b N	to Strong gale	Cloudy	Ditto

1817	Latitude.	Longitude.	THERMOMETER.			BAROMETER.		
			Max.	Min.	Med.	Max.	Min.	Med.
June 16	77°.44′	3.15 W	26	23	24.0	29.52	29.50	29.51
17	77.20	1.25	32	25	29.0	29.75	29.50	29.63
18	77.27*	2.16*	34	29	31.0	30.05	29.75	29.90
19	77.36*	1.15	40	34	36.6	30.15	30.05	30.10
20	77.41*	1. 0 E	37	32	34.5	30.22	30.15	30.18
21	77.58*	0.20	34	30	32.3	30.25	30.09	30.17
22	78.20	1.20 W	33	30	31.4	30.09	30.00	30.05
23	77.30	2.20	35	30	33.0	30.16	30.00	30.08
24	76.30*	3.50	38	33	35.3	30.24	30.16	30.20
25	76.17*	3.10	34	30	32.3	30.24	30.20	30.22
26	76.33	4.40	35	34	34.4	30.20	29.98	30.09
27	76.26	5. 0	35	34	34.3	29.98	29.80	29.89
28	76.30*	5. 5*	34	32	32.7	29.80	29.60	29.70
29	76.24*	5.20	38	32	35.3	29.71	29.68	29.69
30	76. 4	5.40	38	36	37.0	29.72	29.68	29.70
July 1	75.59	7.20	38	36	37.3	29.92	29.72	29.82
2	75.25	8.10	38	35	36.3	29.92	29.92	29.92
3	75.40	7.30	36	35	35.7	29.92	29.85	29.88
4	75.50	5.20	36	33	34.6	29.85	29.80	29.83
5	75.54*	7.10	38	32	35.4	29.80	29.78	29.79
6	75.46	7.20	42	32	36.7	29.88	29.82	29.85
7	75.53	7.40	35	31	33.7	29.88	29.88	29.88
8	75.50	8.35	36	33	34.7	29.88	29.88	29.88
9	75.12	9.10	36	34	35.0	29.88	29.83	29.85
10	75.20	7.10	40	35	37.0	29.83	29.72	29.78
11	75.12*	6.40	40	32	36.0	29 78	29.70	29.74
12	75.20	4.50	35	32	33.6	29.83	29.78	29.80
13	75.18	4.20	33	32	32.3	29.83	29.78	29.81
14	74.59*	2.50	37	33	35.0	29.80	29.78	29.79
15	75.54	1. 0 E	38	33	35.7	29.87	29.80	29.83
16	76.20*	0.33 W	40	35	37.7	29.92	29.87	29.90
17	75.56	3.49 E	36	34	35.3	29.93	29.92	29.92
18	75.45	6.30	40	36	37.4	29.94	29.93	29.94
19	76.20	10.30	37	36	36.5	30.08	29.94	30.01
20	76. 4	13.10	40	38	39.0	30.08	29.95	30.01
21	75.15	12.42	39	37	37.6	29.98	29.97	29.98
22	75. 5	11.38	42	41	41.3	30.01	29.96	29.98
23	74.25	6.58	45	44	44.3	29.96	29.92	29.94
24	73.49	1.58	45	40	42.4	29.92	29.73	29.83
25	73.55	0. 1 W	40	38	39.3	29.97	29.83	29.90
26	73.35	0.30	41	39	40.0	29.97	29.85	29.91
27	73.27	0.35	41	35	38.3	29.85	29.83	29.84
28	73.56*	4.47*	39	35	36.7	29.83	29.65	29.74
29	74. 0	10.37*	36	33	34.7	29.70	29.65	29.67
30	73.46	8.50	38	32	35.0	29.70	29.70	29.70
31	73.46*	8.10	40	33	36.0	29.75	29.70	29.73

1817	WINDS.		Meteors and Weather.	Situation and Remarks.
	Direction.	Force.		
June 16	N W b N	Hard gale	Much snow	Drift ice and floes
17	to N E b N	to Strong breeze	Hazy, clear	Ditto
18	to N W	to Light breeze	Clear	Drift ice
19	N.erly, W.erly	Light airs, calm	Ditto	Much drift ice
20	N N E	Fresh breeze	Clear, cloudy	At sea
21	to N b W	to Strong gale	Much snow	Ice streams
22	N to N W	Very strong gale	Snow	Ditto
23	N W	to Fresh breeze	Cloudy, snow	Ditto
24	N W. var.	Light airs	Clear	At sea
25	S W. b S to S b W	Fresh gales	Hazy, showery	Ice streams
26	S to S b E	Strong gales	Fog or snow	Ice-field, &c.
27	S b E	Strong gale	Thick fog	Ditto
28	Variable	Fresh br. light airs	Hazy, clear	Ditto
29	Ditto	to Calm	Snow showers, hazy	Drift ice and floes
30	S.erly, var.	Moderate breeze	Hazy, thick fog	Ditto
July 1	S.erly, S E	Ditto	Thick fog	Much drift ice
2	S b W, S W b W	Light or mod. br.	Ditto	Ditto
3	S b W	Fresh breeze	Ditto	Ditto
4	S b E to S W	Light airs	Ditto	Drift ice and floes
5	to S b W	Moderate breeze	Fog showers, fog	Ditto
6	Variable.	to Calm	Foggy	Ditto
7	S.erly, to S W	to Moderate breeze	Fog, snow	Crowded ice
8	S W b W to S	Moderate breeze	Fog showers	Much drift ice
9	to S W b W	Ditto	Thick fog	Floes and drift ice
10	to S b W	Fresh breeze	Ditto	Ditto
11	W b S to S W	Moderate breeze	Fog, rain	Ditto
12	S W	Fresh gale	Rain, fog	Ditto
13	W S W	Moderate gales	Constant fog	Ditto
14	to W	Fresh breeze	Fog, clear	Loose ice
15	N W to N b E	Ditto	Fog, cloudy	At sea
16	S W to S b W	to Calm	Thick fog, clear	Floe and loose ice
17	S W, W, var.	Strong breeze	Cloudy, fog	At sea
18	N W, var.	Calm, mod. breeze	Cloudy, clear	No ice
19	S W to W N W	to Strong breeze	Cloudy	Spitzbergen in sight
20	N to W S W	to Moderate breeze	Cloudy, hazy	Ditto
21	W.erly, var.	to Calm	Cloudy	No ice
22	Variable	to Moderate breeze	Cloudy, rain	At sea, no ice
23	E b S to S S W	Fresh breeze	Cloudy, rain, fog	Ditto
24	S to W	Ditto	Rain, fog	Ditto
25	W, var.	Str. br. light airs	Fog	Ditto
26	Variable	Chiefly calm	Thick fog	Ditto
27	N E to E S E	Calm, light airs	Ditto	Ditto
28	E to N E b N	to Strong gale	Fog showers	Ditto
29	N E to N W	Fresh breeze	Ditto	Drift ice and floes
30	N.erly	to Calm	Thick fog	*W. Greenl. in sight*
31	Variable	Calm, moderate br.	Fog, clear	Crowded drift ice

1818	Latitude.	Longitude.	THERMOMETER.					BAROMETER.		
			Max.	Min.	Med.	Deck.	Mast-head.	Max.	Min.	Med.
May 1	70°.50	6.50 W	27	25	26.3	27	24.5	30.45	30.25	30.35
2	71.10	6.20	28	25	26.7	27	†24	30.54	30.45	30.49
3	71.34	5.28*	29	26	27.3	29	†26	30.47	30.44	30.46
4	72. 1*	4.26	31	30	30.4	30	26.5	30.44	30.04	30.24
5	72.30	3. 0	32	30	31.3	32	†30	30.04	29.60	29.82
6	74.40	1.44 E	27	24	25.7	26	†23	29.80	29.60	29.70
7	75.39	2.40	32	29	31.0	32	†30	29.82	29.74	29.78
8	78.10	5.10	29	16	22.3	16	12	29.74	29.40	29.57
9	78.30	6.20	22	19	20.4	22	17	29.70	29.40	29.55
10	78.16	4.10	22	14	17.0	16	12	29.90	29.70	29.80
11	78.10	4. 0	19	14	17.0	18	14	29.90	29.88	29.89
12	78. 6*	3.10	22	13	16.3	14	†10	30.05	29.88	29.96
13	78. 0	3.30	28	20	24.0	24	†20	30.29	30.05	30.17
14	78.27*	1.50	28	24	26.0	24	†20	30.32	30.29	30.31
15	78.35	2.20	30	28	28.6	28	†25	30.34	30.20	30.27
16	78.26	1.40	30	25	28.0	29	†26	30.20	30.14	30.17
17	78.36	1.30	24	24	24.0	24	†20	30.14	30.02	30.08
18	78.26	0.40 W	22	18	19.3	18	†14	30.02	29.80	29.91
19	78.10	0.50	18	12	15.2	14	†10	29.85	29.73	29.79
20	77.55	0.55	20	13	15.8	20	16	29.88	29.85	29.86
21	77.59	0.40	26	19	22.4	22	†18	30.00	29.88	29.94
22	78. 0	1. 0	30	27	28.7	29	†26	30.00	29.90	29.95
23	77.58	1. 2	26	23	25.0	26	23	30.02	29.88	29.95
24	77.55	0.42	22	19	20.3	20	†16	30.06	30.02	30.04
25	77.59	0.30 E	19	18	18.8	19	†15	30.08	30.06	30.07
26	77.40	0.10 W	20	16	18.0	18	†14	30.20	30.08	30.14
27	77.31*	0.40	29	24	25.7	24	†20.5	30.22	30.18	30.20
28	78. 0	0.50	30	30	30.0	30	†28	30.18	29.70	29.94
29	78. 5	1.20 E	30	25	28.4	25	23	29.70	29.30	29.50
30	78.30	0.19	28	24	25.5	28	25	29.30	29.30	29.30
31	78.28	0.30	24	22	22.5	22	20	29.40	29.30	29.35
June 1	78.25	0.10	24	23	23.3			29.50	29.40	29.45
2	78.20	0.10 W	27	25	26.0			29.70	29.50	29.60
3	78.28	1.10 E	27	26	26.3			29.85	29.70	29.77
4	78.35*	0.55	27	26	26.4			29.86	29.85	29.86
5	78.50	0.20 W	28	26	27.0			30.02	29.86	29.94
6	78.22*	0.40 E	29	26	27.7			30.02	30.00	30.01
7	78.28	0.30	33	31	32.0			30.00	29.96	29.98
8	78.25	0.30 W	34	33	33.7			29.96	29.25	29.60
9	78.20	0. 5 E	34	32	33.3			29.63	29.25	29.44
10	78.30	2. 0	33	31	32.3			29.90	29.63	29.77
11	78.34	1.40	32	30	30.6			30.15	29.90	30.02
12	78.50	2.20	40	32	35.4			30.22	30.15	30.19
13	78.47	3. 0	34	31	32.3			30.30	30.20	30.25
14	79.10	3.25	32	30	31.0			30.20	30.20	30.20
15	79.18	3.12	32	13	31.3			30.22	30.16	30.19

1818	WINDS.		Weather and Meteors.	Situation and Remarks.
	Direction.	Force.		
May 1	N E b E to E	Strong breezes	Snow showers	Bay and drift ice
2	E b N	to Light breeze	Cloudy, clear	Ice streams
3	E N E	to Fresh breeze	Cloudy	Ditto
4	to E b S	to Strong gale	Clear, snow	Drift and bay ice
5	S E to S W	Strong gales	Fog showers, cloudy	A little ice
6	to N W	to Light airs	Cloudy	Ice streams
7	Variable, S	to Strong gale	Snow, fog, cloudy	No ice
8	S b W to W	to Fresh breeze	Cloudy, snow show.	Drift ice
9	W b N, W S W, N	Light breezes	Clear, cloudy	Ditto
10	N N W, N	Light airs	Cloudy	Ice streams
11	N N E, N W	Fresh gales	Snow, clear	Much ice
12	N W, var.	to Calm	Clear	Much drift ice
13	S, W S W to N	to Moderate breeze	Ditto	Ice streams
14	N N E to E S E	Light airs	Partially clear	An open pack
15	S E.erly	Near calm	Clear in the N W	Ditto
16	Variable	to Fresh breeze	Cloudy, ditto	Ditto
17	N E b E	Strong gale	Thick snow	Drift and bay ice
18	N E b N	Hard gale	Snow, hazy	Ditto
19	to N b E	Ditto	Clear, snow	Near a west pack
20	N b E	Ditto	Clear	Ditto
21	N to W b N	to Calm	Cloudy, snow	Floes and heavy ice
22	W.erly, var.	Light airs, calm	Snow showers	Ditto
23	Variable	Ditto	Cloudy	Much ice
24	E b N, N E b E	Fresh breeze	Ice blinks, snow	Heavy drift ice
25	N E b N to N b E	Fresh gales	Snow showers	Floes and drift ice
26	to W b N	to Moderate breeze	Ditto	Drift ice
27	to S S W	Fresh gales	Clear, cloudy	Bay and drift ice
28	to S E & S W	Strong ga. light br.	Foggy, hazy, snow	Some ice
29	to W b N	Calm, fresh gale	Hazy, snow	Ice streams
30	to S, var.	to Calm	Clear, snow	Floes near
31	N, N N W	to strong gale	Snow showers	Heavy drift ice
June 1	N	Fresh breeze	Ditto	Ice streams
2	N N W, W N W	Strong breeze	Cloudy	Ditto
3	W b N to N W	Light airs	Hazy, clear	Ditto
4	N N W to N W	to Moderate breeze	Snow, fog, rain	Floes, drift ice
5	W N W, var.	Moderate breeze	Fog or snow show.	Fields, floes, &c.
6	W S W, S W	to Fresh breeze	Fog or snow	Field
7	S S W to S S E	Strong gales	Fog, hail, rain, snow	Ditto
8	to E to N b E	Fresh ga. mod. br.	Snow, rain, sleet, fog	Ditto
9	to N	Fresh gales	Snow or fog show.	Floes, drift ice
10	N N E, N E	Light airs	Cloudy, snow	At sea
11	N N E, var. S	Calm, light breeze	Snow showers	Loose ice
12	S b W to E S E	Light airs	Thick fog, snow	A pack near
13	S S E	to Moderate breeze	Fog shower, cloudy	Ditto
14	to S W	to Fresh breeze	Hazy	Ditto
15	W S W, var.	Gentle breeze	Ditto	Field near

1818	Latitude.	Longitude.	THERMOMETER.			BAROMETER.		
			Max.	Min.	Med.	Max.	Min.	Med.
June 16	79°.26′	2.42 E	34	29	31.7	30.16	30.04	30.10
17	79.30	2.11	34	30	31.7	30.04	30.02	30.03
18	79.28	2.20	34	31	32.4	30.02	29.98	30.00
19	79. 0	4.22	32	29	31.0	29.98	29.96	29.97
20	78.31*	4. 0	34	31	32.0	29.96	29.93	29.94
21	78.10	2. 0	32	31	31.3	29.93	29.87	29.90
22	77.45	3. 4	32	30	31.0	29.87	29.78	29.83
23	77.40	2.44	31	29	30.0	29.78	29.76	29.77
24	77. 1	2.30	34	31	32.3	29.76	29.65	29.70
25	75.40	2.30	35	34	34.4	29.65	29.35	29.50
26	75.44*	0.10 W	38	32	35.3	29.55	29.35	29.45
27	76.10	2. 0	32	31	31.3	29.70	29.55	29.62
28	75.40	3.40	34	30	31.4	29.76	29.70	29.73
29	75.40	8.20	32	30	31.0	29.76	29.70	29.73
30	75.10	8. 0	34	32	33.0	29.70	29.62	29.66
July 1	74.54*	9. 0	36	30	32.7	29.82	29.70	29.76
2	74.20	7. 0	32	30	30.7	29.96	29.82	29.89
3	74.50	8 20	30	34	36.5	29.98	29.96	29.97
4	75.50	5. 0	36	34	34.5	29 98	29.90	29.94
5	76. 0	4.30	36	34	34.6	29.90	29.80	29.85
6	76.10	4. 0	33	30	31.7	29.86	29.80	29.83
7	75.56	3.30	33	32	32.3	29.86	29.78	29.82
8	75.50	3.10	36	34	35.0	29.86	29.78	29.82
9	75.58*	3.40	35	32	34.0	30.06	29.86	29.96
10	76.30	3. 0	35	33	34.0	30.08	30.06	30.07
11	76.30	3.20	35	34	34.3	30.08	30.08	30.08
12	76.30	3.30	35	34	34.4	30.08	29.92	30.00
13	76.25*	2. 0	36	28	32.3	30.08	29.92	30.00
14	76.20	1.10	32	29	30.7	30.08	29.98	30.03
15	77.10	1.30 E	36	34	34.6	29.98	29.88	29.93
16	77.55	1.10	38	35	36.3	29.88	29.74	29.81
17	78.40	7. 0	38	36	37.4	29.74	29.62	29.68
18	79.10	9. 4	36	34	35.0	29.70	29.62	29.66
19	79.15	5.30	38	33	35.7	29.95	29.70	29.83
20	79.22*	5.55	34	34	34.0	30.08	29.95	30.01
21	79.19*	6.10	46	34	40.0 *	30.08	30.08	30.08
22	79.11*	6.10	44	40	42.0	30.08	29.90	29.99
23	79.14*	7.30	44	42	42.7	29.90	29.88	29.89
24	79. 8	9.15	48	44	46.0	29.88	29.80	29.84
25	79. 5	9.22	45	38	41.6	29.80	29.68	29.74
26	79. 5	9.24	38	36	37.3	29.82	29.62	29.72
27	78.55	9.55	46	40	42.3	30.10	29.82	29.96
28	79.10	7.30	41	39	40.0	30.10	29.79	29.94
29	78.40	6. 5	41	39	40.0	20.01	29.38	29.70
30	78.48	6.30	36	34	34.7	39.88	29.38	29.63
31	78.18*	4.30	41	33	38.0	29.98	29.88	29.93

* Thermometer hung over the ship's side, against the black paint work, on which the sun shone, rose to 92° !

1818	WINDS.		Meteors and Weather.	Situation and Remarks.
	Direction.	Force.		
June 16	Variable	Calm, light breeze	Snow showers	Field near
17	Var. N E b N	to Calm	Ditto	Ship inclosed in ice
18	Var. S W.erly	to Moderate breeze	Ditto	Ditto
19	S S W to W S W	to Strong breeze	Ditto	Spitzbergen in sight
20	W b S to S S W	to Moderate breeze	Snow, clear	No ice
21	to W S W, var,	to Fresh breeze	Fog, snow	Ice streams
22	N to N E	to Calm	Snow showers	Ditto
23	N N E	Fresh breeze	Cloudy, snow	Ditto
24	N to E N E	Fresh br Mod. br.	Snow, hazy	At sea
25	to E	Strong gale	Haze, rain	No ice
26	to E S E, var.	to Light airs	Thick fog, cloudy	Ditto
27	E b N to E S E	Strong br. mod. br.	Fog, snow	A pack near
28	to S E b S	to Fresh breeze	Thick fog	Brash ice
29	Var. N E to N b W	to Calm, strong ga.	Fog, snow, rain	Crowded ice
30	to N W b W	to Fresh breeze	Ditto	Ship beset
July 1	Var. W S W	Calm to strong br.	Clear, fog	Near a pack of ice
2	S W b S to W	to Moder. breeze	Thick fog	Ditto
3	to N W, var. S	to Calm	Beautifully clear	In a bay of the ice
4	S b W	to Strong gale	Ditto, cloudy	Ice near
5	to S W, var.	Moder. br. calm	Fog	Ice streams
6	E.erly, N E	Calm, fresh breeze	Fog, rain, snow, hail	Pack near
7	N b E	to Moderate breeze	Ditto	Heavy streams
8	N.erly	to Calm	Fog	Ice streams
9	S b E	to Fresh breeze	Fog, haze, cloudy	Ditto
10	S E to E b S	Fresh breeze	Fog, rain	In an open pack
11	N E b E to S E	to Light breeze	Thick fog, rain	Sailing ice
12	N b E to N b W	Moderate breeze	Thick fog	Crowded ice
13	S W.erly, var.	to Calm	Constant fog	Encl. in a bay of ice
14	S W.erly	Light airs	Fog, snow	At sea
15	S W b S	Fresh breeze	Fog, rain	Ice in sight
16	S W to S E	Fresh gales	Much rain	Ditto
17	to S S W	to Calm	Rain, fog	Near Spitzb. no ice
18	N W	Fresh or mod. br.	Rain, fog, snow	Spitzb. 3 miles off
19	Var. W S W	to Calm	Fog, clear	Loose ice
20	S W	Gentle br. calm	Fog	In open pack
21	E.erly, var.	Light airs, calm	Fog, clear	Ice and land in sig.
22	Var.	Calm, light airs	Clear, rain, fog	Char. Isl. S S E, 25′
23	Ditto	Calm, light breeze	Rain, clear	Ditto, S S E, 20′
24	Ditto	Chiefly calm	Fine clear weather	Mitre Cape, S E 5′
25	Var. S.erly	Calm to strong gale	Clear, rain, fog	Ditto, E 1′
26	W N W to N N W	Fresh br. light airs	Cloudy, clear	Ditto, E ¼′
27	S S W to S S E	Fresh gale	Clear, rain	In King's Bay
28	S to S W	Strong ga. fresh br.	Cloudy. rain, fog	Fair Foreland in sig.
29	S to E N E	to Hard gale	Rain, fog, hazy	At sea
30	S to W & N	Very hard ga. calm	Hazy, cloudy	Ditto
31	N	Calm. gentle breeze	Cloudy, clear	Char. Isl. E b N 60′

REMARKS

ON THE FOREGOING

METEOROLOGICAL TABLES.

THE *winds* in the preceding Tables, are estimated from the true north, being in all cases corrected by the application of the variation of the compass.

In the first three years, 1807, 1808, and 1809, the *day* commences at twelve at noon, according to the usual nautical estimation, and is twelve hours earlier than the day by civil reckoning; but the time, in every succeeding year, is the civil day, commencing at twelve at night.

Those *Latitudes* and *Longitudes*, having an asterisk annexed to them, were deduced from celestial observations, and are consequently accurate. The others, being from estimation, are liable to some error; but nothing sufficient to affect the general results.

In the Tables for the first three years, the column superscribed " *Thermometer*," consists only of a single daily observation; but as this observation was intentionally made at a different hour almost every day, and as often near the hour of mid-night as of mid-day, it is presumed that the mean temperature derived therefrom, will be very nearly the same as if more observations had been registered. In these three Tables also, the *Barometer* is merely marked once a-day, and that at the time of noon.

In the last nine years observations, however, the Tables are more complete; the columns headed " *Barometer*," including the daily extremes, and those entitled " *Thermometer*," consisting of the result of three or four daily observations. But as common Thermometers only were used, the extremes of temperature that occurred may not be always shown, excepting when these extremes were remarkable; in which case, I was very particular in registering them. As all these observations on the temperature, were made at irregular hours of the day and night, they will doubtless afford a very close approximation to the mean temperature. All the thermometers used, were graduated according to Fahrenheit's scale.

For the sake of brevity, in the two columns of " *Winds*," I have distinguished the progressive veering of the

wind between two points, and the progressive change
between two denominations of strength or "*force*," by the
intervention of the particle *to*. Thus when the wind is
marked as having blown from east *to* north, it must be understood to have either veered from the former to the latter, or to have fluctuated between the two extremes; or, in
most instances, to have blown from every intermediate point.
And the same application of the word *to*, has been used to
connect the winds of two contiguous days. Thus on the
24th of April 1807, the wind is registered " N W to E b N,"
and on the following day, " to N;" that is, on the former
day, N. W. progressively to N. N. E., and as far as E. by N.;
and, on the latter, from E. b N. back again to N. On the
other hand, on April 11th, the wind stands E. S. E., E. N. E.
In this case, the change of wind from E. S. E. to E. N. E.
has been sudden, and not progressive, as in the cases where
the particle *to* is placed intermediately. It may also be
right to mention, that whatever may be the interval between two points connected by the particle *to*, the change
in the wind has always been performed in the shortest way
round the compass. Thus April 20. 1811, the wind is
registered W. S. W. to N. N. E.; that is, from W. S. W.
towards the W., N. W., N. and N. N. E., and not from
W. S. W. to S., S. E., E. and N. N. E., because the interval
in the latter instance is above a semicircle.

In the register for May 1818, are introduced two additional columns under " *Thermometer*;" showing the relative temperature of the air near the deck, and of the mast-
head, 90 feet higher, or 106 feet above the surface of the
water. The mean temperature by the deck thermometer,
is 23°.6; but of the mast-head thermometer, the mean is
20°.3, being 3°.3 lower. As this reduction of temperature
is greater by 2°.3 than what is supposed to be the simple
effect of elevation, it may perhaps be occasioned by the comparative warmth of the water, or the radiation of heat from
the ship. If the latter be the cause, the mean results of
the thermometric observations given in the following Table, will be somewhat too high. The figures in the " mast-
head" column of this register, having this mark † prefix-
ed to them, are not actual observations, but are derived
from estimation, by the application of the usual difference
between the temperature of the mast-head and that of the
deck.

In the last six years journals, the state of the Barometer marked each day, is inclusive between the noon

of that and the noon of the preceding day, or an interval corresponding with the day by nautical computation; consequently the " medium" column represents the state of the Barometer (nearly) on the first mid-night, or beginning of each day.

The registers of the first six years, from 1807 to 1812 inclusive, have already been laid before the Public, in the " Memoirs of the Wernerian Natural History Society * " As, on comparison with the present series, there will appear some dissimilarity, to prevent a hasty censure of inconsistency, some explanation seems proper. The " latitudes," " longitudes," " force of wind," and " meteors," as published in the Wernerian Memoirs, will be found to agree with this series, excepting so far as the necessary abridgment in the remarks on the weather, may have caused some things to appear in the one, which do not appear in the other. The thermometrical observations in this series, though extended in their plan, and carried to decimals of a degree in the column " medium," will be found to correspond, as nearly as possible, with the column headed " Thermometer," in the Wernerian Memoirs, excepting in the case of three or four trifling typographical errors, and a few instances where the fractions of a degree had been omitted ; the fraction of one day in excess compensating for the deficiency of a similar fraction on a subsequent day. The means of the two series, however, will be found the same. The plan of the barometrical register being now also altered and extended, occasions some dissimilarity between the two series. The apparent difference is thus produced. In the registers in the Wernerian Memoirs, the state of the Barometer at noon, only is given; but having, in my original journals, inserted the highest and lowest of the mercury at every change, I have been enabled now to give the extremes of pressure during each day, for every year, excepting the first three. Hence, though some of the daily observations seem to disagree in the two series, the means of each month are not essentially different. The direction of the winds will appear to be totally different throughout the two series. This arises from the winds in the Tables first published being quoted according to the magnetic meridian, while those now presented to the public, have, by the application of the variation, been reduced to the true meridian.

---

* Vol. i. p. 249. and 609;—and vol. ii. p. 155, and 167.

No. II.—METEOROLOGICAL RESULTS. —*Table A.*

Year.	Month.	N° of Days.	Extremes of Latitude.	Mean Latitude.	Extremes of Longitude.	OBSERVATION N° of Observ.	Mean Temp.	Maximum.
1807,	April,	30	60. 9—75.36	66°.54	6°.36'W, 13° 10'E	30	33.77	55
1808,	——	30	65.11—76.20	71.49	6.40 W, 10.40 E	29	23.77	36
1811,	——	30	69.40—77. 8	73.34	3.31 W, 16.32 E	89	21.48	37
1813,	——	30	60. 9—80.10	73.12	1. 8 W, 11.18 E	90	26.24	50
1815,	——	30	61.52—78.30	74.34	0.21 W, 10.20 E	94	25.43	55
1816,	——	30	59.10—77. 0	71.43	2. 0 W, 9. 48 E	87	29.12	45
1817,	——	30	54.29—78.23	69.13	1.20 W, 13.22 E	86	29.20	56
1807,	May,	31	74.26—76. 2	75.45	7. 3 E, 12.20 E	31	22.84	34
1808,	——	31	76. 6—78.37	77.48	5. 0 E, 9. 0 E	31	25.64	32
1809,	——	31	73.38—79. 0	75.49	5.40 E, 23. 0 E	31	22.52	36
1810,	——	31	76.58—79.20	78.21	2.50 E, 10.10 E	89	18.30	36
1811,	——	31	76.46—78.34	77.26	5.35 E, 9.50 E	93	19.71	33
1812,	——	31	72.38—76.37	75.30	8. 8 E, 15.13 E	96	23.97	34
1813,	——	31	77. 9—79.54	78.24	1.10 E, 8.15 E	93	22.39	32
1814,	——	31	76.46—78.20	77.43	0. 0 E, 8.30 E	98	20.64	34
1815,	——	31	76.40—78.45	77.46	3.15 E, 9.40 E	100	21.90	34
1816,	——	31	77. 4 – 79.55	78.49	4.50 E, 10.30 E	100	24.57	40
1817,	——	31	75.12—80. 5	77. 7	11.20 W, 5.50 E	94	27.48	38
1818,	——	31	70.50—78.36	76.55	6.50 W, 6.20 E	100	23.80	32
1807—1818, General mean of 12 years observations in May, Sums & Extremes,		†372	(70.50—80. 5)	77.17	— —	†956	22.81	34.6 (40
1809,	June,	30	77.40—79.57	79. 7	5. 4 E, 7.10 E	30	29.96	35
1810,	——	30	70.50—78.34	77.11	3. 0 E, 12.30 E	72	29.12	39
1811,	——	30	78. 0—79.20	78.35	5. 0 E, 8. 0 E	88	31.15	38
1812,	——	30	77.14—79.26	78.19	5.27 E, 9. 5 E	92	29.99	37
1813,	——	30	77.25—78.54	78.23	3.38 E, 6.20 E	90	34.15	48
1814,	——	30	77.45—79. 0	78.27	4. 0 E, 7.30 E	95	31.83	40
1815,	——	30	75.47—79.15	77.45	2.55 E, 8. 0 E	91	30.86	40
1816,	——	30	78. 6—80. 1	79. 6	2. 5 W, 6.50 E	91	33.87	45
1817,	——	30	76. 4—78.34	77.39	5.40 W, 1. 0 E	92	31.09	43
1818,	——	30	75.10—70.30	78. 0	8. 0 W, 4.22 E	90	30.95	40
1809—1818, General mean of 10 years observations in June, Sums and Extremes,		†300	(70.50—80. 1)	78.15	(8.0 W, 12.30 E)	†831	31.297	40.5 (48.
1812,	July,	31	68.24—78.58	77. 0	1 7 E, 6.48 E	96	34.28	45
1813,	——	31	67.10—78.20	75.21	1. 0 E, 10.56 E	94	40.97	62
1814,	——	31	62.45—80.25	74.32	0.10 W, 10.35 E	94	41.62	58
1815,	——	31	58. 6—76.57	70.21	2. 0 W, 14.40 E	92	43.62	58
1817,	——	31	73.27 – 76.20	75. 8	10.37 W, 13.10 E	95	36.79	45
1818,	——	31	74.20—79.22	77.30	9. 0 W, 9.55 E	96	36.30	48

N. B.—Those sums marked thus †, are not means, but the general amount of all the

* Where this mark occurs in the column of " remarkable variations," the change or variation
because, in several of the instances, these extremes occurred in different days, or because the

Abstract of the preceding Series of Meteorological Tables.

| | NS ON THE THERMOMETER | | | | OBSERVATIONS ON THE BAROMETER | | | | | | | | |
Mini-mum.	Range.	Date.	Inter-val.	Quan-tity.	Mean Presure.	Maxi-mum.	Mini-mum.	Range.	Date.	Inter-val.	Quan-tity.	Spaces de-scribed.	Spaces p. day.
			Hou.	Deg.				Inch.					
16	39	9	12	12	29.730	30.16	29.21	0 95	17	24	0.55	5.46	0.182
9	27	*25	16	13	29.736	30.48	28.03	2.45	*4	24	0.92	7.24	0.241
5	32	*19-20	18	22	30.006	30.47	29.50	0.97	*3	12	0.50	4.88	0.163
—4	54	24	22	24	29.538	30.35	28.70	1.65	*13	12	1.02	10.69	0.356
+6	49	*10	15	19	29.718	30.33	28.79	1.54	29	20	0.80	9.42	0.314
12	33	*15-16	9	20	29.730	30.36	29.35	1.01	14-15	16	0,53	6.37	0.212
4	52	3	7	12	29.840	30.72	28.75	1.97	18-19	21	1.12	9.35	0.312
14	20	8	22	14	29.851	30.31	29.46	0.85	12-13	24	0.33	2.44	0.079
18	14	*11	14	8	29.806	30.54	29.23	1.31	11-12	24	0.72	4.55	0.147
10	26	4	24	16	29.876	30.20	29.35	0.85	5-6	24	0.62	4.94	0.159
8	28	31	11	16	29.945	30.40	29.47	0 93	7-8	24	0.50	4.94	0.159
5	28	13	15	20	29.928	30.17	29.63	0.54	22-23	24	0.38	3.82	0.123
10	24	18	10	13	29.931	30.37	29.40	0.97	2	12	0.77	5,02	0.162
12	20	3	9	15	29,782	30.20	29.34	0.86	3	24	0.50	4.27	0.138
7	27	11	12	20	30.019	30.51	29.40	1.11	4	24	0.40	4.22	0.136
8	26	18	10	15	30.046	30.57	29.66	0.91	2	24	0.44	3.59	0.116
8	32	14	14	14	29.844	30.20	29.37	0.83	25	12	0.43	4.94	0.159
10	28	15-16	24	16	29.926	30.25	29.39	0.86	16	12	0.40	5.08	0.164
12	20	8	14	13	29.953	30.54	29.30	1.24	27-28	24	0.48	5.19	0.167
10.2	24.4				29.909	30,36	29.42	0.94	—	—			0.142
5	35)	(11,1814	12	20)	—	(30.57	29.23	1.34)	(2.1812	12	0.77)	†53.00	—
22	13	20	20	15	29.873	30.24	29.50	0.74	18	24	0.28	2·90	0.097
15	24	5	10	12	29.865	30.25	29.60	0.65	*1	24	0.57	3.94	0.131
22	16	5	8	11	29.823	30.10	29.50	0.60	27-28	24	0.41	2.67	0.089
23	14	10	8	8	29.861	30.37	29.50	0.87	24-25	24	0.40	3.47	0.116
25	23	9	10	13	29.993	30.30	29.67	0.63	9	24	0.45	2.97	0.099
21	19	13	8	10	29.841	30.11	29.42	0.69	12	24	0.42	5.23	0.174
16	24	2-3	20	17	29.878	30.21	29 34	0.87	30	24	0.40	3.75	0.125
·27	18	10	9	13	29.813	30.36	29.42	0.94	22	24	0.30	3.65	0.122
20	23	18-19	14	10	29.908	30.25	29.50	0.75	13	24	0.35	3.38	0.113
23	17	11-12	15	10	29.840	30.30	29.25	1.05	8	·24	0.71	4.54	0.151
21.4	19.1				29.869	30.25	29.47	0.79					0.122
15	33)	(10.1816	9	13)	—	(30.37	29.25	1.12)	(8.1818	24	0.71)	†36.50	—
31	14	*13	12·	9	29.906	30.32	29.40	0.92	*17	24	0.50	3.89	0.125
33	29	1	12	11	29.825	30.30	29.50	0.80	4	24	0.45	4.98	0.161
30	28	15	14	16	29.836	30.17	29.32	0.85	31	8	0.42	5.31	0.171
28	30	14	16	12	29.945	30.27	29.66	0.61	20	24	0.23	2.49	0.080
31	14	6	10	10	29.851	30.08	29.65	0.43	24	12	0.19	2.17	0.070
28	·20	21	13	12	29.883	30.10	29.38	0.72	29	12	0.63	4.84	0.156

observations in the respective columns; and those in parentheses are neither means nor sums, referred to, will not appear in the preceding Tables, because the time of the day in which the remarkable variation occurred before the commencement of the journal in the series of Tables.

Abstract of the preceding Series of Meteorological Tables.

| | NS ON THE THERMOMETER. | | | | OBSERVATIONS ON THE BAROMETER. | | | | | | | | |
Mini-mum.	Range.	Remarkable Variations. Date.	Inter-val.	Quan-tity.	Mean Pressure.	Maxi-mum.	Mini-mum.	Range.	Remarkable Variations. Date.	Inter-val.	Quan-tity.	Spaces de-scribed.	Spaces p. day.
			Hou.	Deg.				Inch.					
16	39	9	12	12	29.730	30.16	29.21	0.95	17	24	0.55	5.46	0.182
9	27	*25	16	13	29.736	30.48	28.03	2.45	*4	24	0.92	7.24	0.241
5	32	*19-20	18	22	30.006	30.47	29.50	0.97	*3	12	0.50	4.88	0.163
—4	54	24	22	24	29.538	30.35	28.70	1.65	*13	12	1.02	10.69	0.356
+6	49	*10	15	19	29.718	30.33	28.79	1.54	29	20	0.80	9.42	0.314
12	33	*15-16	9	20	29.730	30.36	29.35	1.01	14-15	16	0.53	6.37	0.212
4	52	3	7	12	29.840	30.72	28.75	1.97	18-19	21	1.12	9.35	0.312
14	20	8	22	14	29.851	30.31	29.46	0.85	12-13	24	0.33	2.44	0.079
18	14	*11	14	8	29.806	30.54	29.23	1.31	11-12	24	0.72	4.55	0.147
10	26	4	24	16	29.876	30.20	29.35	0.85	5-6	24	0.62	4.94	0.159
8	28	31	11	16	29.945	30.40	29.47	0.93	7-8	24	0.60	4.94	0.159
5	28	13	15	20	29.928	30.17	29.63	0.54	22-23	24	0.38	3.82	0.123
10	24	18	10	13	29.931	30.37	29.40	0.97	2	12	0.77	5.02	0.162
12	20	3	9	15	29.782	30.20	29.34	0.86	3	24	0.50	4.27	0.138
7	27	11	12	20	30.019	30.51	29.40	1.11	4	24	0.40	4.22	0.136
8	26	18	10	15	30.046	30.57	29.66	0.91	2	24	0.44	3.59	0.116
8	32	14	14	14	29.844	30.20	29.37	0.83	25	12	0.43	4.94	0.159
10	28	15-16	24	16	29.926	30.25	29.39	0.86	16	12	0.40	5.08	0.164
12	20	8	14	13	29.953	30.54	29.30	1.24	27-28	24	0.48	5.19	0.167
10.2	24.4				29.909	30.36	29.42	0.94		—	—		0.142
5	35)	(11,1814	12	20)	—	(30.57	29.23	1.34)	(2.1812	12	0.77)	†53.00	—
22	13	20	20	15	29.873	30.24	29.50	0.74	18	24	0.28	2.90	0.097
15	24	5	10	12	29.865	30.25	29.60	0.65	*1	24	0.57	3.94	0.131
22	16	5	8	11	29.823	30.10	29.50	0.60	27-28	24	0.41	2.67	0.089
23	14	10	8	8	29.861	30.37	29.50	0.87	24-25	24	0.40	3.47	0.116
25	23	9	10	13	29.993	30.30	29.67	0.63	9	24	0.45	2.97	0.099
21	19	13	8	10	29.841	30.11	29.42	0.69	12	24	0.42	5.23	0.174
16	24	2-3	20	17	29.878	30.21	29 34	0.87	30	24	0.40	3.75	0.125
27	18	10	9	13	29.813	30.36	29.42	0.94	22	24	0.30	3.65	0.122
20	23	18-19	14	10	29.908	30.25	29.50	0.75	13	24	0.35	3.38	0.113
23	17	11-12	15	10	29.840	30.30	29.25	1.05	8	24	0.71	4.54	0.151
21.4	19.1				29.869	30.25	29.47	0.79					0.122
15	33)	(10.1816	9	13)	—	(30.37	29.25	1.12)	(8.1818	24	0.71)	†36.50	—
31	14	*13	12	9	29.906	30.32	29.40	0.92	*17	24	0.50	3.89	0.125
33	29	1	12	11	29.825	30.30	29.50	0.80	4	24	0.45	4.98	0.161
30	28	15	14	16	29.836	30.17	29.32	0.85	31	8	0.42	5.31	0.171
28	30	14	16	12	29.945	30.27	29.66	0.61	20	24	0.23	2.49	0.080
31	14	6	10	10	29.851	30.08	29.65	0.43	24	12	0.19	2.17	0.070
28	20	21	13	12	29.883	30.10	29.38	0.72	29	12	0.63	4.84	0.156

observations in the respective columns; and those in parentheses are neither means nor sums,

referred to, will not appear in the preceding Tables, because the time of the day in which the remarkable variation occurred before the commencement of the journal in the series of Tables.

OBSERVATIONS on the WINDS.

N° of Changes.	N b W to N N E	N E b N to E N E	E b N to E S E	S E b E to S S E	S b E to S S W	S W b S to W S W	W b S to W N W	N W b W to N N W	Variable.	Calm.	Brisk. Days.	Strong. Days.	Boisterous.	N° of Da.	N° of wet Days.
13	9.8	5.5	1.7	0.6	4.6	2.2	2.0	1.6	1.2	0.8	9	3	4	9	17
13	5.2	7.8	5.0	0.8	1.5	0.6	2.6	5.5	0.5	0.5	2	8	5	11.5	18
13	4.6	5.9	1.9	1.3	2.6	2.5	3.6	3.2	2.0	2.4	4	8	8	7	22
15	5.6	2.5	3.1	1.3	3.6	2.3	1.3	4.7	2.6	3.0	2	5.5	10	15.5	24
20	5.7	1.5	2.6	2.2	4.3	3.1	4.2	0.7	3.2	2.5	4	5	8	10.5	22
23	4.2	4.2	6.1	4.3	1.6	0.4	0.4	4.6	2.6	1.6	3.5	5	8	11	28
21	6.9	3.6	0.9	0.4	2.5	3.5	2.9	4.9	2.3	2.1	3.7	4.5	8	12.5	24
15	11.0	4.8	—	—	1.1	1.6	3.7	6.1	1.5	1.2	10	7	1	1	11
15	4.0	1.8	4.4	1.9	1.5	1.9	1.4	7.6	2.2	4.3	4	7	2	2	22
13	7.8	4.1	4.1	2.2	1.4	2.0	2.9	5.1	0.9	0.5	5	7	5	6	17
15	11.1	4.8	0.9	0.8	1.9	1.1	1.4	6.0	1.8	1.2	4	9	6	6.5	25
14	6.2	3.5	2.2	1.9	0.8	0.8	3.8	9.6	1.3	0.9	3.5	6.5	4	7.5	24
13	7.0	2.7	2.8	1.9	1.2	0.5	1.2	8.0	3.9	1.8	2.8	5.4	4	10.5	18
17	6.2	4.6	0.8	1.8	2.3	2.3	2.8	5.4	3.2	1.6	8	7.5	4	6.	16
13	12.8	4.0	1.9	2.0	1.0	1.4	1.6	3.6	1.1	1.6	6	7.	6	7.	20
16	6.6	0.4	0.4	2.0	1.3	2.5	2.2	6.9	5.9	2.8	2.5	5.0	4	5.5	18
19	3.9	1.1	0.2	7.5	9.1	1.4	1.1	3.4	2.1	1.2	1.6	7.4	5	8.8	23
16	8.0	6.4	3.9	4.6	1.2	0.4	0.7	2.3	1.5	2.0	4.0	5	3	4.5	24
13	4.6	6.3	2.7	1.1	2.2	2.6	2.8	3.1	3.4	2.2	2.5	5	5	8.5	18
†179	7.4	3.7	2.0	2.3	2.1	1.6	2.1	5.6	2.4	1.8	4.5	6.6	4.1	6.1	19.7
10	2.2	3.7	2.0	4.7	3.9	2.8	2.0	1.3	4.6	2.8	5	3	1	1	22
16	4.3	1.4	1.3	1.4	4.7	2.5	4.0	6.4	1.4	2.6	1.5	5	2	1.5	19
15	6.6	2.7	2.3	2.3	3.6	1.2	1.2	1.7	5.3	3.1	5.5	3	1	1	25
17	10.5	2.4	0.5	2.8	2.7	1.3	2.3	5.2	1.4	0.9	8.0	4.5	6	6	20
16	4.7	1.6	—	2.9	5.4	4.7	1.0	4.7	1.3	3.7	4.5	5.0	3	3.5	29
23	2.6	0.7	2.5	4.2	8.3	4.7	1.2	1.6	2.5	1.7	5.0	6.5	5	4.0	24
18	5.7	1.3	0.5	2.6	3.2	3.5	1.9	5.8	3.1	2.4	3.5	6.5	4	2.5	22
12	3.8	1.6	1.1	2.0	3.5	6.1	1.8	1.6	4.1	4.4	4.0	5	2	2	28
15	4.7	0.7	0.7	1.6	4.9	1.1	1.6	7.4	5.6	1.7	3.4	3	4	8.3	21
9	5.3	2.5	3.1	2.9	3.0	3.9	1.2	3.1	3.0	2.0	5.0	4	3	3.5	29
15.1 †151	5.1	1.9	1.4	2.7	4.3	3.2	1.8	3.9	3.2	2.5	4.5	4.6	3.1	3.3	239
13	5.2	6.1	4.4	1.0	3.5	3.2	1.2	3.6	1.3	1.5	6.5	4.5	4	6	29
17	1.1	0.5	0.7	2.3	8.1	7.7	2.4	1.4	3.0	3.8	4.3	8.3	4	3.8	27
16	0.7	0.4	1.3	2.6	7.9	5.6	2.3	1.0	3.8	5.4	3.	6.5	3	5	28
9	4.4	3.5	1.6	—	1.4	2.3	4.5	6.7	3.7	2.9	5.5	5.5	1	1	21
15	1.2	1.3	1.0	1.1	5.6	8.5	3.8	1.2	3.6	3.7	9.0	3.5	1	0.5	28
15	3.4	0.9	1.5	1.9	6.5	4.3	0.9	1.9	3.2	6.5	5.5	3.0	4	2.5	26

but the extremes or the most remarkable observations in the whole period,

barometer and thermometer were in certain extremes, is not registered therein ;

TABLE B.

For Determining the mean ANNUAL TEMPERATURE of LATITUDE 78°N, and of the NORTH POLE.

Year.	Interval.	No. of Days.	Thermom. N° of Obs.	Thermom. Sum.	Latitudes. Sum.	N b W to N N E.	N E b N to E N E.	E b N to E S E.	S E b E to S S E.	S b E to S S W.	S W b S to W S W.	W b S to W N W.	N W b W to N N W.	Variable.	Calm.
1804,	April 13. to May 12.	30	30	539°	2311°.7'	3.9	2.9	2.8	1.6	0.8	1.3	3.6	7.1	4.0	2.0
1807,	23. to Apr. 30.	8	8	181	602.3	4.6	1.8	0.4	—	—	0.7	0.3	0.2	—	—
1808,	25. to Apr. 30.	6	6	83	457.47	1.0	2.8	—	—	—	—	1.8	0.4	—	—
1810,	9. to May 16.	38	116	610	2911.59	11.0	5.0	5.1	0.6	0.2	0.7	3.9	5.7	3.6	2.2
1811,	1. to May 24.	84	161	1089	4060.7	7.4	9.4	4.1	3.2	3.4	3.3	7.4	9.4	3.1	3.3
1813,	15. to May 10.	26	78	523	2053.16	4.0	4.4	1.9	1.2	2.7	2.8	1.6	1.6	3.4	2.4
1815,	10. to May 14.	35	113	617	2731.45	8.3	0.9	0.8	1.6	1.7	3.2	4.5	6.8	5.0	2.2
1816,	10. to May 14.	35	108	772	2668.41	9.8	5.3	3.8	4.3	0.8	0.7	1.2	4.9	2.9	1.3
1817,	21. to Apr. 30.	10	30	150	776.10	1.8	1.5	0.8	—	—	0.5	0.9	4.1	0.2	0.2
Sums,		242	656	4564	18572.55	51.8	34.0	19.7	12.5	9.6	13.2	25.2	40.2	22.2	13.6
Means,				18.86	76.45										
Correction for 1°15' of Latitude, See p. 357 of this Volume,				-1.86	+ 1.15										
Mean Temperat. of the year, Lat. 78°,				17.00	78.00										

For the application of this Table to the determination of the Mean Annual Temperature of the North Pole, see p. 363 of this Volume.

TABLE C.

Containing a combination of Meteorological Results for ascertaining the Mean Temperature of the Atmosphere in the Greenland Sea in the month of APRIL, Latitude 78° N.

Year.	Interval.	Nº of Days.	Thermometer. Nº of Obs.	Thermometer. Sum.	Latitudes Sum.
1808,	25 to 30	6	6	83°.0	457°.47'
1810,	9 — 30	28	67	324.2	1666.32
1811,	1 — 30	30	89	644.3	2207.00
1813,	15 — 30	16	48	293.8	1260 30
1815,	10 — 30	21	67	399.5	1632.36
1816,	10 — 30	21	63	509.4	1572.44
1817,	21 — 30	10	30	149.6	776.10
Sum, -		126	370	2403.3	9573.19
Mean, 21st—22d day,				19.07	75.59
Correction for 6 days beyond the middle of the month, -				—1.84	—
Correction for 2° 1' of Latitude; see p. 357. of this Volume, -				—3.00	+2.1
Mean Temp. of APRIL, Lat. 78°, -				14.23	78.0

TABLE D.

Containing a combination of Meteorological Results for ascertaining the Mean Temperature of the Atmosphere in the Greenland Sea in the month of JULY, Latitude 78° N.

Year.	Interval.	Nº of Days.	Thermometer. Nº of Obs.	Thermometer. Sum.	Latitudes Sum.
1777*,	1 to 31	31	86	1272°	2481°.01'
1812,	1 — 31	31	96	1063	2387.15
1813,	1 — 22	22	70	802	1702.00
1814,	1 — 16	16	48	569	1267.49
1815,	1 — 19	19	57	720	1420.52
1817,	1 — 31	31	95	1140	2328.56
1818,	1 — 31	31	96	1125	2402.28
Sum, -		181	548	6691	13990.21
Mean, 13th to 14th day,				36.97	77.18
Correction for 2¼ days short of the middle of the month, -				+0.31	—
Correction for 42' of Latitude; see p. 358. of this Volume,				—0.28	+0.42
Mean Temp. of JULY, Latitude 78°, -				37.00	78.00

* The results for the year 1777 are derived from the thermometrical observations of Captain Phipps, contained in his "Voyage towards the North Pole."

TABLE E.

Abstract of Thermometrical Observations made at the Apartments of the Royal Society of London.

[*Referred to* p. 287. & 356.]

Month.	Mean Temperature.			Mean Temperature.		
	By 20 years Observation.	By Calculation, formula Table G.	Difference.	By 37 years Observation.	By Calculation, formula Table G.	Difference.
January,........	37°.4	37°.4	0°.0	37°.3	37°.3	0°.0
February,....	40.2	38.6	1.6	41.2	38.5	2.7
March,.........	42.2	42.3	0.1	43.4	42.3	1.1
April,.....	48.1	47.6	0.5	48.8	47.7	1.1
May,.	55.5	54.1	1.4	55.7	54.4	1.3
June, ...	59.8	60.0	0.2	60.7	60.4	0.3
July, ...	63.6	63.6	0.0	64.1	64.1	0.0
August,........	63.6	62.1	1.5	64.3	62.6	1.7
September,....	59.1	57.3	1.8	58.8	57.7	1.1
October,.......	51.6	50.8	0.8	51.8	51.0	0.8
November,....	43.6	44.7	1.1	43.8	44.9	1.1
December, ...	39.7	40.2	0.5	40.0	40.2	0.2
Annual Mean,	50.4	49.9	0.5	50.8	50.1	0.7

Explanation.—Column 2d contains the Mean Monthly Temperature, as derived from 20 years' observations, made between the years 1795 and 1814 inclusive. Column 3d is the Calculated Temperature by the formula in Table G, founded on the ratio of increase and decrease of temperature, as obtained from 50 years' observations at Stockholm. In the use of this formula, the temperatures of January and July are all the data requisite. Column 4th is the difference between the calculated and observed temperatures, which, it will be observed, in no instance amounts to 2 degrees. Column 5th contains the Mean Monthly Temperature from 37 years' observations, viz. from 1772 to 1780 inclusive, and from 1787 to 1814 inclusive. Columns 6th and 7th are of the same nature as the 3d and 4th. The greatest difference of the calculated and observed temperatures, month of February (in which there is possibly some error) excepted, is 1°.7, and the average difference is 0°.7.

TABLE F.

Containing an Abstract of 50 years Observations on the Temperature of Stockholm, collated for the purpose of ascertaining the ratio of Increase and Decrease of Temperature with the Advance of the Year.

[Latitude of Stockholm 59° 20′ 31″; Longitude 18° 3′ 51″ E.]

| Month. | Probable mean temperat. of the penthemeron, the middle day of which is the 1st of the month. | Probable mean temperature of each month. | | Decimals of difference of temperat. between January and July. | Mean temperature of each month by Observation. [Fahrenh.] |
		Celsius' Scale.	Fahren. Scale.		
January,.......	— 4.350	— 5.167	22.70	0.000	23.79
February,.....	— 5.216	— 4.169	24.49	0.044 —	25.19
March,.........	— 2.783	— 0.910	30.36	0.188 —	28.11
April,..........	+ 1.318	+ 3.655	38.59	0.388 +	38.37
May,...........	6.407	9.367	48.87	0.639 +	48.63
June,..........	12.273	14.452	58.01	0.861 +	58.69
July,..........	16.483	17.640	63.75	1.000	63.79
August,.......	17.838	16.381	61.48	0.944	61.45
September,....	14.469	12.159	53.89	0.759 —	53.37
October,.......	9.441	6.504	43.70	0.512 +	43.89
November,....	3.563	1.303	34.34	0.283 —	34.67
December,....	0.931	— 2.715	27.10	0.107 —	27.36
Annual Mean,			42.27		

[This Table is referred to in p. 287. 290. 356. & 359.]

This Abstract is derived from an interesting Table in the "Annals of Philosophy," vol. i. p. 113. The last column is the result of 54.750 observations. But as the ratio of increase of temperature from January to July, and the ratio of decrease from July to January, are not exactly regular, the 2d, 3d and 4th columns are taken from the application of the nearest regular ratio to the actual observations, and are considered as being the probable result of the thermometric observations, had they been conducted through a series of several centuries. The difference between the temperature of January and that of July being considered as 1.000, column the 5th shows the proportionate difference between the temperature of January and that of any other month in the year. By the use of these decimals, in connection with the formulæ in the next table, the mean temperature of any month, in any country situated to the northward of the 50th degree of latitude, may be calculated, provided the temperature of the months of January and July, or the mean temperature of the year and that of July be known.

G.

Formula referred to in p. 288, and 358.

Let the mean temperature of the year be called   T
The mean temperature of January,   - b
The mean temperature of July,   - c
The mean temperature of April,   -   - d
And the mean temperature of any other month, t

Then $\overline{c-T} \times 1.907 = cb$.

   or, $c - (\overline{c-T} \times 1.907) = b$.

   $(\overline{c-T} \times 0.172) - T = d$.

   $(\overline{c-b} \times 0.044) + b = t$ February.

   $(\overline{c-b} \times 0.188) + b = t$ March.

And $(\overline{c-b} \times$ decimal col. 5. Table F) $+ b = t$ of the corresponding month; that is, the difference between the mean temperature of January and that of July, multiplied into any decimal of Table F (column 5.), and the amount added to the temperature of January, gives the temperature of the month with which the decimal used corresponds.

Example.—The mean annual temperature of latitude 78° N. is by observation 17°, and the temperature of July 37°; required the mean temperature of January, and of the succeeding months?

Then, (by formula 2d), $37 - (37 - 17 = 20 \times 1.907) =$ — 0°.86, or nearly one degree below zero, the temperature of January.

And, (formula 4th), temperature of July 37°
      Temperature of January, say — 1

Difference, - 38 × 0.044	= 1.67
Temperature of January, (add) -	— 1.00
Mean temperature of February, -	0.67

By these formulæ the following table of the mean monthly temperature of the Greenland Sea, latitude 78°, was calculated.

	Jan.	Feb.	Mar.	April	May	June	July	Aug.	Sept.	Oct.	Nov.	Dec.
Temp. by Calculation,	−1,0	0.7	6.1	13.7	23.3	31.7	37.0	34.9	27.8	18.5	9.0	3.1
Temp. by Observation,	—	—	—	14.2	22.5	31.4	37.0	—	—	—	—	—

By the application of these formulæ, the approximate change of temperature through the course of the year, in London, in Stockholm, and in the Spitzbergen Sea, having been calculated, the curve described by the monthly differences in each place is laid down in Plate II. fig. 3. together with the irregular curve, (the dotted lines), representing the progressive changes of temperature by observation.

No. III. a.

CHRONOLOGICAL ENUMERATION OF VOYAGES UNDERTAKEN BY THE DIFFERENT NATIONS OF THE WORLD IN SEARCH OF A NORTHERN COMMUNICATION BETWEEN THE ATLANTIC AND PACIFIC OCEANS; INCLUDING SUCH OTHER VOYAGES AS HAVE BEEN CONDUCIVE TO THE ADVANCEMENT OF DISCOVERY IN THE NORTH.

ABBREVIATIONS.

Da. Danish.	*F.* French.	*P.* Portugueze.	*Sw.* Swedish.
Du. Dutch.	*Ic.* Icelandic.	*R.* Russian.	*V.* Venetian.
E. English.	*N.* Norwegian.	*Sp.* Spanish.	*W.* Welch.

A. D.

861, *N.* Iceland accidentally discovered by one NADDODD, a Scandinavian pirate, and called by him *Schneeland* or *Snowland*.

864, *Sw.* Iceland visited by a Swede of the name of Gardar Suaffarson, who wintered there.

865 *Sw.* This island was visited again by one Flocke, who na-
to 870,   med it *Iceland*.

874, *N.* Iceland visited by Ingolf and Lief, who formed a settlement there about four years afterwards.

A. D.

Abt 890, *N.* OHTHERE coasted along the west shore of Norway towards the north and east, and discovered the entrance of the *White Sea.*

Abt 970, *Ic. Greenland* discovered by one GUNBIORN.

982, *N.* This country was visited by ERIC RAUDA, who wintered there, and spent part of three years in exploring it. He named it Greenland.

Abt 986, *Ic.* A colonizing voyage undertaken by Eric Rauda to Greenland, with a fleet of 25 vessels, not above one-half of which reached their destination.

1001, *Ic.* BIORN, while on a voyage to Greenland, in search of his father, was driven out of his course by a storm, and accidentally discovered *Winland.*

Abt 1003, *Ic.* Lief, the son of Eric Rauda, with Biorn as pilot, re-visited Winland, and wintered in the country in about the latitude of 50° N.

1006,   *Ic.* Thorwald, the brother of Lief, pursued discoveries in
or   Winland, and in the adjacent country, during three
1008,   years, and then was killed by a party of the natives.

Abt 1010, *Ic.* A voyage to Winland was undertaken by one Thorstein; but being driven upon the coast of Greenland, himself and many of his retinue died.

1170, *W.* Some part of *America* or the *West Indies* said to be discovered by MADOC, son of Owen Guyneth, Prince of North Wales.

Abt 1384, *V.* Nicholas Zeno, in a voyage from Shetland or Feroe, visited the coast of Greenland.

1384,   *Ve.* Antonio Zeno visited Iceland and Greenland, and,
to 1394,   as some suppose, Winland also.

1463,   *P.* John Vaz Costa Cortereal, on a voyage towards the
or   N. W., is said to have discovered the *Terra de Bac-*
1464,   *calhaos,* afterwards named Newfoundland.

1492, *Sp.* COLUMBUS, in a voyage undertaken for the discovery of a western passage to India, discovered the *West Indies.*

1494? *En.* John Cabot and Sebastian his son, are said to have discovered Newfoundland, and called it *Prima Vista* ?

1497, *En. America* discovered by SEBASTIAN CABOT, when on a voyage in search of a N. W. passage to India, and the coast examined from latitude 67½? to 38°.

A. D.

1500. *P.* GASPAR CORTEREAL, with two ships, fitted out for research towards the N. W. visited Greenland and Labrador, and discovered the *River St Lawrence,* together with some islands contiguous to the American
coast.

1501, *P.* Gaspar Cortereal undertook a second voyage in search
of a N. W. passage with two ships; he made the coast
of Greenland, but being separated from his consort in
a storm, was never heard of afterwards.   His consort
returned home safe.

1502, *P.* Michael Cortereal, with three ships, proceeded in search
of his brother Gaspar Cortereal, when himself and
ship's company likewise perished.   The two other ships
under his direction, however, got safe home.

1504, *F.* Newfoundland and Cape Breton visited by the Biscay-
ners and Bretons, for the purpose of fishing.

1506, *F.* Jean Denis, with Camart, a native of Rouen, as pilot,
sailed from Honfleur to Newfoundland, and is said to
have been the first who laid down a chart of this country.

1508, *F.* The coast of Newfoundland examined by one Aubert,
in a ship called the Pensée.

1524, *F.* Juan Verazzani sailed to America, and proceeded along
the coast about 700 leagues.   This part, included
between the parallels of perhaps 30° N. and 56° N.
was named *New France.*

—— *Sp.* Estevan Gomer, towards the N. W.   No discovery appears to have been made.

1527, *En.* Two ships, one of which was called the Dominus Vobiscum, were sent out for discoveries towards the North
Pole.   One of the ships was lost, and little or nothing
accomplished.

1534, *Fr.* Jaques Cartier proceeded in search of a W. or N. W.
passage; sailed up the *Gulf of St Lawrence.*

1535, *Fr.* Jaques Cartier, with three ships, performed a second
voyage up the *River St Lawrence,* which he examined
as high as Montreal.   He wintered in the St Lawrence, where 25 of his crew died of the scurvy.

1536, *En.* A voyage towards the N. W. of the ships Trinitie and
Minion, in which Cape Breton and Newfoundland
were visited.   The crews suffered much from fa-
mine.

2

A. D.

Abt 1537, *Sp.* Francisco Ulloa, under the orders of Cortez, the conqueror of Mexico, appears to have made a voyage, with three ships, for discoveries towards the N. or W. or respecting the Strait of Anian.

1540, *Fr.* Jaques Cartier made a third voyage with five ships, towards the N. W. This, however, was entirely a colonizing expedition. For after remaining two years in North America, he was joined, by appointment, by Roberval, Lieutenant-General and Viceroy of Canada, Newfoundland, Labrador, &c. who established a colony near Quebec.

1542, *Sp.* A journey from Mexico towards the north, undertaken by one Coronado, in search of the Strait of Anian; unsuccessful.

—— *Sp.* Alarcon sent from Mexico in search of the Strait of Anian by sea; unsuccessful.

1542, *Sp.* Juan Rodriguez de Cabrillo, with an object similar to
or   the two last, proceeded along the N. W. coast of Ame-
1544,   rica as high as latitude 44° N.

1553, *En.* Sir HUGH WILLOUGHBY and Richard Chancellor, with three ships, went out for the discovery of foreign countries. Sir H. discovered *Nova Zembla?* and on attempting to winter in Lapland, perished, together with the crews of two of the ships. Chancellor, in the other ship discovered the *White Sea* to near about the *Dwina,* and travelled overland from thence to *Moscow.*

1555, *En.* Richard Chancellor embarked on a trading voyage to the same quarter; he was drowned on his return in 1556.

—— *P.* Martin Chaque: a pretended voyage through North America.

1556, *En.* STEPHEN BURROUGH, proceeded in a small vessel for discovery, &c. towards the N. E. He visited Nova Zembla, and discovered the Island of *Weigats.*

—— *Sp.* Andrea Urdanietta: A pretended voyage.

1564, *Da.* Dithmar Blefkens sailed from Iceland towards the N. E. A feeble attempt.

1576, *En.* MARTIN FROBISHER, with three small vessels, proceeded in search of a N. W. passage; discovered *Frobisher's Strait,* or *Lumley's Inlet,* also the land *Meta Incognita,* and is said to have found gold-ore.

A. D.

1577, *En.* A second voyage was undertaken by Frobisher, in search of a N. W. passage, and gold-ore. Nothing discovered.

—— *En.* Edward Fenton was sent out to attempt the N. W. passage reversed. The voyage was intercepted by enemies.

1578, *En.* Frobisher, with a fleet of 15 ships, proceeded towards the north-west, for forming a settlement, and making discoveries. *Hatton's Headland,* and some other unimportant places, were discovered or visited; but the main objects of the expedition entirely failed. One ship was lost, and ten persons died on the voyage.

1580, *En.* Arthur Pet and Charles Jackman, with two ships, sailed in search of a N. E. passage. One of the ships passed the Weigats Strait; the other, after wintering in Norway, was never heard of.

1582, *Sp.* An attempt was made to reverse the N. W. passage by Francisco Gualle: He sailed from Japan 700 leagues E. N. E. to within 200 leagues of California, and then returned.

1583, *En.* An expedition for colonizing, trading, or making discoveries towards the N. W., was undertaken by Sir Humphrey Gilbert, with five vessels. One vessel, with about 90 men, was lost.

1585, *En.* JOHN DAVIS, with two small vessels, sailed in search of a N. W. passage. He discovered or named the *Land of Desolation, Mount Raleigh, Cumberland Island, Cumberland Strait, Dier's Cape, Cape Walsingham, Cape of God's Mercy, Exeter Sound,* and *Totness Road.*

1586, *En.* A second voyage towards the N. W. for trading and discovery, was undertaken by Davis. He saw more of Greenland and Labrador than any former navigator; but made no discovery of moment. One of his vessels, a pinnace of 10 tons, was lost, and all hands.

1587, *En.* Davis embarked on his third voyage for discovery towards the N. W. On this occasion he discovered *Davis' Strait, London Coast,* &c. and named *Lumley's Inlet, Warwick's Foreland, Cape Chidley,* &c.

1588, *Sp.* A pretended voyage, by Maldonado, through a strait called Anian.

A. D.

1592, *Sp.* Juan de Fuca performed a voyage to the northward along the W. coast of N. America, and imagined he discovered a communication with the Atlantic in an easterly direction.

1594, *Du.* An expedition of four ships under CORNELIS CORNELISON, William Barentz, &c. proceeded in search of a N. E. passage. Some of the ships passed forty leagues beyond Weigats Strait, and Barentz explored the western coast of Nova Zembla.

1595, *Du.* WILLIAM BARENTZ sailed along with another expedition of seven ships, intended for trading and discoveries towards the N. E., which altogether failed.

1596, *Du.* Barentz, on a third voyage, for discovery towards the N. and E., with two ships, discovered *Bear Island,* now called Cherie Island, and *Spitzbergen.* Barentz, with one ship's company, wintered in Nova Zembla; most of his companions got home the next summer in two open boats, but himself and some others died.

—— *Sp.* Sebastiano Vizcaino sailed above 100 leagues to the northward, along the W. coast of America. In one place he lost seventeen men.

1598, *Fr.* The Marquis de la Roche, in a colonizing voyage to the west coast of N. America, made some researches.

1602, *Sp.* Vizcaino, in a second voyage to the west coast of America, sailed as high as 42° or 43° N. in search of harbours.

—— *En.* George Weymouth, with two vessels, for the discovery of a N. W. passage, is said to have sailed 100 leagues to the westward, in a sea nearly corresponding with Hudson's Strait.

1603, *En.* On a voyage towards the N., partly for trading, and partly for discovery, by Stephen Bennet, Bear Island, of Barentz, was visited, and named *Cherie Island.*

1605, *Da.* JAMES HALL, an Englishman, as pilot, and Gotske Lindenau, a Dane, as Admiral of an expedition of three vessels, intended for the recovery of Lost Greenland and research, gave names to several places in Greenland, but discovered nothing.

1606, *Da.* Hall was employed in a second expedition under Lindenau, of five ships, for research, &c. about the coast of Greenland: nothing of consequence was discovered.

A. D.

1606, *En.* In a voyage in search of a N. W. passage, by John Knight, with one small vessel, nothing was discovered : Knight and three of his crew landed on the coast of Labrador, and were never afterwards seen.

1607, *Da.* Hall, in a third voyage, with two ships, in the same direction, only reached Cape Farewell, the crew having mutinied.

—— *En.* HENRY HUDSON, in a voyage towards the North Pole, with one small vessel only, discovered the E. coast of Greenland, as high as latitude 73°. *Young's Cape, Mount of God s Mercy,* and *Hold with Hope,* were positions discovered and named by him : the same voyage he visited Spitzbergen, and sailed to the latitude of about 81°.

1608, *En.* In his second voyage, with one vessel, in search of a N. E. passage, Hudson landed on Nova Zembla.

1609, *Du.* Hudson, in his third voyage, in the Dutch service, sailed to the eastward of the North Cape, then westerly to Newfoundland, and along the American coast to the southward. The design of this curious navigation is not known.

1610, *En.* Hudson's fourth voyage, in search of a N. W. passage, was important. With only one vessel he discovered (?) and passed *Hudson's Strait,* and discovered *Hudson's Bay,* where he wintered. The crew of the vessel afterwards mutinied, and forcing Hudson and eight other persons into a boat, left them to perish.

—— *En.* In a voyage for trade and discovery towards the N. by JONAS POOLE, *Horn Sound, Deer Sound,* and some other positions in Spitzbergen, were discovered and named. The whole of the country he named *Greenland.*

1611, *Du.* A voyage by a ship belonging to Holland, is said to
or   have been made about this time, in which a distance
1614,   of 100 leagues to the eastward of Nova Zembla was
            accomplished (?)

1611, *Du.* The island of *Jan Mayen* is stated to have been discovered in this year, by the person whose name it bears : it is probable, however, that the discovery was not made until a year or two later.

—— *En.* A voyage towards the north, with two vessels, the principal object of which was to attempt the whale fishery, was undertaken by Jonas Pool ; he sailed to lati-

A. D.

tude 80° N. and also to the S. W., from thence until he was 125 leagues to the westward of Cherie Island. Both ships were lost, but the crews were saved. Great part of the W. coast of Spitzbergen was examined, and some bays discovered.

1611, *En.* Our whale-fishers, in their early voyages, had generally
to a discovery-vessel along with them. Their researches
1620, about the coast were productive of several discoveries, among which, besides bays, harbours and headlands, were *Hope, Bear, Abbot's, Edge's, Scott's, Wester, Heling, Sir Thomas Smith's,* and various other islands.

1612, *En.* Sir Thomas Button, with two ships, sailed in search of a N. W. passage by the way of Hudson's Bay. He discovered *Nelson's River, Southampton Island, Mancel's Island,* &c. and gave names to several remarkable headlands.

—— *En.* James Hall embarked towards the N. W. for the discovery of a passage or treasure, being his fourth voyage, and was killed by an Esquimaux. *Cockin Sound* discovered.

1614, *En.* Captain Gibbons, in attempting to find a N. W. passage, got beset, and spent the season in a bay in Labrador: this place is said to have been named in derision " *Gibbons his Hole.*"

—— *En.* Robert Fotherby, having along with him the celebrated Baffin, attempted discoveries in the north and about Spitzbergen; but nothing of consequence was accomplished.

1615, *En.* ROBERT BYLOT, with Baffin as mate, attempted the finding of a N. W. passage. Discovered *Savage Islands, Mill Island,* &c. about Hudson's Bay and Strait.

1616, *En.* WILLIAM BAFFIN, appointed as pilot to a small vessel, of which Bylot was master, in searching for a N. W. passage, discovered and circumnavigated the bay bearing his name. Among other discoveries in this bay that are enumerated, are *Women's Islands, Horn Sound, Sir Dudley Digges' Cape, Wostenholm Sound, Whale Sound, Hakluyt's Island, Sir Thomas Smith's Sound, Carey's Islands, Alderman Jones' Sound, Sir James Lancaster's Sound,* &c.

A. D.

1617, *En. Wiches Land,* afterwards named by the Dutch Ryke Yse's Islands, discovered by one of the English whale fishers.

1619, *Da.* Two vessels, under the direction of Jens Munk, were sent out for the discovery of a N. W. passage. They wintered in Hudson's Bay, where all the people, sixty-four in number, excepting Munk and two others, are stated to have died of the scurvy. These three accomplished their passage home in the smaller vessel.

1620? *En.* In a voyage towards the N. W. by William Hawk-bridge, considerable researches in Hudson's Bay appear to have been made, but nothing was discovered The year in which this voyage was made, and the ships employed in it, are uncertain.

1631, *En.* A considerable exploration of Hudson's Bay was made by LUKE FOX, in which names were given to various islands, promontories and bays. Among the islands, he named *Sir Thomas Rowe's Welcome, Brooke Cobham, Briggs his Mathematics,* &c. among headlands, *Cape Maria, Cape Dorchester, King Charles his Promontorie,* &c.

—— *En.* A similar route to that taken by Fox, was pursued by THOMAS JAMES who passed the winter in Hudson's Bay, yet discovered nothing.

1636, *Da.* Greenland was visited, in search for treasure, by a vessel or vessels, fitted out by the Danish Greenland Company.

—— *Ru.* The navigation of the Frozen Sea commenced by the Russians, who formed establishments on the banks of the Lena.

1643, *Du.* A voyage in the ships Castricom and Breskes, under the command of Martin Herizoom van Vriez, and H. C. Schaep, was undertaken from Japan towards the north. Between the Island of Ternate, from whence they sailed, and the latitude of 47°, beyond which they navigated, several islands, including perhaps the *Kuriles,* were discovered.

1646, *Ru.* The rivers *Jana, Indighirsa, Alasei,* and *Kovyma,* having been discovered within ten years preceding this date, a voyage for trade and research from the Kovima towards the east, the first in this position, was undertaken by Isai Ignatiew, with a party of Promyschleni, under his direction: They traded with the Tchuktchi.

A. D.

1647, *Ru.* A second trading voyage, with four kotches, from the Kovima towards the E., was attempted under the direction of the Kossak, Semoen Deschnew or Deshneff: this altogether failed.

1648, *Ru.* Seven kotches, from the Kovima, &c. in one of which SEMOEN DESCHREW again sailed, were dispatched towards the east. Six, if not all of these vessels, appear to have been wrecked; but one of them, commanded by Deschnew, previously accomplished the passage, it is supposed, round the great promontory of the Tchuktchi *, to the east side of *Kamtchatka*, and was lost near the River Olutora or Aliutori.

1652, *Da.* An expedition of two ships under Captain Danell, was sent out for the discovery of the east side of Greenland. The east coast at intervals, was seen from latitude 65° 30′ to Cape Farewell: but no landing was effected.

1653, *Da.* A second examination by Danell was undertaken. The east coast was again seen, but only at a distance, from Herjolfsness, latitude 64°, to Cape Farewell.

—— *Da.* Three ships, sent out for the discovery of a N. E. passage, passed the Weigatz, but discovered nothing.

1654, *Du.* *Gale Hamkens Land*, on the east coast of Greenland, intimated, by the Dutch charts, as having been discovered by a Greenland trader of the same name.

1655, *Du.* The *Land of Edam*, east side of Greenland, latitude 78°, marked in the Dutch charts as having been discovered.

1660, *Po.* David Melguer, said to have reversed the N. E. passage. A pretended voyage.

1668, *En.* A voyage into Hudson's Bay, and for discovery towards the N. W., was performed by Captain Zacchariah Gillam, accompanied by M. de Grosseliez, a Frenchman, by whom the practicability of making an important settlement in this quarter had been suggested. Gillam wintered in Hudson's Bay, and built a small stone fort. The apparent advantages to be derived from settlements, founded on the examinations

---

* Captain Burney is of opinion, that this voyage might have been accomplished without doubling the great promontory, by taking the vessel in pieces, a practice not uncommon with the Russians, and carrying it over a narrow neck of land between the Koyima and the Anadir.

A. D.

of this voyage, &c. appear to have led to the formation of the *Hudson's Bay Company*, which was char-
tered in the year 1669.

1676, *En.* John Wood and William Flawes, with two ships, proceeded in search of a N. E. passage. Wood's ship
was wrecked on the west coast of Nova Zembla, and
no discovery whatever made.

1696, *Ru. Kamtchatka*, discovered by land, by a troop of sixteen Kossaks.

1707, *Du.* A country to the N. E. of Spitzbergen, named *Gilles'
Land*, intimated by the Dutch charts as having been
discovered.

1712, *Ru.* Mercurei Wagin, a Cossak, with a party of eleven
men, proceeded from the river Jana across a surface
of ice, in sledges drawn by dogs, towards the north,
and is said to have discovered and landed on a large
island. Having suffered great hardships on their return, Wagin, his son, and another Cossak, to whom
their difficulties were attributed, were murdered by
the rest of the party.

1715, *Ru.* A remarkable journey from the Jana towards the
north, was accomplished by ALEXEI MARKOFF. He
travelled by means of sledges drawn by dogs, across a
frozen sea, as far north, it is supposed, as the 78th
degree of latitude, without finding land, and accomplished a journey of about 800 miles in twenty-four
days.

1716, *Ru.* The first voyage from Ochotzk to *Kamtchatka*, was
performed by Henry Busch, a native of Hoorn, in
North Holland.

1719, *En.* Two vessels, under the direction of James Knight,
and commanded by George Barlow and David
Vaughan, were sent out by the Hudson's Bay Company, to search for " the Strait of Anian, in order to
discover gold, &c. to the northward." Neither of
these ships ever returned: Knight and his companions are supposed to have perished at Marble Island in Hudson's Bay.

1721, *Da.* The Greenland Company of Bergen established a
colony on the west coast of Greenland, of which
Hans Egede, the enterprising and zealous missionary,
was a member.

A. D.

1722, *En.* A voyage from Churchill River, Hudson's Bay, was undertaken by John Scroggs, in search of Knight. He examined several parts of the bay without success. He does not appear, indeed, to have paid much attention to the original object of the voyage.

1723, *Da.* A ship sent out by the Bergen Greenland Company, for reconnoitring Davis' Strait, was lost, and all hands it is supposed perished.

1724 *Da.* Two ships fitted out by the Bergen Company for discovery, one for exploring the west side of Davis' Strait, in the 67th parallel, and the other for examining the east coast of Greenland, effected nothing.

—— *Ru.* About this time, several voyages and journeys were made by the Russians, on and about the Frozen Sea, in search of northern lands, in which several islands were discovered.

1728, *Ru.* Captain VITUS BEHRING was employed in a voyage from Kamtchatka, for discoveries towards the north, and for ascertaining whether Asia and America were continuous. He sailed as high as 67° 18′ N. latitude, having passed the place now called *Behring's Strait.*

1729, *Ru.* Behring sailed on his second voyage from Kamtchatka, in search of land towards the east. He did not, however, leave the land above 200 versts, and discovered nothing.

—— *Da.* Lieutenant Richard made an unsuccessful attempt to reach the east coast of Greenland, in the parallel of Iceland.

1730, *Ru.*
or
1731.
A vessel was dispatched under the orders of the Surveyor Gwosdew, and Tryphon Krupischew, a Kossak officer, for the purpose of inviting the Tchuktchi to pay tribute; in this voyage the *West Coast of America,* in the 66th parallel, was discovered.

1734, *Ru.*
and
1735.
The navigation from Archangel to the west coast of the peninsula separating the Gulfs of Kama and Obe, was accomplished by Lieutenant Morovieff.

1735, *Ru.* Lieutenant Lassenius sailed from the Lena towards the east, and wintered in the river Charaulack, where 46 out of 52 persons, composing his crew, died of the scurvy.

1735, *Ru.*
and
Lieutenant Prontschitscheff sailed from the Lena westward, and after wintering in the Olenec, proceeded to

A. D.

1736.   the height of 77° 25′, and westward to the Bay of Taimourska.

—— *Ru.* A voyage from the Lena somewhat to the eastward of the Charaulack, was performed by Dmitri Laptiew.

1737, *En.* Two ships equipped by the Hudson's Bay Company, for discoveries in Hudson's Bay, and towards the N. W., appear to have accomplished little or nothing.

1738, *Ru.* The navigation from Archangel towards the east, by the Russians, commenced in 1734, was continued by Lieutenants Mlyagin and Skuratow, and accomplished as far as the Obe.

—— *Ru.* The voyage from the Obe to the Eniesi, was accomplished by Lieutenants Owzen and Koschelew.

1739, *Ru.* Lieutenant Laptieff, on his second voyage in the Frozen Sea, sailed from the Lena, wintered in the Indig-
and   hirsa, and proceeded the next spring to the Kovima,
1740.   from whence, according to some authors, he crossed the isthmus of the Tchuktchi to the river Anadir, communicating with the sea of Kamtchatka *.

1741, *Ru.* An expedition of two vessels, under Commodore Behring and Captain Tschirikow, was dispatched from Ochotsk in 1740, which, after wintering in Kamtchatka, proceeded towards America, for the purpose of making discoveries about its shores. The ships being separated on the passage, Behring discovered the Continent in latitude 58° 28′, and Tschirikow in 55° 36′. The former, after discovering several islands, lost his ship on one of the Aleutians, called *Behring's Island,* where he died. The latter returned, having lost two boats and their crews on the American coast.

1741, *En.* Some part of the *Welcome,* in Hudson's Bay, examined
and   by Christopher Middleton and William Moor, with
1742.   two vessels, after having wintered in Churchill River. The object of the voyage was the discovery of a N. W. passage.

1743, A reward of L. 20,000 offered by Parliament, for the discovery of a N. W. passage, by the way of Hudson's Bay, (18th Geo. II. c. 17.)

---

* The combined result of these Russian navigations in the Frozen Sea, is briefly traced in chap. I. § 2. of this volume.

2

A. D.

1746, *En.* Two ships, under the command of William Moor and Francis Smith, sent out in search of a N. W. passage, by the way of Hudson's Bay. The first summer they examined some part of the Welcome, and, after wintering in Haye's River, made a good exploration of Wager River, previously supposed to be a strait.

1753, *Am.* Captain Charles Swaine, in the schooner Argo, sailed from Philadelphia for the discovery of a N. W. passage; but being unable to penetrate through Hudson's Strait, he examined a large extent of the Labrador Coast, from 56°, it is said, to latitude 65°.

1760, *Ru.* A most persevering but unsuccessful attempt was made
to   by a Russian merchant of the name of SHALAUROFF,
1763.   to sail from the Lena round the great Tchutkchi promontory. He first wintered in the Jana, and then twice in the Kovima. He discovered some islands and a bay, being the farthest spot he reached, which has been named *Tschaoon Bay.*

1761, *En.* A sloop, under the command of Captain Christopher, was sent by the Hudson's Bay Company to explore *Chesterfield Inlet* in Hudson's Bay, with the expectation that it might be the opening of a N. W. passage. Christopher is said to have penetrated above 150 miles, and then returned.

1762, *En.* Christopher was again sent out to complete the examination of Chesterfield Inlet, when he traced it by a river into a lake, 24 miles long, and 6 or 7 broad; and across this to the westward into another river, until his further progress, even in boats, was interrupted by falls.

1764, *Ru.* The indefatigable Shalauroff made a final attempt to pass from the Lena round the Tchutkchi promontory, in which he is supposed to have perished, as neither himself nor any of his companions ever returned.

1769, *Da.* Baron von Uhlefeld through Hudson's Bay into the Pacific. A pretended voyage.

1669 *En.* A journey by Samuel Hearne, after two unsuccessful
to   attempts, accomplished from Prince of Wales Fort,
1772.   Hudson's Bay, to the *Copper-Mine* River, supposed to fall into the *Northern Ocean.*

1772, *Am.* A second voyage for the discovery of a N. W. passage, seems to have been attempted by the Americans;

A. D.

Captain Wilder, in the brig Diligence, having sailed to latitude 69° 11' with such a design. This vessel was fitted out by means of the subscriptions of some gentlemen of Virginia.

1773, *En.* In a voyage towards the North Pole, with two vessels under the charge of CONSTANTINE JOHN PHIPPS and Skeffington Lutwidge, the latitude of 80° 48' was reached, and some interesting surveys and observations made, but no discoveries.

1775, *Sp.* A voyage for discovery along the west side of North America, made, by order of the Viceroy of Mexico, by Bruno Heceta and others; they reached the latitude of 57° 18' N.

1776, The reward of £20,000 for the discovery of a N. W. passage extended, not by the way of Hudson's Bay and in merchant ships only, but to any ships, even those of his Majesty, which, by a former act, were excluded, and in any northern direction between the Atlantic and Pacific Oceans: Also, an award of £5000 to any ship that should approach within one degree of the North Pole. (16th Geo. III. cap. 6.)

1776, *En.* Richard Pickersgill, in the brig Lion, was sent out to Baffin's Bay for the protection of the whale-fishers, and for the examination of the coasts. He only reached the latitude of 68° 10', and then returned without having accomplished almost any thing.

1777, *En.* The same vessel was again equipped, under the command of Lieutenant Walter Young, who was ordered to examine Baffin's Bay, and attempt to find a N. W. passage, with a view, it seems, of meeting Captain Cook, who was expected about the same time to be trying to reverse the same track. But Young, having reached to the height of 72° 42', though so early as the month of June, tacked, and soon after returned home.

1776 *En.* The adventurous navigator JAMES COOK, with two
to   ships under his direction, being appointed to make
1778.   discoveries towards the reversing of a N. W. passage, passed Behring's Strait on his third voyage, in the summer of 1778, and discovered or named *Cape Prince of Wales, Point Mulgrave, Icy Cape, Cape Lisburne, Cape North*, &c. and advanced to the north-

A. D.

ward as high as latitude 70° 44′ N. ; which limit being unable to pass, he returned to the southward to spend the winter.   In one of the Sandwich Islands, Owhy_hee, this celebrated character lost his life.

1779, *En.* After the death of Captain Cook, a second examination of the icy sea, to the northward of Behring's Strait,· was undertaken by Charles Clerke, in which the same two ships reached the latitude of 70° 33′, beyond which they were unable to advance on account of ice.

1786 *Da.* An expedition under Captain Lowenorn and Lieutenant
and   Egede, was sent out from Copenhagen for the reco-
1787.   very of lost Greenland.   Several attempts were made to reach the coast about the parallel of 65°, without being able to approach nearer than about 50 miles on account of ice; Lowenorn returned to Denmark in July, and Egede to Iceland to refit.   The latter made another attempt in the month of August, when he reached within 10 miles of the land, and then proceeded to Iceland, where he wintered.   The next year, Egede, with two small vessels, one commanded by Lieutenant Rothé, made other trials to approach the Greenland coast, but with less success than before, never being able to reach the land within 30 miles.

1787 *Ru.* Joseph Billings, an Englishman, was employed in the
to   service of Russia for researches about Behring's Strait
1791.   and the Tchutkchi Promontory.   In 1787, he made a short voyage from the Kovima into the Icy Sea; in 1790, he sailed from Kamtchatka to the Alutian Islands ; and from thence, the same year, he sailed to the Bay of St Laurence, on the south side of Cape East, Behring's Strait, where he landed, and traced the coasts to the northward as far as Klutshenic Bay, the eastern side of which is formed by Cape North.   From this place he crossed the country towards the west, and arrived at the Kovima in 1791.

1789, *En.* ALEXANDER MACKENZIE accomplished a river navigation from Fort Chepewyan, on the south side of the Lake of the Hills, as far as latitude 69° 14′, where he was evidently at the borders of the Hyperborean Sea, or near the mouth of a river communicating with it. The river he descended is now named *Mackenzie's River.*

A. D.

1789, *Sp.* Two corvettes, under the orders of Malaspina, were sent to the N. W. of America, to search for a navigable communication from the Pacific to the Atlantic, between the parallels of 53° and 60° N.

1790 *En.* Charles Duncan sailed in one of the Hudson's Bay
to   ships, with the view of being furnished with a small
1792.   vessel on his arrival out, for making investigations towards a N. W. passage; but being disappointed, both in the vessel and crew provided for him, he returned to England without attempting any thing. The following year he proceeded on the adventure towards the N. W. in a small vessel fitted out of London; wintered in Hudson's Bay, then made some slight examination of Chesterfield's Inlet, and again returned to a port in the Bay to winter. After these failures or disappointments, nothing else by him was attempted.

1791 *En.* Two vessels, under the command of GEORGE VANCOUVER,
to   were sent out to the west coast of North America, part-
1795.   ly for receiving back some territories which had been seized by the Spaniards, and partly for discovery in regard of a navigable communication from the Pacific to the Atlantic, between the parallels of 30° and 60° N. The whole of the west coast was accordingly traced from latitude 30° to the head of Cook's Inlet, in about 61° 18'. In this laborious investigation, Vancouver sailed almost 1000 miles in channels, in some places very contracted, between ranges of islands and the main. The non-existence of a passage through the continent, within the limits prescribed, was well established.

1805 *Ru.* Several islands to the northward of that part of Russia,
to   included between the Jana and the Kovima, were dis-
1809.   covered in different brief northern expeditions, among which was an extensive tract of country, now called *New Siberia.*

1815 *Ru.* Lieutenant Kotzebue, in a small vessel called the Ru-
to   rick, was employed for making discoveries to the
1818.   northward of Behring's Strait on the side of America. He passed Behring's Strait in 1816, and after some little time spent in research, returned to the southward to winter. The next summer, Kotzebue proceeded again towards the north; but having met with

A. D.

a personal accident, was obliged to bear up homeward, after reaching the mouth of Behring's Strait.

1818, *En.* JOHN ROSS and William Edward Parry, proceeded
with two well equipped ships, for the discovery of a
N. W. passage.   They circumnavigated Baffin's Bay,
proved the non-existence of Cumberland Island, discovered some part of the west coast that was not seen
by Baffin, and gave names to numerous positions in
the course of their navigation.

—— *En.* DAVID BUCHAN and John Franklin, with two ships,
undertook a voyage for discovery towards the North
Pole.   One of the vessels received damage in the best
part of the season, and occasioned, it is said, the return of the expedition before that research had been
made which was intended.

1818 *En.* Rewards to navigators, for advancing to latitude 83° N.
and   and to longitude 110° W. within the Arctic circle,
1819.   with a progressive increase of premiums for sailing still
nearer to the N. Pole, and making further advances in
the discovery of a N. W. passage, permitted by act of
Parliament, and fixed by an order in Council

1819, *En.* William Edward Parry was again dispatched for discoveries towards the N. W. with two vessels under his
direction.   The issue not yet known.

—— *En.* John Franklin, with others, proceeded to America, for
making researches by land about the shores of the
Frozen Ocean.

In drawing up the preceding abstract of northern voyages, it
is but proper to mention, that I have not been at the pains to con-
sult many originals, having principally been indebted to the writings of Foster, Muller, Coxe, Barrow, and Burney.   The two
voyages of Christopher in 1761 and 1762, of Wilder in 1772, and
of Swaine in 1753, are not noticed, I believe, by any of the above
authors.   Christopher's voyages are mentioned in Goldson's Observations on the Passage between the Atlantic and Pacific Oceans,
and in Macpherson's Annals of Commerce, vol. iii. p. 362 : Wilder's voyage is also given by Macpherson, vol. iii. p. 527 ; and
several particulars respecting Swaine's voyage, are contained in the
Gentleman's Magazine, vol. xxiv. p. 46.

Act 58th Geo. III. c. 20, and London Gazette 23d March 1819.

No. III. *b.*

IN page 47. of this volume, a familiar approximation relating to the effect of the sun's rays, during the summer solstice, in the Arctic Regions, is given in a note. It may be worth while to mention, that in an admirable article on " Climate," in the third volume of the Supplement to the fourth and fifth editions of the Encyclopedia Britannica, this subject, together with several others connected with atmospheric temperature and pressure, is scientifically illustrated.

The effect of elevation, in occasioning a reduction of temperature, forms a part of the investigations in this article. Instead of 90 yards of elevation producing a depression of one degree of Fahrenheit in the lower atmosphere, as stated by the late Professor Playfair in his " Outlines of Natural Philosophy," and by other philosophers; it would appear from the author's (Professor Leslie) researches, that the height producing a change of a degree of temperature is 100 yards. In the higher regions of the atmosphere, a similar change of temperature takes place, under a smaller difference of altitude. Thus, in temperate climates, while the mean temperature at the level of the sea decreases one degree of Fahrenheit during an ascent of 300 feet above the surface, it suffers a similar diminution in 295 feet, at the altitude of a mile; in 277 feet, at the height of 2 miles; in 252 feet, at the height of 3 miles; in 223 feet, at the height of 4 miles; and in 192 feet, at the elevation of 5 miles above the surface. In this ratio, the decrease of temperature, on ascending a mile into the atmosphere from the surface of the sea, would be about 17.7 degrees; on ascending two miles 36.1, three miles 55.9, four miles 78.1, and five miles above the sea 103.5 degrees.

No. IV.

TABLE OF LATITUDES AND LONGITUDES OF CAPES, BAYS, &C. IN
SPITZBERGEN AND JAN MAYEN, DERIVED CHIEFLY FROM
ORIGINAL SURVEYS.

Spitzbergen.

Point Look-out, or South Cape (the high land)	76° 39′	N. 16°	5′	E.
(the S. W. corner of the low land)	76 29½	15	44	
Horn Mount, - - -	76 58	15	20	
Horn Sound, middle of the entrance, -	77 2	15	0	
Cape on the N. side of entrance,	77 4	14	58	
S. W. ditto,	77 0	14	54	
Iceberg Mount, - -	77 13	14	30	
Bell Sound, middle of the entrance, -	77 35	13	42	
Cape on N. side of entrance,	77 38	13	42	
N. W. ditto, -	77 42	13	5	
S. W. ditto, -	77 29	13	18	
S. E. ditto, -	77 32	14	5	
Fair Haven,	77 40	13	53	
Cold Harbour, - -	77 50	15	0	
Bell River, entrance, -	77 45	14	56	
Van Keulen's Bay, - -	77 37	15	0	
Reyniere's River, -	77 38	15	27	
Clean Bay, - -	77 32	14	37	
Ice Sound, middle of the entrance, -	78 9	12	46	
Cape on the N. side of entrance,	78 12	12	42	
S. ditto, -	78 7	12	49	
Safe Haven, - -	78 14	12	48	
Sassen Bay, - -	78 16	13	40	
Green Harbour, -	78 4	13	24	
Foreland or Charles' Island ;—Back Point,	78 13 (?)	10	37	
Middle Hook, -	78 36	9	35	
Cape Sitoe, (?) - -	78 44	9	20	
North end, or Fair Foreland,	78 53 (?)	9	17	
King's Bay ;—Cape at S. W. side of entrance,	78 56	10	18	
N. W. ditto.	79 5	10	37	
N. side within,	78 59	11	0	

Cross Bay ;—Mitre Cape, (the high land)	79° 10′N.	10° 11′E
(the low land)	79 7	10 12
Cape at the W. side of entrance (within) - -	79 13	10 33
N. ditto (within)	79 15	10 44
Seven Icebergs ;—Cape to the southward of 1st,	79 13	9 46
northward of 3d,	79 17	9 27
northward of 7th, or the south point of Hamburgher's Bay, -	79 26	9 24
Hamburgher's Bay, - -	79 28	9 30
Magdalena Bay, middle of entrance,	79 35	9 30
Cape at the S. W. side of entrance, or Magdalena Hook,	79 34	9 23
John Duncan's Bight,	79 34	9 38

Jan Mayen Island.

Young's Foreland, or Cape North-east,	71° 8′ N.	7° 26′ W
Cape Neill, - -	71 3	7 29
Cape South-east, - -	71 2	7 29
Cape Hope, - -	71 1	7 34
Cape Fishburn, - -	71 1	7 37
Jameson Bay, - -	71 0	7 46
Cape Brodrick, - -	70 59	7 50
Esk Mount, - -	71 1	7 46
Beerenberg (altitude 6870 feet), -	71 4	7 36
Cape Traill, - -	70 56	8 8
Cape South, -	70 49	8 41
Cape South-west, - -	70 50 ?	8 45

No. V.

CATALOGUE OF PLANTS FOUND IN SPITZBERGEN *.

HEXANDRIA.
Luzula campestris, Juncus campestris *L.*

DECANDRIA.
Andromeda tetragona, *Linné.*
Saxifraga oppositifolia. *L.*
        cernua. *L.*
        var. nivalis. *L.*
        cæspitosa, β grœnlandica. *Wahlenb. lapp.* 119
Cerastium alpinum, α hirsutum. *Wahlenb. lapp.* 136.

ICOSANDRIA.
Dryas octopetala. *L.*

POLYANDRIA.
Papaver radicatum. *Rottb.* Vix diversum a P. nudicaule. *L.*
Ranunculus sulphureus. *Soland. in Phipps' Voyage.*

DIDYNAMIA.
Pedicularis hirsuta. *L.*

TETRADYNAMIA.
Cochlearia grœnlandica? Vel C. Anglica, *Wahl. lapp.*
Cardamine bellidifolia. *L.*
Draba alpina. *L.*

DIŒCIA.
Salix polaris. *Wahlenb. lapp.* 261.

CRYPTOGAMIA.
Trichostomum lanuginosum.
Hypnum dendroides.
        rufescens?
Bryum ventricosum. *Smith brit.*
      ligulatum?
Dicrani species?
Andræa alpina.
Ulva   ?

---

* This list includes the whole of the plants that I met with, excepting some of the larger fuci, in three or four visits to the shore about King's Bay and Mitre Cape. Some of the specimens being imperfect, or without fructification, their species could not always be determined.

Fucus   forsan nov. sp. prope *alatum*, sed absque
   fructific.

      plumosus.
      sinuatus.

Conferva   ?
      nigra ?

Cenomyce furcata.   *Achar. syn.* 276.
        pocillum.   *Id.* 253.

Solorina crocea.   *Id.* 8.

Alectoria jubata, β chalybeiformis.   *Id.* 291.

Lecanora murorum, var.   *Id.* 181.

Lecidea atrovirens.   *Id.* 24.

Gyrophora hirsuta.   *Id.* 69.
        erosa.   *Id.* 65.
        proboscidea.   *Id.* 64.

Endocarpum sinopicum.   *Id.* 98.

Sphærophoron coralloides.   *Id.* 287.

Parmelia stygia.   *Id.*
        recurva.   *Id.* 206 ?
        sp. nov. ? sed absque fructific.

Peltidea canina ?

Cetraria nivalis.   *Id.* 228.

Cornicularia aculeata, β spadicea.   *Id.* 300.

Usnea ? prope U. melaxantham.   *Id.* 303.

Stereocaulon paschale.   *Id.* 284.

No. VI.

NOTICE RESPECTING THE MINERALS OF SPITZBERGEN.

Specimens of the different rocks met with, when I landed
in Spitzbergen in the summer of 1818, were sent to my friend
Professor Jameson, who observed the following kinds:

   Bluish-grey foliated-granular limestone, of which some
      varieties are minute foliated, passing into splintery;
      and others contain veins and imbedded portions of
      quartz.

   Gneiss.

Mica-slate.

Mica-slate passing into clay-slate.

Quartz-rock.

Rhomboidal calcareous-spar.

The gneiss was of a grey colour, the felspar and quartz being both grey, and the mica dark blackish-brown.   Some varieties were very coarse granular and inclining to granite, but no true granite was met with.   The mica-slate had the usual characters of that rock.   The quartz-rock was grey, small granular, and in some specimens splintery.   Some masses contained disseminated scales of mica, but no felspar. In both varieties of quartz-rock observed, were minutely disseminated iron-pyrites, which decaying of a yellowish-brown, tinged the rock of that colour.   The calcareous-spar occurred in veins in the limestone.   It was found only in the roof of a deep cavern.

From these specimens, which were all the varieties met with in two or three excursions to the shore, it appeared to Professor Jameson that the mountains and shores of Spitzbergen visited by me, are formed of gneiss, mica-slate, and quartz-rock, which contain great and frequent beds of bluish-coloured limestone.   No secondary rocks, such as sandstone, basalt, clinkstone, or others of a similar description, nor any rock of volcanic formation, were met with.   In this respect Spitzbergen is remarkably distinguished from Jan Mayen *, where all the rocks are secondary trap or volcanic.

Nova Zembla is said to have the same geognostical features as Spitzbergen; and West Greenland abounds in primitive rocks, but contains few species of the secondary class.   Probably Spitzbergen and Nova Zembla, were formerly more intimately connected than they are at present.

---

* Cherie Island appears to be composed of the same rocks as Jan Mayen.

No. VII.

STATE OF THE WIND AND WEATHER, FROM AUGUST TO
MAY, IN THE ISLAND OF JAN MAYEN, AS COLLECTED
FROM THE JOURNAL OF SEVEN SAILORS OF HOLLAND WHO
WINTERED THERE IN THE YEAR 1633,–4 *.

[Referred to p. 168.]

1633	WINDS.	REMARKS.
Aug. 26	N E	Strong breeze. The fleet sailed for Holland
27	N E	
28	N E	Snow
29		Clear
30	N W, at night N E	
31	N E	Fresh gale, clear
Sept. 1	N W to N E	Snow
2	N E	Snow
3	N E	Some snow
4	N E	Some snow
5	N E	Some snow
6	N E	rainy
7	N E	Fair. At night S E b S rainy
8	S E	Rainy morning
9	S E	Clear and warm
10	S E	Very stormy, rainy
11	S E b S to S W and N E.	Foggy, rainy
12	N E	Blowing hard, clear
13	S E to N E b N and N W.	Fair, sunshiny
14	W, N W b W	Some snow
15	W	Blowing so hard the sea foamed
16	S W	Fair
17	S W	Blowing very hard, clear
18	S W b S	Rainy
19	W, S E	Clear, starlight at night
20	S E b S, S W	Sunshiny
21	S W	Misty and rainy
22	S W	Blowing hard and rainy
23	E, S E	Cloudy, with rain and mist
24	S E b S	Rainy
25	S E b E	Stormy and rainy
26	E.erly	Frosty weather
27	N E	Fair, at night W Foul weather
28	N, S, S E	Violent storm, snow
29	S E	Blowing hard, with snow
30	S W b W	Ramy, stormy at night

1633	WINDS.	REMARKS.
Oct. 1	N E	Frosty
2	E	Freezing hard
3	E, W	Frost and snow
4	S, S W	Frosty, fog or rain at night
5	S W	Much rain
6	S W b S	Blowing hard
7	S W b W	Very stormy
8	S W b W, N E, N	Very tempestuous
9	N.erly	Tempestuous
10	N E b N	Blowing strong, excessive cold
11	N E	Very cold, snow
12	N E	Blowing hard, very cold
13	N E	Very cold
14	N E	Excessive cold
15	N.erly	Weather tolerable
16	N.erly	Cold, snow
17	N	Blowing hard, frosty
18	N	Frosty
19	N	Some ice a mile off shore
20	N E	Fair, much ice seen
21	E, N E	Blowing and snowing hard
22	N E	Much snow
23	N E	Cloudy
24	N E	Frosty
25	S W	Excesive cold, clear
26	S W, W	Sea full of ice
27	W	Clear
28	W	Clear frosty weather
29	N	Severe cold, sea full of ice, snow
30	N	Freezing hard, tempestuous
31	N	Severe frost, with snow
Nov. 1	N E	Cold vehement
2		Hard frost
3	N E	Tolerable weather
4	N E, W	Freezing hard
5	S	Heavy fall of snow
6	S to E	Tempestuous weather
7	N E	Still weather

* See CHURCHILL's " Collection of Voyages and Travels," Vol. ii. Ed. 1732, p. 369.

1633 WINDS. REMARKS.	1633 WINDS. REMARKS.

Nov.
8 N Excessive cold
9 N Sun ½ an hour above the horizon
10 N
11 N E Wind increased, thick clouds
12 E Thick fogs, gulls seen
13 E Freezing severely
14 E, W Cold weather, bay full of ice
15 W Saw three or four bears
16 W
17 N Dark snowy weather, cold relaxed
18 N E Frost increased
19 N Sun seen just above the sea
20 N, W Dark snowy weather
21 W Sea full of ice
22 W.erly Cold weather
23 N W b N Fair, sea full of ice
24 S E, W Frosty, sea-gulls seen
25 W Frosty
26 S Mild, the ice left the bay
27 S W, E Fair weather
28 S E Fair mild weather
29 S E Land blocked with ice on S side
30 S E Violent rains

Dec.
1 S.erly Rain, S E at night
2 S E Mild rainy wr. ice set off the land
3 S Rainy, blowing strong
4 S Mild, cloudy
5 S Mild calm weather
6 S E Cloudy
7 S E, S Foggy, snow and frost
8 N E, W Frosty
9 W Clear cold weather, sea full of ice
10 W Frosty, nothing but ice at sea
11 W Ditto
12 W Cold weather, calm at night
13 S W Cloudy, S E at night, with snow
14 S Clear frosty day, ice removed off land
15 S Dark wr. ice returned
16 S W Moonlight night
17 S Cloudy dark weather, snow, thaw at night
18 S. E Dark rainy day
19 E Hard frost
20 E Do. calm weather, dark night
21 E, N Frost and snow
22 N Ice returned, coldest day yet experienced
23 E Frost, snow, stormy night
24 E, N E Hard frost and storm at night
25 S Fair day, at night wind N
26 E, N W Clear frosty day
27 N W At night calm, wind E.erly

Dec.
28 E, W Violent snow and wind
29 W Clear cold wr. S E at night, with snow
30 S W Blowing hard
31 S W Calm, snow at night

1634
Jan.
1 S W Dark cold weather
2 N E Clear, ice forced to sea
3 S E, A little rain, at night a S W storm
4 W.erly Fierce wind, cold weather, ice returned ; E.erly wind at night
5 E.erly Thick fog and frost
6 N Increasing wind, with snow
7 N Snowing and freezing hard
8 N E Frosty, excessive cold and stormy at night
9 N E The ice heaped in the bay like huts
10 N E Bright pleasant day, but very cold
11 N E to S & S E. Vast qantity of snow with S E wind
12 S E Vast quantity of snow fell, weather milder
13 S E Do., ice forced to sea, cold wr.
14 E Tolerably clear
15 E.erly, N E. Snow, ice seen off shore
16 S Milder wr. E at night, with frost
17 E Fog, N at night, froze the bay up in a night
18 N to W Cold, foggy, snow
19 W Abundance of snow
20 W.erly Much snow, E at night, snow
21 E Blowing violently, with thick snow, W at night
22 W. A heavy fall of snow
23 W to E Sun visible, clear frosty weather, ice went off
24 W Snowy, S wind at night, cloudy
25 S Strong wind, cold night
26 W Snowing hard, ice returned, S at night
27 W Mild, E at night, snowy weather
28 W to S E Snow, ice carried a great way off
29 S W, W Dark rainy wr. ice returned
30 Calm clear frosty day, sun seen an hour and a half
31 W.erly, N with frost

Feb.
1 W.erly Clear calm wr. bay full of ice
2. N E Clear cold wr. bears grow shy
3 E.rly, S E Cloudy, milder
4 S E to S Milder, snow, ice went off
5 S E and E Cold abated
6 E to S W Clear moonlight night
7 E Blowing strong

1634 WINDS. REMARKS.

Feb.
8 S Calm weather, ice was carried out of sight
9 N.erly Snowed violently ; at night S
10 N to S W Dark and stormy
11 S to E Cloudy
12 E Snow ; not very cold for the season
13 E Snowy, calm weather, moonlight night
14 E Clear day ; stormy cloudy night
15 E Snow so high could not stir out
16 E Mild, saw two fowls like geese and a falcon
17 E Much snow
18 E Cloudy, mild weather
19 E Fair day, no ice
20 E Mild weather
21 N E Fair and calm, frost and snow at night
22 N E Much snow, frosty
23 N E Some ice returned to the bay
24 E.erly Intense frost, N at night
25 N Cloudy, dark night
26 (No remark)
27 Calm mild weather, S wind at night and thaw
28 S Mild wr. ice far off, S W at night

March
1 S W Rainy in the evening
2 W Blowing hard, clear cold weather
3 N E to N Violent wind forced the ice into the bay
4 N E Cloudy calm weather
5 N E Cloudy, cold less severe
6 N E Pleasant, and calm at night
7 N E Do. at night stormy
8 N E Dark cloudy weather
9 N E Sharp frost
10 N E Excessive cold weather
11 N E A south wind brought pleasant weather
12 S, S E Ice went out of sight, do. wr.
13 S E, N E Moderately cold
14 N E Very cold
15 S, S W Milder wr. killed a bear, which was very serviceable, as the scurvy had appeared
16 S W, N at night, cold weather
17 N Cloudy, bay filled with ice
18 N Cloudy frosty day
19 (No remark)
20 S Calm, sunshiny day
21 S Dark rainy weather, ice went to sea
22 S E Scurvy becomes very afflictive

1634 WINDS. REMARKS.

March
23 S E Pleasant day
24 S.erly or calm weather
25 S E, S Ice returned
26 S Fair clear weather
27 S E Cloudy, 10 whales seen in the bay
28 S.erly wind, Innumerable whales appeared
29 S.erly Plenty of whales
30 S.erly Dark night
31 N E Some snow, 4 or 5 whales seen

April
1 E Cloudy, S at night, 4 or 5 whales
2 S E Snow, mild weather
3 W Cloudy, two of the men only in health
4 W.erly Sunshiny day
5 S E Two large whales in the bay
6 N E 4 or 5 whales
7 N E Cold, sunshiny weather
8 N E Do. innumerable whales
9 N Frosty, do.
10 N Cold, ice returned, some whales
11 N No whales or bears
12 N E Clear frosty day
13 N E Do. bay full of ice
14 N E, A south wind at night carried the ice away
15 W Calm mild day, 4 whales seen in the bay
16 W. Clear, *The clerk died.*
17 W Cloudy, bay full of ice
18 (No remark)
19 W The men much afflicted, having no refreshment left
20 S At night E.erly, with snow ; ice drifted away
21 S E A calm day
22 N E Ice closed to the shore ; S wind at night
23 S Ice off land, rain. All the survivors but one rendered helpless by disease ; the captain struggling with death
34 S Cloudy
25 S Sunshiny, some ice, whales seen ; A W wind at night brought the ice in
26 W Cloudy day, calm
27 E Mild weather. Killed a dog for food
28 E Cloudy weather, ice went out of sight, N wind at night
29 N E Blowing hard at night
30 N E A fine clear day

Here the journal terminates with the word *die;* alluding perhaps to other observations which the writer, in his usual way, had been about to set down.   The first man of this unfortunate party died on the 16th of April, the other six seem to have expired in the beginning of May.   The scurvy was evidently the cause of their death, which, it appears, arose more from the want of fresh provisions than from the cold, as they could generally stir abroad at least once in three or four days.

No. VIII.

EXPERIMENTS FOR DETERMINING THE SPECIFIC GRAVITY OF ICE.

[Referred to p. 234.]

Some attempts to obtain the specific gravity of ice, by measuring the proportion of rectangular pieces which floated above the surface in a vessel of water, having given discordant results, a more accurate method was adopted.

Three masses of ice, of different qualities, being drained some time in air when the temperature was 30°, (the most porous in a warmer situation), were washed in pure water, dried, and carefully weighed.   A copper ball, weighing 2515 grains, being then attached alternately to each mass, the weight in a vessel of fresh water, at a freezing temperature, was found.   From these data the following results were obtained.

	WEIGHTS OBTAINED.			Ice less heavy than its bulk of water. *Diff.* of Col. III. and IV.	Weight of a quantity of water of the same bulk as the ice. Sum of col. II. & V.	Specific gravity of the ice compared with fresh water, temp. 32º.
	Ice in ira.	Ice in fresh water, with ball attached.	Copper ball in water.			
I.	II. Grains.	III. Gr.	IV. Gr.	V. Gr.	VI. Gr.	VII. Gr.
1. Transparent fresh water ice, without a visible pore.	3333	1922	2233	311	3644	0.9146
2 Semi-transparent ice from a *tongue* of what is called *salt-water ice*; tasted quite fresh.	3661	1898	2233	335	3996	0.9162
3. Bay ice, porous and opaque; when drained, tasted nearly quite fresh.	4892	1838	2233	395	5287	0.925 +
[Copper ball used for sinking the ice.	2515	——	2233	——	282	8.918]

These experiments with similar kinds of ice, and under similar circumstances, were repeated on another voyage, in which the coincidence of the results are remarkable. The specific gravity, (compared with fresh water, temperature 34º,) of a specimen the same as No. 1. was found to be 0.9165; of a specimen similar to No. 2. 0.9200; and of another corresponding with No. 3. 0.9215. Specimens of the same descriptions of ice compared with sea-water, temperature 34º, gave the specific gravity of No. 2.=0.8942, and of No. 3.= 0.8943.

When all these experiments were made, the temperature of the air being within 2 degrees of the freezing point, was particularly favourable. The experiments were conducted throughout in the open air, and the blocks of ice, when handled, were lifted with a woollen glove. All the apparatus that was used had the temperature of 30º to 34º, so that no loss was likely to take place by the melting of any portion of the ice.

END OF VOLUME FIRST.